This book is dedicated to the many who have helped to train
and develop me along the way, including

My wife: Caroline

My kids: Ray, Tim, and Melissa

My parents: Raymond J. and Mildred Noe

The many close friends who have touched my heart and made
me laugh

The teachers who have shared their wisdom

The graduate students who have worked with me over the years

Raymond A. Noe

Preface

Traditionally, training and development was not viewed as an activity that could help companies create "value" and successfully deal with competitive challenges. Today, that view has changed. Companies that use innovative training and development practices are likely to report better financial performance than their competitors that do not. Training and development also helps a company to meet competitive challenges. Current recessionary economic times have resulted in cuts in training and development budgets. However, companies need to continue to rely on efficient and effective training practices to help employees strengthen or increase their skills in order to improve or make new products, generate new and innovative ideas, and provide high quality customer service. Also, development activities and career management are needed to prepare employees for managerial and leadership positions and to attract, motivate, and retain talented employees at all levels and in all jobs. Training, development, and career management are no longer in the category of "nice to do"—they are a "must do" in order for companies to gain a competitive advantage and meet employees' expectations.

Businesses today must compete in the global marketplace, and the diversity of the work force continues to increase. As a result, companies need to train employees to work with persons from different cultures both in the United States and abroad. New technologies such as Web-based training and iPods reduce the costs associated with bringing employees to a central location for training. At the same time, the challenge is how to ensure that these training methods include the necessary conditions (practice, feedback, self-pacing, etc.) for learning to occur. Also, through the blended learning approach companies are seeking the best balance between private, self-paced, technology-based training (such as online learning), and methods that allow interpersonal interaction among trainees (such as classroom instruction or active learning).

The role of training has broadened beyond training program design. Effective instructional design remains important, but training managers, human resource experts, and trainers are increasingly being asked to create systems to motivate employees to learn, create knowledge, and share that knowledge with other employees in the company. Training has moved from an emphasis on a one-time event to the creation of conditions for learning that can occur through collaboration, online learning, traditional classroom training, or a combination of methods. There is increased recognition that learning occurs outside the boundaries of a formal training course.

Also, the employee-employer relationship has changed. Due to rapidly changing business environments and competition that can quickly cause profits to shrink and skill needs to change, companies are reluctant to provide job security to employees. At the same time, as employees see downsizing take place (or experience it themselves!), they are reluctant to be fully committed to company goals and values. As a result, both employees and companies are concerned with developing future skills and managing careers. Companies want a work force that is motivated and productive, has up-to-date skills, and can quickly learn new skills to meet changing customer and marketplace needs. Employees want to develop skills that not only are useful for their current jobs but also are congruent with their

Employee Training and Development

Fifth Edition

Raymond A. Noe
The Ohio State University

Boston   Burr Ridge, IL   Dubuque, IA   Madison, WI   New York   San Francisco   St. Louis
Bangkok   Bogotá   Caracas   Kuala Lumpur   Lisbon   London   Madrid   Mexico City
Milan   Montreal   New Delhi   Santiago   Seoul   Singapore   Sydney   Taipei   Toronto

The **McGraw·Hill** Companies

EMPLOYEE TRAINING AND DEVELOPMENT
International Edition 2010

Exclusive rights by McGraw-Hill Education (Asia), for manufacture and export. This book cannot be re-exported from the country to which it is sold by McGraw-Hill. This International Edition is not to be sold or purchased in North America and contains content that is different from its North American version.

10 09 08 07 06 05 04 03 02 01
20 15 14 13 12 11 10
CTF   ANL

When ordering this title, use ISBN 978-007-126778-6 or MHID 007-126778-6

Printed in Singapore

www.mhhe.com

personal interests and values. Employees are interested in developing skills that can h them remain employable with either their current employer or a future one. Given th increasing time demands of work, employees are also interested in maintaining balance between work and nonwork interests.

The chapter coverage of *Employee Training and Development* reflects the traditional as well as the broadening role of training and development in organizations. Chapter 1 introduces the student to the role of training and development in companies. Chapter 2, "Strategic Training," discusses how training practices and the organization of the training function can support business goals. Because companies are interested in reducing costs, the amount of resources allocated to training is likely to be determined by how much training and development activities help the company reach business goals. Topics related to designing training programs are covered in Chapters 3 through 6. Chapter 3, "Needs Assessment," discusses how to identify when training is appropriate. Chapter 4, "Learning: Theories and Program Design," addresses the learning process and characteristics of a learning environment, and it provides practical suggestions for designing training to ensure that learning occurs. Chapter 5, "Transfer of Training," emphasizes what should be done in the design of training and the work environment to ensure that training is used on the job. Chapter 6, "Training Evaluation," discusses how to evaluate training programs. Here the student is introduced to the concepts of identifying cost-effective training; evaluating the return on investment of training and learning; and determining if training outcomes related to learning, behavior, or performance have been reached. Chapters 7 and 8 cover training methods. Chapter 7, "Traditional Training Methods," discusses presentational methods (e.g., lecture), hands-on methods (e.g., on-the-job training, behavior modeling), and group methods (e.g., adventure learning). Chapter 8, "E-Learning and Use of Technology in Training," introduces the student to new technologies that are increasingly being used in training. These technology-based training methods include Web-based instruction, distance learning, e-learning, iPods, simulations, virtual worlds, and blended learning. Chapters 7 and 8 both conclude by comparing training methods on the basis of costs, benefits, and learning characteristics.

Chapter 9, "Employee Development," introduces the student to developmental methods (assessment, relationships, job experiences, and formal courses). Topics such as 360-degree feedback and mentoring are discussed. Chapter 10, "Special Issues in Training and Employee Development," discusses cross-cultural training, diversity training, school-to-work programs, and skill-based pay. Chapters 11 and 12 deal with careers and career management. Chapter 11, "Careers and Career Management," emphasizes the protean career and the career management process. Chapter 12, "Special Challenges in Career Management," deals with special issues that trainers, employees, and managers face. These issues include skills obsolescence, plateauing, career breaks, employee orientation and socialization, work-life balance, downsizing, outplacement, and retirement. Last, Chapter 13, "The Future of Training and Development," looks at how training and development might be different 10 or 20 years from now.

Employee Training and Development is based on my more than 20 years of teaching training and development courses to both graduate and undergraduate students. From this experience, I have realized that managers, consultants, trainers, and faculty working in a variety of disciplines (including education, psychology, business, and industrial relations) have contributed to the research and practice of training and development. As a result, the book is based on research conducted in several disciplines while offering a practical perspective. The book is appropriate for students in a number of programs. It suits both undergraduate and master's-level training courses in a variety of disciplines.

DISTINCTIVE FEATURES

This book has several distinctive features. First, my teaching experience has taught me that students become frustrated if they do not see research and theory in practice. As a result, one distinctive feature of the book is that each chapter begins with a vignette of a company practice that relates to the material covered in the chapter. Many examples of company practices are provided throughout the chapters. Each chapter ends with a case and related questions that give students the opportunity to apply the chapter's content to an actual training or development issue.

A second distinctive feature of the book is its topical coverage. The chapters included in Part 2 relate to training design (needs assessment, training methods, learning environment, transfer of training, and evaluation). Instructional design is still the "meat and potatoes" of training. Part 3 covers the more exciting part of training and development, that is, training and development methods. But as the role of managers and trainers broadens, they are increasingly involved in understanding career issues and career management. For example, managers and trainers need to be concerned with understanding generational differences in employees' career needs, career paths, cross-cultural training, diversity, outplacement, skills obsolescence, and succession planning—topics that fall outside the realm of instructional design. These topics are covered in the chapters included in Part 4 of the book.

The book begins with a discussion of the context for training and development. Part 1 includes chapters that cover the economic and workplace factors that are influencing trends in the training profession. In addition, these chapters discuss the need for training, development, and learning to become strategic (i.e., to contribute to business strategy and organizational goals). Why? In successful, effective training, all aspects of training—including training objectives, methods, evaluation, and even who conducts the training—relate to the business strategy. More and more companies are demanding that the training function and training practices support business goals; otherwise training may be outsourced or face funding cuts. Although students in business schools are exposed to strategic thinking, students in psychology and education who go on to become trainers need to understand the strategic perspective and how it relates to the organization of the training function and the type of training conducted.

Not only has technology changed the way we live and the way work is performed, but it also has influenced training practice. As a result, one chapter of the book is devoted entirely to the use of new technologies for training delivery and instruction, such as online learning, blended learning, iPods, virtual worlds, and personal data assistants (PDAs).

The book reflects the latest "hot topics" in the area of training. Some of the new topics discussed in the book are corporate universities, outsourcing training, developing and measuring human capital, learning management systems, competencies, knowledge management, e-learning, the use of mobile technology (such as iPods and PDAs) and virtual worlds (such as Second Life) for training. Each chapter contains the most recent academic research findings and company practices.

FEATURES DESIGNED TO AID LEARNING

Employee Training and Development provides several features to aid learning:

1. Each chapter lists objectives that highlight what the student is expected to learn in that chapter.
2. In-text examples and chapter openers feature companies from all industries including service, manufacturing, and retail, and nonprofit organizations.
3. Discussion questions at the end of each chapter help students learn the concepts presented in the chapter and understand potential applications of the material.
4. Important terms and concepts used in training and development are boldfaced in each chapter. Key terms are identified at the end of each chapter. These key terms are important to help the student understand the language of training.
5. Application assignments are useful for the students to put chapter content into practice. Most chapters include assignments that require the student to use the World Wide Web.
6. Cases at the end of each chapter and part help students apply what they have learned to training and development issues faced by actual companies.
7. Name and subject indexes at the end of the book help in finding key people and topics.

WHAT'S NEW IN THE FIFTH EDITION

I want to personally thank all of you who have adopted this book! Based on the comments of the reviewers of the fourth edition and training research and practice, I have made several improvements. Some important changes in the fifth edition of *Employee Training and Development* stand out:

*   Each chapter has been updated to include the most recent research findings and new best company practices. New examples have been added in each chapter's text.
*   All the chapter opening vignettes are new. For example, the opening vignette for Chapter 8, "E-Learning and use of Technology in Training," highlights how Dunkin' Donuts® is using a blended learning approach to help franchisees run a successful and profitable business.
*   This edition offers new and expanded coverage of such topics as outsourcing training, business-embedded training functions, knowledge management, blended learning, learning management systems, intangible assets and human capital, implications of the aging work force for training and development, new technologies in training, (including virtual worlds such as Second Life), and how to design programs, courses and lessons.
*   Each chapter ends with application assignments, including new and updated Web-based exercises. These assignments are also found on the book's Web site.
*   Each chapter concludes with a brief case that illustrates a training, development, or learning issue faced by a company. The case questions ask students to consider the issue and make recommendations based on the chapter content.
*   To help students better understand the connections between topics, the book is now organized into five different parts. Part 1 focuses on the context for training and development and includes a chapter devoted to strategic training. Part 2 includes coverage related to the fundamentals of designing training programs. Chapters in Part 2 focus on

needs assessment, learning theories and program design, transfer of training, and training evaluation. Part 3 focuses on training and development methods and includes chapters devoted to traditional training methods, e-learning and the use of technology in training, employee development, and special issues in employee development, such as managing diversity, succession planning, and cross-cultural preparation. Chapters in Part 4 cover career issues and how companies manage careers as well as challenges in career management, such as dealing with work-life conflict, retirement, and socialization. Finally, Part 5 provides a look at the future of training and development.

- New to this edition, *BusinessWeek* cases at the end of each of the five parts of the book look at training and development issues companies are facing and encourage students to critically evaluate each problem and apply what they have learned in that part of the text.

Acknowledgments

The author is only one of many important persons involved in writing a textbook. The fifth edition of this book would not have been possible without the energy and expertise of several persons. Editor Laura Spell gave me free rein to write the training book I wanted to write and provided helpful ideas and suggestions regarding how to improve the book. Jolynn Kilburg, developmental editor, and Michelle Gardner, project manager, both deserves kudos for ensuring that my ideas made sense and my writing was clear, concise and easy to understand.

I take full responsibility for any errors, omissions, or misstatements of fact in this book. However, regardless of your impression of the book, it would not have been this good had it not been for the reviewers. Special thanks to the manuscript reviewers who provided me with detailed comments that helped improve the fifth edition of the book for students and instructors. These reviewers include

Linda Matthews
University of Texas Pan American

Shumon Johnson
Columbia Southern University

Cindy Simerly
Lakeland Community College

John Knue
University of North Texas

Richard Wagner
University of Wisconsin—Whitewater

Dwight Frink
University of Mississippi

Raymond A. Noe

About the Author

Raymond A. Noe   *The Ohio State University*

Raymond A. Noe is the Robert and Anne Hoyt Designated Professor of Management at The Ohio State University. He has taught for more than 20 years at Big Ten universities. Before joining the faculty at Ohio State, he was a professor in the Department of Management at Michigan State University and the Industrial Relations Center of the Carlson School of Management, University of Minnesota. He received his B.S. in psychology from The Ohio State University and his M.A. and Ph.D. in psychology from Michigan State University. Professor Noe conducts research and teaches all levels of students—from undergraduates to executives—in human resource management, managerial skills, quantitative methods, human resource information systems, training and development, and organizational behavior. He has published articles in the *Academy of Management Journal, Academy of Management Review, Journal of Applied Psychology, Journal of Vocational Behavior,* and *Personnel Psychology.* Professor Noe is currently on the editorial boards of several journals, including *Journal of Applied Psychology, Personnel Psychology,* and *Journal of Organizational Behavior.* Besides *Employee Training and Development,* he has co-authored two other textbooks: *Fundamentals of Human Resource Management* and *Human Resource Management: Gaining a Competitive Advantage,* both published with McGraw-Hill/Irwin. Professor Noe has received awards for his teaching and research excellence, including the Herbert G. Heneman Distinguished Teaching Award in 1991, the Ernest J. McCormick Award for Distinguished Early Career Contribution from the Society for Industrial and Organizational Psychology in 1993, and the ASTD Outstanding Research Article of the Year Award for 2001. He is also a fellow of the Society of Industrial and Organizational Psychology.

Brief Contents

Contents

PART TWO
DESIGNING TRAINING   101

Chapter Three
Needs Assessment   102

Chapter Four
Learning: Theories and Program Design   138

Chapter Five
Transfer of Training   185

PART FOUR
CAREERS AND CAREER MANAGEMENT 443

Chapter Eleven
Careers and Career Management 444

Chapter Twelve
Special Challenges in Career Management 477

PART FIVE
THE FUTURE   521

Chapter Thirteen
The Future of Training and Development   522

The Context for Training and Development

Part One focuses on issues related to the context for training and development. Chapter 1, Introduction to Employee Training and Development, discusses why training and development are important to help companies successfully compete in today's business environment. The chapter provides an overview of training practices, the training profession, and how to design effective training (a topic that is covered in detail in Part Two, Training Designing). Chapter 2 discusses the strategic training and development process, organizational characteristics that influence training, various models for organizing the training department, how to market training to the rest of the company, and the advantages and disadvantages of outsourcing training.

Part One concludes with a case highlighting how PricewaterhouseCoopers is using training to cope with competitive challenges, reach business goals, and expand learning beyond the classroom and boardroom.

---

1. Introduction to Employee Training and Development
2. Strategic Training

Introduction to Employee Training and Development

Forces Affecting the Workplace Make Training a Key Ingredient for Company Success

Customer service, productivity, safety, employee retention and growth, the downturn in the economy, coping with the retirement of skilled employees—these are some of the issues affecting companies in all industries and sizes and influencing training practices. Four companies—Boston Pizza, Seattle City Light, Starbucks, and US Airways—provide examples of how these concerns have affected business and how training has helped them succeed.

Boston Pizza International, a casual restaurant chain, recognized that most of its managers understood the Boston Pizza concept but lacked the soft skills needed to be successful managers. At Boston Pizza College, managers learn and practice skills needed for successful store management. The learning initiative has paid off. Reports from secret shoppers and quality assurance visits have improved, and the restaurant chain has increased retention in an industry in which turnover can approach 300 percent.

Seattle City Light, the city's municipally owned electric company, expects more than a quarter of its work force to retire within the next five years. Seattle City Light is using training courses and interactions with more experienced employees and mentors to help employees learn new and innovative technologies as well as the electrical system's history to prevent electrical demand from overloading aging dams and power tunnels. Final exams and hands-on field tests are administered after training to ensure that new employees have acquired the knowledge and skills needed to be successful operators. The company also uses apprenticeship programs to develop technical employees such as hydro machinists. They are rotated throughout the plant to ensure they understand how their role and their interactions with other employees contribute to the effective and efficient operation of the utility.

Starbucks believes that the key to company success is its employees or partners. Training is integral to Starbucks's strategy for successfully competing in a weak economy in which customers are spending less. The attitudes and abilities of the partners who greet and serve customers are key to creating positive customer service and repeat business. Every new U.S. employee starts his or her job in paid training called "First Impressions." Store managers serve as trainers. The training focuses on coffee knowledge and how to create a positive experience for customers. Training specialists from headquarters work with store managers to ensure that training is consistent across all stores. The training courses are also frequently updated. Managers and assistant store managers take a 10-week retail management training course. Computer, leadership, and diversity training are available. Most corporate employees begin their careers with Starbucks in immersion training. Immersion training involves working in a Starbucks store and learning the business by experiencing making beverages and interacting with customers. When Starbucks enters a new international market, partners are brought to Seattle for 6 to 12 weeks of training and then sent to other locations to get store experience. To ensure that customers are delighted and that the coffee served meets high quality standards, Starbucks shuts down operations of most of its stores for a full day training event. The training event, known as "Perfect the Art of Espresso," was designed to help baristas deliver high quality espresso. One activity consisted of pulling an espresso shot and then evaluating the process and the product (was it the right color? Did it take too long or too short a time?). Staff discussions about how the training would benefit customers were held at each store. Also, to counter the perception that Starbucks is the home of the $4 cup of coffee, the company is training baristas to tell customers that the average price of a Starbucks beverage is less than $3 and that 90 percent of Starbucks drinks cost less than $4. Baristas are also encouraged to promote the company's new discounted pairing of coffee and breakfast for $3.95.

US Airways Group provides extensive training for flight attendants and pilots. Newly hired flight attendants receive five weeks of training, including an introduction to the aviation industry, and Airbus cabin simulators include "door trainers" to practice opening emergency exits under difficult evacuation conditions, such as total darkness and billowing smoke. Training also includes jumping into a pool and inflating a life raft and helping passengers into and out of a raft. Federal law requires annual classroom safety training for flight attendants and performance drills every two years. Pilot training includes practicing skills in a simulator that presents many different scenarios, such as both engines failing, and recreates the feelings and sounds experienced in flight, including turbulence. Forced landings and water ditchings are taught in the classroom. The pay-off for this type of extensive training was most evident in the spectacularly safe landing of Flight 1549 and its 155 passengers and flight crew in the Hudson River. Based on their almost automatic responses developed through years of training, flight attendants were able to calm passengers, prepare them for a crash landing, and open doors and inflate life rafts to assist in the orderly but quick exit of the slowly sinking airplane. The cockpit crew followed the training they received in how to cope with engine failure and successfully conducted a water landing.

Sources: Based on B. Hall, "The Top Training Priorities for 2006," *Training* (February 2006): 38–42; "Seattle's Strategy, Water Power & Dam Construction," *Training* (February 29, 2009): 36; "Tops of the Trade," *Human Resource Executive* (December 2005): 1, 16–25; G. Weber, "Preserving the Counter Culture," *Workforce Management* (February 2005): 28–34; S. McCartney, "Crash Courses for the Crew," *The Wall Street Journal* (January 27, 2009): D1, D8; J. Adamy, "Schultz's Second Act Jolts Starbucks," *The Wall Street Journal* (May 19, 2008): A1, A11; M. Weinstein, "Fresh Cup of Training," *Training* (May 2008): 10; J. Adamy, "Starbucks Plays Common Joe," *The Wall Street Journal* (February 9, 2009): B3.

INTRODUCTION

Boston Pizza, Seattle City Light, Starbucks, and US Airways illustrate how training can contribute to companies' competitiveness. **Competitiveness** refers to a company's ability to maintain and gain market share in an industry. Although they are different types of businesses, these four companies have training practices that have helped them gain a **competitive advantage** in their markets. That is, the training practices have helped them grow the business and improve customer service by providing employees with the knowledge and skills they need to be successful.

Companies are experiencing great change due to new technologies, rapid development of knowledge, globalization of business, and development of e-commerce. Also, companies have to take steps to attract, retain, and motivate their work forces. Training is not a luxury; it is a necessity if companies are to participate in the global and electronic marketplaces by offering high-quality products and services! Training prepares employees to use new technologies, function in new work systems such as virtual teams, and communicate and cooperate with peers or customers who may be from different cultural backgrounds.

Human resource management refers to the policies, practices, and systems that influence employees' behavior, attitudes, and performance. Human resource practices play a key role in attracting, motivating, rewarding, and retaining employees. Other human resource management practices include recruiting employees, selecting employees, designing work, compensating employees, and developing good labor and employee relations. Chapter 2, Strategic Training, details the importance placed on training in comparison to other human resource management practices. To be effective, training must play a strategic role in supporting the business.

Human resource management is one of several important functions in most companies. Other functions include accounting and finance, production and operations, research and development, and marketing. Keep in mind that although human resource management practices (such as training) can help companies gain a competitive advantage, the company needs to produce a product or provide a service that customers value. Without the financial resources and physical resources (e.g., equipment) needed to produce products or provide services, the company will not survive!

This chapter begins by defining training and discussing how the training function has evolved. Next, the forces that are shaping the workplace and learning are addressed. These forces influence the company's ability to successfully meet stakeholders' needs. The term **stakeholders** refers to shareholders, the community, customers, employees, and all the other parties that have an interest in seeing that the company succeeds. The discussion of the forces shaping the workplace (including technology, globalization, attracting and winning talent) highlights the role of training in helping companies gain a competitive advantage.

The second part of the chapter focuses on current trends in the training area. This section also introduces you to the trainer's role in a business and how the training function is organized. This section should help you understand current training practices, the types of jobs that trainers may perform, and the competencies needed to be a successful trainer (or, if you are a manager, to identify a successful trainer). The chapter concludes with an overview of the topics covered in the book.

WHAT IS TRAINING?

Training refers to a planned effort by a company to facilitate employees' learning of job-related competencies. These competencies include knowledge, skills, or behaviors that are critical for successful job performance. The goal of training is for employees to master the knowledge, skill, and behaviors emphasized in training programs and to apply them to their day-to-day activities. For a company to gain a competitive advantage, its training has to involve more than just basic skill development.[1] That is, to use training to gain a competitive advantage, a company should view training broadly as a way to create intellectual capital. Intellectual capital includes basic skills (skills needed to perform one's job), advanced skills (such as how to use technology to share information with other employees), an understanding of the customer or manufacturing system, and self-motivated creativity. Intellectual capital is discussed further in Chapter 2. Keep in mind that, traditionally, most of the emphasis on training has been at the basic and advanced skill levels. But some experts estimate that soon up to 85 percent of jobs in the United States and Europe will require extensive use of knowledge. Employees will be required not only to understand the service or product development system but also to share knowledge and to creatively use it to modify a product or serve the customer.

Many companies have adopted this broader perspective, which is known as high-leverage training. **High-leverage training** is linked to strategic business goals and objectives, uses an instructional design process to ensure that training is effective, and compares or benchmarks the company's training programs against training programs in other companies.[2]

High-leverage training practices also help to create working conditions that encourage continuous learning. **Continuous learning** requires employees to understand the entire work system, including the relationships among their jobs, their work units, and the company.[3] Employees are expected to acquire new skills and knowledge, apply them on the job, and share this information with other employees. Managers take an active role in identifying training needs and help to ensure that employees use training in their work. To facilitate the sharing of knowledge, managers may use informational maps that show where knowledge lies within the company (for example, directories that list what individuals do as well as the specialized knowledge they possess) and use technology such as groupware or the Internet that allows employees in various business units to work simultaneously on problems and share information.[4] Chapter 8 discusses how technology such as the Internet is being used for training.

The emphasis on high-leverage training has been accompanied by a movement to link training to performance improvement.[5] Companies have lost money on training because it is poorly designed, because it is not linked to a performance problem or business strategy, or because its outcomes have not been properly evaluated.[6] That is, companies have been investing money into training simply because of the belief that it is a good thing to do. The perspective that the training function exists to deliver programs to employees without a compelling business reason for doing so is being abandoned. Today, training is being evaluated not on the basis of the number of programs offered and training activity in the company but on how training addresses business needs related to learning, behavior change, and performance improvement. In fact, training is becoming more performance-focused. That is, training is used to improve employee performance, which leads to improved business results. Training is seen as one of several possible solutions to improve performance. Other solutions include actions such as changing the job or increasing employee motivation through pay and incentives. Today there is a greater emphasis on[7]

- Providing educational opportunities for all employees. These educational opportunities may include training programs, but they also include support for taking courses offered outside the company, self-study, and learning through job rotation.
- Performance improvement as an ongoing process that is directly measurable rather than a one-time training event.
- Demonstrating to executives, managers, and trainees the benefits of training.
- Learning as a lifelong event in which senior management, trainer managers, and employees have ownership.
- Training being used to help attain strategic business objectives, which help companies gain a competitive advantage.

PricewaterhouseCoopers is a good example of a company that uses high-leverage training.[8] Its Learning and Education (L&E) team was restructured to better link it to the business goals related to value and impact. L&E works with the business to understand what it wants education to be. It ensures ongoing innovation in training delivery and instructional methods by evaluating emerging technologies and using them in small pilot projects. The chief learning officer in charge of L&E is a member of the company's leadership team, which gives that individual the opportunity to discuss ideas regarding training methods, delivery, and content with other top-level managers. L&E sponsors traditional and virtual classroom courses, self-study, team-based learning, action learning projects, coaching and mentoring, and conferences, and it has served more than 150,000 users each year, with over 6,000 courses, 12,000 classroom-based training sessions, and 19,000 Web-based training sessions.

PricewaterhouseCoopers uses a learning management system to create a single access point for training activities. To help employees learn on an as-needed basis, the company's e-learning includes video and audio conferencing, virtual classrooms, and webcasting. To evaluate the success of training, L&E considers its influence on outcomes, such as retention of top people. Also, focus groups are used to determine whether trainees and managers are satisfied with the training. A program on sustainability was designed to help partners understand how to provide solutions for their clients. The company's investment in the program has paid off. The company believes it has achieved a return on investment of more than 1,000 percent in new business sold and reputation gains in the marketplace. In the future, L&E plans to further strengthen the relationship between training, development, and the business by focusing on how it can make learning even more accessible and closer to the point where employees need it. L&E wants to integrate learning and knowledge to speed employees' development and improve their competencies.

This discussion is not meant to underestimate the importance of "traditional training" (a focus on acquisition of knowledge, skills, and abilities), but it should alert you that for many companies training is evolving from a focus on skills to an emphasis on learning and creating and sharing knowledge. This evolution of training is discussed in Chapter 2.

DESIGNING EFFECTIVE TRAINING

The **training design process** refers to a systematic approach for developing training programs. Figure 1.1 presents the seven steps in this process. Step 1 is to conduct a needs assessment, which is necessary to identify whether training is needed. Step 2 is to ensure that employees have the motivation and basic skills necessary to master the training content. Step 3 is to create a learning environment that has the features necessary for learning to occur. Step 4 is to ensure that trainees apply the training content to their jobs. This step involves having the trainee understand how to manage skill improvement as well as getting co-worker and manager support.

FIGURE 1.1   Training Design Process

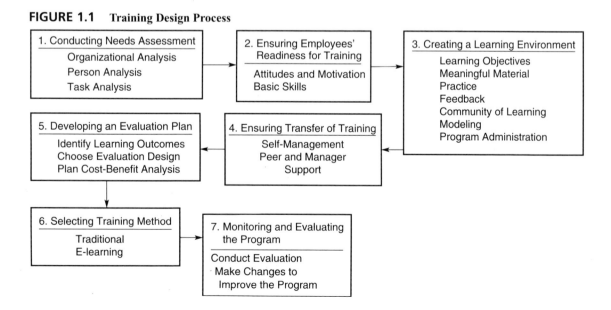

Step 5 is to develop an evaluation plan. Developing an evaluation plan includes identifying what types of outcomes training is expected to influence (for example, learning, behavior, skills), choosing an evaluation design that allows you to determine the influence of training on these outcomes, and planning how to demonstrate how training affects the "bottom line" (that is, using a cost-benefit analysis to determine the monetary benefits resulting from training). Step 6 is to choose the training method based on the learning objectives and learning environment. This step may include a traditional training method of face-to-face interaction with a trainer or e-learning using CD-ROM or Web-based training. Step 7 is to evaluate the program and make changes in it or revisit any of the earlier steps in the process to improve the program so that learning, behavior, change, and the other learning objectives are obtained.

The training design process shown in Figure 1.1 is based on principles of Instructional System Design. **Instructional System Design (ISD)** refers to a process for designing and developing training programs. There is not one universally accepted instructional systems development model. The training design process sometimes is referred to as the ADDIE model because it includes analysis, design, development, implementation, and evaluation.[9] In Figure 1.1, Step 1, conducting needs assessment, and Step 2, ensuring employees' readiness for training, are related to analysis. The next three steps—creating a learning environment, ensuring transfer of training, and developing an evaluation plan—are design issues. Step 6, selecting and using a training method, relates to implementation. Step 7, monitoring and evaluating the program, relates to evaluation. Regardless of the specific ISD approach used, all share the following assumptions:[10]

- Training design is effective only if it helps employees reach instructional or training goals and objectives.
- Measurable learning objectives should be identified before the training program begins.
- Evaluation plays an important part in planning and choosing a training method, monitoring the training program, and suggesting changes to the training design process.

American Infrastructure (AI), located in Worcester, Pennsylvania, uses the ADDIE model to design training for its employees involved in construction and mining.[11] Templates based on the ADDIE model are used to design and develop training and development programs. AI uses the templates to ensure that needs assessment is conducted and evaluation is considered as training and development programs are being designed. The use of the templates also helps to show that training and development programs are aligned with the business strategy and are designed to contribute to important business results—which helps AI get the necessary financial support and encouragement from key organizational stakeholders.

Some training professionals argue that the ISD model is flawed for several reasons.[12] First, in organizations the training design process rarely follows the neat, orderly, step-by-step approach of activities shown in Figure 1.1. Second, in trying to standardize their own ISD method used in the training function, some organizations require trainers to provide detailed documents of each activity found in the model. This adds time and cost to developing a training program. Third, the ISD implies an end point: evaluation. However, good instructional design requires an iterative process of design, execution, evaluation, and reconsideration of the needs that the program was designed to meet as well as the learning environment, the transfer of training, and all the other activities in the ISD process. Despite these criticisms, the ISD model can be considered a set of general guidelines that trainers need to follow to ensure effective training.

The training design process should be systematic yet flexible enough to adapt to business needs. Different steps may be completed simultaneously. Keep in mind that designing training unsytematically will reduce the benefits that can be realized. For example, choosing a training method before determining training needs or ensuring employees' readiness for training increases the risk that the method chosen will not be the most effective one for meeting training needs. Also, training may not even be necessary and may result in a waste of time and money! Employees may have the knowledge, skills, or behavior they need but simply not be motivated to use them.

The introduction of new technologies such as podcasting (discussed in Chapter 8) highlights a shift from trainees having to learn from an instructor in one location to trainees learning independently and not being bound to learn in the workplace. Still, good training design requires determining the trainees' needs, identifying resources so that trainees can learn what they need to know, and providing them with access to reference materials and knowledge bases when they encounter problems, issues, or questions on the job.[13]

The development of a Web-based training program focusing on teaching managers skills needed to run effective business meetings provides a good example of use of the instructional design process. The first step of the process, needs assessment, involved determining that managers lacked skills for conducting effective meetings and helped to identify the type of meetings that managers were involved in. The needs assessment process involved interviewing managers and observing meetings. The needs assessment process also identified the most appropriate training method.

Because the managers were geographically dispersed and had easy access to computers and because the company wanted a self-directed, self-paced program that the managers could complete during free time in their work schedule, the training designers and company management decided that Web-based training was the appropriate method. Because training was going to be conducted over the Web, the designers had to be sure that managers could access the Web and were familiar with tools for using the Web (e.g., Web browsers). This relates to determining the managers' readiness for training.

The next step was to create a positive learning environment on the Web. Designers made sure that the program objectives were clearly stated to the trainees and provided opportunities within the program for exercises and feedback. For example, trainees were asked to prepare an outline for the steps they would take to conduct an effective meeting. The designers built into the program a feedback system that indicated to the managers which of the steps they outlined were correct and which needed to be changed. The designers also built in assessment tests allowing the trainees to receive feedback through the program and to skip ahead or return to earlier material based on their scores on the tests. The assessment included a test of meeting skills that the managers completed both prior to and after completing the program. The assessment tests were stored in a data bank that the company could use to evaluate whether trainees' meeting skills improved from pretraining levels.

THE FORCES INFLUENCING WORKING AND LEARNING

Table 1.1 illustrates the forces that are influencing working and learning. Globalization of business, demographic changes, new technologies, and economic changes are several of the forces shown in Table 1.1 that influence all aspects of our lives: how we purchase products and services, how we learn, how we communicate with each other, and what we value in our lives and on the job.[14] These forces are affecting individuals, communities, businesses, and society. To survive, companies must address these forces—with training playing an important role.

Economic Cycles

The U.S. economy is currently in a recession. In the U.S., the current economic downturn could be the worst since the years following World War II. The economy has lost 5.1 million since the beginning 2008—the most since the end of World War II—and the unemployment rate grew to over 8.5 percent, the highest since 1983.[15] Most consumers have seen their homes lose value, as well as experienced substantial declines in retirement savings and household wealth, due to the collapse of the stock market. The recession has a number of probable causes, including the subprime lending scandals and the collapse and failure of major financial institutions such as Bear Sterns, Lehman Brothers, and Merrill-Lynch.[16] All of the bad news has contributed to a lack of confidence in the economy, making it difficult for businesses and consumers alike to obtain credit and loans. Most industries, especially retailers, automakers, manufacturing, and construction, have not escaped the crisis. Retailers reported record sales declines for the 2008 holiday season as consumers reduced their holiday spending. The Big Three automakers sought money from the government to avoid bankruptcy and the elimination of hundreds of thousands of jobs. The highest unemployment rate at the end of 2008 was 15.3 percent in the construction sector as plans for new homes and office buildings were postponed or canceled. The economic slowdown has not been limited to the U.S. The economies of China and India have slowed and Europe, Mexico, and Japan have slipped into recession. President Obama has proposed and the Congress has passed an economic stimulus plan that is intended to create jobs and increase consumer and investor confidence. However, its impact may not be realized for several years.

The poor economy means more companies are downsizing their work force, delaying plans for new operations and growth, and revisiting training and development and human resource budgets to cut unnecessary programs and costs. For example, just in January 2009 more than 70,000 job cuts were announced, impacting employees from Pfizer, Texas Instruments, Home Depot, General Motors, Boeing, Alcoa, Andersen, and World Wrestling

TABLE 1.1
Forces Influencing Working and Learning

Economic cycles
Globalization
Increased value placed on intangible assets and human capital
Focus on link to business strategy
Changing demographics and diversity of the work force
Talent Management
Customer service and quality emphasis
New technology
High-performance work systems

Entertainment.[17] Employees are delaying retirement and newly retired employees are returning to work out of necessity because of losses affecting their retirement assets.

One estimate is that companies plan to cut their training budgets over 10 percent in response to the economic crisis.[18] However, such economic times also provide an opportunity for companies to take a closer look at training and development to identify those activities that are critical for supporting the business strategy as well as those mandated by law (such as safety training or sexual harassment training). Also, training technologies using iPods and online learning will likely receive more serious consideration to reduce training and development costs (travel costs, instructor costs) and increase employees' access to training. For example, Philips Electronics is cutting its training budget but will continue to offer its Inspire program for high potential employees, emphasizing business strategy and personal leadership topics. Philips believes that investing in leadership development will help the company weather the recession and prepare for economic recovery. Likewise, Estée Lauder Companies, the cosmetics maker, has realized lower profits and sales, resulting in the elimination of over 2,000 jobs over the next two years. But Estée Lauder is continuing its leadership development programs, which will emphasize innovation and managing change in turbulent business conditions. Despite the recession, talent retention is still an important concern. Some companies are creating discretionary bonus pools to reward employees who may be recruited by other companies. To keep employees engaged, Best Buy uses online surveys to get employees' opinions and suggestions regarding how to cut costs.

Globalization

Every business must be prepared to deal with the global economy. Global business expansion has been made easier by technology. The Internet allows data and information to be instantly accessible and sent around the world. The Internet, e-mail, and video conferencing enable business deals to be completed between companies thousands of miles apart.

Globalization is not limited to any particular sector of the economy, product market, or company size.[19] Companies without international operations may buy or use goods that have been produced overseas, hire employees with diverse backgrounds, or compete with foreign-owned companies operating within the United States.

Many companies are entering international markets by exporting their products overseas, building manufacturing facilities or service centers in other countries, entering into alliances with foreign companies, and engaging in e-commerce. Developing nations such as Taiwan, Indonesia, and China may account for over 60 percent of the world economy by 2020.[20] For example, Coca-Cola is trying to build a global juice business through deals in Latin America, Russia, and China.[21] Power Curbers Inc., a small North Carolina manufacturer, sells construction-related machinery to more than 70 countries, including Australia, China, Central America, and Western Europe. Its equipment helped complete the Eurotunnel under the English Channel. Technical Materials, a 250-employee Rhode Island company, has been exporting high-technology materials systems to China. At Texas Instruments (TI), with approximately 30,000 employees worldwide, 80 percent of sales come from customers outside the United States. More than 50 percent of the wireless phones sold worldwide contain TI's digital signal processing.

Global companies are struggling both to find and retain talented employees, especially in emerging markets. Companies are moving into China, India, Eastern Europe, the Middle

East, Southeast Asia, and Latin America, but the demand for talented employees exceeds the supply. Also, companies often place successful U.S. managers in charge of overseas operations but they lack the cultural understanding necessary to attract, motivate, and retain talented employees. To cope with these problems, companies are taking actions to better prepare their managers and their families for overseas assignments and to ensure that training and development opportunities are available for global employees. Cross-cultural training prepares employees and their families to understand the culture and norms of the country to which they are being relocated and assists in their return to their home country after the assignment. Cross-cultural training is discussed in Chapter 10.

IBM obtains more than two-thirds of its revenue from outside the U.S. and is seeking to build team leadership in order to compete in emerging markets around the world. IBM's Corporate Service Program donates the time and services of about 600 employees for projects in countries such as Turkey, Romania, Ghana, Vietnam, the Phillipines, and Tanzania.[22] The goal of the program is to develop a leadership team to learn about the needs and the culture of these countries while at the same time providing valuable community service. For example, eight IBM employees from five countries traveled to Timisoara, Romania. Each employee was assigned to help a different company or non-profit organization. One software-development manager helped GreenForest, a manufacturer of office, hotel, school, and industrial furniture, reach its goal of cutting costs and becoming more efficient by recommending the computer equipment and systems needed to increase production and exports to Western Europe. Another employee worked with a nonprofit organization that offers services to disabled adults. Besides benefiting the companies, the employees have also found that the experience has helped them understand cultural differences, improve their communication and teamwork skills, and gain insight into global marketing and strategy.

A.P. Moller-Maersk Group is a world leader in shipping, transportation, and logistics.[23] A.P. Moller-Maersk has very selective hiring as well as extensive training and development practices. In its entry-level Maersk International Shipping Education program, one employee is hired for approximately every 200 applicants. The new employees receive job assignments that help them understand the entire company and its global operations, not just one functional area. The company also provides extensive coaching and assessment of managerial potential and provides regular feedback to keep employees focused on the things they need to do to reach their career goals.

Globalization also means that employees working in the United States will come from other countries. The United States takes more than 1 million immigrants, some who are illegal. Immigrants provide scientific talent as well as fill low-wage jobs. Immigrants will likely account for an additional million persons in the work force each year through 2012.[24] The impact of immigration will be especially large in certain areas of the United States, including the states on the Pacific Coast, where 70 percent of new entrants to the work force are immigrants.[25] Many of these immigrants will have to be trained to understand the U.S. culture. U.S. employees will need skills to improve their ability to communicate with employees from different cultures. The terrorist attacks of 9/11 have not changed the use of immigrants but have raised security issues, resulting in more deliberate approval of visas (and longer waits for hiring to be approved).

Globalization also means that U.S. companies may move jobs overseas; **offshoring** refers to the process of moving jobs from the United States to other locations in the world.

For example, many technical workers are being asked to train their foreign replacements who return to their home countries once the training is completed.[26] The U.S. workers either lose their jobs or are offered other jobs at lower wages. There are three reasons this is occurring. First, the U.S. visa program allows companies to transfer workers from overseas offices to the United States for seven years. The workers can continue to receive their home country wage, which is usually much less than the wages received by U.S. employees (e.g., Indian workers receive about $10 per hour compared to $60 per hour for U.S. programmers). Second, U.S. colleges are graduating fewer U.S.-born engineers, so companies have to look overseas to hire the best employees. China graduates about four times the number of engineers, although they are not all trained at the same level as U.S. engineers.[27] Japan graduates twice as many engineers and South Korea graduates nearly as many engineers as the U.S. Third, more talented employees may be available outside the United States.

In contrast to the computer and printer manufacturer Hewlett-Packard, which hired its first foreign workers 20 years after its founding in 1939, search engine Google employed people outside the United States just three years after its 1998 start.[28] OfficeTiger, which provides business services to banks, insurance companies, and other clients, has 200 employees in the United States and 2,000 in southern India. Whether its clients need typesetting or marketing research, Indian employees can submit their work over the Internet. Because Indian workers are generally paid only one-fifth of U.S. earnings for comparable jobs, OfficeTiger offers attractive prices. The company is growing and expects that two-thirds of its future hires will be in India, Sri Lanka, and countries other than the United States.[29] Regardless of company size, talent comparable to that in the United States is available overseas at lower costs.[30] GEN3 Partners, a Boston-based product innovation company, has a research and development lab in Saint Petersburg, Russia, that employs 90 scientists and engineers, all with advanced degrees. Russia has a tradition of scientific excellence, and salaries are lower than for comparable talent in the United States. For small companies such as Cobalt Group, a Seattle, Washington, automotive online services company, labor costs for its 50 research and development engineers working in a technology center in India are about one-third of U.S. labor costs.

However, as a result of 9/11 and concerns that American employees should get the first chance at U.S. jobs, new immigration rules have made it difficult for immigrants to seek employment, and the number of visas permitted to be issued has not recently been expanded. For example, in 2008 only 65,000 H-1B visas were made available, and all were taken on the first day they were made available.[31]

Increased Value Placed on Intangible Assets and Human Capital

Today more and more companies are interested in intangible assets and human capital as a way to gain an advantage over competitors. Training and development can help a company's competitiveness by directly increasing the company's value through contributing to intangible assets. A company's value includes three types of assets that are critical for the company to provide goods and services: financial assets (cash and securities), physical assets (property, plant, equipment), and intangible assets. Table 1.2 provides examples of intangible assets, which consist of human capital, customer capital, social capital, and intellectual capital. **Human capital** refers to the sum of the attributes, life experiences, knowledge, inventiveness, energy, and enthusiasm that the company's employees invest in

TABLE 1.2
Examples of Intangible Assets

Source: Based on L. Weatherly, *Human Capital—The Elusive Asset* (Alexandria, VA: SHRM Research Quarterly, 2003); E. Holton and S. Naquin, "New Metrics for Employee Development," *Performance Improvement Quarterly* 17 (2004): 56–80; M. Huselid, B. Becker, and R. Beatty, *The Workforce Scorecard* (Boston, MA: Harvard University Press, 2005).

Human Capital
- Tacit knowledge
- Education
- Work-related know-how
- Work-related competence

Customer Capital
- Customer relationships
- Brands
- Customer loyalty
- Distribution channels

Social Capital
- Corporate culture
- Management philosophy
- Management practices
- Informal networking systems
- Coaching/mentoring relationships

Intellectual Capital
- Patents
- Copyrights
- Trade secrets
- Intellectual property

their work.[32] **Intellectual capital** refers to the codified knowledge that exists in a company. **Social capital** refers to relationships in the company. **Customer capital** refers to the value of relationships with persons or other organizations outside the company for accomplishing the goals of the company (e.g., relationships with suppliers, customers, vendors, government agencies). Intangible assets are equally as valuable as financial and physical assets but they are not something that can be touched and they are nonmonetary.

Intangible assets have been shown to be responsible for a company's competitive advantage. A study by the American Society for Training and Development of more than 500 publicly traded U.S.-based companies found that companies that invested the most in training and development had a shareholder return that was 86 percent higher than companies in the bottom half and 46 percent higher than the market average.[33] Training and development have a direct influence on human and social capital because they affect education, work-related know-how and competence, and work relationships. Training and development can have an indirect influence on customer and social capital by helping employees better serve customers and by providing them with the knowledge needed to create patents and intellectual property.

Intangible assets also contribute to a company's competitive advantage because they are difficult to duplicate or imitate.[34] For example, consider companies in the airline industry. Southwest Airlines consistently is profitable and ranked high in on-time arrivals and other indicators of airline success.[35] One of the distinctions between Southwest Airlines and its competitors is how it treats its employees. For example, Southwest has a policy of no layoffs and was able to maintain this record even during the difficult time for airlines following 9/11. Southwest also emphasizes training and development, which provide its employees with skills to perform multiple jobs. This benefit allows Southwest airplanes to be quickly cleaned and serviced at airports because employees have multiple skill sets that can be applied to various aspects of readying an aircraft for departure. As a result of these human resource policies, Southwest employees are loyal, productive, and flexible (which contributes to the success of the airline). Other airlines may have similar or greater levels of financial assets and may have physical assets that are comparable to Southwest's (e.g., same type of airplanes, similar gates), but what contributes to Southwest's success and gives the company a competitive advantage are its intangible assets in the form of human capital. American Airlines and United Airlines have similar (or greater!) financial and physical assets but have not been successful in competing with Southwest by offering flights on the same routes.

Recognizing the importance of human capital and social capital, John Chambers, CEO of Cisco Systems, has transformed the company from one with one or two primary products, in which the most important decisions are made by the top 10 people in the company, to one where networks of employee councils and boards and Web 2.0 applications encourage executives to work together.[36] Business unit leaders now share responsibilities for each other's success. Cisco's directory is designed to help anyone inside the company find answers to questions, a product demo, or the right person to speak to a customer in any language, anywhere in the world. As a result of its improved face-to-face and electronic collaboration, Cisco Systems has been able to get products to market faster.

Chapters 7, 8, and 9 discuss specific training and development activities that contribute to the development of human and social capital. How to measure human capital is explained in Chapter 6, Training Evaluation. The value of intangible assets and human capital has three important implications:

(1) a focus on knowledge worker,

(2) employee engagement, and

(3) an increased emphasis on adapting to change and continuous learning.

Focus on Knowledge Workers

One way that a company can increase its intangible assets, specifically human capital, is by focusing on attracting, developing, and retaining knowledge workers. **Knowledge workers** are employees who contribute to the company not through manual labor but through what they know, perhaps about customers or a specialized body of knowledge. Employees cannot simply be ordered to perform tasks; they must share knowledge and collaborate on solutions. Knowledge workers contribute specialized knowledge that their managers may not have, such as information about customers, and managers depend on these knowledge workers to share that information. Knowledge workers have many job opportunities. If they choose, they can leave a company and take their knowledge to a competitor. Knowledge workers are in demand because of the growth of jobs requiring them.

Employee Engagement

To fully benefit from employees' knowledge requires a management style that focuses on engaging employees. **Employee engagement** refers to the degree to which employees are fully involved in their work and the strength of their commitment to their job and the company.[37] Employees who are engaged in their work and committed to their companies give those companies a competitive advantage, including higher productivity, better customer service, and lower turnover.[38] What is the state of employee engagement in U.S. companies? One survey of 50,000 employees across different companies showed that about 13 percent of employees are disengaged, poor performers who put minimal effort into the job and are likely to leave the organization and about 76 percent of employees exhibit moderate engagement. That is, they are marginally committed to the company and perform their jobs to the level expected by their manager. Only 11 percent of employees surveyed have high levels of engagement. That is, they exhibit strong commitment to the company and are high performers who help other employees with their work, volunteer for new responsibilities, and are constantly looking for ways to perform their jobs better.[39]

Perhaps the best way to understand engagement is to consider how companies measure employee engagement. Companies measure employees' engagement levels with attitude or opinion surveys. Although the types of questions asked on these surveys vary from company to company, research suggests the questions generally measure themes such as pride in the company, satisfaction with the job, prospects for future growth with the company, and opportunity to perform challenging work.[40] As you probably realize, employees' engagement is influenced by most human resource management practices, including training and development. A survey of senior level human resource and learning professionals conducted by ASTD found that over 50 percent reported engagement was affected by the frequency, quality, and number of workplace learning opportunities, employee orientation programs, and learning that occurred through job assignments (a type of development activity).[41] Training and development gives employees an opportunity for personal growth within the company and helps provide the company with the knowledge and skills it needs to gain a competitive advantage. Using training delivery methods that provide employees with the flexibility to manage their personal learning while balancing other work and nonwork responsibilities, such as online learning, helps build employee commitment to the company.

Change and Continuous Learning

In addition to acquiring and retaining knowledge workers, companies need to be able to adapt to change. **Change** refers to the adoption of a new idea or behavior by a company. Technological advances, changes in the work force or government regulations, globalization, and new competitors are among the many factors that require companies to change. Change is inevitable in companies as products, companies, and entire industries experience shorter life cycles.[42] The characteristics of an effective change process are discussed in Chapter 13.

A changing environment means that all employees must embrace a philosophy of learning. A **learning organization** embraces a culture of lifelong learning, enabling all employees to continually acquire and share knowledge. Improvements in product or service quality do not stop when formal training is completed.[43] Employees need to have the financial, time, and content resources (courses, experiences, development opportunities) available to increase their knowledge. Managers take an active role in identifying training needs and helping to ensure that employees use training in their work. Also, employees should be actively encouraged to share knowledge with colleagues and other work groups across the company using e-mail and the Internet.[44] Chapter 5 discusses learning organizations and knowledge management in detail. For a learning organization to be successful, teams of employees must collaborate to meet customer needs. Managers need to empower employees to share knowledge, identify problems, and make decisions. This allows the company to continuously experiment and improve.

As more companies become knowledge-based, it's important that they promote and capture learning at the employee, team, and company levels. Buckman Laboratories is known for its knowledge management practices.[45] Buckman Laboratories develops and markets specialty chemicals. Buckman's CEO, Robert Buckman, has developed an organizational culture, technology, and work processes that encourage the sharing of knowledge. Employees have laptop computers so they can share information anywhere and anytime using the Internet. The company rewards innovation and knowledge creation and exchange by including the sales of new products as part of employees' performance evaluations. Buckman also changed the focus of the company's information systems department, renaming it *knowledge transfer department* to better match the service it is supposed to provide.

At American Express, the training organization was rebranded from Operations Training into what is now called the American Express Learning Network.[46] The department's new goal is to position the American Express work force so it can better serve its customers. At W.W. Grainger, the Grainger Learning Center is dedicated to developing sales and customer service representatives to better understand the operations of business customers and to better position training program offerings to meet business needs. It sponsors learning experiences based on the company's strategy specifically requested by senior executives.

Focus on Link to Business Strategy

Given the important role that intangible assets and human capital play in a company's competitiveness, managers are beginning to see a more important role for training and development as a means to support a company's business strategy, that is, its plans for meeting broad goals such as profitability, market share, and quality. Managers expect training and development professionals to design and develop learning activities that will help the company successfully implement its strategy and reach business goals. Strategic training will be discussed in greater detail in Chapter 2.

Changing Demographics and Diversity of the Work Force

Companies face several challenges as a result of increased demographics and diversity of the work force. Population is the single most important factor in determining the size and composition of the labor force, which is composed of people who are either working or looking for work. The civilian labor force is projected to increase by 13 million between 2006 and 2016, reaching 164.2 million by 2016. The work force will be older and more culturally diverse than at any time in the past 40 years.

Increase in Ethnic and Racial Diversity

The U.S. labor force will continue to grow more ethnically and racially diverse due to immigration, increased participation of minorities in the work force, and higher minority fertility rates. Between 2006–2016, the labor force growth rates for Hispanics and Asians are expected to be much faster than the rates for white non-Hispanics.[47] By 2016 the work force is projected to be 80 percent white, 12 percent African American, and 8 percent Asian and other ethnic or cultural groups. Approximately 16 percent of the labor force will be of Hispanic origin. The Asian and Hispanic labor force increases are due to immigration trends and higher-than-average birth rates. The labor force participation rates of women in nearly all age groups are projected to increase. Not only must companies face the issues of race, gender, ethnicity, and nationality to provide a fair workplace, but they must also develop training programs to help immigrants acquire the technical and customer service skills required in a service economy.

Aging Work Force

Figure 1.2 compares the projected distribution of the age of the work force in 2006 and 2016. In 2016, baby boomers will be 50 to 68 years old, and this age group will grow significantly between 2006 and 2016. The labor force will continue to age and the size of the 16–24-year-old youth labor force will decrease to its lowest level in 30 years. The 55 years and older segment of the work force is expected to grow by approximately 47 percent between 2006–2016, more than five times the 8.5 percent growth projected for the entire work force.[48] The labor force participation of those 55 years and older is expected to grow because older individuals are leading healthier and longer lives than in the past, providing the opportunity to work more years. In addition, the high cost of health insurance and decrease in health benefits will cause many employees to keep working to maintain their employer-based insurance or will prompt them to return to work after retirement to obtain health insurance through their employer. Also, the trend toward pension plans based on individuals' contributions to them, rather than years of service, will provide yet another incentive for older employees to continue working.

The aging population means that companies are likely to employ a growing share of older workers—many of them in their second or third career. Older people want to work, and many say they plan a working retirement. Despite myths to the contrary, worker performance and learning in most jobs is not adversely affected by aging.[49] Older employees are willing and able to learn new technology. An emerging trend is for qualified older employees to ask to work part-time or for only a few months at a time as a means to transition to retirement. Employees and companies are redefining what it means to be retired to include second careers as well as part-time and temporary work assignments. Another source of work force diversity is greater access to the workplace for people with disabilities.

FIGURE 1.2
Comparison of the Age of the 2006 and 2016 Labor Force

Source: Based on M. Toossi, "Labor Force Projections to 2016: More Workers in Their Golden Years," *Monthly Labor Review* (November 2007): 33–52.

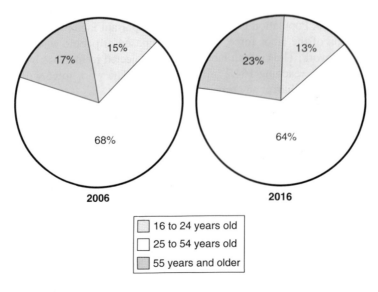

2006

2016

16 to 24 years old
25 to 54 years old
55 years and older

Because of this diversity, it is unlikely that all employees will hold similar work values. Research suggests that to maximize employees' motivation and commitment to company goals, employees should be given the opportunity to develop their skills, meet their interests, and balance work and nonwork activities.

Consider how Borders Group, the bookstore, is capitalizing on older workers through hiring and retention.[50] Because 50 percent of the books purchased in the U.S. are made by customers over age 45, Borders believed that older workers could relate better to its customers. To attract and retain older workers, Borders added medical and dental benefits for part-time workers. The company is planning to add a "passport" program enabling employees to work half-time in one part of the country and half-time at a different store in another part of the country. This accommodates the needs of older employees who may relocate to warmer climates such as Florida during the winter months, but otherwise live in other areas of the U.S. the rest of the year. Sixteen percent of Borders's employees are over the age of 50, over 75 percent more than when the program first started. Borders's investment is having a positive impact on retention. The turnover rate for workers over age 50 is 10 times less than the rate for those under 30 years old, and turnover has dropped 30 percent since the start of the program.

Table 1.3 shows how companies can use this increased diversity to provide a competitive advantage. Training plays a key role in ensuring that employees accept and work more

TABLE 1.3
How Managing Cultural Diversity Can Provide Competitive Advantage

Source: T. H. Cox and S. Blake, "Managing Cultural Diversity: Implications for Organizational Competitiveness," *Academy of Management Executive* 5 (1991): 47; N. Lockwood, *Workplace Diversity: Leveraging the Power of Difference for Competitive Advantage* (Alexandria, VA: Society for Human Resource Management, 2005).

Argument	Rationale
1. Cost	As organizations become more diverse, the cost of a poor job in integrating workers will increase. Companies that handle this well will create cost advantages over those that don't.
2. Employee Attraction and Retention	Companies develop reputations on favorability as prospective employers for women and ethnic minorities. Those with the best reputations for managing diversity will be the most attractive employers for women and other minority groups. As the labor pool shrinks and changes composition, this edge will become increasingly important.
3. Market Share	For multinational organizations, the insight and cultural sensitivity that members with roots in other countries bring to the marketing effort should improve these efforts in important ways. The same rationale applies to marketing to subpopulations within domestic operations.
4. Creativity	Diversity of perspectives and less emphasis on conformity to norms of the past (which characterize the modern approach to management of diversity) should improve the level of creativity.
5. Problem-solving	Heterogeneity in decisions and problem-solving groups potentially produces better decisions through a wider range of perspectives and more thorough critical analysis of issues.
6. Flexibility	Greater adaptability in a rapidly changing market.

effectively with each other. To successfully manage a diverse work force, managers and employees must be trained in a new set of skills, including:

1. Communicating effectively with employees from a wide variety of backgrounds.
2. Coaching, training, and developing employees of different ages, educational backgrounds, ethnicities, physical abilities, and races.
3. Providing performance feedback that is free of values and stereotypes based on gender, ethnicity, or physical handicap.
4. Training managers to recognize and respond to generational differences.
5. Creating a work environment that allows employees of all backgrounds to be creative and innovative.[51]

Johnson & Johnson's analysis of women's leadership programs showed that, although the company was not experiencing greater turnover of women, it had been ineffective in reaching multicultural women and women of color.[52] Johnson & Johnson has since created a program, titled "Crossing the Finish Line," for high-performing, high-potential multicultural women and women of color. The program includes a two and one-half day project assignment in which participants have open conversations with their managers and with executives, including the CEO and the vice chair of the company. The program helps Johnson & Johnson identify women who should be given new development opportunities, as well as help them understand that they must be visible, establish networks, and take the initiative to ask for development assignments. Also, the program educates managers about cultural differences and creates an awareness of how an employee's culture might affect his or her career.

People with disabilities also need greater access to the workplace. Wiscraft Inc., a Milwaukee company, contracts with companies such as Briggs & Stratton Corporation and Harley-Davidson to do assembly, packaging, and machining work.[53] At least 75 percent of Wiscraft's employees are legally blind. But the company is not a charity. It competes with other companies for contracts. It receives no subsidies from local, state, or federal governments. Employees have to rely on public transportation or friends or relatives to get to work. Kathy Walters says she could have worked at another company but chose Wiscraft because of its supportive culture. Walters, who is legally blind, believes she would have had trouble finding a job that offered health benefits and paid as well as her job at Wiscraft. The company has received ISO 9001:2000 certification, evidence that it provides high quality work and can compete internationally.

A survey conducted at Ernst & Young LLC found that generation Y employees (born after 1980) want and ask for more frequent and candid feedback than baby boomers (born 1946–1964).[54] As a result, Ernst & Young developed an online "Feedback Zone" where employees can provide or ask for feedback at any time. Also, the company assigns every employee a mentor and offers training for managers on how to give effective feedback. To make sure employees understand generational differences and how to connect and communicate with employees from different generations, Aflac, the insurance provider, offers a training program called "Connecting Generations."[55] Aflac believes that employees in all age groups are more effective if they understand how members of each generation approach their jobs. The program reviews the characteristics of each generation represented in the workplace. It also describes the effects of family and world events on each generation, analyzes their work styles and employment characteristics, and helps to show connections to bridge generation gaps.

As discussed in Chapter 10, many companies have viewed managing diversity as a way to reduce costs related to discrimination lawsuits rather than to improve company performance. As Table 1.3 shows, management of diversity contributes to a company's bottom line by its influence on creativity, problem solving, employee retention, and creation of new markets for a company's products and services. Companies that do not manage diversity will find that employees' talents are underutilized and their personal and professional needs are not being met. As a result, they will become dissatisfied and leave, resulting in a poorly performing, less competitive organization. Companies that are known for managing diversity also have an edge in attracting talented employees.

Talent Management

Talent management refers to attracting, retaining, developing, and motivating highly skilled employees and managers. Talent management is becoming increasingly more important because of changes in demand for certain occupations and jobs, skill requirements, the anticipated retirement of the baby boomer generation, and the need to develop managerial talent with leadership skills. Also, the results of surveys suggest that opportunities for career growth, learning, and development, and the performance of exciting and challenging work are some of the most important factors in determining employees' engagement and commitment to their current employer.[56] It is important to identify employees who want to develop their skills and seek promotions and to keep them growing through new job experiences and training. For example, Liz Claiborne tries to avoid turnover of the company's best employees by creating jobs with growth potential.[57] These jobs involve new assignments that require employees to apply their skills in different ways or to learn new skills. Sales managers are encouraged to spend more time in operations where they can learn about product flow, delivery, and other technical processes. This helps sales managers become better qualified for general manager jobs. Bristol-Meyers encourages employees in corporate staff positions to exchange jobs with other employees who work in the business units, such as the pharmaceutical business.

Occupational and Job Changes

The labor force is projected to increase from 13 million to 164.2 million in 2016. Most of the growth is expected within the service-providing industries, in which employment is projected to increase 15.8 million, rising to 130.2 million by 2016.[58] Employment in services is expected to account for 86 percent of all jobs. Examples of service-providing industries include educational services, health care, leisure and hospitality, transportation, government, utilities, and wholesale and retail trade. Jobs in goods-producing industries, including mining, construction, and manufacturing, are projected to decrease, falling to 21.8 million in 2016.

Table 1.4 shows examples of the projected fastest-growing occupations between 2006 and 2016. Professional and related occupations and the services occupational group are expected to add the most jobs and have the fastest growth rate between 2006–2016.[59] Health care practitioners and technical occupations are projected to add the most jobs (1.4 million) and computer and mathematical occupations are expected to grow the fastest (24.8 percent growth rate). In the services occupation group, by 2016 food preparation and related services are expected to generate the most new jobs and health care support is expected to grow the fastest (27 percent). Medical and dental assistants, nurses, and home health aides are examples of health care support occupations. Fishery, forestry, and farming occupations and production occupations are expected to have declines in the number of

TABLE 1.4 **Examples of the Fastest-Growing Occupations**

| Occupation | Employment Change, 2006–2016 | | |
	Number (in thousands)	Percent	Most Significant Education or Training
Network systems and data communications analysts	140	54	Bachelor's degree
Personal and home health care aids	389	51	Short-term on-the-job training
Home health care aides	384	49	Short-term on-the-job training
Computer software engineers, applications	226	45	Bachelor's degree
Veterinary technologists and technicians	29	41	Associate degree
Personal financial advisors	72	41	Bachelor's degree
Makeup artists, theatrical and performance	1	40	Postsecondary vocational award
Medical assistants	148	35	Moderate-term on-the-job training
Veterinarians	22	35	First professional degree

Source: Based on A. Dohm and C. Shniper, "Occupational Employment Projections to 2016," *Monthly Labor Review* (November 2007): 86–125.

jobs between 2006–2016. The aging of the population and the labor force means that jobs in health care and social assistance services are expected to have the fastest growth rate between 2006–2016, adding four million new jobs, or 27 percent of all new nonagricultural wage and salary jobs.

Occupations that require a bachelor's degree or higher for an entry-level position will grow faster than average for all occupations. Of the fastest growing occupations, 18 of the 30 are in professional and related occupations, and 10 are in service occupations. Fifteen of the thirty fastest-growing occupations require a bachelor's degree or higher as their most significant source of education and training. Most of the 30 fastest-growing occupations are considered professional and related occupations, which include health care, education, and science-related occupations.

Retirement of Baby Boomers

As the oldest baby boomers begin to retire in the next several years, the implications for the work force could be enormous.[60] This could hinder prospects for economic growth and put a greater burden on those remaining in the work force, perhaps forcing them to work longer hours. Especially in occupations with functions less conducive to technology-driven productivity innovations—many jobs in health services and educational services, for example—service may suffer and needs could go unmet unless older workers can be retained or other sources of workers can be found. Even in occupations in which technological innovations have produced relatively large productivity gains—many of the more complex machining jobs in manufacturing, for example—the learning curves often are steep, meaning that new workers need to enter these occupations soon, so they can become proficient in the necessary skills by the time the baby boomers begin leaving the labor force.

It is also important for companies to try to capture the valuable knowledge that is leaving.[61] To ensure that the expertise of retiring engineers is not lost, NASA is using phone interviews to capture their experiences.[62] These engineers have been designated as NASA Discipline Experts; each has been identified by NASA as an expert in a specific field of study such as propulsion or shuttle life support. The experiences captured on audiotape are turned into courses held at universities that offer graduate programs in aeronautics, such as the University of Maryland. A similar approach is used at the federal Department of Housing and Urban Development, where many employees are now retirement-eligible.[63] Subject matter experts are identified and trained to conduct workshops or make presentations. The agency uses its own studios to videotape the presentations and broadcast the information to Housing and Urban Development sites across the United States. The video is made available on the department's internal Web site. Interviewers who capture knowledge must know what questions to ask and how to get employees to talk about their knowledge. Many experienced employees may not recognize what is special about their personal knowledge and, as a result, have a difficult time speaking about it.

Skill Requirements

As the occupational structure of the U.S. economy has shifted, skill requirements have changed.[64] The demand for specific skills is being replaced by a need for cognitive skills—mathematical and verbal reasoning ability—and interpersonal skills related to being able to work in teams or to interact with "customers" in a service economy (e.g., patients, students, vendors, suppliers). Cognitive and interpersonal skills are important because in the service-oriented economy employees must take responsibility for the final product or service. Variety and customization require employees to be creative and good problem solvers. Continuous innovation requires the ability to learn. To offer novelty and entertainment value to customers, workers must be creative. Most companies relate these skills with educational attainment, so many firms use a college degree as a standard to screen prospective employees.

The future U.S. labor market will be both a knowledge economy and a service economy.[65] There will be many high-education professional and managerial jobs and low-education service jobs. Boundaries between knowledge and service work are blurring, creating "technoservice" occupations which combine service technology and software application. Software application engineers and those in technical support, engineering, and scientific consulting jobs work directly with customers and those customers influence the product design process.

Despite the need for high-level skills, many job applicants lack the necessary skills. In surveys of employers, over half report that high school graduates are deficient in problem solving/critical thinking, written and oral communications, and professionalism/work ethic.[66] Employers are more positive about four-year college graduates, although approximately 25 percent report these graduates are deficient in written communication, writing in English, and leadership skills.

In a 2005 study of American manufacturers, 80 percent reported a shortage of experienced workers, especially production workers, machinists, and craft workers. An online poll of members of the American Society for Training and Development found that 97 percent of respondents indicated a current skill gap in their companies.[67] The most frequently mentioned remedy was to provide training and development for employees with the skill gap. For example, at Whirlpool, building a dishwasher requires that the sheet of steel used on the sides of the machine be the correct width.[68] Employees must be able to ensure that the steel meets specifications by calibrating equipment, which requires algebra-level math knowledge. Whirlpool is finding that employees lack the math problem-solving skills needed to perform the job. As a result, Whirlpool has developed training programs to improve work force skills. About 25 percent of the programs focus on remedial skills. Given the tight labor market and numerous job applicants' lack of basic skills, many companies are unable to hire qualified employees. But they are unwilling or unable to leave jobs open. Therefore, they have to hire employees with skill deficiencies and rely on training and involvement in local school districts to correct the deficiencies. For example, Oberg Industries in Freeport, Pennsylvania, has increased its number of apprentices learning tool and die making, electroplating, and press operations (apprenticeship programs are discussed in Chapter 7, Traditional Training Methods).[69]

Business leaders such as Bill Gates have expressed their concern at the comparatively low numbers of U.S. students in the science and engineering fields.[70] One estimate shows that 70,000 engineers graduated in the U.S. in 2005, compared to 350,000 in India and 600,000 in China. This has resulted in a shortage of engineering and other technical professionals.

IBM, Hewlett-Packard, and Advanced Micro Devices are making efforts to increase the skills of the work force by investing in local secondary schools.[71] IBM's Transition to Teaching program allows employees to take leaves of absence to student teach for three months. Eligible employees must meet certain requirements, such as 10 years of service with IBM, a bachelor's degree in math or science or a higher degree in a related field, and some experience teaching, tutoring, or volunteering in schools. IBM hopes that many of its experienced employees with math and engineering backgrounds will take advantage of the program, providing high quality math and science teachers for public schools. Hewlett-Packard supports about 70 U.S. school districts with plans to enhance math and science programs. HP also helps equip schools with the technologies required for state-of-the-art technical education. Advanced Micro Devices, a company in the semiconductor industry, devotes half of its corporate contributions to education programs, including a summer math and science academy.

Developing Leadership

Companies report that the most important talent management challenges they face are identifying employees with managerial talent and training and developing them for managerial positions.[72] This is attributed to the aging of the work force, globalization, and the need for managers to contribute to employee engagement. Executive, administrative, and managerial occupations will experience the greatest turnover due to death or retirement.[73] Also, many companies do not have employees with the necessary competencies to manage in a global economy.[74] To successfully manage in a global economy, managers need to be self-aware and be able to build international teams, create global management and marketing practices, and interact and manage employees from different cultural backgrounds. Managers contribute to employee engagement by performing basic management functions (planning, organizing, controlling, leading) but also through using good communication skills, helping employees develop, and working collaboratively with employees.

For example, consider The Schwan Food Company and Yum! Brands.[75] The Schwan Food Company, maker of frozen pizzas and pies, is selecting employees with leadership talent to attend programs involving management classes and coaching sessions. These employees, considered "high-potential" managers, also receive challenging job assignments that require them to capitalize on their skill strengths and develop new skill sets (such as helping to launch a new joint venture in Mexico). Yum! Brands has over 35,000 KFC, Pizza Hut, and Taco Bell restaurants worldwide. The company needs to develop a large number of managers to meet demands for new restaurants resulting from growth plans, such as opening two KFC restaurants a day in China. To support and sustain global growth in restaurant operations, Yum! is preparing new managers through identifying and assigning job experiences that involve food innovation, marketing, and the development of general management skills.

Customer Service and Quality Emphasis

Companies' customers judge quality and performance. As a result, customer excellence requires attention to product and service features as well as to interactions with customers. Customer-driven excellence includes understanding what the customer wants and anticipating future needs. Customer-driven excellence includes reducing defects and errors, meeting specifications, and reducing complaints. How the company recovers from defects and errors is also important for retaining and attracting customers.

Due to increased availability of knowledge and competition, consumers are very knowledgeable and expect excellent service. This presents a challenge for employees who interact with customers. The way in which clerks, sales staff, front-desk personnel, and service providers interact with customers influences a company's reputation and financial performance. Employees need product knowledge and service skills, and they need to be clear about the types of decisions they can make when dealing with customers. Customer service as a strategic training and development initiative is discussed in Chapter 2.

To compete in today's economy, whether on a local or global level, companies need to provide a quality product or service. If companies do not adhere to quality standards, their ability to sell their product or service to vendors, suppliers, or customers will be restricted. Some countries even have quality standards that companies must meet to conduct business there. **Total Quality Management (TQM)** is a companywide effort to continuously improve the ways people, machines, and systems accomplish work.[76] Core values of TQM include the following:[77]

- Methods and processes are designed to meet the needs of internal and external customers.
- Every employee in the company receives training in quality.
- Quality is designed into a product or service so that errors are prevented from occurring rather than being detected and corrected.
- The company promotes cooperation with vendors, suppliers, and customers to improve quality and hold down costs.
- Managers measure progress with feedback based on data.

There is no universal definition of quality. The major differences in its various definitions relate to whether the customer, product, or manufacturing process is emphasized. For example, quality expert W. Edwards Deming emphasizes how well a product or service meets customer needs. Phillip Crosby's approach emphasizes how well the service or manufacturing process meets engineering standards.

The emphasis on quality is seen in the establishment of the **Malcolm Baldrige National Quality Award** and the **ISO 9000:2000** quality standards. The Baldrige award, created by public law, is the highest level of national recognition for quality that a U.S. company can receive. To become eligible for the Baldrige, a company must complete a detailed application that consists of basic information about the firm as well as an in-depth presentation of how it addresses specific criteria related to quality improvement. The categories and point values for the Baldrige award are found in Table 1.5. The award is not given for specific products or services. Three awards may be given annually in each of these categories: manufacturing, service, small business, education, and health care. All applicants for the Baldrige Award undergo a rigorous examination process that takes from 300 to 1,000 hours. Applications are reviewed by an independent board of about 400 examiners who come primarily from the private sector. Each applicant receives a report citing strengths and opportunities for improvement.

The Baldrige Award winners usually excel at human resource practices, including training and development. For example, consider two of the 2007 Baldrige Award winners.[78] Sharp HealthCare is San Diego County's largest health care system, serving over 785,000 people each year. Sharp is a not-for-profit organization that employs 14,000 staff members and 2,600 affiliated physicians, operates seven hospitals, three medical groups, and 19 outpatient clinics, and manages its own health insurance plan. Sharp HealthCare

TABLE 1.5
Categories and Point Values for the Malcolm Baldrige National Quality Award Examination

Source: Based on 2008 Baldrige National Quality Program Criteria for Performance Excellence from the Web site for the National Institute of Standards and Technology, www.quality.nist.gov.

Leadership The way senior executives create and sustain corporate citizenship, customer focus, clear values, and expectations and promote quality and performance excellence	120
Measurement, Analysis, and Knowledge Management The way the company selects, gathers, analyzes, manages, and improves its data, information, and knowledge assets	90
Strategic Planning The way the company sets strategic direction, how it determines plan requirements, and how plan requirements relate to performance management	85
Work Force Focus Company's efforts to develop and utilize the work force and to maintain an environment conductive to full participation, continuous improvement, and personal and organizational growth	85
Process Management Process design and control, including customer-focused design, product and service delivery, support services, and supply management	85
Business Results Company's performance and improvement in key business areas (product, service, and supply quality; productivity; and operational effectiveness and related financial indicators)	450
Customer and Market Focus Company's knowledge of the customer, customer service systems, responsiveness to customer, customer satisfaction	85
Total Points	1,000

meets and exceeds patients' expectations by providing high-quality care and services that are accessible, convenient, and cost effective. Sharp has made a considerable investment in its employees, including the use of yearly employee surveys to gauge the satisfaction and engagement of its work force, action teams, performance improvement teams, and lean/Six Sigma teams (discussed later in this chapter) that encourage employee participation in creating change and increasing organizational effectiveness. Sharp's training expenditures per employee exceed those of the best-in-class companies (as identified by the American Society for Training and Development). Sharp University offers training programs for developing current and future leaders. It provides each employee with a $1,000 fund to take advantage of educational opportunities offered outside the organization. PRO-TEC Coating Company, located in rural Leipsic, Ohio, is an industry leader in developing high-strength steel that inhibits corrosion. High-strength steel is used mainly in manufacturing cars, trucks, and sport utility vehicles. From 2002–2006, the company produced an estimated 85 percent of the high-strength steel supply in the U.S. PRO-TEC's 236 employees work in self-directed teams and are empowered to use continuous improvement processes to fix problems as they occur. All employees participate in a profit-sharing plan that provides an average annual payout of 15 percent of employees' base pay. Surveys, meetings, and management "walk arounds" are some of the methods used to obtain employees' feedback. PRO-TEC is committed to lifelong learning for its employees. Employees are given time off to attend classes and are reimbursed for tuition and the cost of books.

The ISO 9000:2000 standards were developed by the International Organization for Standardization (ISO) in Geneva, Switzerland.[79] ISO 9000 is the name of a family of standards (ISO 9001, ISO 9004) that include requirements for dealing with issues such as how to establish quality standards and how to document work processes to help companies understand quality system requirements. ISO 9000:2000 has been adopted as a quality standard in nearly 100 countries including Austria, Switzerland, Norway, Australia, and Japan. The ISO 9000:2000 standards apply to companies in many different industries—for example, manufacturing, processing, servicing, printing, forestry, electronics, steel, computing, legal services, and financial services. ISO 9001 is the most comprehensive standard because it covers product or service design and development, manufacturing, installation, and customer service. It includes the actual specification for a quality management system. ISO 9004 provides a guide for companies that want to improve.

Why are standards useful? Customers may want to check that the product they ordered from a supplier meets the purpose for which it is required. One of the most efficient ways to do this is when the specifications of the product have been defined in an International Standard. That way, both supplier and customer are on the same wavelength, even if they are based in different countries, because they are both using the same references. Today many products require testing for conformance with specifications or compliance with safety or other regulations before they can be put on many markets. Even simpler products may require supporting technical documentation that includes test data. With so much trade taking place across borders, it is more practical for these activities to be carried out not by suppliers and customers but by specialized third parties. In addition, national legislation may require such testing to be carried out by independent bodies, particularly when the products concerned have health or environmental implications. One example of an ISO standard is on the back cover of this book and nearly every other book. On the back cover is something called an ISBN number. ISBN stands for International Standard Book Number. Publishers and booksellers are very familiar with ISBN numbers, since these numbers are the method through which books are ordered and bought. Try buying a book on the Internet, and you will soon learn the value of the ISBN number—there is a unique number for the book you want! And it is based on an ISO standard.

In addition to competing for quality awards and seeking ISO certification, many companies are using the Six Sigma process. The **Six Sigma process** refers to a process of measuring, analyzing, improving, and then controlling processes once they have been brought within the narrow Six Sigma quality tolerances or standards. The objective of Six Sigma is to create a total business focus on serving the customer, that is, to deliver what customers really want when they want it. For example, at General Electric, introducing the Six Sigma quality initiative meant going from approximately 35,000 defects per million operations—which is average for most companies, including GE—to fewer than 4 defects per million in every element of every process GE businesses perform—from manufacturing a locomotive part to servicing a credit card account to processing a mortgage application to answering a phone.[80] Training is an important component of the process. Six Sigma involves highly trained employees known as Champions, Master Black Belts, Black Belts, and Green Belts who lead and teach teams that are focusing on an ever-growing number of quality projects. The quality projects focus on improving efficiency and reducing errors in products and services. Today GE has over 100,000 employees trained in Six Sigma. Employees are working on more than 6,000 quality projects. Since 1996, when the Six Sigma quality initiative was started, it has produced more than $2 billion in benefits for GE.

Training can help companies meet the quality challenge by teaching employees statistical process control and engaging in "lean" processes. Cardinal Fastener & Speciality Company, a Cleveland, Ohio, company, needed to shorten the lead time it required on orders or face losing business to global competition.[81] The company manufactures bolts used in construction, heavy equipment, wind turbine, and other industries. To help improve its competitiveness, Cardinal Fastener engaged in lean thinking, an approach to eliminate "waste." **Lean thinking** involves doing more with less effort, equipment, space, and time, but providing customers with what they need and want. Part of lean thinking includes training workers in new skills or teaching them how to apply old skills in new ways so they can quickly take over new responsibilities or use new skills to help fill customer orders. As a result of lean thinking at Cardinal Fastener, machines were moved so that operators could make a complete bolt or fastener from start to finish, resulting in a decrease in the time it takes to make a finished product. Quality is near perfect and inventory has been reduced 54 percent.

A group within the ISO has drafted a standard for employee training. **ISO 10015** is a quality management tool designed to ensure that training is linked to company needs and performance. ISO 10015 has two key features. First, companies have to determine the return on investment of training to company performance. Second, ISO 10015 requires companies to use appropriate design and effective learning processes. ISO 10015 defines training design as analyzing, planning, doing, and evaluating (recall the discussion of the Instructional System Design model earlier in this chapter). The first companies to have achieved ISO 10015 certification are in China and Switzerland but U.S. companies are likely to soon attempt to achieve certification.[82]

New Technology

Technology has reshaped the way we play (e.g., games on the Internet), communicate (e.g., cell phones, personal digital assistants), and plan our lives (e.g., electronic calendars that include Internet access) and where we work (e.g., small, powerful personal computers allow us to work at home, while we travel, and even while we lie on the beach!). The Internet has created a new business model—**e-commerce,** in which business transactions and relationships can be conducted electronically. The **Internet** is a global collection of computer networks that allows users to exchange data and information. Today more than 79 percent of adults go online spending an average of 11 hours a week on the Internet. Nearly 72 percent access the Internet most often from home, while 37 percent do so from work.[83]

Technology continues to have a large impact on all sectors of the economy. Robotics, computer-assisted design, radio frequency identification, and nanotechnology are transforming manufacturing.[84] Technology has also made equipment easier to operate, helping companies cope with skill shortages and allowing older workers to postpone retirement. For example, consider working a grader construction vehicle, which is used to smooth and level dirt on roadways and other construction projects. Older vehicle models required the operation of as many as 15 levers in addition to a steering wheel and several foot pedals. As a result, working the grader usually left operators with sore backs and shoulders at the end of the day. Caterpillar's latest version of the grader includes redesigned controls that use only two joysticks and eliminate the physical demands of pushing pedals and turning a steering wheel.[85] Besides reducing the physical demands, the redesign of the grader without a steering wheel has resulted in operators having better visibility of the steel blade and the switches for lights, windshield wipers, and the parking brake are now grouped together in one place in the cab.

In yet another example of how technology is being used today, companies can connect with job candidates across the world on www.monster.com and employees can connect with friends, family, and co-workers using MySpace at www.myspace.com.

Influence on Training

Advances in sophisticated technology along with reduced costs for the technology are changing the delivery of training, making training more realistic, and giving employees the opportunity to choose where and when they will work. New technologies allow training to occur at any time and any place.[86] New technologies include the Internet, e-mail, CD-ROMs, DVDs, satellite or cable television, and mobile technology such as personal digital assistants (PDAs) and iPods. The Internet and the Web allow employees to send and receive information as well as to locate and gather resources, including software, reports, photos, and videos. The Internet gives employees instant access to experts whom they can communicate with and to newsgroups, which are bulletin boards dedicated to specific areas of interest, where employees can read, post, and respond to messages and articles. Internet sites also have home pages—mailboxes that identify the person or company and contain text, images, sounds, and video. For example, the organization for training professionals and those interested in training, the American Society for Training and Development (ASTD), has a Web site on the Internet. From its Web site, www.astd.org, users can search for and access articles on training topics, review training programs, purchase training materials, and participate in chat rooms on various training topics such as e-learning or evaluation.

Technology has many advantages including reduced travel costs, greater accessibility to training, consistent delivery, the ability to access experts and share learning with others, and the possibility of creating a learning environment with many positive features such as feedback, self-pacing, and practice exercises. While trainer-led classroom instruction remains the most popular way to deliver training, companies report that they plan on delivering a large portion of training through learning technologies such as CD-ROMs, intranets, and even iPods! For example, consider how training at Kinko's, the world's leading supplier of document solutions and business services with 1,100 locations in nine countries, has changed. Because Kinko's stores are geographically dispersed, the company has had to struggle with costly training programs offered in multiple locations to prepare employees for new products and services. Kinko's adopted a blended learning approach including Internet instruction, job aids, virtual classroom training, and mentoring. Cost savings and greater efficiency occurred as a result of the blended approach. The approach has also resulted in increasing staff skills and reducing their time to competence and in increasing the speed with which new products and services can be brought to market.[87] Capital One, a financial services company, uses an audio learning program that allows employees to learn through their iPods at their own convenience.[88] The company has also developed a mobile audio learning channel. The channel supplements competency-based programs, leadership and management programs, and other existing company training courses. It is also used to ensure that employees receive information when they need it.

Technology is pushing the boundaries of artificial intelligence, speech synthesis, wireless communications, and networked virtual reality.[89] Realistic graphics, dialogue, and sensory cues can now be stored onto tiny, inexpensive computer chips. For example, Second Life is an online virtual world that allows members to develop fictional lives. In Second Life, members can run a business, take a date to a dance club, or visit a training center. Virtual sensations (vibrations and other sensory cues) are being incorporated into training applications. For example, in medical training, machines can replicate the feeling of pushing a needle into an artery, using sound and motion to create different situations such as a baby crying or a patient in pain.

Flexibility in Where and When Work Is Performed

Advances in technology, including more powerful computer chips and increased processing power of PDAs, have the potential for freeing workers from going to a specific location to work and from traditional work schedules. PDAs were originally used only to keep track of contacts, tasks, schedules, and e-mail. Now, PDAs can download software applications, databases, articles, and Web pages and can also be used as phones or global positioning systems. A survey found that 37 percent of employers offer telecommuting on a part-time basis and 23 percent on a full-time basis.[90] More than 23 percent of the U.S. work force worked at home at least one day a month in 2005. This figure was 12 percent in 2000.[91] Telecommuting has the potential to increase employee productivity, encourage family-friendly work arrangements, and help reduce traffic and air pollution. But at the same time technologies may result in employees being on call 24 hours a day, seven days a week. Many companies are taking steps to provide more flexible work schedules to protect employees' free time and to more productively use employees' work time. For example, Best Buy created its Results-Only Work Environment (ROWE) to give employees control over how, when, and where they complete the job as long as they achieve the desired results.[92] The idea is to let employees focus on productivity, rather than whether they are physically present in a meeting or at their desks at a specific time of the day. In divisions that have tried ROWE, employees say they are more engaged at work, are more loyal to the company, and have improved family relationships.

Dow Corning has a no-meetings week once a quarter which allows employees to reduce travel and work without interruptions.[93] The no-meetings week allows employees such as Laura Asiala, a global manager, a break from her normal workday, which starts as early as 5 AM and lasts as late as midnight. The no-meetings week gives her the opportunity to spend evenings with her two sons, free from overseas calls. IBM has "ThinkFridays," a free time on Friday afternoons, during which programmers spread across three continents can research new technologies or work on papers or patents, free from phone calls, e-mails, and instant messaging.

Technology also allows companies greater use of alternative work arrangements. **Alternative work arrangements** include independent contractors, on-call workers, temporary workers, and contract company workers. The Bureau of Labor Statistics estimates that alternative work arrangements make up 11 percent of total employment.[94] There are 10.3 million independent contractors, 2.5 million on-call workers, 1.2 million temporary help agency workers, and approximately 813,000 workers employed by contract firms. Use of alternative work arrangements allows companies to more easily adjust staffing levels based on economic conditions and product and services demand. And when a company downsizes by laying off workers, the damage to the morale of full-time employees is likely to be less severe. Alternative work arrangements also provide employees with flexibility for balancing work and life activities. For example, Willow CSN is a provider of home-based call center agents (CyberAgents).[95] Willow contracts with businesses such as Office Depot, whose call centers need more employees at certain hours. The CyberAgents use a company Web site to choose the shifts they want to work. They work a variable number of hours ranging from 10 to 32 hours per week and are paid based on the number of calls they answer. They take calls at home using the same software and equipment used by the agents at the client's call center. The agents are monitored and calls are recorded just as though the agents were working in a traditional call center. The CyberAgents can get help from supervisors or co-workers in an online chat room. Nike uses 3,700 temporary employees each year as part of its global work force of 28,000.[96] The temporary employees help Nike deal with cyclical labor needs during the business cycle and ongoing needs for specialized talent to meet strategic initiatives, such as new product development or retail store concepts. Companies like BMW are using alternative work arrangements to help staff new production lines and also to take over old production lines while permanent employees train for and move to new production processes.

A key training issue that alternative work arrangements present is to prepare managers and employees to coordinate their efforts so such work arrangements do not interfere with customer service or product quality. The increased use of alternative work arrangements means that managers need to understand how to motivate employees who may actually be employed by a third party such as a temporary employee service or leasing agency.

High-Performance Models of Work Systems

New technology causes changes in skill requirements and work roles and often results in redesigned work structures (e.g., using work teams).[97] For example, computer-integrated manufacturing uses robots and computers to automate the manufacturing process. The computer allows the production of different products simply by reprogramming the computer.

As a result, laborer, material handler, operator/assembler, and maintenance jobs may be merged into one position. Computer-integrated manufacturing requires employees to monitor equipment and troubleshoot problems with sophisticated equipment, share information with other employees, and understand the relationships among all components of the manufacturing process.[98]

Through technology, the information needed to improve customer service and product quality becomes more accessible to employees. This means that employees are expected to take more responsibility for satisfying the customer and determining how they perform their jobs. One of the most popular methods for increasing employee responsibility and control is work teams. **Work teams** involve employees with various skills who interact to assemble a product or provide a service. Work teams may assume many of the activities usually reserved for managers, including selecting new team members, scheduling work, and coordinating activities with customers and other units in the company. To give teams maximum flexibility, cross training of team members occurs. **Cross training** refers to training employees in a wide range of skills so they can fill any of the roles needed to be performed on the team.

Consider the high-performance work system at the Global Engineering Manufacturing Alliance (GEMA) plant in Dundee, Michigan.[99] Compared to most engine plants, GEMA's plant is more automated and employs fewer employees—275 compared to 600–2,000. The goal of the plant is to be the most productive engine plant in the world. The plant's hourly employees rotate jobs and shifts, giving the company greater flexibility. The plant's culture emphasizes problem solving and the philosophy that anyone can do anything, anytime, anywhere. Everyone has the same title: team members or team leaders. By rotating jobs, the plant keeps workers motivated and avoids injuries. Team leaders and engineers don't stay in their offices, they are expected to work on the shop floor as part of six-person teams. Contractors are also seen as part of the team, working alongside assembly workers and engineers and wearing the same uniforms. The GEMA plant gives employees access to technology that helps them monitor productivity. Large electronic screens hanging from the plant ceiling provide alerts of any machinery parts that are ending their lifespan and need to be replaced before they malfunction. A performance management system, available on personal computers as well as a display board, alerts employees to delays or breakdowns in productivity. This is different than in most engine plants, where only the managers have access to this information. The technology at the GEMA plant empowers all employees to fix problems—not just managers or engineers.

Use of new technology and work designs such as work teams needs to be supported by specific human resource management practices. These practices include the following actions:[100]

- Employees choose or select new employees or team members.
- Employees receive formal performance feedback and are involved in the performance improvement process.
- Ongoing training is emphasized and rewarded.
- Rewards and compensation are linked to company performance.
- Equipment and work processes encourage maximum flexibility and interaction between employees.

- Employees participate in planning changes in equipment, layout, and work methods.
- Employees understand how their jobs contribute to the finished product or service.

What role does training play? Employees need job-specific knowledge and basic skills to work with the equipment created by the new technology. Because technology is often used as a means to achieve product diversification and customization, employees must have the ability to listen and communicate with customers. Interpersonal skills, such as negotiation and conflict management, and problem-solving skills are more important than physical strength, coordination, and fine-motor skills—previous job requirements for many manufacturing and service jobs. Although technological advances have made it possible for employees to improve products and services, managers must empower employees to make changes.

Besides changing the way that products are built or services are provided within companies, technology has allowed companies to form partnerships with one or more other companies. **Virtual teams** refer to teams that are separated by time, geographic distance, culture, and/or organizational boundaries and that rely almost exclusively on technology (e-mail, Internet, video conferencing) to interact and complete their projects. Virtual teams can be formed within one company whose facilities are scattered throughout the country or the world. A company may also use virtual teams in partnerships with suppliers or competitors to pull together the necessary talent to complete a project or speed the delivery of a product to the marketplace. The success of virtual teams requires a clear mission, good communications skills, trust between members that they will meet deadlines and complete assignments, and an understanding of cultural differences (if the teams have global members).

At Nissan Motor's U.S. operations, 16 teams, each with 8 to 16 salaried employees from different departments, meet weekly to discuss issues such as quality, diversity, or supply chain management.[101] The team members, chosen by management, are considered to be high performers who have demonstrated that they are receptive to new ideas. The teams are used to challenge the organization and propose new initiatives to make the company more creative and innovative. For example, as a result of one team's discussion of how to save money, a proposal for working at home was developed. The team conducted an experiment to determine the benefits of working at home. A pilot study involving 41 employees found that working at home resulted in reduced operating costs and improved morale, as well as productivity increases. As a result, a virtual office initiative is now in place at Nissan's headquarters in Nashville, Tennessee. The company's employees who analyze market trends and identify concepts for Nissan will now work from their homes in Los Angeles.

Software developers are positioning employees around the world; with clusters of three or four facilities six to eight hours apart, they are able to keep projects moving 24 hours a day.[102] Employees are able to focus continuously on projects by using highly talented engineers who can work in their own time zone and location without having to move to a different country or work inconvenient hours. The result is increased productivity and reduced project completion time. Also, globally distributed projects can draw on employees from many different cultures, backgrounds, and perspectives, helping to produce services and products that better meet the needs of global customers. The challenge is to organize the work so that teams in different locations and different work shifts can share tasks with minimum interaction.

Employees must be trained in principles of employee selection, quality, and customer service. They need to understand financial data so they can see the link between their performance and company performance.

SNAPSHOT OF TRAINING PRACTICES

Training can play a key role in helping companies gain a competitive advantage and successfully deal with competitive challenges. Before you can learn how training can be used to help companies meet their business objectives and before you can understand training design, training methods, and other topics covered in the text, you need to become familiar with the amount and type of training that occurs in the United States. Also, you must understand what trainers do. The next sections of this chapter present data regarding training practices (e.g., how much companies spend on training, what type of training is occurring, who is being trained) as well as the skills and competencies needed to be a trainer.

Training Facts and Figures

The snapshot of training practices provided in this section is based on data collected from a number of sources, including surveys conducted by *Training* magazine, the American Society for Training and Development (ASTD), and the Bureau of Labor Statistics.[103] Note that these data should be viewed as reasonable estimates of practices rather than exact facts. The generalizability of survey results of training practices to U.S. companies is somewhat limited because of potential biases in the survey methods used. For example, the *Training* survey was conducted by a research firm that e-mailed invitations to subscribers to participate in an online survey. The response rate ranged from 30 percent for large firms to 34 percent for small firms. Also, the most recent survey of employer-provided training conducted by the Bureau of Labor Statistics was done in 1995. While this survey is scientifically accurate, it is not current.

You may be asking yourself questions such as, "How much time and money do companies spend on training?" or "Is instructor-delivered training obsolete?" Table 1.6 provides a snapshot of trends in workplace learning found in the annual *State of the Industry Report* prepared by the American Society for Training and Development. U.S. organizations continue to invest large amounts of money in learning initiatives. Here is an overview of some key trends in these investments:

- Direct expenditures, as a percentage of payroll and learning hours, have remained stable over the last several years.
- There is an increased demand for specialized learning that includes professional or industry-specific content.
- The use of technology-based learning delivery has increased from 11 percent in 2001 to 33 percent in 2007.
- Self-paced online learning is the most frequently used type of technology-based learning.
- Technology-based learning has helped improve learning efficiency, as shown by increases in the reuse ration since 2003. (The "reuse ratio" is defined as how much learning content is used or received for every hour of content.)

TABLE 1.6
Questions and Answers about Training Practices

Source: A. Paradise, *2008 State of the Industry Report* (Alexandria, VA: American Society for Training and Development, 2008); "2008 Industry Report: Gauges & Drivers," *Training* (November/December):16–34.

Investment and Distribution of Expenditures
Q: How much do U.S. organizations spend on employee learning and development?
A: Approximately $134 billion
Q: How much is spent per employee?
A: $1,103
Q: What is the percentage of dollars spent on training and development as a percentage of payroll?
A: 2.15%
Q: How much time do employees spend in formal training?
A: 37 hours
Q: Who receives most of the training?
A: 34% of training budgets and dollars are spent on non-exempt employees; 32% on exempt employees; 24% on managers; and 9.5% on executives

Efficiency
Q: What percent of total expenses are for tuition reimbursement?
A: 12.6%
Q: How many training staff members are there for each employee?
A: 1:227
Q: What is the average cost for every learning hour received?
A: $56
Q: What is the average cost of an hour of formal training?
A: $1,135
Q: What is the ratio of learning hours used to learning hours available?
A: 44.8

Delivery Methods
Q: How is training delivered?
A: 71% instructor-led; 32% technology-based; 25% online
Q: What percentage of direct learning expenditures are allocated to outside providers (outsourced)?
A: 25%

- Technology-based learning has resulted in a larger employee–learning staff member ratio.
- The percentage of services distributed by external providers (e.g., consultants, workshops, training programs) dropped from 29 percent in 2004 to 25 percent in 2007.

Of the $134 billion spent on training, 62 percent is for internal costs such as training-staff salaries and course development, 25 percent is for services provided by external providers such as consultants, workshops, or training programs outside the company, and 1 percent is for tuition reimbursement.

Figure 1.3 shows the different types of training provided by companies. Profession or industry-specific content, managerial and supervisory, and processes, procedures, and business practices account for 37 percent of learning content. The least amount learning content is for executive development, sales training, and interpersonal skills.

FIGURE 1.3   **Different Types of Training Provided by Companies**

Note: Data from consolidated responses (companies that submitted their annual data as part of ASTD's benchmarking programs).
Source: Based on A. Paradise, "State of the Industry Report 2008." (Alexandria, VA: American Society for Training and Development, 2008).

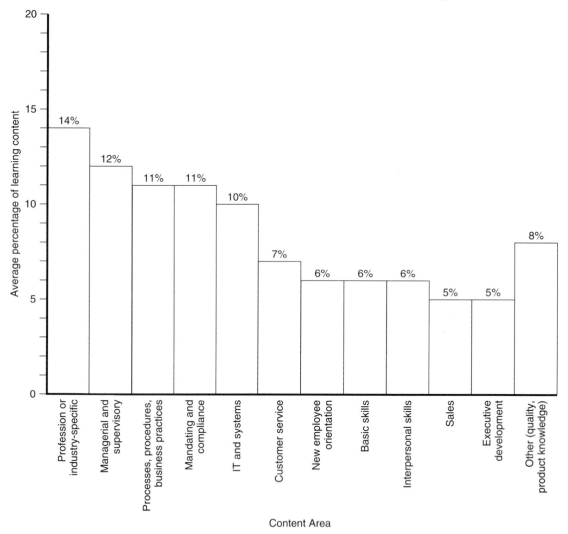

Training Investment Leaders

The chapter's opening vignette illustrates how training can be used by companies to gain a competitive advantage. Higher investment in training by companies in the United States is related to use of innovative training practices and high-performance work practices such as teams, employee stock ownership plans, incentive compensation systems (profit sharing), individual development plans, and employee involvement in business decisions. This spending (along with the use of high-performance work practices) has been shown to be related to improved profitability, customer and employee satisfaction, and the ability to retain employees. For example, companies including Pfizer, Lockheed Martin, Intel, Steelcase, and Booz Allen Hamilton have recognized that training contributes to their competitiveness. They invest 4 percent to 10 percent of payroll in training. Chapter 2 discusses how training can help companies meet their business goals.

How do the training practices of companies that have recognized training's importance in gaining a competitive advantage differ from other companies? ASTD's *2008 State of the Industry Report* compares the training practices of companies that were part of the ASTD Benchmarking Forum with companies that received ASTD BEST Awards (recognizing companies that show a clear link between learning and performance).[104] Benchmarking Forum companies provided ASTD with a standard set of information on their training practices (e.g., number of hours spent on training); these included 25 companies with an average of 64,241 employees. The BEST Award winners were companies that had made a significant investment in training, determined by ranking all companies that participated in the Benchmarking Service on four categories: training investment (expenses for training), total training hours per employee, percentage of employees eligible for training who received it, and percentage of training time delivered through learning technologies (e.g., Web-based training). Table 1.7 shows other characterstics of BEST Award-winning companies. As we will discuss in Chapter 2, the BEST Award winners are engaging in strategic training and development—training and development that supports the business's strategies and has measurable outcomes. The BEST Award winners included 40 companies with an average of 28,763 employees. Table 1.8 compares the BEST Award winners with the Benchmark companies. As the table shows, companies that were BEST Award winners spent 10 percent more money per employee for training than did the Benchmark firms. BEST Award winners also used more learning technologies, such as computer-for Internet-delivered training and spent less time training in the classroom than Benchmark firms. CD-ROMs and company intranets were the two most popular learning technologies used to deliver training.

TABLE 1.7
Characteristics of BEST Award Winners

Source: A. Paradise, *2008 State of the Industry Report* (Alexandria, VA: American Society for Training and Development, 2008).

Alignment of business strategy with training and development

Visible support from senior executives

Efficiency in training and development through internal process improvements, use of technology, outsourcing

Effective practices by aligning training and development to business needs and providing all employees with access to training and development on an as-needed basis

Investment in training and development

Different learning opportunities provided

Measurement of effectiveness and efficiency of training and development activities

Non-training solutions for performance improvement used, including organization development and process improvement

TABLE 1.8   **Comparison of BEST Award Winners and Benchmark Companies**

	Benchmark Company	BEST Award Winner
Amount of training received per employee	43 hours	45 hours
Amount spent on training		
• Percentage of payroll	2%	3%
• Per employee	$1,451	$1,609
Average percent of learning hours used via learning technology	36%	39%
Average percent of live instructor-led training	60%	70%

Source: A. Paradise, *2008 State of the Industry Report* (Alexandria, VA: American Society for Training and Development, 2008).

What types of courses were purchased with training dollars? The learning content did not vary significantly between Benchmarking and BEST Award winners. For Benchmarking Forum companies, the top three learning content areas were profession- or industry-specific content; IT and systems skills; and processes, procedures, and business practices. For BEST Award winners, the top three content areas were profession- or industry-specific content, information technology or systems skills, and mandatory or compliance training.

Roles, Competencies, and Positions of Training Professionals

Trainers can typically hold many jobs, such as instructional designer, technical trainer, or needs analyst. Each job has specific roles or functions. For example, one role of the needs analyst is to summarize data collected via interviews, observation, and even surveys to gain an understanding of training needs of a specific job or job family (a grouping of jobs). Special knowledge, skills, or behaviors—also called competencies—are needed to successfully perform each role. For example, the needs analyst must understand basic statistics and research methods to know what type of data to collect and to summarize data to determine training needs.

The most comprehensive study of training professionals has been conducted by the American Society for Training and Development.[105] Figure 1.4 shows the ASTD competency model. The model describes what it takes for an individual to be successful in the training and development field. The top of the model shows the roles that training and development professionals can take. The learning strategist determines how workplace learning can be best used to help meet the company's business strategy. The business partner uses business and industry knowledge to create training that improves performance. The project manager plans, obtains, and monitors the effective delivery of learning and performance solutions to support the business. The professional specialist designs, develops, delivers, and evaluates learning and performance solutions. These roles are included in jobs such as organizational change agent, career counselor, instructional designer, and classroom trainer. Training department managers devote considerable time to the roles of business partner and learning strategist. Training department managers may be involved in the project manager role but, because of their other responsibilities, they are involved to a smaller extent than are specialists who hold other jobs. Human resource or personnel managers may also be required to complete many of the training roles, although their primary

FIGURE 1.4   The 2004 ASTD Competency Model

Source: Reprinted with permission from the American Society of Training and Development. From P. Davis, J. Naughton, and W. Rothwell, "New Roles and Competencies for the Profession," *TD* (2004): 26–36. Permission conveyed through Copyright Clearance Center, Inc.

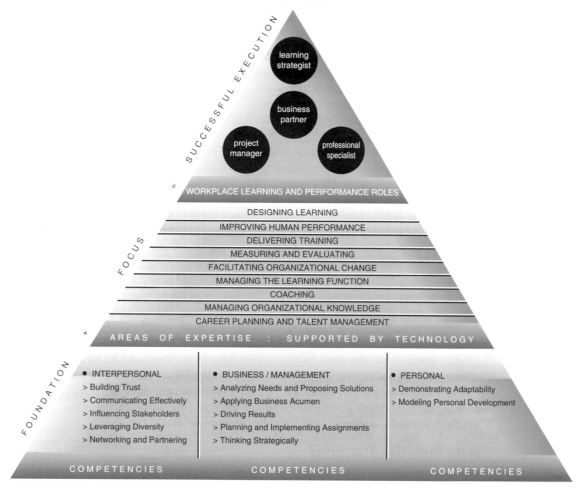

responsibility is in overseeing the human resources functions of the company (e.g., staffing, recruiting, compensation, benefits).

The second tier of the model includes areas of expertise, which are the specific technical and professional skills and knowledge required for success (e.g., designing learning, delivering training, etc.). Although training professionals spend most of their time in designing learning, delivering training, managing the learning function, and coaching, they do spend time in the other areas as well.

The foundational competencies anchor the competency model. The foundational competencies include interpersonal competencies, business and management competencies, and personal competencies. The foundational competencies are important regardless of a trainer's area of expertise or role but are used to a different extent in each role or specialization.

Traditional narrow jobs in the training department focusing on one type of expertise (e.g., instructional designer and technical writer) are changing; having multiple areas of expertise becomes more necessary for training and development to contribute to the business. Project management requires the knowledge of new training technologies (e.g., Web-delivered learning, CD-ROM, knowledge management systems) and the ability to manage managers, engineers, scientists, and others who may have more experience or technical saavy than the trainer. For example, at Hewlett-Packard (HP), new learning professionals need to be project managers.[106] They need to know how to create high-impact training solutions that business units in the company want to buy, and they have to do it in short time frames—about six months. Project managers need a solid background in instructional design and knowledge of new technologies that can be used to deliver training.

Hewlett-Packard recently launched Web Shops, which are 90-minute Web-delivered sessions that employees can participate in from around the globe. Web Shops include slide shows and presentations by HP experts, followed by online discussions among employees and subject-matter experts. HP also relies heavily on third-party vendors and design contractors for developing training programs. Trainers at HP make sure that vendors deliver the promised program on time (i.e., they manage vendors). Although HP continues to put more knowledge on the Web and class time has been reduced, the company realizes that the time in the classroom needs to be well spent. Trainers need to be skilled facilitators who can lead executive dialog discussions, simulations, case studies, and action learning sessions. These training methods are discussed further in Chapters 6 and 7, but for now it is important to know that these are training methods in which the trainee is very actively involved in the learning process. Trainers develop learning content and facilitate hands-on learning experiences. HP trainers are also able to work in global virtual teams that include members from different business functions and locations around the world. Personal interaction, reviews of training content, and project coordination occur through e-mail and the Internet.

Table 1.9 shows median salaries for training professionals. Note that very rarely does anyone hold the highest-paying jobs (training manager, executive-level manager) without having developed competencies in a number of training roles.

Who Provides Training?

In most companies training and development activities are provided by trainers, managers, in-house consultants, and employee experts. However, as the snapshot of training practices suggests, training and development activities are also outsourced. **Outsourcing** means that

TABLE 1.9
Average Salaries for Training Professionals

Source: Based on "The Bucks Stop Here," *Training* (October 2008): 22–28.

Executive-Level Training/Human Resource Development Manager	$106,267
Executive-Level Manager	118,708
Training Department Manager (1–5 trainers report to you)	82,976
Training Department Manager (more than 5 trainers report to you)	89,121
One-Person Training Department	72,297
Classroom Instructor/Trainer	64,213
Instructional Designer	65,932
CBT/Web/Multimedia Programmer Designer/Manager	68,221
Management/Career/Organization Development Specialist	79,841
Human Resource Manager/Specialist	67,003

training and development activities are provided by individuals outside the company. Training providers outside the company include colleges and universities, community and junior colleges, technical and vocational institutions, product suppliers, consultants and consulting firms, unions, trade and professional organizations, and government organizations. Outsourcing is discussed in greater detail in Chapter 2.

Who Is in Charge of Training?

Training and development can be the responsibility of professionals in human resources, human resource development, or organizational development.[107] Companies may also have entire functions or departments called human resources, human resource development, or organizational development that provide training and development.

In small companies training is the responsibility of the founder and all the employees. When organizations grow to 100 employees, typically someone within the company is in charge of human resources, either as part of that person's job or as his or her sole responsibility. At this point, training becomes one of the responsibilities of the employee in charge of human resources. In mid to large organizations, training can be the responsibility of human resource professionals or can come from a separate function known as human resource development or organizational development. As mentioned at the start of this chapter, *human resource management* refers broadly to the policies, practices, and systems that influence employees' behavior, attitudes, and performance. Human resource management includes staffing (recruitment and selection), compensation, employee relations, health and safety, equal employment opportunity, human resource planning, and training.

Human resource development refers to the integrated use of training and development, organizational development, and career development to improve individual, group, and organizational effectiveness. Human resource development professionals might be involved in job and task analysis, instructional systems design, on-the-job training, and individual performance improvement. Organizational development professionals might focus on training as well as team building, conflict avoidance, employee development, and change management. As you can see from these descriptions, training and development activities can be the responsibility of human resource management, human resource development, and organizational development professionals or departments. Keep in mind that regardless of what individual, department, or function is responsible, for training and development to be successful, employees, managers, training professionals, and top managers all have to take ownership for training! Throughout this book the point is made that although training may be a formal responsibility of someone's job, employees at all levels of the company play a role in the success of training. Also, regardless of whether training and development is the responsibility of human resources, human resource development, or organizational development, training and development must be aligned with the business strategy and must support business needs. Professionals in each of the three areas may have specialized areas of expertise, such as change management for organizational development specialists, but they may also have training and development responsibilities. As shown in Figure 1.4, to successfully perform the workplace learning and performance roles, professionals must understand the business and must master the competencies and areas of expertise.

As companies grow and/or recognize the important role of training for business success, they form an entire training function (how training functions can be organized is discussed in Chapter 2). The training function may include instructional designers, instructors, technical training, and experts in instructional technology.

The reporting relationship between human resource management and the training function varies across companies.[108] Some organizations include training as part of the human resource function, believing that this provides strategic partnerships with other business functions and consistent companywide training. For example, at Life Care Centers of America, a Tennessee-based company that operates elder care facilities, training is included in the human resource department because the company believes that training is part of human resource expertise, including the ability to write training curriculum and evaluate learning. Being centrally located in the human resource department makes the best use of resources and helps communicate a common management culture.

Other companies separate training from the human resource function because it allows the training function to be decentralized to better respond to unique needs in different business units. The training and development department at A. G. Edwards has a learning center and develops training programs for its financial consultants and employees.[109] Representatives of the training department regularly meet with the company's management committee at corporate headquarters as well as with regional officers and branch managers to help them understand how training can support business objectives. A new branch manager certification program succeeded because the branch managers were involved in identifying skill gaps and their suggestions were used in the program design. The branch managers took ownership of the program and helped develop the program proposal that they then presented to corporate managers to receive funding and approval for the program. Regardless of the organizational approach used for the training function, it must help meet the training needs of the business.

Preparing to Work in Training

Everyone is a trainer at some point in his or her life! Consider the last time you had to teach some skill to a peer, sibling, spouse, friend, or even your boss. Although some people learn to train by trial and error, the best way is to take courses in training and development or even choose an academic major related to training. For example, training and development courses are usually found in education, business and management, and psychology departments at colleges and universities. Business schools may offer undergraduate and graduate degrees in human resource management with courses in training and development and organizational development. Education departments may have undergraduate and graduate degrees in human resource development. Courses offered with such degrees include instructional design, curriculum development, adult learning, evaluation, and on-the-job training. Psychology departments offer courses in training and development as well. These courses can be part of a degree program in industrial and organizational psychology. If you are fortunate enough to be at a large university, you may have the opportunity to take courses from education, business/management, and the psychology departments that relate to training and development.

To be a successful training professional requires staying up-to-date on current research and training practices. The primary professional organizations for persons interested in training and development include the American Society for Training and Development (ASTD), the Academy of Human Resource Development (AHRD), the Society for Human Resource Management (SHRM), the Society for Industrial and Organizational Psychology (SIOP), the Academy of Management (AOM), and the International Society for Performance Improvement (ISPI). The Web addresses for these organizations are listed inside the front cover of this book. Articles about training practices can be found in the following journals: *Training, T + D, Training and Development, Workforce Management, HR Magazine, Academy of Management Executive,* and *Academy of Management Learning and Education.* Training and development research can be found in the following journals: *Human Resource Development Quarterly, Human Resource Development Review, Performance Improvement, Personnel Psychology, Journal of Applied Psychology, Academy of Management Journal,* and *Human Resource Management.*

ORGANIZATION OF THIS BOOK

This book is organized into five parts. Part One focuses on the context for training and development and includes this chapter which offered a broad perspective on training and helped answer questions such as what is training? Why is it important? Who is receiving training? How much money is spent on training? How should training be designed. Part One also includes Chapter 2 which discusses the strategic training and development process. In Chapter 2, you will see how a company's business strategy influences training practices and the organization of the training department. Chapters 3 through 6 make up Part Two. These chapters discuss the fundamentals of training design and address different aspects of the Instructional System Design model, the model used to guide the development of training (see Figure 1.1). Chapter 3 deals with how to determine training needs. Chapter 4 discusses the important issue of learning—specifically, how to create an environment conducive to learning within the training session. Chapter 5 addresses transfer of training, that is, how to ensure that the training environment and the work setting are conducive to the use of knowledge and skills acquired in training. Chapter 6 explains how to evaluate a training program. Part Three focuses on training and development methods. Chapters 7 and 8 discuss training methods. Chapter 7 looks at traditional training methods such as lecture, behavior modeling simulation, and role play. Chapter 8 examines e-learning and methods that have developed from applications of new technology, for example, Web-based training, iPods, virtual reality, and intelligent tutoring systems.

Chapter 9 addresses the important issue of employee development; it discusses four approaches used to develop employee assessments, assignments, relationships, and courses and formal programs. Chapter 10 deals with special topics in training and development including ethics and legal issues, diversity training, cross-cultural training, and the relationship between training and other human resource management practices. Part Four focuses on careers and career management. Chapters 11 and 12 introduce such career issues as understanding what a career is, the systems companies use to manage careers, and concerns in career management, such as plateauing, socialization, downsizing, and outplacement. Part Five looks at the future of training and development Chapter 13 discusses how the role of training in organizations may change in the future.

Students should be aware of several important features of the book. Each chapter begins with chapter objectives. These objectives (1) highlight what the student should learn from each chapter and (2) preview the topics. Next comes an opening vignette—an example of a company practice related to the chapter topics. Company examples are liberally used throughout each chapter to help students see how theory and research in training are put into practice. Each chapter ends with key terms, discussion questions, application assignments, and a short case. Key terms are related to important concepts emphasized in the chapter. Discussion questions and application assignments can facilitate learning through interacting with other students and actually trying to develop and conduct various training applications. Many application assignments require the use of the Web, a valuable source of information on training practices. Each of the parts concludes with a case from *BusinessWeek* magazine that highlights a company's training and development practices. These cases include questions asking you to apply what you have learned in the chapters.

Key Terms

competitiveness, *4*
competitive advantage, *4*
human resource management, *4*
stakeholders, *5*
training, *5*
high-leverage training, *5*
continuous learning, *5*
training design process, *7*
Instructional System Design (ISD), *8*
offshoring, *12*
human capital, *13*

intellectual capital, *14*
social capital, *14*
customer capital, *14*
knowledge workers, *15*
employee engagement, *15*
change, *16*
learning organization, *16*
talent management, *21*
Total Quality Management (TQM), *25*
Malcolm Baldrige National Quality Award, *26*
ISO 9000:2000, *26*

Six Sigma process, *28*
lean thinking, *28*
ISO 10015, *28*
e-commerce, *29*
Internet, *29*
alternative work arrangements, *31*
work teams, *32*
cross training, *32*
virtual teams, *33*
outsourcing, *40*
human resource development, *41*

Discussion Questions

1. Describe the forces affecting the workplace and learning. How can training help companies deal with these forces?

2. What steps are included in the training design model? What step do you think is most important? Why?

3. What are intangible assets? How do they relate to training and development?

4. How is Starbucks using training to benefit the company during difficult economic times?

5. Training professionals continue to debate whether the ISD model is flawed. Some argue that ISD should be treated as a project management approach rather than a step-by-step recipe for building training programs. Others suggest that ISD is too linear and rigid a process, that it is the primary reason training is expensive, and that it takes too long to develop. ISD focuses on inputs; management wants outputs. Businesses want results, not the use of a design technology. Do you believe that ISD is a useful process? Why or why not? Are there certain situations when it is a more (or less) effective way to design training?

6. Which of the training professionals' roles do you believe is most difficult to learn? Which is easiest?

7. How might technology influence the importance of training professionals' roles? Can technology reduce the importance of any of the roles? Can it result in additional roles?

8. Describe the training courses that you have taken. How have they helped you? Provide recommendations for improving the courses.

9. How does training differ between companies that are considered BEST Award winners and those that are not?

10. What are the implications of the aging work force? What strategies should companies consider from a training and development perspective to best utilize older employees and prepare for their retirement?

11. How has new technology improved training and development? What are some of the limitations of using iPods or PDAs for training?

12. Explain how training relates to attracting new employees, employee retention, and motivation.

13. What is the relationship between talent management and employee engagement? What role can training and development practices play in keeping employee engagement high during poor economic times? Explain.

Application Assignments

1. Go to the American Society for Training and Development (ASTD) home page on the World Wide Web. The address is www.astd.org. Investigate the links on the home page. One link is to *T + D* magazine. Find an article related to training. Summarize the main topic of the article and identify how it relates to course topics or topics covered in this text.

2. Go to www.quality.nist.gov, the Web site for the National Institute of Standards and Technology (NIST). The NIST oversees the Malcolm Baldrige Quality Award. Click on "Criteria for Performance Excellence." Choose either "Criteria for Performance Excellence," "Education," or "Health Care." Download the award criteria. What questions are used to determine a company's education, training, and development focus?

3. For many years General Electric (GE) has been recognized as one of the world's most admired companies. Visit GE's Web site at www.gecareers.com and click on "Why GE" and then "Leadership & Learning Programs." How have training and learning contributed to GE's success?

4. Conduct a phone or personal interview with a manager. Ask this person to describe the role that training plays in his or her company.

5. Conduct a phone or personal interview with a training manager. Ask this person to discuss how training has changed in the past five years and how he or she believes it will change in the future.

6. *Training* identified the Top 125 companies for training (see *Training*, February 2009). The top ten ranked companies were:

    1. PricewaterhouseCoopers
    2. KMPG LLP
    3. SCC Soft Computer

4. EMC Corporation

5. Wyeth Pharmaceuticals

6. Vanguard

7. General Mills

8. Satyam Computer Services Limited

9. Mohawk Industries Inc.

10. Microsoft Corporation

Choose one of these companies to research. Visit the company's Web site, use a Web search engine, or look for references to the company in publications such as *Training, T + D, Workforce,* or *HR Magazine.* Prepare a report (not to exceed three pages) based on your research (*a*) describing why you believe the company was ranked in the top 10 and (*b*) explaining the relationship between training and the company's competitiveness and business goals and objectives. Your instructor will advise you on whether the report should be submitted electronically or in a paper copy. (*Hint:* Possible reasons a company might be ranked include the amount of money it devotes to training, the level of employee involvement in training, and the type of training used.)

Case

Zappos: *Facing Competitive Challenges*

Zappos, based in Las Vegas, is an online retailer. Its initial goal has been to be the best Web site for buying shoes, offering a wide variety of brands, styles, colors, sizes, and widths. The zappos.com brand has grown to offer shoes, handbags, eyewear, watches, and accessories for online purchase. Zappos's vision is that in the future online sales will account for 30 percent of all retail sales in the U.S., and Zappos will be the company with the best service and selection. As a result, Zappos believes it can become the online service leader, drawing customers and expanding into selling other products. Zappos believes that the speed at which a customer receives an online purchase plays a critical role in how that customer thinks about shopping online again in the future, so it is focusing on making sure the items get delivered to customers as quickly as possible.

Zappos CEO Tony Heish has shaped the company's culture, brand, and business strategy around 10 core values. They are:

Deliver WOW through Service

Embrace and Drive Change

Create Fun and a Little Weirdness

Be Adventurous, Creative, and Open-Minded

Pursue Growth and Learning

Build Open and Honest Relationships with Communication

Build a Positive Team and Family Spirit

Do More with Less

Be Passionate and Determined

Be Humble

Deliver WOW through Service means that call center employees need to provide excellent customer service. Call center employees encourage callers to order more than one size or color because shipping and return shipping are free. They are also encouraged to use their imaginations to meet customer needs.

Zappos's employment practices help to perpetuate its company culture. For example, the HR team uses unusual interview questions, such as "How weird are you?" and "What's your theme song?" to find employees who are creative and have strong individuality. Zappos provides free lunch in the cafeteria (cold cuts) and a full-time life coach (employees have to sit on a red velvet throne to complain). Managers are encouraged to spend time with employees outside of the office, and any employee can reward another employee a $50 dollar bonus for good performance. Most employees at Zappos are hourly. All new hires complete four weeks of training, including two weeks working the phones. New recruits are offered $2,000 to leave the company during training to weed out individuals who will not be happy working at the company.

Due to a downturn in sales, Zappos was forced to cut costs, including laying off 124 employees. Heish handled the downsizing in a positive way. Laid-off employees with less than two years of service were paid through the end of the year. Everyone received six months of paid health coverage. Zappos also allowed laid-off employees to keep their 40 percent employee discount through Christmas.

What challenges is Zappos facing that may derail its attempt to be the best online retailer? How can training and development help Zappos meet these challenges? Do you think that employees at Zappos have high levels of engagement? Why? Which of Zappos's 10 core values do you believe training and development can influence the most? The least? Why?

Source: Based on Web site for Zappos, www.zappos.com; J. O'Brien, "Zappos Knows How to Kick It," *Fortune* (February 2, 2009): 55–66.

Endnotes

1. J. B. Quinn, P. Anderson, and S. Finkelstein, "Leveraging Intellect," *Academy of Management Executive* 10 (1996): 7–27.

2. A. P. Carnevale, "America and the New Economy," *Training and Development Journal* (November 1990): 31–52; R. Brinkerhoff and A. Apking, *High-Impact Learning* (Cambridge, MA: Perseus Publishing, 2001).

3. V. Sessa and M. Condan, *Continuous Learning in Organizations* (Mahwah, NJ: Erlbaum, 2006).

4. L. Thornburg, "Accounting for Knowledge," *HR Magazine* (October 1994): 51–56; T. A. Stewart, "Mapping Corporate Brainpower," *Fortune* (October 30, 1995): 209.

5. T. O'Driscoll, "Improving Knowledge Worker Performance," *Performance Improvement* (April 2003): 5–11; F. Wilmouth, C. Prigmore, and M. Bray, "HPT Models: An Overview of the Major Models in the Field," *Performance Improvement* (September 2002): 14–22.

6. B. Pfau and I. Kay, "HR Playing the Training Game and Losing," *HR Magazine* (August 2002): 49–54.

7. D. Zahn, "Training: A Function, Profession, Calling, What?" *Training and Development* (April 2001): 36–41.

8. L. Freifeld, "PWC Does It Again," *Training* (February 2009): 24–28.

9. M. Molenda, "In Search of the Elusive ADDIE Model," *Performance Improvement* (May/June 2003): 34–36; C. Allen (ed.), "ADDIE Training System Revisited," *Advances in Developing Human Resources* 8 (2006): 427–555.

10. G. Snelbecker, "Practical Ways for Using Theories and Innovations to Improve Training," in *The ASTD Handbook of Instructional Technology,* ed. G. Piskurich (Burr Ridge, IL: Irwin/McGraw-Hill, 1993): 19.3–19.26.

11. "American Infrastructure: A Cornerstone for Learning," *T + D* (October, 2008), 66–67.

12. R. Zemke and A. Rosett, "A Hard Look at ISD," *Training* (February 2002): 26–34; Brinkerhoff and Apking, *High-Impact Learning*.

13. H. Dolezalek, "Who Has the Time to Design?" *Training* (January 2006): 25–28.

14. K. Colteryahn and P. Davis, "8 Trends You Need to Know Now," *T + D* (January 2004): 29–36; M. Weinstein, "What Does the Future Hold?" *Training* (January 2006): 18–22; K. Tyler, "Training Revs Up," *HR Magazine* (April 2005): 58–63; B. Hall, "The Top Training Priorities for 2005," *Training* (February 2005): 22–29; Society for Human Resource Management, "HR Insight into the Economy," *Workplace Visions* 4 (2008): 4; Society for Human Resource Management, "Workplace Trends: An Overview of the Findings of the Latest SHRM Workplace Forecast," *Workplace Visions* 3 (2008): 1–6.

15. K. Evans and K. Maher, "Yearly Job Loss Worst Since 1945," *The Wall Street Journal* (January 10–11, 2009): A1–2; S. Reddy; "Jobless rate hits 8.5%," *Wall Street Journal* (April 4 & 5, 2009): A1. S. Reddy, R. Smith, and K. Maher, "Job Losses Are Worst Since '74," *The Wall Street Journal* (December 6–7, 2008): A1, A8; D. DePass, "Factories Can't Stop the Bleeding," *Columbus Dispatch* (December 21, 2008): D3.

16. R. Curran, "Dow Jones Industrials Lost 18% in Their Worst Week Ever," *The Wall Street Journal* (October 11–12, 2008): B3.

17. E. White and S. Thurm, "Layoffs Continue in the New Year," *The Wall Street Journal* (January 10–11, 2009): A2; S. Wartenberg, "44,400 Jobs Gone," *Columbus Dispatch* (January 27, 2009): A1, A4.

18. J. McGregor, "Keeping Talent in the Fold," *BusinessWeek* (November 3, 2008): 51–52; D. Mattioli, "Despite Cutbacks, Firms Invest in Developing Leaders," *The Wall Street Journal* (February 9, 2009): B4.

19. "Manufacturing: Engine of U.S. Innovation," *National Association of Manufacturing* (October 4, 2006), available at Web site www.nam.org (January 21, 2009).

20. C. Hill, *Informational Business* (Burr Ridge, IL: Irwin/McGraw-Hill, 1997).

21. B. McKay, "Coke Bets on Russia for Sales Even as Economy Falls Flat," *The Wall Street Journal* (January 28, 2009): A1, A12.

22. C. Hymowitz, "IBM Combines Volunteer Service, Teamwork to Cultivate Emerging Markets," *The Wall Street Journal* (August 4, 2008): B6.

23. D. Ready and J. Conger, "How to Fill the Talent Gap," *The Wall Street Journal* (September 15–16, 2007): R4, R5.

24. M. Horrigan, "Employment Projections to 2012: Concepts and Contexts," *Monthly Labor Review* 127 (February 2004): 3–22.

25. "The People Problem," *Inc.* (May 29, 2001): 84–85.

26. R. Konrad, "More U.S. Programmers Training Foreign Replacements," *Columbus Dispatch* (September 1, 2003): D1, D2.

27. "Manufacturing: Engine of U.S. Innovation," *National Association of Manufacturing* (October 4, 2006), available at Web site www.nam.org (January 21, 2009). `

28. Jim Hopkins, "To Start Up Here, Companies Hire Over There," *USA Today,* February 10, 2005, downloaded at www.usatoday.com.

29. Ibid.

30. F. Hansen, "U.S. Firms Going Wherever the Knowledge Workers Are," *Workforce Management* (October 2005): 43–44.

31. R. Grossman, "The Truth about the Coming Labor Shortage," *HR Magazine* (March 2005): 47–53.

32. L. Weatherly, *Human Capital—The Elusive Asset* (Alexandria, VA: SHRM Research Quarterly, 2003).

33. L. Bassi, J. Ludwig, D. McMurrer, and M. Van Buren, *Profiting from Learning: Do Firms' Investments in Education and Training Pay Off?* (Alexandria, VA: American Society for Training and Development, September 2000).

34. J. Barney, *Gaining and Sustaining Competitive Advantage* (Upper Saddle River, NJ: Prentice Hall, 2002).

35. W. Zeller, "Southwest: After Kelleher, More Blue Skies," *BusinessWeek* (April 2, 2001): 45; S. McCartney, "Southwest Sets Standards on Costs," *The Wall Street Journal* (October 10, 2002): A2; S. Warren and M. Trottman, "Southwest's Dallas Duel," *The Wall Street Journal* (May 10, 2005): B1, B4.

36. E. McGirt, "Revolution in San Jose," *Fast Company* (January 2009): 89–94, 134–136.

37. R. Vance, *Employee Engagement and Commitment* (Alexandria, VA: Society for Human Resource Management (SHRM) Foundation, 2006).

38. For example, see M. Huselid, "The Impact of Human Resource Management Practices on Turnover, Productivity, and Corporate Financial Performance," *Academy of Management Journal* 38 (1995): 635–672; S. Payne and S. Webber, "Effects of Service Provider Attitudes and Employment Status on Citizenship Behaviors and Customers' Attitudes and Loyalty Behavior," *Journal of Applied Psychology* 91 (2006): 365–368; J. Hartner, F. Schmidt, and T. Hayes, "Business-Unit Level Relationship between Employee Satisfaction, Employee Engagement, and Business Outcomes: A Meta-Analysis," *Journal of Applied Psychology* 87 (2002): 268–279; I. Fulmer, B. Gerhart, and K. Scott, "Are the 100 Best Better? An Empirical

Investigation of the Relationship between Being a "Great Place to Work" and Firm Performance," *Personnel Psychology* 56 (2003): 965–993; "Working Today: Understanding What Drives Employee Engagement," *Towers Perrin Talent Report* (2003).

39. Corporate Leadership Council, "Driving Performance and Retention through Employee Engagement" (Washington, DC: Corporate Executive Board, 2004).

40. Vance, *Employee Engagement and Commitment.*

41. American Society for Training and Development (2008), *2007 State of the Industry Report* (Alexandria, VA), A. Paradise, "Learning Influences Engagement," *T + D* (January 2008): 54–59.

42. P. Drucker, *Management Challenges for the 21st Century* (New York: Harper Business, 1999); Howard N. Fullerton Jr., "Labor Force Projections to 2008: Steady Growth and Changing Composition," *Monthly Labor Review* (November 1999): 19–32.

43. D. Senge, "The Learning Organization Made Plain and Simple," *Training and Development Journal* (October 1991): 37–44.

44. L. Thornburg, "Accounting for Knowledge," *HR Magazine* (October 1994): 51–56.

45. "CIO Panel: Knowledge-Sharing Roundtable," Information Week Online, News in Review, April 26, 1999 (from *Information Week* Web site, www.informationweek.com); Buckman Laboratories Web site, www.buckman.com.

46. P. Harris, "Training Time at the Learning Corral," *T + D* (June 2008): 41–45.

47. M. Toosi, " Labor Force Projections to 2016: More Workers in Their Golden Years," *Monthly Labor Review* 7 (November 2007): 33–52.

48. Ibid.

49. N. Lockwood, *The Aging Workforce* (Alexandria, VA: Society for Human Resource Management, 2003).

50. D. Wessel, "Older Staffers Get Uneasy Embrace," *The Wall Street Journal* (May 15, 2008): A2; J. Marquez, "Novel Ideas at Borders Lure Older Workers," *Workforce Management* (May 2005): 28,30.

51. M. Loden and J. B. Rosener, *Workforce America!* (Burr Ridge, IL: Business One Irwin, (1991); Toosi, "Labor Force Projections to 2014"; Lockwood, *The Aging Workforce.*

52. J. Salopek, "Retaining Women," *T + D* (September 2008): 24–27.

53. M. Johnson, "Blind Workers Find Fulfillment at Wiscraft Inc.," *Columbus Dispatch* (February 18, 2006): F2.

54. B. Hite, "Employers Rethink How They Give Feedback," *The Wall Street Journal* (October 13, 2008): B5; E. White, "Age Is as Age Does: Making the Generation Gap Work for You," *The Wall Street Journal* (June 30, 2008): B3; P. Harris, "The Work War," *T + D* (May 2005): 45–48; C. Hirshman, "Here They Come," *HR Executive* (July 2006): 1, 22–26.

55. M. Rowh, "Older and Wiser," *Human Resource Executive* (August 2008): 35–37.

56. re:SEARCH, "Want to Keep Employees Happy? Offer Learning and Development," *T + D* (April 2005): 18; P. Cappelli, "Talent Management for the Twenty-First Century," *Harvard Business Review* (March 2008): 74–81.

57. C. Hymowitz, "Best Way to Save: Analyze Why Talent Is Going out the Door," *The Wall Street Journal* (September 24, 2007): B1; C. Hymowitz, "They Ponder Layoffs, but Executives Still Face Gaps in Talent," *The Wall Street Journal* (January 28, 2008): B1.

58. E. Figueroa and R. Woods, "Industry Output and Employment Projections to 2016," *Monthly Labor Review* (November 2007): 53–85.

59. A. Dohm and L. Shniper, "Occupational Employment Projections to 2016," *Monthly Labor Review* (November 2007): 86–125.

60. M. Toosi, "Labor Force Projections to 2014: Retiring Boomers," *Monthly Labor Review* (November 2005): 25–44; N. Lockwood, *The Aging Workforce* (Alexandria, VA: Society for Human Resource Management, 2003).

61. J. Salopek, "The New Brain Drain," *T + D* (June 2005): 23–25; P. Harris, "Beware of the Boomer Brain Drain!" *T + D* (January 2006): 30–33; M. McGraw, "Bye-Bye Boomers," *Human Resource Executive* (March 2, 2006): 34–37; J. Phillips, M. Pomerantz, and S. Gully, "Plugging the Boomer Drain," *HR Magazine* (December 2007): 54–58.

62. M. Weinstein, "NASA Training Program Blasts Off," *Training* (December 2005): 8–9.

63. P. Harden, "The Federal Exodus," *Human Resource Executive* (November 2005): 70–73.

64. R. Davenport, "Eliminate the Skills Gap," *T + D* (February 2006): 26–34; M. Schoeff Jr., "Amid Calls to Bolster U.S. Innovation, Experts Lament Paucity of Basic Math Skills," *Workforce Management* (March 2006): 46–49.

65. M. Hilton, "Skills for Work in the 21st Century: What Does the Research Tell Us?" *Academy of Management Executive* (November 2008): 63–78.

66. J. Rossi, "The `Future' of U.S. Manufacturing," *T + D* (March 2006): 12–13; Society for Human Resource Management, Conference Board, Partnership for 21st Century Skills, Corporate Voices for Working Families, *Are They Ready to Work?* (New York, Conference Board, 2006).

67. Davenport, "Eliminate the Skills Gap."

68. Schoeff, "Amid Calls to Bolster U.S. Innovation."

69. K. Maher, "Skills Shortage Gives Training Programs New Life," *The Wall Street Journal* (June 3, 2005): A2.

70. R. Davenport, "Eliminate the Skills Gap," *T + D* (February 2006): 26–34; M. Schoeff, "Amid Calls to Bolster U.S. Innovation."

71. J. Barbian, "Get `Em While They're Young," *Training* (January 2004): 44–46; E. Frauenheim, "IBM Urged to Take Tech Skills to Classrooms," *Workforce Management* (October 24, 2005): 8–9; K. Maher, "Skills Shortage Gives Training Programs New Life," *The Wall Street Journal* (June 3, 2005): A2.

72. Towers-Perrin, *Talent Management: The State of the Art* (Towers-Perrin, 2005).

73. A. Dohm, "Gauging the Labor Force Effects of Retiring Babyboomers," *Monthly Labor Review* (July 2000): 17–25.

74. Society for Human Resource Management, *Workplace Visions* 5 (2000): 3–4.

75. E. White, "Manager Shortage Spurs Small Firms to Grow Their Own," *The Wall Street Journal* (February 5, 2007): B1, B4; P. Galagan, "Talent Management: What Is It, Who Owns It, and Why Should You Care?" *T + D* (May 2008): 40–44.

76. J. R. Jablonski, *Implementing Total Quality Management: An Overview* (San Diego: Pfeiffer, 1991).

77. R. Hodgetts, F. Luthans, and S. Lee, "New Paradigm Organizations: From Total Quality to Learning World-Class," *Organizational Dynamics* (Winter 1994): 5–19.

78. "Malcolm Baldrige 2007 Award Recipient; PRO-TEC Coating Company" and "Malcolm Baldrige 2007 Award Recipient: Sharp HealthCare" available at 2007 Baldrige Award recipients 2007 profiles at www.nist.gov, the Web site for the National Institute of Standards and Technology.

79. S. L. Jackson, "What You Should Know about ISO 9000," *Training* (May 1992): 48–52; Bureau of Best Practices, *Profile of ISO 9000* (Boston: Allyn and Bacon, 1992); "ISO 9000 International Standards for Quality Assurance," *Design Matters* (July 1995): http://www.best.com/ISO 9000/att/ISONet.html/. See www.iso9000y2k.com, a Web site containing ISO 9000:2000 documentation.

80. General Electric 1999 Annual Report. Available at www.ge.com/annual99.

81. D. Arnold, "Cardinal Fastener Soars with Lean Thinking," from www.cardinalfastener.com, January 19, 2008.

82. L. Yiu and R. Saner, "Does It Pay to Train? ISO 10015 Assures the Quality and Return on Investment of Training," *ISO Management Systems* (March–April 2005): 9–13.

83. S. Ho, "Poll Finds Nearly 80 Percent of U.S. Adults Go Online www.reviters.com (March 2, 2009).

84. "Manufacturing: Engine of U.S. Innovation," *National Association of Manufacturing* (October 4, 2006). Available at Web site www.nam.org (January 21, 2009).

85. I. Brat, "A Joy(stick) to Behold," *The Wall Street Journal* (June 23, 2008): R5.

86. D. Gayeski, "Goin' Mobile," *T + D* (November 2004): 46–51; D. Hartley, "Pick Up Your PDA," *T + D* (February 2004): 22–24.

87. B. Manville, "Organizing Enterprise-Wide E-learning and Human Capital Management," *Chief Learning Officer* (May 2003): 50–55.

88. "Outstanding Training Initiatives: Capital One—Audio Learning in Stereo," *Training* (March 2006): 64.

89. A. Weintraub, "High Techs' Future Is in the Toy Chest," *BusinessWeek* (August 26, 2002): 124–26.

90. Society of Human Resource Management, *2002 Benefits Survey* (Alexandria, VA: SHRM Foundation, 2002).

91. C. Rhoads and S. Silver, "Working at Home Gets Easier," *The Wall Street Journal* (December 29, 2005): B4.

92. P. Kiger, "Flexibility to the Fullest," *Workforce Management* (September 25, 2006): 1, 16–23.

93. S. Shellenbarger, "Time-Zoned: Working around the Round-the-Clock Workday," *The Wall Street Journal* (February 15, 2007): D1.

94. Bureau of Labor Statistics, "Contingent and Alternative Employment Arrangements, February 2005" from www.bls.gov, the Web site for the Bureau of Labor Statistics (accessed January 21, 2009).

95. H. Dolezalek, "Virtual Agent Nation," *Training* (June 2004): 12.

96. F. Hansen, "A Permanent Strategy for Temporary Hires,", *Workforce Management* (February 26, 2007): 25–30.

97. P. Choate and P. Linger, *The High-Flex Society* (New York: Knopf, 1986); P. B. Doeringer, *Turbulence in the American Workplace* (New York: Oxford University Press, 1991).

98. K. A. Miller, *Retraining the American Workforce* (Reading, MA: Addison-Wesley, 1989).

99. J. Marquez, "Engine of Change," *Workforce Management* (July 17, 2006): 20–30.

100. J. Neal and C. Tromley, "From Incremental Change to Retrofit: Creating High Performance Work Systems," *Academy of Management Executive* 9 (1995): 42–54; M. Huselid, "The Impact of Human Resource Management Practices on Turnover, Productivity, and Corporate Financial Performance," *Academy of Management Journal* 38 (1995): 635–72.

101. J. Marquez, "Driving Ideas Forward at Nissan," *Workforce Management* (July 17, 2006): 28.

102. A. Gupta, "Expanding the 24-Hour Workplace," *The Wall Street Journal* (September 15–16, 2007): R9, R11.

103. "BLS Reports on the Amount of Employer-Provided Formal Training," press release (July 10, 1996); H. J. Frazis, D. E. Herz, and M. W. Harrigan, "Employer-Provided Training: Results from a New Survey," *Monthly Labor Review* 5 (May 1995): 3–17; "2008 Industry Report: Gauges and Drivers," *Training* (November/December 2008): 16–34; "Training Best Practices 2006," *Training* (March 2006): 60–62; A. Paradise, *2008 State of the Industry* (Alexandria, VA: American Society for Training and Development, 2008).

104. A. Paradise, *2008 State of the Industry.*

105. P. Davis, J. Naughton, and W. Rothwell, "New Roles and Competencies for the Profession," *T + D* (April 2004): 26–36; W. Rothwell and R. Wellins, "Mapping Your Future: Putting New Competencies Together to Work for You," *T + D* (May 2004): 1–8.

106. D. Zielinski, "Training Careers in the 21st Century," *Training* (January 2000): 27–38.

107. W. Ruona and S. Gibson, "The Making of Twenty-First Century HR: An Analysis of the Convergence of HRM, HRD, and OD," *Human Resource Management* (Spring 2004): 49–66.

108. J. Schettler, "Should HR Control Training?" *Training* (July 2002): 32–38.

109. K. Ellis, "The Mindset That Matters Most: Linking Learning to the Business," *Training* (May 2005): 38–43.

Strategic Training

Objectives

After reading this chapter, you should be able to

1. Discuss how business strategy influences the type and amount of training in a company.
2. Explain how the role of training is changing.
3. Describe the strategic training and development process.
4. Discuss how a company's staffing and human resource planning strategies influence training.
5. Explain the training needs created by concentration, internal growth, external growth, and disinvestment business strategies.
6. Discuss the advantages and disadvantages of organizing the training function according to the faculty, customer, matrix, corporate university, and business-embedded models.
7. Discuss what factors need to be considered before making the decision to outsource training.

McCormick & Company Uses Strategic Training to Spice Up Business Results

You may know McCormick & Company from its flavorings and spices that enhance the taste of appetizers, main dishes, and desserts (who doesn't appreciate the great aroma of just-baked chocolate chip cookies?). You should also know that training and development play a strategic role at McCormick & Company. Learning is driven by the company strategy. The company's main strategies include growing sales, fostering innovation, managing the cost base, and planning for succession. These strategies have been translated into several strategic training and development initiatives. One initiative supporting the innovation strategy involves the development of technological innovation centers for scientists and learning and development centers for company leaders. In another initiative, $1 million was spent to teach employees how to use the new SAP business software implemented throughout the company. The company's succession planning process is designed to make good on the promise that all employees have access to the training and development they need to become successors to the current company leaders at all levels. Robert Lawless, chairman and CEO, believes that having a process to grow employees internally gives the company a competitive advantage. Growing employees internally requires challenging employees and providing opportunities for career growth, learning, and development. His commitment to succession planning is evident in the amount of time he spends reviewing development needs, goals, performance, and recent training and development for the top employees in the company.

To ensure that training and development are strategic, the director of learning and development has positioned the training department as a team of performance consultants who serve the needs of the business. Also, McCormick & Company has emphasized teaching at all levels of the organization, with the goal of making the company more agile and able to adapt to change and cope with the loss of expertise due to the retirement of baby boomers. The teaching organization has four roles, each aligned with business plans. *Corporate learning professionals* are found at the company's two learning centers in Maryland and in the United Kingdom. Corporate learning professionals are charged with establishing expertise and then sharing it with others. *Site-specific learning professionals* include employees who have responsibility for learning and development at the company's locations. Each training manager reports directly to each location's human resource or operations function to ensure that training needs are identified and met. *Leader-teachers* include all employees with supervisory responsibilities, regardless of level. Managers are trained to help employees apply the skills they learn in training and senior executives teach classes. To ensure that leaders are teachers, the performance evaluations for all of McCormick's managers include one competency: attracting and developing talent. Attracting and developing talent involves active participation in the growth and development of employees and effective coaching and mentoring. *Peer-teachers* engage in one-on-one training with other employees as well as through the company's multiple management board (MMB) system. The MMB system includes cross-functional, cross-divisional groups of employees from all levels who work on projects that can have a significant impact on the business. The MMB experience provides participating employees with skills and knowledge that are not typically part of their job responsibilities, such as developing strategic thinking or strengthening presentation skills. At any one time, there are approximately 200 employees serving on MMBs.

The strategic importance the company places on training and development is highlighted by the board of directors' decision not to cut the firm's learning budget—despite budget cuts elsewhere due to a decrease in company earnings (attributed to the effects of Hurricane Katrina on business in the southern United States and falling prices in the world market for vanilla). McCormick & Company's board of directors will provide additional funding for training and development initiatives if there is a business case made for additional financial resources. To make the business case for training and development, McCormick & Company evaluates the effectiveness of training and development using metrics such as how many employees have been promoted, how many employees have attended the learning and development center, how many employees are in the MMBs, and the dollar impact of MMB project results on the business.

Sources: T. Bingham and P. Galagan, "Growing Talent and Sales at McCormick," *T + D* (July 2007): 30–34; R. Frattali, "The Company that Teaches Together Performs Together," *T + D* (July 2007): 36–39. Also, go to www.mccormick.com, the Web site for McCormick & Company.

INTRODUCTION

As the chapter opening vignette shows, training and development at McCormick & Company support the business strategy. Recognizing that learning is part of all employees' responsibilities, both managers and peers, along with training professionals, are actively involved in helping other employees gain new skills and perspectives. This helps to reinforce the value of learning and its importance for the business. McCormick & Company recognizes that learning through training and development is critical for meeting its main strategies: growing sales, innovation, managing the cost base, and planning for succession.

Why is the emphasis on strategic training important? Companies are in business to make money, and every business function is under pressure to show how it contributes to business success or face spending cuts and even outsourcing. To contribute to a company's success, training activities should help the company achieve its business strategy. A **business strategy** is a plan that integrates the company's goals, policies, and actions.[1] The strategy influences how the company uses physical capital (e.g., plants, technology, and equipment), financial capital (e.g., assets and cash reserves), and human capital (employees). The business strategy helps direct the company's activities (production, finance, marketing, human resources) to reach specific goals. The **goals** are what the company hopes to achieve in the medium- and long-term future. Most companies' goals include financial goals, such as to maximize shareholder wealth. But companies have other goals related to employee satisfaction, industry position, and community service.

There is both a direct and indirect link between training and business strategy and goals. Training that helps employees develop the skills needed to perform their jobs directly affects the business. Giving employees opportunities to learn and develop creates a positive work environment, which supports the business strategy by attracting talented employees as well as motivating and retaining current employees.

IBM is a company that reinvented itself in 2002.[2] Its business strategy is to reshape its work force so as to better meet clients' needs and expectations as IBM transforms itself from a high-tech industrial-age company to an information- and knowledge-driven company. This new business strategy has required a massive organizational culture change: Employees have had to accept the strategy and make it work. Dedication to clients is the core foundation of IBM's new business strategy. To meet client needs, employees must be adaptable and constantly adjusting. As a result, IBM's training has shifted so that employees learn through work, on location, and based on client needs rather than traveling to a different location for a training course, although formal training courses will still be used to teach managers, executives, and salespeople new skills or product lines at critical moments in their careers. On Demand Learning, as IBM has called it, requires that the learning teams that are responsible for designing the program understand the specific work being done by employees in different roles. IBM has defined over 500 specific roles in the company and the expertise required for each role. The learning team has designed learning opportunities into the work itself, a concept known as "work-embedded learning." Employees work via computer to connect with experts, participate in an online community on a topic, or complete an online learning module. The amount of time spent on learning and training at IBM has grown 32 percent through the expansion of work-embedded learning. The company has committed more than $700 million to its learning initiatives, which it believes are critical for achieving its business strategy.

Business strategy has a major impact on the type and amount of training that occurs and whether resources (money, trainers' time, and program development) should be devoted to training. Also, strategy influences the type, level, and mix of skills needed in the company. Strategy has a particularly strong influence on determining:

1. The amount of training devoted to current or future job skills.
2. The extent to which training is customized for the particular needs of an employee or is developed based on the needs of a team, unit, or division.
3. Whether training is restricted to specific groups of employees (such as persons identified as having managerial talent) or open to all employees.
4. Whether training is planned and systematically administered, provided only when problems occur, or developed spontaneously as a reaction to what competitors are doing.
5. The importance placed on training compared to other human resource management practices such as selection and compensation.[3]

This chapter begins with a discussion of how training is evolving. Traditionally, training has been seen as an event or program to develop specific explicit knowledge and skills. But managers and trainers and human resource professionals have begun to recognize the potential contribution to business goals of knowledge that is based on experience and that is impossible to teach in a training program, and they have broadened the role of training to include learning and designing ways to create and share knowledge. The chapter goes on to discuss the process of strategic training and development, including identifying the business strategy, choosing strategic training and development initiatives that support the strategy, providing training and development activities that support the strategic initiatives, and identifying and collecting metrics to demonstrate the value of training. The chapter next describes organizational factors that influence how training relates to the business strategy. These include the roles of employees and managers; top management support for training; integration of business units; staffing and human resource planning strategy; degree of unionization; and manager, trainer, and employee involvement in training. The chapter then addresses specific strategic types and their implications for training. The chapter ends with a description of several different ways of organizing the training function, emphasizing that the business-embedded and corporate university models are gaining in popularity as companies are aligning training activities with business goals.

THE EVOLUTION OF TRAINING'S ROLE

As more companies such as McCormick & Company recognize the importance of learning for meeting business challenges and providing a competitive advantage, the role of training in companies is changing. Figure 2.1 shows the evolution of training's role from a program focus to a broader focus on learning and creating and sharing knowledge.[4] Training will continue to focus on developing programs to teach specific skills; however, to better relate to improving employees' performance and to help meet business needs and challenges (and be considered strategic), training's role has to evolve to include an emphasis on learning and creating and sharing knowledge. **Learning** refers to the acquisition of knowledge by individual employees or groups of employees who are willing to apply that knowledge in their jobs in making decisions and accomplishing tasks for the company.[5] **Knowledge** refers to

FIGURE 2.1
Evolution of Training's Role

what individuals or teams of employees know or know how to do (human and social knowledge) as well as company rules, processes, tools, and routines (structured knowledge).[6] Knowledge is either tacit knowledge or explicit knowledge.[7] **Explicit knowledge** refers to knowledge that can be formalized, codified, and communicated. That is, it can be found in manuals, formulas, and specifications. **Tacit knowledge** refers to personal knowledge based on individual experience that is difficult to explain to others. Because tacit knowledge is difficult to communicate, it is passed along to others through direct experience (e.g., interacting with other employees, watching other employees). The types of tacit and explicit knowledge that are important for employees include knowledge about the company, knowledge about customers, and knowledge about the company's business processes.[8] Employees need to understand the company's business, strategy, and financial statements as well as how the company is organized. This gives them some idea of where to go with new ideas, how to seek help with problems, and how to create opportunities for cross-functional businesses. Employees must know who the company's customers are, what they need, and why they choose to do business with the company. Finally, employees must have a general understanding of the major business processes and a more detailed understanding of the business processes they are involved in. Well-designed traditional training courses can successfully help employees learn tacit knowledge. But to learn tacit knowledge requires interpersonal interaction and experiences that are usually not found in training programs.

In traditional approaches to training, training is seen as a series of programs or events that employees attend. After attending the training program, employees are responsible for using what they learned in training on the job, and any support they might receive is based on the whims of their manager. Also, traditional training provides no information that would help employees understand the relationship between the training content and individual performance or development objectives or business goals. This type of training usually fails to improve workplace performance and meet business needs. The role of training as a program or event will continue into the future because employees will always need to be taught specific knowledge and skills. This approach assumes that business conditions are predictable, they can be controlled by the company, and the company can control and predict the knowledge and skills that employees need in the future. These assumptions are true for certain skills such as communication and conflict resolution.

However, these training events or programs will need to be more closely tied to performance improvement and business needs to receive support from top management. The training design model presented in Chapter 1 and the different aspects of the model discussed in Chapters 3 though 8 will help you understand how to design training programs that can improve employee performance and meet business needs.

Movement from Training as an Event to Learning

At Walt Disney Company, over the last 10 years training has evolved to include flexible learning delivery, customized learning experiences, and collaborative development with internal training customers.[9] Disney has moved from an instructor-led training approach to an approach that uses face-to-face instruction (classroom, on-the-job) combined with online instruction (game simulation, e-learning). This matches Disney's business strategy, which has always emphasized matching the appropriate technology and methods to the audience regardless of whether the audience is a guest or an employee (cost member).

A single training event or program is not likely to give a company a competitive advantage because explicit knowledge is well-known and programs designed to teach it can be easily developed and imitated. However, tacit knowledge developed through experience and shared through interactions between employees is impossible to imitate and can provide companies with a competitive advantage. Pixar's development of successful computer-animated films such as *WALL-E* (a robot love story in a post-apocalyptic world of trash) and *Ratatouille* (a tale of a French rat who longs to be a chef) requires the cooperation of a team of talented directors, writers, producers, and technology artists who may be located in different buildings, have different priorities, and speak different technical languages.[10] Pixar follows three operating principles: (1) all employees must have the freedom to communicate with other employees, regardless of their position or department, (2) it must be safe for everyone to offer ideas, and (3) the company must stay close to innovations occurring in the academic community. Pixar University offers a collection of in-house courses for training and cross-training employees within their specialty areas. But it also offers optional classes that provide opportunities for employees from different disciplines to meet and learn together. Screenplay writing, drawing, and sculpting are directly related to the business while courses in Pilates and yoga are not. The courses are attended by employees with all levels of expertise—from novices to experts—which reinforces the idea that all employees are learning and it is fun to learn together.

The emphasis on learning has several implications. First, there is a recognition that to be effective, learning has to be related to helping employees' performance improve and the company achieve its business goals. This connection helps ensure that employees are motivated to learn and that the limited resources (time and money) for learning are focused in areas that will directly help the business succeed. Second, unpredictability in the business environment in which companies operate will continue to be the norm. Because problems cannot be predicted in advance, learning needs to occur on an as-needed basis. Companies need to move beyond the classroom and instead use job experiences and Web-based training to teach employees skills while they focus on business problems. Third, because tacit knowledge is difficult to acquire in training programs, companies need to support informal learning that occurs through mentoring, chat rooms, and job experiences. Fourth, learning has to be supported not only with physical and technical resources but also psychologically. The company work environment needs to support learning, and managers and peers need to encourage learning and help employees find ways to obtain learning on the job. Also, managers need to understand employees' interests and career goals to help them find suitable development activities that will prepare them to be successful in other positions in the company or deal with expansion of their current job. Chapter 5 discusses the characteristics of a learning organization and how to create a work environment that supports training and learning.

Creating and sharing knowledge refers to companies' development of human capital. As discussed in Chapter 1, human capital includes cognitive knowledge (know what), advanced skills (know how), system understanding and creativity (know why), and self-motivated creativity (care why).[11] Traditionally, training has focused on cognitive and advanced skills. But the greatest value for the business may be created by having employees understand the manufacturing or service process and the interrelationships between departments and divisions (system understanding) as well as motivating them to deliver high-quality products and services (care why). To create and share knowledge, companies have to provide the physical space and technology (e-mail, Web sites) to encourage employee collaboration and knowledge sharing. Ford Motor Company has communities of practice organized around functions.[12] For example, all the painters in every Ford assembly plant around the world belong to the same community. At each plant, one of the painters serves as a "focal point." If a local painter discovers a better way to improve one of the 60 steps involved in painting, the focal person completes a template describing the improvement and its benefits. The template is submitted electronically to a subject matter expert located at Ford headquarters, who reviews the practice and decides whether it is worth sharing with other assembly plants. If so, the practice is approved and sent online to the other assembly plants. Ford has collected $1.3 billion in projected value for the company and has realized over $800 million of actual value from its communities of practice.

As companies recognize the value of training and development and view them as part of a broader learning strategy, seven key capabilities are needed, according to a survey by Accenture Learning.[13] These capabilities are:

1. Alignment of learning goals to the business goals.
2. Measurement of the overall business impact of the learning function.
3. Movement of learning outside the company to include customers, vendors, and suppliers.
4. A focus on developing competencies for the most critical jobs.
5. Integration of learning with other human resource functions such as knowledge management, performance support, and talent management.
6. Training delivery approaches that include classroom as well as e-learning.
7. Design and delivery of leadership development courses.

THE STRATEGIC TRAINING AND DEVELOPMENT PROCESS

Now that you understand how training is evolving in companies and have been introduced to the concept of business strategy and how training can support a business strategy, you are ready to study the process of strategic training and development. Figure 2.2 shows a model of the strategic training and development process with examples of strategic initiatives, training activities, and metrics.

FIGURE 2.2
The Strategic Training and Development Process

The model shows that the process begins with identifying the business strategy. Next, strategic training and development initiatives that support the strategy are chosen. Translating these strategic training and development initiatives into concrete training and development activities is the next step of the process. The final step involves identifying measures or metrics. These metrics are used to determine whether training has helped contribute to goals related to the business strategy. The following sections detail each step in the process.

Identify the Company's Business Strategy

Three factors influence the company's business strategy. First, the company's mission, vision, values, and goals help to determine the strategy. These are usually determined by the top management team. The **mission** is the company's reason for existing. It may specify the customers served, why the company exists, what the company does, or the values received by the customer. The **vision** is the picture of the future that the company wants to achieve. **Values** are what the company stands for. Second, a **SWOT analysis** (strengths, weaknesses, opportunities, threats) involves an analysis of the company's operating environment (e.g., product markets, new technologies) to identify opportunities and threats as well as an internal analysis of the company's strengths and weaknesses including people, technology, and financial resources. The business challenges identified in Chapter 1 may also represent an opportunity (or threat) to the company. Recall that these business challenges include globalization, the need for leadership, increased value of human capital, change, attracting and winning talent, and a focus on customers and quality. Third, the company has to consider its competition. That is, how will the company successfully compete? The decisions that a company has to make in determining how to compete are shown in Table 2.1.

Although these decisions are equally important, companies often pay less attention to the "with what will we compete" issue, resulting in failure to reach the goals. This decision includes deciding how human, physical, and financial capital will be used. To use human capital to gain a competitive advantage requires linking the company's human resources practices (such as training and development) to the business strategy.

Consider how training contributes to the business strategy at Nokia Corporation. Nokia, the world leader in mobile communications, has over 68,000 employees and net sales of $30 billion. Nokia's business strategy is to build trusted customer relationships

TABLE 2.1

Decisions a Company Must Make about How to Compete to Reach Its Goals

Source: "Strategy-Decisions about Competition," from R. Noe, J. Hollenbeck, B. Gerhart, and P. Wright, *Human Resource Management: Gaining a Competitive Advantage*, 6th ed. (Burr Ridge, IL: Irwin/McGraw-Hill, 2009): 61.

1. Where to compete?
In what markets (industries, products, etc.) will we compete?
2. How to compete?
On what outcome or differentiating characteristic will we compete? Cost? Quality? Reliability? Delivery? Innovativeness?
3. With what will we compete?
What resources will allow us to beat the competition? How will we acquire, develop, and deploy those resources to compete?

by offering compelling and valued consumer solutions that combine the best mobile devices with context-enriched services (business mobility and Internet).[14] Nokia's vision is a world where everyone can be connected and feel close to what is important to them. Nokia consists of the following business units: Devices, Software and Services, Markets (management of supply chains, sales, and brand and marketing activities), Nokia Siemens Networks (infrastructure and related services business), NAVTEQ (provider of digital map data for automotive navigation systems and other mapping applications), and the Corporate Development Office (which focuses on strategy and future growth and supports the other units). Nokia wants to create personalized communication technology that enables people to create their own mobile world. Nokia continues to target and enter segments of the communications market that the company believes will experience faster growth than the industry as a whole. As the demand for wireless access to services increases, Nokia plans to lead the development and commercialization of networks and systems required to make wireless content more accessible and rewarding for customers.

The management approach at Nokia, known as the "Nokia way," consists of the Nokia values, its organizational competencies, and its operations and processes used to maintain operational efficiency. The company has built its current and future strength on the Nokia way. The Nokia way has resulted in a flat, networked company emphasizing speed and flexibility in decision making. Nokia's values include "engaging you" (customer satisfaction and engaging with all stakeholders, including employees), "achieving together" (trust, sharing, working in formal and informal networks), "passion for innovation," and "very human" (understanding that how the company does business impacts people and the environment). Continuous learning provides employees with the opportunity to develop themselves and to stay technologically current. Employees are encouraged to share experiences, take risks, and learn together. Continuous learning goes beyond formal training classes. At Nokia, continuous learning means that employees support each other's growth, developing and improving relationships through the exchange and development of ideas. E-learning is used to provide employees with the freedom to choose the best possible time and place for personal development.

Nokia's top management is committed to continuous learning. Figure 2.3 shows how Nokia links training and development to its business strategy. For example, the business group presidents are the "owners" of all global management and leadership programs for senior managers. They personally provide input into the development of these programs but they also appoint "godfathers" from their management teams. These godfathers participate actively throughout the program and are also designers of program content. Together with

FIGURE 2.3
How Nokia Corporation Links Training and Development to Business Strategy.

Strategy	Strategic Training and Development Initiatives	Training and Development Activities	Metrics that Show the Value of Training
• Build trusted customer relationships by offering compelling and valued consumer solutions that combine the best mobile devices with context-enriched services (business mobility and internet) • Values Engaging You Achieving Together Passion for Innovation Very Human	• Continuous learning	• Action Learning • Employee ownership for learning and development plans • Learning Market Place Internet • On-the-job learning • Manager involvement in program development • Investing in People (IIP)	• Employee reactions • Competence attainment

the training and development staff, the godfathers help the learning processes in the programs. Most of the programs involve strategic projects (action learning) that participants are responsible for completing. Top managers invest time in reviewing the projects and have the authority to take action based on the project team recommendations.

The value of continuous learning translates into personal and professional growth opportunities including a commitment to self-development, coaching, learning solutions and training, management training, a vibrant internal job market, and performance management. Employees are encouraged to create their own development plan and use available learning solutions and methods. Coaching with highly skilled colleagues helps employees develop and gives them the opportunity to share ideas and goals with each other. Nokia employees have access to a wide variety of training and development opportunities, including learning centers and the Learning Market Place Internet, which has information on all the available learning solutions including e-learning and classroom training. Through the learning centers, Nokia has integrated the learning activities of all the business groups into one place. Nokia believes that by mixing participants from across business groups, knowledge is created because traditions and experiences can be shared among employees. In addition to formal programs offered in classrooms or on the Internet, Nokia emphasizes on-the-job learning through job rotation and through managers giving their employees challenging new job assignments. There is also a wide range of opportunities for managers to improve their management and leadership skills. The emphasis on the internal labor market encourages employees to improve their skills by changing jobs. Nokia's performance management process, known as Investing in People (IIP), involves twice yearly discussions between employees and their managers. The IIP process consists of objective setting, coaching and achievement review, competence analysis, and a personal development plan. The entire IIP process is supported electronically. Employees can choose their profile from the company intranet, conduct a self-evaluation, create a personal development plan, and investigate what learning solutions are available at the learning centers.

Nokia uses a combination of measures to evaluate the value of training. Nokia always asks employees for their immediate reactions after they have completed a program. Other measures include attainment of competence and resource strategy in all parts of the company. Top management believes that the largest benefit of the learning is that employees have opportunities to network, creating more knowledge, reinforcing continuous learning, and creating committed employees.

Identify Strategic Training and Development Initiatives That Support the Strategy

Strategic training and development initiatives are learning-related actions that a company should take to help it achieve its business strategy.[15] The strategic training and development initiatives vary by company depending on a company's industry, goals, resources, and capabilities. The initiatives are based on the business environment, an understanding of the company's goals and resources, and insight regarding potential training and development options. They provide the company with a road map to guide specific training and development activities. They also show how the training function will help the company reach its goals (and in doing so, show how the training function will add value).

There is a tendency to have a disconnect between strategy and execution of the strategy. To avoid this, learning professionals need to reach out to managers to ensure that the strategic training initiatives and training activities are aligned with the business strategy and the necessary financial resources and support are provided to carry out the training activities.[16] This requires consideration of people and cultural issues that might inhibit execution of training initiatives. In addition, the success or failure of previous training activities should be identified and addressed to ensure that future training activities support strategic training initiatives and are successfully implemented.

Table 2.2 shows strategic training and development initiatives and their implications for training practices. *Diversify the learning portfolio* means that companies may need to provide more learning opportunities than just traditional training programs. These learning opportunities include informal learning that occurs on the job through interactions with peers; new job experiences; personalized learning opportunities using mentors, coaches, and feedback customized to the employee needs; and the use of technology (including Web-based training). Such training is self-paced and available outside a formal classroom environment (these learning opportunities are discussed in Chapters 5, 7, 8, and 9). Consider how Freddie Mac, the mortgage finance company based in Virginia, provides learning when it is needed.[17] A Freddie Mac employee who has a learning need can go to the learning portal on the Web to find solutions. The learning portal includes online courses, books, videos, discussion groups, and articles. Learning consultants are available to help employees use the learning portal, address special needs, and incorporate learning needs into their personal development plan. Accenture Resources Group, a consulting company in New York, uses informal learning as a way to increase communications between executives, managers, and consultants in the field. Each Accenture consultant is assigned to a community of 100 people that meets four times a year. The community meetings often feature senior executives leading discussions on topics such as leadership and the creation of shareholder value.

Expand who is trained refers to the recognition that because employees are often the customer's primary point of contact, they need as much if not more training than managers do.

TABLE 2.2 **Strategic Training and Development Initiatives and Their Implications**

Strategic Training and Development Initiatives	Implications
Diversify the Learning Portfolio	• Use new technology such as the Internet for training • Facilitate informal learning • Provide more personalized learning opportunities
Expand Who Is Trained	• Train customers, suppliers, and employees • Offer more learning opportunities to nonmanagerial employees
Accelerate the Pace of Employee Learning	• Quickly identify needs and provide a high-quality learning solution • Reduce the time to develop training programs • Facilitate access to learning resources on an as-needed basis
Improve Customer Service	• Ensure that employees have product and service knowledge • Ensure that employees have skills needed to interact with customers • Ensure that employees understand their roles and decision-making authority
Provide Development Opportunities and Communicate to Employees	• Ensure that employees have opportunities to develop • Ensure that employees understand career opportunities and personal growth opportunities • Ensure that training and development addresses employees' needs in current job as well as growth opportunities
Capture and Share Knowledge	• Capture insight and information from knowledgeable employees • Logically organize and store information • Provide methods to make information available (e.g., resource guides, Web Sites)
Align Training and Development with the Company's Strategic Direction	• Identify needed knowledge, skills, abilities, or competencies • Ensure that current training and development programs support the company's strategic needs
Ensure that the Work Environment Supports Learning and Transfer of Training	• Remove constraints to learning, such as lack of time, resources, and equipment • Dedicate physical space to encourage teamwork, collaboration, creativity, and knowledge sharing • Ensure that employees understand the importance of learning • Ensure that managers and peers are supportive of training, development, and learning

Source: Based on S. Tannenbaum, "A Strategic View of Organizational Training and Learning," in *Creating, Implementing, and Managing Effective Training and Development*, ed. K. Kraiger (San Francisco: Jossey-Bass, 2002): 10–52.

Also, to provide better customer service to suppliers, vendors, and consumers, companies need to distribute information about how to use the products and services they offer. Companies are beginning to train suppliers to ensure that the parts that suppliers provide will meet their customers' quality standards. To be successful, companies have to be able to deal with changes in technology, customer needs, and global markets. Training needs have to be quickly identified and effective training provided. That is, companies have to *accelerate the pace of employee learning*. Also, companies are relying on electronic performance support systems (EPSS) that provide employees with immediate access to information, advice, and guidance (EPSS are discussed in more detail in Chapter 5). EPSS can be accessed through personal computers or handheld computers whenever they are needed. Because customers now have access to databases and Web Sites and have a greater awareness of high-quality customer service, they are more knowledgeable, are better prepared, and have higher service expectations than ever before. Employees must be prepared to *improve customer service.* Employees have to be knowledgeable about the product or service, they need to have customer service skills, and they need to understand the types of decisions they can make (e.g., can they make an exception to the policy of no cash refunds?). *Providing development opportunities* and communicating them to employees is important to ensure that employees believe that they have opportunities to grow and learn new skills. Such opportunities are important for attracting and retaining talented employees. *Capturing and sharing knowledge* ensures that important knowledge about customers, products, or processes is not lost if employees leave the company. Also, giving employees access to knowledge that other employees have may quicken response times to customers and improve product and service quality. For example, rather than "reinventing the wheel," service personnel can tap into a database that allows them to search for problems and identify solutions that other service reps have developed. *Aligning training and development with the company's strategic direction* is important to ensure that training contributes to business needs. Companies need to identify what employee capabilities (e.g., knowledge, skills) are needed and whether training programs and services are helping to improve these capabilities. Lastly, *a supportive work environment* is necessary for employees to be motivated to participate in training and learning activities, use what they learn on the job, and share their knowledge with others. Tangible support includes time and money for training and learning as well as work areas that encourage employees to meet and discuss ideas. Psychological support from managers and peers for training and learning is also important. Types of tangible and psychological support for training are discussed in Chapter 5.

How might a company ensure that its training and development initiatives are linked to its business strategy? Table 2.3 shows the questions that a company needs to answer to identify and develop its strategic training and development initiatives. To help answer these questions, trainers need to read the annual reports, strategic plans, earnings releases, and analyst reports for their companies. To understand the business strategy and its implications for training, it may be useful to invite managers to attend training and development

TABLE 2.3 **Questions to Ask to Develop Strategic Training and Development Initiatives** Source: Based on R. Hughes and K. Beatty, "Five Steps to Leading Strategically," *TD* (December 2005): 46–48.	1. What is the vision and mission of the company? Identify the strategic drivers of the business strategy. 2. What capabilities does the company need as a result of the business strategy and business environment challenges? 3. What types of training and development will best attract, retain, and develop the talent needed for success? 4. Which competencies are critical for company success and the business strategy? 5. Does the company have a plan for making the link between training and development and the business strategy understood by executives, managers, and employees or customers? 6. Will the senior management team publicly support and champion training and development? 7. Does the company provide opportunities for training and developing not only individuals but also teams?

staff meetings and present information on the company's business strategy. Also, in companies with multiple divisions, it is important to understand each business, including how it measures effectiveness, how it monitors and reports performance, and what challenges it faces, such as supply chain management, new product development, competitive pressures, or service warranty issues.

Provide Training and Development Activities Linked to Strategic Training and Development Initiatives

After a company chooses its strategic training and development initiatives related to its business strategy, it then identifies specific training and development activities that will enable these initiatives to be achieved. These activities include developing initiatives related to use of new technology in training, increasing access to training programs for certain groups of employees, reducing development time, and developing new or expanded course offerings. For example, one of the strategic training and development initiatives for American Express Financial Advisors, located in Minneapolis, Minnesota, is to prepare employees to offer world-class service.[18] Training the company's customer service representatives is especially important because of the breadth of the job requirements. The customer service representatives have to be able to discuss the content of financial products as well as handle transactions of these products over the phone with both customers and financial experts. Also, the representatives work in the securities industry, which is highly regulated, and some are required to have a license to sell securities. American Express's emphasis on training is related not only to the company needs but also to the basic business principle that it costs less to serve customers well and keep them than to try to replace them after they have left. Providing good customer service and maintaining customer loyalty depend on how well customer service representatives work the phones, take orders, offer assistance, and develop relationships with customers.

When new employees report for work in the customer services section of American Express, they begin an eight-week training program designed to help them succeed in building and solidifying the company's client base. First, they split their days into learning about American Express's investment products and practicing how they will work with the company's financial advisers and clients. After employees complete the initial training and begin to work on the phone with actual clients, they still receive at least two weeks of training each year. The ongoing training includes a mix of classroom and Web-based training on subjects such as new financial products or changes in security regulations. Online training modules are used to teach computer skills such as how to use a new software product or how to reduce the number of screens a representative must go through to retrieve a particular piece of information. American Express's training includes active participation by the trainees. Customer service trainees are given time to review material, ask questions, and practice on the computer systems they will be using.

Sun Microsystems, a manufacturer of computer workstations and workstation software based in Santa Clara, California, has made sure its training function and training activities support its business strategy. Sun's mission statement (shown in Table 2.4) discusses how Sun views computer networks (a vision of network participation driven by shared innovation, community development, and open source leadership). Sun has established a history of innovation and technology leadership, helps companies in every industry leverage the power of the Internet, has established relationships with leading suppliers of computing solutions that Sun can rely on to develop integrated solutions, and is committed to high-quality service and

TABLE 2.4
Sun Microsystems's Vision, Mission, and Strategy

Source: *www.sun.com*, About Sun, Our Company, Mission (February 25, 2009).

Vision: "The Network Is the Computer." Sun drives network participation (the Participation Age) through shared innovation, community development, and open source leadership.

Mission: To create the technologies and fuel the communities that power the Participation Age.

Strategy: We engineer solutions for our customers' biggest, most important problems. We share our solutions to grow communities, increase participation, and create world-changing new market opportunities. We will build and run the world's participation infrastructure, *The network,* to make sure the job is done right.

technical support. In his letter to stockholders in the 2005 annual report, Scott McNealy, then chairman of the board and chief executive officer, identified six priorities: making money; growing; capitalizing on acquisitions; leveraging partners; reenlisting champions (creating passion for Sun in customers, partners, employees, and shareholders); and simplifying the business. The training and development activities that Sun develops can help the company achieve these business priorities.[19]

A good example of how a training function can contribute to business strategy is evident in the changes made by SunU, the training and development organization of Sun Microsystems.[20] SunU realigned its training philosophy and the types of training it conducted to be more linked to the strategy of Sun. Sun was in a constantly evolving business due to new technologies, products, and product markets. SunU found that its customers wanted training services that could be developed quickly, could train many people, and would not involve classroom training. Because of its importance for the business, Sun was also interested in maintaining and improving the knowledge and competence of its current work force.

Table 2.5 presents the questions that SunU used to determine how to better contribute to the business strategy. Note that the questions SunU asked not only deal with the delivery of

TABLE 2.5
SunU's Analysis to Align Training with Business Strategy

Source: Based on P.A. Smith, "Reinventing SunU," *Training and Development* (July 1994): 23–27.

Customers
Who are our customers and how do we work for them?

Organization
What is the nature of practices required to complete our mission?

Products and Services
How do we ensure that our products and services meet strategic requirements?

Research and Development
How do we stay current in the training and learning fields and use our knowledge in these areas?

Business Systems
What are the processes, products, tools, and procedures required to achieve our goals?

Continuous Learning
How do we recognize that learning at Sun Microsystems is continuous, is conscious, and comes from many sources?

Results
How do we obtain results according to our customers' standards?

training, but also attempt to understand internal customer needs and potential business needs as determined by Sun's business strategy.

As a result of the need to better align the training function with the needs generated by the business strategy, SunU took several steps. First, it developed a new approach to determining the knowledge and skills that the employees needed to meet business goals. SunU identified several basic competencies (such as customer relations). A team of trainers at SunU constantly reviews these competencies and discusses them with key senior managers. For example, in the customer service competency, vice presidents and directors of sales and marketing are interviewed to identify training needs. As a result of this process SunU learns more about the business needs and is able to develop relevant training. To help deliver training quickly to a large number of trainees without relying on the classroom, SunU developed videoconferencing programs that allow training to be delivered simultaneously to several sites without requiring trainees to travel to a central location. To help maintain and improve the knowledge and abilities of its employees, SunU developed a desktop library that enables all employees to access CD-ROMs containing up-to-date information on technologies and products as well as profiles on customers and competitors. SunU also delivers Web-based training to more than 400,000 students, and more than 80,000 online training sessions are accessible daily to employees, customers, suppliers, and partners.[21]

In 2001, when SunU was faced with the business need to train and certify all Sun employees in Sun Sigma (Sun's version of Six Sigma quality training) in less than six months, SunU turned to online training. SunU's training program needed to reach employees who worked in 170 different countries and who spoke a variety of languages, and it needed to be tailored to both individuals and groups. The customized course material was incorporated into e-learning, which allowed SunU to train twice as many employees as would have been possible in a classroom approach. The Sun Sigma training initiative was able to save the company approximately $1.2 million.

Identify and Collect Metrics to Show Training Success

How does a company determine whether training and development activities actually contribute to the business goals? This determination involves identifying and collecting outcome measures, or metrics. The metrics that are typically used to identify training success or effectiveness include trainees' satisfaction with the training program; whether the trainees' knowledge, skill, ability, or attitudes changed as a result of program participation (cognitive and skill-based outcomes); and whether the program resulted in business-related outcomes for the company.

The business-related outcomes should be directly linked to the business strategy and goals. Business-related outcomes could evaluate, for example, customer service, employee satisfaction or engagement, employee turnover, number of product defects, time spent in product development, number of patents, or time spent filling management positions. Some companies use the balanced scorecard as a process to evaluate all aspects of the business. The **balanced scorecard** is a means of performance measurement that provides managers with a chance to look at the overall company performance or the performance of departments or functions (such as training) from the perspective of internal and external customers, employees, and shareholders.[22] The balanced scorecard considers four different perspectives: customer, internal, innovation and learning, and financial. The emphasis and type of indicators used to measure each of these perspectives are based on the company's business strategy and goals. The four perspectives and examples of metrics used to measure them include:

- Customer (time, quality, performance, service, cost).
- Internal (processes that influence customer satisfaction).
- Innovation and learning (operating efficiency, employee satisfaction, continuous improvement).
- Financial (profitability, growth, shareholder value).

Metrics that might be used to assess training's contribution to the balanced scorecard include employees trained (employees trained divided by total number of employees), training costs (total training costs divided by number of employees trained), and training costs per hour (total training costs divided by total training hours). For example, EMC Corporation, a technology company, uses a balanced scorecard to track and measure learning.[23] Company performance is tracked quarterly with metrics measuring business alignment, work-force readiness, time-to-market, globalization, and effectiveness. The company has also implemented performance metrics that are directly linked to present and future business needs. Employees are given individual development plans that are based on an analysis of their jobs. Ingersoll Rand requires its business units to make strong business cases for new spending.[24] Following this model, Ingersoll Rand University shows that learning makes a difference and contributes to the business strategy by using metrics such as expected benefits, one-time versus ongoing costs, shelf-life of learning products, and employee participation rates in its programs. Each year Ingersoll Rand University (IRU) provides the company with an annual report communicating accomplishments, challenges, strategic directions, and operational efficiencies. For example, IRU has offered process improvement workshops related to Lean Six Sigma (a quality initiative), which is a business priority. IRU has been able to demonstrate that its workshops have resulted in saving the company hundreds of thousands of dollars by reducing vendor delivery costs by 76 percent. The process of identifying and collecting metrics is related to training evaluation, the final step in Figure 1.1. Chapter 6 discusses the different types of outcomes in greater detail. Of course, showing that training directly relates to the company "bottom line" (e.g., increased service, sales, product quality) is the most convincing evidence of the value of training!

ORGANIZATIONAL CHARACTERISTICS THAT INFLUENCE TRAINING

The amount and type of training as well as the organization of the training function in a company are influenced by employee and manager roles; by top management support for training; by the company's degree of integration of business units; by its global presence; by its business conditions; by other human resource management practices, including staffing strategies and human resource planning; by the company's extent of unionization; and by the extent of involvement in training and development by managers, employees, and human resource staff.[25]

Roles of Employees and Managers

The roles that employees and managers have in a company influence the focus of training, development, and learning activity. Traditionally, employees' roles were to perform their jobs according to the managers' directions. Employees were not involved in improving the quality of the products or services. However, with the emphasis on the creation of intellectual capital and the movement toward high-performance work systems using teams, employees today are performing many roles once reserved for management (e.g., hiring; scheduling work; interacting with customers, vendors, and suppliers).[26] If companies are using teams to manufacture goods and provide services, team members need training in interpersonal problem solving and team skills (e.g., how to resolve conflicts, give feedback). If employees are responsible for the quality of products and services, they need to be trained to use data to make decisions, which involves training in statistical process control techniques. As discussed in Chapter 1, team members may also receive training in skills needed for all positions on the team (cross training), not just for the specific job they are doing. To encourage cross training, companies may adopt skill-based pay systems, which base employees' pay rates on the number of skills they are competent in rather than what skills they are using for their current jobs. Skill-based pay systems are discussed in Chapter 10.

Research suggests that managers in traditional work environments are expected to do the following:[27]

- *Manage individual performance.* Motivate employees to change performance, provide performance feedback, and monitor training activities.
- *Develop employees.* Explain work assignments and provide technical expertise.
- *Plan and allocate resources.* Translate strategic plans into work assignments and establish target dates for projects.
- *Coordinate interdependent groups.* Persuade other units to provide products or resources needed by the work group, and understand the goals and plans of other units.
- *Manage group performance.* Define areas of responsibility, meet with other managers to discuss effects of changes in the work unit on their groups, facilitate change, and implement business strategy.
- *Monitor the business environment.* Develop and maintain relationships with clients and customers, and participate in task forces to identify new business opportunities.
- *Represent one's work unit.* Develop relationships with other managers, communicate the needs of the work group to other units, and provide information on work group status to other groups.

Regardless of their level in the company (e.g., senior management), all managers are expected to serve as spokespersons to other work units, managers, and vendors (i.e., represent the work unit). Of course, the amount of time managers devote to some of these roles is affected by their level. Line managers spend more time managing individual performance and developing employees than midlevel managers or executives do. The most important roles for midlevel managers and executives are planning and allocating resources, coordinating interdependent groups, and managing group performance (especially managing change). Executives also spend time monitoring the business environment by analyzing market trends, developing relationships with clients, and overseeing sales and marketing activities.

The roles and duties of managers in companies that use high-performance work systems (such as teams) are shown in Table 2.6. The managers' duty is to create the conditions necessary to ensure team success. These roles include managing alignment, coordinating

TABLE 2.6 **The Roles and Duties of Managers in Companies That Use High-Performance Work Practices**

Roles	Key Duties
Managing Alignment	Clarify team goals and company goals. Help employees manage their objectives. Scan organization environment for useful information for the team.
Coordinating Activities	Ensure that team is meeting internal and external customer needs. Ensure that team meets its quantity and quality objectives. Help team resolve problems with other teams. Ensure uniformity in interpretation of policies and procedures.
Facilitating Decision-Making Process	Facilitate team decision making. Help team use effective decision-making processes (deal with conflict, statistical process control).
Encouraging Continuous Learning	Help team identify training needs. Help team become effective at on-the-job training. Create environment that encourages learning.
Creating and Maintaining Trust	Ensure that each team member is responsible for his or her work load and customers. Treat all team members with respect. Listen and respond honestly to team ideas.

activities, facilitating the decision-making process, encouraging continuous learning, and creating and maintaining trust.[28]

To manage successfully in a team environment, managers need to be trained in "people skills," including negotiation, sensitivity, coaching, conflict resolution, and communication skills. A lack of people skills has been shown to be related to managers' failure to advance in their careers.[29]

Top Management Support

The CEO, the top manager in the company, plays a key role in determining the importance of training and learning in the company. The CEO is responsible for[30]

- A clear direction for learning (vision).
- Encouragement, resources, and commitment for strategic learning (sponsor).
- Taking an active role in governing learning, including reviewing goals and objectives and providing insight on how to measure training effectiveness (governor).
- Developing new learning programs for the company (subject-matter expert).
- Teaching programs or providing resources online (faculty).
- Serving as a role model for learning for the entire company and demonstrating a willingness to constantly learn (learner).
- Promoting the company's commitment to learning by advocating it in speeches, annual reports, interviews, and other public relations tools (marketing agent).

For example, James Hackett, CEO of Steelcase, a company in the office furniture industry, declared publicly that learning is the core of Steelcase's strategy. The key, said Hackett, is for Steelcase to study space and help companies use it more efficiently and effectively.[31] At Ingersoll Rand, to ensure that top managers understand and support the role that training and development can play in the company, a "ladder of engagement" model has been created.[32] Top managers are engaged in training and development in many different ways, including providing input into learning program development, serving as trainers or co-trainers, visiting courses as executive speakers, or serving as advisory council members for Ingersoll Rand's corporate university.

Integration of Business Units

The degree to which a company's units or businesses are integrated affects the kind of training that takes place. In a highly integrated business, employees need to understand other units, services, and products in the company. Training likely includes rotating employees between jobs in different businesses so they can gain an understanding of the whole business.

Global Presence

As noted in Chapter 1, the development of global product and service markets is an important challenge for U.S. companies. For companies with global operations, training is used to prepare employees for temporary or long-term overseas assignments. Also, because employees are geographically dispersed outside the United States, companies need to determine whether training will be conducted and coordinated from a central U.S. facility or will be the responsibility of satellite installations located near overseas facilities.

Consider how globalization has affected the training practices of KLA-Tencor, a manufacturer of equipment and systems for semiconductor manufacturers.[33] KLA-Tencor has factories in China, Taiwan, Singapore, and India in order to better serve its customers, such as Intel, which also have global locations. At KLA-Tencor, employees are trained in installing and servicing machine tools in its global operations. Employees also need to know how to adjust the machines to maximize productivity so they can educate customers on how to use them more effectively. Technology training is provided regionally because trainees need hands-on experience with the machines. KLA-Tencor finds local instructors who are qualified to teach in the local language. The local instructors are trained in how to deliver the technical training and use the machines. Before teaching courses on their own, the local instructors co-teach a class with another trainer to ensure that they are comfortable and proficient in delivering training. Network Appliances, a data storage technology company, is headquartered in the U.S. but has locations in the Middle East, Asia, and Africa. NetApp University provides training to account managers, systems engineers, technical support employees, customers, and maintenance suppliers. NetApp training centers in overseas locations provide training that is delivered in English. Some courses, such as customer training, are available in 23 different languages.

At Intel, a semiconductor and microprocessor manufacturer, providing for the company's global strategic needs begins with a needs assessment.[34] Regardless of whether employees are in China or Arizona, they are going to receive the same training content. Intel's programs are delivered by local instructors (subject-matter experts, not full-time trainers) who tailor the training content to meet the needs of the learners at each location. Intel uses local instructors to ensure that the training content is not too generic or U.S.-focused. Typically, the content is 80 to 90 percent consistent across the company, but instructors have the flexibility to use examples that are geographically and/or business-unit relevant.

Business Conditions

When unemployment is low and/or businesses are growing at a high rate and need more employees, companies often find it difficult to attract new employees, find employees with necessary skills, and retain current employees.[35] Companies may find themselves in the position of hiring employees who might not be qualified for the job. Also, in these types of business conditions, companies need to retain talented employees. In the knowledge-based economy (including companies in information technology and pharmaceuticals), product development is dependent on employees' specialized skills. Losing a key employee may cause a project to be delayed or hinder a company's taking on new projects. Training plays a key role in preparing employees to be productive as well as motivating and retaining current employees. Studies of what factors influence employee retention suggest that employees rate working with good colleagues, challenging job assignments, and opportunities for career growth and development as top reasons for staying with a company. Across all industries, from high tech to retailing, companies are increasingly relying on training and development to attract new employees and retain current ones. For example, companies such as Eli Lilly (a pharmaceutical company) and Microsoft are successful in terms of financial returns. They are typically found on lists of great places to work (for example, *Fortune* magazine's list of "Best Companies to Work For"). They are quite successful in attracting and retaining employees. Not only do they provide employees with very competitive pay and benefits, but they also are committed to training and development. Retailers such as Macy's and Nordstroms cannot generate sales unless they have enough skilled employees.[36] For example, Macy's begins its employee retention strategy by starting with executives. Executives are accountable for retention of the employees who report to them. Managers have been trained to run meetings and conduct performance evaluations (skills that influence employees' perceptions of how they are treated, which ultimately affects whether they remain with Macy's). Macy's has also provided training programs and courses for employees.

For companies in an unstable or recessionary business environment—one characterized by mergers, acquisitions, or disinvestment of businesses—training may be abandoned, be left to the discretion of managers, or become more short term (such as offering training courses only to correct skill deficiencies rather than to prepare staff for new assignments). These programs emphasize the development of skills and characteristics needed (e.g., how to deal with change) regardless of the structure the company takes. Training may not even occur as a result of a planned effort. Employees who remain with a company following a merger, acquisition, or disinvestment usually find that their job now has different responsibilities requiring new skills. For employees in companies experiencing growth—that is, an increased demand for their products and services—there may be many new opportunities for lateral job moves and promotions resulting from the expansion of sales, marketing, and manufacturing operations or from the start-up of new business units. These employees are usually excited about participating in development activities because new positions often offer higher salaries and more challenging tasks.

During periods when companies are trying to revitalize and redirect their business, earnings are often flat. As a result, fewer incentives for participation in training—such as promotions and salary increases—may be available. In many cases, companies downsize their work forces as a way of cutting costs. Training activities under these conditions focus on ensuring that employees are available to fill the positions vacated by retirement or turnover. Training also involves helping employees avoid skill obsolescence. (Strategies to help employees avoid skill obsolescence are discussed in Chapter 12.)

Other Human Resource Management Practices

Human resource management (HRM) practices consist of the management activities related to investments (time, effort, and money) in staffing (determining how many employees are needed, and recruiting and selecting employees), performance management, training, and compensation and benefits. The type of training and the resources devoted to training are influenced by the strategy adopted for two human resource management practices: staffing and human resource planning.

Staffing Strategy

Staffing strategy refers to the company's decisions regarding where to find employees, how to select them, and the desired mix of employee skills and statuses (temporary, full-time, etc.). For example, one staffing decision a company has to make is how much to rely on the internal labor market (within the company) or external labor market (outside the company) to fill vacancies. Two aspects of a company's staffing strategy influence training: the criteria used to make promotion and assignment decisions (assignment flow) and the places where the company prefers to obtain the human resources to fill open positions (supply flow).[37]

Companies vary in terms of the extent to which they make promotion and job assignment decisions based on individual performance or group or business-unit performance. They also vary in terms of the extent to which their staffing needs are met by relying on current employees (internal labor market) or employees from competitors and recent entrants into the labor market, such as college graduates (external labor market). Figure 2.4 displays the two dimensions of staffing strategy. The interaction between assignment flow and supply flow results in four distinct types of companies: fortresses, baseball teams, clubs, and academies. Each company type places a different emphasis on training activities. For example, some companies (such as medical research companies) emphasize innovation and creativity. These types of companies are labeled baseball teams. Because it may be difficult to train skills related to innovation and creativity, they tend to handle staffing needs by luring employees away from competitors or by hiring graduating students with specialized skills. Figure 2.4 can be used to identify development activities that support a specific staffing strategy. For example, if a company wants to reward individual employee contributions and promote from within (the bottom right quadrant of Figure 2.4), it needs to use lateral, upward, and downward moves within and across functions to support the staffing strategy.

Another staffing strategy is deciding what skills new employees will be expected to possess and what skills the company will develop through training. MidAmerican Energy was having trouble finding skilled, ready-to-hire meter readers and increasing the diversity of its meter readers.[38] Turnover was 50 percent, and customers increasingly complained about incorrect meter reads, which translated into higher bills. These problems were blamed on the company's traditional hiring, which involved employee referrals. As a result, MidAmerican decided to change its hiring practices in order to hire more skilled people. First, MidAmerican identified that the important skills for the job were reading for information, locating information, and observation. Next, MidAmerican Energy

FIGURE 2.4
Implications of
Staffing
Strategy for
Training

Source: Adapted from
J. A. Sonnenfeld and
M. A. Peiperl,
"Staffing Policy as a
Strategic Response: A
Typology of Career
Systems," *Academy of*
Management Review
13 (1988): 588–600.

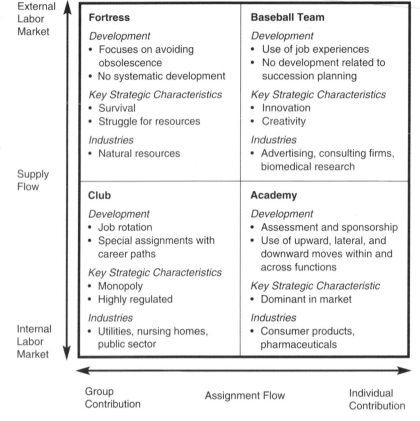

decided to use tests on these skills as part of the hiring process. The tests ask questions that assess these skills in the context of the work of meter readers. As a result of the tests, turnover has been reduced, customer service has improved, the diversity of the work force has increased, and new meter readers are completing MidAmerican's apprenticeship programs more quickly.

Human Resource Planning

Human resource planning includes the identification, analysis, forecasting, and planning of changes needed in the human resource area to help the company meet changing business conditions.[39] Human resource planning allows the company to anticipate the movement of human resources in the company because of turnover, transfers, retirements, or promotions. Human resource plans can help identify where employees with certain types of skills are needed in the company. Training can be used to prepare employees for increased responsibilities in their current job, promotions, lateral moves, transfers, and downward job opportunities that are predicted by the human resource plan.

Extent of Unionization

Unions' interest in training has resulted in joint union-management programs designed to help employees prepare for new jobs. When companies begin retraining and productivity-improvement efforts without involving unions, the efforts are likely to fail. The unions may see the programs as just another attempt to make employees work harder without sharing the productivity gains. Joint union-management programs (detailed in Chapter 10) ensure that all parties (unions, management, employees) understand the development goals and are committed to making the changes necessary for the company to make profits and for employees to both keep their jobs and share in any increased profits.

Staff Involvement in Training and Development

How often and how well a company's training program is used are affected by the degree to which managers, employees, and specialized development staff are involved in the process. If managers are not involved in the training process (e.g., determining training needs, being used as trainers), training may be unrelated to business needs. Managers may also not be committed to ensuring that training is effective (e.g., giving trainees feedback on the job). As a result, training's potential impact on helping the company reach its goals may be limited because managers may feel that training is a "necessary evil" forced on them by the training department rather than a means of helping them to accomplish business goals.

If line managers are aware of what development activity can achieve, such as reducing the time it takes to fill open positions, they will be more willing to become involved in it. They will also become more involved in the training process if they are rewarded for participating. Constellation Energy, located in Baltimore, Maryland, links employee learning to individual and organizational performance.[40] Each summer the company is involved in its business planning process until December, during which time a comprehensive five-year plan detailing organizational and business goals and objectives is developed. The human resources plan, which includes learning, ensures that employee development strategies are aligned with business strategies. Individual development plans and goals jointly established between employees and their managers are established based on the business goals and objectives and human resource needs. Managers are held accountable for developing employees. One of the competencies they are evaluated on is human capital management, which includes employee engagement, talent management, and diversity. Part of each manager's bonus is based on the evaluation he or she receives on this competency.

An emerging trend is that companies expect employees to initiate the training process.[41] Companies with a greater acceptance of a continuous learning philosophy require more development planning. Companies will support training and development activities (such as tuition reimbursement and the offering of courses, seminars, and workshops) but will give employees the responsibility for planning their own development. Training and development planning involve identifying needs, choosing the expected outcome (e.g., behavior change, greater knowledge), identifying the actions that should be taken, deciding how progress toward goal attainment will be measured, and creating a timetable for improvement. To identify strengths and weaknesses and training needs, employees need to analyze what they want to do, what they can do, how others perceive them, and what others expect of them. A need can result from gaps between current capabilities and interests and the type of work or position the employee wants in the future. The needs assessment process is discussed in greater detail in Chapter 3.

TRAINING NEEDS IN DIFFERENT STRATEGIES

Table 2.7 describes four business strategies—concentration, internal growth, external growth, and disinvestment—and highlights the implications of each for training practices.[42] Each strategy differs based on the goal of the business. A **concentration strategy** focuses on increasing market share, reducing costs, or creating and maintaining a market niche for products and services. Southwest Airlines has a concentration strategy. It focuses on providing short-haul, low-fare, high-frequency air transportation. It utilizes one type of aircraft (the Boeing 737), has no reserved seating, and serves no meals. This concentration strategy has enabled Southwest to keep costs low and revenues high. An **internal growth strategy** focuses on new market and product development, innovation, and joint ventures. For example, the merger between two publishing companies, McGraw-Hill and Richard D. Irwin, created one company with strengths in the U.S. and the international college textbook markets. An **external growth strategy** emphasizes acquiring vendors and suppliers or buying businesses that allow the company to expand into new markets. For example, General Electric, a manufacturer of lighting products and jet engines, acquired the National Broadcast Corporation (NBC), a television and communications company. A **disinvestment strategy** emphasizes liquidation and divestiture of businesses. For example, General Mills sold its restaurant businesses.

Preliminary research suggests a link between business strategy and amount and type of training.[43] Table 2.7 shows that training issues vary greatly from one strategy to another. Divesting companies need to train employees in job-search skills and to focus on cross-training remaining employees who may find themselves in jobs with expanding responsibilities. Companies focusing on a market niche (a concentration strategy) need to emphasize skill currency and development of their existing work force. New companies formed from a merger or acquisition need to ensure that employees have the skills needed to help the company reach its new strategic goals. Also, for mergers and acquisitions to be

TABLE 2.7 **Implications of Business Strategy for Training**

Strategy	Emphasis	How Achieved	Key Issues	Training Implications
Concentration	• Increased market share • Reduced operating costs • Market niche created or maintained	• Improve product quality • Improve productivity or innovate technical processes • Customize products or services	• Skill currency • Development of existing work force	• Team building • Cross training • Specialized programs • Interpersonal skill training • On-the-job training
Internal Growth	• Market development • Product development	• Market existing products/add distribution channels	• Creation of new jobs and tasks • Innovation	• High-quality communication of product value • Cultural training

Continued

Strategy	Emphasis	How Achieved	Key Issues	Training Implications
Internal Growth *continued*	• Innovation • Joint ventures	• Expand global market • Modify existing products • Create new or different products • Expand through joint ownership		• Development of organizational culture that values creative thinking and analysis • Technical competence in jobs • Manager training in feedback and communication • Conflict negotiation skills
External Growth (Acquisition)	• Horizontal integration • Vertical integration • Concentric diversification	• Acquire firms operating at same stage in product market chain (new market access) • Acquire business that can supply or buy products • Acquire firms that have nothing in common with acquiring firm	• Integration • Redundancy • Restructuring	• Determination of capabilities of employees in acquired firms • Integration of training systems • Methods and procedures of combined firms • Team building • Development of shared culture
Disinvestment	• Retrenchment • Turnaround • Divestiture • Liquidation	• Reduce costs • Reduce assets • Generate revenue • Redefine goals • Sell off all assets	• Efficiency	• Motivation, goal setting, time management, stress management, cross training • Leadership training • Interpersonal communications • Outplacement assistance • Job-search skills training

successful, employees need to learn about the new, merged organization and its culture.[44] The organization must provide training in systems such as how the phone, e-mail, and company intranet work. Managers need to be educated on how to make the new merger successful (e.g., dealing with resistance to change). For example, EMC's products help companies store, protect, and organize employee, customer, and product information.[45] In five years EMC grew from offering 200 to 300 products to offering more than 4,000 products based on a business strategy that included acquiring 40 companies whose products complemented EMC's product line. The acquisition strategy meant that a necessary strategic training initiative for EMC was to develop and expand its professional certification program (Proven Professionals). The certification program is critical for the company's technical employees and customers to understand the value of its products and how to install and support them. The program includes 10 technologies with certification available, and within each certification area employees and customers can attain associate, specialist, and expert levels.

Companies with an internal growth strategy face the challenge of keeping employees up-to-date on new products and services. For example, Masimo Corporation, located in Orange County, California, develops, licenses, and markets advanced medical signal processing technologies for monitoring patient vital signs.[46] Because employees work with sophisticated technology and because new products are constantly being developed, Masimo is challenged to keep its sales force and distribution partners aware of the latest features, functions, and applications of its monitoring devices. Using an Internet-based corporate university, Masimo has been able to provide programs that enhance revenue by more quickly preparing the sales force to sell new products, and these programs have given the company the ability to bring products to the market faster. Also, the training benefits the clinical staff by increasing brand awareness and product competence among hospital staff and by building a community of users to drive future sales. The Internet-based corporate university is also important because it allows clinical staff who work long hours access to training and because it tracks and documents training as required by government regulations.

Despite the dismal financial picture for automobile companies, instead of cutting worker hours or downsizing, Toyota Motor Corporation is keeping employees at the plants, participating in training programs designed to improve their job skills and find more efficient and effective methods for assembling vehicles.[47] Based on their union contracts, employees at GM, Ford, and Chrysler, are paid for not working when their assembly lines are shut down. If a plant is shut down temporarily, employees receive most of their pay but don't have to show up for work. At its Princeton plant, Toyota uses downtime to improve employees' quality control and productivity skills, keeping good on its pledge never to lay off any of its full-time non-union employees. The training has already resulted in continuous improvements (also known as *kaizen*). One example is a Teflon ring designed by an assembly line employee that helps prevent paint damage when an electrical switch is installed on the edge of a vehicle's door.

A disinvestment strategy resulted in Edwards Lifesciences Corporation being spun off from another company.[48] The new company's management team developed a new strategic plan that described goals for sales growth, new product development, customer loyalty, and employee commitment and satisfaction. The company realized that it had to prepare leaders who could help the company meet its strategic goals. A review of leadership talent showed that leadership development was needed, and a leadership program was created. The program includes 20 participants from different functions and company locations. Part of the week-long program is devoted to a simulation in which teams of managers run their own business and take responsibility for marketing, manufacturing, and financials. The sessions also include classes taught by company executives, who speak about important topics such as the company's business strategy.

MODELS OF ORGANIZING THE TRAINING DEPARTMENT

This section discusses five models that are used to organize the training department: faculty model, customer model, matrix model, corporate university model, and business-embedded model.[49] This review of these structures should help you to understand that the organization of the training department has important consequences for how the training department (and trainers employed in the department) contributes (or fails to contribute) to the business strategy. Keep in mind that—particularly with large, decentralized companies—there may be multiple separate training functions, each organized using a different model. The business-embedded model and the corporate university model (or a blended model that includes both) are the models that companies are moving to in order to ensure that training is used to help the company achieve its business objectives. These models are also being adopted as companies begin to value human capital and view training as part of a learning system designed to create and share knowledge.

Many companies, including Boeing, Cingular Wireless, and Harley-Davidson have centralized their training departments.[50] **Centralized training** means that training and development programs, resources, and professionals are primarily housed in one location and that decisions about training investment, programs, and delivery methods are made from that department. Training at Boeing used to be decentralized because of the company's many geographic locations. Boeing and other companies have found several advantages to centralized training, including the ownership of training to one organization and the elimination of course and program variation and duplication in the training system. Wyeth, a global leader in pharmaceuticals and consumer and animal health care products, uses a centralized training function to ensure that selling skills are adopted across the company. Instead of the four different selling models that were being used, Wyeth businesses in more than 140 countries are now using a consistent selling model.

Also, a centralized training function helps drive stronger alignment with business strategy, allows development of a common set of metrics or scorecards to measure and report rates of quality and delivery, helps to streamline processes, and gives the company a cost advantage in purchasing training from vendors and consultants because of the number of trainees who will be involved. Finally, a centralized training function helps companies better integrate programs for developing leaders and managing talent with training and learning during times of change. At both Cingular Wireless and Harley-Davidson, a centralized training function allows selection of a common technology for delivery of training programs.[51] This policy helps reduce the chances that functional groups will adopt different technologies, for which some training programs and their features, such as video, will work and others will not. The key to the success of a centralized approach is that top managers must believe they are in control of the training function and that the training function is aligned with the business strategy. That is, the business objectives have to be communicated and understood, and training and development have to help drive that strategy. At the same time, centralized training functions must be in touch with the unique needs of the functions and divisions they serve. At ETS, employee education is the responsibility of the learning and development (L&D) unit of strategic work force solutions.[52] The 50 L&D employees are organized around "people processes," including learning and knowledge management. The director and executive director work with the chief learning officer to ensure that training and development and learning strategies are related to ETS's business strategy.

Faculty Model

Training departments organized by the **faculty model** look a lot like the structure of a college. Figure 2.5 shows the faculty model. The training department is headed by a director with a staff of experts who have specialized knowledge of a particular topic or skill area. These experts develop, administer, and update training programs. For example, sales trainers are responsible for sales skills training (cultivating clients, negotiating a sale, closing a sale), and computer experts provide training on topics such as using e-mail and the World Wide Web as well as software design language.

The faculty model has several strengths. First, training staff are clearly experts in the areas in which they train. Second, the training department's plans are easily determined by staff expertise. The content and timing of programs are determined primarily by when they are available and the expertise of the trainers. Organizing by the faculty model also has several disadvantages. Companies that use the faculty model may create a training function that has expertise that does not meet the needs of the organization. Trainers in a faculty model may also be unaware of business problems or unwilling to adapt materials to fit a business need. This can result in demotivated trainees who fail to learn because course content lacks meaning for them—that is, it does not relate to problems or needs of the business. Programs and courses that may be needed may not be offered because trainers are not experts in certain areas. Skill and knowledge emphasized in programs may not match the needs of the company. To overcome these disadvantages of the faculty model, managers need to frequently survey training's customers to ensure that course offerings are meeting their needs. Expert trainers also need to ensure that they adapt course materials so they are meaningful for participants.

FIGURE 2.5
The Faculty Model

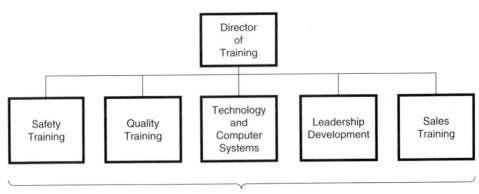

Training Specialty Areas

Customer Model

Training departments organized according to the **customer model** are responsible for the training needs of one division or function of the company. For example, trainers might be responsible for programs related to information systems, marketing, or operations. The trainers might also be human resource generalists whose job responsibilities include a broad range of human resource functions such as training, performance management, hiring, and benefits. Figure 2.6 shows the customer model. This model overcomes a major problem of the faculty model. Training programs are developed more in line with the particular needs of a business group rather than based on the expertise of the training staff. Selection, training, compensation, and development are all based on a common set of knowledges, skills, abilities, or competencies. That is, training is integrated with other human resource responsibilities. Trainers in this model are expected to be aware of business needs and to update courses and content to reflect them. If needs change such that training is no longer available from a source inside the company, the trainers may use outside experts (e.g., consultants). Materials provided by a training staff organized by this model are likely to be meaningful to trainees.

There are several disadvantages to this model. First, trainers have to spend considerable time learning the business function before they can be useful trainers. Second, a large number of programs covering similar topics may be developed by customers. These programs may also vary greatly in effectiveness. It may be difficult for the training director to oversee each function to ensure that (1) a common instructional design process is used or (2) the company's quality philosophy is consistently emphasized in each program. For example, quality training may be developed separately for marketing and for operations employees. This type of structure is likely to be unattractive to trainers who consider presentation and teaching to be their primary job function. In the customer model, trainers are likely to be employees from the functional area (e.g., manufacturing engineers) who have great functional expertise but lack training in instructional design and learning theory. As a result, courses may be meaningful but poor from a design perspective (e.g., have inadequate feedback and practice opportunities).

For example, Transamerica Life Companies has identified skills that are needed companywide.[53] These skills include communications, accountability, initiative, and

FIGURE 2.6
The Customer Model

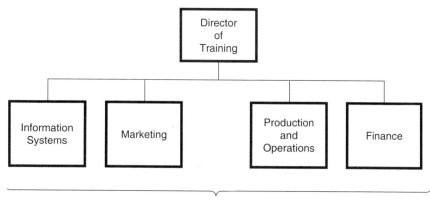

Business Functions

collaboration. Transamerica Life also has identified technical knowledge that is needed only in certain business units of the company. These skills and this knowledge are used to make hiring, promotion, and compensation decisions. All employee training and development activity focuses on knowledge and skills that are needed companywide or within a business unit.

Matrix Model

In the **matrix model,** trainers report to both a manager in the training department and a manager in a particular function. Figure 2.7 shows the matrix model. The trainer has the responsibility of being both a training expert and a functional expert. For example, as Figure 2.7 shows, sales trainers report to both the director of training and the marketing manager. One advantage of the matrix model is that it helps ensure that training is linked to the needs of the business. Another advantage is that the trainer gains expertise in understanding a specific business function. Because the trainer is also responsible to the training director, it is likely that the trainer will stay professionally current (e.g., up-to-date on new training delivery mechanisms such as the Internet). A major disadvantage of the matrix model is that trainers likely will have more time demands and conflicts because they report to two managers: a functional manager and a training director.

Corporate University Model (Corporate Training Universities)

Because of the trend to centralize training, many companies use the corporate university model, as shown in Figure 2.8. The **corporate university model** differs from the other models in that the client group includes not only employees and managers but also stakeholders outside the company, including community colleges, universities, high schools, and grade schools. Training functions organized by the university model tend to offer a wider range of programs and courses than functions organized by the other models. Important culture and

FIGURE 2.7
The Matrix Model

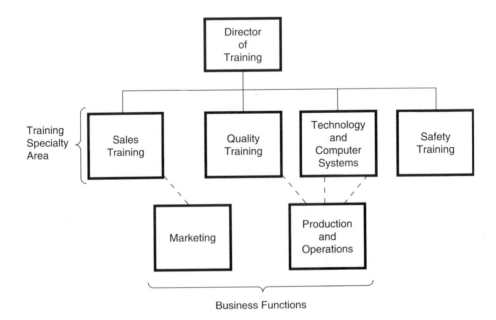

FIGURE 2.8
The Corporate University Model

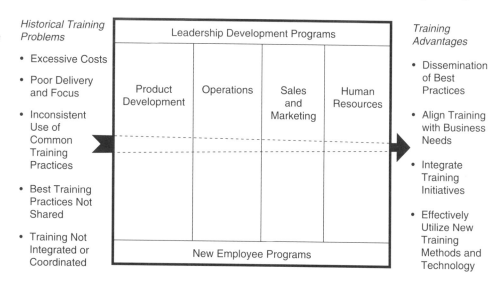

Historical Training Problems

- Excessive Costs
- Poor Delivery and Focus
- Inconsistent Use of Common Training Practices
- Best Training Practices Not Shared
- Training Not Integrated or Coordinated

Leadership Development Programs

| Product Development | Operations | Sales and Marketing | Human Resources |

New Employee Programs

Training Advantages

- Dissemination of Best Practices
- Align Training with Business Needs
- Integrate Training Initiatives
- Effectively Utilize New Training Methods and Technology

values also tend to be emphasized more often in the training curriculum of corporate universities than the other models. The university model centralizes training to make sure that "best training practices" that may be used in one unit of the company are disseminated across the company. Also, the corporate university enables the company to control costs by developing consistent training practices and policies. For example, when Capital One Financial Services created Capital One University, it reduced learning and development costs and training staff by one-third and reduced course offerings by 43 percent.[54] The company consolidated five training organizations into a facility called Town Center, located in Richmond, Virginia. The Capital One University has four goals: meeting business needs, building organizational capability, establishing and sustaining operational excellence, and creating a world-class experience.

Corporate universities also can help effectively utilize new technology. The University of Toyota, a division of Toyota Motor Sales, oversees external vendors' development of classroom and e-learning training for employees and dealerships.[55] Trainees were frustrated because there was considerable variability in course navigation and quality. The group responsible for uploading courses to the company's learning management system and distributing the courses to learners was also frustrated because it had difficulties integrating different software and explaining to users why courses coming from the university had different bandwidth requirements. To ensure that courses meet minimum standards for quality and usability, the University of Toyota has developed a single set of development standards, benchmarks, purchasing specifications, and best practices. The information is housed on e-Source, the university's Web site. Vendors are required to visit e-Source to bid on any e-learning projects for Toyota University. Courses that do not meet the specifications are revised at the vendor's expense. E-mail bulletins are sent to course owners and developers to notify them of any content additions or changes to the Web site.

Both large and small companies have started their own universities to train new employees and to retain and update the skills and knowledge of current employees. Caterpillar University comprises six colleges: leadership, marketing and distribution, technology, business and business processes, Six Sigma, and product support.[56] The deans of the colleges report to the president of the university. Caterpillar's CEO, vice presidents, and two group presidents provide policy guidance, approve budgets, and identify priorities for the university. One priority was to support new business growth goals through the development of leaders who are willing to collaborate with others, have a global mindset, and understand the financial aspects of the business. The College of Marketing and Distribution focuses on providing a comprehensive curriculum for sales professionals and sales marketing managers. It includes product knowledge, sales skills, and management skills. All learning goals are tied to business goals. The College of Product Support focuses on training dealer employees to meet certification standards. Caterpillar University staff members help the business units deal with their learning needs. Lead learning managers in each unit have a dual reporting relationship to the university and to the unit's human resource manager. The learning managers work with the business unit managers to set up learning plans.

Hamburger University, the corporate university for McDonald's Corporation, is charged with continuing to teach the core values that founder Ray Kroc believed were the key to success: quality, service, cleanliness, and value.[57] McDonald's conducts research designed to identify the characteristics of its work force that influence learning. As a result, Hamburger University has transitioned away from teaching courses with a lecture format and is moving toward fewer large group sessions and more interactive learning in classes of 25–35 students, which are then further divided into small groups for discussion and exercises. McDonald's changed its learning format to accommodate how most of its students (who would be considered Generation Y) learn. The typical education level of frontline service workers has influenced curriculum design through the development of more easily understandable coursework. E-learning is used to deliver the basics of restaurant operations or management training and classroom instruction and simulations are used to help the learner apply the basics on the job. Because students come from around the world, learners are provided with headphones that connect them with translators who provide instruction in the learner's native language during class. Besides classroom instruction, Hamburger University includes a simulated kitchen and drive-thru window. Despite having learners at the university who are already familiar with behind-the-counter operations, everyone takes part in the simulation, making real food and filling orders just as they would at a real McDonald's restaurant. Learners have performance goals to meet and receive feedback from fellow learners and trainers.

Are corporate universities effective? Corporate University Xchange surveyed corporate universities at 170 different companies.[58] The top five organizational goals of corporate universities were to improve customer service and retention, improve productivity, reduce costs, retain talented employees, and increase revenue. The survey found that measuring business impact was a high priority. Seventy percent of the companies surveyed measure business impact through product and service quality and customer service, and more than 50 percent measure reductions in operating costs and increased revenues. For example, CoreTech Consulting Group in King of Prussia, Pennsylvania, found that compensaton was less of an issue with its employees than growth opportunities and career development.[59] CoreTech started CoreTech University, which offers short training courses to help employees improve their technical and interpersonal skills. While the company spends approximately $4,500 per employee each year on training, it helps certify employees in different areas of information technology (e.g., a Microsoft certified systems engineer), which is tied directly to the company's mission and goals. CoreTech even used the in-house courses offered by the university to create a separate for-profit training company that offers courses to the public. It has generated $325,000 in revenues through courses offered primarily to chief information officers and information technology managers.

Ritz-Carlton Hotel manages 58 luxury hotels worldwide.[60] The Ritz-Carlton hotels and resorts are renowned for indulgent luxury. Beautiful surroundings and legendary award-winning service are provided to every guest. The Ritz-Carlton Leadership Center is designed to support the growth and expansion of the company's products and services. The Leadership Center includes the School of Performance Excellence, which houses all the training and development for hourly employees; the School of Leadership and Business Excellence, which trains leaders; and the School of Service Excellence, which helps ensure high customer service. Programs at the School of Service Excellence are offered to other companies, which has resulted in yearly revenues for Ritz-Carlton of more than $1 million. These revenues help offset the costs of training and development for employees. For example, a new customized training certification system for housekeeping staff utilizes CD-ROM and Web-based training. The training is linked to the results of room inspections that highlight defects for the day, week, and year. The housekeeper can then identify the correct processes that are needed to remedy the defects. This just-in-time training has helped increase customer satisfaction scores at Ritz-Carlton. One hotel increased its satisfaction with cleanliness from 82 percent to 92 percent within six months.

Steelcase's business is making workspace more effective to facilitate innovation, productivity, efficiency, and creativity. To highlight Steelcase's capabilities for effective workspace design and to facilitate learning, creativity, and collaboration, Steelcase University Learning Center was developed.[61] Many organizations visit annually to benchmark the university, the social network capabilities, and the learning tools. Also, the Steelcase University Learning Center has centralized all of the company's training and development efforts—reducing redundancies, facilitating consistency, and ensuring knowledge sharing. The learning center includes 70 percent formal and 30 percent informal learning space, putting into practice research results regarding how learning and social networking occur. The learning center provides flexible, informal space that allows employees to meet privately as well as interact in groups, facilitating cooperation and collaboration. Nine classrooms and ten breakout areas include flexible furniture and the newest technology. Each room and area can be changed to fit the specific needs of the users. The learning center is also the gathering place for cross-functional teams. Activities held in the learning center include town hall meetings, lunch-and-learn sessions, and virtual teaching sessions. The learning center is also known as the place for employee leadership development. The company's global leadership teams can use the center to meet both physically and virtually.

Creating a Corporate University

Creating a corporate university from scratch involves several steps.[62] First, senior managers and business managers form a governing body with the responsibility of developing a vision for the university. (This group answers questions such as, What are the university's policies, systems, and procedures? What are the key functional areas for which training courses will be developed?) Second, this vision is fleshed out, and the vision statement is linked to the business strategy. For example, Ingersoll Rand has a business goal of obtaining 38 percent of its revenue in 2010 from new product innovation.[63] As a result, most of the programs and courses offered through Ingersoll Rand University discuss how to get close to the customer, innovation, and strategic marketing. The programs are designed for teams working on real business issues. Subject matter experts and managers teach these programs, which are scheduled based on key product launch dates. Third, the company decides how to fund the university. The university can be funded by charging fees to business units and/or by monies allocated directly from the corporate budget. Fourth, the company determines the degree to which all training will be centralized. Many universities centralize the development of a learning philosophy, core curriculum design, and policies and procedures related to registration, administration, measurement, marketing, and distance learning. Local and regional on-site delivery and specialized business-unit curriculum are developed by business units. Fifth, it is important to identify the needs of university "customers" including employees, managers, suppliers, and external customers. Sixth, products and services are developed. The Bank of Montreal uses a service team that includes a client-relationship manager, a subject-matter expert, and a learning manager. The client-relationship manager works with the business units to identify their needs. The subject-matter expert identifies the skill requirements for meeting those needs. The learning manager recommends the best mix of learning, including classroom training as well as training based on, say, the Web or CD-ROM. The seventh step is to choose learning partners including suppliers, consultants, colleges, and companies specializing in education. Eighth, the company develops a strategy for using technology to train more employees, more frequently, and more cost-effectively than instructor-led training. Ninth, learning that occurs as a result of a corporate university is linked to performance improvement. This involves identifying how performance improvement will be measured (tests, sales data, etc.). For example, Sprint's corporate university, the University of Excellence, has developed the Standard Training Equivalent (STE) unit, an evaluation tool for its customers who are internal business units.[64] The STE unit is equal to one hour of the traditional instructor-led classroom time that would be required to deliver a course to a group of employees at a central location. An STE unit consisting of a one-hour course over the company intranet is worth much more than the same amount of time spent in the classroom. The STE program helps the University of Excellence demonstrate its value to Sprint's business units, who fund the university. Finally, the value of the corporate university is communicated to potential "customers." Questions about the types of programs offered, how learning will occur, and how employees will enroll are addressed.

Business-Embedded Model

Many companies are organizing their training function so that they can better control their training costs and ensure that training is aligned with the business strategy but at the same time respond quickly to client needs and provide high-quality services.[65] The **business-embedded (BE) model** is characterized by five competencies: strategic direction, product design, structural versatility, product delivery, and accountability for results. Strategic direction includes a clearly described goal and direction to the department as well as a customer focus that includes customizing training to meet customer needs and continuously improving programs. A BE training function not only views trainees as customers but also views managers as customers who make decisions to send employees to training and views senior-level managers as customers who allocate money for training. Table 2.8 contrasts a BE training function with a traditional training department. Compared to a traditional training department, a BE function is customer focused. It takes more responsibility for learning and evaluating training effectiveness, provides customized training solutions based on customer needs, and determines when and how to deliver training based on customer needs. To ensure

TABLE 2.8   Comparison between a Business-Embedded Training Organization and a Traditional Training Department

Traditional Training Department	Business-Embedded Training
Strategic Direction	
Leaves objectives unstated or vague	Broadly disseminates a clearly articulated mission
Assumes that class participants are its only customers	Recognizes that its customer base is segmented
Limits offerings to predetermined courses	Provides customized solutions to its clients' needs
Continues to supply products that are no longer useful	Understands product life cycles
Organizes its offerings by courses	Organizes its offerings by competencies
Tries to mandate training	Competes for internal customers
Product Design	
Uses rigid and cumbersome design methodologies	Uses benchmarking and other innovative design strategies to develop products quickly
Views suppliers as warehouses of materials	Involves suppliers strategically
Structural Versatility	
Employs trainers who serve primarily as facilitators and classroom instructors	Employs professionals who serve as product managers and internal consultants
Operates with a fixed number of staff	Leverages resources from many areas
Relies solely on training staff to determine the department's offerings	Involves line managers in determining direction and content
Product Delivery	
Distributes a list of courses	Offers a menu of learning options
Offers courses on a fixed schedule at fixed locations	Delivers training at the work site
Accountability for Results	
Believes that the corporation manages employee development	Believes individual employees must take responsibility for their personal growth
Ends its involvement with participants when courses end	Provides follow-up on the job to ensure that learning takes place
Considers the instructor the key player in supporting learning	Considers the manager the key player in supporting learning
Relies on course critiques as its primary source of feedback	Evaluates the strategic effects of training and its bottom-line results
Vaguely describes training outcomes	Guarantees that training will improve performance

Source: S. S. McIntosh, "Envisioning Virtual Training Organization," *Training and Development* (May 1995): 47.

that EMC's business strategy is supported by training, the company uses learning councils and development frameworks.[66] Every business unit, including sales, technical, and engineering units, has education and development performance consultants who serve on the unit's learning council. The consultants report to EMC's central training organization, thus ensuring that the needs of the business units are discussed when training delivery or design is discussed. EMC uses a consistent training design framework, which makes it easier for managers and employees in all business units to understand how training leads to skill development and career advancement.

The most noticeable difference between a BE function and a traditional training department is its structure. The traditional training organization tends to operate with a fixed staff of trainers and administrators who perform very specific functions such as instructional design. In traditional training departments developers and instructors often take a "silo" approach, focusing only on their particular responsibilities.[67] This approach can hinder the development of successful training programs. In BE training functions all persons who are involved in the training process communicate and share resources. Trainers—who are responsible for developing training materials, delivering instruction, and supporting trainees—work together to ensure that learning occurs. For example, access to project managers and subject-matter experts can be provided by developers to instructors who usually do not have contact with these groups. The number of trainers in BE training functions varies according to the demand for products and services. The trainers not only have specialized competencies (e.g., instructional design) but can also serve as internal consultants and provide a wide range of services (e.g., needs assessment, content improvement, customization of programs, results measurement).

Current Practice: Business-Embedded Model with Centralized Training

Because many companies are recognizing training's critical role in contributing to the business strategy, there is an increasing trend for the training function, especially in companies that have separate business units, to be organized by a blend of the BE model with centralized training that often includes a corporate university. This approach allows the company to gain the benefits of centralized training but at the same time ensure that training can provide programs, content, and delivery methods that meet the needs of specific businesses.

At Carter & Burgess, a professional services company, every learning program is aligned with the business strategy.[68] Because the company has federal contracts, employees must complete yearly compliance training and professional education courses to maintain their licenses. Other learning programs are determined based on an annual needs analysis, exit interviews, and information from focus groups and stakeholders. The training and development team lets offices determine their training needs based on business needs. Office managers review the training programs and decide which ones they want to invest in. The training and development team monitors the usage of training and consults with the office on strategy and delivery. Allowing customization based on office needs, while at the same time centralizing strategy and training delivery, has helped to decrease costs. A companywide commitment to a single external vendor of training practices has resulted in a savings of more than 34 percent in the first year.

Nextel Communications provides wireless communications services in the United States.[69] The company offers a suite of advanced wireless services that include digital wireless mobile telephone service; walkie-talkie features, including its Nextel Direct Connect; Nextel Nationwide Direct Connect; Nextel International Direct Connect; and wireless data transmission services. To stay ahead of the changing business environment, Nextel's training organization embeds business training managers (BTM) in every business function. The BTMs report to the training organization but they are expected to contribute to the business teams and to earn their trust and respect as a way to appreciate the businesses' learning needs. The BTMs are also learning experts for the business units. Because the BTMs have a detailed understanding of the business units they support, they are better able to take into account long- and short-term business goals when choosing or designing training and to identify metrics that show how the training impacts the business.

Prior to the formation of a strategic training organization and Nextel University, business functions determined their own training needs and funded their own training initiatives. The result was limited knowledge-sharing across the company, costly redundancies in training programs, and training that was developed simply as a response to business function management requests without a consideration of how training fit into the business function's strategy or whether training really was appropriate. Now, all company programs with significant impact or cost must be accepted by Nextel's program oversight committee. Committee members include representatives from information technology, engineering, new product development, marketing, legal, and the human resource development (HRD) organization. By involving HRD in the program approval process, Nextel ensures that any training and development needs are included at the beginning rather than at the end of the project and that adequate training funds are allocated to programs and products. Training and development are linked directly to critical business decisions, and new products and programs are cost-effective, timely, and support the business strategy.

At Nextel, all funding for training and development is controlled by the HRD organization. To reduce training and development costs and to ensure that these activities are linked to business needs and are of high quality, each employee has a development plan. The Business Management Institute is responsible for Nextel's core business literacy. Its functions include all business management training and new-hire orientation. Nextel's Leadership Institute provides services to 150 employees who are viewed as the next company leaders. Nextel University enables efficiency and quality in training program design, development, and implementation. It provides a variety of technical, management, and sales training. Besides creating training on an as-needed basis, Nextel University increases the company's talent pool by participating in programs that develop the company's future leaders.

Is Nextel's HRD organization paying dividends? Recent surveys suggest that internal customers are satisfied and that more than 90 percent of business function leaders believe that HRD is doing a good job of supporting company business objectives and goals.

MARKETING THE TRAINING FUNCTION

Despite the increased recognition of the importance of training and learning on achieving business goals, many managers and employees may not recognize the value of training. Internal marketing involves making employees and managers excited about training and learning. Internal marketing is especially important for trainers who act as internal consultants to business units. For internal consultants to survive, they must generate fees for their services. Some if not all of their operating expenses come from fees paid for their services. Here are some successful internal marketing tactics.[70]

- Involve the target audience in developing the training or learning effort.
- Demonstrate how a training and development program can be used to solve specific business needs.
- Showcase an example of how training has been used within the company to solve specific business needs.
- Identify a "champion" (e.g., top-level manager) who actively supports training.
- Listen and act on feedback received from clients, managers, and employees.

- Advertise on e-mail, on company Web sites, and in employee break areas.

- Designate someone in the training function as an account representative who will interact between the training designer or team and the business unit that is the customer.

- Determine what financial numbers—such as return on assets, cash flow from operations, or net profit or loss—top-level executives are concerned with and show how training and development will help improve those numbers.

- Speak in terms that employees and managers understand. Translate jargon.

At Constellation Energy, there was no standard sales methodology and no organized way to communicate product knowledge other than on-the-job learning.[71] Constellation New Energy, one of the business units, developed a new-hire sales program that focused on developing selling skills within an energy company. The program includes pre-training work, classroom instruction, lab sessions where salespersons prepare tools and materials to market to their target segments (industries, consumers, etc.), and role plays. The program has been so successful that it is now being used across the company with sales employees in other business units.

At IKON Office Solutions, the learning and development group publishes a strategic document each year that demonstrates what it has delivered, how its efforts align with the company business strategy, and what the group plans to do to help business leaders achieve their future goals.[72] At the end of each year, the document is used to measure the learning and development group's successes, and this information is shared with senior management to make a case for continued investment in training.

The training department at Booz Allen Hamilton, a consulting firm in McLean, Virginia, develops a marketing plan every year that includes a branding strategy (how the department will be recognized, including logos and slogans); overall marketing objectives; techniques for communications with employees, managers, and all internal customers; and plans for launching all new learning programs.[73] One marketing objective is to increase awareness of the company's Center for Performance Excellence and to make it a tool for employee recruitment and retention. The marketing effort communicates the message that training programs will help workers in their jobs and their careers. Also, Booz Allen's accomplishments, such as a listing on *Training* magazine's top 100 training companies, are communicated to prospective hires to show them that the company takes training and development seriously.

Training functions are beginning to become profit centers by selling training courses or seats in training courses to other companies.[74] Companies sell training services for a number of reasons. Some businesses are so good at a particular aspect of their operations that other companies are asking for their expertise. Other companies aim training at their own customers or dealers. In some cases, the training department sells unused seats in training programs or e-learning courses. For example, Walt Disney Company sells training on customer service and organizational creativity at the Disney Institute in Florida. The institute gives employees from other companies the opportunity to understand how Disney developed its business strengths, including leadership development, service, customer loyalty, and team building. Dell Educational Services, a division of Dell Computer, sells basic training to product users and sells professional training to software engineers, developers, systems administrators, and dealership salespeople. Courses are delivered via traditional classroom instruction, on CDs, and online in self-paced and virtual classrooms. When Ohio Savings Bank has extra seats in its team dynamics or time management courses, the training function recovers costs by selling the seats to other companies. For example, Sherwin-Williams, the Cleveland, Ohio–based paint company, sent its information technology employees through a team-building program with bank employees. Randstad sells online training to its customers, who employ Randstad's workers in customer service call centers.[75] Although Randstad makes revenue by selling the training, its greater benefit is realized from building relationships with its clients. Within a one-year period, Randstad was able to show that $45 million in company business was influenced by providing training to clients who chose the company (or stayed with the company).

OUTSOURCING TRAINING

Outsourcing refers to the use of an outside company (an external services firm) that takes complete responsibility and control of some training or development activities or that takes over all or most of a company's training including administration, design, delivery, and development.[76] **Business process outsourcing** refers to the outsourcing of any business process, such as human resource management, production, or training. A recent survey from the Society for Human Resource Management (SHRM) found that 57 percent of human resource and training professionals surveyed outsource all or portions of their training and development programs.[77] Training experts predict that within 10 years, half of all trainers will work for outsourcing providers. Why would companies outsource training? Some of the reasons are cost savings; time savings that allow a company to focus on business strategy; improvements in compliance and accuracy in training mandated to comply with federal, state, or local rules (e.g., safety training); the lack of capability within the company to meet learning demands; or the desire to access best training practices. Some companies choose a comprehensive approach, outsourcing all training activities. For example, consider the outsource providers Accenture Learning and Convergys.[78] Accenture Learning operates Avaya University for Avaya, a global leader in communication systems, applications, and services.[79] Convergys offers corporations either a comprehensive learning outsourcing partnership or selective outsourcing of specific learning-related tasks.[80] Convergys provides a wide range of learning-related functions including planning, content development and delivery, administration, operations, and technology. Convergys helped SonicWALL, an Internet security company that sells complicated and technical products, transition from instructor-led workshops to e-learning and provided Web-based training for SonicWALL's customers and employees.

Although some companies are beginning to outsource and the trend appears to be growing, most companies outsource only smaller projects and not the complete training and development function. Two reasons companies do not outsource their training are (1) the inability of outsourcing providers to meet company needs and (2) companies' desire to maintain control over all aspects of training and development, especially delivery and learning content. Table 2.9 shows some of the questions that should be considered when a company is deciding whether to outsource. Any decision to outsource training is complex. Training functions that do not add any value to the company are likely candidates for outsourcing (see Table 2.9, questions 1–4 and 9). Many companies have training functions that do add value to the business but still may not be capable of meeting all training needs.

TABLE 2.9

Questions to Ask When Considering Outsourcing

Source: Based on G. Johnson, "To Outsource or Not to Outsource . . . That Is the Question," *Training* (August 2004): 26–29; K. Tyler, "Carve Out Training?" *HR Magazine* (February 2004): 52–57.

1. What are the capabilities of your in-house training function? Does the staff know enough that you can grow the training skills you need, or do you need to hire training skills from the outside?
2. Can your in-house training function take on additional training responsibilities?
3. Is training key to your company's strategy? Is it proprietary?
4. Does your company value its training organization?
5. Does the training content change rapidly?
6. Are outsourced trainers viewed as experts? Or are they viewed with cynicism?
7. Do you understand the strengths and weaknesses of your current training programs?
8. Do you want to outsource the entire training function?
9. Are executives trying to minimize training's impact in your company? Does your company accept responsibility for building skills and talent?
10. Is a combination of internal and external training the best solution?

For example, a company that has a strong skilled training function and that values training and views it as important to the business strategy probably doesn't need to outsource its entire training function. However, that company may turn to outsourcing providers for special training needs beyond staff capabilities or for certain training content that changes rapidly. Consider the case of Texas Instruments (TI).[81] TI contracts General Physics, a training outsource provider, to conduct all its open-enrollment courses for professional development and technical training. These courses are offered often by TI and in areas in which knowledge changes quickly. As a result, these courses were seen as the best candidates for outsourcing, and TI wanted to achieve cost savings by outsourcing them. TI is still in charge of its customized professional development offerings. In the outsourcing agreement, TI was careful to include contract language that allowed it to raise and lower the amount of training it was buying as needed. Given the cyclical nature of the semiconductor business, the ability to raise and lower the amount of training yet still keep customized programs that add significant value to the business was an important reason that TI decided to outsource some of its training programs. Research suggests that company satisfaction with the outsourcing of training and development depends on company-supplier trust (e.g., managers of both the company and the outsource provider are loyal to each other and look out for each other's interests) and the specificity of the contract (e.g., whether the contract clearly outlines responsibilities).[82]

Summary

For training to help a company gain a competitive advantage, it must help the company reach business goals and objectives. This chapter emphasized how changes in work roles, organizational factors, and the role of training influence the amount and type of training as well as the organization of the training functions. The process of strategic training and development was discussed. The chapter explained how different strategies (concentration, internal growth, external growth, and disinvestment) influence the goals of the business and create different training needs. The chapter included a discussion of different models of the training function. As training makes a greater contribution to the achievement of business strategies and goals, the business-embedded and corporate university models will become more prevalent. The chapter concluded with information about marketing and outsourcing the training function.

Key Terms

business strategy, *54*
goals, *54*
learning, *55*
knowledge, *55*
explicit knowledge, *56*
tacit knowledge, *56*
mission, *59*
vision, *59*
values, *59*
SWOT analysis, *59*
strategic training and
development initiatives, *62*

balanced scorecard, *67*
human resource
management (HRM)
practices, *73*
staffing strategy, *73*
human resource
planning, *74*
concentration strategy, *76*
internal growth
strategy, *76*
external growth
strategy, *76*

disinvestment strategy, *76*
centralized training, *79*
faculty model, *80*
customer model, *81*
matrix model, *82*
corporate university
model, *82*
business-embedded (BE)
model, *86*
outsourcing, *91*
business process
outsourcing, *91*

Discussion Questions

1. How would you expect the training activities of a company that is dominant in its product market to differ from those of a company that emphasizes research and development?

2. What do you think is the most important organizational characteristic that influences training? Why?

3. Which model or combination of models is best for organizing the training function? Why?

4. Shering-Plough HealthCare Products Inc. decided several years ago to expand its product line by developing pocket-size sticks and sprays of Coppertone sunblocks, previously only available as lotions packaged in squeeze bottles. The company placed a strategic emphasis on developing markets for this product. The company knew from market research studies that its Coppertone customers were already using the product in its original squeeze container to prevent sunburn. Due to increased awareness of the dangers of excessive skin exposure, consumers who had not previously used sunblock except when at the beach were looking for a daily sunblock product. Company managers reasoned that their market could be expanded significantly if the product were repackaged to fit conveniently in consumers' pockets, purses, and gym bags. Identify the business strategy. What training needs result from this strategy? What are the training implications of this decision for (1) manufacturing and (2) the sales force?

5. Which strategic training and development initiatives do you think all companies should support in today's economic climate? Why?

6. Are any of the strategic training and development initiatives more important for small business? Explain.

7. Evaluate Nextel Communications's training organization using the five competencies of the business-embedded model. Would you consider Nextel Communications's training organization to be a BE training function?

8. Compare and contrast the corporate university model with the faculty model. How are they similar? How do they differ?

9. What is human capital? How is human capital influencing the changing role of training from skill and knowledge acquisition to creating and sharing knowledge?

10. How could SWOT analysis be used to align training activities with business strategies and goals?

11. What are the training implications of the increased use of teams to manufacture products or provide services?

12. How would you design a corporate university? Explain each step you would take.

13. What are the advantages and disadvantages of a centralized training function?

14. What factors should a company consider in deciding whether to outsource its entire training function? Are the considerations different if the company wants to outsource a training program? Explain.

Application Assignments

1. Go to www.pfizer.com, the Web site for Pfizer, a company that researches, develops, manufactures, and markets leading prescription medicines for humans and animals. Identify Pfizer's mission statement, vision, and values. Go to the Careers section of the Web site. Click on Working for Pfizer. Review the links on this page. Describe how education supports Pfizer's vision and values.

2. Find a company's annual report by using the World Wide Web or visiting a library. Using the annual report, do the following:
   a. Identify the company's mission, values, and goals.
   b. Find any information provided in the report regarding the company's training practices and how they relate to the goals and strategies. Be prepared to give a brief presentation of your research to the class.

3. Go to www.orkin.com, the Web site for Orkin, a company committed to providing the world's best pest and termite control. Click on About Orkin to learn more about the company. Click on Press at the bottom of Orkin's home page. Then Click on "Orkin, Inc. Named to Training Magazine's Top 125 for Seventh Straight Year." What type of training does Orkin offer employees? Is training strategic? Why or why not? How does Orkin use training to contribute to the company's competitive advantage?

4. www.milliken.com is the Web site for Milliken and Company, which produces high-quality textiles and chemical products. Click on Industry Leadership and then Education. What is the mission of Milliken University? What learning resources are used? What courses and curricula are offered? How does the university relate to the company's business strategy, mission, and goals?

5. www.corpu.com is the Web site for Corporate University Xchange, a corporate education and research and consulting firm that is an expert on corporate universities. What kind of information about corporate universities is available on this site? Why is it useful?

6. Go to www.adayanaauto.com, the Web site for Adayana Automotive, an outsourcing company that specializes in training for the automotive industry. What services does Adayana Automotive provide? If you worked as a human resource professional in the automotive industry, what would be the advantages and disadvantages of outsourcing training to Adayana Automotive?

Case: *Training and Development Help Rubber Hit the Road at Tires Plus*

The mission at Tires Plus's headquarters and its 500 stores in 22 states is to encourage employees to be the same at work as they are in every other area of their lives. Tires Plus sells and repairs tires and provides other car repair services. Employees at Tires Plus include managers, various levels of automobile technicians/mechanics, retail sales people, and tire maintenance technicians. Tires Plus has the philosophy, "We won't sell you tires, we help you buy them," encouraging customers to be confident that tires and services will never be recommended unless they are needed. This straightforward, honest approach is the basis of Tires Plus's success and has helped make it part of the largest tire retailing group in the country. At Tires Plus, customer satisfaction is simply not good enough; rather, guest enthusiasm

must be the goal. Tires Plus believes a customer who leaves satisfied will come back, but a guest who leaves enthused may tell everyone they know. Therefore, Tires Plus not only demands guests be treated courteously but also guarantees the lowest price on every tire it sells. One of the company's most important goals is to promote employees' growth and loyalty and fairness as social and economic concepts.

What do you think are the most important business goals for Tires Plus? If you were going to establish Tires Plus University, what types of strategic training and development initiatives would you create?

Source: Based on K. Dobbs, "Tires Plus Takes the Training High Road," *Training* (April 2000): 57–63.

Endnotes

1. J. Meister, "The CEO-Driven Learning Culture," *Training and Development* (June 2000): 52–70.
2. R. Davenport, "A New Shade of Big Blue," *T + D* (May 2005): 35–40.
3. R. S. Schuler and S. F. Jackson, "Linking Competitive Strategies with Human Resource Management Practices," *Academy of Management Executive* 1 (1987): 207–19.
4. T. T. Baldwin, C. Danielson, and W. Wiggenhorn, "The Evolution of Learning Strategies in Organizations: From Employee Development to Business Redefinition," *Academy of Management Executive* 11 (1997): 47–58; J. J. Martocchio and T. T. Baldwin, "The Evolution of Strategic Organizational Training," in *Research in Personnel and Human Resource Management* 15, ed. G. R. Ferris (Greenwich, CT: JAI Press, 1997): 1–46; R. Brinkerhoff and A. Apking, *High Impact Learning* (Cambridge, MA: Perseus, 2001).
5. D. Miller, "A Preliminary Typology of Organizational Learning: Synthesizing the Literature," *Strategic Management Journal* 22 (1996): 484–505; S. Jackson, M. Hitt, and A. DeNisi (eds.), *Managing Knowledge for Sustained Competitive Advantage* (San Francisco: Jossey-Bass, 2003).
6. D. DeLong and L. Fahey, "Diagnosing Cultural Barriers to Knowledge Management," *Academy of Management Executive* 14 (2000): 113–27; A. Rossett, "Knowledge Management Meets Analysis," *Training and Development* (May 1999): 71–78.
7. I. Nonaka and H. Takeuchi, *The Knowledge Creating Company* (New York: Oxford University Press, 1995).
8. D. Tobin, *The Knowledge-Enabled Organization* (New York: AMACOM, 1998).
9. M. Weinstein, "Managing the Magic," *Training* (July/August 2008): 20–22.
10. E. Catmull, "How Pixar Fosters Collective Creativity," *Harvard Business Review* (September 2008): 64–72.
11. J. B. Quinn, P. Andersen, and S. Finkelstein, "Leveraging Intellect," *Academy of Management Executive* 10 (1996): 7–39.
12. K. Ellis, "Share Best Practices Globally," *Training* (July 2001): 32–38.
13. R. Hughes and K. Beatty, "Five Steps to Leading Strategically," *T + D* (December 2005): 46–48.
14. www.nokia.com, February 27, 2009; L. Masalin, "Nokia Leads Change through Continuous Learning," *Academy of Management Learning and Education* 2 (2003): 68–72.

15. S. Tannenbaum, "A Strategic View of Organizational Training and Learning," in *Creating, Implementing, and Managing Effective Training and Development,* ed. K. Kraiger (San Francisco: Jossey-Bass, 2002): 10–52.

16. M. Lippitt, "Fix the Disconnect between Strategy and Execution," *T + D* (August 2007): 54–56.

17. K. Ellis, "Top Training Strategies," *Training* (July/August 2003): 30–36.

18. F. Jossi, "Lesson Plans," *HR Magazine* (February 2003): 72–76.

19. *www.sun.com*, Chairman's Letter, FY06 Priorities.

20. P. A. Smith, "Reinventing SunU," *Training and Development* (July 1994): 23–27; *www.sun.com*, "Life at Sun: Training and Development" (April 4, 2006).

21. "Case Study—Sun Microsystems: Portal Solution for Key Constituencies," available from *www.sun.com/service/about/success/sun3.html* (April 21, 2005).

22. R. Kaplan and D. Norton, "The Balanced Scorecard—Measures That Drive Performance," *Harvard Business Review* (January–February 1992): 71–79; R. Kaplan and D. Norton, "Putting the Balanced Scorecard to Work," *Harvard Business Review* (September–October 1993): 134–47.

23. J. Salopek, "Best 2005: EMC Corporation," *T + D* (October 2005): 42–43.

24. R. Smith, "Aligning Learning with Business Strategy," *T + D* (November 2008): 40–43.

25. R. J. Campbell, "HR Development Strategies," in *Developing Human Resources,* ed. K. N. Wexley (Washington, DC: BNA Books, 1991): 5-1–5-34; J. K. Berry, "Linking Management Development to Business Strategy," *Training and Development* (August 1990): 20–22.

26. D. F. Van Eynde, "High Impact Team Building Made Easy," *HR Horizons* (Spring 1992): 37–41; J. R. Hackman, ed., *Groups That Work and Those That Don't: Creating Conditions for Effective Teamwork* (San Francisco: Jossey-Bass, 1990); D. McCann and C. Margerison, "Managing High-Performance Teams," *Training and Development* (November 1989): 53–60.

27. A. I. Kraut, P. R. Pedigo, D. D. McKenna, and M. D. Dunnette, "The Role of the Manager: What's Really Important in Different Managerial Jobs," *Academy of Management Executive* 4 (1988): 36–48; F. Luthans, "Successful versus Effective Real Managers," *Academy of Management Executive* 2 (1988): 127–32; H. Mintzberg, *The Nature of Managerial Work* (New York: Harper and Row, 1973); S. W. Floyd and B. Wooldridge, "Dinosaurs or Dynamos? Recognizing Middle Management's Strategic Role," *Academy of Management Executive* 8 (1994): 47–57.

28. B. Gerber, "From Manager into Coach," *Training* (February 1992): 25–31; C. Carr, "Managing Self-Managed Workers," *Training and Development* (September 1991): 37–42.

29. P. Kizilos, "Fixing Fatal Flaws," *Training* (September 1991): 66–70; F. S. Hall, "Dysfunctional Managers: The Next Human Resource Challenge," *Organizational Dynamics* (August 1991): 48–57.

30. J. Meister, "The CEO-Driven Learning Culture."

31. T. Bingham and P. Galagan, "At C Level: A Conversation with James P. Hackett," *T + D* (April 2005): 22–26.

32. R. Smith, "Aligning Learning with Business Strategy," *T + D* (November 2008): 40–43.

33. H. Dolezalek, "It's a Small World," *Training* (January 2008): 22–26.

34. M. Weinstein, "Taking the Global Initiative," *Training* (January 2009): 28–31.

35. K. Dobbs, "Winning the Retention Game," *Training* (September 1999): 50–56.

36. N. Breuer, "Shelf Life," *Workforce* (August 2000): 28–32.

37. J. A. Sonnenfeld and M. A. Peiperl, "Staffing Policy as a Strategic Response: A Typology of Career Systems," *Academy of Management Review* 13 (1988): 588–600.

38. H. Johnson, "The Economy," *Training* (November 2004): 39–41.

39. V. R. Ceriello and C. Freeman, *Human Resource Management Systems: Strategies, Tactics, and Techniques* (Lexington, MA: Lexington Books, 1991).

40. Constellation Energy, "Shining Stars," *T + D* (October 2008): 35–36.

41. D. T. Jaffe and C. D. Scott, "Career Development for Empowerment in a Changing Work World," in *New Directions in Career Planning and the Workplace,* ed. J. M. Kummerow (Palo Alto, CA: Consulting Psychologist Press, 1991): 33–60; L. Summers, "A Logical Approach to Development Planning," *Training and Development* 48 (1994): 22–31; D. B. Peterson and M. D. Hicks, *Development First* (Minneapolis, MN: Personnel Decisions, 1995).

42. A. P. Carnevale, L. J. Gainer, and J. Villet, *Training in America* (San Francisco: Jossey-Bass, 1990); L. J. Gainer, "Making the Competitive Connection: Strategic Management and Training," *Training and Development* (September 1989): s1–s30.

43. S. Raghuram and R. D. Arvey, "Business Strategy Links with Staffing and Training Practices," *Human Resource Planning* 17 (1994): 55–73.

44. K. Featherly, "Culture Shock," *Training* (November 2005): 24–29.

45. H. Dolezalek, "EMC's Competitive Advantage," *Training* (February 2009): 42–46.

46. B. Manville, "Organizing Enterprise-Wide E-Learning and Human Capital Management," *Chief Learning Officer* (May 2003): 50–55.

47. K. Linebaugh, "Idle Workers Busy at Toyota," *The Wall Street Journal* (October 13, 2008): B1, B3.

48. K. Ellis, "The Mindset That Matters: Linking Learning to the Business," *Training* (May 2005): 38–43.

49. M. London, *Managing the Training Enterprise* (San Francisco: Jossey-Bass, 1994); D. Laird, *Approaches to Training and Development,* 2d ed. (Boston: Addison-Wesley, 1985); J. Barbazette, *Managing the Training Function for Bottom Line Results* (San Francisco: Pfeiffer, 2008).

50. K. Oakes, "Grand Central Training," *T + D* (May 2005): 30–32.

51. K. Oakes, "Grand Central Training, Part 2" *T + D* (July 2005): 22–25.

52. ETS: Princeton, New Jersey, "A Tested Commitment to Learning," *T + D* (October 2008): 38–40.

53. S. Caudron, "Integrate HR and Training," *Workforce* (May 1998): 89–91.

54. K. Ellis, "Corporate University on a Budget," *Training* (April 2005): 20–25.

55. M. Morrison, "Leaner E-Learning," *Training* (January 2008): 16–18.

56. "Identify Needs, Meet Them," *T + D* (October 2005): 30–32.

57. M. Weinstein, "Getting McSmart," *Training* (May 2008): 44–47.

58. "Training Today: Update on Corporate Universities," *Training* (April 2005): 8.

59. D. Fenn, "Corporate Universities for Small Companies," *Inc.* (February 1999): 95–96.

60. "Ritz-Carlton: #9," *Training* (March 2005): 45–46.

61. G. Wolfe, "Leveraging the Learning Space," *T + D* (July 2007): 40–44.

62. J. Meister, "Ten Steps to Creating a Corporate University," *Training and Development* (November 1998): 38–43.

63. L. Freifeld, "CU There," *Training* (May 2008): 48–49.

64. G. Johnson, "Nine Tactics to Take Your Corporate University from Good to Great," *Training* (July/August 2003) 38–42.

65. S. S. McIntosh, "Envisioning Virtual Training Organization," *Training and Development* (May 1995): 46–49.

66. H. Dolezalek, "EMC's Competitive Advantage," *Training* (February 2009): 42–46.

67. B. Mosher, "How 'Siloed' Is Your Training Organization?" *Chief Learning Officer* (July 2003): 13.

68. "Carter & Burgess," *T + D* (October 2008): 55–56.

69. R. Davenport, "Beyond Reactive," *T + D* (August 2005): 29–31; *www.businessweek.com,* "The Information Technology" 100: 9, Nextel Communications.

70. W. Webb, "Who Moved My Training?" *Training* (January 2003): 22–26; T. Seagraves, "The Inside Pitch," *T + D* (February 2005): 40–45; K. Oakes, "Over the Top or On the Money," *T + D* (November 2005): 20–22.

71. Constellation Energy, "Shining Stars," *T + D* (October 2008): 35–36.

72. S. Boehle, "Get Your Message Out," *Training* (February 2005): 36–41.

73. Ibid.

74. J. Gordon, "Selling It on the Side," *Training* (December 2005): 34–39.

75. D. Sussman, "What HPLOs Know," *T + D* (August 2005); 35–39.

76. N. DeViney and B. Sugrue, "Learning Outsourcing: A Reality Check," *T + D* (December 2004): 40–45.

77. G. Johnson, "To Outsource or Not to Outsource . . . That Is the Question," *Training* (August 2004): 26–29.

78. P. Harris, "Outsourced Training Begins to Find Its Niche," *T + D* (November 2004); DeViney and Sugrue, "Learning Outsourcing."

79. Harris, "Outsourced Training Begins."

80. "Convergys Learning Vaults into Training BPO's Top Tier," available from *www.Training Outsourcing.com*, "Supplier Spotlight" (February 22, 2006).

81. C. Cornell, "Changing the Supply Chain," *Human Resource Executive* (March 2, 2005): 32–35.

82. T. Gainey and B. Klass, "The Outsourcing of Training and Development: Factors Affecting Client Satisfaction," *Journal of Management* 29, no. 2 (2003): 207–29.

It Takes a Village—And a Consultant: *PricewaterhouseCoopers Tests Partners by Sending Them to Work in Poor Nations*

Last summer, accounting-and-consulting giant Price-waterhouseCoopers tapped partner Tahir Ayub for a consulting gig unlike anything he had done before. His job: helping village leaders in the Namibian outback grapple with their community's growing AIDS crisis. Faced with language barriers, cultural differences, and scant access to electricity, Ayub, 39, and two colleagues had to scrap their PowerPoint presentations in favor of a more low-tech approach: face-to-face discussion. The village chiefs learned that they needed to garner community support for programs to combat the disease, and Ayub learned an important lesson as well: Technology isn't always the answer. "You better put your beliefs and biases to one side and figure out new ways to look at things," he said.

Ayub may never encounter as extreme a cultural disconnect at PwC as he did in Namibia. But for the next generation of partners, overcoming barriers and forging a connection with clients the world over will be a crucial part of their jobs. It's those skills that PwC hopes to foster in partners who take part in the Ulysses Program, which sends top mid-career talent to the developing world for eight-week service projects. For a fairly modest investment—$15,000 per person, plus salaries—Ulysses both tests the talent and expands the worldview of the accounting firm's future leaders. Since the company started the program four years ago, it has attracted the attention of Johnson & Johnson (**JNJ**), Cisco Systems (**CSCO**), and other big companies considering their own programs.

While results are hard to quantify, PwC is convinced that the program works. All two dozen graduates are still working at the company. Half of them have been promoted, and most have new responsibilities. Just as important, all 24 people say they have a stronger commitment to PwC—in part because of the commitment the firm made to

them and in part because of their new vision of the firm's values. Says Global Managing Partner Willem Bröcker: "We get better partners from this exercise."

The Ulysses Program is PwC's answer to one of the biggest challenges confronting professional services companies: identifying and training up-and-coming leaders who can find unconventional answers to intractable problems. By tradition and necessity, new PwC leaders are nurtured from within. But with 8,000 partners, identifying those with the necessary business savvy and relationship-building skills isn't easy. Just as the program gives partners a new view of PwC, it also gives PwC a new view of them, particularly their ability to hold up under pressure.

For mid-career partners who were weaned on e-mail and the Blackberry, this was no walk in the park. They had become accustomed to a world of wireless phones, sleek offices, and Chinese take-out—so the rigors of the developing world came as quite a shock. Brian P. McCann, 37, a mergers and acquisitions expert from PwC's Boston office, had never been to a Third World country before his stint in Belize, where he encountered dirt-floored houses, sick children, and grinding poverty.

Ayub, having been born in Africa, considered himself worldly. Even so, long days spent among Africa's exploding HIV-positive population took their psychological toll. With his work confined to daylight house—there was often no electricity—Dinu Bumbacea, a 37-year-old partner in PwC's Romanian office who spent time in Zambia working with an agricultural center, had plenty of time to dwell on the misery all around him. "Africa is poor, and we all know that," says Bumbacea. "But until you go there, you don't understand how poor it is. We take so much for granted."

For more than 15 years, companies have used social-responsibility initiatives to develop leaders. But PwC takes the concept to a new level. Participants spend eight weeks in developing countries lending their business skills to local aid groups—from an ecotourism collective in Belize to small organic farmers in Zambia to AIDS groups in Namibia. Ulysses also presents participants with the challenge of collaborating across cultures with local clients as well as with PwC colleagues from other global regions. Ayub, for example, was paired with partners from Mexico and the Netherlands.

BEYOND ACCOUNTING

PwC says the program, now in its third cycle, gives participants a broad, international perspective that's crucial for a company that does business around the world. Traditional executive education programs turn out men and women who have specific job skills but little familiarity with issues outside their narrow specialty, according to Douglas Ready, director of the International Consortium for Executive Development Research. PwC says Ulysses helps prepare participants for challenges that go beyond the strict confines of accounting or consulting and instills values such as community involvement that are fundamental to its corporate culture.

Ulysses is also a chance for partners to learn what they can accomplish without their usual resources to lean on. The program forces them to take on projects well outside their expertise. In the summer of 2003, for example, McCann developed a business plan for an ecotourism group in Belize. The experience was an eye-opener. McCann's most lasting memory is a dinner he shared in the home of a Mayan farmer after they spent a day discussing their plan. "He didn't even have electricity," McCann recalls, "but he made do."

PwC partners say they've already adapted their experiences to the task of managing people and clients. Malaysian partner Jennifer Chang says her team noticed a shift in her managerial style after the Belize trip. She listened more and became more flexible. "Once you see how slowly decisions are made in other places, you gain patience for the people you work with," she says. Ayub, who was promoted in June, now manages 20 partners. He says he favors face-to-face conversations over e-mail because the low-tech approach builds trust. "It made the difference in Namibia," he says.

If insights like those ripple out across the firm, Ulysses will be more than a voyage of personal discovery for a handful of partners. It could help build leaders capable of confronting the challenges of an increasingly global business. And that, says PwC, is the whole point.

Questions

1. What competitive challenges motivated PwC to develop the Ulysses Program?

2. Do you think the Ulysses Program contributes to PwC's business strategy and goals? Explain.

3. How would you determine if the Ulysses Program was effective? What metrics or outcomes would you collect? Why?

4. What are the advantages and disadvantages of the Ulysses Program compared to more traditional ways of training leaders such as formal courses (e.g., MBA) or giving them more increased job responsibility?

Source: J. Hempel and S. Porges, "It Takes a Village—And a Consultant: PricewaterhouseCoopers Tests Partners by Sending Them to Work in Poor Nations," *Business Week* (September 6, 2004), retrieved from *www.businessweek.com* February 23, 2009.

Designing Training

Part Two focuses on how to systematically design effective training. Chapter 3, Needs Assessment, discusses the process used to determine whether training is necessary. Needs assessment includes organizational, person, and task analysis. Chapter 4, Learning: Theories and Program Design, discusses learning theories and their implications for creating an environment that will help trainees learn the desired outcomes from training such as knowledge, skills, or competencies. The chapter also reviews practical issues in training program design, including developing training courses and programs and how to choose and prepare a training site. Chapter 5, Transfer of Training, discusses how the work environment, managers, peers, and even trainees influence whether what is learned in training is used on the job. The role of knowledge management in transfer of training is also discussed. Chapter 6, Training Evaluation, provides an overview of how to evaluate training programs, including the types of outcomes that need to be measured and the types of evaluation designs available.

Part Two concludes with a case on the use of on-the-job video gaming for training.

Needs Assessment

Objectives

After reading this chapter, you should be able to

1. Discuss the role of organization analysis, person analysis, and task analysis in needs assessment.

2. Identify different methods used in needs assessment and identify the advantages and disadvantages of each method.

3. Discuss the concerns of upper-level and mid-level managers and trainers in needs assessment.

4. Explain how person characteristics, input, output, consequences, and feedback influence performance and learning.

5. Create conditions to ensure that employees are receptive to training.

6. Discuss the steps involved in conducting a task analysis.

7. Analyze task analysis data to determine the tasks for which people need to be trained.

8. Explain competency models and the process used to develop them.

Needs Assessment at NetApp

Network Appliances (NetApp) creates innovative storage and data management solutions that help customers accelerate business breakthroughs and achieve outstanding cost efficiencies. NetApp is one of the fastest-growing storage and data management providers, with over 8,000 employees in 130 offices around the world. NetApp was rated among the top 15 best workplaces in 2008 in *Fortune* magazine's "100 Best Companies to Work For" annual report and has been on the list for six consecutive years. NetApp is known for several of its training and development programs, including its "Training On All Special Things" (TOAST), a new-hire orientation program with top-level NetApp executives and NetApp University.

As a result of company growth, NetApp needed to develop recently hired support engineers in order to provide world-class services. Existing training programs were inadequate; NetApp needed training that would cover troubleshooting skills for all aspects of support, including process, systems, operations, and soft skills. These skills were needed to ensure that NetApp's newly hired suppport engineers would be competent in meeting demands for NetApp's services. To conduct a needs assessment,

NetApp asked its best performers to participate in focus groups. The focus groups were asked to consider what types of support engineers needed to know to perform their jobs. From the focus groups, more than 1,400 tasks were identified. The tasks were ranked according to difficulty, frequency, and importance. Five hundred tasks were identified as being critical for support engineers to perform within their first year on the job. To address these tasks, a new-hire training program was developed. It includes self-paced e-learning, hands-on work in the classroom, and cases based on the company's computerized support system or initiated by customers on the Web.

Source: Based on S. Varman and B. Collins, "On Ramp to Success at Network Appliances," *T + D* (July 2007): 58–61; www.netapp.com.

INTRODUCTION

As discussed in Chapter 1, effective training practices involve the use of a training design process. The design process begins with a needs assessment. Subsequent steps in the process include ensuring that employees have the motivation and basic skills necessary to learn, creating a positive learning environment, making sure that trainees use learned skills on the job, choosing the training method, and evaluating whether training has achieved the desired outcomes. As the NetApp example highlights, before you choose a training method, it is important to determine what type of training is necessary and whether trainees are willing to learn. **Needs assessment** refers to the process used to determine whether training is necessary.

Needs assessment typically involves organizational analysis, person analysis, and task analysis.[1] An organizational analysis considers the context in which training will occur. That is, **organizational analysis** involves determining the appropriateness of training, given the company's business strategy, its resources available for training, and support by managers and peers for training activities. You are already familiar with one aspect of organizational analysis. Chapter 2 discussed the role of the company's business strategy in determining the frequency and type of training.

Person analysis helps to identify who needs training. **Person analysis** involves (1) determining whether performance deficiencies result from a lack of knowledge, skill, or ability (a training issue) or from a motivational or work-design problem, (2) identifying who needs training, and (3) determining employees' readiness for training. **Task analysis** identifies the important tasks and knowledge, skills, and behaviors that need to be emphasized in training for employees to complete their tasks.

WHY IS NEEDS ASSESSMENT NECESSARY?

Needs assessment is the first step in the instructional design process, and if it is not properly conducted any one or more of the following situations could occur:

- Training may be incorrectly used as a solution to a performance problem (when the solution should deal with employee motivation, job design, or a better communication of performance expectations).
- Training programs may have the wrong content, objectives, or methods.

- Trainees may be sent to training programs for which they do not have the basic skills, prerequisite skills, or confidence needed to learn.
- Training will not deliver the expected learning, behavior change, or financial results that the company expects.
- Money will be spent on training programs that are unnecessary because they are unrelated to the company's business strategy.

Figure 3.1 shows the three types of analysis involved in needs assessment and the causes and outcomes resulting from needs assessment. There are many different "pressure points" that suggest that training is necessary. These pressure points include performance problems, new technology, internal or external customer requests for training, job redesign, new legislation, changes in customer preferences, new products, or employees' lack of basic skills. Note that these pressure points do not guarantee that training is the correct solution. For example, consider, a delivery truck driver whose job is to deliver anesthetic gases to medical facilities. The driver mistakenly hooks up the supply line of a mild anesthetic to the supply line of a hospital's oxygen system, contaminating the hospital's oxygen supply. Why did the driver make this mistake, which is clearly a performance problem? The driver may have made this mistake because of a lack of knowledge about the appropriate line hookup for the anesthetic, because of anger over a requested salary increase that the driver's manager recently denied, or because of mislabeled valves for connecting the gas supply. Only the lack of knowledge can be addressed by training. The other pressure points require addressing issues related to the consequence of good performance (pay system) or the design of the work environment.

What outcomes result from a needs assessment? Needs assessment provides important input into most of the remaining steps in the training design. As shown in Figure 3.1, the needs assessment process results in information related to who needs training and what trainees need to learn, including the tasks in which they need to be trained plus knowledge, skill, behavior, or other job requirements. Needs assessment helps to determine whether the

FIGURE 3.1 **Causes and Outcomes of Needs Assessment**

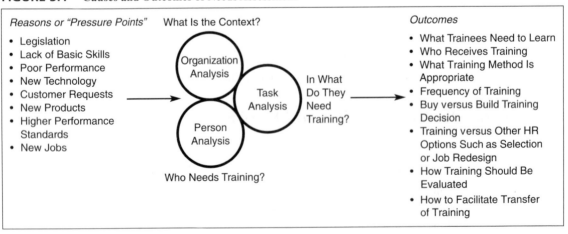

company will outsource its training, that is, purchase training from a vendor or consultant, or develop training through internal resources. Determining exactly what trainees need to learn is critical for the next step in the instructional design process: identifying learning outcomes and objectives. Chapter 4 explores identifying learning outcomes and learning objectives and creating a training environment so that learning occurs. Through identifying the learning outcomes and resources available for training, the needs assessment also provides information that helps the company choose the appropriate training or development method (discussed in Part Three of the book). Needs assessment also provides information regarding the outcomes that should be collected to evaluate training effectiveness. Training evaluation is discussed in Chapter 6.

WHO SHOULD PARTICIPATE IN NEEDS ASSESSMENT?

Because the goal of needs assessment is to determine whether a training need exists, who it exists for, and for what tasks training is needed, it is important to include managers, trainers, and employees in the needs assessment process. Traditionally, only trainers were concerned with the needs assessment process. But, as Chapter 2 showed, as training increasingly becomes used to help the company achieve its strategic goals, both upper- and top-level managers are involved in the needs assessment process.

Table 3.1 shows the questions that upper-level managers, mid-level managers, and trainers are interested in answering for organizational analysis, person analysis, and task analysis. Upper-level managers include directors, chief executive officers (CEOs), and vice

TABLE 3.1 Key Concerns of Upper-Level and Mid-Level Managers and Trainers in Needs Assessment

	Upper-Level Managers	Mid-Level Managers	Trainers
Organizational Analysis	Is training important to achieve our business objectives? How does training support our business strategy? What are the threats to our talent base?	Do I want to spend money on training? How much? How will training and development help meet my business goals? Are we retaining top talent	Do I have the budget to buy training services? Will managers support training?
Person Analysis	What functions or business units need training? What do employees need to do to accomplish our business objectives?	Who should be trained? Managers? Professionals? Core employees?	How will I identify which employees need training?
Task Analysis	Does the company have people with the knowledge, skills, and abilities or competencies needed to compete in the marketplace?	For what jobs can training make the biggest difference in product quality or customer service?	For what tasks should employees be trained? What knowledge, skills, ability, or other characteristics are necessary?

presidents. Upper-level managers view the needs assessment process from the broader company perspective. They do not focus on specific jobs. Upper-level managers are involved in the needs assessment process to identify the role of training in relation to other human resource practices in the company (e.g., selection, compensation). That is, upper-level managers help to determine if training is related to the company's business strategy—and if so, what type of training is required. Upper-level managers are also involved in identifying what business functions or units need training (person analysis) and in determining if the company has the knowledge, skills, and abilities in the work force that are necessary to meet its strategy and be competitive in the marketplace. Mid-level managers are more concerned with how training may affect the attainment of financial goals for the units they supervise. As a result, for mid-level managers, organizational analysis focuses on identifying (1) how much of their budgets they want to devote to training, (2) the types of employees who should receive training (e.g., engineers, or core employees who are directly involved in producing goods or providing services), and (3) for what jobs training can make a difference in terms of improving products or customer service.

As discussed in Chapter 2, trainers (including training managers and instructional designers) need to consider whether training is aligned with the business strategy. However, trainers are primarily interested in needs assessment to provide them with information that they need to administer, develop, and support training programs. This information includes determining if training should be purchased or developed in-house, identifying the tasks for which employees need to be trained, and determining top-level and mid-level managers' interest in and support for training.

Upper-level managers are usually involved in determining whether training meets the company's strategy and then providing appropriate financial resources. Upper-level managers are not usually involved in identifying which employees need training; the tasks for which training is needed; or the knowledge, skills, abilities, and other characteristics needed to complete those tasks. This is the role of subject-matter experts (SMEs). **Subject-matter experts (SMEs)** are employees, academics, managers, technical experts, trainers, and even customers or suppliers who are knowledgeable in regard to (1) training issues including tasks to be performed; (2) knowledge, skills, and abilities required for successful task performance; (3) necessary equipment; and (4) conditions under which the tasks have to be performed. A key issue with SMEs is making sure they are knowledgeable about the content that training must cover as well as realistic enough to be able to prioritize what content is critical to cover in the time allotted for the subject in the training curriculum. SMEs also must have information that is relevant to the company's business and have an understanding of the company's language, tools, and products. There is no rule regarding how many types of employees should be represented in the group conducting the needs assessment. Still, it is important to get a sample of job incumbents involved in the process because they tend to be most knowledgeable about the job and can be a great hindrance to the training process if they do not feel they have had input into the needs assessment. **Job incumbents** are employees who are currently performing the job.

For example, Netg, an Illinois company that develops courseware for training information technology skills, uses academics or trainers who are familiar with course content.[2] To develop the courseware, Netg's development team includes a project manager; one or more SMEs; a curriculum planner who determines what the course will cover; an instructional designer who makes sure the course development covers all aspects of the instructional system design model; and writers, programmers, and graphic artists who build the simulations included in the course. The SME leads a group training session to determine what the subject matter is for the course, the different elements the course needs to cover, and the goals for the course. The instructional designer meets with the SMEs to review the learning objectives. To keep the SMEs on track, Netg asks them to consider not only the value of the information that is being communicated to the trainee but also what trainees need to know at the end of the course.

METHODS USED IN NEEDS ASSESSMENT

Several methods are used to conduct needs assessment, including observing employees performing the job, utilizing online technology, reading technical manuals and other documentation, interviewing SMEs, conducting focus groups with SMEs, and asking SMEs to complete questionnaires designed to identify tasks and knowledge, skills, abilities, and other characteristics required for a job. Table 3.2 presents advantages and disadvantages of each method. Texas Instruments was trying to determine how to train engineering experts to become trainers for new engineers.[3] All the engineers had technical expertise. The problem was that their level of instructional expertise varied. Some had no experience teaching, whereas others taught courses at local colleges. When new engineers became inexperienced instructors, both the trainees and the instructors were frustrated. In assessing the engineers' training needs, training and development specialists used five of the six methods shown in Table 3.2. They collected information that was useful for organization and task analysis. Training course listings and mission statements were used to identify the engineering department mission, and current and previous course offerings were used to develop engineers. Competency studies and project checklists were used to identify relevant tasks. Classroom observation of new and experienced instructors was used to identify strengths and weaknesses of instructors' presentations (person analysis). Both instructors and noninstructors were interviewed to validate the information gathered through the written documentation and surveys. Another example is Boeing, which uses a process borrowed from the field of artificial intelligence. Experts are observed and interviewed to identify their thinking processes for solving problems, dealing with uncertainty, and minimizing risks. The expert practices that are uncovered are then included in the training curriculum.[4]

For newly created jobs, trainers often do not have job incumbents to rely on for this information. Rather, technical diagrams, simulations, and equipment designers can provide information regarding the training requirements, tasks, and conditions under which the job is performed. Another source of information for companies that have introduced a new technology is the help desk that companies often set up to deal with calls regarding problems, deficiencies in training, or deficiencies in documentation, software, or systems.[5] Help desk management software can categorize and track calls and questions by application, by caller, or by vendor. Report creation capability built into the software makes it easy to generate documents on user problems and identify themes among calls. Analyzing these calls is practical for identifying gaps in training. For example, common types of call problems can be analyzed to determine if they are due to inadequate coverage in the training program and/or inadequate written documentation and job aids used by trainees.

TABLE 3.2   Advantages and Disadvantages of Needs Assessment Techniques

Technique	Advantages	Disadvantages
Observation	• Generates data relevant to work environment • Minimizes interruption of work	• Needs skilled observer • Employees' behavior may be affected by being observed
Questionnaires	• Inexpensive • Can collect data from a large number of persons • Data easily summarized	• Requires time • Possible low return rates, inappropriate responses • Lacks detail • Only provides information directly related to questions asked
Interviews	• Good at uncovering details of training needs as well as causes of and solutions to problems • Can explore unanticipated issues that come up • Questions can be modified	• Time consuming • Difficult to analyze • Needs skilled interviewer • Can be threatening to SMEs • Difficult to schedule • SMEs only provide information they think you want to hear
Focus Groups	• Useful with complex or controversial issues that one person may be unable or unwilling to explore • Questions can be modified to explore unanticipated issues	• Time-consuming to organize • Group members only provide information they think you want to hear • Group members may be reluctant to participate if status or position differences exist among members
Documentation (Technical Manuals, Records)	• Good source of information on procedure • Objective • Good source of task information for new jobs and jobs in the process of being created	• You may be unable to understand technical language • Materials may be obsolete
Online Technology (Software)	• Objective • Minimizes interruption of work • Requires limited human involvement	• May threaten employees • Manager may use information to punish rather than train • Limited to jobs requiring interaction with customers via computer or phone

Source: Based on S. V. Steadham, "Learning to Select a Needs Assessment Strategy," *Training and Development Journal* (January 1980): 56–61; R. J. Mirabile, "Everything You Wanted to Know about Competency Modeling," *Training and Development* (August 1997): 74; K. Gupta, *A Practical Guide to Needs Assessment* (San Francisco: Jossey-Bass, 1999); M. Casey and D. Doverspike "Training Needs Analysis and Evaluation for New Technologies through the Use of Problem-Based Inquiry," *Performance Improvement Quarterly* 18, no. 1 (2005): 110–24.

Online technology is available to monitor and track employee performance. This information is useful for identifying training needs and providing employees with feedback regarding their skill strengths and weaknesses. In call centers, for example, technology provides an ongoing assessment of performance.[6] An employee who triggers the online system by failing to meet a defined standard, such as receiving more than five callbacks on an unresolved issue, is automatically referred to the appropriate job aid or training event. As shown in Table 3.2, online technology has several advantages: It provides an objective report of behaviors, the data can be quickly summarized into reports, it does not require a trainer or SME to observe or interview employees, and it minimizes work interruptions. However the use of online technology in needs assessment is best suited for only a small number of jobs requiring interactions with customers through the use of a computer or telephone.[7] Also, for online technology to be effective, managers need to ensure that the information is used to train and not to punish employees. Otherwise, employees will feel threatened, which will contribute to employee dissatisfaction and turnover.

Because no one method of conducting needs assessment is superior to the others, multiple methods are usually used. The methods vary in the type of information as well as the level of detail provided. The advantage of questionnaires is that information can be collected from a large number of persons. Also, questionnaires allow many employees to participate in the needs assessment process. However, when using questionnaires it is difficult to collect detailed information regarding training needs. Face-to-face and telephone interviews are time consuming, but more detailed information regarding training needs can be collected. **Focus groups** are a type of SME interview that involves a face-to-face meeting with groups of SMEs in which the questions that are asked relate to specific training needs. It is important to verify the results of interviews and observations because what employees and managers say they do and what they really do may differ. For example, the author was involved in a needs assessment project for the educational services division of a financial services company. The company wanted to determine the training needs of 3,000 employees including managers, nonmanagers, and regional trainers in the needs assessment process. The company had five regional sites geographically dispersed across the United States (e.g., Midwest region, West region).

One of the potential training needs identified by the corporate training staff was that employees were unable to use new technologies such as the Internet to access training programs. Questionnaires administered to all 3,000 employees to help determine their training needs included questions related to skills in using new technology. Because there were too many skills and tasks related to the use of technology to include all of them on the questionnaire (e.g., how to use the personal computer operating system, Web browsers, CD-ROM, spreadsheets), several general questions were included—for instance, "To what extent do you believe you need training to use new technologies that the company is implementing at your workplace?" Phone interviews were conducted with a small sample of the employees to gather more detailed information regarding specific skill needs.

With the increasing emphasis on Total Quality Management, many companies are also using information about other companies' training practices (a process known as **benchmarking**) to help determine the appropriate type, level, and frequency of training.[8] For example, Chevron, Federal Express, GTE, Xerox, and several other companies are members of the American Society for Training and Development (ASTD) benchmarking forum. A common survey instrument is completed by each company. The survey includes questions on training costs, staff size, administration, design, program development, and delivery. The information is summarized and shared with the participating companies.

THE NEEDS ASSESSMENT PROCESS

This section examines the three elements of needs assessment: organizational analysis, person analysis, and task analysis. Figure 3.2 illustrates the needs assessment process. In practice, organizational analysis, person analysis, and task analysis are not conducted in any

FIGURE 3.2   **The Needs Assessment Process**

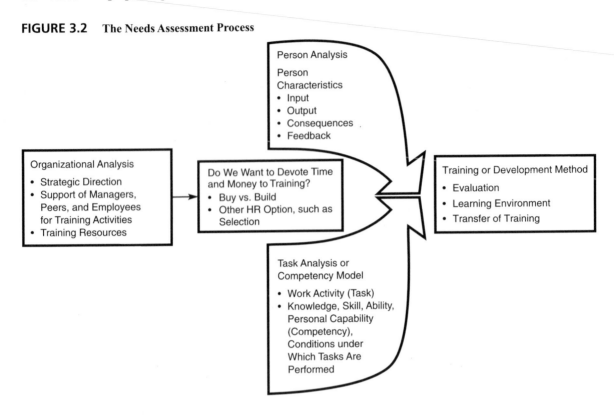

order. Whether time and money are devoted to training is contingent on the results of organizational, person, and task analyses. While any one analysis can indicate the need for training, companies need to consider the information from all three types of analysis before the decision is made to devote time and money to training. Because organizational analysis is concerned with identifying whether training fits with the company's strategic objectives and whether the company has the budget, time, and expertise for training (the context for training), it is usually conducted first. Person analysis and task analysis are often conducted at the same time because it is difficult to determine whether performance deficiencies are a training problem without understanding the tasks and the work environment. An initial organizational analysis may suggest that a company does not want to spend financial resources on training. However, if person analysis reveals that a large number of employees lack a skill in an important area that is related to the company's business objectives (such as customer service), upper-level managers may decide to reallocate financial resources for training.

Organizational Analysis

Organizational analysis involves identifying whether training supports the company's strategic direction; whether managers, peers, and employees support training activity; and what training resources are available. Table 3.3 provides questions that trainers should answer in an organizational analysis. Some combination of documentation, interviews, or focus groups of managers and individuals in the training function should be used to answer these questions.

TABLE 3.3   **Questions to Ask in an Organizational Analysis**

How might the training content affect our employees' relationship with our customers?
What might suppliers, customers, or partners need to know about the training program?
How does this program align with the strategic needs of the business?
Should organizational resources be devoted to this program?
What do we need from managers and peers for this training to succeed?
What features of the work environment might interfere with training (e.g., lack of equipment, no time to use new skills)?
Do we have experts who can help us develop the program content and ensure that we understand the needs of the business as we develop the program?
Will employees perceive the training program as an opportunity? reward? punishment? waste of time?
Which persons or groups (employees, managers, vendors, suppliers, program developers) have an interest in seeing training succeed? Whose support do we need?

Source: Based on F. Nickols, "Why a Stakeholder Approach to Evaluating Training," *Advances in Developing Human Resources* (February 2005): 121–134; S. Tannenbaum, "A Strategic View of Organizational Training and Learning," in *Creating, Implementing, and Managing Effective Training and Development,* ed. K. Kraiger (San Francisco: Jossey-Bass, 2002): 10–52.

Company's Strategic Direction

How the company's business strategy influences training was discussed in Chapter 2. The strategic role of training influences the frequency and type of training and how the training function is organized in the company. In companies in which training is expected to contribute to the achievement of business strategies and goals, the amount of money allocated to training and the frequency of training will likely be higher than in companies in which training is done haphazardly or with no strategic intent in mind. For example, companies that believe learning contributes to their competitive advantage or that have adopted high-performance work systems (e.g., teams) are likely to have greater training budgets and conduct more training. The business strategy also influences the type of training. For example, as noted in Chapter 2, companies that have adopted a disinvestment strategy are more likely to focus on outplacement assistance and job search skills training than are companies with other strategic initiatives. Last, the greater the strategic role of training, the more likely the company will organize the training function using the business-embedded or corporate university models. Both these models emphasize that training is used to help solve business problems.

Support of Managers, Peers, and Employees for Training Activities

A number of studies have found that peer and manager support for training is critical, along with employee enthusiasm and motivation to attend training. The key factors for success are a positive attitude among peers, managers, and employees about participation in training activities; managers' and peers' willingness to provide information to trainees about how they can more effectively use knowledge, skill, or behaviors learned in training on the job; and opportunities for trainees to use training content in their jobs.[9] If peers' and managers' attitudes and behaviors are not supportive, employees are not likely to apply training content to their jobs.

Training Resources

It is necessary to identify whether the company has the budget, time, and expertise for training. For example, if the company is installing computer-based manufacturing equipment in one of its plants, it has three possible strategies for dealing with the need to have computer-literate employees. First, the company can decide that, given its staff expertise and budget, it can use internal consultants to train all affected employees. Second, the company may decide that it is more cost-effective to identify employees who are computer-literate by using tests and work samples. Employees who fail the test or perform below standards on the work sample can be reassigned to other jobs. Choosing this strategy suggests that the company has decided to devote resources to selection and placement rather than training. Third, because it lacks time or expertise, the company may decide to purchase training from a consultant.

One way to identify training resources is for companies that have similar operations or departments located across the country or the world to share practices.[10] For example, Pfizer Pharmaceuticals created a "virtual learning team" to promote the sharing of "best practices" in technical training among its U.S. manufacturing sites. Training managers from New York, New Jersey, Missouri, Nebraska, Indiana, Puerto Rico, and Belgium serve on the team. The team members meet face-to-face once every business quarter and also have a regular conference call every six weeks. The objectives of the team are to (1) provide a centralized focus to Pfizer's training strategies, (2) enable training managers to mentor peers and exchange training practices, and (3) establish training standards for each of the manufacturing sites. The team has made some valuable contributions, including the development of a new operator training standard, a 10-step method for teaching and evaluating the skills of employees who make drug products or operate machinery. The team based the standard on an existing practice at one of the manufacturing sites. Another accomplishment was that the New York and Puerto Rico team representatives found that they had similar work areas in their plants, so they decided to each create one module of a new training plan and transfer each module to the other location.

Choosing a Vendor or Consultant   If a company decides to purchase a training program from a consultant or vendor rather than build the program in-house, it is important to choose a high-quality provider. Training providers may include individual consultants, consulting firms, or academic institutions. Many companies identify vendors and consultants who can provide training services by using requests for proposals.[11] A **request for proposal (RFP)** is a document that outlines for potential vendors and consultants the type of service the company is seeking, the type and number of references needed, the number of employees who need to be trained, funding for the project, the follow-up process used to determine level of satisfaction and service, the expected date of completion of the project, and the date when proposals must be received by the company. The RFP may be mailed to potential consultants and vendors or posted on the company's Web site. The RFP is valuable because it provides a standard set of criteria against which all consultants will be evaluated. The RFP also helps eliminate the need to evaluate outside vendors that cannot provide the needed services.

Usually the RFP helps to identify several vendors who meet the criteria. The next step is to choose the preferred provider. Table 3.4 provides examples of questions to ask vendors. Managers and trainers should check the vendor's reputation by contacting prior clients and professional organizations (such as the American Society for Training and Development). The consultant's experience should be evaluated. (For example, in what industry has the vendor worked?) Managers should carefully consider the services, materials, and fees outlined in the consulting contract. For example, it is not uncommon for

TABLE 3.4   **Questions to Ask Vendors and Consultants**

How much and what type of experience does your company have in designing and delivering training?

What are the qualifications and experiences of your staff?

Can you provide demonstrations or examples of training programs you have developed?

Can you provide references of clients for whom you have worked?

What evidence do you have that your programs work?

What instructional design methods do you use?

How do your products or services fit our needs?

Source: Based on R. Zemke and J. Armstrong, "Evaluating Multimedia Developers," *Training* (November 1996): 33–38; B. Chapman, "How to Create the Ideal RFP," *Training* (January 2004): 40–43.

training materials, manuals, and handouts to remain the property of the consultant. If the company wishes to use these materials for training at a later date, it would have to pay additional fees to the consultant.

When using a consultant or other outside vendor to provide training services, it is also important to consider the extent to which the training program will be customized based on the company's needs or whether the consultant is going to provide training services based on a generic framework that it applies to many different organizations. For example, Towers Perrin, a well-known, successful New York consulting firm, told several clients that it would study their companies in detail and provide a customized diversity training program to fit their needs. However, six companies (including Nissan USA, Thompson Consumer Electronics, and Harris Bank) were given the same 18 recommendations (e.g., separate the concept of affirmative action from that of managing diversity)![12]

How long should it take a vendor or consultant to develop a training program? The answer is, "It depends."[13] Some consultants estimate that development time ranges from 10 to 20 hours for each hour of instruction. Highly technical content requiring more frequent meetings with SMEs can add an additional 50 percent more time. For training programs using new technology (such as a CD-ROM), development time can range from 300 to 1,000 hours per hour of program time depending on how much animation, graphics, video, and audio are included; how much new content needs to be developed; the number of practice exercises and the type of feedback to be provided to trainees; and the amount of "branches" to different instructional sequences. Chapter 8 details the use of new technologies in training.

Person Analysis

Person analysis helps to identify employees who need training, that is, whether employees' current performance or expected performance indicates a need for training. The need for training may result from the pressure points in Figure 3.1, including performance problems, changes in the job, or use of new technology. Person analysis also helps determining employees' readiness for training. **Readiness for training** refers to whether (1) employees have the personal characteristics (ability, attitudes, beliefs, and motivation) necessary to learn program content and apply it on the job and (2) the work environment will facilitate learning and not interfere with performance. This process includes evaluating person characteristics, input, output, consequences, and feedback.[14]

A major pressure point for training is poor or substandard performance. Poor performance is indicated by customer complaints, low performance ratings, or on-the-job incidents such as accidents and unsafe behavior. Another potential indicator of the need for training is if the job changes such that current levels of performance need to be improved or employees must be able to complete new tasks.

Process for Person Analysis

Figure 3.3 shows a process for analyzing the factors that influence performance and learning. **Person characteristics** refer to the employees' knowledge, skill, ability, and attitudes. **Input** relates to the instructions that tell employees what, how, and when to perform. Input also refers to the resources that the employees are given to help them perform. These resources may include equipment, time, or budget. **Output** refers to the job's performance standards. **Consequences** refer to the type of incentives that employees receive

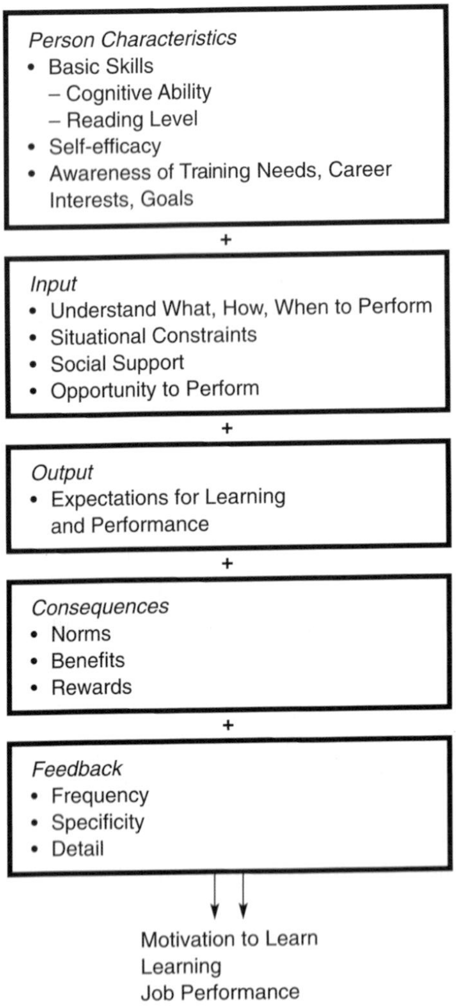

FIGURE 3.3
Process for Analyzing the Factors That Influence Employee Performance and Learning

Source: G. Rummler, "In Search of the Holy Performance Grail," *Training and Development* (April 1996): 26–31; C. Reinhart, "How to Leap over Barriers to Performance," *Training and Development* (January 2000): 20–24; G. Rummler and K. Morrill, "The Results Chain," *T + D* (February 2005): 27–35.

```
┌─────────────────────────────────────────┐
│ Person Characteristics                    │
│  • Basic Skills                           │
│     – Cognitive Ability                   │
│     – Reading Level                       │
│  • Self-efficacy                          │
│  • Awareness of Training Needs, Career    │
│    Interests, Goals                       │
└─────────────────────────────────────────┘
                    +
┌─────────────────────────────────────────┐
│ Input                                     │
│  • Understand What, How, When to Perform  │
│  • Situational Constraints                │
│  • Social Support                         │
│  • Opportunity to Perform                 │
└─────────────────────────────────────────┘
                    +
┌─────────────────────────────────────────┐
│ Output                                    │
│  • Expectations for Learning              │
│    and Performance                        │
└─────────────────────────────────────────┘
                    +
┌─────────────────────────────────────────┐
│ Consequences                              │
│  • Norms                                  │
│  • Benefits                               │
│  • Rewards                                │
└─────────────────────────────────────────┘
                    +
┌─────────────────────────────────────────┐
│ Feedback                                  │
│  • Frequency                              │
│  • Specificity                            │
│  • Detail                                 │
└─────────────────────────────────────────┘
                    ↓ ↓
            Motivation to Learn
            Learning
            Job Performance
```

for performing well. **Feedback** refers to the information that employees receive while they are performing.

Interviews or questionnaires can be used to measure person characteristics, input, output, consequences, and feedback. For example, a package delivery company believed that lead drivers were valuable for providing on-the-job training for new employees.[15] The company employed 110 lead drivers. The lead driver job involved driving, delivery, and bookkeeping duties. The lead drivers benefited from training because coaching and training made their jobs more interesting. The company benefited because on-the-job training was relatively inexpensive and effective. Lead drivers often quickly spotted and corrected performance problems with new trainees. Lead drivers knew the technical aspects of the delivery job quite well. Although many of the lead drivers were good trainers and coaches, the company believed they needed to learn how to coach and train the new drivers. The company used interviews to identify what type of coaching and training skills the lead drivers needed. Interviews were conducted with 14 lead drivers, six supervisors, and two regional vice presidents. The interview for the lead drivers consisted of questions such as

- What types of situations call for coaching on your part?
- What keeps you from being a good coach on the job?
- How do you encourage or motivate other lead drivers? Do you use incentives or rewards? Do you try other things (compliments, personal attention)?
- What common types of performance problems do new hires have?
- What were the biggest problems you encountered as a new coach and trainer? What mistakes did you make? What lessons have you learned over time?
- Tell me about a successful coaching experience and an unsuccessful coaching experience.

Recurring trends in the interview data were noted and categorized. For example, interview questions on obstacles to coaching related to three themes: lack of time to coach, the physical environment (no privacy), and reluctance to coach peers. These three topics were covered in the coaching course.

Person characteristics, input, output, consequences, and feedback influence the motivation to learn. **Motivation to learn** is trainees' desire to learn the content of training programs.[16] Consider how your motivation to learn may be influenced by personal characteristics and the environment. You may have no problem understanding and comprehending the contents of this textbook. But your learning may be inhibited because of your attitude toward the course. That is, perhaps you do not believe the course will be important for your career. Maybe you are taking the course only because it fits your schedule or is required in your degree program. Learning may also be inhibited by the environment. For example, maybe you want to learn, but your study environment prevents you from doing so. Every time you are prepared to read and review your notes and the textbook, your roommates could be having a party. Even if you do not join them, the music may be so loud that you cannot concentrate!

Marriott International, the hotel and restaurant chain, found that personal characteristics were having a significant influence on the success rate of the company's welfare-to-work program.[17] This program involved training welfare recipients for jobs in the company's hotels and restaurants. (These types of programs are discussed in greater detail in Chapter 10.) Many trainees were unable to complete the training program because of poor attendance resulting from unreliable child care, drug problems, or abusive husbands or boyfriends. As a result, Marriott has instituted tight standards for selecting welfare recipients for the training program. These standards include requiring trainees to have child care, transportation, and housing arrangements. Also, Marriott plans to add an additional drug test during training. Currently, trainees are tested for drugs only at the beginning of training.

A number of research studies have shown that motivation to learn is related to knowledge gained, behavior change, or skill acquisition resulting from training.[18] Besides considering the factors of person characteristics, input, output, consequences, and feedback in determining whether training is the best solution to a performance problem, managers should also consider these factors prior to selecting which employees will attend a training program. These factors relate to the employees' motivation to learn. The following sections describe each of these factors and its relationship to performance and learning.

Person Characteristics

Basic skills refer to skills that are necessary for employees to successfully perform on the job and learn the content of training programs. Basic skills include cognitive ability and reading and writing skills. For example, one assumption that your professor is making in this course is that you have the necessary reading level to comprehend this textbook and the other course materials such as overhead transparencies, videos, or readings. If you lacked the necessary reading level, you likely would not learn much about training in this course. As Chapter 1 mentioned, recent forecasts of skill levels of the U.S. work force indicate that managers will likely have to work with employees who lack basic skills. A literacy audit can be used to determine employees' basic skill levels. Table 3.5 shows the activities involved in conducting a literacy audit.

TABLE 3.5 Steps in Performing a Literacy Audit Source: U.S. Department of Education, U.S. Department of Labor, *The Bottom Line: Basic Skills in the Workplace* (Washington, DC: 1988): 14–15.	Step 1: Observe employees to determine the basic skills they need to be successful in their job. Note the materials the employee uses on the job, the tasks performed, and the reading, writing, and computations completed by the employee. Step 2: Collect all materials that are written and read on the job and identify computations that must be performed to determine the necessary level of basic skill proficiency. Materials include bills, memos, and forms such as inventory lists and requisition sheets. Step 3: Interview employees to determine the basic skills they believe are needed to do the job. Consider the basic skill requirements of the job yourself. Step 4: Determine whether employees have the basic skills needed to successfully perform the job. Combine the information gathered by observing and interviewing employees and evaluating materials they use on their job. Write a description of each job in terms of the reading, writing, and computation skills needed to perform the job successfully. Step 5: Develop or buy tests that ask questions relating specifically to the employees' job. Ask employees to complete the tests. Step 6: Compare test results (from step 5) with the description of the basic skills required for the job (from step 4). If the level of the employees' reading, writing, and computation skills does not match the basic skills required by the job, then a basic skills problem exists.

It is important to note that possession of a high school diploma or a college degree is no guarantee that an employee has basic skills. If participants do not have the fundamental reading, writing, and math skills to understand the training, they will not be able to learn, they will not apply their training to the job (a process known as transfer, which is discussed in Chapter 5), and the company will have wasted money on training that does not work. Trainers need to evaluate the strengths and weaknesses of trainees before designing a training program. The skill weaknesses that are identified can be used to determine prerequisites that trainees need or must acquire before entering a training program. How do trainers identify skills gaps?[19] First, trainers collect general information through position-specific training materials and job descriptions. They also observe the job to become familiar with the necessary skills. Next, trainers meet with SMEs including employees, managers, engineers, or others who are familiar with the job. With the help of the SMEs, trainers identify a list of regularly performed activities and prioritize the list according to importance. Finally, trainers identify the skills and skill levels that are needed to perform the activities or job tasks. For example, nurses must watch for changes in patient conditions, reactions, and comfort levels; they need to identify and recall details when observing patients. These activities require good observation skills, and the trainer needs to find a test to measure those skills. Once the skills analysis is complete, trainers conduct a basic (or pretraining) skills evaluation to identify skills gaps that need to be addressed prior to enrolling employees in a training session.

Cognitive Ability   Research shows that cognitive ability influences learning and job performance. **Cognitive ability** includes three dimensions: verbal comprehension, quantitative ability, and reasoning ability.[20] Verbal comprehension refers to the person's capacity to understand and use written and spoken language. Quantitative ability refers to how fast and accurately a person can solve math problems. Reasoning ability refers to the person's capacity to invent solutions to problems. Research shows that cognitive ability is related to successful performance in all jobs.[21] The importance of cognitive ability for job success increases as the job becomes more complex.

For example, a supermarket cashier needs low to moderate levels of all three dimensions of cognitive ability to successfully perform that job. An emergency room physician needs higher levels of verbal comprehension, quantitative ability, and reasoning ability than the cashier. The supermarket cashier needs to understand basic math operations (addition, subtraction, etc.) to give customers the correct amount of change. The cashier also needs to invent solutions to problems. (For example, how does the cashier deal with items that are not priced that the customer wants to purchase?) The cashier also needs to be able to understand and communicate with customers (verbal comprehension). The physician also needs quantitative ability, but at a higher level. For example, when dealing with an infant experiencing seizures in an emergency situation, the physician needs to be able to calculate the correct dosage of medicine (based on an adult dosage) to stop the seizures after considering the child's weight. The physician has to be able to quickly diagnose the situation and determine what actions (blood tests, X-rays, respiratory therapy) are necessary. The physician also needs to communicate clearly to the patient's parents the treatment and recovery process.

Cognitive ability influences job performance and ability to learn in training programs. If trainees lack the cognitive ability level necessary to perform job tasks, they will not perform well. Also, trainees' level of cognitive ability can influence how well they can learn in training programs.[22] Trainees with low levels of cognitive ability are more likely to fail to complete training or (at the end of training) receive lower grades on tests to measure how much they have learned.

To identify employees without the cognitive ability to succeed on the job or in training programs, companies use paper-and-pencil cognitive ability tests. For example, consider the actions taken by the Federal Aviation Administration (FAA) to identify potential air traffic controllers who will successfully complete training.[23] Due to retirements, the FAA, which trains all the nation's air traffic controllers, has to replace over 75 percent of 14,717 air traffic controllers. Air traffic control work requires quick analytical thinking and strong communications skills. The FAA estimates that in the past it spent $10 million per year on unsuccessful trainees, which resulted in a doubling of training costs. To reduce its training costs and increase the number of new controllers who will be successful, the FAA is using new tests that are designed to better identify those people who have the skills to be successful air traffic controllers. Previously, potential air traffic controllers were given an aptitude test and nine weeks of training and were then sent out into the field for on-the-job training. Now, the FAA uses an eight-hour test of cognitive skills that could help identify whether applicants can think spatially, have good short- and long-term memory, and can work well under pressure—skills that are needed by successful air traffic controllers. In addition to classroom training, air traffic controllers also receive training through computer-based simulations of airport towers and en route centers, which direct planes between airports. Determining a job's cognitive ability requirement is part of the task analysis process discussed later in this chapter.

Reading Ability Lack of the appropriate reading level can impede performance and learning in training programs. Material used in training should be evaluated to ensure that its reading level does not exceed that required by the job. **Readability** refers to the difficulty level of written materials.[24] A readability assessment usually involves analysis of sentence length and word difficulty.

If trainees' reading level does not match the level needed for the training materials, four options are available. First, trainers can determine whether it is feasible to lower the reading level of training materials or use video or on-the-job training, which involves learning by watching and practicing rather than by reading. Second, employees without the necessary reading level could be identified through reading tests and reassigned to other positions more congruent with their skill levels. Third, again using reading tests, trainers can identify employees who lack the necessary reading skills and provide them with remedial training. Fourth, trainers can consider whether the job can be redesigned to accommodate employees' reading levels. The fourth option is certainly the most costly and least practical. Therefore, alternative training methods need to be considered, or managers can elect a nontraining option. Nontraining options include selecting employees for jobs and training opportunities on the basis of reading, computation, writing, and other basic skill requirements.

Many companies are finding that employees lack the basic skills needed to successfully complete training programs. For example, a training program for 1,800 hourly employees at Georgia-Pacific (a paper manufacturer) was ineffective.[25] Employees reported that they understood training content but once they left training and returned to their jobs, they couldn't successfully perform maintenance tasks. In trying to determine the cause of the failed training, employees' basic skills were tested. Tests revealed that many employees had difficulty reading and writing. As a result, they were unable to understand the materials used in training. This translated into reduced learning and poor job performance.

To help ensure that employees have the necessary basic skills needed to succeed in training, Georgia-Pacific developed a basic skills assessment and training program. The first step involved assessment (or measurement) of employees' basic skills. A test of reading and math skills was given to employees. People who scored at or above a ninth-grade reading level were eligible to attend training programs. Those with literacy levels below ninth grade were counseled to attend basic skills training. Because Georgia-Pacific's primary concern was how to convince employees to attend training, the company had to establish trust with the employees. In general, employees who lack basic skills are embarrassed to admit they have difficulty and are afraid that their lack of literacy will cost them their jobs. To alleviate these fears, employees received confidential counseling about their test results, they were not required to start basic skills training immediately after the assessment, and the company did not put information regarding test results (pass or fail) in employees' personnel files.

A local community college supplied the basic skills training. Classes were set up close to Georgia-Pacific's plants so employees could attend classes before or after their work shifts. There was no charge for the classes. Now the work force has the necessary basic skills. To ensure that new employees do not lack basic skills, Georgia-Pacific has changed its hiring qualifications. The company does not accept applications from anyone who has not completed a specific 18-month schedule of courses at the community college.

Another approach to improving basic skills is incorporating basic skills instruction into training programs. An example is the electronics technician training program developed by the Ford Foundation.[26] Before the start of the program, students are given information about electronic technician jobs. Students are told they will learn how to think about operating, maintaining, and repairing electrical equipment that they are familiar with such as flashlights, curling irons, and lamps. These appliances were selected because they are useful for introducing basic electronic concepts and procedures.

Trainees are given a book that covers the basic literacy skills needed to read training and job-related material in electronics. The book's exercises and worksheets help the trainee master "reading-to-do" and "reading-to-learn" skills that have been identified as required in the majority of jobs.[27] Reading-to-do involves searching for and reading information in manuals, books, or charts (e.g., looking up information such as repair specifications in a technical manual or scanning tables and graphs to locate information). Reading-to-learn involves reading information to apply it in the future, such as reading instructions on how to use a piece of equipment (e.g., paraphrasing and summarizing information).

Besides learning reading skills related to electronics, trainees study how electronics is used in flashlights and table lamps. The textbook introduces students to math concepts and their applications, including scientific notation needed to understand waves that appear on an oscilloscope. This training program has prepared competent electronic technicians for entry-level positions.

Self-Efficacy   **Self-efficacy** is employees' belief that they can successfully perform their job or learn the content of the training program. The job environment can be threatening to many employees who may not have been successful performers in the past. For example, as you will see in Chapter 10, people who are hired through a welfare-to-work program—a program designed to help find jobs for welfare recipients—may lack self-efficacy. The training environment can also be threatening to people who have not received training or formal education for some length of time, lack education, or are not experienced in the training program's subject matter. For example, training employees to use equipment for computer-based manufacturing may represent a potential threat, especially if they are intimidated by new technology and lack confidence in their ability to master the skills needed to use a computer. Research has demonstrated that self-efficacy is related to performance in training programs.[28] Employees' self-efficacy level can be increased by

1. Letting employees know that the purpose of training is to try to improve performance rather than to identify areas in which employees are incompetent.
2. Providing as much information as possible about the training program and the purpose of training prior to the actual training.
3. Showing employees the training success of their peers who are now in similar jobs.
4. Providing employees with feedback that learning is under their control and they have the ability and the responsibility to overcome any learning difficulties they experience in the program.

Awareness of Training Needs, Career Interests, and Goals   To be motivated to learn in training programs, employees must be aware of their skill strengths and weaknesses and of the link between the training program and improvement of their weaknesses.[29] Managers should make sure that employees understand why they have been asked to attend training programs, and they should communicate the link between training and improvement of skill weaknesses or knowledge deficiencies. This can be accomplished by sharing performance feedback with employees, holding career development discussions, or having employees complete a self-evaluation of their skill strengths and weaknesses as well as career interests and goals. For example, Reynolds and Reynolds, an Ohio information services company, uses surveys to obtain sales employees' opinions about what kinds of training they want.[30] The survey asks questions about what additional training the company could provide to improve sales effectiveness and productivity and how employees want to receive training. Sixty percent of the employees felt they needed more training on how to create and present credible estimates of return on investments for each solution they offer customers. Time management training, working in a virtual environment, problem-solving decision making, and listening skills were personal development areas identified by the employees as needing improvement. Most employees preferred classroom training but they also mentioned webcasts, on-the-job training, or CDs. The internal training director shares the results with the sales leadership teams, including vice presidents and service directors. The results are being used as part of the process for setting goals for the training department.

If possible, employees need to be given a choice of what programs to attend and must understand how actual training assignments are made to maximize motivation to learn. Several studies have suggested that giving trainees a choice regarding which programs to attend and then honoring those choices maximizes motivation to learn. Giving employees choices but not necessarily honoring them can undermine motivation to learn.[31]

Input

Employees' perceptions of two characteristics of the work environment—situational constraints and social support—are determinants of performance and motivation to learn. **Situational constraints** include lack of proper tools and equipment, materials and supplies, budgetary support, and time. **Social support** refers to managers' and peers' willingness to provide feedback and reinforcement.[32] If employees have the knowledge, skills, attitudes, and behavior needed to perform but do not have the proper tools and equipment needed, their performance will be inadequate.

To ensure that the work environment enhances trainees' motivation to learn, managers should take the following steps:

1. Provide materials, time, job-related information, and other work aids necessary for employees to use new skills or behavior before participating in training programs.
2. Speak positively about the company's training programs to employees.
3. Let employees know they are doing a good job when they are using training content in their work.
4. Encourage work-group members to involve each other in trying to use new skills on the job by soliciting feedback and sharing training experiences and situations in which training content has been helpful.
5. Provide employees with time and opportunities to practice and apply new skills or behaviors to their work.

Output

Poor or substandard performance can occur on the job because employees do not know at what level they are expected to perform. For example, they may not be aware of quality standards related to speed or the degree of personalization of service that is expected. Employees may have the knowledge, skill, and attitudes necessary to perform and yet fail to perform because they are not aware of the performance standards. Lack of awareness of the performance standards is a communications problem, but it is not a problem that training can "fix."

Understanding the need to perform is important for learning. Trainees need to understand what specifically they are expected to learn in the training program. To ensure that trainees master training content at the appropriate level, trainees in training programs also need to understand the level of proficiency that is expected of them. For example, for tasks, level of proficiency relates to how well employees are to perform a task. For knowledge, level of proficiency may relate to a score on a written test. The standards or the level of performance is part of the learning objectives (discussed in Chapter 4).

Consequences

If employees do not believe that rewards or incentives for performance are adequate, they will be unlikely to meet performance standards even if they have the necessary knowledge, behavior, skill, or attitudes. Also, work-group norms may encourage employees not to meet performance standards. **Norms** refer to accepted standards of behavior for work-group members. For example, during labor contract negotiations baggage handlers for Northwest Airlines worked slowly loading and unloading baggage from airplanes. As a result, many passenger departures and arrivals were delayed. The baggage handlers had the knowledge, skills, and behaviors necessary to unload the planes more quickly, but they worked slowly because they were trying to send a message to management that the airlines could not perform effectively if their contract demands were not met.

Consequences also affect learning in training programs. Employees' motivation to learn can be enhanced by communicating to them the potential job-related, personal, and career benefits they may receive as a result of attending training and learning the content of the training program. These benefits may include learning a more efficient way to perform a process or procedure, establishing contacts with other employees in the company (also known as networking), or increasing their opportunity to pursue other jobs in the company. It is important that the communication from the manager about potential benefits be realistic. Unmet expectations about training programs can hinder motivation to learn.[33]

Feedback

Performance problems can result when employees do not receive feedback regarding the extent to which they are meeting performance standards. Training may not be the best solution to this type of problem if employees know what they are supposed to do (output), but do not understand how close their performance is to the standard. Employees need to be given specific, detailed feedback of effective and ineffective performance. For employees to perform to standard, feedback needs to be given frequently, not just during a yearly performance evaluation.

In Chapter 4 the role of feedback in learning is discussed in detail. Keep in mind that feedback is critical for shaping trainees' behaviors and skills.

Determining Whether Training Is the Best Solution

To determine whether training is needed to solve a performance problem, managers need to analyze characteristics of the performer, input, output, consequences, and feedback. How might this be done?[34] Managers should assess the following:

1. Is the performance problem important? Does it have the potential to cost the company a significant amount of money from lost productivity or customers?
2. Do the employees know how to perform effectively? Perhaps they received little or no previous training or the training was ineffective. (This problem is a characteristic of the person.)
3. Can the employees demonstrate the correct knowledge or behavior? Perhaps employees were trained but they infrequently or never used the training content (knowledge, skills, etc.) on the job. (This is an input problem.)
4. Were performance expectations clear (input)? Were there any obstacles to performance such as faulty tools or equipment?
5. Were positive consequences offered for good performance? Was good performance not rewarded? For example, if employees are dissatisfied with their compensation, their peers or a union may encourage them to slow down their pace of work. (This involves consequences.)
6. Did employees receive timely, relevant, accurate, constructive, and specific feedback about their performance (a feedback issue)?
7. Were other solutions—such as job redesign or transferring employees to other jobs—too expensive or unrealistic?

If employees lack the knowledge and skill to perform a job and the other factors are satisfactory, training is needed. If employees have the knowledge and skill to perform but input, output, consequences, or feedback is inadequate, training may not be the best solution. For example, if poor performance results from faulty equipment, training cannot solve this problem but repairing the equipment will. If poor performance results from lack of feedback, then employees may not need training, but their managers may need training on how to give performance feedback!

It is also important to consider the relationships among a critical job issue (a problem or opportunity that is critical to the success of a job within the company), a critical process issue (a problem or opportunity that is critical to the success of a business process), and a critical business issue (a problem or opportunity that is critical to the success of the company).[35] If the critical job issue, process issue, and business issue are related, training should be a top priority because it will have a greater effect on business outcomes and results and will likely receive greater management support. Table 3.6 shows the relationships among the critical job, process, and business issues for a sales representative. This analysis resulted from a request from a top manager who suggested that sales representatives needed more training because incomplete sales orders were being submitted to production.

Task Analysis

Task analysis results in a description of work activities, including tasks performed by the employee and the knowledge, skills, and abilities required to complete the tasks. A **job** is a specific position requiring the completion of certain tasks. (The job exemplified in Table 3.7 is that of an electrical maintenance worker.) A **task** is the employee's work activity in a specific job. Table 3.7 shows several tasks for the electrical maintenance worker job. These tasks include replacing light bulbs, electrical outlets, and light switches. To complete tasks, employees must have specific levels of knowledge, skill, ability, and other considerations (KSAOs). **Knowledge** includes facts or procedures (e.g., the chemical properties of gold). **Skill** indicates competency in performing a task (e.g., negotiation skill, a skill in getting another person to agree to take a certain course of action). **Ability** includes the physical and mental capacities to perform a task (e.g., spatial ability, the ability to see the relationship between objects in physical space). **Other** refers to the conditions under which tasks are performed. These conditions include identifying the equipment and environment that the employee works in (e.g., the need to wear an oxygen mask, work in extremely hot conditions), time constraints for a task (e.g., deadlines), safety considerations, or performance standards.

TABLE 3.6

Example of the Relationships among a Critical Job Issue, a Critical Process Issue, and a Critical Business Issue

Critical Job Issue	Critical Process Issue	Critical Business Issue
Desired Results No incomplete order forms 100% accurate orders	*Desired Results* Order cycle time of 3 days	*Desired Results* Market share of 60%
Current Results 10% incomplete order forms 83% accurate orders	*Current Results* Order cycle time of 30 days	*Current Results* Market Share of 48%

Source: Based on G. A. Rummler and K. Morrill, "The Results Chain," *T + D* (February 2005): 27–35.

TABLE 3.7   **Sample Items from Task Analysis Questionnaires for the Electrical Maintenance Job**

Job: Electrical Maintenance Worker				
		Task Performance Ratings		
Task #s	Task Description	Frequency of Performance	Importance	Difficulty
199–264	Replace a light bulb	0 1 2 3 4 5	0 1 2 3 4 5	0 1 2 3 4 5
199–265	Replace an electrical outlet	0 1 2 3 4 5	0 1 2 3 4 5	0 1 2 3 4 5
199–266	Install a light fixture	0 1 2 3 4 5	0 1 2 3 4 5	0 1 2 3 4 5
199–267	Replace a light switch	0 1 2 3 4 5	0 1 2 3 4 5	0 1 2 3 4 5
199–268	Install a new circuit breaker	0 1 2 3 4 5	0 1 2 3 4 5	0 1 2 3 4 5
		Frequency of Performance 0 = never 5 = often	**Importance** 1 = negligible 5 = extremely high	**Difficulty** 1 = easiest 5 = most difficult

Source: E. F. Holton III and C. Bailey, "Top to Bottom Curriculum Redesign," *Training and Development* (March 1995): 40–44.

Task analysis should be undertaken only after the organizational analysis has determined that the company wants to devote time and money for training. Why? Task analysis is a time-consuming, tedious process that involves a large time commitment to gather and summarize data from many different persons in the company, including managers, job incumbents, and trainers.

Steps in a Task Analysis

A task analysis involves four steps:[36]

1. Select the job or jobs to be analyzed.
2. Develop a preliminary list of tasks performed on the job by (1) interviewing and observing expert employees and their managers and (2) talking with others who have performed a task analysis.
3. Validate or confirm the preliminary list of tasks. This step involves having a group of SMEs (job incumbents, managers, etc.) answer in a meeting or on a written survey several questions regarding the tasks. The types of questions that may be asked include the following: How frequently is the task performed? How much time is spent performing each task? How important or critical is the task for successful performance of the job? How difficult is the task to learn? Is performance of the task expected of entry-level employees?

Table 3.8 presents a sample task analysis questionnaire. This information is used to determine which tasks will be focused on in the training program. The person or committee conducting the needs assessment must decide the level of ratings across dimensions that will determine that a task should be included in the training program.

TABLE 3.8   **Sample Task Statement Questionnaire**

Name	Date

Position

Please rate each of the task statements according to three factors: (1) the *importance* of the task for effective performance, (2) how *frequently* the task is performed, and (3) the degree of *difficulty* required to become effective in the task. Use the following scales in making your ratings.

Importance

4 = Task is critical for effective performance.
3 = Task is important but not critical for effective performance.
2 = Task is of some importance for effective performance.
1 = Task is of no importance for effective performance.
0 = Task is not performed.

Frequency

4 = Task is performed once a day.
3 = Task is performed once a week.
2 = Task is performed once every few months.
1 = Task is performed once or twice a year.
0 = Task is not performed.

Difficulty

4 = Effective performance of the task requires extensive prior experience and/or training (12–18 months or longer).
3 = Effective performance of the task requires minimal prior experience and training (6–12 months).
2 = Effective performance of the task requires a brief period of prior training and experience (1–6 months).
1 = Effective performance of the task does not require specific prior training and/or experience.
0 = This task is not performed.

Task	Importance	Frequency	Difficulty
1. Ensuring maintenance on equipment, tools, and safety controls			
2. Monitoring employee performance			
3. Scheduling employees			
4. Using statistical software on the computer			
5. Monitoring changes made in processes using statistical methods			

Tasks that are important, frequently performed, and of moderate-to-high level of difficulty are tasks for which training should be provided. Tasks that are not important and are infrequently performed should not involve training. It is difficult for managers and trainers to decide if tasks that are important but are performed infrequently and require minimal difficulty should be included in training. Managers and trainers must determine whether or not important tasks—regardless of how frequently they are performed or their level of difficulty—will be included in training.

4. Once the tasks have been identified, it is important to identify the knowledge, skills, or abilities necessary to successfully perform each task. This information can be collected through interviews and questionnaires. Recall this chapter's discussion of how ability influences learning. Information concerning basic skill and cognitive ability

requirements is critical for determining if certain levels of knowledge, skills, and abilities will be prerequisites for entrance to the training program (or job) or if supplementary training in underlying skills is needed. For training purposes, information concerning how difficult it is to learn the knowledge, skill, or ability is important—as is whether the knowledge, skill, or ability is expected to be acquired by the employee before taking the job.[37]

Table 3.9 summarizes key points to remember regarding task analysis.

Example of a Task Analysis

Each of the four steps of a task analysis can be seen in this example from a utility company. Trainers were given the job of developing a training system in six months.[38] The purpose of the program was to identify tasks and knowledge, skills, abilities, and other considerations that would serve as the basis for training program objectives and lesson plans.

The first phase of the project involved identifying potential tasks for each job in the utility's electrical maintenance area. Procedures, equipment lists, and information provided by SMEs were used to generate the tasks. SMEs included managers, instructors, and senior technicians. The tasks were incorporated into a questionnaire administered to all technicians in the electrical maintenance department. The questionnaire included 550 tasks. Table 3.7 shows sample items from the questionnaire for the electrical maintenance job. Technicians were asked to rate each task on importance, difficulty, and frequency of performance. The rating scale for frequency included zero. A zero rating indicated that the technician rating the task had never performed the task. Technicians who rated a task zero were asked not to evaluate the task's difficulty and importance.

Customized software was used to analyze the ratings collected via the questionnaire. The primary requirement used to determine whether a task required training was its importance rating. A task rated "very important" was identified as one requiring training regardless of its frequency or difficulty. If a task was rated moderately important but difficult, it also was designated for training. Tasks rated as unimportant, not difficult, or done infrequently were not designated for training.

The list of tasks designated for training was reviewed by the SMEs to determine if it accurately described job tasks. The result was a list of 487 tasks. For each of the

TABLE 3.9 **Key Points to Remember When Conducting a Task Analysis** Source: Adapted from A. P. Carnevale, L. J. Gainer, and A.S. Meltzer, *Workplace Basics Training Manual* (San Francisco: Jossey-Bass, 1990).	A task analysis should identify both what employees are actually doing and what they should be doing on the job. Task analysis begins by breaking the job into duties and tasks. Use more than two methods for collecting task information to increase the validity of the analysis. For task analysis to be useful, information needs to be collected from subject-matter experts (SMEs). SMEs include job incumbents, managers, and employees familiar with the job. In deciding how to evaluate tasks, the focus should be on tasks necessary to accomplish the company's goals and objectives. These may not be the tasks that are the most difficult or take the most time.

487 tasks, two SMEs identified the necessary knowledge, skills, abilities, and other factors required for performance. This included information on working conditions, cues that initiate the task's start and end, performance standards, safety considerations, and necessary tools and equipment. All data were reviewed by plant technicians and members of the training department. More than 14,000 knowledge, skill, ability, and other considerations were grouped into common areas and assigned an identification code. These groups were then combined into clusters. The clusters represented qualification areas. That is, the task clusters were related to linked tasks that the employees must be certified in to perform the job. The clusters were used to identify training lesson plans and course objectives. Trainers also reviewed the clusters to identify prerequisite skills for each cluster.

COMPETENCY MODELS

In today's global and competitive business environment, many companies are finding that it is difficult to determine whether employees have the capabilities needed for success. The necessary capabilities may vary from one business unit to another and even across roles within a business unit. As a result, many companies are using competency models to help them identify the knowledge, skills, and personal characteristics (attitudes, personality) needed for successful performance in a job. Competency models are also useful for ensuring that training and development systems are contributing to the development of such knowledge, skills, and personal characteristics.

Traditionally, needs assessment has involved identifying knowledge, skills, abilities, and tasks. However, a current trend in training is for needs assessment to focus on competencies. A **competency** refers to an area of personal capability that enables employees to successfully perform their jobs by achieving outcomes or accomplishing tasks.[39] A competency can be knowledge, skills, attitudes, values, or personal characteristics. A **competency model** identifies the competencies necessary for each job as well as the knowledge, skills, behavior, and personality characteristics underlying each competency.[40] Table 3.10 shows a competency model for a systems engineer. The left side of the table lists technical competencies within the technical cluster (systems architecture, data migration, documentation). The right side shows behaviors that might be used to determine a systems engineer's level of proficiency for each competency.

One way to understand competency models is to compare them to job analysis. As you may recall from other classes or experiences, **job analysis** refers to the process of developing a description of the job (tasks, duties, and responsibilities) and the specifications (knowledge, skills, and abilities) that an employee must have to perform it. How does job analysis compare to competency models? Job analysis is more work- and task-focused (what is accomplished), whereas competency modeling is worker-focused (how objectives are met or how work is accomplished). Focusing on "how" versus "what" provides valuable information for training and development. A recent study asked competency modeling experts (consultants, HR practitioners, academics, industrial psychologists) to compare and contrast competency modeling to job analysis.[41] The study found several differences between job analysis and competency models. Competency models are more likely to link

TABLE 3.10 Example of Competencies and a Competency Model

Technical Cluster	Proficiency Ratings
Systems Architecture Ability to design complex software applications, establish protocols, and create prototypes.	**0**—Is not able to perform basic tasks. **1**—Understands basic principles; can perform tasks with assistance or direction. **2**—Performs routine tasks with reliable results; works with minimal supervision. **3**—Performs complex and multiple tasks; can coach or teach others. **4**—Considered an expert in this task; can describe, teach, and lead others.
Data Migration Ability to establish the necessary platform requirements to efficiently and completely coordinate data transfer.	**0**—Is not able to perform basic tasks. **1**—Understands basic principles; can perform tasks with assistance or direction. **2**—Performs routine tasks with reliable results; works with minimal supervision. **3**—Performs complex and multiple tasks; can coach or teach others. **4**—Considered an expert in this task; can describe, teach, and lead others.
Documentation Ability to prepare comprehensive and complete documentation including specifications, flow diagrams, process control, and budgets.	**0**—Is not able to perform basic tasks. **1**—Understands basic principles; can perform tasks with assistance or direction. **2**—Performs routine tasks with reliable results; works with minimal supervision. **3**—Performs complex and multiple tasks; can coach or teach others. **4**—Considered an expert in this task; can describe, teach, and lead others.

Source: R. J. Mirabile, "Everything You Wanted to Know about Competency Modeling," *Training and Development* (August 1997): 73–77.

competencies and the company's business goals. Competency models provide descriptions of competencies that are common for an entire occupational group, level of jobs, or an entire organization. Job analysis describes what is different across jobs, occupational groups, or organization levels. Finally, job analysis generates specific knowledge, skills, and abilities for particular jobs. It is used to generate specific requirements to be used for employee selection. The competencies generated by competency modeling are more general and believed to have greater application to a wider variety of purposes, including selection, training, employee development, and performance management.

Another way to think about competency models is by considering performance management.[42] Unfortunately, many performance management systems suffer from a lack of agreement on what outcomes should be used to evaluate performance. Manager-employee discussions about performance deficiencies tend to lack specificity. By identifying the areas of personal capability that enable employees to successfully perform their jobs, competency models ensure an evaluation of both what gets done and how it gets done. Performance feedback can be directed toward specific concrete examples of behavior; and knowledge, skills, ability, and other characteristics that are necessary for success are clearly described.

How are competencies identified and competency models developed? Figure 3.4 shows the process used to develop a competency model. First, any changes in the business strategy are identified. The implications of business strategy for training were discussed in Chapter 2. Changes in the business strategy might cause new competencies to be needed or old competencies to be altered. Second, the job or position to be analyzed is identified. Third, effective and ineffective performers are identified. Fourth, the competencies responsible for effective and ineffective performance are identified. There are several approaches for identifying competencies. These include analyzing one or several "star" performers, surveying persons who are familiar with the job (SMEs), and investigating benchmark data of good performers in other companies.[43] Fifth, the model is validated. That is, a determination is made as to whether the competencies included in the model truly are related to effective performance. In Table 3.10's example of the technical competencies for the systems engineer, it is important to verify that (1) these three competencies are necessary for job success and (2) the level of proficiency of the competency is appropriate.

Following the development process outlined in Figure 3.4 will ensure that competencies and competency models are valid. However, trainers, employees, managers, and other experts should be trained (especially inexperienced raters) in how to make accurate competency ratings. Training should ensure that raters understand each competency and the differences between them and can distinguish between low, medium, and high levels of proficiency.[44]

Competency models are useful for training and development in several ways:[45]

- They identify behaviors needed for effective job performance. These models ensure that feedback given to employees as part of a development program (such as 360-degree feedback) relate specifically to individual and organizational success.
- They provide a tool for determining what skills are necessary to meet today's needs as well as the company's future skill needs. They can be used to evaluate the relationship between the company's current training programs and present needs. That is, they help align training and development activities with the company's business goals. They can be used to evaluate how well the offerings relate to anticipated future skill needs.
- They help to determine what skills are needed at different career points.
- They provide a framework for ongoing coaching and feedback to develop employees for current and future roles. By comparing their current personal competencies to those required for a job, employees can identify competencies that need development and choose actions to develop those competencies. These actions may include courses, job experiences, and other types of development. (Development methods are detailed in Chapter 9.)
- They create a "road map" for identifying and developing employees who may be candidates for managerial positions (succession planning).

FIGURE 3.4. **Process Used in Developing a Competency Model**

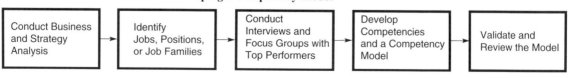

For example, at American Express, competency models are used to help managers lead their own teams by providing a framework their employees can use to capitalize on strengths and improve weaknesses.[46] At the company level, competencies are used to determine the talent level of the entire company, including capabilities, strengths, and opportunities. This information is provided to managers who use the data to identify key needs and plan actions to ensure that current and future competencies are developed in employees.

Sharp Electronics was interested in developing a competency model because of the need to adapt to a more competitive market with many new products and customer requirements.[47] Sharp wanted to clarify the knowledge, skills, and behaviors that would help employees achieve organizational goals. Executive managers wanted the competency system to provide objective criteria to identify high-potential employees. The human resource department wanted to use the competencies as part of an employee development system which employees could use on their own or with their managers to identify strengths and weaknesses. HR also wanted to use the competencies in the performance management process to help employees understand their performance results. That is, to use the competencies as the basis for feedback about how employees' performance results were achieved.

To develop the competencies, interviews were conducted with senior managers to identify the company's strategic direction, anticipated changes in the business, and the knowledge, skills, and behaviors needed to achieve the company's goals. Other competency models and best practices were reviewed. Interviews were conducted with top performers and examples of outstanding performance were analyzed. Focus groups at all levels of the company provided additional information regarding knowledge and skills required for certain competencies. Competencies and a competency model were developed and interviews and focus groups were again conducted to ensure the validity or correctness of the model and to ensure that employees felt they had ownership of the model and were committed to using it. Table 3.11 shows the 14 competencies developed by Sharp. Each competency has a behavioral definition and includes five stages of development that identify performance from low to high.

TABLE 3.11
Sharp's Competencies

Source: From R. Montier, D. Alai, and D. Kramer, "Competency Models Develop Top Performance," *T + D* (July 2006): 47–50.

- Demonstrates creativity
- Learns continuously
- Establishes high standards
- Uses information technology
- Communicates effectively
- Partners with others
- Understands the organization
- Drives change
- Focuses on the customer
- Knows the global business
- Thinks strategically
- Delegates authority
- Develops and coaches
- Leads others

SCOPE OF NEEDS ASSESSMENT

Up to this point, the chapter has discussed the various aspects of needs assessment, including organizational, person, and task analyses. This involves interviews, observations, and potentially even surveying employees. You might be saying to yourself, This sounds good, but it appears to be a very elaborate process that takes time. What happens if I don't have time to conduct a thorough needs assessment? Should I abandon the process?

Time constraints can limit the length and detail obtained from a needs assessment. However, even if managers demand a training course right now, needs assessment should still be conducted. There are several ways to conduct a rapid needs assessment. A **rapid needs assessment** refers to a needs assessment that is done quickly and accurately, but without sacrificing the quality of the process or the outcomes.[48] There are several ways to conduct a rapid needs assessment. First, the scope of needs assessment depends on the size of the potential pressure point. If the pressure point seems to be local and has a potentially small impact on the business, then the information-gathering part of needs assessment could consist of only a few interviews with managers or job incumbents. If the pressure point will have a large impact on the business, then more information gathering should be conducted. If, after interviewing SMEs and job incumbents, you can tell that you are not learning anything new about the job, then interviewing could be stopped. Second, consider using already available data collected for other purposes. For example, error data, sales data, customer complaints, and exit interviews might provide valuable clues as to the source of performance problems. The Web may be a useful source for quickly conducting interviews with SMEs in different locations. Finally, if you are attuned to the business problems, technological developments, and other issues facing the organization, you will be able to anticipate training needs. For example, if the company is opening sales offices in an international location and introducing new technology in the manufacturing plants, cross-cultural training and training designed to help employees use the new technology undoubtedly will be needed. Be prepared by understanding the business!

Needs Assessment in Practice

The manufacturing operations of the Owens-Corning Insulation Business were interested in increasing the productivity, product quality, and safety performance of the business. This was consistent with the companywide strategy of trying to increase shareholder value, ensure individual dignity, and deliver customer service. To help meet the strategic goals, plant-based specialists in human resources, training, organization development, and project management created a group to direct training activities. The first priority of this group was to establish supervisor training. At that time there was no formal training for manufacturing supervisors. Therefore, the group worked on developing such a program. Interviews with plant human resource managers and trainers suggested that creation of a generic training program would not be effective. As a result, the group developed a survey that was administered to employees in all the plants. The survey asked specific questions about the supervisors' skill needs—for example, "The supervisor actively listens to individuals or teams to check for understanding" and "The supervisor meets all deadlines on projects, action items, and special requests." The data collected from the survey indicated that supervisors' greatest skill deficiencies included two-way communications, active listening skills, setting performance expectations, providing feedback, handling conflict, and time management. The design of each plant supervisor training program was based on these needs, taking into account the uniqueness of the facility and its culture.

This example illustrates several aspects of the needs assessment process. First, training was viewed as critical for helping the company meet its strategic objectives. As a result, resources and time were allocated for needs assessment and training. Second, the person analysis consisted of a survey of supervisor skills. This information was used to identify overall skill deficiencies across the plants. Third, training programs were developed to improve the identified skill deficiencies through methods that were congruent with the plant environment and culture. For example, one plant used a three-day skills workshop, a one-day quarterly leadership skills conference (which updates and refreshes supervisors' skills), and an informal once-per-month leadership discussion.

Summary

The first step in a successful training effort is to determine that a training need exists through a process known as needs assessment. Needs assessment involves three steps: organizational analysis, person analysis, and task analysis. Various methods—including observation, interviews, and surveys or questionnaires—are used to conduct a needs assessment. Each has advantages and disadvantages. Organizational analysis involves determining (1) the extent to which training is congruent with the company's business strategy and resources and (2) if peers and managers are likely to provide the support needed for trainees to use training content in the work setting.

Person analysis focuses on identifying whether there is evidence that training is the solution, who needs training, and whether employees have the prerequisite skills, attitudes, and beliefs needed to ensure they master the content of training programs. Because performance problems are one of the major reasons that companies consider training for employees, it is important to investigate how personal characteristics, input, output, consequences, and feedback relate to performance and learning. Managers and trainers need to be concerned about employees' basic skill levels, attitudes, and the work environment in determining if performance problems can be solved using training.

Training is likely the best solution to a performance problem if employees don't know how to perform. If employees have not received feedback about their performance, if they lack the equipment needed to perform the job, if the consequences for good performance are negative, or if they are unaware of an expected standard for performance, then training is not likely to be the best solution.

To maximize employees' motivation to learn in training programs, managers and trainers need to understand these factors prior to sending employees to training. For example, lack of basic skills or reading skills can inhibit both job performance and learning.

A task analysis involves identifying the task and the training that employees will require in terms knowledge, skills, and abilities. Competency modeling is a new approach to needs assessment that focuses on identifying personal capabilities, including knowledge, skills, attitudes, values, and personal characteristics.

Key Terms

needs assessment, *103*

organizational
analysis, *103*

person analysis, *103*

task analysis, *103*

subject-matter experts
(SMEs), *106*

job incumbent, *106*

focus groups, *109*

benchmarking, *109*

request for proposal
(RFP), *112*

readiness for
training, *113*

person characteristics, *114*

input, *114*

output, *114*

consequences, *114*

feedback, *115*

motivation to learn, *115*

basic skills, *116*

cognitive ability, *117*

readability, *118*

self-efficacy, *119*

situational
constraints, *121*

social support, *121*

norms, *121*

job, *123*

task, *123*

knowledge, *123*

skill, *123*

ability, *123*

other, *123*

competency, *127*

competency model, *127*

job analysis, *127*

rapid needs
assessment, *131*

Discussion Questions

1. Which of the factors that influence performance and learning do you think is most important? Which is least important?

2. If you had to conduct a needs assessment for a new job at a new plant, describe the method you would use.

3. If you were going to use online technology to identify training needs for customer service representatives for a Web-based clothing company, what steps would you take to ensure that the technology was not threatening to employees?

4. Needs assessment involves organization, person, and task analyses. Which one of these analyses do you believe is most important? Which is least important? Why?

5. Why should upper-level managers be included in the needs assessment process?

6. Explain how you would determine if employees had the reading level necessary to succeed in a training program. How would you determine if employees had the necessary computer skills needed to use a Web-based training program?

7. What conditions would suggest that a company should buy a training program from an outside vendor? Which would suggest that the firm should develop the program itself?

8. Assume you have to prepare older employees with little computer experience to attend a training course on how to use the World Wide Web. How will you ensure that they have high levels of readiness for training? How will you determine their readiness for training?

9. Review the accompanying sample tasks and task ratings for the electronic technician's job. What tasks do you believe should be emphasized in the training program? Why?

Task	Importance	Frequency	Learning Difficulty
1. Replaces components	1	2	1
2. Repairs equipment	2	5	5
3. Interprets instrument readings	1	4	5
4. Uses small tools	2	5	1

Explanation of ratings:
Frequency: 1 = very infrequently to 5 = very frequently.
Importance: 1 = very important to 5 = very unimportant.
Learning difficulty: 1 = easy to 5 = very difficult.

10. Discuss the types of evidence that you would look for in order to determine whether a needs analysis has been improperly conducted.

11. How is competency modeling similar to traditional needs assessment? How does it differ?

12. What is a rapid needs assessment? How would you conduct a rapid needs assessment so that it is valuable and accurately identifies training needs?

Application Assignments

1. Develop a competency model for a job held by a friend, spouse, or roommate (someone other than yourself). Use the process discussed in this chapter to develop your model. Note the most difficult part of developing the model. How could the model be used?

2. The Department of Social Services represents a large portion of your county's budget and total number of employees. The job of eligibility technician is responsible for all client contact, policy interpretation, and financial decisions related to several forms of public aid (e.g., food stamps, aid to families with dependent children). Eligibility technicians must read a large number of memos and announcements of new and revised policies and procedures. Eligibility technicians were complaining they had difficulty reading and responding to this correspondence. The county decided to send the employees to a speed reading program costing $250 per person. The county has 200 eligibility technicians.

   Preliminary evaluation of the speed reading program was that trainees liked it. Two months after the training was conducted, the technicians told their managers that they were not using the speed reading course in their jobs, but were using it in leisure reading at home. When their managers asked why they weren't using it on the job, the typical response was, "I never read those memos and policy announcements anyway."

   a. Evaluate the needs assessment process used to determine that speed reading was necessary. What was good about it? Where was it faulty?
   b. How would you have conducted the needs assessment? Be realistic.

3. Consider the interview questions for the lead drivers that are shown on page 115. Write questions that could be used to interview the six lead driver supervisors and the two regional vice presidents. How do these questions differ from those for the lead drivers? How are they similar?

4. Several companies are known for linking their values and human resource practices in ways that have led to business success as well as employee satisfaction. These companies include Southwest Airlines (*www.iflyswa.com*), Cisco Systems (*www.cisco.com*), SAS Institute (*www.sas.com*), the Men's Wearhouse (*www.menswearhouse.com*), Intel (*www.intel.com*), Steelcase (*www.steelcase.com*), whole foods (*www.wholefoods.com*), and Nokia (*www.nokia.com*). Choose one of these companies' Web sites and perform an organizational needs analysis. Read about the company's values and vision; look for statements about the importance of training and personal development. Is training important in the company? Why or why not? Provide supporting evidence from the Web site.

5. Go to *wdr.doleta.gov/SCANS/*, a Web site for the U.S. Department of Labor Employee and Training Administration that includes reports of the SCANS commission (Secretary's Commission on Achieving Necessary Skills). Look at the report, "What Work Requires of Schools." What competencies does the report identify as being necessary for effective job performance? What foundational skills underlie these competencies? Identify a company that you, a friend, a neighbor, or a relative works for. Set up an interview with a manager, trainer, or human resource representative at the company. Ask this person to discuss with you the extent to which he or she believes that the employees at this company possess these five competencies. Which competencies are most strongly represented in the work force? Which competencies are weaknesses in the work force?

Case: *Determining Training Needs at Union Pacific Railroad*

Union Pacific Railroad is the largest railroad in North America, operating in the western two-thirds of the United States. The railroad serves 23 states, linking every major West Coast and Gulf Coast port, and provides service to the East through its four major gateways in Chicago, Memphis, St. Louis, and New Orleans. Additionally, Union Pacific operates key North/South corridors, connects with the Canadian and Mexican rail systems, and is the only railroad to serve all six gateways to Mexico. The railroad transports a large number of products, including chemical, coal, food and food products, forest products, grain and grain products, metals and minerals, and automobiles and parts. Union Pacific has been ranked first among railroads in *Fortune* magazine's published list of "America's Most Admired Companies."

In an attempt to improve its 70 percent rate of timeliness and accuracy of shipping to customers, Union Pacific plans to install computers and satellites on the railroad engines, which would give conductors a better ability to communicate and locate railcars that need to be delivered.

How would you conduct a needs assessment to determine what types of training conductors need to effectively use the new system?

Source: Based on D. Goldwasser, "First Things First," *Training* (January 2001): 88.

Endnotes

1.   I. L. Goldstein, E. P. Braverman, and H. Goldstein, "Needs Assessment," in *Developing Human Resources,* ed. K. N. Wexley (Washington, DC: Bureau of National Affairs, 1991): 5–35 to 5–75.

2.   L. Simpson, "In Search of Subject Matter Excellence," *Training* (January 2003): 44–47.

3.   J. Wircenski, R. Sullivan, and P. Moore, "Assessing Training Needs at Texas Instruments," *Training and Development* (April 1989).

4.   L. Overmyer-Day and G. Benson, "Training Success Stories," *Training and Development* (June 1996): 24–29.

5. M. Casey and D. Doverspike, "Training Needs Analysis and Evaluation for New Technologies through the Use of Problem-Based Inquiry," *Performance Improvement Quarterly* 18, no. 1 (2005):110–24.

6. K. Ellis, "The Right Track," *Training* (September 2004): 40–45.

7. K. Mahler, "Big Employer Is Watching," *The Wall Street Journal* (November 4, 2003): B1 and B6.

8. L. E. Day, "Benchmarking Training," *Training and Development* (November 1995): 27–30.

9. J. Rouiller and I. Goldstein, "The Relationship between Organizational Transfer Climate and Positive Transfer of Training," *Human Resource Development Quarterly* 4 (1993): 377–90; R. Noe and J. Colquitt, "Planning for Training Impact," in *Creating, Implementing, and Managing Effective Training and Development,* ed. K. Kraiger (San Francisco: Jossey-Bass, 2002): 53–79.

10. D. Zielinski, "Have You Shared a Bright Idea Today?" *Training* (July 2000): 65–68.

11. B. Gerber, "How to Buy Training Programs," *Training* (June 1989): 59–68.

12. D. A. Blackmon, "Consultants' Advice on Diversity Was Anything but Diverse," *The Wall Street Journal,* March 11, 1997: A1, A16.

13. R. Zemke and J. Armstrong, "How Long Does It Take? (The Sequel)," *Training* (May 1997): 69–79.

14. G. Rummler, "In Search of the Holy Performance Grail," *Training and Development* (April 1996): 26–31; D. G. Langdon, "Selecting Interventions," *Performance Improvement* 36 (1997): 11–15.

15. K. Gupta, *A Practical Guide to Needs Assessment* (San Francisco: Jossey-Bass/Pfeiffer, 1999).

16. R. A. Noe, "Trainee Attributes and Attitudes: Neglected Influences on Training Effectiveness," *Academy of Management Review* 11 (1986): 736–49; R. Noe and J. Colquitt, "Planning for Training Impact."

17. D. Milibank, "Marriott Tightens Job Program Screening," *The Wall Street Journal* (July 15, 1997): A1, A12.

18. T. T. Baldwin, R. T. Magjuka, and B. T. Loher, "The Perils of Participation: Effects of Choice on Trainee Motivation and Learning," *Personnel Psychology* 44 (1991): 51–66; S. I. Tannenbaum, J. E. Mathieu, E. Salas, and J. A. Cannon-Bowers, "Meeting Trainees' Expectations: The Influence of Training Fulfillment on the Development of Commitment, Self-Efficacy, and Motivation," *Journal of Applied Psychology* 76 (1991): 759–69; J. Colquitt, J. LePine, and R. Noe, "Toward an Integrative Theory of Training Motivation: A Meta-analytic Path Analysis of 20 Years of Research," *Journal of Applied Psychology* 85 (2000): 678–707.

19. M. Eisenstein, "Test, Then Train," *T + D* (May 2005): 26–27.

20. J. Nunally, *Psychometric Theory* (New York: McGraw-Hill, 1978).

21. L. Gottsfredson, "The g Factor in Employment," *Journal of Vocational Behavior* 19 (1986): 293–96.

22. M. J. Ree and J. A. Earles, "Predicting Training Success: Not Much More Than g," *Personnel Psychology* 44 (1991): 321–32.

23. S. McCartney, "The Air-Traffic Cops Go to School," *The Wall Street Journal* (March 29, 2005): D1, D7.

24. D. R. Torrence and J. A. Torrence, "Training in the Face of Illiteracy," *Training and Development Journal* (August 1987): 44–49.

25. M. Davis, "Getting Workers Back to the Basics," *Training and Development* (October 1997): 14–15.

26. J. M. Rosow and R. Zager, *Training: The Competitive Edge* (San Francisco: Jossey-Bass, 1988), chap. 7 ("Designing Training Programs to Train Functional Illiterates for New Technology").

27. A. P. Carnevale, L. J. Gainer, and A. S. Meltzer, *Workplace Basics Training Manual, 1990* (San Francisco: Jossey-Bass, 1990).

28. M. E. Gist, C. Schwoerer, and B. Rosen, "Effects of Alternative Training Methods on Self-Efficacy and Performance in Computer Software Training," *Journal of Applied Psychology* 74 (1990): 884–91; J. Martocchio and J. Dulebohn, "Performance Feedback Effects in Training: The Role of Perceived Controllability," *Personnel Psychology* 47 (1994): 357–73; J. Martocchio, "Ability Conceptions and Learning," *Journal of Applied Psychology* 79 (1994): 819–25.

29. R. A. Noe and N. Schmitt, "The Influence of Trainee Attitudes on Training Effectiveness: Test of a Model," *Personnel Psychology* 39 (1986): 497–523.

30. H. Johnson, "The Whole Picture," *Training* (July 2004): 30–34.

31. M. A. Quinones, "Pretraining Context Effects: Training Assignments as Feedback," *Journal of Applied Psychology* 80 (1995): 226–38; Baldwin, Magjuka, and Loher, "The Perils of Participation."

32. L. H. Peters, E. J. O'Connor, and J. R. Eulberg, "Situational Constraints: Sources, Consequences, and Future Considerations," in *Research in Personnel and Human Resource Management,* ed. K. M. Rowland and G. R. Ferris (Greenwich, CT: JAI Press, 1985), : 79–114; E. J. O'Connor, L. H. Peters, A. Pooyan, J. Weekley, B. Frank, and B. Erenkranz, "Situational Constraints Effects on Performance, Affective Reactions, and Turnover: A Field Replication and Extension," *Journal of Applied Psychology* 69 (1984): 663–72; D. J. Cohen, "What Motivates Trainees?" *Training and Development Journal* (November 1990): 91–93; J. S. Russell, J. R. Terborg, and M. L. Power, "Organizational Performance and Organizational Level Training and Support," *Personnel Psychology* 38 (1985): 849–63.

33. W. D. Hicks and R. J. Klimoski, "Entry into Training Programs and Its Effects on Training Outcomes: A Field Experiment," *Academy of Management Journal* 30 (1987): 542–52.

34. R. F. Mager and P. Pipe, *Analyzing Performance Problems: Or You Really Oughta Wanna,* 2d ed. (Belmont, CA: Pittman Learning, 1984); Carnevale, Gainer, and Meltzer, *Workplace Basics Training Manual;* Rummler, "In Search of the Holy Performance Grail"; C. Reinhart, "How to Leap over Barriers to Performance," *Training Development* (January 2000): 46–49.

35. G. A. Rummler and K. Morrill, "The Results Chain," *T + D* (February 2005): 27–35; D. LaFleur, K. Smalley, and J. Austin, "Improving Performance in a Nuclear Cardiology Department," *Performance Improvement Quarterly* 18, no. 1 (2005): 83–109.

36. C. E. Schneier, J. P. Guthrie, and J. D. Olian, "A Practical Approach to Conducting and Using Training Needs Assessment," *Public Personnel Management* (Summer 1988): 191–205 ; J. Annett and N. Stanton, "Task Analysis," in G. Hodgkinson and J. Ford, *International Review of Industrial and Organizational Psychology* 21 (John Wiley and Sons, 2006): 45–74.

37. I. Goldstein, "Training in Organizations," in *Handbook of Industrial/Organizational Psychology,* 2d ed., ed. M. D. Dunnette and L. M. Hough (Palo Alto, CA: Consulting Psychologists Press, 1991) : 507–619.

38. E. F. Holton III and C. Bailey, "Top-to-Bottom Curriculum Redesign," *Training and Development* (March 1995): 40–44.

39. A. Reynolds, *The Trainer's Dictionary: HRD Terms, Abbreviations, and Acronyms* (Amherst, MA: HRD Press, 1993).

40. M. Dalton, "Are Competency Models a Waste?" *Training and Development* (October 1997): 46–49.

41. J. S. Shippmann, R. A. Ash, M. Battista, L. Carr, L. D. Eyde, B. Hesketh, J. Kehoe, K. Pearlman, and J. I. Sanchez, "The Practice of Competency Modeling," *Personnel Psychology* 53 (2000): 703–40.

42. A. Lucia and R. Lepsinger, *The Art and Science of Competency Models* (San Francisco: Jossey-Bass, 1999).

43. J. Kochanski, "Competency-Based Management," *Training and Development* (October 1997): 41–44; D. Dubois and W. Rothwell, "Competency-Based or a Traditional Approach to Training," *T + D* (April 2004): 46–57; E. Kahane, "Competency Management: Cracking the Code," *T + D* (May 2008): 71–76.

44. F. Morgeson, K. Delaney-Klinger, M. Mayfield, P. Ferrara, and M. Campion, "Self-Presentation Processes in Job Analysis: A Field Experiment Investigating Inflation in Abilities, Tasks, and Competencies," *Journal of Applied Psychology* 89 (2004): 674–686; F. Lievens and J. Sanchez, "Can Training Improve the Quality of Inferences Made by Raters in Competency Modeling? A Quasi-Experiment," *Journal of Applied Psychology* 92 (2007): 812–819; F. Lievens, J. Sanchez, and W. DeCorte, "Easing the Inferential Leap in Competency Modeling: The Effects of Task-Related Information and Subject Matter Expertise," *Personnel Psychology* 57 (2004): 881–904.

45. Lucia and Lepsinger, *The Art and Science of Competency Models;* M. Derven, "Lessons Learned," *T + D* (December 2008) 68–73.

46. M. Derven, "Lessons Learned," *T + D* (December 2008): 68–73.

47. R. Montier, D. Alai, and D. Kramer, "Competency Models Develop Top Performance," *T + D* (July 2006): 47–50.

48. Gupta, *A Practical Guide to Needs Assessment;* R. Zemke, "How to Do a Needs Assessment When You Don't Have the Time," *Training* (March 1998): 38–44; G. Piskurich, *Rapid Instructional Design* (San Francisco, CA: Pfeiffer, 2006).

Learning: Theories and Program Design

Objectives

After reading this chapter, you should be able to

1. Discuss the five types of learner outcomes.
2. Explain the implications of learning theory for instructional design.
3. Incorporate adult learning theory into the design of a training program.
4. Describe how learners receive, process, store, retrieve, and act upon information.
5. Discuss the internal conditions (within the learner) and external conditions (learning environment) necessary for the trainee to learn each type of capability.
6. Be able to choose and prepare a training site.
7. Explain the four components of program design: design document template, course or lesson plan, and course or lesson plan overview.

A Positive Learning Environment Energizes Training!

Boring lectures, lack of meaningful content in e-learning, and on-the-job training that doesn't give employees the opportunity to practice and receive feedback—all of these methods demotivate trainees and make it difficult for them to learn. However, many companies are using innovative instructional methods to make training more interesting and to help trainees learn.

ArchivesOne, a records management company, encourages employees to learn outside the classroom. The company has started a book club in which two to three business books are read by employees who then meet in six-person groups for half-hour sessions to discuss the books. The books provided to employees are intended to reinforce company values and customer service. The book discussions are led by general managers and regional vice-presidents who are provided with facilitator guides that help them respond to questions about concepts in the books. The facilitators also challenge the employees to consider how they can apply the concepts and ideas in the books to improve ArchivesOne.

The training offered to truck technicians at ArvinMeritor was revised to get learners more involved. Technicians complete online prework that helps them learn about rear drive axle components, operations, and preventative maintenance. Next, in-person class time is used for hands-on work such as disassembling and reassembling drive axle parts and making adjustments to drive axles. After training, learners complete post-work which reviews the concepts covered in the hands-on sessions. Every four to six months, learners are asked to go online to practice using simulation technology that allows them to select tools from their tool box to measure or adjust or otherwise work with drive axle components using their computer mouse.

The Toshiba America Group specializes in advanced electronics and is a recognized leader in products that enhance the home, the office, and industry and health care environments. Toshiba markets and manufactures information and communication systems, electronic components, heavy electrical apparatus, consumer products, and medical diagnostic imaging equipment. At Toshiba America Business Solutions in Irvine, California, a mobile flexible training program was developed to train new dealers who had no experience with the company's products. Training To Go is a blended learning approach with work-based and classroom learning sessions. Delivering the information in multiple ways engages the learners and aids in retention.

Colorado Springs Utilities, a community-owned utility, provides natural gas, water, and electric services to more than 600,000 customers. All the company executives issue public statements in support of learning, participate in learning events as instructors or speakers, and include learning objectives as part of their performance goals. Every training program begins with a brainstorming session to identify themes and activities; this beginning engages trainees and helps them enjoy training and retain more of what they have learned. In a safety training class, students experience a simulated emergency and have to respond using skills they have learned along with their knowledge of an evacuation plan. The trainees perform different roles and activities in response to a power shutdown. Afterward, the trainer critiques their performance, and trainees discuss what they have learned (or still need to learn). Trainees complete a written exam and review to ensure their knowledge retention.

Source: Based on J. Salopek, "Toshiba America Business Solutions: 2005 BEST Award Winner," *T + D* (October 2005): 67; J. Salopek, "Colorado Springs Utilities: 2005 BEST Award Winner," *T + D* (October 2005): 38–40; M. Weinstein, "Wake-up Call," *Training* (June 2007): 48–50.

INTRODUCTION

Although they use different methods, the purpose of the training at the four companies just described is to help employees learn so they can successfully perform their jobs. Regardless of the training method, certain conditions must be present for learning to occur. These include (1) providing opportunities for trainees to practice and receive feedback, (2) offering meaningful training content, (3) identifying any prerequisites that trainees need to successfully complete the program, and (4) allowing trainees to learn through observation and experience. For example, feedback from trainers and coaches is provided at Colorado Springs Utilities. The meaningfulness of training content is enhanced at both Colorado Springs Utilities and ArvinMeritor by having trainees perform tasks and work on problems that are identical to those they will encounter on the job. Toshiba America Group delivers training content in multiple ways, which helps maintain trainees' attention and helps them commit training content to memory.

For learning to occur it is important to identify *what* is to be learned—that is, to identify learning outcomes. Learning outcomes should be related to what is required to successfully perform the job. As the previous company examples highlight, this may include selling products or services, providing quality customer service, or even climbing a utility pole to make repairs! As a student you are probably most familiar with one type of learning outcome: intellectual skills. However, training programs often focus on other outcomes such as motor skills (e.g., climbing) and attitudes. Understanding learning outcomes is crucial because they influence the characteristics of the training environment that are necessary for learning to occur. For example, if trainees are to master motor skills such as climbing a pole, they must have opportunities to practice climbing and receive feedback about their climbing skills.

Also, the design of the training program is important for learning to occur. This includes creating the program schedule, providing a physically comfortable training environment, and arranging the seating in the training environment to facilitate interaction among trainees and between trainer and trainees.

This chapter begins by defining learning and acquainting you with the different learning outcomes. Next is a discussion of various theories of learning and their implications for creating a learning environment designed to help the trainee learn the desired outcomes. The last section of the chapter looks at practical issues in training program design, including selecting and preparing a training site and developing lesson plans.

WHAT IS LEARNING? WHAT IS LEARNED?

Learning is a relatively permanent change in human capabilities that is not a result of growth processes.[1] These capabilities are related to specific learning outcomes, as Table 4.1 shows.

TABLE 4.1   **Learning Outcomes**

Type of Learning Outcome	Description of Capability	Example
Verbal Information	State, tell, or describe previously stored information	State three reasons for following company safety procedures
Intellectual Skills	Apply generalizable concepts and rules to solve problems and generate novel products	Design and code a computer program that meets customer requirements
Motor Skills	Execute a physical action with precision and timing	Shoot a gun and consistently hit a small moving target
Attitudes	Choose a personal course of action	Choose to respond to all incoming mail within 24 hours
Cognitive Strategies	Manage one's own thinking and learning processes	Selectively use three different strategies to diagnose engine malfunctions

Source: R. Gagne and K. Medsker, *The Conditions of Learning* (New York: Harcourt-Brace, 1996).

Verbal information includes names or labels, facts, and bodies of knowledge. Verbal information includes specialized knowledge that employees need in their jobs. For example, a manager must know the names of different types of equipment as well as the body of knowledge related to Total Quality Management.

Intellectual skills include concepts and rules. These concepts and rules are critical to solve problems, serve customers, and create products. For example, a manager must know the steps in the performance appraisal process (e.g., gather data, summarize data, prepare for appraisal interview with employee) in order to conduct an employee appraisal.

Motor skills include coordination of physical movements. For example, a telephone repair person must have the coordination and dexterity necessary to climb ladders and telephone poles.

Attitudes are a combination of beliefs and feelings that predispose a person to behave a certain way. Attitudes include a cognitive component (beliefs), an affective component (feeling), and an intentional component (the way a person intends to behave in regard to the subject of the attitude). Important work-related attitudes include job satisfaction, commitment to the organization, and job involvement. Suppose you say that an employee has a "positive attitude" toward her work. This means the person likes her job (the affective component). She may like her job because it is challenging and provides an opportunity to meet people (the cognitive component). Because she likes her job, she intends to stay with the company and do her best at work (the intentional component). Training programs may be used to develop or change attitudes because attitudes have been shown to be related to physical and mental withdrawal from work, turnover, and behaviors that impact the well-being of the company (e.g., helping new employees).

Cognitive strategies regulate the processes of learning. They relate to the learner's decision regarding what information to attend to (i.e., pay attention to), how to remember, and how to solve problems. For example, a physicist recalls the colors of the light spectrum through remembering the name "Roy G. Biv" (red, orange, yellow, green, blue, indigo, violet).

As this chapter points out, each learning outcome requires a different set of conditions for learning to occur. Before this chapter investigates the learning process in detail, it looks at the theories that help to explain how people learn.

LEARNING THEORIES

Several theories relate to how people learn. Each theory relates to different aspects of the learning process. Many of the theories also relate to trainees' motivation to learn, which was discussed in Chapter 3.

Reinforcement Theory

Reinforcement theory emphasizes that people are motivated to perform or avoid certain behaviors because of past outcomes that have resulted from those behaviors.[2] There are several processes in reinforcement theory. Positive reinforcement is a pleasurable outcome resulting from a behavior. Negative reinforcement is the removal of an unpleasant outcome. For example, consider a machine that makes screeching and grinding noises unless the operator holds levers in a certain position. The operator will learn to hold the levers in that position to avoid the noises. The process of withdrawing positive or negative reinforcers to eliminate a behavior is known as extinction. Punishment is presenting an unpleasant outcome after a behavior, leading to a decrease in that behavior. For example, if a manager yells at employees when they are late, they may avoid the yelling by being on time (but they may also call in sick, quit, or trick the boss into not noticing when they arrive late).

From a training perspective, reinforcement theory suggests that for learners to acquire knowledge, change behavior, or modify skills, the trainer needs to identify what outcomes the learner finds most positive (and negative). Trainers then need to link these outcomes to learners' acquiring knowledge or skills or changing behaviors. As was mentioned in Chapter 3, learners can obtain several types of benefits from participating in training programs. The benefits may include learning an easier or more interesting way to perform their job (job-related), meeting other employees who can serve as resources when problems occur (personal), or increasing opportunities to consider new positions in the company (career-related). According to reinforcement theory, trainers can withhold or provide these benefits to learners who master program content. The effectiveness of learning depends on the pattern or schedule for providing these reinforcers or benefits. Schedules of reinforcement are shown in Table 4.2.

Behavior modification is a training method that is primarily based on reinforcement theory. For example, a training program in a bakery focused on eliminating unsafe behaviors such as climbing over conveyor belts (rather than walking around them) and sticking hands into equipment to dislodge jammed materials without turning off the equipment.[3] Employees were shown slides depicting safe and unsafe work behaviors. After viewing the slides, employees were shown a graph of the number of times safe behaviors were observed during past weeks. Employees were encouraged to increase the number of safe

TABLE 4.2 **Schedules of Reinforcement**

Type of Schedule	Description	Effectiveness
Ratio Schedules		
Fixed-Ratio Schedule	Reinforcement whenever target behavior has taken place a given number of times	Rapid learning; frequent instances of target behavior; rapid extinction
Continuous Reinforcement	Reinforcement after each occurrence of target behavior	Same direction of behavior as with fixed-ratio schedules but more extreme
Variable-Ratio Schedule	Reinforcement after several occurrences of target behavior; number of occurrences before reinforcement may differ each time	Target behavior less susceptible to extinction than with fixed-ratio schedules
Interval Schedules		
Fixed-Interval Schedule	Reinforcement at a given time interval after performance of target behavior	Lower performance of target behavior than with ratio schedules; lower effectiveness if time interval is long
Variable-Interval Schedule	Reinforcement occurring periodically after performance of target behavior; time intervals may differ each time	Target behavior less susceptible to extinction than with fixed-interval schedules; lower performance of target behavior than with ratio schedules

Source: P. Wright and R. A. Noe, *Management of Organizations* (Burr Ridge, IL: Irwin/McGraw-Hill, 1996).

behaviors they demonstrated on the job. They were given several reasons for doing so: for their own protection, to decrease costs for the company, and to help their plant get out of last place in the safety rankings of the company's plants. Immediately after the training, safety reminders were posted in employees' work areas. Data about the number of safe behaviors performed by employees continued to be collected and displayed on the graph in the work area following the training. Employees' supervisors were also instructed to recognize the workers whenever they saw them perform a safe work behavior. In this example, the data of safe behavior posted in the work areas and supervisors' recognition of safe work behavior represent positive reinforcers.

Social Learning Theory

Social learning theory emphasizes that people learn by observing other persons (models) whom they believe are credible and knowledgeable.[4] Social learning theory also recognizes that behavior that is reinforced or rewarded tends to be repeated. The models' behavior or skill that is rewarded is adopted by the observer. According to social learning theory, learning new skills or behaviors comes from (1) directly experiencing the consequences of using that behavior or skill, or (2) the process of observing others and seeing the consequences of their behavior.[5]

According to social learning theory, learning also is influenced by a person's self-efficacy. **Self-efficacy** is a person's judgment about whether he or she can successfully learn knowledge and skills. Chapter 3 emphasizes self-efficacy as an important factor to consider in the person analysis phase of needs assessment. Why? Self-efficacy is one determinant of readiness to learn. A trainee with high self-efficacy will put forth effort to learn in a training program and is most likely to persist in learning even if an environment is not conducive to learning (e.g., noisy training room). In contrast, a person with low self-efficacy will have self-doubts about mastering the content of a training program and is more likely to withdraw psychologically and/or physically (daydream or fail to attend the program). These persons believe that they are unable to learn, and regardless of their effort level, they will be unable to learn.

A person's self-efficacy can be increased using several methods: verbal persuasion, logical verification, observation of others (modeling), and past accomplishments.[6] **Verbal persuasion** means offering words of encouragement to convince others they can learn. **Logical verification** involves perceiving a relationship between a new task and a task already mastered. Trainers and managers can remind employees when they encounter learning difficulties that they have been successful at learning similar tasks. **Modeling** involves having employees who already have mastered the learning outcomes demonstrate them for trainees. As a result, employees are likely to be motivated by the confidence and success of their successful peers. **Past accomplishments** refers to allowing employees to build a history of successful accomplishments. Managers can place employees in situations where they are likely to succeed and provide training so that employees know what to do and how to do it.

Social learning theory suggests that four processes are involved in learning: attention, retention, motor reproduction, and motivational processes (see Figure 4.1).

Attention suggests that persons cannot learn by observation unless they are aware of the important aspects of a model's performance. Attention is influenced by characteristics of the model and the learner. Learners must be aware of the skills or behavior they are supposed to observe. The model must be clearly identified and credible. The learner must have

FIGURE 4.1   **Processes of Social Learning Theory**

Source: Based on A. Bandura, *Social Foundations of Thoughts and Actions* (Englewood Cliffs, NJ: Prentice Hall, 1986); P. Taylor, D. Russ-Eft, and D. Chan, "A Meta-analytic Review of Behavior Modeling Training," *Journal of Applied Psychology* 90 (2005): 692–709.

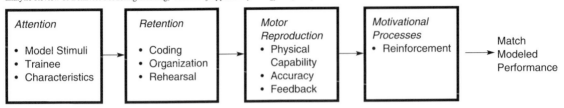

the physical capability (sensory capability) to observe the model. Also, a learner who has successfully learned other skills or behavior by observing the model is more likely to attend to the model.

Learners must remember the behaviors or skills that they observe. This is the role of *retention*. Learners have to code the observed behavior and skills in memory in an organized manner so they can recall them for the appropriate situation. Behaviors or skills can be coded as visual images (symbols) or verbal statements.

Motor reproduction involves trying out the observed behaviors to see if they result in the same reinforcement that the model received. The ability to reproduce the behaviors or skills depends on the extent to which the learner can recall the skills or behavior. The learner must also have the physical capability to perform the behavior or exhibit the skill. For example, a firefighter can learn the behaviors necessary to carry a person away from a dangerous situation, but he may be unable to demonstrate the behavior because he lacks upper body strength. Note that performance of behavior is usually not perfect on the first attempt. Learners must have the opportunity to practice and receive feedback to modify their behavior to be similar to the model's behavior.

Learners are more likely to adopt a modeled behavior if it results in positive outcomes. Social learning theory emphasizes that behaviors that are reinforced (a *motivational process*) will be repeated in the future. For example, a major source of conflict and stress for managers often relates to the performance appraisal interview. A manager may, through observing successful managers, learn behaviors that allow employees to be more participative in a performance appraisal interview (e.g., give employees the opportunity to voice their concerns). If the manager uses this behavior in the performance appraisal interview and the behavior is rewarded by employees (e.g., they make comments such as "I really felt the feedback meeting was the best we have ever had") or the new behavior leads to reduced conflicts with employees (e.g., negative reinforcement), the manager will more likely use this behavior in subsequent appraisal interviews.

As you will see in the discussion of training methods in Chapters 7 and 8, social learning theory is the primary basis for behavior modeling training and has influenced the development of multimedia training programs. For example, in the training program called "Getting Your Ideas Across," trainees are first presented with the five key behaviors for getting their ideas across: (1) state the point and purpose of the message, (2) present points to aid understanding, (3) check the audience for reactions and understanding, (4) handle reactions from the audience to what was presented, and (5) summarize the main point. The trainer provides a rationale for each key behavior. Next, trainees view a video of a business meeting in which a manager is having difficulty getting subordinates to accept his ideas regarding how to manage an impending office move. The manager, who is the model, is ineffective in getting his ideas across to his subordinates. As a result, the video shows that the subordinates are dissatisfied with the manager and his ideas. The video is turned off and the trainer leads the trainees in a discussion of what the manager did wrong in trying to get his ideas across. Trainees again view the video. But this time the manager, in the same situation, is shown using the key behaviors. As a result, subordinates react quite positively to their boss (the model). Following this video segment, the trainer leads a discussion of how the model used the key behaviors to successfully get his ideas across.

After observing the model and discussing the key behaviors, each trainee is paired with another trainee for practice. Each group is given a situation and message to communicate. The trainees take turns trying to get their ideas across to each other using the key behaviors. Each trainee is expected to provide feedback regarding the partner's use of the key behaviors. The trainer also observes and provides feedback to each group. Before leaving training, the trainees are given a pocket-size card with the key behaviors, which they take back with them to the job. Also, they complete a planning guide in which they describe a situation where they want to use the key behaviors and how they plan to use them.

Goal Theories

Goal Setting Theory

Goal setting theory assumes that behavior results from a person's conscious goals and intentions.[7] Goals influence a person's behavior by directing energy and attention, sustaining effort over time, and motivating the person to develop strategies for goal attainment.[8] Research suggests that specific challenging goals result in better performance than vague, unchallenging goals.[9] Goals have been shown to lead to high performance only if people are committed to the goal. Employees are less likely to be committed to a goal if they believe it is too difficult.

An example of how goal setting theory influences training methods is seen in a program designed to improve pizza deliverers' driving practices.[10] The majority of pizza deliverers are young (age 18 to 24), inexperienced drivers, who are compensated based on the number of pizzas they can deliver. This creates a situation in which deliverers are rewarded for fast but unsafe driving practices—for example, not wearing a safety belt, failing to use turn signals, and not coming to complete stops at intersections. These unsafe practices have resulted in a high driving accident rate.

Prior to goal setting, pizza deliverers were observed by their managers leaving the store and then returning from deliveries. The managers observed the number of complete stops at intersections over a one-week period. In the training session, managers and trainers presented the deliverers with a series of questions for discussion. Here are examples: In what situations should you come to a complete stop? What are the reasons for coming to a complete stop? What are the reasons for not coming to a complete stop?

After the discussion, pizza deliverers were asked to agree on the need to come to a complete stop at intersections. Following the deliverers' agreement, the managers shared the data they collected regarding the number of complete stops at intersections they had observed the previous week. (Complete stops were made 55 percent of the time.) The trainer asked the pizza deliverers to set a goal for complete stopping over the next month. They decided on a goal of 75 percent complete stops.

After the goal setting session, managers at each store continued observing their drivers' intersection stops. The following month in the work area, a poster showed the percentages of complete stops for every four-day period. The current percentage of total complete stops was also displayed.

Goal setting theory also is used in training program design. Goal setting theory suggests that learning can be facilitated by providing trainees with specific challenging goals and objectives. Specifically, the influence of goal setting theory can be seen in the development of training lesson plans. As explained later in the chapter, these lesson plans begin with specific goals providing information regarding the expected action that the learner will demonstrate, conditions under which learning will occur, and the level of performance that will be judged acceptable.

Goal Orientation

Goal orientation refers to the goals held by a trainee in a learning situation. Goal orientation can include a learning orientation or a performance orientation. **Learning orientation** relates to trying to increase ability or competence in a task. People with a learning orientation believe that training success is defined as showing improvement and making progress, prefer trainers who are more interested in how trainees are learning than in how they are performing, and view errors and mistakes as part of the learning process. **Performance orientation** refers to learners who focus on task performance and how they compare to others. Persons with a performance orientation define success as high performance relative to others, value high ability more than learning, and find that errors and mistakes cause anxiety and want to avoid them.

Goal orientation is believed to affect the amount of effort a trainee will expend in learning (motivation to learn). Learners with a high learning orientation will direct greater attention to the task and learn for the sake of learning in comparison to learners with a performance orientation. Learners with a performance orientation will direct more attention to performing well and less effort to learning. Research has shown that trainees with a learning orientation exert greater effort to learn and use more complex learning strategies than do trainees with a performance orientation.[11] There are several ways to create a learning orientation in trainees.[12] These include setting goals around learning and experimenting with new ways of having trainees perform trained tasks rather than emphasizing trained-task performance; deemphasizing competition among trainees; creating a community of learning (discussed later in the chapter); and allowing trainees to make errors and to experiment with new knowledge, skills, and behaviors during training.

Need Theories

Need theories help to explain the value that a person places on certain outcomes. A **need** is a deficiency that a person is experiencing at any point in time. A need motivates a person to behave in a manner to satisfy the deficiency. Maslow's and Alderfer's need theories focused on physiological needs, relatedness needs (needs to interact with other persons), and growth needs (self-esteem, self-actualization).[13] Both Maslow and Alderfer believed that persons start by trying to satisfy needs at the lowest level, then progress up the hierarchy as lower-level needs are satisfied. That is, if physiological needs are not met, a person's behavior will focus first on satisfying these needs before relatedness or growth needs receive attention. The major difference between Alderfer's and Maslow's hierarchies of needs is that Alderfer allows the possibility that if higher-level needs are not satisfied, employees will refocus on lower-level needs.

McClelland's need theory focused primarily on needs for achievement, affiliation, and power.[14] According to McClelland, these needs can be learned. Need for achievement relates to a concern for attaining and maintaining self-set standards of excellence. Need for affiliation involves concern for building and maintaining relationships with other people and for being accepted by others. The need for power is a concern for obtaining responsibility, influence, and reputation.

Need theories suggest that to motivate learning, trainers should identify trainees' needs and communicate how training program content relates to fulfilling these needs. Also, if certain basic needs of trainees (e.g., physiological and safety needs) are not met, they are unlikely to be motivated to learn. For example, consider a word processing training class for secretaries in a downsizing company. It is doubtful that even the best designed training class will result in learning if employees believe their job security is threatened (unmet need for security) by the company's downsizing strategy. Also, it is unlikely the secretaries will be motivated to learn if they believe that word processing skills emphasized in the program will not help them keep their current employment or increase their chances of finding another job inside or outside the company.

Another implication of need theory relates to providing employees with a choice of training programs to attend. As Chapter 3 mentioned, giving employees a choice of which training course to attend can increase their motivation to learn. This occurs because trainees are able to choose programs that best match their needs.

Expectancy Theory

Expectancy theory suggests that a person's behavior is based on three factors: expectancy, instrumentality, and valence.[15] Beliefs about the link between trying to perform a behavior and actually performing well are called **expectancies.** Expectancy is similar to self-efficacy. In expectancy theory, a belief that performing a given behavior (e.g., attending a training program) is associated with a particular outcome (e.g., being able to better perform your job) is called **instrumentality**. **Valence** is the value that a person places on an outcome (e.g., how important it is to perform better on the job).

According to expectancy theory, various choices of behavior are evaluated according to their expectancy, instrumentality, and valence. Figure 4.2 shows how behavior is determined based on finding the mathematical product of expectancy, instrumentality, and valence. People choose the behavior with the highest value.

FIGURE 4.2   **Expectancy Theory of Motivation**

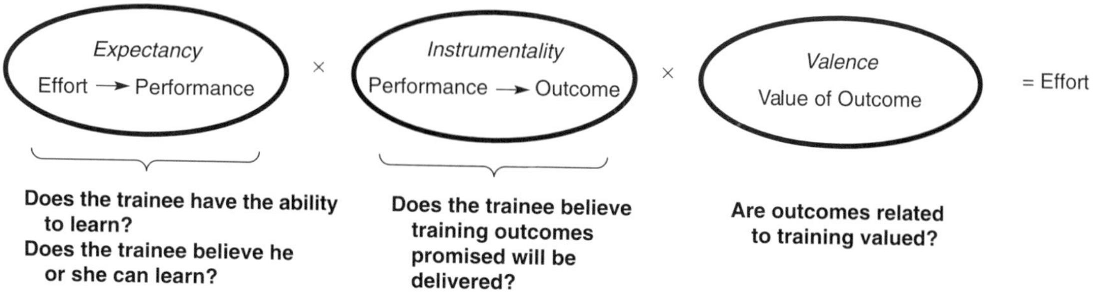

$$\underbrace{\begin{array}{c} \textit{Expectancy} \\ \text{Effort} \longrightarrow \text{Performance} \end{array}}_{} \times \underbrace{\begin{array}{c} \textit{Instrumentality} \\ \text{Performance} \longrightarrow \text{Outcome} \end{array}}_{} \times \begin{array}{c} \textit{Valence} \\ \text{Value of Outcome} \end{array} = \text{Effort}$$

Does the trainee have the ability to learn?
Does the trainee believe he or she can learn?

Does the trainee believe training outcomes promised will be delivered?

Are outcomes related to training valued?

From a training perspective, expectancy theory suggests that learning is most likely to occur when employees believe they can learn the content of the program (expectancy); learning is linked to outcomes such as better job performance, a salary increase, or peer recognition (instrumentality); and employees value these outcomes (valence).

Adult Learning Theory

Adult learning theory was developed out of a need for a specific theory of how adults learn. Most educational theories as well as formal educational institutions have been developed exclusively to educate children and youth. Pedagogy, the art and science of teaching children, has dominated educational theory. Pedagogy gives the instructor major responsibility for making decisions about learning content, method, and evaluation. Students are generally seen as (1) being passive recipients of directions and content and (2) bringing few experiences that may serve as resources to the learning environment.[16]

Educational psychologists, recognizing the limitations of formal education theories, developed **andragogy,** the theory of adult learning. Malcolm Knowles is most frequently associated with adult learning theory. Knowles's model is based on several assumptions:[17]

1. Adults have the need to know why they are learning something.
2. Adults have a need to be self-directed.
3. Adults bring more work-related experiences into the learning situation.
4. Adults enter into a learning experience with a problem-centered approach to learning.
5. Adults are motivated to learn by both extrinsic and intrinsic motivators.

Adult learning theory is especially important to consider in developing training programs because the audience for many such programs tends to be adults, most of whom have not spent a majority of their time in a formal education setting. Table 4.3 shows implications of adult learning theory for learning. For example, many adults are intimidated by math and finance.[18] In a day-long seminar to teach basic accounting principles, the course designers considered the trainees' readiness. They created a program, filled with fun and music, in which participants start their own lemonade stand. This reduced trainees' anxiety, which could have inhibited their learning. Many adults believe that they learn through experience. As a result, trainers need to provide opportunities for trainees to experience something new and discuss it or review training materials based on their experiences.

Note that a common theme in these applications is mutuality. That is, the learner and the trainer are both involved in creating the learning experience and making sure that learning occurs.

TABLE 4.3
Implications of Adult Learning Theory for Training

Source: Based on M. Knowles, *The Adult Learner,* 4th ed. (Houston, TX: Gulf Publishing, 1990).

Design Issue	Implications
Self-Concept	Mutual planning and collaboration in instruction
Experience	Use learner experience as basis for examples and applications
Readiness	Develop instruction based on the learner's interests and competencies
Time Perspective	Immediate application of content
Orientation to Learning	Problem-centered instead of subject-centered

Information Processing Theory

Compared to other learning theories, information processing theories give more emphasis to the internal processes that occur when training content is learned and retained. Figure 4.3 shows a model of information processing. Information processing theories propose that information or messages taken in by the learner undergo several transformations in the human brain.[19] Information processing begins when a message or stimuli (which could be sound, smell, touch, or pictures) from the environment is received by receptors (ears, nose, skin, eyes). The message is registered in the senses and stored in short-term memory. The message is then transformed or coded for storage in long-term memory. A search process occurs in memory during which time a response to the message or stimulus is organized. The response generator organizes the teamers response and tells the effectors (muscles) what to do. The "what to do" relates to one of the five learning outcomes: verbal information, cognitive skills, motor skills, intellectual skills, or attitudes. The final link in the model is feedback from the environment. This feedback provides the learner with an evaluation of the response given. This information can come from another person or the learner's own observation of the results of his or her action. A positive evaluation of the response provides reinforcement that the behavior is desirable and should be stored in long-term memory for use in similar situations.

Besides emphasizing the internal processes needed to capture, store, retrieve, and respond to messages, the information processing model highlights how external events influence learning. These events include:[20]

1. Changes in the intensity or frequency of the stimulus that affect attention.
2. Informing the learner of the objectives to establish an expectation.
3. Enhancing perceptual features of the material (stimulus), drawing the attention of the learner to certain features.
4. Verbal instructions, pictures, diagrams, and maps suggesting ways to code the training content so that it can be stored in memory.
5. Meaningful learning context (examples, problems) creating cues that facilitate coding.
6. Demonstration or verbal instructions helping to organize the learner's response as well as facilitating the selection of the correct response.

FIGURE 4.3
A Model of Human Information Processing

Source: Adapted from R. Gagne, "Learning Processes and Instruction," *Training Research Journal* 1 (1995/96):17–28.

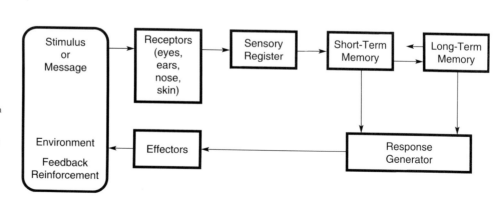

THE LEARNING PROCESS

Now that you have reviewed learning theories, you are ready to address three questions: What are the physical and mental processes involved in learning? How does learning occur? Do trainees have different learning styles?

Mental and Physical Processes

Table 4.4 shows the learning processes. These processes include expectancy, perception, working storage, semantic encoding, long-term storage, retrieval, generalizing, and gratification.[21] Table 4.4 emphasizes that learning depends on the learner's cognitive processes,

TABLE 4.4 The Relationship among Learning Processes, Instructional Events, and Forms of Instruction

Processes of Learning	External Instructional Events	Forms of Instruction
1. Expectancy	1. Informing the learner of the lesson objective	1a. Demonstrate the expected performance. 1b. Indicate the kind of verbal question to be answered.
2. Perception	2. Presenting stimuli with distinctive features	2a. Emphasize the features of the subject to be perceived. 2b. Use formatting and figures in text to emphasize features.
3. Working Storage	3. Limiting the amount to be learned	3a. Chunk lengthier material. 3b. Provide a visual image of material to be learned. 3c. Provide practice and overlearning to aid the attainment of automaticity.
4. Semantic Encoding	4. Providing learning guidance	4a. Provide verbal cues to proper combining sequence. 4b. Provide verbal links to a larger meaningful context. 4c. Use diagrams and models to show relationships among concepts.
5. Long-Term Storage	5. Elaborating the amount to be learned	5a. Vary the context and setting for presentation and recall of material. 5b. Relate newly learned material to previously learned information. 5c. Provide a variety of contexts and situations during practice.
6. Retrieval	6. Providing cues that are used in recall	6a. Suggest cues that elicit the recall of material. 6b. Use familiar sounds or rhymes as cues.
7. Generalizing	7. Enhancing retention and learning transfer	7a. Design the learning situation to share elements with the situation to which learning applies. 7b. Provide verbal links to additional complexes of information.
8. Gratifying	8. Providing feedback about performance correctness	8a. Provide feedback on degree of accuracy and timing of performance. 8b. Confirm whether original expectancies were met.

Source: R. Gagne, "Learning Processes and Instruction," *Training Research Journal* 1 (1995/96): 17–28.

including attending to what is to be learned (learning content), organizing the learning content into a mental representation, and relating the learning content to existing knowledge from long-term memory.[22] **Expectancy** refers to the mental state that the learner brings to the instructional process. This includes factors such as readiness for training (motivation to learn, basic skills) as well as an understanding of the purpose of the instruction and the likely benefits that may result from learning and using the learned capabilities on the job. **Perception** refers to the ability to organize the message from the environment so that it can be processed and acted upon. Both working storage and semantic encoding relate to short-term memory. In **working storage,** rehearsal and repetition of information occur, allowing material to be coded for memory.

Working storage is limited by the amount of material that can be processed at any one time. Research suggests that not more than five messages can be prepared for storage at any one time. **Semantic encoding** refers to the actual coding process of incoming messages.

Different learning strategies influence how training content is coded. Learning strategies include rehearsal, organizing, and elaboration.[23] **Rehearsal,** the simplest learning strategy, focuses on learning through repetition (memorization). **Organizing** requires the learner to find similarities and themes in the training material. **Elaboration** requires the trainee to relate the training material to other, more familiar knowledge, skills, or behaviors. Trainees use a combination of these strategies to learn. The "best" strategy depends on the learning outcome. For knowledge outcomes, rehearsal and organization are most appropriate. For skill application, elaboration is necessary. After messages have been attended to, rehearsed, and coded, they are ready for storage in long-term memory.

To use learned material (e.g., cognitive skills, verbal information), it must be retrieved. **Retrieval** involves identifying learned material in long-term memory and using it to influence performance. An important part of the learning process is not only being able to reproduce exactly what was learned but also being able to adapt the learning for use in similar but not identical situations. This is known as **generalizing.** Finally, **gratifying** refers to the feedback that the learner receives as a result of using learning content. Feedback is necessary to allow the learner to adapt responses so they are more appropriate. Feedback also provides information about the incentives or reinforcers that may result from performance.

The Learning Cycle

Learning can be considered a dynamic cycle that involves four stages: concrete experience, reflective observation, abstract conceptualization, and active experimentation.[24] First, a trainee encounters a concrete experience (e.g., a work problem). This is followed by thinking (reflective observation) about the problem, which leads to generation of ideas of how to solve the problem (abstract conceptualization) and finally to implementation of the ideas directly to the problem (active experimentation). Implementing the ideas provides feedback as to their effectiveness, so the learner can see the results and start the learning process over again. Trainees continually develop concepts, translate them into ideas, implement them, and adapt them as a result of their personal observations about their experiences.

Researchers have developed questionnaires to measure trainees' weak and strong points in the learning cycle. Some people have a tendency to over- or underemphasize one stage of the learning cycle or to avoid certain stages. The key to effective learning is to be competent in each of the four stages. Four fundamental learning styles are believed to exist. These learning styles combine elements of each of the four stages of the learning cycle. Table 4.5 shows the characteristics and dominant learning stage of these styles, called Divergers, Assimilators, Convergers, and Accommodators.[25] Although the questionnaires have been widely used as part of training programs, few studies have investigated the reliability and validity of the learning styles.

Trainers who are aware of trainees' learning styles can try to customize instruction to match their preferences. If a group of trainees tends to prefer hands-on learning, trying to teach the mechanics of a technical application online by having them read it will not result in learning. They need applications and the ability to get feedback from an instructor. (Effective online learning is discussed in Chapter 8.)

For example, AmeriCredit, an auto finance company located in Fort Worth, Texas, is trying to modify training to better match employees' learning styles.[26] The company has created a database to identify and track each employee's learning style. Also, employees' learning styles are being considered in course design. In a new e-learning class, employees who prefer learning by action will receive information in bullet points and will complete activities that help them learn. Employees who prefer thought and reasoning will receive more conceptual material during the course and be involved in fewer experiences. The company plans to compare the new e-learning class that takes into account learning styles with one that does not to determine whether the adaptation to learning styles makes a difference in trainee satisfaction and learning.

TABLE 4.5 **Learning Styles**

Learning Style Type	Dominant Learning Abilities	Learning Characteristics
Diverger	• Concrete experience • Reflective observation	• Is good at generating ideas, seeing a situation from multiple perspectives, and being aware of meaning and value • Tends to be interested in people, culture, and the arts
Assimilator	• Abstract conceptualization • Reflective observation	• Is good at inductive reasoning, creating theoretical models, and combining disparate observations into an integrated explanation • Tends to be less concerned with people than with ideas and abstract concepts
Converger	• Abstract conceptualization • Active experimentation	• Is good at decisiveness, practical application of ideas, and hypothetical deductive reasoning • Prefers dealing with technical tasks rather than interpersonal issues
Accommodator	• Concrete experience • Active experimentation	• Is good at implementing decisions, carrying out plans, and getting involved in new experiences • Tends to be at ease with people but may be seen as impatient or pushy

Source: Based on D. Kolb, *Learning Style Inventory, Version 3* (Boston, MA: Hay/McBer Training Resources Group, 1999).

Age Influences on Learning

There is biological evidence that certain mental capacities decrease from age 20 to age 70.[27] Short-term memory and the speed at which people process information decline as we age. However, with age comes experience, which can compensate for the loss of memory and mental quickness. Although mental quickness and memory losses diminish at a steady pace, at older ages the memory loss is much greater because mental resources are more depleted than at earlier ages. Some trainers believe that there are four generations of employees with distinct attitudes toward work and preferred ways to learn. Those generations have been called millenniums (or nexters), Gen Xers, baby boomers, and traditionalists.

But note that members of the same generation are no more alike than members of the same gender or race. Each generation may be characterized by certain characteristics that can influence learning. Also note that there has been no research that follows different generations of employees over their life spans to identify differences. Trainers should consider generational differences in designing learning environments but keep in mind that definite conclusions regarding generational differences cannot be made.

The terms **millenniums** and **nexters** refer to people born after 1980. They are optimistic, willing to work and learn, and technology-literate; they appreciate diversity. The term **Gen Xers** refers to people born from 1961 to 1980. Gen Xers need feedback and flexibility; they dislike close supervision. They have experienced change all their lives (in terms of parents, homes, and cities). Gen Xers value a balance between work and nonwork. **Baby boomers** are people born between 1945 and 1960. They are competitive, hard working, and concerned that all employees be fairly treated. **Traditionalists** are people born between 1920 and 1944. They are patriotic and loyal, and they have a great deal of knowledge of the history of organizations and work life. Each generation may have specific preferences for the arrangement of the learning environment, type of instruction, and learning activities.[28] (Chapter 11 discusses implications of generational differences for career management.)

Traditionalists prefer a traditional training room with a stable, orderly learning environment. They do not like to be put on the spot in front of other trainees. They value direct presentation of information and training materials that are organized logically. They like trainers to ask them to share their experiences or anecdotes. But they also look to the trainer to provide expertise.

Baby boomers respond well to interactive training activities—they like group activities. They like well-organized training materials with an overview of the information and an easy way to access more detailed information. Compared to the other groups, they are especially motivated to learn if they believe training content will benefit them personally. Baby boomers need to work on translating the knowledge they have into skills.

Gen Xers prefer a self-directed learning environment. They respond best to training methods that allow them to work at their own pace: videos, CD-ROMs, and Web-based training. Gen Xers are highly motivated learners who view training as a way to increase their employability. They like to learn by doing, through experimentation and feedback. They respond best to training materials that provide visual stimulation with relatively few words.

Although they are techno-saavy, millenniums like to learn by working alone and helping others. They prefer a blended learning approach that involves self-paced online learning for acquiring basic concepts, ideas, and knowledge followed by group activities and hands-on practice in which they work with others on questions, cases, and role plays.[29] They are motivated to learn skills and acquire knowledge that will help make their working lives less stressful and increase their employability. They place a high value on money so linking training to monetary incentives may facilitate learning. Nexters (like Gen Xers) prefer entertaining training activities. Training needs to be interactive and to utilize music, art, and games. UPS was experiencing much higher than normal failure rates among its millennium drivers. The initial idea was to train millenniums using video games and simulations. However, needs assessment found that while these employees wanted to use technology in their training they also wanted hands-on training in the skills needed to be successful drivers. As a result, UPS's new Integrad learning facility for driver trainees in Maryland includes online learning, podcasts, and videos, along with classroom training and simulations involving driving delivery trucks and delivering packages on the streets of a fictitious town named Clarksville.[30]

The potential for generational differences to affect learning suggests that trainers need to be aware of trainees' ages before the session so they can try to create a learning environment and develop materials that meet their preferences. Recent research summarizing the findings of studies on the influence of age on performance in training found that self-paced training had the largest influence on training performance of trainees over 40 years of age.[31] Self-pacing gives older trainees time to assume responsibility for their learning, to focus on what is required to learn, and to understand the training and its importance. Also, training that occurred in small groups was advantageous for older trainees. Most training groups probably have a mix of generations. Employees can learn much from cross-generation interaction if it is managed well. Trainees of all age groups need to feel that participation in the session through questioning, providing answers, and discussing issues is valued and rewarded. If a group of trainees includes all generations, the training must take a blended approach—use examples that include people from different generations and use different training approaches (experts, audience involvement, group work, self-directed learning activities).

Implications of the Learning Process for Instruction

Instruction refers to the trainer's manipulation of the environment in order to help trainees learn.[32] The right side of Table 4.4 shows the forms of instruction that support learning. To provide trainees with the best chance to learn, it is important to ensure that these forms of instruction are included in training. Table 4.6 summarizes the features of good instruction that facilitate the learning process. The features of a positive learning environment need to be designed into training courses, programs, or specific training methods that might be

TABLE 4.6
Features of Good Instruction That Facilitate Learning

- Objectives: Employees need to know why they should learn
- Meaningful content
- Opportunities to practice
- Methods for committing training content to memory
- Feedback
- Observation, experience, and social interaction
- Proper coordination and arrangement of the training program
- Careful selection of instructors

used, whether lectures, e-learning, or on-the-job training. Below and in the rest of the chapter we discuss these features.

Employees Need to Know Why They Should Learn

Employees learn best when they understand the objective of the training program. The **objective** refers to the purpose and expected outcome of training activities. There may be objectives for each training session as well as overall objectives for the program. Recall the discussion of goal setting theory earlier in the chapter. Because objectives can serve as goals, trainees need to understand, accept, and be committed to achieving the training objectives for learning to occur. Training objectives based on the training needs analysis help employees understand why they need training and what they need to learn. Objectives are also useful for identifying the types of training outcomes that should be measured to evaluate a training program's effectiveness.

A training objective has three components:[33]

1. A statement of what the employee is expected to do (performance or outcome).
2. A statement of the quality or level of performance that is acceptable (criterion).
3. A statement of the conditions under which the trainee is expected to perform the desired outcome (conditions).

The objective should not describe performance that cannot be observed, such as "understand" or "know." Table 4.7 shows verbs that can be used for cognitive, affective, and psychomotor (physical abilities and skills) outcomes. For example, a training objective for a customer-service training program for retail salespeople might be "After training, the employee will be able to express concern [performance] to all irate customers by a brief

TABLE 4.7   **Examples of Performance or Outcomes for Objectives**

Domain	Performance
Knowledge (recall of information)	Arrange, define, label, list, recall, repeat
Comprehension (interpret in own words)	Classify, discuss, explain, review, translate
Application (apply to new situation)	Apply, choose, demonstrate, illustrate, prepare
Analysis (break down into parts and show relationships)	Analyze, categorize, compare, diagram, test
Synthesis (bring together to form a whole)	Arrange, collect, assemble, propose, set up
Evaluation (judgments based on criteria)	Appraise, attack, argue, choose, compare
Receiving (pay attention)	Listen to, perceive, be alert to
Responding (minimal participation)	Reply, answer, approve, obey
Valuing (preferences)	Attain, assume, support, participate
Organization (development of values)	Judge, decide, identify with, select
Characterization (total philosophy of life)	Believe, practice, carry out
Reflexes (involuntary movement)	Stiffen, extend, flex
Fundamental movements (simple movements)	Crawl, walk, run, reach
Perception (response to stimuli)	Turn, bend, balance, crawl
Physical abilities (psychomotor movements)	Move heavy objects, make quick motions
Skilled movements (advanced learned movements)	Play an instrument, use a hand tool

Source: Based on H. Sredl and W. Rothwell, "Setting Instructional Objectives," Chapter 16 in *The ASTD Reference Guide to Professional Training Roles and Competencies, Vol. II* (New York: Random House, 1987); and R. Mager, *Preparing Instructional Objectives,* 3rd ed. (Atlanta, GA: Center for Effective Performance, 1997).

(fewer than 10 words) apology, only after the customer has stopped talking [criteria] and no matter how upset the customer is [conditions]." Table 4.8 shows the characteristics of good training objectives.

Employees Need Meaningful Training Content

Employees are most likely to learn when the training is linked to their current job experiences and tasks—that is, when it is meaningful to them.[34] To enhance the meaningfulness of training content, the message should be presented using concepts, terms, and examples familiar to trainees. Also, the training context should mirror the work environment. The **training context** refers to the physical, intellectual, and emotional environment in which training occurs. For example, in a retail salesperson customer-service program, the meaningfulness of the material will be increased by using scenarios of unhappy customers actually encountered by salespersons in stores. Some useful techniques for convincing trainees that the training program content is meaningful include:[35]

- Telling stories about others' success in applying training content, especially former trainees.
- Showing how training relates to company goals and strategy.
- Showing how trainees can use training content ideas at work.
- Discussing examples or cases that remind trainees of the good and poor work they have seen.
- Repeating the application of ideas in different contexts.
- Presenting evidence of the effectiveness of knowledge, skills, and behaviors.
- Showing how the conditions that trainees face in training are similar to those on the job.
- Providing practice or application activities that can be used on the job.
- Providing hard copies or electronic access to well-organized materials so trainees can refer to them on the job or use them to teach others.
- Allowing trainees to choose their practice strategy and how they want training content presented (e.g., verbally, visually, problem-based, a combination of approaches).

Employees Need Opportunities to Practice

Practice refers to the physical or mental rehearsal of a task, knowledge, or skill to achieve proficiency in performing the task or skill or demonstrating the knowledge. Practice involves having the employee demonstrate the learned capability (e.g., cognitive strategy,

TABLE 4.8 **Characteristics of Good Training Objectives**	• Provide a clear idea of what the trainee is expected to be able to do at the end of training. • Include standards of performance that can be measured or evaluated. • State the specific resources (e.g., tools, equipment) that the trainee needs to perform the action or behavior specified. • Describe the conditions under which performance of the objective is expected to occur (e.g., the physical work environment, such as at night or in high temperatures; mental stresses, such as angry customers; equipment failure, such as malfunctioning computer equipment).

verbal information) emphasized in the training objectives under conditions and performance standards specified by the objectives. For practice to be effective, it needs to actively involve the trainee, include overlearning (repeated practice), take the appropriate amount of time, and include the appropriate unit of learning (amount of material). Practice also needs to be relevant to the training objectives. It is best to include a combination of examples and practice rather than all practice.[36] This helps to avoid overloading trainees' memory so they can engage in the cognitive processes needed for learning to occur (selecting, organizing, and integrating content). Viewing examples helps learners develop a new mental model of skills which they can then use in practice. Some examples of ways to practice include case studies, simulations, role plays, games, and oral and written questions.

Pre-practice Conditions   Trainers need to focus not just on training content but also on how to enable trainees to process information in a way that will facilitate learning and the use of training on the job. There are several steps trainers can take within the training course prior to practice to enhance trainees' motivation to learn and facilitate retention of training content. Before practice, trainers can[37]

1. Provide information about the process or strategy that will result in the greatest learning. For example, let trainees in a customer service class know about the types of calls they will receive (irate customer, request for information on a product, challenge of a bill), how to recognize such calls, and how to complete the calls.

2. Encourage trainees to develop a strategy (metacognition) to reflect on their own learning process. **Metacognition** refers to individual control over one's thinking. Two ways that individuals engage in metacognition are monitoring and control.[38] *Monitoring* includes identifying the problem or task, evaluating one's own learning progress, and predicting what will occur as a result of learning. *Control* includes identifying the specific steps for completing a task or solving a problem, deciding how quickly or how much attention to devote to the task, and deciding how to prioritize learning. Trainees who engage in metacognition ask themselves questions such as, Why am I choosing this type of action? Do I understand the relationship between this material and my job? What is the next step in the task? Metacognition helps trainees monitor learning and decide what content needs more energy and attention.

3. Provide **advance organizers**—outlines, texts, diagrams, and graphs that help trainees organize the information that will be presented and practiced.

4. Help trainees set challenging mastery or learning goals.

5. Create realistic expectations for the trainees by communicating what will occur in training.

6. When training employees in teams, communicate performance expectations and clarify roles and responsibilities of team members.

Practice Involves Experience   Learning will not occur if employees practice only by talking about what they are expected to do. For example, using the objective for the customer service course previously discussed, practice would involve having trainees participate in role playing with unhappy customers (customers upset with poor service, poor merchandise, or unsatisfactory exchange policies). Training should involve an active learning approach in which trainees must explore and experiment to determine the rules, principles, and strategies for effective performance.[39] Trainees need to continue to practice even if they have been able to perform the objective several times **(overlearning).** Overlearning helps the trainee become more comfortable using new knowledge and skills and increases the length of time the trainee will retain the knowledge, skill, or behavior.

Conventional wisdom is that we all learn the most from our errors. However, most people feel that errors are frustrating and lead to anger and despair. Research suggests that from a training perspective, errors can be useful.[40] **Error management training** refers to giving trainees opportunities to make errors during training. In error management training, trainees are instructed that errors can help learning, and they are encouraged to make errors and learn from them. Trainees may actually commit more errors and may take longer to complete training that incorporates error management training. However, error management training helps improve employee performance on the job (a concept known as transfer of training, which is discussed in Chapter 5).

Error management training is effective because it provides the opportunity for trainees to engage in metacognition, that is, to plan how to use training content, to monitor use of training content, and to evaluate how training content was used. This results in a deeper level of cognitive processing, leading to better memory and recall of training. Trainers should consider using error management training in the training program along with traditional approaches by giving trainees the opportunity to make errors when they work alone on difficult problems and tasks while encouraging them to use errors as a way to learn.

It is important to note that allowing trainees simply to make errors does not help learning. For errors to have a positive influence on learning, trainees need to be taught to use errors as a chance to learn. Error management training may be particularly useful whenever the training content to be learned cannot be completely covered during a training session. As a result, trainees have to discover on their own what to do when confronted with new tasks or problems.

Massed versus Spaced Practice   The frequency of practice has been shown to influence learning, depending on the type of task being trained.[41] **Massed practice** conditions are those in which individuals practice a task continuously without rest. Massed practice also involves having trainees complete practice exercises at one time within a lesson or class versus distributing the exercises within the lesson. In **spaced practice** conditions, individuals are given rest intervals within the practice session. Spaced practice is superior to massed practice. However, the effectiveness of massed versus spaced practice varies by the characteristics of the task. Task characteristics include overall task complexity, mental requirements, and physical requirements. **Overall task complexity** refers to the degree to which a task requires a number of distinct behaviors, the number of choices involved in performing the task, and the degree of uncertainty in performing the task. **Mental requirements** refers to the degree to which the task requires the subject to use or demonstrate mental skills or cognitive skills or abilities to perform the task. **Physical requirements** refers to the degree to which the task requires the person to use or demonstrate physical skills and abilities to perform and complete the task. Table 4.9 shows how tasks can differ.

For more complex tasks (including those that are representative of training settings such as Web-based instruction, lecture, and distance learning), relatively long rest periods appear to be beneficial for task learning.

After practice, trainees need specific feedback to enhance learning. This includes feedback from the task or job itself, trainers, managers, and peers.

TABLE 4.9 **Mental and Physical Requirements and Overall Complexity for Tasks**

Mental Requirements	Overall Complexity	Physical Requirements	Tasks
Low	Low	High	Rotary pursuit, typing, ball toss, ladder climb, peg reversal, bilateral transfer, crank turning
High	Average	Low	Free recall task, video games, foreign language, slide bar task, voice recognition, classroom lecture, sound localization, word processing, stoop task, verbal discrimination, maze learning, connecting numbers, upside down alphabet printing, distance learning, Web training
Low	High	High	Gymnastic skills, balancing task
High	High	High	Air traffic controller simulation, milk pasteurization simulation, airplane control simulation, hand movement memorization, puzzle box task, music memorization and performance

Source: J. Donovan and D. Radosevich, "A Meta-analytic Review of the Distribution of Practice Effect: Now You See It, Now You Don't," *Journal of Applied Psychology* 84 (1999):795–805.

Whole versus Part Practice   A final issue related to practice is how much of the training should be practiced at one time. One option is that all tasks or objectives should be practiced at the same time **(whole practice)**. Another option is that an objective or task should be practiced individually as soon as each is introduced in the training program **(part practice)**. It is probably best to employ both whole and part practice in a training session. Trainees should have the opportunity to practice individual skills or behaviors. If the skills or behaviors introduced in training are related to one another, the trainee should demonstrate all of them in a practice session after they have been practiced individually.

For example, one objective of the customer service training for retail salespeople is learning how to deal with an unhappy customer. Salespeople are likely to have to learn three key behaviors: (1) greeting disgruntled customers, (2) understanding their complaints, and then (3) identifying and taking appropriate action. Practice sessions should be held for each of the three behaviors (part practice). Then another practice session should be held so that trainees can practice all three skills together (whole practice). If trainees are only given the opportunity to practice the behaviors individually, it is unlikely that they will be able to deal with an unhappy customer.

Effective Practice Conditions   For practice to be relevant to the training objectives, several conditions must be met.[42] Practice must involve the actions emphasized in the training objectives, be completed under the conditions specified in the training objectives, help trainees perform to meet the criteria or standard that was set, provide some means to evaluate the extent to which trainees' performance meets the standards, and allow trainees to correct their mistakes.

Practice must be related to the training objectives. The trainer should identify what trainees will be doing when practicing the objectives (performance), the criteria for attainment of the objective, and the conditions under which they may perform. These conditions should be present in the practice session. Next, the trainer needs to consider the adequacy of the trainees' performance. That is, how will trainees know whether their performance meets performance standards? Will they see a model of desired performance? Will they be provided with a checklist or description of desired performance? Can the trainees decide if their performance meets standards, or will the trainer or a piece of equipment compare their performance with standards?

The trainer must also decide—if trainees' performance does not meet standards—whether trainees will be able to understand what is wrong and how to fix it. That is, trainers need to consider whether trainees will be able to diagnose their performance and take corrective action or if they will need help from the trainer or a fellow trainee.

Employees Need to Commit Training Content to Memory

Memory works by processing stimuli we perceive through our senses into short-term memory. If the information is determined to be "important," it moves to long-term memory, where new interconnections are made between neurons or electrical connections in the brain. There are several ways that trainers can help employees store knowledge, skills, behavior, and other training in long-term memory.[43] One way is to make trainees aware of how they are creating, processing, and accessing memory. It is important for trainees to understand how they learn. A presentation of learning styles (discussed earlier in this chapter) can be a useful way to determine how trainees prefer to learn.

To create long-term memory, training programs must be explicit on content and elaborate on details. There are several ways to create long-term memory. One approach trainers use is to create a concept map to show relationships among ideas. Another is to use multiple forms of review including writing, drawings, and role plays to access memory through multiple methods. Teaching key words, a procedure, or a sequence, or providing a visual image gives trainees another way to retrieve information. Reminding trainees of knowledge, behavior, and skills that they already know that are relevant to the current training content creates a link to long-term memory that provides a framework for recalling the new training content. External retrieval cues can also be useful. Consider a time when you misplaced your keys or wallet. In trying to remember, we often review all the information we can recall that was close in time to the event or preceded the loss. We often go to the place where we were when we last saw the item because the environment can provide cues that aid in recall.

Research suggests that no more than four or five items can be attended to at one time. If a lengthy process or procedure is to be taught, instruction needs to be delivered in relatively small chunks or short sessions in order to not exceed memory limits.[44] Long-term memory is also enhanced by going beyond one-trial learning. That is, once trainees correctly demonstrate a behavior or skill or correctly recall knowledge, it is often assumed that they have learned it, but this is not always true. Making trainees review and practice over multiple days (overlearning) can help them retain information in long-term memory. Overlearning also helps to automize a task.

Automatization refers to making performance of a task, recall of knowledge, or demonstration of a skill so automatic that it requires little thought or attention. Automatization also helps reduce memory demands. The more that automatization occurs, the more that memory is freed up to concentrate on other learning and thinking. The more active a trainee is in rehearsal and practice, the greater the amount of information retained in long-term memory and the less memory decay occurs over time.

Another way to avoid overwhelming trainees with complex material is to give them pre-training work that can be completed online or using workbooks.[45] For example, trainees can become familiar with the "basics" such as names, definitions, principles, and characteristics of components before they are trained in how the principles are applied (e.g., dealing with angry customers) or how a process works (e.g., testing for pathogens in a blood sample, changing a car's water pump).

Employees Need Feedback

Feedback is information about how well people are meeting the training objectives. To be effective, feedback should focus on specific behaviors and be provided as soon as possible after the trainees' behavior.[46] Also, positive trainee behavior should be verbally praised or reinforced. Videotape is a powerful tool for giving feedback. Trainers should view the videotape with trainees, provide specific information about how behaviors need to be modified, and praise trainee behaviors that meet objectives. Feedback can also come from tests and quizzes, on-the-job observation, performance data, a mentor or coach, written communications, or interpersonal interactions.

The specificity of the level of feedback provided to trainees needs to vary if trainees are expected to understand what leads to poor performance as well as good performance.[47] For example, employees may need to learn how to respond when equipment is malfunctioning as well as when it is working properly; therefore, feedback provided during training should not be so specific that it leads only to employee knowledge about equipment that is working properly. Less specific feedback can cause trainees to make errors that lead to equipment problems, providing trainees with opportunities to learn which behaviors lead to equipment problems and how to fix those problems. Difficulties encountered during practice as a result of errors or reduced frequency of feedback can help trainees engage more in exploration and information processing to identify correct responses.

Employees Learn through Observation, Experience, and Social Interaction

As mentioned earlier in the chapter, one way employees learn is through observing and imitating the actions of models. For the model to be effective, the desired behaviors or skills need to be clearly specified and the model should have characteristics (e.g., age or position) similar to the target audience.[48] After observing the model, trainees should have the opportunity in practice sessions to reproduce the skills or behavior shown by the model. According to adult learning theory, employees also learn best if they learn by doing.[49] This involves giving employees hands-on experiences or putting them with more experienced employees and providing them with the tools and materials needed to manage their knowledge gaps.

Learning also occurs through interacting with other trainees in small groups during the training session as well as back at work. By working in small groups, trainees can obtain diverse perspectives on problems and issues, perspectives they would never hear if they learned alone. Problem-based learning may be useful for stimulating and holding trainees' attention.[50] In problem-based learning, trainees are divided into small groups. (Action learning, a type of problem-based learning, will be discussed in Chapter 7.) The groups are presented with a problem such as a real problem the company is facing or a case study. In each group, trainees are asked to identify the problem and to identify what they know and do not know (learning issues). Each group has to decide how it will better understand the learning issues. Part of the training program is designed to allow trainees to access the Web, experts in the field, and company records and documents to solve the learning issues. After trainees gather information, they discuss what they have learned and how to use that information to solve the problem. Table 4.10 shows the types of situations, with examples, in which learning through observation, experience, and interacting with others may be most valuable.

Communities of practice refers to groups of employees who work together, learn from each other, and develop a common understanding of how to get work accomplished.[51] The idea of communities of practice suggests that learning occurs on the job as a result of social interaction. Every company has naturally occurring communities of practice that arise as a result of relationships employees develop to accomplish work and as a result of the design of the work environment. For example, at Siemens Power Transmission in Wendell, North Carolina, managers were wondering how to stop employees from gathering in the employee cafeteria for informal discussions.[52] But that was before the managers discovered that the informal discussions actually encouraged learning. In the discussions, employees were developing problem-solving strategies, sharing product and procedural information, and providing career counseling to each other. Now Siemens is placing pads of paper and overhead projectors in the lunchroom as aids for informal meetings. Managers who were previously focused on keeping workers on the job are now encouraging employees by providing essential tools and information and giving employees the freedom to meet.

Communities of practice also take the form of discussion boards, list servers, or other forms of computer-mediated communication in which employees communicate electronically. In doing so, each employee's knowledge can be accessed in a relatively quick manner. It is as if employees are having a conversation with a group of experts. Wyeth Pharmaceuticals has 11 communities of practice (COP) focusing on maintenance, shop floor excellence.[53] The COP's make it easy for employees to share best practices, learn from one another, and improve business processes. The maintenance function used its COP to deliver more than 600 hours of training on new technology and maintenance processes. This has resulted in more reliable equipment and higher productivity, such as increasing equipment use in one manufacturing plant from 72 to 92 percent.

Despite the benefits of improved communication, a drawback to these communities is that participation is often voluntary, so some employees may not share their knowledge unless the organizational culture supports participation. That is, employees may be reluctant to participate without an incentive or may be fearful that if they share their knowledge with others, they will give away their personal advantage in salary and promotion

TABLE 4.10   Situations, Skills, and Knowledge Best Learned through Observation, Experience, and
Interacting with Others

Situations/Knowledge	Examples
Interpersonal Skills	Negotiating a merger, handling a problem employee
Personal Knowledge Based on Experience	Closing a sale, creating a new candy bar, reducing tension between employees
Context-Specific Knowledge	Managing in an international location, handling union grievances, manufacturing with special equipment
Uncertainty or New Situations	Marketing a new product or service, using a new technology for service or manufacturing

Source: Based on D. Leonard and W. Swap, "Deep Smarts," *Harvard Business Review* (September 2004): 88–97.

decisions.[54] (The role of organizational culture in learning is discussed in Chapter 5.) Another potential drawback is information overload. Employees may receive so much information that they fail to process it. This may cause them to withdraw from the community of practice.

Employees Need the Training Program to Be Properly Coordinated and Arranged

Training coordination is one of several aspects of training administration. **Training administration** refers to coordinating activities before, during, and after the program.[55] Training administration involves:

1. Communicating courses and programs to employees.
2. Enrolling employees in courses and programs.
3. Preparing and processing any pretraining materials such as readings or tests.
4. Preparing materials that will be used in instruction (e.g., copies of overheads, cases).
5. Arranging for the training facility and room.
6. Testing equipment that will be used in instruction.
7. Having backup equipment (e.g., paper copy of slides, an extra overhead projector bulb) should equipment fail.
8. Providing support during instruction.
9. Distributing evaluation materials (e.g., tests, reaction measures, surveys).
10. Facilitating communications between trainer and trainees during and after training (e.g., coordinating exchange of e-mail addresses).
11. Recording course completion in the trainees' training records or personnel files.

Good coordination ensures that trainees are not distracted by events (such as an uncomfortable room or poorly organized materials) that could interfere with learning. Activities before the program include communicating to trainees the purpose of the program, the place it will be held, the name of a person to contact if they have questions, and any pre-program work they are supposed to complete. Books, speakers, handouts, and videotapes need to be prepared. Any necessary arrangements to secure rooms and equipment (such as DVD players) should be made. The physical arrangement of the training room should complement the training technique. For example, it would be difficult for a team-building session to be effective if the seats could not be moved for group activities. If visual aids will be used, all trainees should be able to see them. Make sure that the room is physically comfortable with adequate lighting and ventilation. Trainees should be informed of starting and finishing times, break times, and location of bathrooms. Minimize distractions such as phone messages; request that trainees turn off cell phones and pagers. If trainees will be asked to evaluate the program or take tests to determine what they have learned, allot time for this activity at the end of the program. Following the program, any credits or recording of the names of trainees who completed the program should be done. Handouts and other training materials should be stored or returned to the consultant. The end of the program is also a good time to consider how the program could be improved if it will be offered again. Practical issues in selecting and preparing a training site and designing a program are discussed later in the chapter.

An interesting example that illustrates many of the features of good instruction that have just been explained can be found in the training programs of the Culinary Institute of America (CIA), located in the rolling hills of the Hudson River Valley, a 90-minute drive from New York City. The CIA, the world's finest training facility for chefs, has approximately 2,000 full-time students in its degree programs. CIA graduates are chefs in some of the best restaurants in the world and in prestigious private dining rooms (such as the White House), and they direct food service operations for large hotel chains such as the Marriott, Hyatt, Radisson, and Hilton. Besides offering degree programs, the CIA also hosts more than 6,000 trainees from a wide variety of companies that have food service operations.

Whether an instructor is teaching meat-cutting or sautéing techniques, the programs' learning environments are basically the same. A lecture is followed by demonstration and several hours of guided hands-on practice. The trainee then receives feedback from the instructor. The trainer moves from a show-and-tell approach to become a coach over the course of the training session. Videos are produced for every class that a student will take. They can be viewed from residence halls or can be seen at the video learning center where students can review the tapes at their own pace; the students control what they see.

CIA programs deal not only with cognitive learning but also with physical and emotional learning. In addition to cooking and baking courses, students are required to study psychology, Total Quality Management, languages, marketing, communications, restaurant management, and team supervision. Physical fitness and stress management are required parts of the curriculum. Why? Running a commercial kitchen involves long hours and high levels of stress—it is very physically demanding. Thanks to the learning environment created at CIA, the institute is recognized as the world leader in gastronomic training as it provides a foundation of basic knowledge for chefs from around the world.[56]

INSTRUCTIONAL EMPHASIS FOR LEARNING OUTCOMES

The discussion of the implications of the learning process for instruction provide general principles regarding how to facilitate learning. However, you should understand the relationship between these general principles and the learning process. Different internal and external conditions are necessary for learning each outcome. **Internal conditions** refer to processes within the learner that must be present for learning to occur. These processes include how information is registered, stored in memory, and recalled. **External conditions** refer to processes in the learning environment that facilitate learning. These conditions include the physical learning environment as well as opportunities to practice and receive feedback and reinforcement. The external conditions should directly influence the design or form of instruction. Table 4.11 shows what is needed during instruction at each step of the learning process. For example, during the process of committing training content to memory, verbal cues, verbal links to a meaningful context, and diagrams and models are necessary. If training content is not coded (or is incorrectly coded), learning will be inhibited.

TABLE 4.11 Internal and External Conditions Necessary for Learning Outcomes

Learning Outcome	Internal Conditions	External Conditions
Verbal Information		
Labels, facts, and propositions	Previously learned knowledge and verbal information Strategies for coding information into memory	Repeated practice Meaningful chunks Advance organizers Recall cues
Intellectual Skills		
Knowing how		Link between new and previously learned knowledge
Cognitive Strategies		
Process of thinking and learning	Recall of prerequisites, similar tasks, and strategies	Verbal description of strategy Strategy demonstration Practice with feedback Variety of tasks that provide opportunity to apply strategy
Attitudes		
Choice of personal action	Mastery of prerequisites Identification with model Cognitive dissonance	Demonstration by a model Positive learning environment Strong message from credible source Reinforcement
Motor Skills		
Muscular actions	Recall of part skills Coordination program	Practice Demonstration Gradual decrease of external feedback

Source: Based on R. M. Gagne and K. L. Medsker, *The Conditions of Learning* (Fort Worth, TX: Harcourt-Brace College Publishers, 1996).

CONSIDERATIONS IN DESIGNING EFFECTIVE TRAINING PROGRAMS

This chapter has discussed implications of learning theory for instruction. The importance of objectives, meaningful material, properly coordinated and arranged training, and opportunities for practice and feedback has been emphasized. How do trainers ensure that these conditions are present in training programs? This last section of the chapter discusses the practical steps involved in designing effective training programs, courses, and lessons. This includes selecting and preparing the training site, selecting trainers, creating a positive learning environment and program design.

Selecting and Preparing the Training Site

The **training site** refers to the room where training will be conducted. A good training site offers the following features:[57]

1. It is comfortable and accessible.
2. It is quiet, private, and free from interruptions.

3. It has sufficient space for trainees to move easily around in, offers enough room for trainees to have adequate work space, and has good visibility for trainees to see each other, the trainer, and any visual displays or examples that will be used in training (e.g., videos, product samples, charts, slides).

Details to Be Considered in the Training Room

Table 4.12 presents characteristics of the meeting room that a trainer, program designer, or manager should use to evaluate a training site. Keep in mind that many times trainers do not have the luxury of choosing the "perfect" training site. Rather, they use their evaluation of the training site to familiarize themselves with the site's strengths and weaknesses in order to adjust the training program and/or physical arrangements of the site (e.g., rearrange the trainer's position so it is closer to electrical outlets needed to run equipment).

Because of technology's impact on the delivery of training programs, many training sites include instructor- and trainee-controlled equipment. For example, at Microsoft's customer briefing center in Chicago, Illinois, 16 different computer platforms, ranging from laptops to mainframe systems, are available to use for training. Two seminar rooms include videoconferencing technology, which allows training sessions to be transmitted from Microsoft's corporate headquarters in Redmond, Washington, to Chicago. The Chicago site can link up to any of 25 Microsoft locations or a combination of 11 sites at once. Presenters have access to a VCR, CD player, cassette decks, and document camera. The seminar

TABLE 4.12 **Details to Consider When Evaluating a Training Room** Source: Based on C. L. Finkel, "Meeting Facilities," in *The ASTD Training and Development Handbook,* 3d ed., ed. R. L. Craig (New York: McGraw-Hill, 1996): 978–89.	*Noise.* Check for noise from heating and air conditioning systems, from adjacent rooms and corridors, and from outside the building. *Colors.* Pastel hues such as oranges, greens, blues, and yellows are warm colors. Variations of white are cold and sterile. Blacks and brown shades will close the room in psychologically and become fatiguing. *Room structure.* Use rooms that are somewhat square in shape. Long, narrow rooms make it difficult for trainees to see, hear, and identify with the discussion. *Lighting.* Main source of lighting should be fluorescent lights. Incandescent lighting should be spread throughout the room and used with dimmers when projection is required. *Wall and floor covering.* Carpeting should be placed in the meeting area. Solid colors are preferable because they are not distracting. Only meeting-related materials should be on the meeting room walls. *Meeting room chairs.* Chairs should have wheels, swivels, and backs that provide support for the lower lumbar region. *Glare.* Check and eliminate glare from metal surfaces, TV monitors, and mirrors. *Ceiling.* Ten-foot-high ceilings are preferable. *Electrical outlets.* Outlets should be available every six feet around the room. A telephone jack should be next to the outlets. Outlets for the trainer should be available. *Acoustics.* Check the bounce or absorption of sound from the walls, ceiling, floor, and furniture. Try voice checks with three or four different people, monitoring voice clarity and level.

rooms have touchscreen systems controlling both the audiovisual equipment and the room environment.[58]

Although the use of technology in training is discussed in more detail in Chapter 8, it is important to note that laptop computers create a desktop training environment that is replacing trainers as the primary way to present training content. For example, at Ernst & Young, an accounting and consulting firm, laptops are used by employees in tax, finance, consulting, and auditing training courses to view visuals, work on case-study exercises, ask questions, and access other information stored on the company's intranet.[59] The laptop connects employees to Web-based training designed to help them gain prerequisites for training sessions as well as provide follow-up information after they attend training. Instead of playing a major role as presenters of content, trainers devote their time to coaching, providing feedback, and monitoring the progress of trainees. Trainers can "see" how trainees are working and provide individualized feedback and coaching. Trainers can use the computer to ask questions about what trainees are finding difficult in a particular training session. These responses can be shared with other trainees or used to guide the trainer to hold special "help" sessions or provide supplemental learning modules. The desktop training environment can handle different sizes of training groups even if they are in assorted geographical areas.

Seating Arrangements   Seating arrangements at the training site should be based on an understanding of the desired type of trainee interaction and trainee-trainer interaction.[60] Figure 4.4 shows several types of seating arrangements.

Fan-type seating is conducive to allowing trainees to see from any point in the room. Trainees can easily switch from listening to a presentation to practicing in groups, and trainees can communicate easily with everyone in the room. Fan-type seating is effective for training that includes trainees working in groups and teams to analyze problems and synthesize information.

If the training primarily involves knowledge acquisition, with lecture and audiovisual presentation being the primary training method used, traditional classroom-type seating is appropriate. Traditional classroom instruction allows for trainee interaction with the trainer but makes it difficult for trainees to work in teams (particularly if the seats are not movable to other locations in the room).

If training emphasizes total-group discussion with limited presentation and no small-group interaction, a conference-type arrangement may be most effective. If the training requires both presentation and total-group instruction, the horseshoe arrangement is useful.

Choosing Trainers

Selecting professional trainers or consultants is one obvious possibility for companies. Trainers, whether from inside or outside the company, should have expertise in the topic and experience in training.[61] Train-the-trainer programs are necessary for managers, employees, and "experts" who may have content knowledge but need to improve presentation and communications skills, gain an understanding of the key components of the learning process (e.g., feedback, practice), or learn to develop lesson plans. This may involve having employees and managers earn a certificate that verifies they have the skills needed to be effective trainers. To increase their chances of success in their first courses, new trainers should be observed and should receive coaching and feedback from more experienced trainers. When companies use in-house experts for training, it is important to

FIGURE 4.4
**Examples of
Seating
Arrangements**

Source: Based on
F. H. Margolis and
C. R. Bell, *Managing
the Learning Process*
(Minneapolis, MN:
Lakewood
Publications, 1984).

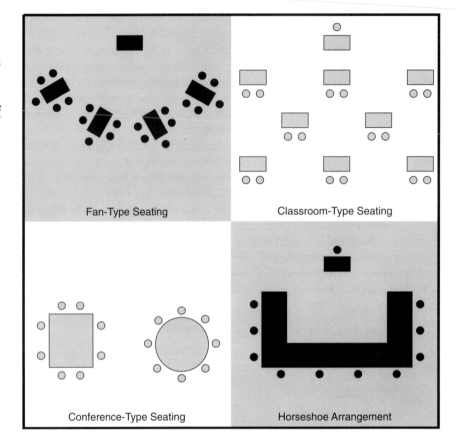

emphasize that these experts convey training content in as concrete a manner as possible (e.g., use examples), especially if the audience is unfamilar with the content. Experts may have a tendency to use more abstract and advanced concepts that may confuse trainees.[62]

Using managers and employees as trainers may help increase the perceived meaningfulness of the training content. Because they understand the company's business, employee and manager trainers tend to make the training content more directly applicable to the trainees' work. Also, use of managers and employees can help increase their support for learning and reduce the company's dependency on expensive outside consultants. Serving as trainers can be rewarding for employees and managers if they are recognized by the company or if the training experience is linked to their personal development plans.

For example, when MasterCard became a public corporation it staged the largest training event in the history of the company.[63] The training event included a series of four and one-half hour seminars in 36 cities involving most of the employees within a three-week time period. The seminars involved using learning maps to help employees understand the competitive marketplace that the company was entering, how MasterCard makes money, and MasterCard's business strategy and the competencies and actions needed to support the strategy. To ensure that all employees would be involved in the training sessions, the seminars were planned so that no more than 10 employees were seated at each table with a learning map. Each table required a facilitator who understood the training content and the instructor's guide and was skilled at facilitating group processes such as dealing with talkative trainees. This instructional strategy required more than 200 trainers. The trainers (HR professionals) participated in a simulated seminar that showed them how the training would work and how to perform their required duties. The trainers needed to be comfortable with facilitation and handling groups. They also learned how to teach the table coach's role to local managers in the same way it was taught to them: by reviewing the actual training experience. Follow-up online sessions and Web sites were also developed for the trainers to review and prepare for the seminars. The Web sites included planning checklists, sign-up sheets, people to call for help, and sneak previews of the video presentations to be given by the CEO.

At Alltell, a wireless communications company, new trainers take a series of classes to learn what they need to know and do.[64] They can also work toward a higher level senior trainer certification. In the senior trainer program, participants attend training either at the company or through a vendor and their performance is evaluated. For example, at the end of call center training, the trainer is evaluated in two ways. First, a training manager observes the course and evaluates the new trainer's instructional skills. Second, the new trainer is evaluated based on the number of trainees who pass the test, certifying they have the skills needed to work in a call center.

How Trainers Can Make the Training Site and Instruction Conducive to Learning

As a trainer, you can take several steps to make the room and instruction conducive to learning.[65]

Creating a Learning Setting

Before choosing a training room, consider how the trainees are expected to learn. That is, determine the extent to which trainees decide when, where, and how they will learn (self-direction) and whether learning will occur by interactions with others (collaboration).[66] Table 4.13 describes the types of training rooms that are appropriate for the amount of self-direction and collaboration necessary for learning. For example, a classroom with easy-to-move furniture supports high collaboration but low self-direction; this classroom can be used for lectures, presentations, discussions, and small groups. A distance learning room

TABLE 4.13
Matching Training Rooms with Learning Requirements

Source: Based on "Workplace Issues: One in a Series. Learning Environments for the Information Age," available from the Steelcase Web site, *www.steelcase.com* (March 1, 2006).

For Learning that Requires:	Suggested Training Rooms
High Collaboration, Low Self-Direction	Classroom with breakout rooms Lecture hall with breakout rooms
High Collaboration, High Self-Direction	Breakout rooms Project room Conference room
Low Collaboration, Low Self-Direction	Classroom Computer classroom Lecture hall
Low Collaboration, High Self-Direction	Distance learning room Media lab Computer lab

that includes computers, cameras, and data equipment supports learning that requires low collaboration but high self-direction. Self-directed learning that requires little collaboration is best suited for labs equipped with computers and software that supports online learning, computer-based training, or software instruction. Of course, a dedicated training space may not be necessary for these learning requirements because trainees can work from their own personal computer at home or at work. The advantages and disadvantages of online learning are discussed in Chapter 8, but be aware that employees may not like the lack of face-to-face collaboration that occurs in online learning programs.

Think about the physical requirements of the training room. Do the trainees need to be able to concentrate and write? Do they need to be able to see detailed visuals? Choose a room large enough to meet your purpose, not just to accommodate a certain number of trainees. Avoid putting 25 people in a room that can seat 250. A small number of trainees in a large room makes it impersonal and leaves people feeling insignificant. Consider the room design well in advance of the session and work with the training site coordinator to design a setting that meets your learning needs.

Preparation

You need to know your content very well. Use mental and physical rehearsals to help build confidence and to evaluate the pace and timing of material. Observe master trainers to get new ideas. Design the training from the audience's perspective—ask "So what?" about everything you plan to do. If you are using computers, CD-ROMs, the Internet, distance learning, or other technologies, make sure you know how to work the equipment and have backup materials in case the technology fails. Make sure your visuals are available in at least two formats (e.g., PowerPoint slides and overheads). Arrive at the training room at least 15 minutes early to make sure the room is set up correctly, materials are available, and technology is functioning. Greet the trainees as they enter the room.

Classroom Management

Monitor the room for extra chairs, overflowing trash cans, and piles of materials left over from previous training sessions. A messy, disorganized, uninviting training room creates learning distractions. Give trainees frequent breaks so they can leave the room and return ready to learn.

Interacting with Trainees

You as a trainer carry the responsibility for the trainees' learning experience. You need to communicate the topics that will be covered, the learning approach that will be used, and the expectations for trainees. You need to be dramatic to draw attention to important points. Research suggests that trainees have the best recall of training content when the trainer is enthusiastic and avoids vocal distractions (e.g., use of "er" and "um").[67] Also, you should use a relaxed style and make learners comfortable.[68] As a trainer, you should recognize that your expectations for trainees' learning and your stereotypes can result in learners confirming those expectations (i.e., a self-fulfilling prophecy).[69] Negative expectations held by instructors can lead to learners' negative evaluation of the training and the trainer.[70]

How you should engage trainees is based on both the size of the room and the number of trainees. The larger the room, the more your gestures and movements must be exaggerated to get the audience's attention. To create intimacy with the training group, you must move close to them. Standing in the front of the room is a way to establish authority. One of the best ways to gain trainees' attention is to facilitate discussion from different places in the room. Strive to lead the instruction but focus on the trainees. Help trainees develop their own answers, apply tools and techniques, and use reference materials to reach solutions that are effective in training and on the job. Use questions that lead trainees to answers or points you want to make. Continually strive for interaction with trainees— trainees may have more real-life experiences, exposure to, or applications related to training topics than you do. Create a training environment where trainees can learn from each other. Listen to trainees, summarize learning points, and provide feedback. Table 4.14 provides examples of how to get trainees involved in a training session.

Dealing with Disruptive Trainees

How can you deal with employees who don't want to be trained despite being informed in advance of the course and how it relates to the business?[71] First, take charge of the session immediately, communicate your credentials, and in a friendly but assertive way tell employees why the training is important and how it will help them. Then let them vent their frustrations. Useful methods for this activity are to have trainees describe what they would be doing if they were not in the program, have trainees draw pictures of how the person next to them feels about attending the training, or have trainees break into groups and then ask some groups to make a list of the top 10 reasons not to be in the class and the other groups to list 10 reasons to be in the class. Reassemble the class and discuss first the reasons not to be in the class, and then end with the reasons why the trainees should be in the class. For trainees who disrupt, sleep through, or constantly interrupt the training sessions, consider using activities that get trainees moving, engaged, and energized.

Managing Group Dynamics

To ensure an even distribution of knowledge or expertise in groups, ask trainees to indicate whether they consider themselves novices, experienced, or experts on a topic. Arrange the groups so that they contain a mix of novice, experienced, and expert trainees. Group dynamics can be changed by changing learners' positions in the room. Pay attention to group dynamics by wandering through the room and noticing which groups are frustrated or stalled, who is withdrawn, and who is dominating the group. Your role is to make sure that everyone in a group has an opportunity to contribute. Seating arrangements such as rectangular tables often give trainees authority based on where they are seated. For example, the end of a rectangular table is the position of authority. Putting a quiet person in the "power seat" creates an opportunity for that person to assume a leadership role within the group.

TABLE 4.14
Examples of How to Get Trainees Involved

Source: Based on J. Curtis, "Engage Me, Please!" *T + D* (November 2008): 68–73.

- Prepare and distribute content-related, open-ended questions to be discussed in breakout groups.
- Use creative activities or games that relate to the training content.
- Use assessment or measures that allow the trainees to learn about themselves and each other.
- Incorporate role-playing.
- Conclude the training session by asking trainees either individually or in teams from the same company or work group to consider the following question: "As a result of this session, what do you plan to start, stop, or continue doing? On what topic would you like to have more information?"

Program Design

For learning to occur, training programs require meaningful material, clear objectives, and opportunities for practice and feedback. However, even if a training program contains all these conditions, it still may not result in learning for several reasons. Proper equipment and materials may not be available during the session, trainers may be rushed to present content and fail to allow adequate time for practice, or the actual activities that occur in the training session may not relate to the learning objectives. **Program design** refers to the organization and coordination of the training program. A training program may include one or several courses. Each course may contain one or more lessons. Program design includes considering the purpose of the program as well as designing specific lessons within the program. Effective program design includes a design document template, a course or lesson plan, and a course or lesson plan overview.[72]

Keep in mind that although the responsibility for designing the training program may belong to the instructional designer, human resource professional, or manager, the "clients" of the program should also be involved in program design. As already discussed in Chapter 3, managers and employees should be involved in the needs assessment process. In addition, their role may include reviewing prototypes of the program, providing examples and program content, and participating in the program as instructors.[73]

The following explanations of each feature of effective program design are accompanied by an example that is based on a training program developed by a company to increase its managers' effectiveness in conducting performance appraisal feedback interviews. Performance appraisal feedback sessions are meetings between managers and subordinates during which the strengths and weaknesses of an employee's performance are discussed and improvement goals are usually agreed upon. Based on a needs assessment, this company discovered that its managers were uncomfortable conducting performance appraisal feedback sessions. These managers often were very authoritarian in the sessions. That is, they tended to tell employees what aspects of their job performance needed to be improved rather than allowing the employees to participate in the session or working with them to identify and solve performance problems.

Design Document

A design document can be used to guide the development of training and to explain the training to managers, subject matter experts, reviewers, or other trainers. Table 4.15 shows a design document template.[74] Information for the design document is based on the information obtained from the needs assessment discussed in Chapter 3.

The level of detail in the design document can vary. *Scope of project* includes the goals, outcomes, or what trainees are expected to achieve; a description of the trainees; a description of how long it will take to develop the course and the checkpoints or tasks that need to be completed as the course is developed; and the length of the course. The length of a course is determined by considering trainees' abilities and their availability for training, the resources needed for training, whether the course is part of a larger curriculum or is a stand-alone course, and the need to develop modules in order to provide an opportunity for trainees to practice concepts and skills to avoid being overwhelmed. *Delivery* includes what the course will cover, how it will be delivered (e.g., face-to-face, online), an estimate of the training time, and the identification of any special conditions or issues that may affect the course (e.g., problems getting equipment to video role-plays and provide feedback).

TABLE 4.15
Design
Document
Template

Source: Based on
G. Piskurich, *Rapid
Instructional Design*
(San Francisco: Pfeif-
fer, 2006).

Scope of Project

- Goal
- Audience
- Design time and checkpoints
- Length of the course

Delivery

- Content
- Method
- Training time
- Problems and opportunities

Objectives

Resources

Who Is Involved

Topical Outline

Administration and Evaluation

Links to Other Programs

Objectives refers to the course objectives. It is important to realize that within a training program there are usually different types of objectives that vary in specificity and detail. **Program objectives** refer to broader summary statements of the purpose of the program. They are usually included on the design template. **Course objectives** or **lesson objectives** refer to the goals of the course or the lesson. These objectives are more specific in terms of expected behaviors, content, conditions, and standards.

Resources refers to the materials—cases, DVDs, videos, models, process maps, podcasts, lesson plans, or guides for use by the facilitator or participants—that need to be purchased or developed for the course. *Who is involved* includes trainers, program designers, and individuals who will be involved in the design, delivery, and evaluation of the program. The *topical outline* includes a brief outline of the topics that will be covered in the program. *Administration and evaluation* refers to who will be in charge of course scheduling, how trainees will enroll, how the course will be evaluated, and who will review and update the course. *Links to other programs* refers to any other needs, such as a train-the-trainer program or manager introduction or kick-off for the program. Table 4.16 shows a simple design document for the performance appraisal feedback course.

Course or Lesson Plan

Lesson plans are typically more detailed than the design document. They include the specific steps involved in the lesson, instructor and trainee activities, and the time allocated to each topic included in the lesson.

Lesson plans can be designed for programs lasting a day, a week, or several hours. If training takes place over several days, a separate lesson plan is prepared for each day.

The **detailed lesson plan** translates the content and sequence of training activities into a guide that is used by the trainer to help deliver the training. That is, lesson plans include the sequence of activities that will be conducted in the training session and identify the

TABLE 4.16
Design
Document

Purpose: To prepare managers to conduct effective performance feedback sessions with their direct reports
Goals: Managers will be able to conduct a performance feedback session using the problem-solving approach
Target audience: Managers
Training time: 1 day
Method: Lecture, video, role plays
Number of participants per session: 20–25
Locations: Various
Prerequisites: None
Problems and opportunities: New Performance appraisal system introduced; manager dislikes conducting feedback sessions
Instructor: Caroline O'Connell and facilitators

administrative details. Table 4.17 shows a lesson plan. The lesson plan provides a table of contents for the training activity. This helps to ensure that training activities are consistent regardless of the trainer. Lesson plans also help to ensure that both the trainee and the trainer are aware of the course and program objectives. Most training departments have written lesson plans that are stored in notebooks or in electronic databases. Because lesson plans are documented, they can be shared with trainees and customers of the training department (i.e., managers who pay for training services) to provide them with detailed information regarding program activities and objectives.

Table 4.18 shows the features of an effective lesson plan. The lesson plan includes the learning objectives, topics to be covered, target audience, time of session, lesson outline, the activity involved, any required preparation or prerequisites, how learning will be evaluated, and steps to insure transfer of training.[75]

In developing the lesson outline, trainers need to consider the proper sequencing of topics. Trainers must answer questions such as, "What knowledge and skills need to be learned first?" "In what order should the knowledge, skills, and behavior be taught?" "What order will make sense to the trainees?" It is also important to consider the target audience. Any information about their training and experience, their motivation for taking the course, and their interests, learning styles, and background (e.g., education, work experience) will be useful for choosing meaningful examples, determining program content, deciding on support materials, and building the credibility of the training. Information about the target audience should be available from the person analysis of the needs assessment (see Chapter 3). Additional information can be collected by talking to the "clients" (e.g., managers) who requested the training program and to past program participants, if available. Support materials include any equipment needed for delivery of instruction, such as computers, overhead projectors, or DVD, CD, or video players. Trainers should arrange for the purchase of any whiteboards, flip charts, or markers that may be used in instruction. Any exercises needed for trainees' practice or preparation, such as readings, role-play exercises, assessments, or pretests, need to be ordered or reproduced (after copyright permission is obtained). In considering instructor and trainee activity, the focus should be on ensuring that the lesson has

TABLE 4.17   Sample of a Detailed Lesson Plan

Course title: Conducting an Effective Performance Feedback Session

Lesson title: Using the problem-solving style in the feedback interview

Lesson length: Full day

Learning objectives:
1. Describe the eight key behaviors used in the problem-solving style of giving appraisal feedback without error
2. Demonstrate the eight key behaviors in an appraisal feedback role play without error

Target audience: Managers

Prerequisites:

   Trainee: None

   Instructor: Familiarity with the tell-and-sell, tell-and-listen, and problem-solving approaches used in performance appraisal feedback interviews

Room arrangement: Fan-type

Materials and equipment needed: VCR, overhead projector, pens, transparencies, VCR tape titled "Performance Appraisal Interviews," role-play exercises

Evaluation and assignments: Role-play; read article titled, "Conducting Effective Appraisal Interviews"

Comment: Article needs to be distributed two weeks prior to session

Lesson Outline	Instructor Activity	Trainee Activity	Time
Introduction	Presentation	Listening	8–8:50 A.M.
View videos of three styles		Watching	8:50–10 A.M.
Break			10–10:20 A.M.
Discussion of strengths and weaknesses of each style	Facilitator	Participation	10:20–11:30 A.M.
Lunch			11:30 A.M.–1 P.M.
Presentation and video of eight key behaviors of problem-solving style	Presentation	Listening	1–2 P.M.
Role plays	Watch exercise	Practice using key behaviors	2–3 P.M.
Wrap-up	Answer questions	Ask questions	3–3:15 P.M.

as many features of a positive learning process as possible, including communication of objectives, feedback, opportunities for practice, opportunities for trainees to share experiences and ask questions, and modeling or demonstration. Transfer and retention strategies might include chat rooms, follow-up meetings with the manager, and action planning. Transfer and retention strategies are discussed in Chapter 5.

The two learning objectives for the course, "Conducting an Effective Performance Feedback Session," are shown in Table 4.17. The eight key behaviors referred to in the learning objectives section are as follows: (1) explain the purpose of the meeting; (2) ask the employee to describe what he has done to deserve recognition; (3) ask the employee to describe what he should stop doing, start doing, or do differently; (4) ask the employee for areas in which you can provide assistance; (5) give the employee your opinion of his performance; (6) ask for and listen to the employee's concerns about your evaluation; (7) agree on steps/actions to be taken by each of you; and (8) agree to a follow-up date.[76]

TABLE 4.18 Features of an Effective Lesson Plan

Feature	
Learning Objectives or Outcomes	What is the lesson designed to accomplish? What is the standard for successful learning?
Target Audience	Who is in the lesson? What are the characteristics of the audience?
Prerequisites (trainees and instructor)	What will trainees need to be able to do before they can benefit from the course? Who is qualified to be in the program? Who is qualified to be an instructor?
Time	How much time is devoted to each part of the lesson?
Lesson Outline	What topics will be covered? In what sequence?
Activity	What will trainees' and instructor's role be during each topic covered?
Support Materials	What materials and/or equipment is needed for delivery of instruction or to facilitate instruction?
Physical Environment	Is a certain size or arrangement of room necessary?
Preparation	Do the trainees have homework that needs to be completed before the lesson? What does the instructor need to do?
Lesson Topic	What topic is the lesson going to cover?
Evaluation	How will learning be evaluated (e.g., tests, role plays)?
Transfer and Retention	What will be done to ensure that training content is used on the job?

Source: Based on R. Vaughn, *The Professional Trainer* (Euclid, OH: Williams Custom Publishing, 2000); R. F. Mager, *Making Instruction Work,* 2d ed. (Atlanta, GA: Center for Effective Performance, 1997); L. Nadler and Z. Nadler, *Designing Training Programs,* 2d ed. (Houston, TX: Gulf Publishing, 1992); Big Dog's Human Resource Development page, *www.nwlink.com/donclark/hrd.html.*

The prerequisites include (1) arrangement of the training site, equipment, and materials needed; (2) instructor preparation; and (3) trainee prerequisites. In the example, the trainer needs a VCR to show a video of performance appraisal feedback styles. The trainer also needs an overhead projector to record points made by the trainees during the planned discussion of the strengths and weaknesses of the appraisal styles presented on the video. The room needs to be fan-shaped so trainees can see the trainer and each other. Also, the fan arrangement is good for role-play exercises that involve trainees working in groups of two or three.

Trainee prerequisites refer to any preparation, basic skills, or knowledge that the trainee needs prior to participating in the program. Trainee prerequisites may include basic math and reading skills, completion of prior training sessions, or successful completion of tests or certificate or degree programs. Instructor prerequisites indicate what the instructor needs to do to prepare for the session (e.g., rent equipment, review previous day's training session) and any educational qualifications the instructor needs. Lesson plans also may cover how the lesson will be evaluated and any assignments that the trainees need to complete. In the example, trainees are required to read an article on effective performance appraisal feedback interviews. The instructor needs to be familiar with the eight key behaviors for conducting problem-solving appraisal feedback interviews.

TABLE 4.19

Sample Lesson Overview

8–8:50 A.M.	Introduction
8:50–10 A.M.	Watch videos of three styles of appraisal feedback
10–10:20 A.M.	Break
10:20–11:30 A.M.	Discussion of strengths and weaknesses of each style
11:30 A.M.–1 P.M.	Lunch
1–2 P.M.	Presentation and video of eight key behaviors of problem-solving approach
2–3 P.M.	Role plays
3–3:15 P.M.	Wrap-up (questions and answers)

Lesson Plan Overview

The **lesson plan overview** matches major activities of the training program and specific times or time intervals.[77] Table 4.19 provides an example of a lesson plan overview for the performance appraisal feedback training.

Completing a lesson plan overview helps the trainer determine the amount of time that needs to be allocated for each topic covered in the program. The lesson plan overview is also useful in determining when trainers are needed during a program; time demands on trainees; program breaks for snacks, lunch, and dinner; and opportunities for practice and feedback. For the performance appraisal feedback training, the lesson plan shows that approximately half of the training time is devoted to active learning by the trainees (discussion, role plays, question-and-answer session).

The experience of Health Partners, which administers Medicaid and Medicare coverage for patients in and around Philadelphia, Pennsylvania, illustrates the importance of lesson planning and program design.[78] The company installed a major upgrade to its data processing system, but the program was unfamiliar to most employees. To conduct the training, Health Partners identified employees who were familiar with the program and asked them to be part-time instructors. Instead of providing day-long classes that would likely be boring and overwhelming, the company's training staff broke the training into a series of 45-minute sessions that employees could easily fit into their work schedules. The curriculum was organized by department rather than by tasks, and staff from other departments were invited to attend the program so they could understand how the entire company used the system. Portions of the training time were devoted to discussing with employees the stress of change in the workplace and the benefits of the new system. The management teams also met periodically with the instructors to keep them up-to-date on the types of problems that employees faced in working with the new system so those issues could be incorporated into the training.

Summary

Learning must occur for training to be effective. This chapter began by defining learning and identifying the capabilities that can be learned: verbal information, intellectual skills, motor skills, attitudes, and cognitive strategies. To explain how these capabilities can be learned, the chapter discussed several theories of learning: reinforcement theory, social learning theory, goal setting theory, need theories, expectancy theory, adult learning theory, and information processing theory. Next, the chapter investigated the learning process and the implications of how people learn. The section on learning process emphasized that internal processes (expectancy, storage, and retrieval) as well as external processes (gratifying) influence learning. The potential influence of learning styles and age differences in learning was examined. The chapter then discussed the relationship between the implications of the learning process and the design of instruction. Important design elements include providing learners with an understanding of why they should learn, meaningful content, practice opportunities, feedback, a model, a coordinated program, and a good physical learning environment. The chapter concluded by discussing how to select and prepare a training site, choosing good trainers, and ensure effective program design. Effective program design includes using a design document to develop course lesson plans and overview.

Key Terms

learning, *140*
verbal information, *141*
intellectual skills, *141*
motor skills, *141*
attitudes, *141*
cognitive strategies, *141*
reinforcement theory, *141*
social learning theory, *143*
self-efficacy, *143*
verbal persuasion, *143*
logical verification, *143*
modeling, *143*
past accomplishments, *143*
goal setting theory, *145*
goal orientation, *146*
learning orientation, *146*
performance orientation, *146*
need, *146*
expectancies, *147*
instrumentality, *147*
valence, *147*

andragogy, *148*
expectancy, *151*
perception, *151*
working storage, *151*
semantic encoding, *151*
rehearsal, *151*
organizing, *151*
elaboration, *151*
retrieval, *151*
generalizing, *151*
gratifying, *151*
millennium (nexter), *153*
Gen Xers, *153*
baby boomers, *153*
traditionalists, *153*
instruction, *154*
objective, *155*
training context, *156*
practice, *156*
metacognition, *157*
advance organizers, *157*
overlearning, *158*
error management training, *158*

massed practice, *158*
spaced practice, *158*
overall task complexity, *158*
mental requirements, *158*
physical requirements, *158*
whole practice, *159*
part practice, *159*
automatization, *160*
feedback, *161*
communities of practice, *162*
training administration, *163*
internal conditions, *164*
external conditions, *164*
training site, *165*
program design, *172*
program objectives, *173*
course objectives (lesson objectives), *173*
detailed lesson plan, *173*
lesson plan overview, *177*

Discussion Questions

1. Compare and contrast any two of the following learning theories: expectancy theory, social learning theory, reinforcement theory, information processing theory.

2. What learning condition do you think is most necessary for learning to occur? Which is least critical? Why?

3. What value would it be to know that you were going to be training a class of persons between the ages of 20 and 35? Would it influence the approach you would take? How?

4. Consider the ages of persons in the class mentioned in the previous question. What suggestions would you make to the instructor or trainer as to how to better teach the course, given the generations represented in the class?

5. How do instructional objectives help learning to occur?

6. Assume you are training an employee to diagnose and repair a loose wire in an electrical socket. After demonstrating the procedure to follow, you let the trainee show you how to do it. The trainee correctly demonstrates the process and repairs the connection on the first attempt! Has learning occurred? Justify your answer.

7. Your boss says, "Why do I need to tell you what type of learning capability I'm interested in? I just want a training program to teach employees how to give good customer service!" Explain to the boss how "good customer service" can be translated into different learning outcomes.

8. How does practice help learning? What could a trainer do in a training session to ensure that trainees engage in metacognition?

9. Can allowing trainees to make errors in training be useful? Explain.

10. What learning conditions are necessary for short- and long-term retention of training content to occur?

11. Under what circumstances might a traditional seating arrangement be superior to a fan-type seating arrangement?

12. Detailed lesson plans have important information for trainers. List the different types of information found in a detailed lesson plan. Also, indicate the importance of each type of information for learning.

13. What is a design document? What is included in a design document? How is it useful for training?

14. You have a one-day classroom experience in which you need to help a group of engineers and software programmers learn to become project managers. After training, they will have to manage some significant projects. Discuss the instructional characteristics and activities you will use to ensure that the engineers and software programmers learn project management. Complete a design document for the course and develop a sample lesson overview.

Application Assignments

1. Using any source possible (magazines, journals, personal conversation with a trainer), find a description of a training program. Consider the learning process and the implications of the learning process for instruction discussed in the chapter. Evaluate the

degree to which the program facilitates learning. Provide suggestions for improving the program.

2. You are the training director of a hotel chain, Noe Suites. Each Noe Suites hotel has 100 to 150 rooms, a small indoor pool, and a restaurant. Hotels are strategically located near exit ramps of major highways in college towns such as East Lansing, Michigan, and Columbus, Ohio. You receive the following e-mail message from the vice president of operations. Prepare an answer.

To: You, Training Director

From: Vice President of Operations, Noe Suites

As you are probably aware, one of the most important aspects of quality service is known as "recovery"—that is, the employee's ability to respond effectively to customer complaints. There are three possible outcomes to a customer complaint: The customer complains and is satisfied by the response, the customer complains and is dissatisfied with the response, and the customer does not complain but remains dissatisfied. Many dissatisfied customers do not complain because they want to avoid confrontation, there is no convenient way to complain, or they do not believe that complaining will do much good.

I have decided that to improve our level of customer service we need to train our hotel staff in the "recovery" aspect of customer service. My decision is based on the results of recent focus groups we held with customers. One theme that emerged from these focus groups was that we had some weaknesses in the recovery area. For example, last month in one of the restaurants, a waiter dropped the last available piece of blueberry pie on a customer as he was serving her. The waiter did not know how to correct the problem other than offer an apology.

I have decided to hire two well-known consultants in the service industry to discuss recovery as well as to provide an overview of different aspects of quality customer service. These consultants have worked in service industries as well as manufacturing industries.

I have scheduled the consultants to deliver a presentation in three training sessions. Each session will last three hours. There will be one session for each shift of employees (day, afternoon, and midnight shifts).

The sessions will consist of a presentation and question-and-answer session. The presentation will last one and a half hours and the question-and-answer session approximately 45 minutes. There will be a half-hour break.

My expectations are that following this training, the service staff will be able to successfully recover from service problems.

Because you are an expert on training, I want your feedback on the training session. Specifically, I am interested in your opinion regarding whether our employees will learn about service recovery from attending this program. Will they be able to recover from service problems in their interactions with customers? What recommendations do you have for improving the program?

3. Identify what is wrong with each of the following training objectives. Then rewrite it.

   a. To be aware of the safety rules for operating the ribbon-cutting machine in three minutes.

b. Given a personal computer, a table, and a chair, enter the data into a Microsoft Excel spreadsheet.

c. Use the World Wide Web to learn about training practices.

d. Given a street address in the city of Dublin, Ohio, be able to drive the ambulance from the station to the address in less than 10 minutes.

4. Go to www.nwlink.com/~donclark/hrd/sat.html, Big Dog's ISD (Instructional System Design) page. This Web site is an excellent resource that describes all aspects of the Instructional System Design model. Click on "Learning" and scroll to the concept map or list of terms under the map. Click on "Learning Styles" and take the VAK survey. What are the implications of your learning style for how you best learn? What type of learning environment is best suited for your style? Be as specific as possible.

5. Go to cs.gmu.edu/cne/modules/dau/stat, the Web site for an interactive tutorial that provides a refresher on probability and statistics. Click on Index. Choose a topic (such as Data Analysis). Review the module for the topic. What does the module include that can help make the learning process effective? Why?

6. Go to http://agelesslearner.com/intros/adultlearning.html, a site authored by Marcia L. Conner about how adults learn. Scroll down to the bottom of the page and click on Learning Styles Assessment. Complete the assessment. What are the assessment's implications for the way that you learn best?

7. Go to www.schneider.com, the Web site for Schneider National, a transportation management company that provides logistics and trucking services. Click on "Drivers." Scroll down the page and click on "Inexperienced Drivers." On the left side of the page, click on "Videos." Watch the video, "The Training Is Great." What types of learning outcomes are emphasized in training? Considering the features of good instruction discussed in the chapter, identify the features of Schneider's training program that contribute to learning. Explain how each feature you identify contributes to learning.

Case: *Plastics Make Perfect*

A small group of U.S. plastics companies have enacted the Global Standards for Plastic Certification (GSPC) training program. The program is modeled after a series of globally recognized protocols, to make certain workers have an in-depth knowledge of manufacturing, safety, quality, and other elements of a business. GSPC is the sole structured certification program in the world for the plastics sector. It is available for numerous processing strategies and has three levels of certification. Level 1 concentrates on general knowledge of a company, with limited processing instruction. Level II focuses more on the manufacturing procedures and the ability to track and maintain product quality. Finally, Level III focuses on advanced knowledge of injection molding and the ability to use this information on the manufacturing floor. Every level mandates a larger comprehension of and responsibility for the business's specific procedure and the facility overall, and to move on to the next level a worker must pass an oral standardized test.

Describe the different types of instructional characteristics that you believe each level of this program should have for learning to occur and workers to pass the oral standardized test.

Source: Based on P. Katen and D. Snyder, "U.S. Manufacturers Adopt Training Program," *Plastics News* (July 14, 2008): 7.

Endnotes

1. R. M. Gagne and K. L. Medsker, *The Conditions of Learning* (Fort Worth, TX: Harcourt-Brace, 1996).

2. B. F. Skinner, *Science and Human Behavior* (New York: Macmillan, 1953).

3. J. Komaki, K. D. Barwick, and L. R. Scott, "A Behavioral Approach to Occupational Safety: Pinpointing and Reinforcing Safe Performance in a Food Manufacturing Plant," *Journal of Applied Psychology* 63 (1978): 434–45.

4. A. Bandura, *Social Foundations of Thought and Action* (Englewood Cliffs, NJ: Prentice Hall, 1986); A. Bandura, "Self-Efficacy Mechanisms in Human Behavior," *American Psychologist* 37 (1982): 122–47.

5. Bandura, *Social Foundations of Thought and Action.*

6. M. E. Gist and T. R. Mitchell, "Self-Efficacy: A Theoretical Analysis of Its Determinants and Malleability," *Academy of Management Review* 17 (1992): 183–221.

7. E. A. Locke and G. D. Latham, *A Theory of Goal Setting and Task Performance* (Englewood Cliffs, NJ: Prentice Hall, 1990).

8. Ibid.

9. E. A. Locke, K. N. Shaw, L. M. Saari, and G. P. Latham, "Goal Setting and Task Performance," *Psychological Bulletin* 90 (1981): 125–52.

10. T. D. Ludwig and E. S. Geller, "Assigned versus Participative Goal Setting and Response Generalization: Managing Injury Control among Professional Pizza Drivers," *Journal of Applied Psychology* 82 (1997): 253–61.

11. S. Fisher and J. Ford, "Differential Effects of Learner Effort and Goal Orientation on Two Learning Outcomes," *Personnel Psychology* 51 (1998): 397–420.

12. D. VandeWalle, D. W. Cron, and J. Slocum, "The Role of Goal Orientation Following Performance Feedback," *Journal of Applied Psychology* 86 (2001): 629–40; R. Noe and J. Colquitt, "Planning for Impact Training: Principles of Training Effectiveness," in *Creating, Implementing, and Managing Effective Training and Development,* ed. K. Kraiger (San Francisco: Jossey-Bass, 2002): 53–79; A. Schmidt and J. Ford, "Learning within a Learner Control Training Environment: The Interactive Effects of Goal Orientation and Metacognitive Instruction on Learning Outcomes," *Personnel Psychology* 56 (2003): 405–29.

13. A. H. Maslow, "A Theory of Human Motivation," *Psychological Reports* 50 (1943): 370–96; C. P. Alderfer, "An Empirical Test of a New Theory of Human Needs," *Organizational Behavior and Human Performance* 4 (1969): 142–75.

14. D. McClelland, "Managing Motivation to Expand Human Freedom," *American Psychologist* 33 (1978): 201–10.

15. V. H. Vroom, *Work and Motivation* (New York: John Wiley, 1964).

16. M. S. Knowles, "Adult Learning," in *The ASTD Training and Development Handbook,* ed. R. L. Craig (New York: McGraw-Hill): 253–65.

17. M. Knowles, *The Adult Learner,* 4th ed. (Houston: Gulf Publishing, 1990).

18. S. Caudron, "Learners Speak Out," *Training and Development* (April 2000): 52–57.

19. Gagne and Medsker, *The Conditions of Learning;* W. C. Howell and N. J. Cooke, "Training the Human Information Processor: A Review of Cognitive Models," in *Training and Development in Organizations,* ed. I. L. Goldstein and Associates (San Francisco: Jossey-Bass, 1991): 121–82.

20. R. M. Gagne, "Learning Processes and Instruction," *Training Research Journal* 1 (1995/96): 17–28.

21. Ibid.

22. R. Mayer, "Applying the Science of Learning: Evidence-based Principles for the Design of Multimedia Instruction," *American Psychologist* (November 2008): 760–769; R. Clark and R. Mayer, "Learning by Viewing versus Learning by Doing: Evidence-based Guidelines for Principled Learning Environments," *Performance Improvement* 47 (2008): 5–13.

23. "Cognitive Strategies," Chapter 6 in Gagne and Medsker, *The Conditions of Learning;* M. Gist, "Training Design and Pedagogy: Implications for Skill Acquisition, Maintenance, and Generalization," in *Training for a Rapidly Changing Workplace,* ed. R. Quinches and A. Ehrenstein (Washington, DC: American Psychological Association, 1997): 201–22.

24. D. Kolb, "Management and the Learning Process," *California Management Review* 18 (1996): 21–31.

25. See D. Kolb, I. Rubin, and J. McIntyre, *Organizational Psychology: An Experimental Approach,* 3d ed. (Englewood Cliffs, NJ: Prentice Hall, 1984): 27–54; M. Delahousaye, "The Perfect Learner: An Expert Debate on Learning Styles," *Training* (March 2002): 28–36.

26. H. Dolezalek, "AmeriCredit," *Training* (March 2003): 46–47.

27. R. Boyd, "Steady Drop in Brain's Prowess Starts in 20s," *Columbus Dispatch,* November 17, 2000: A5.

28. R. Zemke, C. Raines, and B. Filipczak, "Generation Gaps in the Classroom," *Training* (November 2000): 48–54; J. Salopek, "The Young and the Rest of Us," *Training and Development* (February 2000): 26–30.

29. K. Tyler, "Generation Gaps," *HR Magazine* (January 2008): 69–72.

30. P. Ketter, "What Can Training Do for Brown?" *T + D* (May 2008): 30–36.

31. J. Callahan, D. Kiker, and T. Cross, "Does Method Matter? A Meta-analysis of the Effects of Training Method on Older Learner Training Performance," *Journal of Management* 29 (2003): 663–80.

32. Gagne, "Learning Processes and Instruction."

33. B. Mager, *Preparing Instructional Objectives,* 5th ed. (Belmont, CA: Lake Publishing, 1997); B. J. Smith and B. L. Delahaye, *How to Be an Effective Trainer,* 2d ed. (New York: John Wiley and Sons, 1987); S. Moore, J. Ellsworth, and R. Kaufman, "Objectives—Are They Useful? A Quick Assessment," *Performance Improvement Quarterly* 47 (2008): 41–47.

34. K. A. Smith-Jentsch, F. G. Jentsch, S. C. Payne, and E. Salas, "Can Pre-training Experiences Explain Individual Differences in Learning?" *Journal of Applied Psychology* 81 (1996): 110–16; Caudron, "Learners Speak Out."

35. J. K. Ford, D. A. Weissbein, S. M. Guly, and E. Salas, "Relationship of Goal Orientation, Metacognitive Activity, and Practice Strategies with Learning Outcomes and Transfer," *Journal of Applied Psychology* 83 (1998): 218–33; Schmidt and Ford, "Learning within a Learner Control Training Environment"; S. Yelon, L. Sheppard, and J. Ford, "Intention to Transfer: How Do Autonomous Professionals Become Motivated to Use New Ideas?" *Performance Improvement Quarterly* 17, no. 2 (2004): 82–103; M. Hequet, "Training No One Wants," *Training* (January 2004): 22–28.

36. R. Clark and R. Mayer, "Learning by Viewing versus Learning by Doing: Evidence-based Guidelines for Principled Learning Environments," *Performance Improvement* 47 (2008): 5–13.

37. J. Cannon-Bowers, L. Rhodenizer, E. Salas, and C. Bowers, "A Framework for Understanding Pre-practice Conditions and Their Impact on Learning," *Personnel Psychology* 51 (1998): 291–320.

38. Schmidt and Ford, "Learning within a Learner Control Training Environment."

39. B. S. Bell and S.W.J. Kozlowski, "Active Learning: Effects of Core Training Design Elements on Self-Regulatory Processes, Learning, and Adaptability," *Journal of Applied Psychology* 93 (2008): 296–316.

40. D. Heimbeck, M. Frese, S. Sonnentag, and N. Keith, "Integrating Errors into the Training Process: The Function of Error Management Instructions and the Role of Goal Orientation," *Personnel Psychology* 56 (2003): 333–61; N. Keith and M. Frese, "Self-Regulation in Error Management Training: Emotion Control and Metacognition as Mediators of Performance Effects," *Journal of Applied Psychology* 90 (2005): 677–91; N. Keith and M. Frese, "Effectiveness of Error Management Training: A Meta-analysis," *Journal of Applied Psychology* 93 (2008): 59–69.

41. J. Donovan and D. Radosevich, "A Meta-analytic Review of the Distribution of Practice Effect: Now You See It, Now You Don't," *Journal of Applied Psychology* 84 (1999): 795–805.

42. R. M. Mager, *Making Instruction Work* (Belmont, CA: David Lake, 1988).

43. R. Weiss, "Memory and Learning," *Training and Development* (October 2000): 46–50; R. Zemke, "Toward a Science of Training," *Training* (July 1999): 32–36.

44. J. C. Naylor and G. D. Briggs, "The Effects of Task Complexity and Task Organization on the Relative Efficiency of Part and Whole Training Methods," *Journal of Experimental Psychology* 65 (1963): 217–24.

45. R. Mayer, "Applying the Science of Learning: Evidence-based Principles for the Design of Multimedia Instruction," *American Psychologist* (November 2008): 760–769.

46. Gagne and Medsker, *The Conditions of Learning.*

47. J. Goodman and R. Wood, "Feedback Specificity, Learning Opportunities, and Learning," *Journal of Applied Psychology* 89 (2004): 809–21.

48. P. J. Decker and B. R. Nathan, *Behavior Modeling Training: Principles and Applications* (New York: Praeger, 1985).

49. Caudron, "Learners Speak Out."

50. S. Mierson and K. Freiert, "Problem-Based Learning," *T + D* (October 2004): 15–17.

51. D. Stamps, "Communities of Practice," *Training* (February 1997): 35–42.

52. D. Goldwasser, "Me, a Trainer," *Training* (April 2001): 61–66.

53. M. Weinstein, "Rx for Excellence," *Training* (February 2009): 48–52.

54. R. Williams and J. Cothrel, "Four Smart Ways to Run On-Line Communities," *Sloan Management Review* (Summer, 2000): 81–91.

55. Smith and Delahaye, *How to Be an Effective Trainer;* M. Van Wart, N. J. Cayer, and S. Cook, *Handbook of Training and Development for the Public Sector* (San Francisco: Jossey-Bass, 1993).

56. R. Zemke, "Cooking Up World-Class Training," *Training* 34 (1997): 52–58.

57. Smith and Delahaye, *How to Be an Effective Trainer;* Van Wart, Cayer, and Cook, *Handbook of Training and Development for the Public Sector.*

58. "Top Training Facilities," *Training* (March 1995): special section.

59. Harrison Conference Centers, "Outlook 2000," *Training* (February 2000): S1–S21.

60. L. Nadler and Z. Nadler, *Designing Training Programs,* 2d ed. (Houston: Gulf Publishing Company, 1994); T. W. Goad, "Building Presentations: A Top-Down Approach," in *Effective Training Delivery* (Minneapolis: Lakewood Publishing, 1989): 21–24; F. H. Margolis and C. R. Bell, *Managing the Learning Process* (Minneapolis: Lakewood, 1984).

61. M. Welber, "Save by Growing Your Own Trainers," *Workforce* (September 2002): 44–48; T. Adams, A. Kennedy, and M. Marquart, "The Reluctant Trainer," *T + D* (March 2008): 24–27.

62. P. Hinds, M. Patterson, and J. Pfeffer, "Bothered by Abstraction: The Effects of Expertise on Knowledge Transfer and Subsequent Novice Performance," *Journal of Applied Psychology* 86 (2001) 1232–43; S. Merrill, "Training the Trainer 101," *T + D* (June 2008): 28–31.

63. J. Gordon, "MasterCard's MASTER PLAN," *Training* (October 2007): 58–62.

64. H. Dolezalek, "Certify Me," *Training* (June 2008): 54–59.

65. D. Booher, "Make the Room Work for You," *Training and Development,* S5–S7; D. Abernathy, "Presentation Tips from the Pros," *Training and Development* (October 1999): 19–25.

66. Steelcase, "Workplace Issues: One in a Series. Learning Environments for the Information Age," available from the Steelcase Web site, *www.steelcase.com* (March 1, 2006).

67. A. Towler and R. Dipboye, "Effects of Trainer Expressiveness, Organizations, and Trainee Goal Orientation on Training Outcomes," *Journal of Applied Psychology* 86 (2001): 664–73.

68. A. Towler and R. Dipboye, "Effects of Trainer Expressiveness, Organization, and Trainee Goal Orientation on Training Outcomes," *Journal of Applied Psychology* 86 (2001): 664–673; T. Sitzmann, K. Brown, W. Casper, K. Ely, and R. Zimmerman, "A Review and Meta-analysis of the Nomological Network of Trainee Reactions," *Journal of Applied Psychology* 93 (2008): 280–295.

69. D. Eden and A. Shani, "Pygmalion Goes to Boot Camp: Expectancy, Leadership, and Trainee Performance," *Journal of Applied Psychology* 67 (1982): 194–199.

70. J. Shapiro, E. King, and M. Quinones, "Expectation of Obese Trainees: How Stigmatized Trainee Characteristics Influence Training Effectiveness," *Journal of Applied Psychology* 92 (2007): 239–249.

71. Hequet, "Training No One Wants."

72. Van Wart, Cayer, and Cook, *Handbook of Training and Development for the Public Sector.*

73. P. Kirschner, C. Carr, and P. Sloep, "How Expert Designers Design," *Performance Improvement Quarterly* 15 (2002): 86–104.

74. G. Piskurich, *Rapid Instructional Design* (San Francisco: Pfeiffer, 2006).

75. Van Wart, Cayer, and Cook, *Handbook of Training and Development for the Public Sector.*

76. G. P. Latham and K. N. Wexley, *Increasing Productivity through Performance Appraisal,* 2d ed. (Reading, MA: Addison-Wesley, 1994).

77. Ibid.

78. P. Kiger, "Health Partners Delivers Training That Works," *Workforce* (November 2002): 60–64.

Transfer of Training

Objectives

After reading this chapter, you should be able to

1. Diagnose and solve a transfer of training problem.
2. Create a work environment that will facilitate transfer of training.
3. Explain to a manager how to ensure that transfer of training occurs.
4. Discuss the implications of identical elements, stimulus generalization, and cognitive theories for transfer of training.
5. Develop a self-management module for a training program.
6. Discuss the technologies that can be used to support transfer of training.
7. Discuss the key features of the learning organization.
8. Provide recommendations for how to manage knowledge.

Transfer of Training and Knowledge Sharing Are Important for Nonprofits

Nonprofit organizations such as the United Nations Children's Fund (UNICEF) and government agencies such as the Peace Corps routinely send workers to some of the most dangerous, underdeveloped nations in the world. They rely upon temporary and short-term field workers and volunteers and have small training budgets compared to those of private, for-profit companies. Despite the difficulties they face, nonprofits still manage to train their workers successfully so they can be effective in their mission. It is especially important that what is emphasized in training is used on the job (transfer of training) and that the valuable knowledge that volunteers have gained about a location, its people, and the assistance needed is not lost when they leave the organization (i.e., knowledge sharing occurs).

For example, consider the online course used by Darkness to Light (D2L), an international child abuse prevention, education, and public awareness organization. "Stewards of Children Online" is designed to teach adults how to prevent and recognize signs of sexual abuse in children. The training was developed around "universal truths" to ensure that the basic principles emphasized in the course would be relevant for everyone, regardless of their culture, socioeconomic background, or location. For example, one of the "universal truths" is that it is healthy and good for parents to talk to their children about their personal boundaries.

UNICEF, which provides humanitarian and development assistance to children and mothers in developing countries, uses a blended learning approach. The majority of e-learning programs offered by UNICEF include both CD-ROM and Internet formats, which allows trainees without dependable access to the Internet to train using personal computers available at their location. Course content is broken into modules so individual regions can easily customize content to local culture and situations.

At the Peace Corps, more than 90 percent of training is conducted by local staff in the field. The Peace Corps trains volunteers in the actual performance situations in which they will be working, based on the belief that skills taught in training better transfer to the work environment. For example, trainees in the Dominican Republic acquire many skills, including technical expertise, medical and security skills, and foreign language proficiency. Trainees are given real-world assignments—such as going into a community to purchase a loaf of bread—in order to use what they are learning.

Medecins Sans Frontieres (MSF), also known as Doctors Without Borders, is challenged by the need to manage knowledge gained by aid workers and logisticians who typically spend only six months to one year on a mission before leaving the organization. To help foster knowledge sharing, MSF requires volunteers who are completing an overseas mission to complete a "handover report" that documents their experiences and lessons learned in the field. Also, to ensure knowledge transfer, MSF rotates staff in and out of mission positions so that workers who are leaving can spend one to two weeks in the field training their replacements. In a mission of five or six persons, one person per month will rotate out over a period of six months. Similarly, to ensure the freshness of the staff, approximately 1,500 U.S. full-time staff members who are in charge of recruiting, training, program support, health assistance, and logistical coordination for the agency's volunteers are required by law (an amendment to the Peace Corps Act) to leave the agency after five years of service. To ensure knowledge sharing for new volunteers, the Peace Corps training programs include well-documented learning objectives and competencies as well as content and lesson plans.

Source: Based on S. Boehle, "Going to Extremes," *Training* (March/April 2008): 26–29.

INTRODUCTION

The training experiences of nonprofit organizations such as UNICEF, the Peace Corps, and MSF highlight the importance of ensuring that the design of training leads to learning as well as the use of training on the job. Also, these nonprofit organizations are taking steps to ensure that what trainees learn is shared with their peers. In many training programs, most of the attention (and money) is focused on developing the program, but just as important is the follow-up, which ensures that learning is put into practice.[1] As you will see in this chapter, trainee motivation to learn as well as manager support for training are key issues for ensuring learning and the application of training to the job.

Recall the Instructional System Design model presented in Chapter 1. After conducting a needs assessment, ensuring that employees are ready for training, and creating a learning environment, the next step is to ensure that what is learned in training is applied on the job. **Transfer of training** refers to trainees' effectively and continually applying what they learned in training (knowledge, skills, behaviors, cognitive strategies) to their jobs.[2] As the nonprofit organizations in the opening vignette illustrate, the work environment and trainee characteristics play an important role in ensuring that transfer of training occurs. Transfer of training is also influenced by training design. Despite the importance of transfer of training and the emphasis that some companies are placing on it, research suggests that only 62 percent of employees transfer training immediately after completing training programs. This statistic decreases to 34 percent one year after training.[3]

Figure 5.1 presents a model of the transfer process. This model is useful for considering what you can do to ensure that trainee characteristics, training design, and the work environment are conducive to transfer of training. The chapter is organized based on this model. As the model shows, transfer of training includes both the generalization of training to the job and the maintenance of learned material. **Generalization** refers to a trainee's ability to apply learned capabilities (verbal knowledge, motor skills, etc.) to on-the-job work problems and situations that are similar but not identical to those problems and situations encountered in the learning environment. **Maintenance** refers to the process of continuing to use newly acquired capabilities over time.

For generalization and maintenance to occur, capabilities must be learned and retained. The model shows three factors that influence learning and transfer of training. Training design, trainee characteristics, and the work environment influence learning, retention, maintenance, and generalization. **Training design** refers to the characteristics of the learning environment. Chapter 4 covered important features of the learning environment— including meaningful material, opportunities to practice, feedback, learning objectives, program, organization and physical features of the training site. Another factor that influences learning and retention is **trainee characteristics.** Trainee characteristics include ability and motivation. The influence of trainee characteristics on learning was discussed in Chapters 3 and 4. If trainees lack the basic skills needed to master learned capabilities (e.g., cognitive ability, reading skills), are not motivated to learn, and do not believe that they can master the learned capabilities (low self-efficacy), it is doubtful that learning and

FIGURE 5.1
A Model of the Transfer Process

Source: Adapted from T. T. Baldwin and J. K. Ford, "Transfer of Training: A Review and Directions for Future Research," *Personnel Psychology* 41 (1988): 63–103.

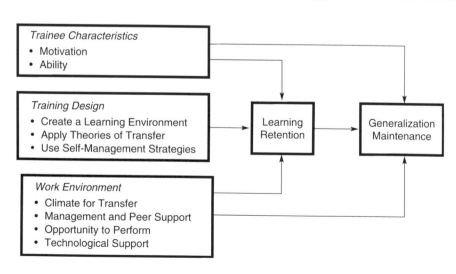

transfer of training will occur. The third factor that influences learning, retention, and transfer is the work environment. The **work environment** includes factors on the job that influence transfer of training, such as managers' support, peer support, technology support, the climate for transfer, and the opportunity to use newly acquired capabilities on the job.

Although transfer of training sounds like something to be considered *after* training occurs, it should be planned for *before* the training. Recall from Chapter 3 that assessment of trainee characteristics and the work environment is part of the needs assessment. Transfer of training does occur after the training occurs. However, the conditions that facilitate transfer need to be provided before the training actually occurs. For example, to motivate trainees to attend a training program, communications about the program need to emphasize the benefit of the training. Design of the learning process needs to include desirable features such as objectives, meaningful material, and opportunities to practice and receive feedback (recall the learning process from Chapter 4). Managers' and peers' attitudes toward training can influence trainees' level of motivation to learn. This chapter focuses on identifying additional factors—besides the learning environment and trainee characteristics already discussed—that influence transfer of training. This chapter includes a detailed discussion of transfer of training theories and how the work environment influences transfer of training.

The chapter begins with a discussion of training design issues related to transfer of training, including (1) the application of theories of transfer of training to training design and (2) an emphasis on self-management as part of the training program. Next, the chapter addresses how the work environment influences the transfer of training process. Trainees', managers', and trainers' roles in ensuring that transfer of training occurs are emphasized. Through discussions of learning organizations and knowledge management, you will gain a perspective on how the work climate can influence transfer of training. The chapter also points out that transfer of training can be enhanced by holding trainees accountable for using information learned in training and sharing that information with their colleagues. The chapter concludes with a discussion of learning organizations—a multifaceted approach for encouraging learning and transfer of training.

TRAINING DESIGN

Training design refers to factors built into the training program to increase the chances that transfer of training will occur. Chapter 4 discussed the important factors needed for learning to occur (objectives, practice, feedback, meaningful material, etc.). For transfer of training to occur, managers need to apply transfer of training theories and encourage trainees to take responsibility for learning and to engage in self-management strategies.

Applications of Transfer of Training Theory

Three theories of transfer of training have implications for training design (the learning environment): the theory of identical elements, the stimulus generalization approach, and the cognitive theory of transfer.[4] Table 5.1 shows each theory's primary emphasis and the conditions under which it is most appropriate to consider.

TABLE 5.1

Transfer of Training Theories

Theory	Emphasis	Appropriate Conditions	Type of Transfer
Identical Elements	Training environment is identical to work environment.	Work environment features are predictable and stable. *Example:* training to use equipment.	Near
Stimulus Generalization	General principles are applicable to many different work situations.	Work environment is unpredictable and highly variable. *Example:* training in interpersonal skills.	Far
Cognitive Theory	Meaningful material and coding schemes enhance storage and recall of training content.	All types of training and environments.	Near and far

Theory of Identical Elements

The **theory of identical elements** proposes that transfer of training occurs when what is being learned in the training session is identical to what the trainee has to perform on the job.[5] Transfer will be maximized to the degree that the tasks, materials, equipment, and other characteristics of the learning environment are similar to those encountered in the work environment.

The use of identical elements theory is shown in the hostage training simulation used by the Baltimore Police Department. The Baltimore Police Department needed to teach police sergeants the skills to handle hostage-barricade situations in which lives are at stake—skills such as negotiating with a troubled husband holding his wife and/or children hostage. The first hour of a hostage situation is critical. The sergeant must quickly organize resources to achieve a successful end to the situation with minimal or no injuries. A simulation was chosen because it provides a model of reality, a mock-up of a real situation without the danger. Multiple scenarios can be incorporated into the simulation, allowing the sergeants to practice the exact skills they will need when faced with a hostage crisis.

The simulation begins by having the trainees briefed on the hostage situation. Then they are directed to take charge of resolving the incident in the presence of an instructor who has personally been involved in similar real-life incidents. Each trainee supervises one difficult and one easy scenario. The simulation is designed to emphasize the importance of clear thinking and decision making in a situation in which time is critical. It is essential that the trainees take actions according to a set of priorities. These priorities place the greatest value on minimizing the risks to the hostages and isolating suspects before communicating with them. The simulation scenarios include elements of many actual hostage incidents such as forced entry, taking persons against their will, the presence of a weapon, and threats. As trainees work in the simulation, their actions are evaluated by the instructor. The instructor provides feedback to the trainees in writing after they complete the simulation or the instructor can correct mistakes as they happen.

The training simulation mirrors the exact circumstances of actual hostage situations encountered by police officers. Also, the checklist of activities and behaviors that the sergeants are provided with in training is the exact checklist used in hostage situations that occur on the street. Evidence of generalization is provided by police sergeants who have successfully dealt with a bank-hostage situation by using the skills emphasized in the simulation. The Baltimore Police Department is also concerned with maintenance. At the conclusion of the simulation, officers may be able to demonstrate how to successfully free hostages. However, the incidence of hostage situations is fairly low compared to other tasks that police officers perform (e.g., issuing traffic citations, investigating burglaries). As a result, the police department is concerned that officers may forget what they learned in training and therefore have difficulties in hostage situations. To ensure that officers have opportunities to practice these infrequently used but important skills, the training department occasionally schedules mock hostage situations.[6]

Another application of the theory of identical elements is found in the use of simulators for training airline pilots. Pilots are trained in a simulator that looks exactly like the cockpit of a commercial aircraft. All aspects of the cockpit in the simulator (e.g., gauges, dials, lights) are the same as in a real aircraft. In psychological terms, the learning environment has complete fidelity with the work environment. **Fidelity** refers to the extent to which the training environment is similar to the work environment. If skills in flying, taking off, landing, and dealing with emergency situations are learned in the simulator, they will be transferred to the work setting (commercial aircraft).

The identical elements approach has also been used to develop instruments designed to measure the similarity of jobs.[7] Job similarity can be used as one measure of the extent to which training in the knowledge and skills required for one job prepares an employee to perform a different job.

The theory of identical elements has been applied to many training programs, particularly those that deal with the use of equipment or that involve specific procedures that must be learned. Identical elements theory is particularly relevant in making sure that near transfer occurs. **Near transfer** refers to trainees' ability to apply learned capabilities exactly to the work situation. Programs that emphasize near transfer should include the following training designs:[8]

- The program should teach specific concepts and procedures.
- Trainees should be given an explanation as to any differences between training tasks and work tasks.
- Trainees should be encouraged to focus only on important differences between training tasks and work tasks (e.g., speed of completion) rather than unimportant differences (e.g., equipment with the same features but a different model).
- Behaviors or skills that trainees learn in the program should contribute to effective performance.

For example, in police officer training, new hires (cadets) practice shooting targets. During practice sessions, cadets fire a round of shells, empty the cartridges into their hands, and dispose of the empty cartridges into the nearest garbage can. This process is repeated several times. After graduation from the police academy, one new officer was involved in a shooting. He fired his gun, emptied the cartridges into his hand, and proceeded to look for a garbage can for the empty cartridges. As a result, he was seen by the gunman, shot, and killed!

Identical elements theory does not encourage transfer where the learning environment and the training environment are not necessarily identical. This situation arises particularly in interpersonal skills training. For example, a person's behavior in a conflict situation is not easily predictable. Therefore, trainees must learn general principles of conflict resolution that they can apply to a wide variety of situations as the circumstances dictate (e.g., an irate customer versus a customer who lacks product knowledge).

Stimulus Generalization Approach

The **stimulus generalization approach** suggests that the way to understand the transfer of training issue is to construct training so that the most important features or general principles are emphasized. It is also important to identify the range of work situations in which these general principles can be applied. The stimulus generalization approach emphasizes far transfer. **Far transfer** refers to the trainee's ability to apply learned capabilities to the work environment, even though the work environment (equipment, problems, tasks) is not identical to that of the training session. Programs that emphasize far transfer should include the following training designs:[9]

- The program should teach general concepts and broad principles.
- Trainees should be made aware of examples from their experiences that are similar to those emphasized in training so that connections can be made among strategies that have been effective in different situations.
- The program should emphasize that the general principles might be applied to a greater set of contexts than those presented in the training setting.

The stimulus generalization approach can be seen in the design of managerial skill training programs, known as behavior modeling training, which are based on social learning theory. Recall from the discussion of social learning theory in Chapter 4 that modeling, practice, feedback, and reinforcement play key roles in learning. One step in developing behavior modeling programs is to identify key behaviors that are needed to be successful in a situation. **Key behaviors** refer to a set of behaviors that can be used successfully in a wide variety of situations. The model demonstrates these key behaviors on a video, and trainees have opportunities to practice the behaviors. In behavior modeling training, the key behaviors are believed to be applicable to a wide variety of situations. In fact, the practice sessions in behavior modeling training require the trainee to use the behaviors in a variety of situations that are not identical.

Cognitive Theory of Transfer

The cognitive theory of transfer is based on the information processing theory of learning discussed in Chapter 4. Recall that the storage and retrieval of information are key aspects of this model of learning. According to the **cognitive theory of transfer,** the likelihood of transfer depends on the trainees' ability to retrieve learned capabilities. This theory suggests that the likelihood of transfer is increased by providing trainees with meaningful material that enhances the chances that they will link what they encounter in the work environment to the learned capability. Also important is providing the trainee with cognitive strategies for coding the learned capabilities in memory so that they are easily retrievable. (These strategies were discussed in Chapter 4.)

The influence of cognitive theory is seen in training design that encourages trainees, as part of the program, to consider potential applications of the training content to their jobs. Many training programs include having trainees identify a work problem or situation and discuss the potential application of training content. Application assignments increase the likelihood that trainees will recall the training content and apply it to the work setting when they encounter the appropriate cues (problems, situations) in the environment. **Application assignments** are work problems or situations in which trainees are asked to apply training content to solve them. The use of application assignments in training helps the trainee understand the link between the learned capability and real-world application, which makes it easier to recall the capability when needed.

Encourage Trainee Responsibility and Self-Management

Trainees need to take responsibility for learning and transfer.[10] This includes preparing for training, being involved and engaged during training, and using training content back on the job. Before training, trainees need to consider why they are attending training and set specific learning goals (either alone or, preferably, in a discussion with their manager) as part of completing an action plan (action plans are discussed in more detail later in the chapter). Also, trainees need to complete any assigned pre-training assignments. During training, trainees need to be involved. That is, they need to participate and share experiences in discussions, to practice, and to ask questions if they are confused. After training, trainees need to review and work toward reaching the goals established in their action plan. They need to be willing to change (e.g., try new behaviors, apply new knowledge) and ask peers and managers for help if they need it.

Self-management refers to a person's attempt to control certain aspects of decision making and behavior. Training programs should prepare employees to self-manage their use of new skills and behaviors on the job. Self-management involves:

1. Determining the degree of support and negative consequences in the work setting for using newly acquired capabilities.
2. Setting goals for using learned capabilities.
3. Applying learned capabilities to the job.
4. Monitoring use of learned capabilities on the job.
5. Engaging in self-reinforcement.[11]

Research suggests that trainees exposed to self-management strategies exhibit higher levels of transfer of behavior and skills than do trainees who are not provided with self-management strategies.[12] Self-management is important because the trainee is likely to encounter several obstacles in the work environment that inhibit transfer of training. Table 5.2 shows these obstacles. They include (1) lack of support from peers and managers and (2) factors related to the work itself (e.g., time pressure). Given the restructuring, downsizing, and cost cutting occurring in many companies, these obstacles are often a reality for trainees.

For example, new technologies allow employees to gain access to resources and product demonstrations using the World Wide Web or personal computers equipped with CD-ROM drives. But while employees are being trained to use these resources with state-of-the-art technology, they often become frustrated because comparable technology is not available to them at their work site. Employees' computers may lack sufficient memory or links to the World Wide Web for them to use what they have learned.

TABLE 5.2   Examples of Obstacles in the Work Environment That Inhibit Transfer of Training

Obstacle	Description of Influence
Work Conditions	
Time pressures Inadequate equipment Few opportunities to use skills Inadequate budget	Trainee has difficulty using new knowledge, skills, or behavior.
Lack of Peer Support **Peers:**	
Discourage use of new knowledge and skills on the job Are unwilling to provide feedback See training as waste of time	Peers do not support use of new knowledge, skills, or behavior.
Lack of Management Support **Management:**	
Does not accept ideas or suggestions that are learned in training Does not discuss training opportunities Opposes use of skills learned in training Communicates that training is a waste of time Is unwilling to provide reinforcement, feedback, and encouragement needed for trainees to use training content	Managers do not reinforce training or provide opportunities to use new knowledge, skills, or behavior.

Source: Based on R. D. Marx, "Self-Managed Skill Retention," *Training and Development Journal* (January 1986): 54–57.

These obstacles inhibit transfer because they cause lapses. **Lapses** take place when the trainee uses previously learned, less effective capabilities instead of trying to apply the capability emphasized in the training program. Lapses into old behavior and skill patterns are common. Trainees should try to avoid a consistent pattern of slipping back or using old, ineffective learned capabilities (e.g., knowledge, skills, behaviors, strategies). Also, trainees should understand that lapses are common and be prepared to cope with them. Trainees who are unprepared for lapses may give up trying to use new capabilities—especially trainees with low self-efficacy and self-confidence.

One way to prepare trainees to deal with these obstacles is to provide instruction in self-management techniques at the end of the training program. Table 5.3 shows an example of self-management instruction. The module begins with a discussion of lapses, emphasizing that lapses are not evidence of personal inadequacy; rather, they result from habits of usage of knowledge and skill that have developed over time. Lapses provide information necessary for improvement. They help identify the circumstances that will have the most negative influence on transfer of training. Next, a specific behavior, skill, or strategy is targeted for transfer. The skill should be measurable and countable. Then, obstacles that inhibit transfer of training are identified; these can include both work environment characteristics and personal characteristics (such as low self-efficacy). Trainees are then provided with an overview of coping skills or strategies that they can use to deal with these obstacles. These skills and strategies include time management,

TABLE 5.3 **Sample Content of Self-Management Module**

1. Discuss lapses. • Note evidence of inadequacy • Provide direction for improvement	**5. Identify when lapses are likely.** • Situations • Actions to deal with lapses
2. Identify skills targeted for transfer. • Specify the skills • Make them measurable and countable	**6. Discuss resources to ensure transfer of skills.** • Manager • Trainer • Other trainees
3. Identify personal or environment factors contributing to lapse. • Low self-efficacy • Time pressure • Lack of manager or peer support	
4. Discuss coping skills and strategies. • Time management • Setting priorities • Self-monitoring • Self-rewards • Creating a personal support network	

Source: Adapted from R. D. Marx, "Improving Management Development through Relapse Prevention Strategies," *Journal of Management Development* 5 (1986): 27–40; M. L. Broad and J. W. Newstrom, *Transfer of Training* (Reading, MA: Addison-Wesley, 1992); R. D. Marx and L. A. Burke, "Transfer Is Personal," in *Improving Learning Transfer in Organizations,* ed. E. Holton and T. Baldwin (San Francisco: Jossey-Bass, 2003): 227–42.

creating a personal support network (persons to talk with about how to transfer skills to the work setting), and self-monitoring to identify successes in transferring skills to the job. Next, to deal with lapses trainees are instructed to be aware of where the situations are most likely to occur. The final part of the module deals with the use of resources to aid transfer of training. These resources may include communications with the trainer or fellow trainees via e-mail as well as discussions with their boss.

For example, a manager may have attended a training program designed to increase her leadership skills. After a discussion of lapses, the manager identifies a target skill, say, participative decision making—that is, discussing problems and potential solutions with subordinates before making decisions that will affect the work group. The manager defines the skill and how to measure it: "Discussing problems and solutions with my subordinates at least two times each week." Next, the manager identifies factors that may contribute to a lapse. One factor may be the manager's lack of confidence in being able to deal with subordinates who disagree with her view. Potential coping strategies that the manager identifies may include (1) scheduling time on the calendar to meet with subordinates (time management), (2) communicating to the boss the transfer goal and asking for help (create a support group), and (3) taking an assertiveness training course. In what situation may the manager be especially likely to experience a lapse? The manager identifies that she may be most likely to lapse back into an autocratic style when faced with a short time frame for making a decision (time pressure being an obstacle). The manager recognizes that it may be inappropriate to try to gain consensus for a decision when time constraints are severe and subordinates lack expertise. In the last step of the module, the manager suggests that she will (1) meet with her mentor to review her progress, (2) talk with other managers about how they effectively use participative decision making, and (3) resolve to communicate with other managers who attended the training session with her. The manager also commits to monitoring her use of participative decision making, noting successes and failures in a diary.

WORK ENVIRONMENT CHARACTERISTICS THAT INFLUENCE TRANSFER

As Figure 5.1 showed, several work environment characteristics influence transfer of training, including the climate for transfer, managerial and peer support, opportunity to perform, and technological support.

Climate for Transfer

Climate for transfer refers to trainees' perceptions about a wide variety of characteristics of the work environment that facilitate or inhibit use of trained skills or behavior. These characteristics include manager and peer support, opportunity to use skills, and the consequences for using learned capabilities.[13] Table 5.4 shows characteristics of a positive climate for transfer of training. Research has shown that transfer of training climate is significantly related to positive changes in managers' administrative and interpersonal behaviors following training. To support the transfer of financial training emphasizing Southwest Airlines's key business metrics, cost checklists explaining how employees can contribute to the company's bottom line are distributed companywide following training.[14] Flip charts showing highlights from manager-employee question-and-answer sessions are posted in work areas. All managers receive large posters displaying the company's four "magic numbers" (net income, unit cost measure, net margin, and invested capital). The posters include blank columns that managers are expected to complete and regularly update to show the past year's performance, the current year's goals, year-to-date numbers, and quarterly results.

Consider how Vanderbilt University Medical Center's work environment supports transfer of training. VUMC's team training program is designed to teach participants about patient safety mistakes and ways to avoid them, team building, cross-checking and communications, decision making, and performance feedback.[15] Several steps are taken to ensure that transfer of training occurs. Before the training starts, VUMC leaders are prepared to help the training succeed. Senior administrators, medical directors, and nursing staff attend a boot camp that highlights the team training program. A safety climate survey is conducted to determine how each department perceives the VUMC attitudes toward safety practices and patient safety issues. Then, each department is reviewed to find built-in errors that are system problems and to evaluate how the team communicates and deals with conflict. After the training, medical supervisors provide observation, coaching, and feedback. Checklists are provided for certain procedures, such as patient handoffs, medication administration, and briefing and debriefing sessions. These checklists help participants use the strategies emphasized in training to improve patient safety and the quality of patient care. Patients also help ensure safety. VUMC has created a video that patients are asked to watch when they are admitted to the hospital. The video emphasizes the importance of asking questions about medications and medical procedures.

TABLE 5.4   **Characteristics of a Positive Climate for Transfer of Training**

Characteristic	Example
Supervisors and co-workers encourage and set goals for trainees to use new skills and behaviors acquired in training.	Newly trained managers discuss how to apply their training on the job with their supervisors and other managers.
Task cues: Characteristics of a trainee's job prompt or remind him or her to use new skills and behaviors acquired in training.	The job of a newly trained manager is designed in such a way as to allow him or her to use the skills taught in training.
Feedback consequences: Supervisors support the application of new skills and behaviors acquired in training.	Supervisors notice newly trained managers who use their training.
Lack of punishment: Trainees are not openly discouraged from using new skills and behaviors acquired in training.	When newly trained managers fail to use their training, they are not reprimanded.
Extrinsic reinforcement consequences: Trainees receive extrinsic rewards for using new skills and behaviors acquired in training.	Newly trained managers who successfully use their training will receive a salary increase.
Intrinsic reinforcement consequences: Trainees receive intrinsic rewards for using new skills and behaviors acquired in training.	Supervisors and other managers appreciate newly trained managers who perform their job as taught in training.

Source: Adapted from J. B. Tracey, S. I. Tannenbaum, and M. J. Kavanagh, "Applying Trained Skills on the Job: The Importance of the Work Environment," *Journal of Applied Psychology* 80 (1995): 235–52; E. Holton, "What's *Really* Wrong: Diagnosis for Learning Transfer System Change," in *Improving Learning Transfer in Organizations,* ed. E. Holton and T. Baldwin (San Francisco: Jossey-Bass, 2003): 59–79.

Manager Support

Manager support refers to the degree to which trainees' managers (1) emphasize the importance of attending training programs and (2) stress the application of training content to the job. Managers can communicate expectations to trainees as well as provide the encouragement and resources needed to apply training on the job. One company asked trainees and their bosses to prepare and send memos to each other. The memos described what the other person should "start to do," "continue to do," "do less," or "stop doing" to improve learning transfer.[16]

Managers can provide different levels of support for training activities, as illustrated in Figure 5.2.[17] The greater the level of support, the more likely that transfer of training will occur. Managers should be actively involved in the design and delivery of training programs. The basic level of support that a manager can provide is acceptance, allowing trainees to attend training. The greatest level of support is to participate in training as an instructor (teaching in the program). Managers who serve as instructors are more likely to provide many of the lower-level support functions, such as reinforcing use of newly learned capabilities, discussing progress with trainees, and providing opportunities to practice. To maximize transfer of training, trainers need to achieve the highest level of support possible. Managers can also facilitate transfer through reinforcement (use of action plans). An **action plan** is a written document that includes the steps that the trainee and manager will take to ensure that training transfers to the job (see Figure 5.3). The action plan includes (1) a goal identifying what training content will be used and how it

FIGURE 5.2

Levels of Management Support for Training

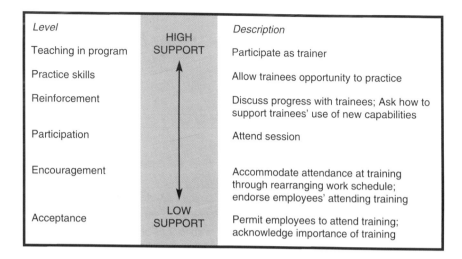

Level		Description
Teaching in program	HIGH SUPPORT	Participate as trainer
Practice skills		Allow trainees opportunity to practice
Reinforcement		Discuss progress with trainees; Ask how to support trainees' use of new capabilities
Participation		Attend session
Encouragement		Accommodate attendance at training through rearranging work schedule; endorse employees' attending training
Acceptance	LOW SUPPORT	Permit employees to attend training; acknowledge importance of training

will be used (project, problem), (2) strategies for reaching the goal (including what the trainee will do differently, resources needed, and type of support from managers and peers), (3) strategies for receiving feedback, and (4) expected results. The action plan also provides a progress check schedule of specific dates and times when the manager and trainee agree to meet to discuss the progress being made in using learned capabilities on the job. The action planning process should start by identifying the goal and the strategies for reaching the goal. Once those are determined, strategies for obtaining feedback and identifying what goal accomplishment will look like are completed. To complete their action plans, trainees may need additional technical support, such as access to experts who can answer questions or reference materials. Trainers or project managers can help trainees get the resources they need to complete their action plans through either face-to-face or electronic meetings.

Table 5.5 presents a checklist that can be used to determine the level of manager support for training. The more statements that managers agree with, the greater their level of support for the training program. There are several ways to gain managers' support for training.[18] First, managers need to be briefed on the purpose of the program and its relationship to business objectives and the business strategy. Managers should be given the schedule of topics and a checklist of what they should do after the training to ensure that transfer occurs. Second, trainees should be encouraged to bring to the training session work problems and situations they face on the job. These can be used as practice exercises or put into action plans. Trainees should jointly identify the problems and situations with their manager. Third, information regarding the benefits of the course collected from past participants should be shared with managers. Fourth, trainers can assign trainees to complete action plans with their managers. Fifth, if possible, use managers as trainers. That is, train the managers first, and then give them responsibility to train their subordinates.

Mac's Convenience Stores in Toronto, Ontario, Canada, wanted market managers to provide more business consulting to the stores as well as to make sure the stores looked good, the employees were wearing clean uniforms, good customer service was being provided, and health and safety information was being posted.[19] Financial understanding was made a key competency for the position and market managers were trained. To help ensure

FIGURE 5.3
Sample Action Plan

Training Topic _____
Goal *Include training content (knowledge, skill, behavior, competency, etc.) and application (project, problem, etc.)*

Strategies for reaching goal
Modifying behavior (What will I do differently?)
_____
_____
_____
_____

Resources needed (equipment, financial)
_____
_____
_____
_____

Support from peers and manager (Be as specific as possible.)
_____
_____
_____
_____

Strategies for receiving feedback about my progress *(Include meetings with peers and managers, self-monitoring of progress, customer reactions, etc.)*
_____
_____
_____
_____

Expected Results *(When I reach the goal, what will be different? Who will notice the difference? What will they notice?)*

What will be different?
_____
_____
_____

Who will notice?
_____
_____
_____

What will they notice?
_____
_____
_____

Progress Date Checks _____ _____ _____

transfer of training, working with store operators to build sales was made an important job requirement as well as a part of market managers' performance evaluation and pay. Also, market managers were held accountable for providing financial training to store operators. The training has resulted in profitability increases and a reduction in costs related to employee theft and shoplifting ("shrink") throughout Ontario.

At a minimum, special sessions should be scheduled with managers to explain the purpose of the training and to set expectations that they will encourage attendance at the

TABLE 5.5
**Checklist for
Determining
Level of
Manager
Support for
Training**

Source: Based on
A. Rossett, "That
Was a Great Class,
But . . . ," *Training
and Development*
(July 1997): 21.

	Agree	Disagree
I have a good sense of what the class is about.		
I know how the training matches what I need employees to do.		
There are tangible ways that the training will help employees.		
There are tangible ways that the training will help our unit.		
I can see why the organization is interested in providing the training.		
In performance appraisals, I can evaluate employees on what they learn in the class.		
I know enough about the training to support employees when they return to work.		
We have the tools and technologies that will be discussed in the class.		
I'm glad employees are attending the class.		
I've discussed the topic and the class with the employees who will participate.		
Employees know that I care about what will be taught in the class.		
I am accountable for employees using the training content in their jobs.		

training session, provide practice opportunities, reinforce use of training, and follow up with trainees to determine the progress in using newly acquired capabilities.

Alltel Corporation, a telecommunications company, uses managers as trainers.[20] When changes in systems, products, or policies occur, managers are the primary trainers for employees. Alltel uses a series of monthly teleconferences to educate managers in the field about new marketing strategies, new rate plans, new wireless or data services, and new offerings in products such as telephone headsets. The emphasis in the sessions is not only on communicating changes but also on teaching the managers to effectively use learning principles to train employees. For example, the teleconferences might have managers participate in a role play designed to teach salespeople how to talk to customers about an equipment upgrade.

KLA-Tencor, a supplier of process control solutions for the semiconductor industry, values training and development, invests in training and development, and ties it to the business strategy. For example, the company was recently ranked fifth in *Training* magazine's Top 100. Because of the high level of investment in training, KLA-Tencor takes several steps with employees and managers to ensure that training is taken seriously and is used on the job.[21]

One of the company's concerns was that too many employees were viewing training as a vacation from their job. To deal with this concern, KLA-Tencor has incorporated a pass/fail policy into its training curriculum. If an employee fails any section within a training course, management action is immediately taken. The employee is removed from the course, and a performance improvement plan is developed that requires the employee to retake the course. The pass/fail policy has resulted in improved employee competency levels, a reduction in marginally performing employees, and savings of $1.4 million. But the most important result has been that the policy has changed employees' view of training. Instead of quickly leaving when a training session has ended, trainees are staying late and forming study groups to complete homework and assignments. The class tardiness rate has dropped from 20 percent to zero. The pass/fail policy has also boosted the morale of the technical instructors because they can see that students are actually learning and are interested in the courses.

Managers pay attention to the development of their staff because part of their incentive plan is based on training and development. The incentive plan comprises fiscal, productivity, and strategic goals. Training and development is considered a strategic goal. Typically, 10 percent to 30 percent of a manager's bonus pay is based on development. For some managers, as much as 75 percent of their bonus pay can be based on staff development as measured by employee training and certification levels. The percentage varies depending on how critical the training is for business operations. The incentive plans also help the employees receive bonuses, which are tied to productivity goals. Only employees who maintain training and certification levels are eligible for productivity bonuses. For some jobs, such as service engineer, bonuses can range from 10 percent to 15 percent. This incentive plan makes training the responsibility of not only the managers but also each employee.

Peer Support

Transfer of training can also be enhanced by a support network among the trainees.[22] A **support network** is a group of two or more trainees who agree to meet and discuss their progress in using learned capabilities on the job. This may involve face-to-face meetings or communications via e-mail. Trainees may share successful experiences in using training content on the job. They might also discuss how they obtained resources needed to use training content or how they coped with a work environment that interfered with use of training content. One midwestern company scheduled a series of meetings with each training group between 2 and 12 weeks following their training session.[23] The more peer meetings that trainees attended, especially trainees who felt there was weak management support for training, the more learning transferred to the workplace.

Trainers might also use a newsletter to show how trainees are dealing with transfer of training issues. Distributed to all trainees, the newsletter might feature interviews with trainees who have been successful in using new skills. Trainers may also provide trainees with a mentor—a more experienced employee who previously attended the same training program, or a peer. The mentor can provide advice and support related to transfer of training issues (e.g., how to find opportunities to use the learned capabilities).

Opportunity to Use Learned Capabilities

Opportunity to use learned capabilities **(opportunity to perform)** refers to the extent to which the trainee is provided with or actively seeks experiences that allow for application of the newly learned knowledge, skill, and behaviors from the training program. Opportunity to perform is influenced by both the work environment and trainee motivation. One way trainees have the opportunity to use learned capabilities is through assigned work experiences (e.g., problems, tasks) that require their use. The trainees' manager usually plays a key role in determining work assignments. Opportunity to perform is also influenced by the degree to which trainees take personal responsibility to actively seek out assignments that allow them to use newly acquired capabilities.

Opportunity to perform is determined by breadth, activity level, and task type.[24] *Breadth* includes the number of trained tasks performed on the job. *Activity level* is the number of times or the frequency with which trained tasks are performed on the job. *Task type* refers to the difficulty or criticality of the trained tasks that are actually performed on the job. Trainees who are given opportunities to use training content on the job are more likely to maintain learned capabilities than trainees given few opportunities.[25]

Opportunity to perform can be measured by asking former trainees to indicate (1) whether they perform a task, (2) how many times they perform the task, and (3) the extent to which they perform difficult and challenging tasks. Individuals who report low levels of opportunity to perform may be prime candidates for "refresher courses" (courses designed to let trainees practice and review training content). Refresher courses are necessary because these persons have likely experienced a decay in learned capabilities because they have not had opportunities to perform. Low levels of opportunity to perform may also indicate that the work environment is interfering with using new skills. For example, the manager may not support training activities or give the employee the opportunity to perform tasks using skills emphasized in training. Finally, low levels of opportunity to perform may indicate that training content is not important for the employee's job.

Technological Support

Electronic performance support systems (EPSSs) are computer applications that can provide, as requested, skills training, information access, and expert advice.[26] An EPSS may be used to enhance transfer of training by providing trainees with an electronic information source that they can refer to on an as-needed basis while they attempt to apply learned capabilities on the job. EPSS use in training is discussed in detail in Chapter 8.

Cagle's, an Atlanta-based poultry processor, uses EPSS for employees who maintain the chicken-processing machines.[27] Because the machines that measure and cut chickens are constantly increasing in sophistication, it is impossible to continually train technicians so that they know the equipment's details. However, technicians are trained on the basic procedures they need to know to maintain these types of machines. When the machines encounter a problem, the technicians rely on what they have learned in training as well as the EPSS, which provides more detailed instructions about the repairs. The EPSS system also tells technicians the availability of parts and where in inventory to find replacement parts. The EPSS consists of a postage-stamp–size computer monitor attached to a visor that magnifies the screen. The monitor is attached to a three-pound computer about half the size of a portable CD player. Attached to the visor is a microphone that the technician uses to give verbal commands to the computer. The EPSS helps employees diagnose and fix the machines very quickly. This speed is important, given that the plant processes more than 100,000 chickens a day and chicken is a perishable food product!

Trainers can also monitor trainees' use of EPSS, which provides the trainer with valuable information about the transfer of training problems that trainees are encountering. These problems might relate to the training design (e.g., lack of understanding of process or procedure) or work environment (e.g., trainees either not having or not being able to find resources or equipment needed to complete an assignment).

ORGANIZATIONAL ENVIRONMENTS THAT ENCOURAGE TRANSFER

To ensure that trainees have the opportunity to perform, that managers and peers support training activities, that trainees are motivated to learn, and that the work environment is favorable for learning, many companies are attempting to become learning organizations and are concerned with knowledge management.

The Learning Organization

A **learning organization** is a company that has an enhanced capacity to learn, adapt, and change.[28] Training processes are carefully scrutinized and aligned with company goals. In a learning organization, training is seen as one part of a system designed to create human capital. Recall from Chapter 2 that human capital includes not only teaching employees basic capabilities needed to perform their current jobs but also stimulating creativity and innovation plus motivating employees to acquire and apply knowledge. King Arthur Flour Company encourages its 160 employees to learn about baking to motivate them to perform their jobs and to help customers better understand its product.[29] Employees are offered about 15 "Brain Food" classes each year. In these classes, their peers teach topics ranging from how to bake whole-grain breads to how to read company financial statements and manage their personal finances. All employees are encouraged to attend the classes, which are voluntary and held during work hours. Employees can also attend classes the company offers for professional and home bakers.

The essential features of a learning organization appear in Table 5.6. Note that the learning organization emphasizes that learning occurs not only at the individual employee level (as we traditionally think of learning), but also at the group and organizational levels. The learning organization emphasizes knowledge management.

To become a successful learning organization, companies may be required not only to place a greater emphasis on training but also to change human resource management systems to support learning. Skandia Sweden is the world's 10th largest life insurance company; it operates in more than 20 countries.[30] Skandia has many of the features of a learning organization. It supports training and development, which is linked to the company's business goals. As part of Skandia's continuous learning efforts, the company developed a corporate university, provides tuition reimbursement, and encourages employees to take advantage of learning opportunities. But despite the encouragement, Skandia noticed an increase in turnover. Interviews revealed that employees were burned out from the pressure to both work and learn. Employees were having difficulties meeting their personal obligations at home because they were busy developing new competencies at work. Skandia came up with a solution to support both learning and work. The company created a new benefit: a competency savings account in which, like a 401(k) account, Skandia matches the employee contribution. Employees can take time off to learn while still receiving a full salary, and the company uses the funds in the competency account to hire a temporary employee to fill the position. Skandia matches, at a rate of 3 to 1, the contributions by employees with minimum education, employees with 15 or more years experience, or employees who are more than 45 years old. The company views these employees as being at risk because their knowledge or skill is inadequate for current and future business. Skandia also created a Web site where employees can develop and manage their own growth plans.

TABLE 5.6   Key Features of a Learning Organization

Supportive Learning Environment

- Employees feel safe expressing their thoughts about work, asking questions, disagreeing with managers, or admitting mistakes.
- Different functional and cultural perspectives are appreciated.
- Employees are encouraged to take risks, innovate, and explore the untested and unknown, such as trying new processes and developing new products and services.
- Thoughtful review of the company's processes is encouraged.

Learning Processes and Practices

- Knowledge creation, dissemination, sharing, and application are practiced.
- Systems are developed for creating, capturing, and sharing knowledge.

Managers Reinforce Learning

- Managers actively question and listen to employees, encouraging dialogues and debate.
- Managers are willing to consider alternative points of view.
- Time is devoted to problem identification, learning processes and practices, and post-performance audits.
- Learning is rewarded, promoted, and supported.

Source: Based on D. Garvin, A. Edmondson, and F. Gino, "Is Yours a Learning Organization?" *Harvard Business Review* (March 2008): 109–116; M. Gephart, V. Marsick, M. Van Buren, and M Spiro, "Learning Organizations Come Alive," *Training and Development* 50 (1996): 34–45.

Knowledge and Knowledge Management

Recall from Chapter 2 that knowledge refers to what individuals or teams of employees know or know how to do (human and social knowledge) as well as a company's rules, processes, tools, and routines (structured knowledge). Knowledge is either tacit knowledge or explicit knowledge. Tacit knowledge is personal knowledge based on individual experience and influenced by perceptions and values. The communication of tacit knowledge requires personal communications through discussion and demonstrations. Explicit knowledge refers to manuals, formulas, and specifications that are described in formal language. Explicit knowledge can be managed by placing it in a knowledge database or it can be managed by a knowledge management system. For example, Fluor Corporation has a Web-based knowledge system that gives employees access to all procedures, guidelines, standards, and best practices needed for their specific job function.[31]

There are four modes of knowledge sharing: socialization, externalization, combination, and internalization. These are shown in Figure 5.4. **Socialization** involves sharing tacit knowledge by sharing experiences. Knowledge is shared and learning occurs through observation, imitation, and practice. **Externalization** involves translating tacit knowledge into explicit knowledge. This takes the form of metaphors, models, concepts, and equations. **Combination** involves systematizing explicit concepts into a knowledge system by analyzing, categorizing, and using information in a new way. Formal courses and seminars convert knowledge in this way. **Internalization** refers to converting explicit knowledge to tacit knowledge. Training methods such as simulations, action learning, and on-the-job experiences are used to create tacit knowledge from explicit knowledge.

As mentioned in Chapter 1, many companies are trying to find ways to capture and share the explicit and tacit knowledge of experienced older employees.[32] LyondellBasell, a

FIGURE 5.4

Four Modes of Knowledge Sharing

Source: I. Nonaka and H. Takeuchi, *The Knowledge Creating Company* (New York: Oxford University Press, 1995).

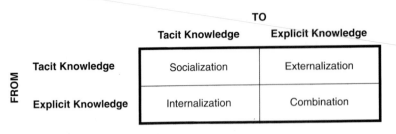

	TO	
	Tacit Knowledge	**Explicit Knowledge**
FROM Tacit Knowledge	Socialization	Externalization
Explicit Knowledge	Internalization	Combination

polymer manufacturer based in Clinton, Iowa, started a knowledge management program because the company projected that many employees would soon be retiring. The first step was asking key employees to take notes on what they had learned during their tenure, especially regarding knowledge that they knew was not already documented. The company also hired a consulting firm to help its knowledge management efforts. Carefully structured interviews were conducted with employees to better understand difficult tasks that lacked well-documented procedures. For example, an interview with a chemical specialist revealed that when a chemical reaches a specific fluidity and color it is ready to be used. That portion of the interview was videotaped so that future employees would have a reference to the correct color of the solution.

Motivated by the expected high retirement rates of technical-service engineers across the U.S., 3M has also taken several steps to manage knowledge. First, 3M has a searchable knowledge base, known as Maven, that gives all 3M employees access to job information from 2,000 technical-service engineers around the world. Second, 3M has a corporate wiki that employees use to categorize and share expertise. Third, 3M uses a technique known as storytelling. Storytelling involves having a 3M department identify important business situations that can adversely affect the business (such as a repair to production equipment that makes it unavailable). Groups of experts, including production, maintenance, and engineering employees, are asked to attend meetings where they explain how they have dealt with the situation. Their diagnosis is captured and published so that other less experienced employees can access their solutions on an as-needed basis.

Knowledge management refers to the process of enhancing company performance by designing and implementing tools, processes, systems, structures, and cultures to improve the creation, sharing, and use of knowledge.[33] Knowledge management can help companies get products to market quicker, better serve customers, develop innovative products and services, and attract new employees and retain current ones by giving people the opportunity to learn and develop.

How might knowledge management occur? There are several ways to help create, share, and use knowledge:[34]

1. Use technology, e-mail, and social networking sites (such as Facebook or MySpace) or portals on the company intranet that allow people to store information and share it with others.

2. Publish directories that list what employees do, how they can be contacted, and the type of knowledge they have.

3. Develop informational maps that identify where specific knowledge is stored in the company.

4. Create chief information officer and chief learning officer positions for cataloging and facilitating the exchange of information in the company.

5. Require employees to give presentations to other employees about what they have learned from training programs they have attended.

6. Allow employees to take time off from work to acquire knowledge, study problems, attend training, and use technology.

7. Create an online library of learning resources such as journals, technical manuals, training opportunities, and seminars.

8. Design office space to facilitate interaction between employees.

9. Create communities of practice using face-to-face meetings, wikis, or blogs for employees who share a common interest in a subject (e.g., product, service, customer, type of problem) where they can collaborate and share ideas, solutions, and innovations.

10. Use "after-action reviews" at the end of each project to review what happened and what can be learned from it.

Consider the following examples of how companies use different ways to share and create knowledge. Nokia Corporation, the mobile phone maker, takes advantange of local innovations around the world by setting up Web sites and wikis to encourage employees to share what they know.[35] Researchers are invited to record their findings in blogs and collaborate with universities, design firms, and telecommunications industry partners. Nokia's technical know-how and broader understanding of the way different cultures address mobility have helped the firm remain competitive in the world's mobile phone market. At Choice Hotels International, departments hold "Link and Learns" and open houses to help employees understand what their department does and how they can collaborate with employees across the company.[36]

Knowledge sharing can involve reviews or audits of projects after they are completed, followed by sharing insights gained from the review with other employees. For example, the U.S. Army's "After Action Review" process, adopted by many companies, involves a review of every mission, project, or critical activity.[37] The review involves considering four questions: (1) What did we set out to do? (2) What actually happened? (3) Why did it happen? and (4) What do we do (stop doing, continue to do, consider doing) next? Lessons learned are made available through Web sites and debriefings up and down the Army leadership command. Steelcase University Learning Center provides the physical space necessary for sharing knowledge.[38] It provides "information zones" that include whiteboards and tack boards throughout the space. It has flexible furniture arrangements that can accommodate new technologies and can offer individual privacy or can promote group work or collaborative learning.

At MWH Global, an engineering and environmental consulting company, a software program was used to analyze data from employees about which colleagues they most frequently interacted with and whom they turned to for expertise.[39] The program plotted a web of interconnecting nodes and lines representing people and relationships. The web provides a corporate map of how work gets done and who the well-connected technical experts are, and it helps identify informal connections among people that are missing on a traditional organizational chart. Solvay, a Belgian pharmaceutical and chemical company, uses maps to facilitate innovation. After inviting university researchers to the company, Solvay mapped its scientists' internal and external networks before and after the event to see where research overlapped and where the potential existed for collaboration.

Caterpillar has moved toward becoming a learning organization with the help of knowledge management.[40] Thirty years ago Caterpillar, a manufacturer of construction and mining equipment, engines, and gas turbines, had most of its value in plants and physical equipment. Today, intangible assets such as human capital account for most of the company's value. In 2001, Caterpillar began to make the transition to a learning organization in response to new technology, a changing market, and an older work force that would begin retiring. The centerpiece of the movement to a learning organization is Caterpillar University and its learning philosophy, which includes an emphasis on building leadership, sharing knowledge, and creating a learning culture.

Caterpillar's knowledge sharing system, a Web-based system known as Knowledge Network, has 3,000 communities of practice. They range in size from small teams to hundreds of employees from across the world. The communities of practice are used to distribute information, post questions, provide space for reference materials, and provide links to standards and regulations relevant to the community. One community of practice focuses on bolted joints and fasteners. The community of practice gives specialized engineers who generally work alone in manufacturing facilities the ability to ask other engineers questions or get second opinions on designs and problems. Caterpillar also has external communities of practice made up of dealers, suppliers, and customers.

Caterpillar's communities of practice using the Knowledge Network have resulted in improved decision making, increased collaboration and teamwork, improved work quality, and better product design and development. For example, members of the Bolted Joints and Fasteners community and the Dealer Service Training community saved more than $1.5 million from online discussions. The company also tracks participation using metrics such as the number of discussions and the number of people logged into the system, with the goal of increasing the amount of discussion and activity in the system.

Keys for Effective Knowledge Management

There are several key considerations for effective knowledge management. They include collaboration between training and the information technology department, creating leadership positions in charge of knowledge management, providing easy-to-use technology, and ensuring employee trust and willingness to share knowledge.

Training and Information Technology Collaboration   For knowledge management to be effective, the training department and information technology department must collaborate.[41] Training can help develop the culture as well as the content and learning strategies. Information technology develops the systems for accessing, sharing, and storing knowledge and delivering training. For example, the Royal Bank of Canada intranet serves as the central depository for information about initiatives completed, planned, or under way in the company. It also contains templates and other tools for training project managers. A separate Web site features summaries posted by employees who have attended conferences and courses. Technologists developed the infrastructure and trainers recommended what features should be included.[42] After every U.S. Army mission, project, or critical activity, the lessons learned are identified, codified, and made accessible through Web sites.[43] The lessons learned include an evaluation of the four simple but critical questions described earlier (What did we set out to do? What happened? Why did it happen? and What will we do again the next time and what will we try to improve?) The Center for Army Lessons Learned (CALL) has created a lessons learned network which has disseminated more than 265,000 products, briefed more than 54,000 soldiers and leaders, and transferred more than 24,000 lessons from military and civilian analysts to forces both in combat and stationed in the United States.

Create Knowledge Management Leadership Positions   Some companies, such as IBM, General Mills, and Randstad of North America, have created leadership positions to foster continuous learning and knowledge management.[44] For example, the chief learning officer at Ernst & Young is responsible for all formal training in North and South America. He is the main client for Intellinex, a subsidiary spun off from Ernst & Young's internal training operation. The chief learning officer also works with internal managers responsible for organizational development and knowledge management. By creating a position that is considered to be part of the company's top management team, a signal is sent to all employees that learning is valued and knowledge management is seen as being related to business strategy and critical for the company's success. **Chief learning, or knowledge, officers (CLOs)** are leaders of a company's knowledge management efforts. The CLO's job is to develop, implement, and link a knowledge/learning culture with the company's technology infrastructure, including databases and intranet. CLOs locate knowledge and find ways to create, capture, and distribute it. The CLO has to ensure that trainers, information technologists, and business units support and contribute to the development of knowledge management practices. The CLO also is responsible for actively supporting strategic business objectives by providing management direction and support for learning and development activities and by ensuring that knowledge management translates into visible benefits for the business.[45] For example, the CLO at Computer Sciences Corporation sponsors a Learning Officer Council that includes learning officers from the business units who help her understand the training and development needs of the company.[46] Her Department of Global Learning and Development recently created a development program designed to meet the learning needs of 1,800 senior executives and managers with high potential. The program is sponsored by the company's board of directors, chief operating officer, and chief executive officer. At Whirlpool, an appliance company, knowledge management has led to the development of "innovation mentors" around the world who encourage employees to try out new ideas.[47]

Easy-to-Use Technology   Knowledge management systems fail for two reasons: the technology is too complicated or companies don't give enough consideration to how to motivate employees to share knowledge.[48] Knowledge management systems can make it harder, not easier, for employees to perform their jobs. If the system asks employees to use multiple search engines, collaboration tools, and document management software all on different computer systems, the knowledge management system won't be used. It is important to build the correct technology infrastructure and make it easy for employees to access and share information within the context of their job. A new approach to knowledge management imbeds knowledge into the work flow of the job. For example, to help physicians keep up with the many new articles on diseases, medication, and research that are added to the medical literature each year, Partners HealthCare imbeds knowledge though an online patient order management system.[49] The system links the most current clinical knowledge and the patient's history to the management system. The system may question physicians' actions, and they have to respond with a reason. Of course, the physicians still have the ability to override the system.

The sales support staff at ExactTarget Inc., a software company, was having difficulty answering all of the questions about products and clients from its 75 sales representatives.[50] Some of the technical questions took many hours to answer and many of the same questions were asked by different sales representatives. To answer the questions, ExactTarget started getting sales representatives to answer each other's questions using a Web site where all posted questions and answers are stored. The Web site is accessible from a computer, hand-held device, or mobile phone. Sales representatives can subscribe to e-mail alerts every time a new question is posted. The sales representatives currently using the system are accessing it on average three times a week. Twelve sales reps who have found the system to be effective in their work are encouraging and showing others how to use it. Sales representatives can rank each others' questions and answers using a five-star scale to identify the most useful posts or to identify inaccurate or incorrect postings. The search function on the site shows the postings with the highest rankings. Besides posting questions and answers, the sales reps can post useful information or documents they find in their work. ExactTarget is combining the informal information exchange between sales representatives with formal training. The company has posted 25 training videos and case studies and plans to post more sales training information, client case studies, and videos with online quizzes that the sales reps will be required to pass in order to become certified as competent to sell certain software products or services.

Employee Trust and Willingness to Share Information   Trust and a willingness to share information are key personal factors that relate to knowledge sharing. Employees may not know or trust other employees, may hoard knowledge to have power over others, may fear that their ideas will be ridiculed or challenged, or may see knowledge sharing as involving too much work and additional responsibility.[51] To encourage knowledge sharing, companies must recognize and promote employees who learn, teach, and share. For example, the incentive for Xerox field technicians around the world to contribute to the company's maintenance tips database is that they become known as a thought leader or expert.[52] When the system was first available, technicians did not find it natural to submit what they knew. To overcome the engineers' anxiety, managers submitted suggestions from engineers at company headquarters and offered rewards such as cash and T-shirts for submitting tips. Managers also featured the names of people who did contribute, resulting in submitters' receiving notes from individuals who found their submissions to be helpful. Today, the system holds 70,000 suggestions and saves the company millions of dollars a year in repair costs. Other ways to encourage knowledge sharing are to show that ideas that are shared are used by the company and to show successes. AT&T used knowledge sharing to help global sales force teams share competitive information, which was useful in closing sales.

Because knowledge management can potentially improve a company's competitive position, companies that are managing knowledge use several measures to evaluate the effectiveness of their knowledge management practices. (Evaluation is discussed in detail in Chapter 6.) These measures are related to company and customer benefits. They include the ability to attract and retain key employees; employee commitment to the company; the encouragement and facilitation of effective teamwork; the use of best practices and the review and updating of these practices; new product introductions; customer satisfaction; and repeat relationships with customers.[53]

Summary

Learning is an important aspect of any training program. But equally important is encouraging trainees to use learned capabilities on the job (transfer of training). This chapter discussed how trainee characteristics, training design features, and the work environment influence transfer of training. The chapter emphasized that good program design requires consideration of identical elements, stimulus generalization, and cognitive theories related to transfer of training. Trainees may need self-management skills to cope with a work environment that is not always conducive to transfer of training. The climate for transfer, manager and peer support, technology support, and opportunity to perform are features of the work environment that influence transfer of training. Transfer of training is an important issue to companies that consider themselves to be learning organizations. Recognizing the value of human, social, and structural knowledge, many companies are attempting to become learning organizations and to manage knowledge in order to develop better products and improve customer service.

Key Terms

transfer of training, *187*
generalization, *187*
maintenance, *187*
training design, *187*
trainee characteristics, *187*
work environment, *188*
theory of identical elements, *189*
fidelity, *190*
near transfer, *190*
stimulus generalization approach, *191*
far transfer, *191*

key behaviors, *191*
cognitive theory of transfer, *191*
application assignments, *192*
self-management, *192*
lapses, *193*
climate for transfer, *195*
manager support, *196*
action plan, *196*
support network, *200*
opportunity to perform, *200*

electronic performance support systems (EPSSs), *201*
learning organization, *202*
socialization, *203*
externalization, *203*
combination, *203*
internalization, *203*
knowledge management, *204*
chief learning, or knowledge, officers (CLOs), *207*

Discussion Questions

1. Consider three time periods (pretraining, during training, and after training) and three parties involved in transfer of training (manager, trainer, trainee). Construct a matrix showing what each party can do to facilitate transfer of training at each time period.

2. Distinguish between the following: (1) maintenance and generalization and (2) learning and transfer.

3. What could be done to increase the likelihood of transfer of training if the work environment conditions are unfavorable and cannot be changed?

4. Discuss how trainees can support each other so that transfer of training occurs.

5. Which is the most important feature of the learning organization? Which is least important? Why?

6. What technologies might be useful for ensuring transfer of training? Briefly describe each technology and how it could be used.

7. How might you motivate managers to play a more active role in ensuring transfer of training?

8. Is training transfer an important issue in the companies where you have worked? How is transfer evaluated in those companies?

9. Discuss the major emphases of the identical elements, stimulus generalization, and cognitive theories of transfer.

10. What is knowledge? Why is knowledge important? How can companies manage knowledge?

Application Assignments

1. Develop a questionnaire to measure the degree to which the work environment supports transfer of training. Include the questions and the rating scales you would use. Use the checklist in Table 5.5 as an example.

2. Listed here are questions designed to measure trainees' motivation to transfer training. Ask several working friends, colleagues, or fellow employees these questions. Also, ask them to discuss why they responded the way they did.

   For each of the following statements, indicate whether you strongly agree, somewhat agree, somewhat disagree, or strongly disagree.

   a. The skills and knowledge I have obtained by attending training programs have been helpful in solving work-related problems.

   b. Before I attend training programs, I usually consider how I will use the content of the program.

   c. I believe my job performance will likely improve if I use the knowledge and skills acquired in training programs.

   d. It is unrealistic to believe that mastering the content of training programs can improve my work productivity.

   e. I am usually able to use skills or knowledge acquired in training programs in my work.

   f. There are usually more problems than the trainers realize in applying training program content in my daily work activities.

   g. Before I attend training programs, I usually identify particular problems or projects that I would like the training to help me with.

   Prepare a written summary of what you learned about motivation to transfer training.

3. Design an action planning sheet that a manager and employee could use to facilitate transfer of training. Justify each category included in the action plan.

4. Develop specific recommendations that the instructor could use to make this class a learning organization.

5. This assignment relates to Application Assignment 2 in Chapter 4. You now receive the following e-mail from the vice president of operations. Prepare an answer.

Thanks for your recommendations regarding how to make the "Improving Service Quality Program" a success. To improve hotel staff ability to respond effectively to customer complaints (that is, "recovery"), we have incorporated many of your ideas into the program, including

a. Having trainees bring an example of a customer problem to class.

b. Giving trainees the opportunity to practice dealing with irate customers.

c. Providing trainees with feedback during role plays.

d. Having trainers identify and communicate objectives of the program to trainees.

e. Having trainers communicate to the trainees specific key behaviors related to customer service.

I am now concerned about how to make sure our training investments pay off. That is, I am really interested in seeing the employees effectively and continuously apply in their jobs the skills and knowledge they have gained in training. What recommendations do you have?

6. Go to www.buckman.com, the Web site for Buckman Laboratories. Buckman Laboratories works with industries worldwide, providing advanced chemical treatment technologies and extensive technical service to help solve complex industrial problems. Its expertise spans a broad range of specialty chemicals including microbiocides, scale inhibitors, corrosion inhibitors, polymers, dispersants, and defoamers. Buckman has been recognized as a leader in knowledge management practices. Click on About Us. At the bottom of the page, click on Knowledge-Nurture, and then click on Resources. Read the presentations at this link. How does Buckman Laboratories manage knowledge? How has knowledge management contributed to the business?

7. Go to www.boozallenhamilton.com, the Web site for Booz Allen Hamilton, a consulting firm. Click on Careers. Review the links in this section of the Web site. Find out information about the company's training programs. Does the company have a work environment that supports training? Explain.

8. One way to diagnose transfer of training problems or to ensure that transfer of training occurs is to complete the matrix shown below. This matrix considers the responsibilities of the manager, the trainer, and the trainee for transfer of training before, during, and after training. Complete each cell of the matrix.

	Before Training	During Training	After Training
Manager			
Trainer			
Trainee			

Case: *Patagonia's Culture*

Patagonia sells outdoors sports clothes and sporting equipment through specialty retailers, a catalog, and stores in North America, Europe, Australia, and Japan. Patagonia is known for having a culture that emphasizes quality products and environmental awareness, and it gives employees the opportunity to grow and develop. This culture has attracted employees who have causal tastes, a motivation and passion to learn, and an active lifestyle. All of Patagonia's human resource management practices, including training and development, support the company's mission. For example, the company hires "dirtbags"—passionate outdoor people who are customers. Patagonia believes that it is easier to teach these people business than it is to turn a business salesperson into someone with a passion for the outdoors.

Patagonia hires primarily from within its current work force. Employee education is emphasized as much as product research and promotion. Patagonia provides employees with a minimum of 45 hours of training per year. The wide range of classes offered are designed to keep employees learning but are not necessarily related to employees' current jobs. These courses include an introduction to French culture, business and communications, Japanese style, and beginning sewing. Patagonia also has an internship program that allows employees to take time off from work.

How do Patagonia's practices contribute to creating a positive climate for learning and transfer of training?

Source: Based on J. Laabs, "Mixing Business with Passion," *Workforce* (March 2000): 80–87. Also, see Patagonia's Web site at www.patagonia.com.

Endnotes

1. J. Zenger, J. Folkman, and R. Sherwin, "Phase 3," *T + D* (January 2005): 30–35; L. Burke and H. Hutchins, "Training Transfer: An Integrative Review," *Human Resource Development Review* 6 (2007): 263–296.

2. M. L. Broad and J. W. Newstrom, *Transfer of Training* (Reading, MA: Addison-Wesley, 1992).

3. A. Saks and M. Belcourt, "An Investigation of Training Activities and Transfer of Training in Organizations," *Human Resource Management* 45 (2006): 629–648.

4. J. M. Royer, "Theories of the Transfer of Learning," *Educational Psychologist* 14 (1979): 53–69.

5. E. L. Thorndike and R. S. Woodworth, "The Influence of Improvement of One Mental Function upon the Efficiency of Other Functions," *Psychological Review* 8 (1901): 247–61.

6. J. F. Reintzell, "When Training Saves Lives," *Training and Development* 51 (1997): 41–42.

7. J. A. Sparrow, "The Measurement of Job Profile Similarity for the Prediction of Transfer of Learning," *Journal of Occupational Psychology* 62 (1989): 337–41.

8. M. Machin, "Planning, Managing, and Optimizing Transfer of Training," in *Creating, Implementing, and Managing Effective Training and Development,* ed. K.Kraiger (San Francisco: Jossey-Bass, 2002): 263–301; J.Kim and C.Lee, "Implications of Near and Far Transfer of Training on Structured On-the-Job Training," *Advances in Developing Human Resources* (November 2001): 442–51; S. L. Yelon and J. K. Ford, "Pursuing a Multidimensional View of Transfer," *Performance Improvement Quarterly* 12 (1999): 58–78.

9. Ibid.

10. J. Barbazette, *Managing the Training Function for Bottom Line Results* (San Francisco: Pfeiffer, 2008).

11. C. A. Frayne and J. M. Geringer, "Self-Management Training for Joint Venture General Managers," *Human Resource Planning* 15 (1993): 69–85; L. Burke and T. Baldwin, "Workforce Training Transfer: A Study of the Effect of Relapse Prevention Training and Transfer Climate," *Human Resource Management* (Fall 1999): 227–42; C. Frayne and J. Geringer, "Self-Management Training for Improving Job Performance: A Field Experiment Involving Salespeople," *Journal of Applied Psychology* (2000): 361–72.

12. A. Tziner, R. R. Haccoun, and A. Kadish, "Personal and Situational Characteristics Influencing the Effectiveness of Transfer of Training Strategies," *Journal of Occupational Psychology* 64 (1991): 167–77; R. A. Noe, J. A. Sears, and A. M. Fullenkamp, "Release Training: Does It Influence Trainees' Post-Training Behavior and Cognitive Strategies?" *Journal of Business and Psychology* 4 (1990): 317–28; M. E. Gist, C. K. Stevens, and A. G. Bavetta, "Effects of Self-Efficacy and Post-Training Intervention on the Acquisition and Maintenance of Complete Interpersonal Skills," *Personal Psychology* 44 (1991): 837–61; M. J. Tews and J. B. Tracey, "An Empirical Examination of Post Training On-the-Job Supplements for Enhancing the Effectiveness of Interpersonal Skills Training," *Personnel Psychology* 61 (2008): 375–401.

13. J. B. Tracey, S. I. Tannenbaum, and M. J. Kavanaugh, "Applying Trained Skills on the Job: The Importance of the Work Environment," *Journal of Applied Psychology* 80 (1995): 239–52; P. E. Tesluk, J. L. Farr,

J. E. Mathieu, and R. J. Vance, "Generalization of Employee Involvement Training to the Job Setting: Individual and Situational Effects,"*Personnel Psychology* 48 (1995): 607–32; J. K. Ford, M. A. Quinones, D. J. Sego, and J. S. Sorra, "Factors Affecting the Opportunity to Perform Trained Tasks on the Job," *Personnel Psychology* 45 (1992): 511–27; E. Holton, R. Bates, and W. Ruona, "Development of a Generalized Learning Transfer System Inventory,"*Human Resource Development Quarterly* 11 (2001): 333–60; K. Bunch, "Training Failure as a Consequence of Organizational Culture," *Human Resource Development Review* 6 (2007): 142–163.

14. S. Boehle, "Dollars and Sense," *Training* (June 2007): 42–45.

15. P. Keller, "Soaring to New Safety Heights," *T + D* (January 2006): 51–54.

16. H. Martin, "Lessons Learned," *The Wall Street Journal* (December 15, 2008): R11.

17. J. M. Cusimano, "Managers as Facilitators," *Training and Development* 50 (1996): 31–33; R. Bates, "Managers as Transfer Agents," in *Improving Learning Transfer in Organizations,* ed. E. Holton and T. Baldwin (San Francisco: Jossey-Bass, 2003): 243–70.

18. S. B. Parry, "Ten Ways to Get Management Buy-In,"*Training and Development* (September 1997): 21–22; Broad and Newstrom, *Transfer of Training.*

19. Boehle, "Dollars and Sense."

20. J. Gordon, "Getting Serious about Supervisory Training,"*Training* (February 2006): 27–29.

21. K. Ellis, "Developing for Dollars,"*Training* (May 2003): 34–39; G. Johnson, "KLA-Tencor,"*Training* (March 2003): 48–49.

22. C. M. Petrini, ed., "Bringing It Back to Work,"*Training and Development Journal* (December 1990): 15–21.

23. Martin, "Lessons Learned."

24. Ford, Quinones, Sego, and Sorra, "Factors Affecting the Opportunity to Perform Trained Tasks on the Job."

25. Ibid.; M. A. Quinones, J. K. Ford, D. J. Sego, and E. M. Smith, "The Effects of Individual and Transfer Environment Characteristics on the Opportunity to Perform Trained Tasks,"*Training Research Journal* 1 (1995/96): 29–48.

26. G. Stevens and E. Stevens, "The Truth about EPSS,"*Training and Development* 50 (1996): 59–61.

27. 'In Your Face EPSs,"*Training* (April 1996): 101–2.

28. M. A. Gephart, V. J. Marsick, M. E. Van Buren, and M. S. Spiro, "Learning Organizations Come Alive,"*Training and Development* 50 (1996): 35–45; C. M. Solomon, "HR Facilitates the Learning Organization Concept,"*Personnel Journal* (November 1994): 56–66; T. A. Stewart, "Getting Real about Brainpower,"*Fortune* (November 27, 1995): 201–3; L. Thornburg, "Accounting for Knowledge,"*HR Magazine* (October 1994): 51–56; V. Sessa and M. London, *Continuous Learning in Organizations* (Mahwah, NJ: Erlbaum, 2006).

29. *The Wall Street Journal* (October 13, 2008): R6. K. Spors, "Top Small Workplaces 2008: King Arthur Floor Co.

30. S. Hawkins, "The Competence Marketplace," *T + D* (December 2002): 60–62.

31. T. Davenport, L. Prusak, and B. Strong, "Putting Ideas to Work," *The Wall Street Journal* (March 10, 2008): R11.

32. J. Thilmany, "Passing on Knowledge," *HR Magazine* (June 2008): 100–104.

33. D. DeLong and L. Fahey, "Diagnosing Cultural Barriers to Knowledge Management," *Academy of Management Executive* 14 (2000): 113–27; A. Rossett, "Knowledge Management Meets Analysis," *Training and Development* (May 1999): 63–68; M. Van Buren, "A Yardstick for Knowledge Management," *Training and Development* (May 1999): 71–78.

34. Gephart, Marsick, Van Buren, and Spiro, "Learning Organizations Come Alive; Davenport, Prusak, and Strong, "Putting Ideas to Work."

35. Davenport, Prusak, and Strong, "Putting Ideas to Work."

36. K. Tyler, "15 Ways to Train on the Job," *HR Magazine* (September 2008): 105–108.

37. "Center for Army Lessons Learned Named in Info World 100 for 2008 Top IT Solutions," at http://usacac.army.mil/cacz/call/index.asp, Web site for the Ceater For Army Lessons Learned, accessed March 30, 2009.

38. "A Recipe for Sharing Knowledge,"*OD/Leadership Network News* (December 2005). Available at *www.steelcase.com/na/* (February 28, 2006).

39. J. MacGregor, "The Office Chart That Really Counts,"*BusinessWeek* (February 27, 2006): 48–49.

40. V. Powers, "Virtual Communities at Caterpillar Foster Knowledge Sharing," *T + D* (June 2004): 40–45.

41. J. Gordon, "Intellectual Capital and You," *Training* (September 1999): 30–38; D. Zielinski, "Have You Shared a Bright Idea Today?"*Training* (July 2000): 65–68.

42. K. Ellis, "Share Best Practices Globally," *Training* (July 2001): 32–38.

43. D. Garvin, A. Edmondson, and F. Gino, "Is Yours a Learning Organization?" *Harvard Business Review* (March 2008): 109–116; "Center For Army Lessons Learned Named in Info World 100 for 2008 Top IT Solutions."

44. D. Bonner, "Enter the Chief Knowledge Officer,"*Training and Development* (February 2000): 36–40; J. Gordon, "CLO: A Strategic Player?"*Training* (April 2005): 14–19.

45. T. O'Driscoll, B.Sugrue, and M. Vona, "The C-Level and the Value of Learning," *T + D* (October 2005): 70–77.

46. J. Salopek, "Computer Sciences Corporation," *T + D* (October 2005): 58.

47. D. Pringle, "Learning Gurus Adapt to Escape Corporate Axes,"*The Wall Street Journal,* (January 7, 2003): B1, B4.

48. P. Babcock, "Shedding Light on Knowledge Management,"*HR Magazine* (May 2004): 46–50; R. Davenport, "Does Knowledge Management Still Matter?" *T + D* (February 2005): 19–25.

49. Babcock, "Shedding Light on Knowledge Management."

50. K. Spors, "Getting Workers to Share Their Know-how with Their Peers," *The Wall Street Journal* (April 3, 2008): B6.

51. T. Aeppel, "On Factory Floor, Top Workers Hide Secrets to Success," *The Wall Street Journal* (July 1, 2002): A1, A10; D. Lepak and S. Snell, "Managing Human Resource Architecture for Knowledge-Based Competition," in *Managing Knowledge for Sustained Competitive Advantage,* ed. S. Jackson, M. Hitt, and A. DeNisi (San Francisco: Jossey-Bass, 2003): 127–54.

52. Thurm, "Companies Struggle to Pass On Knowledge That Workers Acquire,"*The Wall Street Journal,* (January 23, 2006): B1.

53. Van Buren, "A Yardstick for Knowledge Management"; L. Bassi and D. McMumer, "Developing Measurement Systems for Managing in the Knowledge Era," *Organizational Dynamics* 34 (2005): 185–96.

Training Evaluation

Objectives

After reading this chapter, you should be able to

1. Explain why evaluation is important.
2. Identify and choose outcomes to evaluate a training program.
3. Discuss the process used to plan and implement a good training evaluation.
4. Discuss the strengths and weaknesses of different evaluation designs.
5. Choose the appropriate evaluation design based on the characteristics of the company and the importance and purpose of the training.
6. Conduct a cost-benefit analysis for a training program.

Training and Leadership Development: A Healthy Investment at Sisters of Charity Providence Hospital

At Sisters of Charity Providence Hospital, a 304-bed hospital in Columbia, South Carolina, a training function that addresses performance gaps and supports quality service is a top priority. Training and development programs are linked to the hospital's strategic goals: to become an employer of choice and to provide service and operational excellence. It is not only important to develop programs supporting the strategy but also to provide evidence as to how they contribute. One priority has been to develop leaders from its current managers. The hospital's first program, Leading Edge, included a curriculum that focused on financial and performance management, identifying and recruiting top talent, and change management. The focus of the training was based on the middle managers' performance needs and weaknesses. The training used a variety of methods but each program included a set of team building activities and a performance review of the organization. Formal processes were implemented to hold leaders accountable for the performance of their area. The principle objectives included (1) increased earnings before interest, depreciation, and amortization and (2) improvement of employee and patient satisfaction. Each goal was met during the first year of the program and improvements have continued. For example, to measure a behavior change in manager feedback, questions were added to employee surveys. Results indicate that there has been a significant increase in feedback by leaders who have attended the training program.

Another priority has been to use training to improve patient care. This has led to the hospital's investment in a clinical simulation training program that recreates real patient experiences in a safe practice environment. Five practice patient rooms have been constructed, each with patient simulators. The "patients" can cough, vomit, and reproduce other bodily functions as well as communicate their medical needs. Employees can work alone or in teams during the simulations to improve their patient care and problem-solving skills. Trainers provide time for reflection and provide feedback to help employees learn. The realistic work environments have improved patient care and employee satisfaction has increased. Also, the retention rate for new first-year nurse graduates has increased 18 percent.

Source: Based on Sisters of Charity Providence Hospitals, "The Healthy Glow of Learning" *T + D* (October 2008): 63–64.

INTRODUCTION

As the opening vignette illustrates, the Sisters of Charity Providence Hospital training function wanted to show that the time, money, and effort devoted to training actually made a difference. That is, the training function was interested in assessing the effectiveness of training programs. **Training effectiveness** refers to the benefits that the company and the trainees receive from training. Benefits for trainees may include learning new skills or behavior. Benefits for the company may include increased sales and more satisfied customers. A training evaluation measures specific outcomes or criteria to determine the benefits of the program. **Training outcomes** or **criteria** refer to measures that the trainer and the company use to evaluate training programs. To determine the effectiveness of the program, the hospital had to conduct an evaluation. **Training evaluation** refers to the process of collecting the outcomes needed to determine whether training is effective. For Sisters of Charity Providence Hospital, some of the outcomes included an increase in feedback by leaders, financial indicators (e.g., increased earnings before interest), and an improvement in patient care satisfaction. The hospital also had to be confident that its information-gathering process was providing it with accurate conclusions about the effectiveness of its training programs. The **evaluation design** refers to the collection of information—including what, when, how, and from whom—that will be used to determine the effectiveness of the training program. Information about the evaluation design used by the hospital is not provided in the opening vignette. However, any organization that evaluates training has to be confident that training—rather than same other factor—is responsible for changes in the outcomes of interest (e.g., patient care and satisfactory earnings).

Recall the Instructional Systems Design model shown in Figure 1.1 and the topics covered in Chapters 2 through 5. The information from the needs assessment, the characteristics of the learning environment, and the steps taken to ensure transfer of training should all be used to develop an evaluation plan. In order to identify appropriate training outcomes, a company needs to look at its business strategy, its organizational analysis (Why are we conducting training? How is it related to the business?), its person analysis (Who needs training?), its task analysis (What is the training content?), the learning objectives of the training, and its plan for training transfer.

This chapter will help you understand why and how to evaluate training programs. The chapter begins by discussing the types of outcomes used in training program evaluation.

The next section of the chapter discusses issues related to choosing an evaluation design. An overview of the types of designs is presented. The practical factors that influence the type of design chosen for an evaluation are discussed. The chapter concludes by reviewing the process involved in conducting an evaluation.

REASONS FOR EVALUATING TRAINING

Companies are investing millions of dollars in training programs to help gain a competitive advantage. Companies invest in training because learning creates knowledge; often, it is this knowledge that distinguishes successful companies and employees from those who are not. Research summarizing the results of studies that have examined the linkage between training and human resource outcomes (attitudes and motivation, behaviors, human capital), organizational performance outcomes (performance and productivity), or financial outcomes (profits and financial indicators) has found that companies that conduct training are likely to have more positive human resource outcomes and greater performance outcomes.[1] The influence of training is largest for organizational performance outcomes and human resource outcomes and weakest for financial outcomes. This result is not surprising, given that training can least affect an organization's financial performance and may do so through its influence on human resource practices. As emphasized in Chapter 2, Strategic Training, training is more strongly related to organizational outcomes when it is matched with the organization's business strategy and capital intensity. Because companies have made large dollar investments in training and education and view training as a strategy to be successful, they expect the outcomes or benefits related to training to be measurable.

For example, consider CompUSA.[2] CompUSA's goal was to focus its human resource strategy by aligning it with the strategies for improving the business. Senior management believed that one way to promote growth was through building engagement with team members. Employee engagement includes employees' feelings toward support, recognition, development, and sharing the company's goals. Employee engagement results in satisfied employees, which translates into better customer service. CompUSA administered an engagement survey to more than 200 stores. The engagement survey results were used to build a strategic training plan. Each year the training function meets to discuss training priorities based on the survey results. Regional human resource managers as well as store managers set improvement goals. All employees are linked to the idea of creating a winning culture that promotes customer satisfaction. The engagement measure is used to track the influence of training programs. It is linked to company strategy, tracks progress over time, and has a direct link to training. The common use of engagement builds accountability for managers and provides a valued progress measure for the entire company.

Training evaluation provides a way to understand the investments that training produces and provides information needed to improve training.[3] If the company receives an inadequate return on its investment in training, the company will likely reduce its investment in training or look for training providers outside the company who can provide training experiences that improve performance, productivity, customer satisfaction, or whatever other outcomes the company is interested in achieving. Training evaluation provides the data needed to demonstrate that training does offer benefits to the company. Training evaluation involves both formative and summative evaluation.[4]

Formative Evaluation

Formative evaluation refers to the evaluation of training that takes place during program design and development. That is, formative evaluation helps to ensure that (1) the training program is well organized and runs smoothly and (2) trainees learn and are satisfied with the program. Formative evaluation provides information about how to make the program better; it usually involves collecting qualitative data about the program. Qualitative data include opinions, beliefs, and feelings about the program. Formative evaluations ask customers, employees, managers, and subject-matter experts their opinions on the description of the training content and objectives and the program design. These people are also asked to evaluate the clarity and ease of use of a part of the training program that is provided to them in the way that it will be delivered (e.g., online, face-to-face, video).[5] The formative evaluation is conducted either individually or in groups before the program is made available to the rest of the company. Trainers may also be involved to measure the time requirements of the program. As a result of the formative evaluation, training content may be changed to be more accurate, easier to understand, or more appealing. The training method can be adjusted to improve learning (e.g., provide trainees with more opportunities to practice or give feedback). Also, introducing the training program as early as possible to managers and customers helps in getting them to buy into the program, which is critical for their role in helping employees learn and transfer skills. It also allows their concerns to be addressed before the program is implemented.

Pilot testing refers to the process of previewing the training program with potential trainees and managers or with other customers (persons who are paying for the development of the program). Pilot testing can be used as a "dress rehearsal" to show the program to managers, trainees, and customers. It should also be used for formative evaluation. For example, a group of potential trainees and their managers may be asked to preview or pilot test a Web-based training program. As they complete the program, trainees and managers may be asked to provide their opinions as to whether graphics, videos, or music used in the program contributed to (or interfered with) learning. They may also be asked how easy it was to move through the program and complete the exercises, and they may be asked to evaluate the quality of feedback the training program provided after they completed the exercises. The information gained from this preview would be used by program developers to improve the program before it is made available to all employees. St. George Bank developed a new Web-based training system for bank tellers.[6] Before the program was provided to all bank tellers, it was reviewed by a small group of bank tellers considered to be typical users of the program. The tellers provided suggestions for improvement, and the instructional designers incorporated their suggestions into the final version of the program.

Summative Evaluation

Summative evaluation refers to an evaluation conducted to determine the extent to which trainees have changed as a result of participating in the training program. That is, have trainees acquired knowledge, skills, attitudes, behavior, or other outcomes identified in the training objectives? Summative evaluation may also include measuring the monetary benefits (also known as return on investment) that the company receives from the program. Summative evaluation usually involves collecting quantitative (numerical) data through tests, ratings of behavior, or objective measures of performance such as volume of sales, accidents, or patents.

From the discussion of summative and formative evaluation, it is probably apparent to you why a training program should be evaluated:

1. To identify the program's strengths and weaknesses. This includes determining if the program is meeting the learning objectives, if the quality of the learning environment is satisfactory, and if transfer of training to the job is occurring.

2. To assess whether the content, organization, and administration of the program— including the schedule, accommodations, trainers, and materials—contribute to learning and the use of training content on the job.

3. To identify which trainees benefit most or least from the program.

4. To assist in marketing programs through the collection of information from participants about whether they would recommend the program to others, why they attended the program, and their level of satisfaction with the program.

5. To determine the financial benefits and costs of the program.

6. To compare the costs and benefits of training versus nontraining investments (such as work redesign or a better employee selection system).

7. To compare the costs and benefits of different training programs to choose the best program.

OVERVIEW OF THE EVALUATION PROCESS

Before the chapter explains each aspect of training evaluation in detail, you need to understand the evaluation process, which is summarized in Figure 6.1. The previous discussion of formative and summative evaluation suggests that training evaluation involves scrutinizing the program both before and after the program is completed. Figure 6.1 emphasizes that training evaluation must be considered by managers and trainers before training has actually occurred. As was suggested earlier in this chapter, information gained from the training design process shown in Figure 1.1 is valuable for training evaluation.

The evaluation process should begin with determining training needs (as discussed in Chapter 3). Needs assessment helps identify what knowledge, skills, behavior, or other

FIGURE 6.1
The Evaluation Process

Source: Based on D. A. Grove and C. Ostroff, "Program Evaluation," in *Developing Human Resources,* ed. K. N. Wexley (Washington, DC: Bureau of National Affairs, 1991): 5–185 to 5–220; K. Kraiger, D. McLinden, and W. Casper, "Collaborative Planning for Training Impact," *Human Resource Management* (Winter 2004): 337–51.

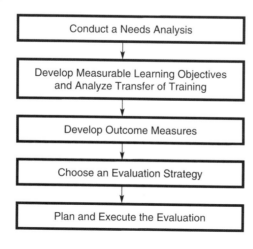

learned capabilities are needed. Needs assessment also helps identify where the training is expected to have an impact. Needs assessment helps focus the evaluation by identifying the purpose of the program, the resources needed (human, financial, company), and the outcomes that will provide evidence that the program has been effective.[7] The next step in the process is to identify specific, measurable training objectives to guide the program. The characteristics of good objectives are discussed in Chapter 4. The more specific and measurable these objectives are, the easier it is to identify relevant outcomes for the evaluation. Besides considering the learning and program objectives in developing learning outcomes, it is also important to consider the expectations of those individuals who support the program and have an interest in it (stakeholders such as trainees, managers, and trainers).[8] If the needs assessment was done well, the stakeholders' interests likely overlap considerably with the learning and program objectives. Analysis of the work environment to determine transfer of training (discussed in Chapter 5) can be useful for determining how training content will be used on the job. Based on the learning objectives and analysis of transfer of training, outcome measures are designed to assess the extent to which learning and transfer have occurred.

Once the outcomes have been identified, the next step is to determine an evaluation strategy. Factors such as expertise, how quickly the information is needed, change potential, and the organizational culture should be considered in choosing a design. Planning and executing the evaluation involves previewing the program (formative evaluation) as well as collecting training outcomes according to the evaluation design. The results of the evaluation are used to modify, market, or gain additional support for the program. The results of the evaluation should also be used to encourage all stakeholders in the training process—including managers, employees, and trainers—to design or choose training that helps the company meet its business strategy and helps managers and employees meet their goals.[9]

OUTCOMES USED IN THE EVALUATION OF TRAINING PROGRAMS

To evaluate its training program, a company must decide *how* it will determine the program's effectiveness; that is, it must identify what training outcomes or criteria it will measure.

One of the original frameworks for identifying and categorizing training outcomes was developed by Kirkpatrick. Table 6.1 shows Kirkpatrick's four-level framework for categorizing training outcomes.[10]

TABLE 6.1
Kirkpatrick's Four-Level Framework of Evaluation Criteria

The hierarchical nature of Kirkpatrick's framework suggests that higher level outcomes should not be measured unless positive changes occur in lower level outcomes. For example, if trainees do not like a course, no learning will occur. Also, the framework implies that changes at a higher level (e.g., results) are more beneficial than

Source: Based on D. L. Kirkpatrick, "Evaluation" in *The ASTD Training and Development Handbook* (2d ed.), ed. R. L. Craig (New York: McGraw-Hill, 1996): 294–312.

Level	Criteria	Focus
4	Results	Business results achieved by trainees
3	Behavior	Improvement of behavior on the job
2	Learning	Acquisition of knowledge, skills, attitudes, behavior
1	Reactions	Trainee satisfaction

changes at a lower level (e.g., learning). However, the framework has been criticized for a number of reasons. First, research has not found that each level is caused by the level that precedes it in the framework, nor does evidence suggest that the levels differ in importance.[11] Second, the approach does not take into account the purpose of the evaluation. The outcomes used for evaluation should relate to the training needs, the program learning objectives, and the strategic reasons for training. Third, use of the approach suggests that outcomes can and should be collected in an orderly manner, that is, measures of reaction followed by measures of learning, behavior, and results. Realistically, learning measures need to be collected at approximately the same time as reaction measures, near the end of the training program, in order to determine whether learning has occurred.

As a result of these criticisms, both training practitioners and academic researchers have developed a more comprehensive model of training criteria; that is, additional training outcomes have been added to Kirkpatrick's original framework. Accordingly, training outcomes have been classified into six categories, as shown in Table 6.2: reaction outcomes, learning or cognitive outcomes, behavior and skill-based outcomes, affective outcomes, results, and return on investment.[12]

Table 6.2 shows training outcomes, D.L. Kirkpatrick's five-level framework for categorizing training outcomes, and a description of each of the outcomes and how they are measured. Both level 1 and level 2 outcomes (reactions and learning) are collected at the completion of training, before trainees return to the job. Level 3 outcomes (behavior/skills) can also be collected at the completion of training to determine trainees' behavior or skill level at the completion of training. To determine whether trainees are using training content back on the job (i.e., whether transfer of training has occurred), level 3, level 4, and/or level 5 outcomes can be collected. Level 3 criteria can be collected to determine whether behavior/skills are being used on the job. Level 4 and level 5 criteria (results and return on investment) can also be used to determine whether training has resulted in an improvement in business results such as productivity or customer satisfaction. These criteria also help to determine whether the benefits of training exceed their costs.

Reaction Outcomes

Reaction outcomes refer to trainees' perceptions of the program, including the facilities, trainers, and content. (Reaction outcomes are often referred to as a measure of "creature comfort.") They are often called class or instructor evaluations. This information is typically collected at the program's conclusion. You probably have been asked to complete class or instructor evaluations either at the end of a college course or a training program at work. Reactions are useful for identifying what trainees thought was successful or what inhibited learning. Reaction outcomes are level 1 (reaction) criteria in Kirkpatrick's framework.

Reaction outcomes are typically collected via a questionnaire completed by trainees. A reaction measure should include questions related to the trainee's satisfaction with the instructor, training materials, and training administration (ease of registration, accuracy of course description) as well as the clarity of course objectives and usefulness of the training content.[13] Table 6.3 shows a reaction measure that contains questions about these areas.

TABLE 6.2   Evaluation Outcomes

Outcome or Criteria	Level	What Is Measured	Example	Method of Measurement
Reactions	1	Learners' satisfaction	Comfortable training room Useful materials and program content	Surveys Interviews
Learning or Cognitive	2	Principles, facts, techniques, procedures, or processes the learners have acquired	Electrical principles Safety rules Steps in interviewing	Tests Work samples
Behavior and skills	2 or 3	Technical or motor skills or behaviors acquired by learners	Preparing a dessert Sawing wood Landing an airplane Listening	Tests Observations Self, peer, customer, and/or managers' ratings Work samples
Affective	2 or 3	Learners' attitudes and motivation	Tolerance for diversity Safety attitudes Customer service orientation	Attitude surveys Interviews Focus groups
Results	4	Payoffs for the company	Productivity Quality Costs Repeat customers Customer satisfaction Accidents	Observation Performance data from records or company databases
Return on Investment	5	Identification and comparison of learning benefits with costs	Dollar value of productivity divided by training costs	Economic value

Source: Based on K. Kraiger, J. K. Ford, and E. Salas, "Application of Cognitive, skill-Based, and Affective Theories of Learning Outcomes to New Methods of Training Evaluation," *Journal of Applied Psychology* 78 (2) (1993): 311–328; K. Kraiger, "Decision-Based Evaluation," in K. Kraiger (ed.), *Creating, Implementing, and Managing Effective Training and Development* (San Francisco: Jossey-Bass, 2002): 331–375; D. Kirkpatrick, "Evaluation," in *The ASTD Training and Development Handbook*, 2nd ed., ed. R. L. Craig (New York: McGraw-Hill, 1996): 294–312.

TABLE 6.3 **Sample Reaction Measure**

Read each statement below. Indicate the extent to which you agree or disagree with each statement using the scale below.

Strongly Disagree	Disagree	Neither	Agree	Strongly Agree
1	2	3	4	5

1. I had the knowledge and skills needed to learn in this course.
2. The facilities and equipment made it easy to learn.
3. The course met all of the stated objectives.
4. I clearly understood the course objectives.
5. The way the course was delivered was an effective way to learn.
6. The materials I received during the course were useful.
7. The course content was logically organized.
8. There was enough time to learn the course content.
9. I felt that the instructor wanted us to learn.
10. I was comfortable asking the instructor questions.
11. The instructor was prepared.
12. The instructor was knowledgeable about the course content.
13. I learned a lot from this course.
14. What I learned in this course is useful for my job.
15. The information I received about the course was accurate.
16. Overall, I was satisfied with the instructor.
17. Overall, I was satisfied with the course.

An accurate evaluation needs to include all the factors related to a successful learning environment.[14] Most instructor or class evaluations include items related to the trainer's preparation, delivery, ability to lead a discussion, organization of the training materials and content, use of visual aids, presentation style, ability and willingness to answer questions, and ability to stimulate trainees' interest in the course. These items come from trainer's manuals, trainer certification programs, and observation of successful trainers. Conventional wisdom suggests that trainees who like a training program (who have positive reactions) learn more and are more likely to change behaviors and improve their performance (transfer of training). Is this the case? Recent research results suggest that reactions have the largest relationship with changes in affective learning outcomes.[15] Also, research has found that reactions are significantly related to changes in declarative and procedural knowledge, which challenges previous research suggesting that reactions are unrelated to learning. For courses such as diversity training or ethics training, trainee reactions are especially important because they affect learners' receptivity to attitude change. Reactions have been found to have the strongest relationship with post-training motivation, trainee self-efficacy, and declarative knowledge when technology is used for instructional delivery. This suggests that for online or e-learning training methods, it is important to ensure that it is easy for trainees to access them and the training content is meaningful, i.e., linked to their current job experiences, tasks, or work issues.

Learning or Cognitive Outcomes

Cognitive outcomes are used to determine the degree to which trainees are familiar with principles, facts, techniques, procedures, or processes emphasized in the training program. Cognitive outcomes measure what knowledge trainees learned in the program. Cognitive outcomes are level 2 (learning) criteria in Kirkpatrick's framework. Typically, pencil-and-paper tests are used to assess cognitive outcomes. Table 6.4 provides an example of items from a pencil-and-paper test used to measure trainees' knowledge of decision-making skills. These items help to measure whether a trainee knows how to make a decision (the process he or she would use). They do not help to determine if the trainee will actually use decision-making skills on the job.

Behavior and Skill-Based Outcomes

Skill-based outcomes are used to assess the level of technical or motor skills and behaviors. Skill-based outcomes include acquisition or learning of skills (skill learning) and use of skills on the job (skill transfer). Skill-based outcomes relate to Kirkpatrick's level 2 (learning) and level 3 (behavior). The extent to which trainees have learned skills can be evaluated by observing their performance in work samples such as simulators. Skill transfer is usually determined by observation. For example, a resident medical student may perform surgery while the surgeon carefully observes, giving advice and assistance as needed. Trainees may be asked to provide ratings of their own behavior or skills (self-ratings). Peers, managers, and subordinates may also be asked to rate trainees' behavior or skills based on their observations. Because research suggests that the use of only self-ratings likely results in an inaccurately positive assessment of skill or behavior transfer of training, it is recommended that skill or behavior ratings be collected from multiple perspectives (e.g., managers and subordinates or peers).[16] Table 6.5 shows a sample rating form. This form was used as part of an evaluation of a training program developed to improve school principals' management skills.

Affective Outcomes

Affective outcomes include attitudes and motivation. Affective outcomes that might be collected in an evaluation include tolerance for diversity, motivation to learn, safety attitudes, and customer service orientation. Affective outcomes can be measured using surveys. Table 6.6 shows an example of questions on a survey used to measure career goals, plans, and interests. The specific attitude of interest depends on the program objectives. Affective outcomes relate to Kirkpatrick's level 2 (learning) or level 3 (behavior) depending on how they are evaluated. If trainees were asked about their attitudes on a survey, that

TABLE 6.4
Sample Test Items Used to Measure Learning

Source: Based on A. P. Carnevale, L. J. Gainer, and A. S. Meltzer, *Workplace Basics Training Manual* (San Francisco: Jossey-Bass, 1990): 8.12.

For each question, check all that apply.

1. If my boss returned a piece of work to me and asked me to make changes on it, I would:
___ Prove to my boss that the work didn't need to be changed.
___ Do what the boss said, but show where changes are needed.
___ Make the changes without talking to my boss.
___ Request a transfer from the department.
2. If I were setting up a new process in my office, I would:
___ Do it on my own without asking for help.
___ Ask my boss for suggestions.
___ Ask the people who work for me for suggestions.
___ Discuss it with friends outside the company.

TABLE 6.5 **Sample Rating Form Used to Measure Behavior**

Rating task: Consider your opportunities over the past three months to observe and interact with the principal/assistant principal you are rating. Read the definition and behaviors associated with the skill. Then complete your ratings using the following scale:

Always	Usually	Sometimes	Seldom	Never
1	2	3	4	5

I. *Sensitivity:* Ability to perceive the needs, concerns, and personal problems of others; tact in dealing with persons from different backgrounds; skill in resolving conflict; ability to deal effectively with people concerning emotional needs; knowing what information to communicate to whom.

To what extent in the past three months has the principal or assistant principal:

__ 1. Elicited perceptions, feelings, and concerns of others?
__ 2. Expressed verbal and nonverbal recognition of the feelings, needs, and concerns of others?
__ 3. Taken actions that anticipated the emotional effects of specific behaviors?
__ 4. Accurately reflected the point of view of others by restating it, applying it, or encouraging feedback?
__ 5. Communicated all information to others that they needed to perform their job?
__ 6. Diverted unnecessary conflict with others in problem situations?

II. *Decisiveness:* Ability to recognize when a decision is required and act quickly. (Disregard the quality of the decision.)

To what extent in the past three months has this individual:

__ 7. Recognized when a decision was required by determining the results if the decision was made or not made?
__ 8. Determined whether a short- or long-term solution was most appropriate to various situations encountered in the school?
__ 9. Considered decision alternatives?
__10. Made a timely decision based on available data?
__11. Stuck to decisions once they were made, resisting pressures from others?

would be considered a learning measure. For example, attitudes toward career goals and interests might be an appropriate outcome to use to evaluate training focusing on employees self-managing their careers.

Results

Results are used to determine the training program's payoff for the company. Examples of results outcomes include increased production and reduced costs related to employee turnover, accidents, and equipment downtime as well as improvements in product quality or customer service.[17] Results outcomes are level 4 (results) criteria in

TABLE 6.6
Example of Affective Outcomes: Career Goals, Plans, and Interests

1. At this time I have a definite career goal in mind.
2. I have a strategy for achieving my career goals.
3. My manager is aware of my career goals.
4. I have sought information regarding my specific areas of career interest from friends, colleagues, or company career sources.
5. I have initiated conversations concerning my career plans with my manager.

Kirkpatrick's framework. For example, Kroger, the supermarket chain, hires more than 100,000 new employees each year who need to be trained.[18] Kroger collected productivity data for an evaluation comparing cashiers who received computer-based training to those who were trained in the classroom and on the job. The measures of productivity included rate of scanning grocery items, recognition of produce that had to be identified and weighed at the checkout, and the amount of time that store offices spent helping the cashiers deal with more complex transactions such as food stamps and checks.

LQ Management LLC, the parent company of La Quinta Inns and Suites, is responsible for training for the hotels.[19] The company recently implemented a new sales strategy designed to generate the best available rate for each hotel location based on customer demand and occupancy rates. A training program involving an experiential game ("Buddy's View") was used to engage staff in understanding how the new sales strategy would impact the business as well as to improve customer service. To evaluate the effectiveness of the program, the company collects business results (Kirkpatrick's level 4 criteria), specifically, percent changes in service quality and customers' intent to return before and after the program.

Return on Investment

Return on investment (ROI) refers to comparing the training's monetary benefits with the cost of the training. ROI is often referred to as level 5 evaluation (see Table 6.2). Training costs can be direct and indirect.[20] **Direct costs** include salaries and benefits for all employees involved in training, including trainees, instructors, consultants, and employees who design the program; program material and supplies; equipment or classroom rentals or purchases; and travel costs. **Indirect costs** are not related directly to the design, development, or delivery of the training program. They include general office supplies, facilities, equipment, and related expenses; travel and expenses not directly billed to one program; training department management and staff salaries not related to any one program; and administrative and staff support salaries. **Benefits** are the value that the company gains from the training program.

The Northwest Airlines technical operations training department includes 72 instructors who are responsible for training thousands of aircraft technicians and more than 10,000 outside vendors who work on maintaining the Northwest aircraft fleet.[21] Each of the training instructors works with one type of aircraft, such as the Airbus 320. Most of the department's training is instructor-led in a classroom, but other instruction programs use a simulator or take place in an actual airplane.

By tracking department training data, which allowed for training evaluation, the technical operations department was able to demonstrate its worth by showing how its services contribute to the airline's business. For example, the technical operations department reduced the cost of training an individual technician by 16 percent; increased customer satisfaction through training; increased training productivity; made the case for upper management to provide financial resources for training; and improved postcourse evaluations, knowledge, and performance gains.

To achieve these results, the technical operations training department developed the Training Quality Index (TQI). The TQI is a computer application that collects data about training department performance, productivity, budget, and courses and allows for detailed analysis of the data. TQI tracks all department training data into five categories: effectiveness, quantity, perceptions, financial impact, and operational impact. The quality of training is included under the effectiveness category. For example, knowledge gain relates to the difference in trainees' pretraining and posttraining knowledge measured by exams. The system can provide performance reports that relate to budgets and the cost of training per student per day and other costs of training. The measures that are collected are also linked to department goals, to department strategy, and ultimately, to Northwest Airline's overall strategy. Questions that were often asked before TQI was developed but couldn't easily be answered—such as how can the cost of training be justified, what is the operational impact of training, and what amount of training have technicians received—can now be answered through the TQI system. Training demand can be compared against passenger loads and the number of flying routes to determine the right number of trainers in the right locations to support business needs. These adjustments increase customer satisfaction and result in positive views of the training operations.

DETERMINING WHETHER OUTCOMES ARE APPROPRIATE

An important issue in choosing outcomes is to determine whether they are appropriate. That is, are these outcomes the best ones to measure to determine whether the training program is effective? Appropriate training outcomes need to be relevant, reliable, discriminative, and practical.[22]

Relevance

Criteria relevance refers to the extent to which training outcomes are related to the learned capabilities emphasized in the training program. The learned capabilities required to succeed in the training program should be the same as those required to be successful on the job. The outcomes collected in training should be as similar as possible to what trainees learned in the program. That is, the outcomes need to be valid measures of learning. One way to ensure the relevancy of the outcomes is to choose outcomes based on the learning objectives for the program. Recall from Chapter 4 that the learning objectives show the expected action, the conditions under which the trainee is to perform, and the level or standard of performance.

Figure 6.2 shows two ways that training outcomes may lack relevance. **Criterion contamination** refers to the extent that training outcomes measure inappropriate capabilities or are affected by extraneous conditions. For example, if managers' evaluations of job performance are used as a training outcome, trainees may receive higher ratings of job performance simply because the managers know they attended the training program, believe the program is valuable, and therefore give high ratings to ensure that the training looks like it positively affects performance. Criteria may also be contaminated if the conditions under which the outcomes are measured vary from the learning environment. That is, trainees may be asked to perform their learned capabilities using equipment, time constraints, or physical working conditions that are not similar to those in the learning environment.

For example, trainees may be asked to demonstrate spreadsheet skills using a newer version of spreadsheet software than they used in the training program. This demonstration

FIGURE 6.2
Criterion
Deficiency,
Relevance, and
Contamination

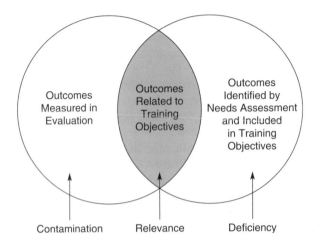

likely will result in no changes in their spreadsheet skills from pretraining levels. In this case, poor-quality training is not the cause for the lack of change in their spreadsheet skills. Trainees may have learned the necessary spreadsheet skills, but the environment for the evaluation differs substantially from the learning environment, so no change in skill level is observed.

Criteria may also be deficient. **Criterion deficiency** refers to the failure to measure training outcomes that were emphasized in the training objectives. For example, the objectives of a spreadsheet skills training program emphasize that trainees both understand the commands available on the spreadsheet (e.g., compute) and use the spreadsheet to calculate statistics using a data set. An evaluation design that uses only learning outcomes such as a test of knowledge of the purpose of keystrokes is deficient, because the evaluation does not measure outcomes that were included in the training objectives (e.g., use spreadsheet to compute the mean and standard deviation of a set of data).

Reliability

Reliability refers to the degree to which outcomes can be measured consistently over time. For example, a trainer gives restaurant employees a written test measuring knowledge of safety standards to evaluate a safety training program they attended. The test is given before (pretraining) and after (posttraining) employees attend the program. A reliable test includes items for which the meaning or interpretation does not change over time. A reliable test allows the trainer to have confidence that any improvements in posttraining test scores from pretraining levels are the result of learning that occurred in the training program, not test characteristics (e.g., items are more understandable the second time) or the test environment (e.g., trainees performed better on the posttraining test because the classroom was more comfortable and quieter).

Discrimination

Discrimination refers to the degree to which trainees' performance on the outcome actually reflects true differences in performance. For example, a paper-and-pencil test that measures electricians' knowledge of electrical principles must detect true differences in trainees' knowledge of electrical principles. That is, the test should discriminate on the basis of trainees' knowledge of electrical principles. (People who score high on the test have a better understanding of the principles of electricity than do those who score low.)

Practicality

Practicality refers to the ease with which the outcome measures can be collected. One reason companies give for not including learning, performance, and behavior outcomes in their evaluation of training programs is that collecting them is too burdensome. (It takes too much time and energy, which detracts from the business.) For example, in evaluating a sales training program, it may be impractical to ask customers to rate the salesperson's behavior because this would place too much of a time commitment on the customer (and probably damage future sales relationships).

EVALUATION PRACTICES

Figure 6.3 shows outcomes used in training evaluation practices. Surveys of companies' evaluation practices indicate that reactions (an affective outcome) and cognitive outcomes are the most frequently used outcomes in training evaluation.[23] Despite the less frequent use of cognitive, behavioral, and results outcomes, research suggests that training can have a positive effect on these outcomes.[24] Keep in mind that while most companies are conducting training evaluations, some surveys indicate that 20 percent of all companies are not!

Which Training Outcomes Should Be Collected?

From our discussion of evaluation outcomes and evaluation practices you may have the mistaken impression that it is necessary to collect all five levels of outcomes to evaluate a training program. While collecting all five levels of outcomes is ideal, the training program objectives determine which ones should be linked to the broader business strategy,

FIGURE 6.3
Training Evaluation Practices

Note: Respondents were companies that participated in ASTD Benchmarking Forum.
Source: Based on B. Sugrue and R. Rivera, *2005 State of the Industry* (Alexandria, VA: American Society for Training and Development, 2005): 15.

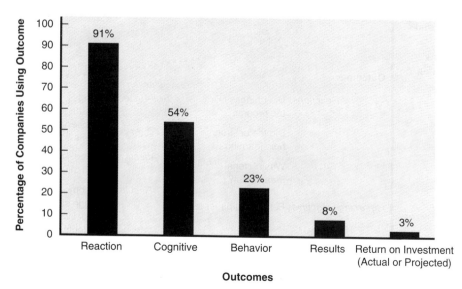

as discussed in Chapter 2. To ensure adequate training evaluation, companies should collect outcome measures related to both learning (levels 1 and 2) and transfer of training (levels 3, 4, or 5).

It is important to recognize the limitations of choosing to measure only reaction and cognitive outcomes. Consider the previous discussions of learning (Chapter 4) and transfer of training (Chapter 5). Remember that for training to be successful, learning *and* transfer of training must occur. Figure 6.4 shows the multiple objectives of training programs and their implication for choosing evaluation outcomes. Training programs usually have objectives related to both learning and transfer. That is, they want trainees to acquire knowledge and cognitive skill and also to demonstrate the use of the knowledge or strategy in their on-the-job behavior. As a result, to ensure an adequate training evaluation, companies must collect outcome measures related to both learning and transfer.

Ernst Young's training function uses knowledge testing (level 2) for all of the company's e-learning courses, which account for 50 percent of training.[25] New courses and programs use behavior transfer (level 3) and business results (level 4). Regardless of the program, the company's leaders are interested in whether the trainees feel that training has been a good use of their time, money, and whether they would recommend it to other employees (level 1). The training function automatically tracks these outcomes. Managers use training and development to encourage observable behavior changes in employees that will result in business results such as client satisfaction and lower turnover, which they also monitor.

Note that outcome measures are not perfectly related to each other. That is, it is tempting to assume that satisfied trainees learn more and will apply their knowledge and skill to the job, resulting in behavior change and positive results for the company. However, research indicates that the relationships among reaction, cognitive, behavior, and results outcomes are small.[26]

FIGURE 6.4

Training Program Objectives and Their Implications for Evaluation

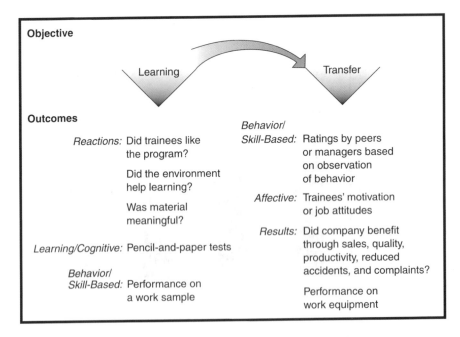

Which training outcomes measure is best? The answer depends on the training objectives. For example, if the instructional objectives identified business-related outcomes such as increased customer service or product quality, then results outcomes should be included in the evaluation. As Figure 6.4 shows, both reaction and cognitive outcomes may affect learning. Reaction outcomes provide information regarding the extent to which the trainer, facilities, or learning environment may have hindered learning. Learning or cognitive outcomes directly measure the extent to which trainees have mastered training content. However, reaction and cognitive outcomes do not help determine how much trainees actually use the training content in their jobs. As much as possible, evaluation should include behavior or skill-based, affective, or results outcomes to determine the extent to which transfer of training has occurred—that is, whether training has influenced a change in behavior, skill, or attitude or has directly influenced objective measures related to company effectiveness (e.g., sales).

How long after training should outcomes be collected? There is no accepted standard for when the different training outcomes should be collected. In most cases, reactions are usually measured immediately after training.[27] Learning, behavior, and results should be measured after sufficient time has elapsed to determine whether training has had an influence on these outcomes. Positive transfer of training is demonstrated when learning occurs and positive changes in skill-based, affective, or results outcomes are also observed. No transfer of training is demonstrated if learning occurs but no changes are observed in skill-based, affective, or learning outcomes. Negative transfer is evident when learning occurs but skills, affective outcomes, or results are less than at pretraining levels. Results of evaluation studies that find no transfer or negative transfer suggest that the trainer and the manager need to investigate whether a good learning environment (e.g., opportunities for feedback and practice) was provided in the training program, trainees were motivated and able to learn, and the needs assessment correctly identified training needs.

EVALUATION DESIGNS

The design of the training evaluation determines the confidence that can be placed in the results, that is, how sure a company can be that training is either responsible for changes in evaluation outcomes or has failed to influence the outcomes. No evaluation design can ensure that the results of the evaluation are completely due to training. What the evaluator strives for is to use the most rigorous design possible (given the circumstances under which the evaluation occurs) to rule out alternative explanations for the results of the evaluation.

This discussion of evaluation designs begins by identifying these "alternative explanations" that the evaluator should attempt to control for. Next, various evaluation designs are compared. Finally, this section discusses practical circumstances that the trainer needs to consider in selecting an evaluation design.

Threats to Validity: Alternative Explanations for Evaluation Results

Table 6.7 presents threats to validity of an evaluation. **Threats to validity** refer to factors that will lead an evaluator to question either (1) the believability of the study results or (2) the extent to which the evaluation results are generalizable to other groups of trainees

TABLE 6.7 **Threats to Validity**

Threats to Internal Validity	Description
Company	
History	Event occurs, producing changes in training outcomes.
Persons	
Maturation	Changes in training outcomes result from trainee's physical growth or emotional state.
Mortality	Study participants drop out of study (e.g., leave company).
Initial group differences	Training group differs from comparison group on individual differences that influence outcomes (knowledge, skills, ability, behavior).
Outcome Measures	
Testing	Trainees are sensitized to perform well on posttest measures.
Instrumentation	Trainee interpretation of outcomes changes over course of evaluation.
Regression toward the mean	High-and low-scoring trainees move toward middle or average on posttraining measure.
Threats to External Validity	**Description**
Reaction to pretest	Use of test before training causes trainee to pay attention to material on test.
Reaction to evaluation	Being evaluated causes trainee to try harder in training program.
Interaction of selection and training	Characteristics of trainee influence program effectiveness.
Interaction of methods	Results of trainees who received different methods can be generalized only to trainees who receive same training in the same order.

Source: Based on T. D. Cook, D. T. Campbell, and L. Peracchio, "Quasi-Experimentation," in *Handbook of Industrial and Organizational Psychology,* 2d ed., Vol. 1, eds. M. D. Dunnette and L. M. Hough (Palo Alto, CA: Consulting Psychologists Press, 1990): 491–576.

and situations.[28] The believability of study results refers to **internal validity.** The internal threats to validity relate to characteristics of the company (history), the outcome measures (instrumentation, testing), and the persons in the evaluation study (maturation, regression toward the mean, mortality, initial group differences). These characteristics can cause the evaluator to reach the wrong conclusions about training effectiveness. An evaluation study needs internal validity to provide confidence that the results of the evaluation (particularly if they are positive) are due to the training program and not to another factor. For example, consider a group of managers who have attended a communication skills training program. At the same time that they attend the program, it is announced that the company will be restructured. After the program, the managers may become better communicators simply because they are scared that otherwise they will lose their jobs. Perhaps no learning actually occurred in the training program!

Trainers are also interested in the generalizability of the study results to other groups and situations (i.e., they are interested in the **external validity** of the study). As shown in Table 6.7, threats to external validity relate to how study participants react to being included in the study and the effects of multiple types of training. Because evaluation usually does not involve all employees who have completed a program (or who may take training in the future), trainers want to be able to say that the training program will be effective in the future with similar groups.

Methods to Control for Threats to Validity

Because trainers often want to use evaluation study results as a basis for changing training programs or demonstrating that training does work (as a means to gain additional funding for training from those who control the training budget), it is important to minimize the threats to validity. There are three ways to minimize threats to validity: the use of pretests and posttests in evaluation designs, comparison groups, and random assignment.

Pretests and Posttests   One way to improve the internal validity of the study results is to first establish a baseline or **pretraining measure** of the outcome. Another measure of the outcomes can be taken after training. This is referred to as a **posttraining measure.** A comparison of the posttraining and pretraining measures can indicate the degree to which trainees have changed as a result of training.

Use of Comparison Groups   Internal validity can be improved by using a control or comparison group. A **comparison group** refers to a group of employees who participate in the evaluation study but do not attend the training program. The comparison employees have personal characteristics (e.g., gender, education, age, tenure, skill level) as similar to the trainees as possible. Use of a comparison group in training evaluation helps to rule out the possibility that changes found in the outcome measures are due to factors other than training. The **Hawthorne effect** refers to employees in an evaluation study performing at a high level simply because of the attention they are receiving. Use of a comparison group helps to show that any effects observed are due specifically to the training rather than the attention the trainees are receiving. Use of a comparison group helps to control for the effects of history, testing, instrumentation, and maturation because both the comparison group and the training group are treated similarly, receive the same measures, and have the same amount of time to develop.

For example, consider an evaluation of a safety training program. Safe behaviors are measured before and after safety training for both trainees and a comparison group. If the level of safe behavior improves for the training group from pretraining levels but remains relatively the same for the comparison group at both pretraining and posttraining, the reasonable conclusion is that the observed differences in safe behaviors are due to the training and not some other factor, such as the attention given to both the trainees and the comparison group by asking them to participate in the study.

Random Assignment   **Random assignment** refers to assigning employees to the training or comparison group on the basis of chance. That is, employees are assigned to the training program without consideration of individual differences (ability, motivation) or prior experiences. Random assignment helps to ensure that trainees are similar in individual differences such as age, gender, ability, and motivation. Because it is often impossible to identify and measure all the individual characteristics that might influence the outcome measures, random assignment ensures that these characteristics are equally distributed in the comparison group and the training group. Random assignment helps to reduce the effects of employees dropping out of the study (mortality) and differences between the training group and comparison group in ability, knowledge, skill, or other personal characteristics.

Keep in mind that random assignment is often impractical. Companies want to train employees who need training. Also, companies may be unwilling to provide a comparison group. One solution to this problem is to identify the factors in which the training and comparison groups differ and control for these factors in the analysis of the data (a statistical procedure known as analysis of covariance). Another method is to determine trainees' characteristics after they are assigned and ensure that the comparison group includes employees with similar characteristics.

Types of Evaluation Designs

A number of different designs can be used to evaluate training programs.[29] Table 6.8 compares each design on the basis of who is involved (trainees, comparison group), when measures are collected (pretraining, posttraining), the costs, the time it takes to conduct the evaluation, and the strength of the design for ruling out alternative explanations for the results. As shown in Table 6.8, research designs vary based on whether they include pretraining and posttraining measurement of outcomes and a comparison group. In general, designs that use pretraining and posttraining measures of outcomes and include a comparison group reduce the risk that alternative factors (other than the training itself) are responsible for the results of the evaluation. This increases the trainer's confidence in using the results to make decisions. Of course, the trade-off is that evaluations using these designs are more costly and take more time to conduct than do evaluations not using pretraining and posttraining measures or comparison groups.

Posttest Only

The **posttest-only** design refers to an evaluation design in which only posttraining outcomes are collected. This design can be strengthened by adding a comparison group (which helps to rule out alternative explanations for changes). The posttest-only design is appropriate when trainees (and the comparison group, if one is used) can be expected to have similar levels of knowledge, behavior, or results outcomes (e.g., same number of sales, equal awareness of how to close a sale) prior to training.

Consider the evaluation design that Mayo Clinic used to compare two methods for delivering new manager training.[30] Mayo Clinic is one of the world's leading centers of

TABLE 6.8 **Comparison of Evaluation Designs**

Design	Groups	Pretraining	Posttraining	Cost	Time	Strength
			Measures			
Posttest only	Trainees	No	Yes	Low	Low	Low
Pretest/posttest	Trainees	Yes	Yes	Low	Low	Med.
Posttest only with comparison group	Trainees and comparison	No	Yes	Med.	Med.	Med.
Pretest/posttest with comparison group	Trainees and comparison	Yes	Yes	Med.	Med.	High
Time series	Trainees	Yes	Yes, several	Med.	Med.	Med.
Time series with comparison group and reversal	Trainees and comparison	Yes	Yes, several	High	Med.	High
Solomon Four-Group	Trainees A	Yes	Yes	High	High	High
	Trainees B	No	Yes			
	Comparison A	Yes	Yes			
	Comparison B	No	Yes			

medical education and research. Recently, Mayo has undergone considerable growth because a new hospital and clinic have been added in the Phoenix area (Mayo Clinic is also located in Rochester, Minnesota). In the process, employees who were not fully prepared were moved into management positions, which resulted in increased employee dissatisfaction and employee turnover rates. After a needs assessment indicated that employees were leaving because of dissatisfaction with management, Mayo decided to initiate a new training program designed to help the new managers improve their skills. There was some debate whether the training would be best administered in a classroom or one-on-one with a coach. Because of the cost implications of using coaching instead of classroom training (the costs were higher for coaching), Mayo decided to conduct an evaluation using a posttest comparison group design. Before training all managers, Mayo held three training sessions. No more than 75 managers were included in each session. Within each session managers were divided into three groups: a group that received four days of classroom training, a group that received one-on-one training from a coach, and a group that received no training (a comparison group). Mayo collected reaction (did the trainees like the program?), learning, transfer, and results outcomes. The evaluation found no statistically significant differences in the effects of the coaching compared to classroom and no training. As a result, Mayo decided to rely on classroom courses for new managers and to consider coaching only for managers with critical and immediate job issues.

Pretest/Posttest

The **pretest/posttest** refers to an evaluation design in which both pretraining and posttraining outcome measures are collected. There is no comparison group. The lack of a comparison group makes it difficult to rule out the effects of business conditions or other factors as explanations for changes. This design is often used by companies that want to evaluate a training program but are uncomfortable with excluding certain employees or that only intend to train a small group of employees.

Pretest/Posttest with Comparison Group

The **pretest/posttest with comparison group** refers to an evaluation design that includes trainees and a comparison group. Pretraining and posttraining outcome measures are collected from both groups. If improvement is greater for the training group than the comparison group, this finding provides evidence that training is responsible for the change. This type of design controls for most of the threats to validity.

Table 6.9 presents an example of a pretest/posttest comparison group design. This evaluation involved determining the relationship between three conditions or treatments and learning, satisfaction, and use of computer skills.[31] The three conditions or treatments (types of computer training) were behavior modeling, self-paced study, and lecture. A comparison group was also included in the study. Behavior modeling involved watching a video showing a model performing key behaviors necessary to complete a task. In this case the task was procedures on the computer. (Behavior modeling is discussed in detail in Chapter 7.)

Forty trainees were included in each condition. Measures of learning included a test consisting of 11 items designed to measure information that trainees needed to know to operate the computer system (e.g., "Does formatting destroy all data on the disk?"). Also, trainees' comprehension of computer procedures (procedural comprehension) was measured by presenting trainees with scenarios on the computer screens and asking them what

TABLE 6.9

Example of a Pretest/Posttest Comparison Group Design

Source: Based on S. J. Simon and J. M. Werner, "Computer Training through Behavior Modeling, Self-Paced, and Instructional Approaches: A Field Experiment," *Journal of Applied Psychology* 81 (1996): 648–59.

	Pretraining	Training	Posttraining Time 1	Posttraining Time 2
Lecture	Yes	Yes	Yes	Yes
Self-paced study	Yes	Yes	Yes	Yes
Behavior modeling	Yes	Yes	Yes	Yes
No training (Comparison)	Yes	No	Yes	Yes

would appear next on the screen. Use of computer skills (skill-based learning outcome) was measured by asking trainees to complete six computer tasks (e.g., changing directories). Satisfaction with the program (reaction) was measured by six items (e.g., "I would recommend this program to others").

As shown in Table 6.9, measures of learning and skills were collected from the trainees prior to attending the program (pretraining). Measures of learning and skills were also collected immediately after training (posttraining time 1) and four weeks after training (posttraining time 2). The satisfaction measure was collected immediately following training.

The posttraining time 2 measures collected in this study help to determine the occurrence of training transfer and retention of the information and skills. That is, immediately following training, trainees may have appeared to learn and acquire skills related to computer training. Collection of the posttraining measures four weeks after training provides information about trainees' level of retention of the skills and knowledge.

Statistical procedures known as analysis of variance and analysis of covariance were used to test for differences between pretraining measures and posttraining measures for each condition. Also, differences between each of the training conditions and the comparison group were analyzed. These procedures determine whether differences between the groups are large enough to conclude with a high degree of confidence that the differences were caused by training rather than by chance fluctuations in trainees' scores on the measures.

Time Series

Time series refers to an evaluation design in which training outcomes are collected at periodic intervals both before and after training. (In the other evaluation designs discussed here, training outcomes are collected only once after and maybe once before training.) The strength of this design can be improved by using **reversal,** which refers to a time period in which participants no longer receive the training intervention. A comparison group can also be used with a time series design. One advantage of the time series design is that it allows an analysis of the stability of training outcomes over time. Another advantage is that using both the reversal and comparison group helps to rule out alternative explanations for the evaluation results. The time series design is frequently used to evaluate training programs that focus on improving readily observable outcomes (such as accident rates, productivity, and absenteeism) that vary over time.

Table 6.10 shows a time series design that was used to evaluate how much a training program improved the number of safe work behaviors in a food manufacturing plant.[32] This plant was experiencing an accident rate similar to that of the mining industry, the most dangerous area of work. Employees were engaging in unsafe behaviors such as putting their hands into conveyors to unjam them (resulting in crushed limbs).

TABLE 6.10

Example of a Time Series Design

Source: J. Komaki, K. D. Badwick, and L. R. Scott, "A Behavioral Approach to Occupational Safety: Pinpointing Safe Performance in a Food Manufacturing Plant," *Journal of Applied Psychology* 63 (1978). Copyright 1978 by the American Psychological Association. Adapted by permission.

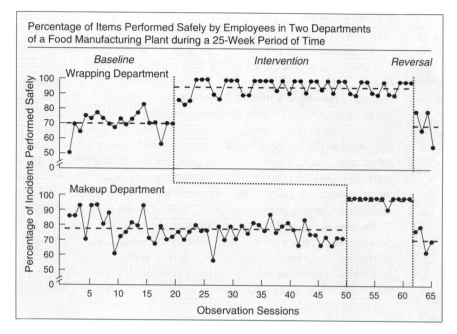

To improve safety, the company developed a training program that taught employees safe behaviors, provided them with incentives for safe behaviors, and encouraged them to monitor their own behavior. To evaluate the program, the design included a comparison group (the Makeup Department) and a trained group (the Wrapping Department). The Makeup Department is responsible for measuring and mixing ingredients, preparing the dough, placing the dough in the oven and removing it when it is cooked, and packaging the finished product. The Wrapping Department is responsible for bagging, sealing, and labeling the packaging and stacking it on skids for shipping. Outcomes included observations of safe work behaviors. These observations were taken over a 25-week period.

The baseline shows the percentage of safe acts prior to introduction of the safety training program. Training directed at increasing the number of safe behaviors was introduced after approximately five weeks (20 observation sessions) in the Wrapping Department and 10 weeks (50 observation sessions) in the Makeup Department. Training was withdrawn from the Wrapping and Makeup Departments after approximately 62 observation sessions. The withdrawal of training resulted in a reduction of the work incidents performed safely (to pretraining levels). As shown, the number of safe acts observed varied across the observation period for both groups. However, the number of safe behaviors increased after the training program was conducted for the trained group (Wrapping Department). The level of safe acts remained stable across the observation period. (See the intervention period.) When the Makeup Department received training (at 10 weeks, or after 50 observations), a similar increase in the percentage of safe behaviors was observed.

Solomon Four-Group

The **Solomon four-group** design combines the pretest/posttest comparison group and the posttest-only control group design. In the Solomon four-group design, a training group and a comparison group are measured on the outcomes both before and after training. Another training group and control group are measured only after training. This design controls for most threats to internal and external validity.

An application of the Solomon four-group design is shown in Table 6.11. This design was used to compare the effects of training based on integrative learning (IL) with traditional (lecture-based) training of manufacturing resource planning. Manufacturing resource planning is a method for effectively planning, coordinating, and integrating the use of all resources of a manufacturing company.[33] The IL-based training differed from the traditional training in several ways. IL-based training sessions began with a series of activities intended to create a relaxed, positive environment for learning. The students were asked what manufacturing resource planning meant to them, and attempts were made to reaffirm their beliefs and unite the trainees around a common understanding of manufacturing resource planning. Students presented training material and participated in group discussions, games, stories, and poetry related to the manufacturing processes.

Because the company was interested in the effects of IL related to traditional training, groups who received traditional training were used as the comparison group (rather than groups who received no training). A test of manufacturing resource planning (knowledge test) and a reaction measure were used as outcomes. The study found that participants in the IL-based learning groups learned slightly less than participants in the traditional training groups. However, IL-group participants had much more positive reactions than did those in the traditional training program.

Considerations in Choosing an Evaluation Design

There is no one appropriate evaluation design. An evaluation design should be chosen based on an evaluation of the factors shown in Table 6.12. There are several reasons why no evaluation or a less rigorous evaluation design may be more appropriate than a more rigorous design that includes a comparison group, random assignment, or pretraining and posttraining measures. First, managers and trainers may be unwilling to devote the time and effort necessary to collect training outcomes. Second, managers or trainers may lack the expertise to conduct an evaluation study. Third, a company may view training as an investment from which it expects to receive little or no return. A more rigorous evaluation design (pretest/posttest with comparison group) should be considered if any of the following conditions are true:[34]

1. The evaluation results can be used to change the program.
2. The training program is ongoing and has the potential to have an important influence on (employees or customers).
3. The training program involves multiple classes and a large number of trainees.
4. Cost justification for training is based on numerical indicators. (Here the company has a strong orientation toward evaluation.)

TABLE 6.11
Example of a Solomon Four-Group Design

Source: Based on R. D. Bretz and R. E. Thompsett, "Comparing Traditional and Integrative Learning Methods in Organizational Training Programs," *Journal of Applied Psychology* 77 (1992): 941–51.

	Pretest	Training	Posttest
Group 1	Yes	IL-based	Yes
Group 2	Yes	Traditional	Yes
Group 3	No	IL-based	Yes
Group 4	No	Traditional	Yes

TABLE 6.12
Factors That Influence the Type of Evaluation Design

Source: Based on S. I. Tannenbaum and S. B. Woods, "Determining a Strategy for Evaluating Training: Operating within Organizational Constraints," *Human Resource Planning* 15 (1992): 63–81.

Factor	How the Factor Influences the Type of Evaluation Design
Change potential	Can program be modified?
Importance	Does ineffective training affect customer service, safety, product development, or relationships among employees?
Scale	How many trainees are involved?
Purpose of training	Is training conducted for learning, results, or both?
Organization culture	Is demonstrating results part of company norms and expectations?
Expertise	Can a complex study be analyzed?
Cost	Is evaluation too expensive?
Time frame	When is the information needed?

5. Trainers or others in the company have the expertise (or the budget to purchase expertise from outside the company) to design and evaluate the data collected from an evaluation study.

6. The cost of the training creates a need to show that it works.

7. There is sufficient time for conducting an evaluation. Here, information regarding training effectiveness is not needed immediately.

8. There is interest in measuring change (in knowledge, behavior, skill, etc.) from pretraining levels or in comparing two or more different programs.

For example, if the company is interested in determining how much employees' communications skills have changed as a result of a training program, a pretest/posttest comparison group design is necessary. Trainees should be randomly assigned to training and no-training conditions. These evaluation design features offer a high degree of confidence that any communication skill change is the result of participation in the training program.[35] This type of evaluation design is also necessary if the company wants to compare the effectiveness of two training programs.

Evaluation designs without pretest or comparison groups are most appropriate in situations in which the company is interested in identifying whether a specific level of performance has been achieved. (For example, are employees who participated in training able to adequately communicate their ideas?) In these situations, companies are not interested in determining how much change has occurred but rather in whether the trainees have achieved a certain proficiency level.

One company's evaluation strategy for a training course delivered to the company's tax professionals shows how company norms regarding evaluation and the purpose of training influence the type of evaluation design chosen.[36] This accounting firm views training as an effective method for developing human resources. Training is expected to provide a good return on investment. The company used a combination of affective, cognitive, behavior, and results criteria to evaluate a five-week course designed to prepare tax professionals to understand state and local tax law. The course involved two weeks of self-study and three weeks of classroom work. A pretest/posttest comparison design was used. Before they took the course, trainees were tested to determine their knowledge of state and local tax laws, and they completed a survey designed to assess their self-confidence in preparing accurate tax returns. The evaluators also identified the trainees' (accountants') billable hours related to calculating state and local tax returns and the revenue generated by the activity. After the course, evaluators again identified billable hours and surveyed trainees' self-confidence. The results of the evaluation indicated that the accountants were spending more time doing state and local tax work than before training. Also, the trained accountants produced more revenue doing state and local tax work than did accountants who had not yet received the training (comparison group). There was also a significant improvement in the accountants' confidence following training, and they were more willing to promote their expertise in state and local tax preparation. Finally, after 15 months, the revenue gained by the company more than offset the cost of training. On average, the increase in revenue for the trained tax accountants was more than 10 percent.

DETERMINING RETURN ON INVESTMENT

Return on investment (ROI) is an important training outcome. This section discusses how to calculate ROI through a cost-benefit analysis. **Cost-benefit analysis** in this situation is the process of determining the economic benefits of a training program using accounting methods that look at training costs and benefits. Training cost information is important for several reasons:[37]

1. To understand total expenditures for training, including direct and indirect costs.
2. To compare the costs of alternative training programs.
3. To evaluate the proportion of money spent on training development, administration, and evaluation as well as to compare monies spent on training for different groups of employees (exempt versus nonexempt, for example).
4. To control costs.

There is an increased interest in measuring the ROI of training and development programs because of the need to show the results of these programs to justify funding and to increase the status of the training and development function.[38] Most trainers and managers believe that there is a value provided by training and development activities, such as productivity or customer service improvements, cost reductions, time savings, and decreased employee turnover. ROI provides evidence of the economic value provided by training and development programs. However, it is important to keep in mind that ROI is not a substitute for other program outcomes that provide data regarding the success of a program based on trainees' reactions and whether learning and training transfer have occurred.

Consider the use of ROI at LensCrafters. LensCrafters brings the eye doctor, a wide selection of frames and lenses, and the lens-making laboratory together in one location.[39] LensCrafters has convenient locations and hours of operations, and it has the ability to make eyewear on-site. Emphasizing customer service, the company offers a one-stop location and promises to make eyewear in one hour. Dave Palm, a training professional at LensCrafters, received a call from a concerned regional manager. He told Palm that although company executives knew that LensCrafters employees had to be well trained to design eyewear and that employees were satisfied with the training, the executives wanted to know whether the money they were investing in training was providing any return. Palm decided to partner with the operations people to identify how to link training to measurable outcomes such as profitability, quality, and sales. After conversations with the operations employees, he decided to link training to waste from mistakes in quality and remakes, store performance and sales, and customer satisfaction. He chose two geographic regions for the evaluation study and compared the results from these two regions with results from one that had not yet received the training. Palm found that all stores in the two regions that received training reduced waste, increased sales, and improved customer satisfaction. As a result, LensCrafters allotted its training department more financial resources—$10 million a year for training program development and administration—than any other optical retail competitor. Because the training department demonstrated that it does contribute to business operations, it also received money to develop a multimedia-based training system.

The process of determining ROI begins with an understanding of the objectives of the training program.[40] Plans are developed for collecting data related to measuring these objectives. The next step is to isolate, if possible, the effects of training from other factors that might influence the data. Last, the data are converted to a monetary value and ROI is calculated. Choosing evaluation outcomes and designing an evaluation that helps isolate the effects of training were explained earlier in the chapter. The following sections discuss how to determine costs and benefits and provide examples of cost-benefit analysis and ROI calculations.

Because ROI analysis can be costly, it should be limited only to certain training programs. ROI analysis is best for training programs that are focused on an operational issue (measurable identifiable outcomes are available), are linked to a companywide strategy (e.g., better customer service), are expensive, are highly visible, have management interest, are attended by many employees, and are permanent.[41] At Deloitte & Touche, the tax and auditing firm, managers don't require analysis of ROI for many training programs.[42] Because knowledge is the product at Deloitte & Touche, investment in training is seen as an important part of the business. Deloitte & Touche makes money through the billable hours its consultants provide to clients. Training helps prepare the consultants to serve clients' needs. ROI is primarily calculated for courses or programs that are new or expensive. For example, ROI analysis was conducted for a simulation designed to help new employees learn more quickly how to service clients. At Deloitte & Touche use of the simulation has resulted in new hires being 30 to 40 percent faster in serving clients—resulting in an ROI of over $66 billion after subtracting program costs.

Determining Costs

One method for comparing costs of alternative training programs is the resource requirements model.[43] The resource requirements model compares equipment, facilities, personnel, and materials costs across different stages of the training process (needs assessment, development, training design, implementation, and evaluation). Use of the resource requirements model can help determine overall differences in costs among training programs. Also, costs incurred at different stages of the training process can be compared across programs.

Accounting can also be used to calculate costs.[44] Seven categories of cost sources are costs related to: program development or purchase, instructional materials for trainers and trainees, equipment and hardware, facilities, travel and lodging, salary of trainer and support staff, and the cost of lost productivity while trainees attend the program (or the cost of temporary employees who replace the trainees while they are at training). This method also identifies when the costs are incurred. One-time costs include those related to needs assessment and program development. Costs per offering relate to training site rental fees, trainer salaries, and other costs that are realized every time the program is offered. Costs per trainee include meals, materials, and lost productivity or expenses incurred to replace the trainees while they attend training.

Determining Benefits

To identify the potential benefits of training, the company must review the original reasons that the training was conducted. For example, training may have been conducted to reduce production costs or overtime costs or to increase the amount of repeat business. A number of methods may be helpful in identifying the benefits of training:

1. Technical, academic, and practitioner literature summarizes the benefits that have been shown to relate to a specific training program.
2. Pilot training programs assess the benefits from a small group of trainees before a company commits more resources.
3. Observance of successful job performers helps a company determine what successful job performers do differently than unsuccessful job performers.[45]
4. Trainees and their managers provide estimates of training benefits.

For example, a training and development consultant at Apple Computer was concerned with the quality and consistency of the training program used in assembly operations.[46] She wanted to show that training was not only effective but also resulted in financial benefits. To do this, the consultant chose an evaluation design that involved two separately trained groups—each consisting of 27 employees—and two untrained groups (comparison groups). The consultant collected a pretraining history of what was happening on the production line in each outcome she was measuring (productivity, quality, and labor efficiency). She determined the effectiveness of training by comparing performance between the comparison and training groups for two months after training. The consultant was able to show that the untrained comparison group had 2,000 more minutes of downtime than the trained group did. This finding meant that the trained employees built and shipped more products to customers—showing definitively that training was contributing to Apple's business objectives.

To conduct a cost-benefit analysis, the consultant had each employee in the training group estimate the effect of a behavior change on a specific business measure (e.g., breaking down tasks will improve productivity or efficiency). The trainees assigned a confidence percentage to the estimates. To get a cost-benefit estimate for each group of trainees, the consultant multiplied the monthly cost-benefit by the confidence level and divided by the number of trainees. For example, one group of 20 trainees estimated a total overall monthly cost benefit of $336,000 related to business improvements and showed an average 70 percent confidence level with that estimate. Seventy percent multiplied by $336,000 gave a cost-benefit of $235,200. This number was divided by 20 ($235,200/20 trainees) to give an average estimated cost benefit for each of the 20 trainees ($11,760). To calculate return on investment, follow these steps:[47]

1. Identify outcomes (e.g., quality, accidents).
2. Place a value on the outcomes.
3. Determine the change in performance after eliminating other potential influences on training results.
4. Obtain an annual amount of benefits (operational results) from training by comparing results after training to results before training (in dollars).
5. Determine the training costs (direct costs + indirect costs + development costs + overhead costs + compensation for trainees).
6. Calculate the total savings by subtracting the training costs from benefits (operational results).
7. Calculate the ROI by dividing benefits (operational results) by costs. The ROI gives an estimate of the dollar return expected from each dollar invested in training.

Example of a Cost-Benefit Analysis

A cost-benefit analysis is best explained by an example.[48] A wood plant produced panels that contractors used as building materials. The plant employed 300 workers, 48 supervisors, 7 shift superintendents, and a plant manager. The business had three problems. First, 2 percent of the wood panels produced each day were rejected because of poor quality. Second, the production area was experiencing poor housekeeping, such as improperly stacked finished panels that would fall on employees. Third, the number of preventable accidents was higher than the industry average. To correct these problems, the supervisors, shift superintendents, and plant manager attended training in (1) performance management and interpersonal skills related to quality problems and poor work habits of employees and (2) rewarding employees for performance improvement. Training was conducted in a hotel close to the plant. The training program was a purchased videotape, and the instructor for the program was a consultant. Table 6.13 shows each type of cost and how it was determined.

The benefits of the training were identified by considering the objectives of the training program and the type of outcomes the program was to influence. These outcomes included the quality of panels, housekeeping in the production area, and the accident rate. Table 6.14 shows how the benefits of the program were calculated.

Once the costs and benefits of the program are determined, ROI is calculated by dividing return or benefits by costs. In this example, ROI was 6.7. That is, every dollar invested in the program returned approximately seven dollars in benefits. How can the company determine if the ROI is acceptable? One way is for managers and trainers to agree on what level of ROI is acceptable. Another method is to use the ROI that other companies obtain from similar types of training. Table 6.15 provides examples of ROI obtained from several types of training programs.

Recall the discussion of the new manager training program at Mayo Clinic.[49] To determine Mayo's return on investment, the human resource department calculated that one-third of the 84 employees retained (29 employees) would have left Mayo as a result of dissatisfaction. The department believed that this retention was due to the impact of the training. Mayo's cost of a single employee turnover was calculated to be 75 percent of average total compensation, or $42,000 per employee. Multiplying $42,000 by the 29 employees retained equals a savings of $609,000. However, the cost of the training program needs to be considered. If the annual cost of the training program ($125,000) is subtracted from the savings,

TABLE 6.13
Determining
Costs for a
Cost-Benefit
Analysis

Direct Costs	
Instructor	$ 0
In-house instructor (12 days @ $125 per day)	1,500
Fringe benefits (25% of salary)	375
Travel expenses	0
Materials ($60 × 56 trainees)	3,360
Classroom space and audiovisual equipment	
(12 days @ $50 per day)	600
Refreshments ($4 per day × 3 days × 56 trainees)	672
Total direct costs	$ 6,507
Indirect Costs	
Training management	$ 0
Clerical and administrative salaries	750
Fringe benefits (25% of salary)	187
Postage, shipping, and telephone	0
Pre- and posttraining learning materials ($4 × 56 trainees)	224
Total indirect costs	$ 1,161
Development Costs	
Fee for program purchase	$ 3,600
Instructor training	
Registration fee	1,400
Travel and lodging	975
Salary	625
Benefits (25% of salary)	156
Total development costs	$ 6,756
Overhead Costs	
General organizational support, top management time	
(10% of direct, indirect, and development costs)	$ 1,443
Total overhead costs	$ 1,443
Compensation for Trainees	
Trainees' salaries and benefits (based on time away from job)	$ 16,969
Total training costs	$ 32,836
Cost per trainee	$ 587

the new savings amount is $484,000. These numbers are based on estimates, but even if the net savings figure were cut in half, the ROI is still over 100 percent. By being able to quantify the benefits delivered by the program, Mayo's human resource department achieved greater credibility within the company.

Other Methods for Cost-Benefit Analysis

Other more sophisticated methods are available for determining the dollar value of training. For example, **utility analysis** is a cost-benefit analysis method that involves assessing the dollar value of training based on estimates of the difference in job performance between trained and untrained employees, the number of individuals trained, the length of time a training program is expected to influence performance, and the variability in job performance in the untrained group of employees.[50] Utility analysis requires the use of a

TABLE 6.14 **Determining Benefits for a Cost-Benefit Analysis**

Operational Results Area	How Measured	Results before Training	Results after Training	Differences (+ or –)	Expressed in Dollars
Quality of panels	Percentage rejected	2 percent rejected— 1,440 panels per day	1.5 percent rejected— 1,080 panels per day	.5 percent— 360 panels	$720 per day, $172,800 per year
Housekeeping	Visual inspection using 20-item checklist	10 defects (average)	2 defects (average)	8 defects	Not measurable in $
Preventable accidents	Number of accidents	24 per year	16 per year	8 per year	$48,000 per year
	Direct cost of accidents	$144,000 per year	$96,000 per year	$48,000 per year	

$$ROI = \frac{Return}{Investment} = \frac{Operational\ results}{Training\ costs} = \frac{\$220,800}{\$32,836} = 6.7$$

Total savings: $187,964

pretest/posttest design with a comparison group to obtain an estimate of the difference in job performance for trained versus untrained employees. Other types of economic analyses evaluate training as it benefits the firm or the government using direct and indirect training costs, government incentives paid for training, wage increases received by trainees as a result of completion of training, tax rates, and discount rates.[51]

Practical Considerations in Determining Return on Investment

As mentioned earlier in the discussion, ROI analysis may not be appropriate for all training programs. Training programs best suited for ROI analysis have clearly identified outcomes, are not one-time events, are highly visible in the company, are strategically focused, and have effects that can be isolated. In the examples of ROI analysis in this chapter, the outcomes were very measurable. That is, in the wood plant example, it was easy to see changes in quality, to count accident rates, and to observe housekeeping behavior. For training programs that focus on soft outcomes (e.g., attitudes, interpersonal skills), it may be more difficult to estimate the value.

TABLE 6.15
Examples of Return on Investment

Source: Based on J.J. Philips, "ROI: The Search for Best Practices," *Training and Development* (February 1996): 45.

Industry	Training Program	ROI
Bottling company	Workshops on managers' roles	15:1
Large commercial bank	Sales training	21:1
Electric and gas utility	Behavior modification	5:1
Oil company	Customer service	4.8:1
Health maintenance organization	Team training	13.7:1

Showing the link between training and market share gain or other higher level strategic business outcomes can be very problematic. These outcomes can be influenced by too many other factors not directly related to training (or even under the control of the business), such as competitors' performance and economic upswings and downturns. Business units may not be collecting the data needed to identify the ROI of training programs on individual performance. Also, the measurement of training can often be very expensive. Verizon Communications employs 240,000 people.[52] The company estimates that it spends approximately $5,000 for an ROI study. Given the large number of training programs the company offers, it is too expensive to conduct an ROI for each program.

Companies are finding that, despite these difficulties, the demand for measuring ROI is still high. As a result, companies are using creative ways to measure the costs and benefits of training.[53] For example, to calculate ROI for a training program designed to cut absenteeism, trainees and their supervisors were asked to estimate the cost of an absence. The values were averaged to obtain an estimate. Cisco Systems tracks how often its partners return to its Web site for additional instruction. A. T. Kearney, a management consulting firm, tracks the success of its training by how much business is generated from past clients. Rather than relying on ROI, Verizon Communications uses training ROE, or return on expectations. Prior to training, the senior managers who are financially accountable for the training program are asked to identify their expectations regarding what the training program should accomplish as well as a cost estimate of the current issue or problem. After training, the senior managers are asked whether their expectations have been met, and they are encouraged to attach a monetary value to those met expectations. The ROE is used as an estimate in an ROI analysis. Verizon Communications continues to conduct ROI analysis for training programs and courses in which objective numbers are available (e.g., sales training) and in which the influence of training can be better isolated (evaluation designs that have comparison groups and that collect pretraining and posttraining outcomes).

Statistical analyses of costs and benefits are desirable; however, they are not the only way to demonstrate that training delivers bottom-line results. Success cases can also be used. **Success cases** refer to concrete examples of the impact of training that show how learning has led to results that the company finds worthwhile and the managers find credible.[54] Success cases do not attempt to isolate the influence of training but rather to provide evidence that it was useful. For example, Federated Department Stores wanted to show the effectiveness of its Leadership Choice program, which was designed to increase sales and profit performance in Federated stores by helping leaders enhance personal effectiveness, develop a customer-focused plan to improve business performance, and recognize the impact of decisions on business results.[55] At the conclusion of the program, participants were asked to set a business and leadership goal to work on in the next three months. Because the managers in the program had a wide range of responsibilities in Federated's various divisions, it was necessary to show that the program produced results for different managers with different responsibilities. As a result, concrete examples were used to illustrate the value of the program to management. Recall from Table 6.12 that a company may want to consider its organizational culture when choosing an evaluation design. Because story telling is an important part of Federated's culture, using success cases was an acceptable way to show senior managers the impact of the leadership program.

Participants who reported good progress toward their goals were interviewed, and case studies were written to highlight the program's impact in management's priority areas, which were categories such as "in-store shopping experience" and "differentiated assortment of goods." Because the case studies told a retailing story, they communicated the kind of results that the program was designed to achieve. For example, one manager set a goal of increasing sales by designing new neckware assortments so that the selling floor would be visually exciting. He directed a new associate buyer to take more ownership of the neckware business, he reviewed future buying strategies, and he visited competitors' stores. As a result, this manager exceeded his goal of increasing sales 5 percent.

MEASURING HUMAN CAPITAL AND TRAINING ACTIVITY

So far this chapter has focused on how to evaluate training programs. As mentioned in Chapter 1, training and development contributes to a company's intangible assets such as human capital. Besides learning how to evaluate training and development programs, you also need to understand how to evaluate the training and development function and how to measure human capital.

Each year the American Society of Training and Development (ASTD) prepares a report that summarizes company-provided training in the United States.[56] This report provides companies with information about training hours and delivery methods that they can use to benchmark, or compare, themselves to other companies in similar industries or with the same number of employees. Table 6.16 provides examples of different measurements, or metrics. These metrics are valuable for benchmarking purposes, for understanding the current amount of training activity in a company, and for tracking historical trends in training activity. However, collecting these metrics does not address such issues as whether training is effective or whether the company is using the data to make strategic training decisions.[57]

Although there are a number of metrics to choose from, each company needs to choose metrics that are related to its business strategy or goals (see Chapter 2). Consider how A. G. Edwards and Accenture measure and determine the value of human capital.[58] A. G. Edwards, a securities and financial services firm based in Saint Louis, Missouri, provided 813,000 hours of training to the company's 15,413 employees located throughout the United States and Europe. Although all human capital investment initiatives are evaluated carefully by A. G. Edwards, they are not part of an annual budgeting process. The chairman of A. G. Edwards wants to make the company stronger in the future by doing whatever it takes to get the best-trained financial planners in the business. One of the metrics that the firm uses to measure progress toward this goal is to count the number of employees who have earned

TABLE 6.16
Training Metrics

Source: Based on A. Paradise, *2008 State of the Industry Report* (Alexandria, VA: American Society for Training and Development, 2008); L. Weatherly, *The Value of People: The Challenges and Opportunities of Human Capital Measurement and Reporting* (Alexandria, VA: Society for Human Resource Management, 2003).

Expenditure per employee
Learning hours received per employee
Expenditure as a percentage of payroll
Expenditure as a percentage of revenue
Cost per learning hour received
Percentage of expenditures for external services
Learning hours received per training and development staff member
Average percentage of learning activities outsourced
Average percentage of learning content by content area (e.g., basic skills, customer service, executive development)
Average percentage of learning hours provided via different delivery methods (instructor-led, technology-based)

industrywide professional credentials such as becoming a certified financial planner. Accenture, a global management consulting and technology services company, invested about $400 million in employee development in 2004. The company found that there was a 17 percent to 20 percent increase in demand for consultants who took the most training, and retention rates for these employees were 14 percent greater than for employees who had not taken the highest levels of training available.

There is no one accepted method for measuring intellectual or human capital. Skandia Corporation, a financial services company, is well known for trying to measure its intellectual capital.[59] Skandia believes that the total value of a company (market value) is based on financial capital *and* intellectual capital. This attitude differs from traditional accounting practices, which value a company based only on financial capital. Intellectual capital includes human capital and structural capital. Recall from the discussion in Chapter 1 that structural capital includes information systems, operating procedures, patents, copyrights, and trade secrets. Skandia uses metrics that assess the focus of training (e.g., training expense per employee, time in training, and annual cost of training, communications, and support programs for full-time employees), renewal and development (e.g., share of training hours, share of development hours), and growth and renewal (e.g., value added per employee, total competence of experts per year). Although Skandia's approach has made a contribution to valuing human capital development, it is not frequently used. One of its limitations is that the metrics are not totally complete for companies that have large investments in plants and equipment. Human capital is important in these companies but financial capital also plays a large role in their ability to invest in plants and equipment.

McBassi and Company, a consulting firm that helps companies measure "return on people," takes a broader approach to measuring human capital.[60] Five human capital indicators are used: leadership and managerial practices (e.g., communications, performance feedback), work-force optimization (e.g., processes for getting work done, good hiring choices), learning capacity (e.g., a company's ability to learn, innovate, and improve), knowledge accessibility (e.g., ability to make knowledge and ideas available to employees), and talent engagement (e.g., job design, how employee time is used).

Summary

Evaluation provides information used to determine training effectiveness. Evaluation involves identifying the appropriate outcomes to measure. The chapter notes that a good evaluation requires thinking about evaluation before conducting training. Information from the needs assessment and specific and measurable learning objectives help identify outcomes that should be included in the evaluation design. The outcomes used in evaluating training programs include trainees' satisfaction with the training program, learning of knowledge or skills, use of knowledge and skills on the job, and results such as sales, productivity, or accident prevention. Evaluation may also involve comparing the costs of training to the benefits received (return on investment). Outcomes used in training evaluation help to determine the degree to which the program has resulted in both learning and transfer of training. Evaluation also involves choosing the appropriate design to maximize the confidence that can be placed in the results. The design is based on a careful analysis of how to minimize threats to internal and external validity as well as the purpose, expertise, and other company and training characteristics. The types of designs used for evaluation vary on the basis of whether they include pretraining and posttraining measures of outcomes and use of a training and a comparison group. The chapter concludes with a discussion of how to measure training's contribution to a company's human capital assets.

Key Terms

training effectiveness, *216*
training outcomes
(criteria), *216*
training evaluation, *216*
evaluation design, *216*
formative evaluation, *218*
pilot testing, *218*
summative evaluation, *218*
reaction outcomes, *221*
cognitive outcomes, *223*
skill-based outcomes, *224*
affective outcomes, *224*
results, *225*
return on investment
(ROI), *226*

direct costs, *226*
indirect costs, *226*
benefits, *226*
criteria relevance, *227*
criterion contamina-
tion, *227*
criterion deficiency, *228*
reliability, *228*
discrimination, *228*
practicality, *229*
threats to validity, *231*
internal validity, *232*
external validity, *232*
pretraining measure, *233*
posttraining measure, *233*

comparison group, *233*
Hawthorne effect, *233*
random assignment, *233*
posttest-only, *234*
pretest/posttest, *235*
pretest/posttest with
comparison group, *235*
time series, *236*
reversal, *236*
Solomon four-group, *237*
cost-benefit analysis, *240*
utility analysis, *244*
success cases, *246*

Discussion Questions

1. What can be done to motivate companies to evaluate training programs?

2. What do threats to validity have to do with training evaluation? Identify internal and external threats to validity. Are internal and external threats similar? Explain.

3. What are the strengths and weaknesses of each of the following designs: posttest-only, pretest/posttest with comparison group, and pretest/posttest only?

4. What are results outcomes? Why do you think most organizations don't use results outcomes for evaluating their training programs?

5. This chapter discussed several factors that influence the choice of evaluation design. Which of these factors would have the greatest influence on your choice of an evaluation design? Which would have the smallest influence? Explain your choices.

6. How might you estimate the benefits of a training program designed to teach employees how to use the World Wide Web to monitor stock prices?

7. A group of managers ($N = 25$) participated in the problem-solving module of a leadership development program two weeks ago. The module consisted of two days in which the group focused on the correct process to use in problem solving. Each manager supervises 15 to 20 employees. The company is willing to change the program, and there is an increasing emphasis in the company to show that training expenses are justifiable. You are asked to evaluate this program. Your boss would like the results of the evaluation no later than six weeks from now. Discuss the outcomes you would collect and the design you would use. How might your answer change if the managers had not yet attended the program?

8. What practical considerations need to be taken into account when calculating a training program's ROI?

9. What metrics might be useful for evaluating the effectiveness of a company's training function? Discuss and rate their importance.

10. What acceptable methods can be used to show the costs and benefits of training without collecting statistics and conducting analyses? Explain these methods and their strengths and weaknesses compared to a cost-benefit analysis.

Application Assignments

1. Consider this course as a training program. In teams of up to five students, identify (*a*) the types of outcomes you would recommend to use in evaluating this course and (*b*) the evaluation design you would use. Justify your choice of a design based on minimizing threats to validity and practical considerations.

2. Domino's Pizza was interested in determining whether a new employee could learn how to make a pizza using a computer-based training method (CD-ROM). The CD-ROM application addresses the proper procedure for "massaging" a dough ball and stretching it to fit a 12-inch pizza pan. Domino's quality standards emphasize the roundness of the pizza, an even border, and uniform thickness of the dough. Traditionally, on-the-job training is used to teach new employees how to stretch pizza dough to fit the pizza pan.

   a. What outcomes or criteria should Domino's Pizza measure to determine if CD-ROM training is an effective method for teaching new employees how to stretch pizza dough to fit a 12-inch pan? Who would be involved in the evaluation?

   b. Describe the evaluation design you would recommend using to determine if CD-ROM training is more effective than on-the-job training.

3. Ask your instructor for a copy of the evaluation form, survey, or rating sheet that is used by your college, university, or business to evaluate the course or program in which you are using this text. As you look over the evaluation, answer the following questions:

   a. What are the strengths and weaknesses of the evaluation form?

   b. What changes would you suggest to improve the evaluation form (e.g., different questions, additional questions)?

   c. How should the evaluation be used to actually improve the instruction that you receive?

4. Sears designed a training program to improve tool and hardware sales. The two-hour program involved distance learning and was broadcast from the Sears training facility to 50 salespersons at 10 store locations in the United States. The salespersons are paid $15 per hour. The program involved training salespeople in how to set up merchandise displays so they attract buyers' attention. Sales of tools and merchandise at the 10 stores included in the program averaged $5,000 per week before the program and $6,500 per week after the program. Program costs included:

Instructor	$10,000
Distance learning (satellite space rental)	5,000
Materials ($100 per trainee @ 50 trainees)	5,000
Trainees' salaries and benefits (50 trainees with wages of $15 per hour in a 2-hour training program)	1,500

   What is the return on investment (ROI) from this program?

5. Cablevision developed an e-learning course that taught salespersons how to increase the number of cable television subscribers, thereby increasing revenue. The company wants to know if salespersons will increase upselling of cable television services (e.g., premium channels) and will try to sell other products (e.g., e-mail and Web access). The company also wants to know the ROI of this training program.

a. What training outcomes should the company collect? From whom should the outcomes be collected?

b. What evaluation design would you recommend? Defend your recommendation.

c. Show how Cablevision can conduct an ROI analysis. Describe the information the company should collect and how it should be collected.

6. The 100-employee information technology department of a financial services company had a high turnover rate. A survey of employees revealed that the reason most left was dissatisfaction with the level of training. The average turnover rate was 23 percent per year. The cost to recruit and train one new employee was $56,625. To address the turnover problem, the company developed a skills training program that averaged 80 hours per year per employee. The average employee wage was $35 per hour. Instructor, classroom, and other costs were $170,000.

a. What is the total cost of training? The total cost of turnover?

b. If the turnover rate dropped 8 percent (from 23 percent to 15 percent), what was the financial benefit of the training program?

c. What was the ROI of the training program?

d. How much would the turnover rate have to be reduced (from 23 percent) for the training program to show a benefit?

7. Go to www.roiinstitute.net, the web site for ROI Institute, Inc., the leading resource on research, training, and networking for practitioners of the Phillips ROI Methodology.™ Click on "Tools." Review the "Nations Hotels—Measuring the ROI in Business Coaching." What are the strengths of this approach for determining ROI? What are the weaknesses?

Case: *Evaluating the Returns on Leadership Development at BP*

Through mergers and acquisitions, BP, a global energy company, has doubled in size in just five years. BP has more than 97,000 employees who work in over 100 countries throughout the world. BP is involved in gas stations and the exploration and production of crude oil and natural gas; in refining marketing, supply, and transportation; in the manufacture and marketing of petrochemicals; and in solar power generation. You may be familiar with some of BP's brands, which include the Wild Bean Café, am/pm, Castrol, ARCO, Amoco, and ARAL (in Germany).

BP developed a First Level Leaders Development Program to provide a common skill set for BP's leaders. First-level leaders work in every BP business, including retail operations, chemical plants, refineries, and drilling platforms. They also lead different numbers of employees. Some lead teams of more than 10 employees, others work with just a few employees in functional areas such as research and development. Despite these differences, the decisions the first-level leaders make influence BP's turnover, costs, quality, safety, innovation, and environmental performance. The program includes a four-day leadership course that focuses on how to lead teams, the role of first-level leaders, and expectations of leaders at BP. E-learning modules were used for helping first-level leaders understand safety, health, security legislation, ethics, and financial decisions. A two and one-half day course focused on performance goals, BP's company structure, an understanding of the BP brand, and BP's global and regional strategy.

What outcomes should BP collect to determine the effectiveness of the First Level Leaders Development Program? What evaluation design should it use?

Source: Based on J. Brown, R. Eagar, and P. Lawrence, "BP Refines Leadership," *T + D* (March 2005): 33–41; also see www.bp.com, the Web site for BP.

Endnotes

1. P. Tharenou, A. Saks, and C. Moore, "A Review and Critique of Research on Training and Organizational-Level Outcomes," *Human Resource Management Review* 17 (2007): 251–273.

2. P. Bernthal, "Measurement Gets Strategic," *T + D* (May 2005): 53–56.

3. A. Purcell, "20/20 ROI," *Training and Development* (July 2000): 28–33.

4. M. Van Wart, N. J. Cayer, and S. Cook, *Handbook of Training and Development for the Public Sector* (San Francisco: Jossey-Bass, 1993).

5. K. Brown and M. Gerhardt, "Formative Evaluation: An Integrative Practice Model and Case Study," *Personnel Psychology* 55 (2002): 951–83.

6. J. Salopek, "BEST 2005: St. George Bank," *T + D* (October 2005): 68.

7. D. Russ-Eft and H. Preskill, "In Search of the Holy Grail: Return on Investment Evaluation in Human Resource Development," *Advances in Developing Human Resources* 7 (February 2005): 71–85.

8. K. Kraiger, D. McLinden, and W. Casper, "Collaborative Planning for Training Impact," Human Resource Management 43 (4) (2004): 337–351; F. Nickols, "Why a Stakeholder Approach to Evaluating Training," *Advances in Developing Human Resources* (February 2005): 121–134.

9. K. Kraiger, D. McLinden, and W. Casper, "Collaborative Planning for Training Impact," *Human Resource Management* (Winter 2004): 337–51; R. Brinkerhoff, "The Success Case Method: A Strategic Evaluation Approach to Increasing the Value and Effect of Training," *Advances in Developing Human Resources* 7 (February 2005): 86–101.

10. D. L. Kirkpatrick, "Evaluation," in *The ASTD Training and Development Handbook,* 2d ed., ed. R. L. Craig (New York: McGraw-Hill, 1996): 294–312.

11. K. Kraiger, J. K. Ford, and E. Salas, "Application of Cognitive, Skill-Based, and Affective Theories of Learning Outcomes to New Methods of Training Evaluation," *Journal of Applied Psychology* 78 (1993): 311–28; J. J. Phillips, "ROI: The Search for Best Practices," *Training and Development* (February 1996): 42–47; G. M. Alliger, S. I. Tannenbaum, W. Bennet, Jr., H. Traver, and A. Shortland, "A Meta-analysis of the Relations among Training Criteria," *Personnel Psychology* 50 (1997): 341–55; K. Kraiger, "Decision-Based Evaluation," in *Creating, Implementing, and Managing Effective Training and Development,* ed. K. Kraiger (San Francisco: Jossey-Bass, 2002): 331–75; G. Alliger and E. Janek, "Kirkpatrick's Levels of Training Criteria: Thirty Years Later," *Personnel Psychology* 42 (1989): 331–42.

12. Kraiger, Ford, and Salas, "Application of Cognitive, Skill-Based, and Affective Theories"; Phillips, "ROI: The Search for Best Practices"; D. L. Kirkpatrick, "Evaluation of Training," in *Training and Development Handbook,* 2d ed., ed. R. L. Craig (New York: McGraw-Hill, 1976): 18-1 to 18-27.

13. R. Morgan and W. Casper, "Examining the Factor Structure of Participant Reactions to Training: A Multidimensional Approach," *Human Resource Development Quarterly* 11 (2000): 301–17; K. Brown, "An Examination of the Structure and Nomological Network of Trainee Reactions: A Closer Look at 'Smile Sheets,'" *Journal of Applied Psychology* 90 (2005): 991–1001; G. Vellios, "On the Level," *T + D* (December 2008): 26–29.

14. G. Hopkins, "How to Design an Instructor Evaluation," *Training and Development* (March 2000): 51–53.

15. T. Sitzmann, K. Brown, W. Casper, K. Ely, and R. Zimmerman, "A review and Meta-analysis of the Nomological Network of Trainee Reactions," *Journal of Applied Psychology* 93 (2008): 280–295.

16. P. Taylor, D. Russ-Eft, and H. Taylor, "Transfer of Management Training from Alternative Perspectives," *Journal of Applied Psychology* 94 (2009): 104–121.

17. J. J. Phillips, "Was It the Training?" *Training and Development* (March 1996): 28–32.

18. T. Murphy and S. Zandvakili, "Data- and Metrics-Driven Approach to Human Resource Practices: Using Customers, Employees, and Financial Metrics," *Human Resource Management* 39 (Spring 2000): 93–105.

19. "LQ Management LLC," *T + D* (October 2008): 76–77.

20. Phillips, "ROI: The Search for Best Practices."

21. J. Schettler, "Homegrown Solutions," *Training* (November 2002): 76–79.

22. D. A. Grove and C. Ostroff, "Program Evaluation," in *Developing Human Resources,* ed. K. N. Wexley (Washington, DC: Bureau of National Affairs, 1991): 5-185 to 5-220.

23. H. J. Frazis, D. E. Herz, and M. W. Horrigan, "Employer-Provided Training: Results from a New Survey," *Monthly Labor Review* 118 (1995): 3–17.

24. W. Arthur, Jr., W. Bennett, P. Edens, and S. Bell, "Effectiveness of Training in Organizations: A Meta-analysis of Design and Evaluation Features," *Journal of Applied Psychology* 88 (2003): 234–45.

25. J. Gordon, "Eye on ROI," *Training* (May 2007): 43–45.

26. Alliger and Janak, "Kirkpatrick's Levels of Training Criteria: Thirty Years Later."

27. W. Arthur, Jr., W. Bennett, P. Edens, and S. Bell, "Effectiveness of Training in Organizations: A Meta-analysis of Design and Evaluation Features," *Journal of Applied Psychology* 88 (2003): 234–45.

28. T. D. Cook, D. T. Campbell, and L. Peracchio, "Quasi Experimentation," in *Handbook of Industrial and Organizational Psychology,* 2d ed., Vol. 1, eds. M. D. Dunnette and L. M. Hough (Palo Alto, CA: Consulting Psychologists Press, 1990): 491–576.

29. Ibid.; J. J. Phillips, *Handbook of Training Evaluation and Measurement Methods,* 2d ed. (Houston, TX: Gulf Publishing, 1991).

30. D. Sussman, "Strong Medicine Required," *T + D* (November 2005): 34–38.

31. S. J. Simon and J. M. Werner, "Computer Training through Behavior Modeling, Self-Paced, and Instructional Approaches: A Field Experiment," *Journal of Applied Psychology* 81 (1996): 648–59.

32. J. Komaki, K. D. Bardwick, and L. R. Scott, "A Behavioral Approach to Occupational Safety: Pinpointing and Reinforcing Safe Performance in a Food Manufacturing Plant," *Journal of Applied Psychology* 63 (1978): 434–45.

33. R. D. Bretz and R. E. Thompsett, "Comparing Traditional and Integrative Learning Methods in Organizational Training Programs," *Journal of Applied Psychology* 77 (1992): 941–51.

34. S. I. Tannenbaum and S. B. Woods, "Determining a Strategy for Evaluating Training: Operating within Organizational Constraints," *Human Resource Planning* 15 (1992): 63–81; R. D. Arvey, S. E. Maxwell, and E. Salas, "The Relative Power of Training Evaluation Designs under Different Cost Configurations," *Journal of Applied Psychology* 77 (1992): 155–60.

35. P. R. Sackett and E. J. Mullen, "Beyond Formal Experimental Design: Toward an Expanded View of the Training Evaluation Process," *Personnel Psychology* 46 (1993): 613–27.

36. B. Gerber, "Does Your Training Make a Difference? Prove It!" *Training* (March 1995): 27–34.

37. A. P. Carnevale and E. R. Schulz, "Return on Investment: Accounting for Training," *Training and Development Journal* (July 1990): S1–S32.

38. J. Phillips and P. Phillips, "Distinguishing ROI Myths from Reality," *Performance Improvement* (July 2008): 12–17.

39. Purcell, "20/20 ROI."

40. J. Phillips and P. Phillips, "Using Action Plans to Measure ROI," *Performance Improvement* 42 (2003): 22–31.

41. K. Ellis, "What's the ROI of ROI?" *Training* (January 2005): 16–21; B. Worthen, "Measuring the ROI of Training," *CIO* (February 15, 2001): 128–36; D. Russ-Eft and H. Preskill, "In Search of the Holy Grail: Return on Investment Evaluation in Human Resource Development," *Advances in Developing Human Resources* (February 2005): 71–85.

42. J. Gordon, "Eye on ROI," *Training* (May 2007): 43–45.

43. Carnevale and Schulz, "Return on Investment: Accounting for Training"; G. Kearsley, *Costs, Benefits, and Productivity in Training Systems* (Boston: Addison-Wesley, 1982).

44. S. D. Parry, "Measuring Training's ROI," *Training and Development* (May 1996): 72–77.

45. D. G. Robinson and J. Robinson, "Training for Impact," *Training and Development Journal* (August 1989): 30–42; J. J. Phillips, "How Much Is the Training Worth?" *Training and Development* (April 1996): 20–24.

46. Purcell, "20/20 ROI."

47. Phillips, *Handbook of Training Evaluation and Measurement Methods;* Phillips. "ROI: The Search for the Best Practices."

48. Robinson and Robinson, "Training for Impact."

49. Sussman, "Strong Medicine Required."

50. J. E. Matheiu and R. L. Leonard, "Applying Utility Analysis to a Training Program in Supervisory Skills: A Time-Based Approach," *Academy of Management Journal* 30 (1987): 316–35; F. L. Schmidt, J. E. Hunter, and K. Pearlman, "Assessing the Economic Impact of Personnel Programs on Work-Force Productivity," *Personnel Psychology* 35 (1982): 333–47; J. W. Boudreau, "Economic Considerations in Estimating the Utility of Human Resource Productivity Programs," *Personnel Psychology* 36 (1983): 551–76.

51. U. E. Gattiker, "Firm and Taxpayer Returns from Training of Semiskilled Employees," *Academy of Management Journal* 38 (1995): 1151–73.

52. Worthen, "Measuring the ROI of Training."

53. D. Abernathy, "Thinking Outside the Evaluation Box," *Training and Development* (February 1999): 19–23; E. Krell, "Calculating Success," *Training* (December 2002): 47–52; D. Goldwater, "Beyond ROI," *Training* (January 2001): 82–90.

54. Brinkerhoff, "The Success Case Method: A Strategic Evaluation Approach."

55. C. Wick and R. Pollock, "Making Results Visible," *T + D* (June 2004): 46–51.

56. A. Paradise, *2008 State of the Industry Report* (Alexandria, VA: American Society for Training and Development, 2008).

57. E. Holton and S. Naquin, "New Metrics for Employee Development," *Performance Improvement Quarterly* 17 (2004): 56–80.

58. R. Stolz, "The Capital Idea," *Human Resource Executive* (February 2005): 1, 24–29.

59. Holton and Naquin, "New Metrics for Employee Development."

60. L. Bassi and D. McMurrer, *What to Do When People Are Your Most Important Asset* (Golden, CO: McBassi and Company, May 2004/updated October 2004).

On-the-Job Video Gaming

Laura Holshouser's favorite video games include *Halo, Tetris,* and an online training game developed by her employer. A training game? That's right. The 24-year-old graduate student, who manages a Cold Stone Creamery ice-cream store in Riverside, California, stumbled across the game on the corporate Web site in October.

It teaches portion control and customer service in a cartoon-like simulation of a Cold Stone store. Players scoop cones against the clock and try to avoid serving too much ice cream. The company says more than 8,000 employees, or about 30 percent of the total, voluntarily downloaded the game in the first week. "It's so much fun," says Holshouser. "I e-mailed it to everyone at work."

The military has used video games as a training tool since the 1980s. Now the practice is catching on with companies, too, ranging from Cold Stone to Cisco Systems Inc. to Canon Inc. Corporate trainers are betting that games' interactivity and fun will hook young, media-savvy employees like Holshouser and help them grasp and retain sales, technical, and management skills. "Video games teach resource management, collaboration, critical thinking, and tolerance for failure," says Ben Sawyer, who runs Digitalmill Inc., a game consultancy in Portland, Me.

The market for corporate training games is small but it's growing fast. Sawyer estimates that such games make up 15 percent of the "serious," or nonentertainment, market, which also includes educational and medical training products. Over the next five years, Sawyer sees the serious-games market more than doubling, to $100 million, with trainers accounting for nearly a third of that. It's numbers like those that prompted Cyberlore Studios Inc., maker of *Playboy: The Mansion,* to refocus on training games—albeit based on its Playboy title. And training games will be top of mind at the Game Developers Conference in San Jose, California, this month.

Companies like video games because they are cost effective. Why pay for someone to fly to a central training campus when you can just plunk them down in front of a computer? Even better, employees often play the games at home on their own time. Besides, by industry standards, training games are cheap to make. A typical military game costs up to $10 million, while sophisticated entertainment games can cost twice that. Since the corporate variety don't require dramatic, warlike explosions or complex 3D graphics, they cost a lot less. BreakAway Games Ltd., which designs simulation games for the military, is finishing its first corporate product, V-bank, to train bank auditors. Its budget? Just $500,000.

DRAG AND DROP

Games are especially well-suited to training technicians. In one used by Canon, repairmen must drag and drop parts into the right spot on a copier. As in the board game *Operation,* a light flashes and a buzzer sounds if the repairman gets it wrong. Workers who played the game showed a 5 percent to 8 percent improvement in their training scores compared with older training techniques such as manuals, says Chuck Reinders, who trains technical support staff at Canon. This spring, the company will unveil 11 new training games.

Games are also being developed to help teach customer service workers to be more empathetic. Cyberlore, now rechristened Minerva Software Inc., is developing a training tool for a retailer by rejiggering its *Playboy Mansion* game. In the original, guests had to persuade models to pose topless. The new game requires players to use the art of persuasion to sell products, and simulates a store, down to the carpet and point-of-purchase display details.

Don Field, director of certifications at Cisco, says games won't entirely replace traditional training methods such as videos and classes. But he says they should be part of the toolbox. Last year, Cisco rolled out six new training games—some of them designed to teach technicians how to build a computer network. It's hard to imagine a drier subject. Not so in the virtual world. In one Cisco game, players must put the network together on Mars. In a sandstorm. "Our employees learn without realizing they are learning," says Field. Sounds suspiciously like fun.

Questions

1. How can video games be used to enhance learning? Transfer of training?

2. What features does a video game need to have to be an effective training method?

3. Do you believe that some generations (e.g., baby boomers, Generation Y, Generation X) of employees will react more positively to video games used for training than other generations? Why? Explain your answer.

4. The article discusses the use of video gaming by Cold Stone and Canon. How would you evaluate the effectiveness of video gaming (choose either Cold Stone or Canon)? What outcomes would you collect? What evaluation design would you use?

Source: R. Jana, "On-the-Job Video Gaming: Interactive Training Tools Are Captivating Employees and Saving Companies Money," www.businessweek.com (March 27, 2006), retrieved February 24, 2009.

Training and Development Methods

Part Three covers the different types of training and development methods and special issues in training and development. Chapter 7, Traditional Training Methods, introduces you to presentational, hands-on, and group training methods. These include on-the-job training, simulations and games, lecture, and various group building methods such as action learning and team training. Chapter 8, E-Learning and Use of Technology in Training, focuses on some of the newest technology-based methods that are being used for training and development. E-learning, or online learning, distance learning, virtual reality, virtual worlds such as Second Life, collaboration tools such as blogs and wikis, and mobile learning using personal data assistants (PDAs) and iPods are examples of some of the methods discussed in Chapter 8. Chapters 7 and 8 both show you how the method is used and help you understand the potential strengths and weaknesses of each method as well as important research results. Many companies are moving toward a blended learning approach to take advantage of the strengths of both face-to-face and technology-aided instruction. Blended learning is discussed in Chapter 8. Chapter 9, Employee Development, covers development planning and different types of development activities, including assessment, formal courses and programs, experiences, and interpersonal relationships involving mentoring and coaching. Chapter 9 also provides you with examples of companies' development systems. Chapter 10, Special Issues in Training and Employee Development, introduces you to a range of important topics such as legal issues in training, managing diversity, cross-cultural training, and succession planning.

The Part Three case, Secrets of an HR Superstar, illustrates how companies can identify and develop leadership talent.

Traditional Training Methods

Objectives

After reading this chapter, you should be able to

1. Discuss the strengths and weaknesses of presentational, hands-on, and group building training methods.

2. Provide recommendations for effective on-the-job training.

3. Develop a case study.

4. Develop a self-directed learning module.

5. Discuss the key components of behavior modeling training.

6. Explain the conditions necessary for adventure learning to be effective.

7. Discuss what team training should focus on to improve team performance.

Training at LaQuinta Hotels Helps Delight Guests

The 11-person training department at LaQuinta Hotels is responsible for call center, reservations, and franchise-opening training, retraining, and education for managers and owners at more than 600 hotels—a work force that includes 10,000 employees. In 2008, the company focused training on employees who have the most contact with the customer and the most influence on whether they return or choose to stay in other LaQuinta Hotels as they travel. These employees include housekeepers, maintenance employees, and front-desk employees. Although most of the training was formerly online, the training department found that face-to-face instructor-led training resulted in greater improvement in guest satisfaction and intent-to-return scores.

One type of training method used is a game similar to Monopoly that guides employees through front-desk operations and helps them learn how to deliver superior service. The training program involves small groups working with a facilitator to review different service scenarios and situations that occur. The groups are asked to consider how employees can deliver the best service in the scenario. The use of small groups help the employees learn from each other. Front-desk employees are better "experts" at customer service than any trainer. For housekeeping and maintenance employees, LaQuinta uses DVDs for training. Employees are provided with small portable DVD players when they need to learn tasks that they frequently perform on the job. For example, DVDs for cleaning the bathroom review the entire cleaning cycle. Employees take the DVD into the bathroom and watch the process of cleaning a bathroom before they try it themselves. They can fast-forward and review the DVD as needed to learn at their own pace. DVDs are available in both English and Spanish to accommodate the employee's language. LaQuinta also uses games that include employees from different functions and levels, including maintenance workers, front-desk employees, housekeepers, and supervisors. The purpose of the game is to help employees work together and understand the need to communicate with each other to solve guest problems. Based on a photograph of a room, employees are asked to determine which small detail might lead to a larger problem. For example, if the TV remote requires batteries and it hasn't been checked to see if it works correctly, the next guest in the room will not be able to watch TV. The guest will be inconvenienced by having to wait for new batteries to be delivered to the room.

Source: Based on "LaQuinta Hotels: Hands-On Training," *Training* (March/April 2008): 38–39.

INTRODUCTION

LaQuinta uses a combination of training methods to ensure that its housekeepers, maintenance employees, and front-desk employees deliver excellent customer service. Like LaQuinta, for most companies training methods have to be developed or purchased within a budget, there usually is a sense of urgency for the training, and training must be made available to those employees who need it.

Figure 7.1 provides an overview of the frequency with which various training methods are used. Instructor-led classroom training still remains the most frequently used method.

Regardless of whether the training method is traditional or technology-based, for training to be effective it needs to be based on the training design model shown in Figure 1.1. Needs assessment, a positive learning environment, and transfer of training are critical for training program effectiveness. Recall the discussions of needs assessment, learning, and transfer of training in Chapters 3, 4, and 5.

FIGURE 7.1
Overview of Use of Training Methods

Source: From "2008 Industry Report: Gauges & Drivers," *Training* (November/December 2008): 24.

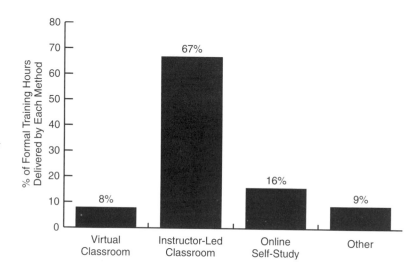

Chapters 7 and 8 present various training methods. Chapter 7 focuses on traditional training methods, methods that do not require new technology (e.g., Internet) for delivery. However, most methods discussed in this chapter can be delivered using CD-ROM or the Internet. For example, a classroom lecture can occur face-to-face with trainees (traditional training) or can be delivered through a virtual classroom in which the instructor is not in the same room as the trainees. Also, instruction can be real-time (synchronous) or time-delayed (asynchronous). Through technology, a lecture can be attended live although the trainees are not in the same classroom as the trainer, or the lecture can be videotaped or burned onto a CD-ROM or DVD. The lecture can be viewed by the trainees at their convenience on a personal computer that gives them access to the appropriate medium for viewing the lecture (e.g., CD-ROM player, DVD player, or Internet connection). Chapter 8 discusses technology-based training methods, including Web-based training, e-learning, and virtual reality. The increased use of technology-based training for delivery of instruction is occurring because of the potential increases in learning effectiveness as well as the reductions in training costs.

Keep in mind that many companies' training programs use a combination of methods to capitalize on each method's strengths for learning and transfer. For example, Colorado Springs Utilities's training program begins with a brainstorming session to engage trainees and help them enjoy the training and retain more of what they learn.[1] In a safety training class, students experience a simulated emergency and have to respond using their new skills along with their knowledge of an evacuation plan. The trainees perform different roles and activities in response to a power shut-down. Afterward, the trainer critiques their performance and trainees discuss what they have learned (or still need to learn). Trainees complete a written exam and review to ensure knowledge retention. Whataburger, a family-owned business that includes 700 restaurants in 10 states, hosts its annual WhataGames training activity to boost employee loyalty, pride in their work, and productivity.[2] The WhataGames training includes a quiz show that tests employees' knowledge of menu items, procedures, and company history (e.g., At what temperature does chicken have to reach to be properly cooked? 165 degrees). To prepare for the competition, employees review company history as well as operations manuals. During the What's Cooking competition, employee teams are tested in a simulated lunch rush. Inspectors examine every order prepared for accuracy and presentation. Besides benefiting the company, winning teams split more than $140,000 in prize money.

The traditional training methods discussed in this chapter are organized into three broad categories: presentation methods, hands-on methods, and group building methods.[3] The following sections provide a description of each method, a discussion of its advantages and disadvantages, and tips for the trainer who is designing or choosing the method. The chapter concludes by comparing methods based on several characteristics including the learning outcomes influenced; the extent to which the method facilitates learning; and transfer, cost, and effectiveness.

PRESENTATION METHODS

Presentation methods are methods in which trainees are passive recipients of information. This information may include facts, processes, and problem-solving methods. Lectures and audiovisual techniques are presentation methods. It is important to note that instructor-led classroom presentation methods may include lectures, video, workbooks and manuals, CD-ROMs, and games. That is, a mix of methods can actively engage trainees in learning and can help transfer of training to occur.

Lecture

In a **lecture,** trainers communicate through spoken words what they want the trainees to learn. The communication of learned capabilities is primarily one-way—from the trainer to the audience. As Figure 7.1 shows, instructor-led classroom presentation remains a popular training method despite new technologies such as interactive video and computer-assisted instruction.

A lecture is one of the least expensive, least time-consuming ways to present a large amount of information efficiently in an organized manner.[4] The lecture format is also useful because it is easily employed with large groups of trainees. Besides being the primary means to communicate large amounts of information, lectures are also used to support other training methods such as behavior modeling and technology-based techniques. For example, a lecture may be used to communicate information regarding the purpose of the training program, conceptual models, or key behaviors to trainees prior to their receiving training that is more interactive and customized to their specific needs.

Table 7.1 describes several variations of the standard lecture method. All have advantages and disadvantages.[5] Team teaching brings more expertise and alternative perspectives to the training session. Team teaching does require more time on the part of trainers to not only prepare their particular session but also coordinate with other trainers, especially when there is a great deal of integration between topics. Panels are good for showing trainees different viewpoints in a debate. A potential disadvantage of a panel is that trainees who are relatively naive about a topic may have difficulty understanding the important points. Guest speakers can motivate learning by bringing to the trainees relevant examples and applications. For guest speakers to be effective, trainers need to set expectations with speakers regarding how their presentation should relate to the course content. Student presentations may increase the material's meaningfulness and trainees' attentiveness, but it can inhibit learning if the trainees do not have presentation skills.

The lecture method has several disadvantages. Lectures tend to lack participant involvement, feedback, and meaningful connection to the work environment—all of which inhibit learning and transfer of training. Lectures appeal to few of the trainees' senses because trainees focus primarily on hearing information. Lectures also make it difficult for the trainer to judge quickly and efficiently the learners' level of understanding. To overcome these problems, the lecture is often supplemented with question-and-answer periods, discussion, video,

TABLE 7.1
Variations of the Lecture Method

Method	Description
Standard Lecture	Trainer talks while trainees listen and absorb information.
Team Teaching	Two or more trainers present different topics or alternative views of the same topic.
Guest Speakers	Speaker visits the session for a predetermined time period. Primary instruction is conducted by the instructor.
Panels	Two or more speakers present information and ask questions.
Student Presentations	Groups of trainees present topics to the class.

games, or case studies. These techniques allow the trainer to build into the lecture more active participation, job-related examples, and exercises, which facilitate learning and transfer of training.

At Sony Pictures' Imageworks, training takes many different forms.[6] For example, employees are retrained before starting a new project. The company creates digital visual effects and animation, and for every project, it uses new methods and technology to create animation that fits each movie's characters and feel. Employees take classes for several hours each day to update their skills. Then they work at developing a frame of animation from a completed film. For example, the frame might include the characters but the employees have to develop the environment, the hair, or the animation, depending on what they are learning. Imageworks has online tutorials that employees can access to learn about other disciplines such as lighting. The online tutorials help employees learn the basic terminology so employees can communicate and work with employees from disciplines other than their own. To showcase good work, employees or teams whose work has received exemplary peer review are asked to give lunchtime lectures to teach techniques to others. At Constellation New Energy, new-hire training involves 30 hours of pretraining work plus two weeks of classroom instruction that focuses on developing sales skills relevant to an energy company.[7] Trainees learn about the issues their potential customers face and learn models to help customers manage costs and risks over time. They also prepare tools and materials for their target markets and participate in role plays. Finally, trainees meet with their managers at the end of training to develop a plan to implement what they have learned.

Audiovisual Techniques

Audiovisual instruction includes overheads, slides, and video. Video is a popular instructional method.[8] It has been used for improving communications skills, interviewing skills, and customer-service skills and for illustrating how procedures (e.g., welding) should be followed. Video is, however, rarely used alone. It is usually used in conjunction with lectures to show trainees real-life experiences and examples. Here is how one company is using video in its training program.

At 5:30 A.M. the Morse Bros. drivers prepare to deliver the first of many loads of concrete. In the concrete business, a perishable product needs to be delivered on a timely basis to construction sites. Morse Bros., located in Tangent, Oregon, is one of only a few ready-mix firms in the Northwest that provide regular training for their drivers. Drivers play a key role in determining the success of the business. Morse Bros. has been able to reduce costs and raise customer satisfaction by providing drivers with product training and by instructing drivers to avoid rollovers and excessive idling at construction sites.

What method does Morse Bros. use to train its drivers? The company produces training videos that are presented by mentor-drivers. The mentor-driver's job is to select the weekly video, schedule viewing sessions, keep attendance records, and guide a wrap-up discussion following each video. The mentor-drivers are trained to call attention to key learning points covered in the video and relate the topic to issues the drivers deal with on the job. Because training sessions are scheduled early in the morning at the beginning of the drivers' shift, time is limited. Videos seldom run more than 10 minutes. For example, one called *Another Pair of Eyes* trains drivers to observe test procedures used by testing agencies at job sites. Samples are tested several times a month. A sample that fails can leave the company liable for demolition and removal of the concrete structure. Morse Bros. provides training on test procedures because samples often fail a test due to contamination (e.g., dirt) that gets into the test cylinder. Another video emphasizes cold-weather precautions: Drain all tanks and hoses at the end of the day, park the drum in neutral. At each training session, drivers are asked to answer several questions related to the content of the program. At the end of a session, drivers and the mentor-driver discuss anything that might be interfering with the quality of the product or timeliness of delivery. Mentor-drivers then share this information with company managers.[9]

Video is also a major component of behavior modeling and, naturally, interactive video instruction. The use of video in training has a number of advantages.[10] First, trainers can review, slow down, or speed up the lesson, which gives them flexibility in customizing the session depending on trainees' expertise. Second, trainees can watch the video multiple times if they have access to it during and after the training session. This gives them control over their learning. Third, trainees can be exposed to equipment, problems, and events that cannot be easily demonstrated, such as equipment malfunctions, angry customers, or emergencies. Fourth, trainees are provided with consistent instruction. Program content is not affected by the interests and goals of a particular trainer. Fifth, videotaping trainees allows them to see and hear their own performance without the interpretation of the trainer. That is, video provides immediate objective feedback. As a result, trainees cannot attribute poor performance to the bias of external evaluators such as the trainer or peers. Sixth, video requires minimal knowledge of technology and equipment. Most trainers and trainees can easily use a VCR or DVD player.

Most problems in video result from the creative approach used.[11] These problems include too much content for the trainee to learn, poor dialogue between the actors (which hinders the credibility and clarity of the message), overuse of humor or music, and drama that makes it confusing for the trainee to understand the important learning points emphasized in the video.

HANDS-ON METHODS

Hands-on methods are training methods that require the trainee to be actively involved in learning. These methods include on-the-job training, simulations, case studies, business games, role plays, and behavior modeling. These methods are ideal for developing specific skills, understanding how skills and behaviors can be transferred to the job, experiencing all aspects of completing a task, or dealing with interpersonal issues that arise on the job.

On-the-Job Training (OJT)

On-the-job training (OJT) refers to new or inexperienced employees learning in the work setting and during work by observing peers or managers performing the job and trying to imitate their behavior. OJT is one of the oldest and most used types of informal training.[12] It is considered informal because it does not necessarily occur as part of a training program and because managers, peers, or mentors serve as trainers. If OJT is too informal, learning will not occur. OJT can be useful for training newly hired employees, upgrading experienced employees' skills when new technology is introduced, cross-training employees within a department or work unit, and orienting transferred or promoted employees to their new jobs.

OJT takes various forms, including apprenticeships and self-directed learning programs. (Both are discussed later in this section.) OJT has several advantages over other training methods.[13] It can be customized to the experiences and abilities of trainees. Training is immediately applicable to the job because OJT occurs on the job using actual tools and equipment. As a result, trainees are highly motivated to learn. Both trainees and trainers are at the job site and continue to work while training occurs. This means that companies save the costs related to bringing trainees to a central location, hiring trainers, and renting training facilities. OJT can be offered at any time, and trainers will be available because they are peers or managers. Finally, OJT uses actual job tasks and occurs at work. As a result, skills learned in OJT more easily transfer to the job.

Reliance Industries, one of India's largest businesses, uses on-the-job training in its Nagothane Manufacturing Division (a refinery that makes polymers and chemicals).[14] Because of rapid company growth and the demand for experienced employees, the company needed to decrease the length of time required for new engineers to contribute. In response to this need, the training staff identified mentors who would help accelerate learning for the new engineers. The mentors and new hires are carefully matched based on an assessment of the mentor's training style and the new employee's learning style. Mentors are paired with up to three new employees each for nine months. The mentors and new employees work together on four learning modules, each of which takes two months to complete. Each module includes predetermined lesson plans and progress is tracked using an online portal. As a result, the length of time it takes new engineers to contribute at work has decreased from 12 to 6 months.

At Sweets Candy, a Salt Lake City, Utah, candy maker, new employees receive training in basic safety and emergency evacuation procedures in an orientation session and then are assigned a mentor.[15] The mentor works with the new employee for two weeks, providing hands-on one-on-one training. Teams hold weekly meetings and managers provide training on safety issues throughout the year. Employees also receive a weekly safety contact card on which they note safety hazards they have encountered on their job and how they have fixed the problem. The safety contact cards are turned in and each month the company has a safety celebration where the cards are put into a drawing. Employees win prizes such as a day off or a $10 gift card. All of the safety contact cards are reviewed to identify safety issues and hazards, which are then communicated to the employees.

OJT is an attractive training method because compared to other methods, it needs less investment in time or money for materials, the trainer's salary, or instructional design. Managers or peers who are job knowledge experts are used as instructors. As a result, it may be tempting to let them conduct the training as they believe it should be done.

There are several disadvantages to this unstructured approach to OJT. Managers and peers may not use the same process to complete a task. They may pass on bad habits as well as useful skills. Also, they may not understand that demonstration, practice, and feedback are important conditions for effective on-the-job training. Unstructured OJT can result in poorly trained employees, employees who use ineffective or dangerous methods to produce a product or provide a service, and products or services that vary in quality.

OJT must be structured to be effective. Table 7.2 shows the principles of structured OJT. Because OJT involves learning by observing others, successful OJT is based on the principles emphasized by social learning theory. These include the use of a credible trainer, a manager or peer who models the behavior or skill, communication of specific key behaviors, practice, feedback, and reinforcement. For example, at Rochester Gas and Electric in Rochester, New York, radiation and chemistry instructors teach experienced employees how to conduct OJT.[16] While teaching these employees how to demonstrate software to new employees, the trainer may ask the employees to watch other OJT instructors as they train new recruits so they can learn new teaching techniques. Regardless of the specific type, effective OJT programs include:

1. A policy statement that describes the purpose of OJT and emphasizes the company's support for it.
2. A clear specification of who is accountable for conducting OJT. If managers conduct OJT, this is mentioned in their job descriptions and is part of their performance evaluations.
3. A thorough review of OJT practices (program content, types of jobs, length of program, cost savings) at other companies in similar industries.
4. Training of managers and peers in the principles of structured OJT (see Table 7.2).
5. Availability of lesson plans, checklists, procedure manuals, training manuals, learning contracts, and progress report forms for use by employees who conduct OJT.
6. Evaluation of employees' levels of basic skills (reading, computation, writing) before OJT.[17]

For example, the OJT program utilized by Borden's North American Pasta Division has many of these characteristics.[18] Not all managers and peers are used as trainers. Borden's invests in trainer selection, training, and rewards to ensure OJT's effectiveness. Employees and managers interested in being instructors are required to apply for the position. Those chosen as instructors are required to complete a demanding train-the-trainer course that involves classroom training as well as time on the manufacturing floor to learn how to operate machinery such as pasta machines and to correctly teach other employees to use the equipment. Borden's also builds accountability into the OJT program. Trainees are responsible for completing a checklist that requires them to verify that the trainer helped them learn the skills needed to operate the equipment and used effective instructional techniques.

TABLE 7.2 **Principles of On-the-Job Training**

Preparing for Instruction

1. Break down the job into important steps.
2. Prepare the necessary equipment, materials, and supplies.
3. Decide how much time you will devote to OJT and when you expect the employees to be competent in skill areas.

Actual Instruction

1. Tell the trainees the objective of the task and ask them to watch you demonstrate it.
2. Show the trainees how to do it without saying anything.
3. Explain the key points or behaviors. (Write out the key points for the trainees, if possible.)
4. Show the trainees how to do it again.
5. Have the trainees do one or more single parts of the task and praise them for correct reproduction (optional).
6. Have the trainees do the entire task and praise them for correct reproduction.
7. If mistakes are made, have the trainees practice until accurate reproduction is achieved.
8. Praise the trainees for their success in learning the task.

Source: Based on W. J. Rothwell and H. C. Kazanas, "Planned OJT Is Productive OJT," *Training and Development Journal* (October 1990): 53–55; P. J. Decker and B. R. Nathan, *Behavior Modeling Training* (New York: Praeger Scientific, 1985).

Self-Directed Learning

Self-directed learning has employees take responsibility for all aspects of learning—including when it is conducted and who will be involved.[19] Trainees master predetermined training content at their own pace without an instructor. Trainers may serve as facilitators. That is, trainers are available to evaluate learning or answer questions for the trainee. The trainer does not control or disseminate instruction. The learning process is controlled by the trainee. Self-directed learning for salespersons could involve reading newspapers or trade publications, talking to experts, or surfing the Internet to find new ideas related to the salesperson industry.[20] Also, self-directed learning could involve the company providing salespersons with information such as databases, training courses, and seminars while still holding the employees responsible for taking the initiative to learn. Because the effectiveness of self-directed learning is based on an employee's motivation to learn, companies may want to provide seminars on the self-directed learning process, self-management, and how to adapt to the environment, customers, and technology.

For example, at Corning Glass, new engineering graduates participate in an OJT program called SMART (Self-Managed, Awareness, Responsibility, and Technical competence).[21] Each employee is responsible for seeking the answers to a set of questions (e.g., "Under what conditions would a statistician be involved in the design of engineering experiments?") by visiting plants and research facilities and meeting with technical engineering experts and managers. After employees complete the questions, they are evaluated by a committee of peers who have already completed the SMART program. Evaluations have shown that the program cuts employees' start-up time in their new jobs from six weeks to three. The program is effective for a number of reasons. It encourages new employees' active involvement in learning and allows flexibility in finding time for training. A peer-review evaluation component motivates employees to complete the questions correctly. And, as a result of participating in the program, employees make contacts throughout the company and gain a better understanding of the technical and personal resources available within the company.

Self-directed learning has several advantages and disadvantages.[22] It allows trainees to learn at their own pace and receive feedback about the learning performance. For the company, self-directed learning requires fewer trainers, reduces costs associated with travel and meeting rooms, and makes multiple-site training more realistic. Self-directed learning provides consistent training content that captures the knowledge of experts. Self-directed learning also makes it easier for shift employees to gain access to training materials. For example, Four Seasons hotels faced the challenge of opening a new hotel in Bali, Indonesia.[23] It needed to teach English skills to 580 employees, none of whom spoke English or understood Western cuisine or customs. Four Seasons created a self-directed learning center that enables employees to teach themselves English. The center emphasizes communications, not simply learning to speak English. As a result of this emphasis, the center features video recorders, training modules, books, and magazines. Monetary incentives are provided for employees to move from the lowest to the highest level of English skills. Besides English, the center also teaches Japanese (the language of 20 percent of the Bali hotel's visitors) and provides training for foreign managers in Bahasa Indonesian, the native language of Indonesia.

A major disadvantage of self-directed learning is that trainees must be willing to learn on their own and feel comfortable doing so. That is, trainees must be motivated to learn.

From the company perspective, self-directed learning results in higher development costs, and development time is longer than with other types of training programs.

Several steps are necessary to develop effective self-directed learning:[24]

1. Conduct a job analysis to identify the tasks that must be covered.
2. Write trainee-centered learning objectives directly related to the tasks. Because the objectives take the place of the instructor, they must indicate what information is important, what actions the trainee should take, and what the trainee should master.
3. Develop the content for the learning package. This involves developing scripts (for video) or text screens (for computer-based training). The content should be based on the trainee-centered learning objectives. Another consideration in developing the content is the media (e.g., paper, video, computer, Web site) that will be used to communicate the content.
4. Break the content into smaller pieces ("chunks"). The chunks should always begin with the objectives that will be covered and include a method for trainees to evaluate their learning. Practice exercises should also appear in each chunk.
5. Develop an evaluation package that includes evaluation of the trainee and evaluation of the self-directed learning package. Trainee evaluation should be based on the objectives (a process known as criterion referencing). That is, questions should be developed that are written directly from the objectives and can be answered directly from the materials. Evaluation of the self-directed learning package should involve determining ease of use, how up-to-date the material is, whether the package is being used as intended, and whether trainees are mastering the objectives.

Self-directed learning is likely to become more common in the future as companies seek to train staff flexibly, take advantage of technology, and encourage employees to be proactive in their learning rather than driven by the employer.

Apprenticeship

Apprenticeship is a work-study training method with both on-the-job and classroom training.[25] To qualify as a registered apprentice under state or federal guidelines, apprentices in most cases must complete at least 144 hours of classroom instruction and must obtain 2,000 hours, or one year, of on-the-job experience.[26] Once their training is complete, apprentices are called journey workers and they earn certification from the U.S. Department of Labor or a state apprenticeship agency. Table 7.3 shows the top occupations for apprentices. Apprenticeships can be sponsored by individual companies or by groups of companies cooperating with a union. As Table 7.3 shows, the majority of apprenticeship programs are in the skilled trades such as plumbing, carpentry, electrical work, and pipe fitting. Table 7.4 is an example of an apprenticeship program for a machinist.

In an apprenticeship program, the hours and weeks that must be devoted to completing specific skill units are clearly defined. The on-the-job training involves assisting a certified tradesperson (a journeyworker) at the work site. The OJT portion of the apprenticeship follows the guidelines for effective OJT by including modeling, practice, feedback, and evaluation.[27] First, the employer verifies that the trainee has the required knowledge of the operation or process. Next, the trainer (who is usually a more experienced, licensed employee) demonstrates each step of the process, emphasizing safety issues and key steps. The senior employee provides the apprentice with the opportunity to perform the process until all are satisfied that the apprentice can perform it properly and safely.

TABLE 7.3

Top 25 Occupations for Active Apprentices

Source: Based on "Top 25 Apprenticeship Occupations Ranked by Total as of September 30, 2005," from U.S. Department of Labor, Employment and Training Administration. Available at www.doleta.gov/atels_bat/top-25-occupations-2005.cfm.

Rank	Occupation	Total Active Enrolled	Number of Active Programs
1	Electrician	38,706	3,280
2	Carpenter	22,434	481
3	Plumber	15,787	2,353
4	Pipe fitter (construction)	8,460	794
5	Sheet metal worker	7,629	582
6	Structural-steel worker	4,724	131
7	Elevator constructor	4,475	55
8	Roofer	4,397	140
9	Sprinkler fitter	4,271	85
10	Bricklayer (construction)	4,148	217
11	Construction craft laborer	4,136	71
12	Painter (construction)	3,937	245
13	Operating engineer	3,370	126
14	Child care development specialist	2,953	1,017
15	Boilermaker	2,556	31
16	Heating/Air-conditioner installer	2,442	622
17	Powerline maintainer	2,418	268
18	Powerline installer and repairer	2,289	78
19	Correction officer	2,269	55
20	Millwright	2,261	438
21	Cook (hotel and restaurant)	1,837	404
22	Electrician (maintenance)	1,828	915
23	Machinist	1,739	1,346
24	Tool and die maker	1,733	1,486
25	Insulation workers	1,732	104
	All occupations	198,876	26,411*

*Includes programs with multiple occupations.

A major advantage of apprenticeship programs is that learners can earn pay while they learn. This is important because programs can last several years. Learners' wages usually increase automatically as their skills improve. Also, apprenticeships are usually effective learning experiences because they involve learning why and how a task is performed through classroom instruction provided by local trade schools, high schools, or community colleges. Apprenticeships also usually result in full-time employment for trainees when the program is completed. From the company's perspective, apprenticeship programs meet specific business training needs and help attract talented employees. At its manufacturing facility in Toledo, Ohio, Libbey Glass has apprenticeship programs in mold making, machine repair, millwrighting, and maintenance repair.[28] These programs are viewed as the best jobs within the company because the wage rates are high and because most apprentices are scheduled to work day shifts instead of afternoon or midnight shifts. The apprenticeship program has been costly for the company but has paid dividends. Each apprentice requires the support of a journeyworker for each work assignment. This means that work is being performed by two employees when only one worker is normally required. The program also requires apprentices to be evaluated every 1,000 hours to meet Department of Labor standards. The reviews are conducted by a committee that includes management and

TABLE 7.4

Example of a Machinist Apprenticeship

Source: A. H. Howard III, "Apprenticeship," in *The ASTD Training and Development Handbook*, 4th ed., ed. R. L. Craig (New York: McGraw-Hill, 1996): 808.

Hours	Weeks	Unit
240	6.0	Bench work
360	9.0	Drill press
240	6.0	Heat treat
200	5.0	Elementary layout
680	17.0	Turret lathe (conventional and numerical control)
800	20.0	Engine lathe
320	8.0	Tool grind
640	16.0	Advanced layout
960	24.0	Milling machine
280	7.0	Profile milling
160	4.0	Surface grinding
240	6.0	External grinding
280	7.0	Internal grinding
200	5.0	Thread grinding
520	13.0	Horizontal boring mills
240	6.0	Jig bore/jig grinder
160	4.0	Vertical boring
600	15.0	Numerical control milling
240	6.0	Computer numerical control
640	16.0	Related training
8,000	200.0	TOTAL

Probationary: The following hours are included in the totals above, but must be completed in the first 1,000 hours of apprenticeship:

Hours	Weeks	Unit
80	2.0	Drill press (probation)
280	7.0	Lathe work (probation)
360	9.0	Milling machine (probation)
40	1.0	Elementary layout (probation)
80	2.0	Related training (probation)
840	21.0	TOTAL

department journeyworkers. The committee also develops tests and other evaluation materials. The committee members cannot perform their normal duties during the time they are reviewing apprentices, so their workload has to be spread among other employees or rescheduled for some other time. The program offers many benefits to Libbey: The company is developing employees who are more receptive to change in the work environment; work can be performed at Libbey so the company does not have to outsource jobs to contract labor; and Libbey is given an edge in attracting talented employees who like the idea that after completing an apprenticeship they are eligible for promotions to other positions in the company, including management positions. Also, the apprenticeship program helps Libbey tailor training and work experiences to meet specific needs in maintenance repair, which is necessary to create and repair production mold equipment used in making glass products.

Apprentice-like programs are also used to prepare new managers. The president and chief executive officer of Goldcorp, a company in the mining industry, offers the chance for MBAs to apply for a nine-month apprenticeship.[29] The apprentice shadows Goldcorp's CEO and observes board meetings, negotiations, mine acquisitions, and other important aspects of the mine industry. Goldcorp hopes the apprenticeships will attract more MBAs to the mining industry, which is viewed by many graduates as an unsafe and dirty business. Hyatt Hotels offers several programs in which management trainees complete training in the areas of facilities, culinary arts, sales, hotel operations, accounting, and catering.[30] Trainees rotate through all parts of the hotel and perform all aspects of each job, ranging from washing dishes to catering, and then spend the rest of the training time in their specialty area. Employees who complete the training are placed in entry-level management positions.

Besides the development costs and time commitment that management and journey-workers have to make to apprenticeship programs, another disadvantage of many programs is limited access for minorities and women.[31] Also, there is no guarantee that jobs will be available when the program is completed. Finally, apprenticeship programs prepare trainees who are well trained in one craft or occupation. Due to the changing nature of jobs (thanks to new technology and use of cross-functional teams), many employers may be reluctant to employ workers from apprenticeship programs. Employers may believe that because apprentices are narrowly trained in one occupation or with one company, program graduates may have only company-specific skills and may be unable to acquire new skills or adapt their skills to changes in the workplace.

Simulations

A **simulation** is a training method that represents a real-life situation, with trainees' decisions resulting in outcomes that mirror what would happen if they were on the job. A common example of the use of simulators for training is flight simulators for pilots. Simulations, which allow trainees to see the impact of their decisions in an artificial, risk-free environment, are used to teach production and process skills as well as management and interpersonal skills. As you will see in Chapter 8, new technology has helped in the development of virtual reality, a type of simulation that even more closely mimics the work environment.

Simulators replicate the physical equipment that employees use on the job. For example, Time Warner cable installers learn how to correctly install cable and high-speed Internet connections by crawling into two-story houses that have been built inside the company's training center.[32] Trainees drill through the walls and crawl around inside these houses, learning how to work with different types of homes. New call center employees at American Express learn in a simulated environment that replicates a real call center.[33] Trainees go to a lab that contains cubicles identical to those in the call center. All materials (binders, reference materials, supplies) are exactly the same as they would be in the call center. The simulator uses a replica of the call center database and includes a role play that uses speech recognition software to simulate live calls. After the call center trainees learn transactions, they answer simulated calls that require them to practice the transactions. The simulator gives them feedback about errors they made during the calls and shows them the correct action. The simulator also tracks the trainees' performance and alerts the instructors if a trainee is falling behind. The simulator prepares call center employees in 32 days, an improvement over the previous 12-week program of classroom and on-the-job training. Turnover among call center employees is 50 percent lower since employees began training in the simulated environment. American Express believes that the reduction in turnover is because the training environment better prepares new employees to deal with the noise and pace of a real call center.

Simulations are also used to develop managerial skills. Looking Glass is a simulation designed to develop both teamwork and individual management skills.[34] In this program, participants are assigned different roles in a glass company. On the basis of memos and correspondence, each participant interacts with other members of the management team over the course of six hours. The simulation records and evaluates participants' behavior and interactions in solving the problems described in correspondence. At the conclusion of the simulation, participants are given feedback regarding their performance.

A key aspect of simulators is the degree to which they are similar to the equipment and situations that the trainee will encounter on the job. Recall the discussion of near transfer in Chapter 5. Simulators need to have elements identical to those found in the work environment. The simulator needs to respond exactly like the equipment would under the conditions and response given by the trainee. For example, flight simulators include distractions that pilots have to deal with, such as hearing chimes in the cockpit from traffic alerts generated by an onboard computer warning system while listening to directions from an air traffic controller.[35] For this reason simulators are expensive to develop and need constant updating as new information about the work environment is obtained.

Case Studies

A **case study** is a description about how employees or an organization dealt with a difficult situation. Trainees are required to analyze and critique the actions taken, indicating the appropriate actions and suggesting what might have been done differently.[36] A major assumption of the case study approach is that employees are most likely to recall and use knowledge and skills if they learn through a process of discovery.[37] Cases may be especially appropriate for developing higher order intellectual skills such as analysis, synthesis, and evaluation. These skills are often required by managers, physicians, and other professional employees. Cases also help trainees develop the willingness to take risks given uncertain outcomes, based on their analysis of the situation. To use cases effectively, the learning environment must give trainees the opportunity to prepare and discuss their case analyses. Also, face-to-face or electronic communication among trainees must be arranged. Because trainee involvement is critical for the effectiveness of the case method, learners must be willing and able to analyze the case and then communicate and defend their positions.

Table 7.5 presents the process used for case development. The first step in the process is to identify a problem or situation. It is important to consider if the story is related to the instructional objectives, will provoke a discussion, forces decision making, can be told in a reasonable time period, and is generalizable to the situations that trainees may face. Information on the problem or situation must also be readily accessible. The next step is to research documents, interview participants, and obtain data that provide the details of the case. The third step is to outline the story and link the details and exhibits to relevant points in the story. Fourth, the media used to present the case should be determined. Also, at this point in case development, the trainer should consider how the case exercise will be conducted. This may involve determining if trainees will work individually or in teams, and how the students will report results of their analyses. Finally, the actual case materials need to be prepared. This includes assembling exhibits (figures, tables, articles, job descriptions, etc.), writing the story, preparing questions to guide trainees' analysis, and writing an interesting, attention-getting case opening that will attract trainees' attention and provide a quick orientation to the case.

TABLE 7.5

Process for Case Development

Source: Based on J. Alden and J. K. Kirkhorn, "Case Studies," in *The ASTD Training and Development Handbook*, 4th ed., ed. R. L. Craig (New York: McGraw-Hill, 1996): 497–516.

1. Identify a story.
2. Gather information.
3. Prepare a story outline.
4. Decide on administrative issues.
5. Prepare case materials.

There are a number of available sources for preexisting cases. A major advantage of preexisting cases is that they are already developed. A disadvantage is that the case may not actually relate to the work situation or problem that the trainee will encounter. It is especially important to review preexisting cases to determine how meaningful they will be to the trainee. Preexisting cases on a wide variety of problems in business management (e.g., human resource management, operations, marketing, advertising) are available from Harvard Business School, the Darden Business School at the University of Virginia, Ivey Business School at the University of Western Ontario, and various other sources.

One organization that has effectively used case studies is the Central Intelligence Agency (CIA).[38] The cases are historically accurate and use actual data. For example, "The Libyan Attack" is used in management courses to teach leadership qualities. "The Stamp Case" is used to teach new employees about the agency's ethics structure. The CIA uses approximately 100 cases. One-third are focused on management; the rest focus on operations training, counterintelligence, and analysis. The cases are used in the training curriculum where the objectives include teaching students to analyze and resolve complex, ambiguous situations. The CIA found that for the cases used in training programs to be credible and meaningful to trainees, the material had to be as authentic as possible and had to stimulate students to make decisions similar to those they must make in their work environment. As a result, to ensure case accuracy, the CIA uses retired officers to research and write cases. The CIA has even developed a case writing workshop to prepare instructors to use the case method.

Business Games

Business games require trainees to gather information, analyze it, and make decisions. Business games are primarily used for management skill development. Games stimulate learning because participants are actively involved and because games mimic the competitive nature of business. The types of decisions that participants make in games include all aspects of management practice: labor relations (agreement in contract negotiations), ethics, marketing (the price to charge for a new product), and finance (financing the purchase of new technology).

Typical games have the following characteristics.[39] The game involves a contest among trainees or teams of trainees or against an established criterion such as time or quantity. The game is designed to demonstrate an understanding of or application of a knowledge, skill, or behavior. Several alternative courses of action are available to trainees, and trainees can estimate the consequences of each alternative, but only with some uncertainty. Trainees do not know for certain what the consequences of their actions will be because the consequences are partially based on the decisions of other game participants. Finally, rules limit participant behavior.

To ensure learning and transfer of training, games used in training should be simple enough that trainees can play them in a short period of time. The best games generate excitement among the participants and interest in the game. Meaningfulness of the game is enhanced if it is realistic. Trainees need to feel that they are participating in a business and acquiring knowledge, skills, and behaviors that are useful on the job.[40] Debriefing from a trainer can help trainees understand the game experience and facilitate learning and transfer. Debriefing can include feedback, discussions of the concepts presented during the game, and instructions in how to use at work the knowledge, skills, or behavior emphasized in the game. Table 7.6 contains some questions that can be used for debriefing.

The University of Texas at Austin has created Executive Challenge, a three-day game in which teams of students are divided into three companies, each given a limited amount of production capacity and employees with different skills.[41] The intent of the game is to teach students how to balance business and ethics and how to interpret the results of too much cost cutting. Teams compete for $11,000 and the chance to perform in front of an executive panel. Companies can borrow money, spend money to increase production capacity, or add products or employees. Companies also have to nurture existing projects and make decisions about whether to spend resources on diversity training or on quality programs.

Many companies are using board games to teach employees finance because employee pay is based on the financial performance of the business function employees work in.[42] In pay-for-performance plans, companies must ensure that employees understand basic financial concepts such as how to read balance sheets and income statements. Employees also need to understand how their actions and decisions affect profits. Most of the board games are similar to the game Monopoly. Trainees guide their companies through a series of decisions challenged by various obstacles such as a rival introducing a competing product or a strike by plant workers. Trainees have to track key financial measures over two years.

Harley-Davidson, the motorcycle company, uses a business game to help prospective dealers understand how dealerships make money.[43] The game, which involves 15 to 35 people working in teams, consists of five simulated rounds, each round challenging a team to manage a Harley dealership in competition with other teams. Between rounds of the game, lectures and case studies reinforce key concepts. The facilitators change the business situation in each round of the game. The facilitators can increase or decrease interest rates, add new products, cause employee turnover, or even set up a bad event such as a fire at the business. The game helps dealers develop skills needed for business success. Participants must work well as a team, listen to each other, and think strategically.

Documentation of learning from games is anecdotal.[44] Games may give team members a quick start at developing a framework for information and may help develop cohesive groups. For some groups (such as senior executives), games may be more meaningful

TABLE 7.6
Questions to Use for Debriefing a Game

Source: Based on S. Sugar, "Using Games to Energize Dry Material," in *The ASTD Handbook of Training Design and Delivery*, ed. G. Piskurich, P. Beckschi, and B. Hall (New York: McGraw-Hill, 2000): 107–20.

How did the score of the game affect your behavior and the behavior of the team?
What did you learn from the game?
What aspects of the game remind you of situations at work?
How does the game relate to your work?
What did you learn from the game that you plan to use at work?

training activities (because the game is realistic) than are presentation techniques such as classroom instruction.

Role Plays

Role plays have trainees act out characters assigned to them.[45] Information regarding the situation (e.g., work or interpersonal problem) is provided to the trainees. Role plays differ from simulations on the basis of response choices available to the trainees and the level of detail of the situation given to trainees. Role plays may provide limited information regarding the situation, whereas the information provided for simulation is usually quite detailed. A simulation focuses on physical responses (e.g., pull a lever, move a dial). Role plays focus on interpersonal responses (e.g., ask for more information, resolve conflict). In a simulation, the outcome of the trainees' response depends on a fairly well-defined model of reality. (If a trainee in a flight simulator decreases the angle of the flaps, that action influences the direction of the aircraft.) In a role play, outcomes depend on the emotional (and subjective) reactions of the other trainees.

At Wequassett Resort and Golf Club in Chatham, Massachusetts, the training schedule considers both the need to make guests happy and the need to help both new and returning employees learn to do that.[46] From April to October the resort is closed but 340 employees start work in the spring before the resort opens. Half of the employees are receiving training for the first time while the returning employees need refresher training. Wequassett Academy offers 70 courses in four schools (customer intimacy, technical training, information and technology, and management). The goal of training is to provide the kind of service that will encourage guests to come back again as well as recommend the resort to their friends. The resort's training is in step with its business, which requires a personal touch. Training involves classroom instruction with role plays as well as the use of DVDs. Employees have to successfully complete competency checklists before they are able to work. For example, food servers may have to take courses in menu knowledge, food service, and wine knowledge.

For role plays to be effective, trainers need to engage in several activities before, during, and after the role play. Before the role play, it is critical to explain the purpose of the activity to the trainees. This increases the chances that they will find the activity meaningful and be motivated to learn. Second, the trainer needs to clearly explain the role play, the characters' roles, and the time allotted for the activity. A short video may also be valuable for quickly showing trainees how the role play works. During the activity, the trainer needs to monitor the time, degree of intensity, and focus of the group's attention. (Is the group playing the roles or discussing other things unrelated to the exercise?) The more meaningful the exercise is to the participants, the less trouble the trainer should have with focus and intensity. At the conclusion of the role play, debriefing is critical. Debriefing helps trainees understand the experience and discuss their insights with each other. Trainees should also be able to discuss their feelings, what happened in the exercise, what they learned, and how the experience, their actions, and resulting outcomes relate to incidents in the workplace.

Behavior Modeling

Behavior modeling presents trainees with a model who demonstrates key behaviors to replicate and provides trainees with the opportunity to practice the key behaviors. Behavior modeling is based on the principles of social learning theory (discussed in Chapter 4), which emphasize that learning occurs by (1) observation of behaviors demonstrated by a model and (2) vicarious reinforcement. **Vicarious reinforcement** occurs when a trainee sees a model receiving reinforcement for using certain behaviors.

Behavior modeling is more appropriate for teaching skills and behaviors than for teaching factual information. Research suggests that behavior modeling is one of the most effective techniques for teaching interpersonal and computer skills.[47]

Table 7.7 presents the activities in a behavior modeling training session. These activities include an introduction, skill preparation and development, and application planning.[48] Each training session, which typically lasts four hours, focuses on one interpersonal skill such as coaching or communicating ideas. Each session includes a presentation of the rationale behind the key behaviors, a videotape of a model performing the key behaviors, practice opportunities using role playing, evaluation of a model's performance in the videotape, and a planning session devoted to understanding how the key behaviors can be used on the job. In the practice sessions, trainees are provided with feedback regarding how closely their behavior matches the key behaviors demonstrated by the model. The role playing and modeled performance are based on actual incidents in the employment setting in which the trainee needs to demonstrate success.

Well-prepared behavior modeling training programs identify the key behaviors, create the modeling display, provide opportunities for practice, and facilitate transfer of training.[49] The first step in developing behavior modeling training programs is to determine (1) the tasks that are not being adequately performed due to lack of skill or behavior and (2) the key behaviors that are required to perform the task. A **key behavior** is one of a set of behaviors that are necessary to complete a task. In behavior modeling, key behaviors are typically performed in a specific order for the task to be completed. Key behaviors are identified through a study of the skills and behaviors necessary to complete the task and the skills or behaviors used by employees who are effective in completing the task.

Table 7.8 presents key behaviors for a behavior modeling training program on problem analysis. The table specifies behaviors that the trainee needs to engage in to be effective in problem analysis skills. Note that the key behaviors do not specify the exact behaviors needed at every step of solving a problem. Rather, the key behaviors in this skill module specify more general behaviors that are appropriate across a wide range of situations. If a task involves a clearly defined series of specific steps that must be accomplished in a specific

TABLE 7.7
Activities in a Behavior Modeling Training Program

Introduction (45 mins.)
- Watch video that presents key behaviors.
- Listen to rationale for skill module.
- Discuss experiences in using skill.

Skill Preparation and Development (2 hrs., 30 mins.)
- View model.
- Participate in role plays and practice.
- Receive oral and video feedback on performance of key behaviors.

Application Planning (1 hr.)
- Set improvement goals.
- Identify situations in which to use key behaviors.
- Identify on-the-job applications of the key behaviors.

TABLE 7.8

Example of Key Behaviors in Problem Analysis

Get all relevant information by:
- Rephrasing the question or problem to see if new issues emerge.
- Listing the key problem issues.
- Considering other possible sources of information.

Identify possible causes.

If necessary, obtain additional information.

Evaluate the information to ensure that all essential criteria are met.

Restate the problem considering new information.

Determine what criteria indicate that the problem or issue has been resolved.

order, then the key behaviors that are provided are usually more specific and explained in greater detail. For example, tennis players learning how to serve must follow a detailed sequence of activities (e.g., align feet on service line, take the racquet back over the head, toss the ball, bring the racquet over the head, pronate the wrist, and strike the ball). People learning interpersonal skills must develop more general key behaviors because there is always more than one way to complete the task. The development of general key behaviors promotes far transfer (discussed in Chapter 5). That is, trainees are prepared to use the key behaviors in a variety of situations.

Another important consideration in developing behavior modeling programs is the modeling display. The **modeling display** provides the key behaviors that the trainees will practice to develop the same set of behaviors. Videotape is the predominant method used to present modeling displays, although computerized modeling displays are also being used. (The use of new technology in training is discussed in Chapter 8.) Effective modeling displays have six characteristics:[50]

1. The display clearly presents the key behaviors. The music and the characteristics of the situation shown in the display do not interfere with the trainee seeing and understanding the key behaviors.
2. The model is credible to the trainees.
3. An overview of the key behaviors is presented.
4. Each key behavior is repeated. The trainee is shown the relationship between the behavior of the model and each key behavior.
5. A review of the key behaviors is included.
6. The display presents models engaging in both positive use of key behaviors and negative use (ineffective models not using the key behaviors).

Providing opportunities for practice involves (1) having trainees cognitively rehearse and think about the key behaviors and (2) placing trainees in situations (such as role plays) in which they have to use the key behaviors. Trainees may interact with one other person in the role play or in groups of three or more in which each trainee can practice the key behaviors. The most effective practice session allows trainees to practice the behaviors multiple times, in a small group of trainees where anxiety or evaluation apprehension is reduced, with other trainees who understand the company and the job.

Practice sessions should include a method for providing trainees with feedback. This feedback should provide reinforcement to the trainee for behaviors performed correctly as well as information needed to improve behaviors. For example, if role plays are used, trainees can receive feedback from the other participants who serve as observers when not playing the role. Practice sessions may also be videotaped and played back to the trainees. The use of video objectively captures the trainees' behavior and provides useful, detailed feedback. Having the trainees view the video shows them specifically how they need to improve their behaviors and identifies behaviors they are successfully replicating.

Behavior modeling helps ensure that transfer of training occurs by using application planning. **Application planning** prepares trainees to use the key behaviors on the job (i.e., enhances transfer of training). Application planning involves having all participants prepare a written document identifying specific situations in which they should use the key behaviors. Some training programs actually have trainees complete a "contract" outlining the key behaviors they agree to use on the job. The trainer may follow up with the trainees to see if they are performing according to the contract. Application planning may also involve preparing trainees to deal with situational factors that may inhibit their use of the key behaviors (similar to relapse prevention, discussed in Chapter 5). As part of the application planning process, a trainee may be paired with another participant, with the stated expectation that the two should periodically communicate with each other to discuss successes and failures in the use of key behaviors.

GROUP BUILDING METHODS

Group building methods are training methods designed to improve team or group effectiveness. Training is directed at improving the trainees' skills as well as team effectiveness. In group building methods, trainees share ideas and experiences, build group identity, understand the dynamics of interpersonal relationships, and get to know their own strengths and weaknesses and those of their co-workers. Group techniques focus on helping teams increase their skills for effective teamwork. A number of training techniques are available to improve work group or team performance, to establish a new team, or to improve interactions among different teams. All involve examination of feelings, perceptions, and beliefs about the functioning of the team; discussion; and development of plans to apply what was learned in training to the team's performance in the work setting. Group building methods include adventure learning, team training, and action learning.

Group building methods often involve experiential learning. **Experiential learning** training programs have four stages: (1) gain conceptual knowledge and theory; (2) take part in a behavioral simulation; (3) analyze the activity; and (4) connect the theory and activity with on-the-job or real-life situations.[51]

For experiential training programs to be successful, several guidelines should be followed. The program needs to tie in to a specific business problem. The trainees need to be moved outside their personal comfort zones but within limits so as not to reduce trainee motivation or ability to understand the purpose of the program. Multiple learning modes should be used, including audio, visual, and kinesthetic. When preparing activities for an experiential training program, trainers should ask trainees for input on the program goals. Clear expectations about the purpose, expected outcomes, and trainees' role in the program are important. Finally, the training program needs to be evaluated. Training programs that include experiential learning should be linked to changes in employee attitudes, behaviors, and other business results. If training programs that involve experiential learning do not follow these guidelines, they may be questioned. For example, the U.S. Postal Inspector resigned after criticisms surfaced about postal team training activities. Current and former postal employees complained to several senators about training activities that included having employees wrap each other in toilet paper and dress as cats and hold signs that spelled "teamwork."[52]

California-based Quantum Corporation developed a project to overhaul the company's online infrastructure across global operations.[53] The project included a diverse group of team members from the information technology, engineering, marketing, and graphic design departments. The team consisted of very talented employees who were not used to working with each other. Many of the team members were geographically dispersed, which increased the difficulties of working together. Quantum hired an actors group to lead the team through a series of improvisational activities designed to get the team members to share personal stories. Using music, props, lighting, and costumes, the actors interpreted the stories told by team members. The actors portrayed team members who, for example, expressed isolation and frustration. Other times, team members would play the parts. The sessions allowed each team member to ask questions of the actors or each other. The team came away from the activity with more empathy and understanding for each other. Development of the personal relationships created positive interpersonal bonds that helped the team meet deadlines and complete projects.

Adventure Learning

Adventure learning focuses on the development of teamwork and leadership skills through structured activities.[54] Adventure learning includes wilderness training, outdoor training, drum circles, and even cooking classes. Adventure learning appears to be best suited for developing skills related to group effectiveness such as self-awareness, problem solving, conflict management, and risk taking. Adventure learning may involve strenuous, challenging physical activities such as dogsledding or mountain climbing. Adventure learning can also use structured individual and group outdoor activities such as wall climbing, rope courses, trust falls, ladder climbing, and traveling from one tower to another using a device attached to a wire that connects the two towers.

For example, "The Beam" requires team members to cross a six-foot-high beam placed between two trees using only help from the team. Trainees can help by shouting advice and encouragement.[55] Rope-based activities may be held 3 to 4 feet or 25 to 30 feet above the ground. The high-ropes course is an individual-based exercise whose purpose is to help the trainee overcome fear. The low-ropes course requires the entire team of trainees to complete the course successfully. The purpose is to develop team identity, cohesiveness, and communication skills.

In one adventure learning program, a Chili's restaurant manager was required to scale a three-story-high wall.[56] About two-thirds of the way from the top of the wall, the manager became very tired. She successfully reached the top of the wall using the advice and encouragement shouted from team members on the ground below. When asked to consider what she learned from the experience, she reported that the exercise made her realize that reaching personal success depends on other people. At her restaurant, everyone has to work together to make the customers happy.

Adventure learning can also include demanding activities that require coordination but place less of a physical strain on team members. In drum circles, each team member is given a drum, and facilitators work with the team to create a drumming orchestra. The car company Toyota spent $20,000 for drums to accommodate 40 people at its training center in Torrance, California.[57] Drum circles are held twice a week. Toyota believes that the drum circles are metaphors for how high-performance teams should operate: cooperatively and smoothly. Cookin' Up Change is one of many team-building courses offered around the United States by chefs, caterers, hotels, and cooking schools.[58] These courses have been used by companies such as Honda and Microsoft. The idea is that cooking classes help strengthen communications and networking skills by requiring team members to work together to create a full-course meal (a culinary feast!). Each team has to decide who does what kitchen tasks (e.g., cooking, cutting, cleaning) and who prepares the main course, salads, and dessert. Often, team members are required to switch assignments in mid-preparation to see how the team reacts to change.

For adventure learning programs to be successful, exercises should relate to the types of skills that participants are expected to develop. Also, after the exercises a skilled facilitator should lead a discussion about what happened in the exercise, what was learned, how events in the exercise relate to the job situation, and how to set goals and apply what was learned on the job.[59] Trust falls require each trainee to stand on a platform five to six feet above the ground and fall backward into the arms of fellow group members. If trainees are reluctant to fall, this suggests they don't trust the team members. After completing the trust fall, the facilitator may question trainees to identify sources of their anxiety and to relate this anxiety to specific workplace incidents (e.g., a project delegated to a peer was not completed on time, resulting in distrust of the peer).

The physical demands of some types of adventure learning and the requirement that trainees often touch each other in the exercises may increase a company's risk for negligence claims due to personal injury, intentional infliction of emotional distress, and invasion of privacy. Also, the Americans with Disabilities Act raises questions about requiring disabled employees to participate in physically demanding training experiences.[60]

Given the physically demanding nature of adventure learning, it is important to consider when to use it instead of another training method. Adventure learning allows trainees to interact interpersonally in a situation not governed by formal business rules. This type of environment may be important for employees to mold themselves into a cohesive work team. Also, adventure learning exercises allow trainees to share a strong emotional experience. Significant emotional experiences can help trainees break difficult behavior patterns and open trainees to change their behaviors. One of the most important characteristics of adventure learning is that the exercises can serve as metaphors for organizational behavior. That is, trainees will behave in the same way in the exercises that they would when working as a team (e.g., developing a product launch plan). As a result, by analyzing behaviors that occur during the exercise, trainees gain insight into ineffective behaviors.

Does adventure learning work? Rigorous evaluations of its impact on productivity or performance have not been conducted. However, former participants often report that they gained a greater understanding of themselves and how they interact with co-workers.[61] One key to an adventure learning program's success may be the insistence that whole work groups participate together so that group dynamics that inhibit effectiveness can emerge and be discussed.

Team Training

Team training coordinates the performance of individuals who work together to achieve a common goal. Figure 7.2 shows the three components of team performance: knowledge, attitudes, and behavior.[62] The behavioral requirement means that team members must perform

FIGURE 7.2
Components of Team Performance

Source: Based on E. Salas and J. A. Cannon-Bowers, "Strategies for Team Training," in *Training for 21st Century Technology: Applications of Psychological Research,* eds. M. A. Quinones and A. Dutta (Washington, DC: American Psychological Association, 1997): 249–81.

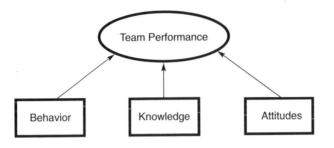

actions that allow them to communicate, coordinate, adapt, and complete complex tasks to accomplish their objective. The knowledge component requires team members to have mental models or memory structures that allow them to function effectively in unanticipated or new situations. Team members' beliefs about the task and feelings toward each other relate to the attitude component. Team morale, cohesion, and identity are related to team performance. For example, in the military as well as the private sector (e.g., nuclear power plants, commercial airlines), much work is performed by crews, groups, or teams. Successful performance depends on coordination of individual activities to make decisions, on team performance, and on readiness to deal with potentially dangerous situations (e.g., an overheating nuclear reactor). Research suggests that teams that are effectively trained develop procedures to identify and resolve errors, coordinate information gathering, and reinforce each other.[63]

Figure 7.3 illustrates the four main elements of the structure of team training (tools, methods, strategies, and team training objectives). Several tools help to define and

FIGURE 7.3
Main Elements of the Structure of Team Training

Source: Based on E. Salas and J. A. Cannon-Bowers, "Strategies for Team Training," in *Training for 21st Century Technology: Applications of Psychological Research,* eds. M. A. Quinones and A. Dutta (Washington, DC: American Psychological Association, 1997): 270.

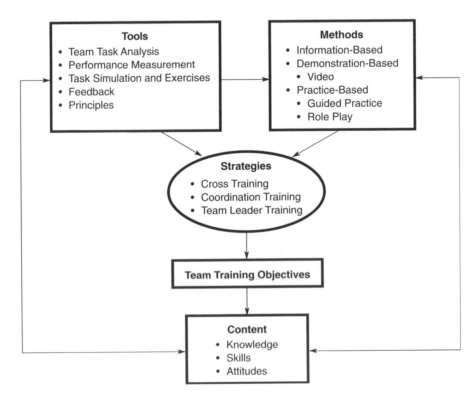

organize the delivery of team training.[64] These tools also provide the environment (e.g., feedback) needed for learning to occur. These tools work in combination with different training methods to help create instructional strategies. These strategies are a combination of the methods, tools, and content required to perform effectively.

The strategies include cross training, coordination training, and team leader training. **Cross training** has team members understand and practice each other's skills so that members are prepared to step in and take the place of a member who may temporarily or permanently leave the team. Research suggests that most work teams would benefit from providing members with at least enough understanding of teammates' roles to discuss trade-offs of various strategies and behaviors that affect team performance.[65] **Coordination training** instructs the team in how to share information and decision-making responsibilities to maximize team performance. Coordination training is especially important for commercial aviation or surgical teams who are in charge of monitoring different aspects of equipment and the environment but who must share information to make the most effective decisions regarding patient care or aircraft safety and performance. **Team leader training** refers to training that the team manager or facilitator receives. This may involve training the manager on how to resolve conflict within the team or helping the team coordinate activities or other team skills.

Employees obviously need technical skills that can help the team accomplish its task. But team members also need skills in communication, adaptability, conflict resolution, and other teamwork issues.[66] Team training usually involves multiple methods. For example, a lecture or video may be used to disseminate knowledge regarding communication skills to trainees. Role plays or simulations may be used to give trainees the opportunity to put into practice the communication skills emphasized in the lecture. Regardless of the method chosen, opportunities for practice and feedback need to be included.

United Airlines is sending its supervisor, or lead, ramp employees to Pit Instruction and Training (Pit Crew U), which focuses on the preparation, practices, and teamwork of NASCAR pit crews. United is using the training to develop standardized methods to safely and more efficiently unload, load, and send off its airplanes.[67] Pit Instruction and Training, located outside Charlotte, North Carolina, has a quarter-mile race track and a pit road with places for six cars. The school offers programs to train new racing pit crews, but most of its business comes from companies interested in teaching their teams to work as safely, efficiently, and effectively as NASCAR pit crews do. NASCAR pit crews work safely, quickly, and efficiently because each crew member knows what tasks to do (change tires, use air gun, add gasoline, clean up spills), and after the crew members have finished servicing the race car, they move new equipment into position in anticipation of the next pit stop. At Pit Crew U, trainees actually work as pit crews. They learn how to handle jacks, change tires, and fill fuel tanks on race cars. They are videotaped and timed just like real pit crews, and they receive feedback from trainers and from professional pit crew members who work on NASCAR teams. Also, the program requires trainees to deal with unforeseen circumstances similar to what they may encounter on the job. For example, at one pit stop, lug nuts had been sprinkled intentionally in the area where the race car stops, and the United employees were observed to see whether they noticed the lug nuts and cleaned them up. On their jobs, ramp employees are responsible for removing debris from the tarmac so it is not sucked into jet engines or does not harm equipment. At another pit stop, United teams had to work with fewer members, which sometimes occurs when ramp crews are understaffed due to absences.

United's training is part of a multimillion-dollar investment that includes updating equipment and providing bag scanners. The purpose of the training is to standardize the tasks of ramp team members, to reinforce the need for ramp teams to be orderly and communicative, and to increase morale. Training has been optional for ramp employees, and they have survived layoffs and have been asked to make wage concessions to help pull the company out of bankruptcy. United has already started scheduling shorter ground times at some airports, anticipating the positive results of the program. With shorter ground times, United can offer more daily flights without having to buy more airplanes. United hopes to make the airline more competitive by cutting the average airplane ground time by eight minutes.

Action Learning

Action learning gives teams or work groups an actual problem, has them work on solving it and committing to an action plan, and then holds them accountable for carrying out the plan.[68] Companies use action learning to solve important problems, develop leaders, quickly build high-performance teams, and transform the organizational culture. Table 7.9 shows the steps involved in action learning. Several types of problems are addressed in action learning, including how to change the business, better utilize technology, remove barriers between the customer and company, and develop global leaders. Typically, action learning involves between 6 and 30 employees. It may also include customers and vendors. There are several variations in the composition of the group. One variation is that the group includes a single customer for the problem being dealt with. Sometimes the groups include cross-functional representatives who all have a stake in the problem. For example, Novartis, a company that has business in pharmaceuticals (such as Sandoz) and in consumer and animal health care, uses action learning to work on issues such as marketing that are important to all of the company's core businesses.[69] Or the group may involve employees from multiple functions who all focus on their own functional problems, each contributing to solving the problems identified. Employees are asked to develop novel ideas and solutions in a short period of time. The teams usually need to gather data for problem solving by visiting customers, employees, academics, and/or industry leaders. Once the teams have

TABLE 7.9
Steps in Action Learning

Source: Based on M. Marquardt, "Harnessing the Power of Action Learning," *T + D* (June 2004): 26–32; D. Dotlich and J. Noel, *Action Learning* (San Francisco: Jossey-Bass, 1998).

- Identification of the sponsors of action learning, including CEOs and top managers
- Identification of the problem or issue
- Identification and selection of the group who can address the problem
- Identification of coaches who can help the group reframe the problem and improve its problem solving by listening, giving feedback, offering assumptions, and so on
- Presentation of the problem to the group
- Group discussion that includes reframing the problem and agreement on what the problem is, what the group should do to solve the problem, and how the group should proceed
- Data gathering and analysis relevant to solving the problem, done by the group as a whole as well as by individual members
- Group presentation on how to solve the problem, with the goal of securing a commitment from the sponsors to act on the group's recommendations
- Self-reflection and debriefing (e.g., What have the group and group members learned? What might they have done differently?)

gathered data and developed their recommendations they are required to present them to top-level executives.

ATC, a public transportation services management company in Illinois, used action learning to help boost profitability by reducing operating costs.[70] Employees were divided into Action Workout Teams to identify ways of reducing costs and to brainstorm effective solutions. The process assumed that employees closest to where the work gets done have the best ideas about how to solve problems. Teams of five to seven employees met once a week for a couple of hours for 45 to 60 days. For example, a team working on parts inventory might have had a parts clerk, a couple of people from maintenance, a supervisor, and an operations employee. These teams studied problems and issues such as overtime, preventive maintenance, absenteeism, parts inventory, and inefficient safety inspection procedures. The teams brainstormed ideas, prioritized them according to their highest potential, developed action plans, installed them, tested them, and measured the outcomes. The solutions that the teams generated resulted in more than $1.8 million in savings for the company.

Six Sigma and Black Belt Training

Six Sigma and black belt training programs involve principles of action learning. Six Sigma provides employees with measurement and statistical tools to help reduce defects and to cut costs.[71] Six Sigma is a quality standard with a goal of only 3.4 defects per million processes. Six Sigma was born at Motorola. It has saved the company an estimated $15 billion since the early 1990s. There are several levels of Six Sigma training, resulting in employees becoming certified as green belts, champions, or black belts.[72] To become black belts, trainees must participate in workshops and written assignments coached by expert instructors. The training involves four 4-day sessions over about 16 weeks. Between training sessions, candidates apply what they learn to assigned projects and then use them in the next training session. Trainees are also required to complete not only oral and written exams but also two or more projects that have a significant impact on the company's bottom line. After completing black belt training, employees are able to develop, coach, and lead Six Sigma teams; mentor and advise management on determining Six Sigma projects; and provide Six Sigma tools and statistical methods to team members. After black belts lead several project teams, they can take additional training and be certified as master black belts. Master black belts can teach other black belts and help senior managers integrate Six Sigma into the company's business goals.

McKesson Corporation trained 15 to 20 black belts and reassigned them to their original business units as their team's Six Sigma representatives.[73] When the two-year commitment ends, the black belts return to the business at higher positions, helping to spread the approach throughout the organization and ensuring that key leaders are committed to the Six Sigma philosophy. In most divisions of the company, Six Sigma training is mandated for senior vice presidents, who attend training that introduces Six Sigma and details how to identify a potential Six Sigma project. Across the company, every manager and director is expected to attend basic training. The Six Sigma effort has shown benefits every year since the program started in 1999.

Although action learning has not been formally evaluated, the process appears to maximize learning and transfer of training because it involves real-time problems that employees are facing. Also, action learning can be useful for identifying dysfunctional team dynamics that can get in the way of effective problem solving. Action learning at General Electric has required employees to use and apply skills to team building, problem solving, change management, conflict resolution, communications, coaching, and facilitation. General Electric believes that action learning has resulted in such benefits as greater speed in decision making and implementation, employees who work more easily across borders and business units, management that is willing to take more risks, and an increase in open dialogue and trust among employees.[74]

CHOOSING A TRAINING METHOD

As a trainer or manager, you will likely be asked to choose a training method. Given the large number of training methods available to you, this task may seem difficult. One way to choose a training method is to compare methods. Table 7.10 evaluates each training method discussed in this chapter according to a number of characteristics. The types of learning outcomes related to each method are identified. Also, for each method, a high, medium, or low rating is provided for each characteristic of the learning environment, for transfer of training, for cost, and for effectiveness.

How might you use this table to choose a training method? The first step in choosing a method is to identify the type of learning outcome that you want training to influence. As discussed in Chapter 4, these outcomes include verbal information, intellectual skills, cognitive strategies, attitudes, and motor skills. Training methods may influence one or several learning outcomes. Research on specific learning methods has shown that for learning to be effective, the instructional method needs to match the desired learning outcome. For example, research on behavior modeling and role play shows that these methods lead to positive results, but their effectiveness varies according to the evaluation criteria used.[75] This emphasizes that the particular learning *method* used to deliver learning is not what is most important. Rather, the choice of the learning method should be based on the desired learning outcomes and the features that facilitate learning and transfer of training. Once you have identified a learning method, the next step is to consider the extent to which the method facilitates learning and transfer of training, the costs related to development and use of the method, and its effectiveness.

As Chapter 4 said, for learning to occur, trainees must understand the objectives of the training program, training content should be meaningful, and trainees should have the opportunity to practice and receive feedback. Also, a powerful way to learn is through observing and interacting with others. As you may recall from Chapter 5, transfer of training refers to the extent to which training will be used on the job. In general, the closer the training content and environment prepare trainees for use of learning outcomes on the job, the greater the likelihood that transfer will occur. As discussed in Chapter 6, two types of costs are important: development costs and administrative costs. Development costs relate to design of the training program, including costs to buy or create the program. Administrative costs are incurred each time the training method is used. These include costs related to consultants, instructors, materials, and trainers. The effectiveness rating is based on both academic research and practitioner recommendations.

Several trends in Table 7.10 are worth noting. First, there is considerable overlap between learning outcomes across the training methods. Group building methods are

TABLE 7.10 Comparison of Training Methods

	Presentation				Hands-On						Group Building		
	Lecture	Video	OJT	Self-Directed Learning	Apprenticeship	Simulation	Case Study	Business Games	Role Play	Behavior Modeling	Adventure Learning	Team Training	Action Learning
Learning Outcome													
Verbal information	Yes	Yes	Yes	Yes	Yes	No	Yes	Yes	No	No	No	No	No
Intellectual skills	Yes	No	No	Yes	Yes	Yes	Yes	Yes	No	No	No	Yes	No
Cognitive strategies	Yes	No	Yes	Yes	No	Yes	Yes	Yes	Yes	Yes	Yes	Yes	Yes
Attitudes	Yes	Yes	No	No	No	No	No	No	Yes	No	Yes	Yes	Yes
Motor skills	No	Yes	Yes	No	Yes	Yes	No	No	No	Yes	No	No	No
Learning Environment													
Clear objective	Medium	Low	High	High	High	High	Medium	High	Medium	High	Medium	High	High
Practice	Low	Low	High	High	High	High	Medium	Medium	Medium	High	Medium	High	Medium
Meaningfulness	Medium	Medium	High	Medium	High	High	Medium	Medium	Medium	Medium	Low	High	High
Feedback	Low	Low	High	Medium	High	High	Medium	High	Medium	High	Medium	Medium	High
Observation and interaction with others	Low	Medium	High	Medium	High	High	High	High	High	High	High	High	High
Transfer of Training	Low	Low	High	Medium	High	High	Medium	Medium	Medium	High	Low	High	High
Cost													
Development	Medium	Medium	Medium	High	High	High	Medium	High	Medium	Medium	Medium	Medium	Low
Administrative	Low	Low	Low	Medium	High	Low	Low	Medium	Medium	Medium	Medium	Medium	Medium
Effectiveness	High for verbal information	Medium	High for structured OJT	Medium	High	High	Medium	Medium	Medium	High	Low	Medium	High

unique because they focus on individual as well as team learning (e.g., improving group processes). If you are interested in improving the effectiveness of groups or teams, you should choose one of the group building methods (e.g., adventure learning, team training, action learning). Second, comparing the presentation methods to the hands-on methods illustrates that most hands-on methods provide a better learning environment and transfer of training than do the presentation methods. The presentation methods are also less effective than the hands-on methods. If you are not limited by the amount of money that can be used for development or administration, choose a hands-on method over a presentation method. The training budget for developing training methods can influence the method chosen. If you have a limited budget for developing new training methods, use structured on-the-job training—a relatively inexpensive yet effective hands-on method. If you have a larger budget, you might want to consider hands-on methods that facilitate transfer of training, such as simulators. Keep in mind that many of the methods discussed in this chapter can be adapted for use in online learning, e-learning, or distance learning. These training methods are discussed in Chapter 8.

If possible, you may want to use several different methods within a single training program to capitalize on the different strengths of each method for facilitating learning and transfer. For example, the Home Depot uses self-paced materials, a video-based course, and instructor-led training to train appliance salespersons.[76] Self-paced training is used to instruct employees about an appliance category (e.g., dishwashers) and to help them understand the products available at the store. The video-based program teaches salespersons to emphasize each product's features and benefits to customers. Salespersons participate in role plays and are evaluated on their ability to follow the company's selling strategies. All salespersons must also complete an eight-hour instructor-led course that helps them evaluate customers' needs, answer questions, and make the sale. The instructor-led course includes role plays so salespersons can practice selling to customers.

Summary

This chapter discussed presentation, hands-on, and group building training methods. Presentation methods (such as lecture) are effective for efficiently communicating information (knowledge) to a large number of trainees. Presentation methods need to be supplemented with opportunities for the trainees to practice, discuss, and receive feedback to facilitate learning. Hands-on methods get the trainee directly involved in learning. Hands-on methods are ideal for developing skills and behaviors. Hands-on methods include on-the-job training, simulations, self-directed learning, business games, case studies, role plays, and behavior modeling. These methods can be expensive to develop but incorporate the conditions needed for learning and transfer of training to occur. Group building methods such as team training, action learning, and adventure learning focus on helping teams increase the skills needed for effective teamwork (e.g., self-awareness, conflict resolution, coordination) and help build team cohesion and identity. Group building techniques may include the use of presentation methods as well as exercises during which team members interact and communicate with each other. Team training has a long history of success in preparing flight crews and surgical teams, but its effectiveness for developing management teams has not been clearly established.

Key Terms

presentation methods, *260*
lecture, *261*
audiovisual instruction, *262*
hands-on methods, *263*
on-the-job training
(OJT), *263*
self-directed learning, *266*
apprenticeship, *267*
simulation, *270*

case study, *271*
business games, *272*
role plays, *274*
behavior modeling, *274*
vicarious reinforce-
ment, *275*
key behavior, *275*
modeling display, *276*
application planning, *277*

group building
methods, *277*
experiential learning, *277*
adventure learning, *278*
team training, *279*
cross training, *281*
coordination training, *281*
team leader training, *281*
action learning, *282*

Discussion Questions

1. What are the strengths and weaknesses of the lecture, the case study, and behavior modeling?
2. If you had to choose between adventure learning and action learning for developing an effective team, which would you choose? Defend your choice.
3. Discuss the process of behavior modeling training.
4. How can the characteristics of the trainee affect self-directed learning?
5. What are the components of effective team performance? How might training strengthen these components?
6. Table 7.10 compares training methods on a number of characteristics. Explain why simulation and behavior modeling receive high ratings for transfer of training.
7. What are some reasons why on-the-job training can prove ineffective? What can be done to ensure its effectiveness?
8. Why are apprenticeship programs attractive to employees? Why are they attractive to companies?
9. Discuss the steps of an action learning program. Which aspect of action learning do you think is most beneficial for learning? Which aspect is most beneficial for transfer of training? Explain why. Defend your choices.

Application Assignments

1. Choose a job with which you are familiar. Develop a self-directed learning module for a skill that is important for that job.
2. Go to www.sabrehq.com, the Web site for Sabre Corporate Development. Click on Team Building Events. Choose one of the activities and events found on this page, and review it. Discuss what you would do to ensure that the team building event you selected is successful.
3. Divide into teams of two students. One student should be designated as a "trainer," the other as a "trainee." The trainee should briefly leave the room while the trainer reads the instructions for folding a paper cup (see p. 288). After the trainers have read the instructions, the trainees should return to the room. The trainers should then train the trainees in how to fold a paper cup (about 15 minutes). When the instructor calls time, the trainers

SUPPLEMENT TO APPLICATION ASSIGNMENT 3
Steps and Key Points in Folding a Paper Cup:

	Steps in the Operation	Key Points
	Step: A logical segment of the operation in which something is done to advance the work.	Key point: Any directions or bits of information that help to perform the step correctly, safely, and easily.
8½" 11"	Place 8½" × 11" sheet of paper in front of you on flat surface.	1. Be sure surface is flat—free of interfering objects.
	Fold lower left corner up.	2a. Line up the right edges. b. Make a sharp crease.
	Turn paper over.	3a. Pick up lower right corner with right hand and place it at the top. b. Folded flap should not be underneath.
	Fold excess lower edge up.	4a. Line up right edges. b. Fold should line up with bottom edge. c. Make sharp crease.
"C" "B" "A"	Fold lower left corner flush with edge "A."	5a. Keep edges "B" and "C" parallel. b. Hold bottom edge in the center with finger while making fold.
"D"	Fold upper corner to point "D."	6a. Hold cup firmly with left hand. b. Bring upper corner down with right hand.
	Separate lower right corner and fold back.	7a. Hold cup with left hand. b. Fold back with right hand. c. Make sharp creases.
	Turn cup over and fold remaining flap back.	8. Make sharp creases.
	Check cup to be sure it will hold water.	9. Open cup and look inside.

Source: From P. Decker and B. Nathan, *Behavior Modeling Training* (New York: Praeger Scientific, 1985).

should note the steps they followed to conduct the training. The trainees should record their evaluations of the strengths and weaknesses of the training session (5–10 minutes). If time allows, switch roles.

Be prepared to discuss the training process and your reactions as a trainer or trainee. Also, be prepared to discuss the extent to which the training followed the steps for effective on-the-job training.

4. Review one of the following Web sites, which feature simulations: www.income-outcome.com or www.celemi.com.

   Describe the situation that the simulation is designed to represent. What elements in the simulation replicate the work environment? How could the simulation be improved to ensure that learning and transfer of training occur?

5. Go to www.doleta.gov/atels_bat/, the U.S. Department of Labor's Registered Apprenticeship Web site. Complete one of the following activities by writing a short paper and/or discussing your answers in class.

   a. Click on High Growth Job Training Initiative. Choose and click on one of the apprenticeship programs listed under the menu on the left side of the page. What are the purpose and goals of the program you chose?

   b. Click on For Employers. Using information found within this location, discuss what a company needs to do to set up an apprenticeship program. What are the potential benefits of apprenticeship programs? What do you believe is the most important benefit? Defend your choice.

6. Go to www.drumcafe.com, a company that specializes in corporate team building through the use of drum circles. Review the Web site and answer the following questions:

   a. What are drum circles? What skills can participants develop?

   b. What recommendations would you make to a company that uses drum circles to train teams regarding how to ensure that transfer of training occurs?

   c. Do you think that drum circles are good for team training? Why or why not?

7. Go to www.5off5on.com, the Web site for Pit Instruction and Training, a company that provides training for racing pit crews as well as team training. Enter the site. Click on Lean Performance U and read the description of the program. Next, click on Video Tours and Media. Click on Lean Performance U/Team Building and watch the YouTube video of the training. The other video clips are also interesting, so watch them if you have time.

   a. What skills can this type of training improve?

   b. What can be done to ensure transfer of training?

   c. How would you go about evaluating the effectiveness of this program?

Case: *Training Methods for Bank Tellers*

BB&T Corporation, headquartered in Winston-Salem, North Carolina, is among the nation's top financial holding companies, with $152 billion in assets. Its bank subsidiaries operate approximately 1,500 financial centers in the Carolinas, Virginia, West Virginia, Kentucky, Georgia, Maryland, Tennessee, Florida, Alabama, Indiana, and Washington, D.C. BB&T's operating strategy distinguishes it from other financial holding companies. BB&T's banking subsidiaries are organized as a group of community banks, each with a regional president, which allows decisions to be made locally, close to the client. This also makes BB&T's client service more responsive, reliable, and empathetic. BB&T was experiencing a 30 percent annual turnover rate for bank tellers and decided that its on-the-job training was ineffective. The bank tellers' tasks include:

- Balance currency, coin, and checks in cash drawers at the end of each shift, and calculate daily transactions using computers, calculators, or adding machines.
- Cash checks and pay out money after verifying that signatures are correct, that written and numerical amounts agree, and that accounts have sufficient funds.
- Receive checks and cash for deposit, verify amounts, and check accuracy of deposit slips.
- Examine checks for endorsements and to verify other information such as dates, bank names, identification of the persons receiving payments, and the legality of the documents.
- Enter customers' transactions into computers to record transactions and issue computer-generated receipts.
- Count currency, coins, and checks received, either by hand or using a currency-counting machine, to prepare them for deposit or shipment to branch banks or the Federal Reserve Bank.
- Identify transaction mistakes when debits and credits do not balance.
- Prepare and verify cashier's checks.
- Arrange monies received in cash boxes and coin dispensers according to denomination.
- Process transactions such as term deposits, retirement savings plan contributions, automated teller transactions, night deposits, and mail deposits.

Tellers' daily work activities include:

- *Communicating with supervisors, peers, or subordinates*—Providing information to supervisors, co-workers, and subordinates either by telephone, in written form, e-mail, or in person.

- *Establishing and maintaining interpersonal relationships*—Developing constructive and cooperative working relationships with others, and maintaining them over time.
- *Performing for or working directly with the public*—Performing for people or dealing directly with the public. This includes providing services for bank customers.
- *Interacting with computers*—Using computers and computer systems (including hardware and software) to program, write software, set up functions, enter data, or process information.
- *Documenting/recording information*—Entering, transcribing, recording, storing, or maintaining information in written or electronic/magnetic form.
- *Evaluating information to determine compliance with standards*—Using relevant information and individual judgment to determine whether events or processes comply with laws, regulations, or standards.
- *Getting information*—Observing, receiving, and otherwise obtaining information from all relevant sources.
- *Making decisions and solving problems*—Analyzing information and evaluating results to choose the best solution and solve problems.
- *Processing information*—Compiling, coding, categorizing, calculating, tabulating, auditing, or verifying information or data.
- *Communicating with persons outside organization*—Communicating with people outside the organization, as well as representing the organization to customers, the public, government, and other external sources, either in person, in writing, or by telephone or e-mail.

Describe the training method or combination of training methods you would recommend to train BB&T's bank tellers. Justify your choice of methods.

Source: Based on "BB&T Winston-Salem, North Carolina, Channeling Aristotle," *T + D* (October 2008): 50–52; www.bbt.com, Web site for BB&T. Tasks and work responsibilities are taken from http://onlinecenter.onet.org, O*Net online summary report for bank tellers (43-0071.00).

Endnotes

1. J. Salopek, "Colorado Springs Utility: 2005 BEST Award Winner," *T + D* (October 2005): pp. 38–40.
2. J. Breal, "Secret Sauce," *Fast Company* (May 2007): 61–63.
3. D. McMurrer, M. Van Buren, and W. Woodrell Jr., *The 2000 ASTD State of the Industry Report* (Alexandra, VA: American Society for Training and Development, 2000); "Industry Report 2000," *Training* (October 2000): 57–66; A. P. Carnevale, L. J. Gainer, and A. S. Meltzer, *Workplace Basics Training Manual* (San Francisco: Jossey-Bass, 1990).
4. M. Van Wart, N. J. Cayer, and S. Cook, *Handbook of Training and Development for the Public Sector* (San Francisco: Jossey-Bass, 1993); R. S. House, "Classroom Instruction," in *The ASTD Training and Development Handbook,* 4th ed., ed. R. L. Craig (New York: McGraw-Hill, 1996): 437–52.
5. Van Wart, Cayer, and Cook, *Handbook of Training and Development for the Public Sector.*
6. K. Tyler, "15 Ways to Train on the Job," *HR Magazine* (September 2008): 105–108.
7. "Constellation Energy," *T + D* (October 2008): 35–36.
8. H. Dolezalek, "Industry Training Report," *Training* (October 2004): 33–34.
9. T. Skylar, "When Training Collides with a 35-Ton Truck," *Training* (March 1996): 32–38.
10. L. Ford, "Caught on Tape," *T + D* (December 2005): 63–64.
11. R. B. Cohn, "How to Choose a Video Producer," *Training* (July 1996): 58–61.
12. R. DeRouin, T. Parrish, and E. Salas, "On-the-Job Training: Tips for Ensuring Success," *Ergonomics in Design* 13 (Spring 2005): 23–26; D. Gallup and K. Beauchemin, "On-the-Job Training," in *The ASTD Handbook of Training Design and Delivery,* ed. G. Piskurich, P. Beckschi, and B. Hall (New York: McGraw-Hill, 2000): 121–132.
13. DeRouin, Parrish, and Salas, "On-the-Job Training: Tips for Ensuring Success"; C. Aik, "The Synergies of the Learning Organization, Visual Factory Management, and On-the-Job Training," *Performance Improvement* 44 (2005): 15–20.
14. "Reliance Industries Limited, Nagothane Manufacturing Division," *T + D* (October) 2008: 78.
15. N. Woodward, "Making Safety Job No. 1," *HR Magazine* (January 2007): 60–65.
16. B. Filipczak, "Who Owns Your OJT?" *Training* (December 1996). 44–49; DeRouin, Parrish, and Salas, "On-the-Job Training: Tips for Ensuring Success"; Gallup and Beauchemin, "On-the-Job Training."
17. W. J. Rothwell and H. C. Kazanas, "Planned OJT Is Productive OJT," *Training and Development Journal* (October 1996): 53–56.
18. Filipczak, "Who Owns Your OJT?"
19. G. M. Piskurich, *Self-Directed Learning* (San Francisco: Jossey-Bass, 1993).
20. S. Boyer and B. Lambert, "Take the Handcuffs Off Sales Team Development with Self-Directed Learning" *T + D* (November 2008): 62–66.
21. D. B. Youst and L. Lipsett, "New Job Immersion without Drowning," *Training and Development Journal* (February 1989): 73–75.
22. G. M. Piskurich, "Self-Directed Learning," in *The ASTD Training and Development Handbook:* 453–72; G. M. Piskurich, "Developing Self-Directed Learning," *Training and Development* (March 1994): 31–36.
23. C. M. Solomon, "When Training Doesn't Translate," *Workforce* (March 1997): 40–44.
24. P. Warr and D. Bunce, "Trainee Characteristics and the Outcomes of Open Learning," *Personnel Psychology* 48 (1995): 347–75; T. G. Hatcher, "The Ins and Outs of Self-Directed Learning," *Training and Development* (February 1997): 35–39.
25. R. W. Glover, *Apprenticeship Lessons from Abroad* (Columbus, OH: National Center for Research in Vocational Education, 1986).
26. Commerce Clearing House, *Orientation-Training* (Chicago: Personnel Practices Communications, Commerce Clearing House, 1981): 501–5.
27. A. H. Howard III, "Apprenticeships," in *The ASTD Training and Development Handbook:* 803–13.
28. M. Rowh, "The Rise of the Apprentice," *Human Resource Executive* (February 2006): 38–43.

29. A. Ciaccio, "'You're Hired': Goldcorp Stint Touts Opportunities in Mining," *The Wall Street Journal,* September 25, 2005: B6.

30. Rowh, "The Rise of the Apprentice."

31. *Eldredge v. Carpenters JATC* (1981), 27 Fair Employment Practices (Bureau of National Affairs):479.

32. M. Pramik, "Installers Learn on Practice Dwellings," *Columbus Dispatch,* February 7, 2003: F1.

33. H. Dolezalek, "Pretending to Learn," *Training* (July/August 2003): 20–26.

34. M. W. McCall Jr. and M. M. Lombardo, "Using Simulation for Leadership and Management Research," *Management Science* 28 (1982): 533–49.

35. S. McCartney, "Addressing Small Errors in the Cockpit," *The Wall Street Journal* (September 13, 2005): D5.

36. J. Alden and J. Kirkhorn, "Case Studies," in *The ASTD Training and Development Handbook:* 497–516.

37. H. Kelly, "Case Method Training: What It Is and How It Works," in *Effective Training Delivery,* ed. D. Zielinski (Minneapolis: Lakewood Books, 1989): 95–96.

38. T. W. Shreeve, "On the Case at the CIA," *Training and Development* (March 1997): 53–54.

39. S. Wiebenga, "Guidelines for Selecting, Using, and Evaluating Games in Corporate Training," *Performance Improvement Quarterly* 18 (2004): 19–36; S. Sugar, "Using Games to Energize Dry Material," in *The ASTD Handbook of Training Design and Delivery:* 107–20.

40. D. Schwartz, J. Bransford, and D. Sears, "Efficiency and Innovation in Transfer," in *Transfer of Learning: Research and Perspectives,* ed. J. Mestre (Greenwich, CT: Information Age Publishing, 2004).

41. S. McCartney, "A Delicate Balance," *The Wall Street Journal* (May 10, 2005): R7, R9.

42. E. Krell, "Learning to Love the P&L," *Training* (September 1999): 66–72.

43. "Business War Games," *Training* (December 2002): 18.

44. M. Hequet, "Games That Teach," *Training* (July 1995): 53–58.

45. S. Thiagarajan, "Instructional Games, Simulations, and Role Plays," in *The ASTD Training and Development Handbook:* 517–33.

46. "Wequassett Resort and Golf Club: Heroic Customer Service," *Training* (March/April 2008): 36–37.

47. S. J. Simon and J. M. Werner, "Computer Training through Behavior Modeling, Self-Paced, and Instructional Approaches: A Field Experiment," *Journal of Applied Psychology* 81 (1996): 648–59; P. Taylor, D. Russ-Eft, and D. Chan, "A Meta-analytic Review of Behavior Modeling Training," *Journal of Applied Psychology* 90, no. 4 (2005): 692–709.

48. W. C. Byham and A. Pescuric, "Behavior Modeling at the Teachable Moment," *Training* (December 1996): 51–56.

49. P. Decker and B. Nathan, *Behavior Modeling Training* (New York: Praeger Scientific, 1985).

50. Ibid.; T. T. Baldwin, "Effects of Alternative Modeling Strategies on Outcomes of Interpersonal/Skills Training," *Journal of Applied Psychology* 77 (1992): 147–54.

51. D. Brown and D. Harvey, *An Experiential Approach to Organizational Development* (Englewood Cliffs, NJ: Prentice Hall, 2000); J. Schettler, "Learning by Doing," *Training* (April 2002): 38–43; P. Mirvis, "Executive Development through Consciousness Raising Experiences," *Academy of Management Learning & Education* (June 2008): 173–188.

52. S. Lueck, "Postal Service's Top Inspector Should Be Fired, Senators Say," *The Wall Street Journal,* (May 2, 2003): A2.

53. Schettler, "Learning by Doing."

54. R. J. Wagner, T. T. Baldwin, and C. C. Rowland, "Outdoor Training: Revolution or Fad?" *Training and Development Journal* (March 1991): 51–57; C. J. Cantoni, "Learning the Ropes of Teamwork," *The Wall Street Journal,* (October 2, 1995): A14.

55. C. Steinfeld, "Challenge Courses Can Build Strong Teams," *Training and Development* (April 1997): 12–13.

56. Ibid.

57. M. Regan, "Execs Scale New Heights in the Name of Teamwork," *Columbus Dispatch,* (February 15, 2004): F2.

58. D. Mishev, "Cooking for the Company," *Cooking Light* (August 2004): 142–47.

59. G. M. Tarullo, "Making Outdoor Experiential Training Work," *Training* (August 1992): 47–52.

60. C. Clements, R. J. Wagner, and C. C. Roland, "The Ins and Outs of Experiential Training," *Training and Development* (February 1995): 52–56.

61. G. M. McEvoy, "Organizational Change and Outdoor Management Education," *Human Resource Management* 36 (1997): 235–50.

62. E. Salas and J. A. Cannon-Bowers, "Strategies for Team Training," in *Training for 21st Century Technology: Applications for Psychological Research,* ed. M. A. Quinones and A. Dutta (Washington, DC: American Psychological Association, 1997).

63. R. L. Oser, A. McCallum, E. Salas, and B. B. Morgan Jr., "Toward a Definition of Teamwork: An Analysis of Critical Team Behaviors," Technical Report 89-004 (Orlando, FL: Naval Training Research Center, 1989).

64. Salas and Cannon-Bowers, "Strategies for Team Training."

65. M. Marks, M. Sabella, C. Burke, and S. Zaccaro, "The Impact of Cross-Training on Team Effectiveness," *Journal of Applied Psychology* 87 (2002): 3–13.

66. E. Salas, C. Burke, and J. Cannon-Bowers, "What We Know about Designing and Delivering Team Training: Tips and Guidelines," *Creating, Implementing, and Managing Effective Training and Development,* ed. K. Kraiger (San Francisco: Jossey-Bass, 2002): 234–62.

67. S. Carey, "Racing to Improve," *The Wall Street Journal,* (March 24, 2006): B1, B6.

68. D. Dotlich and J. Noel, *Active Learning: How the World's Top Companies Are Recreating Their Leaders and Themselves* (San Francisco: Jossey-Bass, 1998).

69. M. Marquardt, "Harnessing the Power of Action Learning," *T + D* (June 2004): 26–32; *www.novartis.com/careers/en/talent_management/learning_development.shtml,* Novartis Web site (April 7, 2006).

70. "A Team Effort," *Training* (September 2002): 18.

71. H. Lancaster, "This Kind of Black Belt Can Help You Score Some Points at Work," *The Wall Street Journal,* (September 14, 1999): B1; S. Gale, "Building Frameworks for Six Sigma Success," *Workforce* (May 2003): 64–66.

72. J. DeFeo, "An ROI Story," *Training and Development* (July 2000): 25–27.

73. S. Gale, "Six Sigma Is a Way of Life," *Workforce* (May 2003): 67–68.

74. Marquardt, "Harnessing the Power of Action Learning."

75. M. Burke and R. Day, "A Cumulative Study of the Effectiveness of Managerial Training," *Journal of Applied Psychology* 71 (1986): 232–245.

76. "Outstanding Training Initiatives. The Home Depot: Appliance Within."

E-Learning and Use of Technology in Training

Objectives

After reading this chapter, you should be able to

1. Explain how new technologies are influencing training.
2. Discuss potential advantages and disadvantages of multimedia training.
3. Evaluate a Web-based training site.
4. Explain how learning and transfer of training are enhanced by new training technologies.
5. Explain the strengths and limitations of e-learning, mobile technology training methods (such as iPods), and simulations.
6. Describe to a manager the different types of distance learning.
7. Recommend what should be included in an electronic performance support system.
8. Compare and contrast the strengths and weaknesses of traditional training methods versus those of technology-based training methods.
9. Identify and explain the benefits of learning management systems.

Blended Learning Is the Key to Tasty Donuts and Hot Coffee

The restaurant business is well known for its high failure rate. But most franchises do *not* fail, due to a number of factors including consumer brand recognition, support from the franchisor, and national advertising. Franchisors (the corporate office that oversees the brand) want their franchisees (the persons who buy the restaurants and runs them) to succeed . . . and training plays a key role in their success.

Consider Dunkin' Donuts, the world's largest coffee and baked goods chain, serving more than 3 million customers per day. Dunkin' Donuts sells 52 varieties of donuts and more than a dozen coffee beverages as well as an array of bagels, breakfast sandwiches, and other baked goods. Dunkin' Donuts is America's largest retailer of coffee-by-the-cup, serving nearly 1 billion cups of brewed coffee each year. At the end of 2008, there were 8,835 Dunkin' Donuts stores worldwide, including 6,395 franchised restaurants in 34 states in the U.S. and 2,440 international shops in 30 countries.

In 2008, global systemwide sales were $5.5 billion. Dunkin' Donuts invests time and money in training because the company believes it is an important investment that supports the brand and helps franchisees be successful and profitable.

Training at Dunkin' Donuts is based on a blended learning approach that involves online, classroom, and on-site work with follow-up and reinforcement. Franchisees attend an introductory course that focuses on the business as well as their roles and responsibilities and those of the franchisor. This helps the franchisees learn from and build relationships with important individuals and teams at the corporation. Franchisees then complete 60 hours of online training on their own time in how donuts are made, equipment maintenance, food safety, and shift management. A five and one-half week instructor-led course and certification program runs at the same time as the online training. The online and the instructor-led courses are both designed to simulate restaurant experiences, with the goal of facilitating on-the-job practice which occurs in the restaurant. Practice sessions are supported with skills checklists so trainees can monitor their progress and review training materials.

Before opening the restaurant, franchisees train their new staffs working side-by-side with regional market trainers or operations managers from Dunkin' Donuts. The goal is to have all employees working efficiently and effectively when the new restaurant opens. Extensive training also occurs after the restaurant opens. Market and network trainers and operations managers visit the store to evaluate them and provide ongoing training, support, and coaching. Based on the store evaluations, new training programs are developed to improve problem areas.

Dunkin' Donuts measures the success of its training programs in several different ways. Each of the training programs measures learning through the franchisee's ability to perform skills in restaurant operations. Dunkin' Donuts also asks franchisees for feedback on the training programs.

Source: Based on W. Webb, "Training = Franchise Success," *Training* (October 2008): 54–55 and the Dunkin' Donuts Web site at www.dunkindonuts.com.

INTRODUCTION

As the opening vignette illustrates, technology is having a major impact on the delivery of training programs. Dunkin' Donuts is using a combination of traditional and new technology training methods (a blended learning approach). Online learning provides trainees with access to training at any time and place. The use of technology such as online learning requires collaboration among the areas of training, information technology, and top management. In addition, needs assessment, design, transfer, and evaluation (training design) are critical components of the effective use of training technology. Although technologies such as MP3 players, iPods, and virtual reality provide exciting capabilities and possibilities, it is critical that companies use training technologies that support the business and learner needs.

Dunkin' Donuts is not alone in its use of new training technologies. Technology is changing learning and training in corporate settings as well as in grade schools, high schools, colleges, and universities. At Ohio State University, students taking its Women,

Culture, and Society course find themselves immersed in Second Life, a computer-based, three-dimensional virtual classroom.[1] Students explore the realities of how race, class, sexual orientation, economic equality, physical ability, violence, and the environment are experienced in a virtual society in which they can choose and change their identity, gender, and race. For example, one student studying disabilities was able to meet a Second Life resident who has cerebral palsy in real life. The Second Life resident gave her a wheelchair, allowing her to tour the virtual world in it, learning about people's attitudes regarding disability. The Second Life simulation includes a replica of an actual university building, display space, oceantop and hillside gathering places for discussion groups, and a virtual women's studies library. At the College of Medicine, students use the iPod Touch in classrooms and clinics.[2] The iPod Touch provides students with an opportunity to access a wide variety of online materials, including lecture recordings, readings, materials, and videos from the university's learning management system, as well as download high-quality images.

Several surveys of company training practices suggest that although face-to-face classroom instruction is used by almost all companies, new technologies are gaining in popularity. Table 8.1 provides a snapshot of the use of technology in training. The use of training technologies is expected to increase dramatically in the next decade as technology improves, the cost of technology decreases, companies recognize the potential cost savings of training via desktop and personal computers (PCs), and the need for customized training increases.[3] As you will see later in this chapter, new training technologies are unlikely to totally replace face-to-face instruction. Rather, face-to-face instruction will be combined with new training technologies (a combination known as blended training) to maximize learning.

This chapter begins by discussing the influence of new technology on training delivery, support, and administration. How technology has changed the learning environment also is addressed. Next, the chapter explores emerging multimedia training techniques (computer-based training, CD-ROM, interactive video, the Internet). E-learning, a comprehensive training strategy that can include several multimedia training techniques (Internet, CD-ROM), is discussed. E-learning emphasizes learning through interaction with training content, sharing with other trainees, and using Internet

TABLE 8.1 **Use of New** **Technology in** **Training** Source: Based on "2008 Industry Report: Gauges & Drivers," *Training* (November/December): 16–34; American Society for Training and Development, *2007 State of the Industry Report* (Alexandria, VA: American Society for Training and Development, 2008).	• 10 percent of training is delivered in a virtual classroom and 18 percent is delivered online. • 71 percent of companies use structured collaboration such as communities of practice. • Communities of practice are the most frequently used collaborative learning tool (22 percent), followed by podcasts and mobile learning (14 percent), blogs (8 percent), and wikis (7 percent). • 32.1 percent of learning hours involve technology-based training methods. • 38 percent of companies use learning management systems. Broken down by size, 79 percent of large (10,000 or more employees), 57 percent of midsize (1,000–9,999 employees), and 36 percent of small companies (100–999 employees) use learning management systems. • 21 percent of large companies (10,000 or more employees) use e-learning to deliver training, compared to 17 percent of midsize (1,000–9,999 employees) and small (100 or less employees) companies.

resources. More sophisticated technologies that are just beginning to be marketed commercially for training delivery (expert systems, virtual reality, virtual worlds, intelligent tutoring systems) are introduced. The use of expert systems and groupware exemplifies how technology supports training through its role as a storage place for intellectual capital (information and learned capabilities), which facilitates access to information and communication of knowledge among employees. The chapter also shows how technology such as interactive voice responses and imaging is used in training administration. The last section of the chapter compares the various training methods that are based on new technology, employing the characteristics used to evaluate the traditional training methods discussed in Chapter 7. As you will see, several training methods discussed in this chapter can replace or be substituted for traditional training methods under certain conditions.

TECHNOLOGY'S INFLUENCE ON TRAINING AND LEARNING

Chapters 1 and 2 discussed the role that training and development should play in helping companies to execute their business strategy and deal with forces influencing the workplace. For training to help a company gain a competitive advantage, it needs to support business goals and be delivered as needed to geographically dispersed employees who may be working at home or in another country. Training costs (such as travel costs) should be minimized and maximum benefits gained, including learning and transfer of training. For learning and transfer to occur (i.e., for the benefits of training to be realized), the training environment must include learning principles such as practice, feedback, meaningful material, and the ability to learn by interacting with others.

New technologies have made it possible to reduce the costs associated with delivering training to employees, to increase the effectiveness of the learning environment, and to help training contribute to business goals. New training delivery and instructional methods include online learning (also called e-learning), distance learning, simulations, virtual reality, expert systems, electronic support systems, and learning management systems. New technologies have influenced the delivery of training, training administration, and training support. Technology has made several benefits possible:[4]

- Employees can gain control over when and where they receive training.
- Employees can access knowledge and expert systems on an as-needed basis.
- Through the use of avatars, virtual reality, and simulations, the learning environment can look, feel, and sound just like the work environment.
- Employees can choose the type of media (print, sound, video) they want to use in a training program.
- Course enrollment, testing, and training records can be handled electronically, reducing the paperwork and time needed for administrative activities.
- Employees' accomplishments during training can be monitored.
- Traditional training methods such as classroom instruction and behavior modeling can be delivered to trainees rather than requiring them to come to a central training location.

Consider how technology has influenced training at IBM and UPS.[5] At IBM, the learning strategy is for employees to learn every day in a dynamic way based on their current job and what they need to do in the future. To better prepare the company's next generation of leaders and to best utilize its global work force, IBM is using new technology—such as collaborative online learning platforms that allow employees to learn from their peers—and virtual tools that give them instant access to experts. Peer learning can occur spontaneously online just as it would if all of IBM's employees were located in the same building. IBM employees participating in the company's virtual 3D online environment create avatars (computer depictions of humans) to interact with each other and discuss and share ideas. At UPS, technology has made the driver's job more complex. Drivers have to handle the truck safely, be proficient on the DIAD (handheld computer), and understand how to stay safe during a package delivery. As a result, UPS developed the Integrad training center in Maryland. Integrad includes a simulator designed to teach new hires how to load and unload packages from shelves, the floor, and the rear door while also meeting company time standards for such activities and minimizing the stress and strain that cause injuries. On average, drivers have to step off and on the truck at least 120 times on their routes—which can strain ankles if done incorrectly. At Integrad, trainees deliver packages while trainers and trainees serve as customers in a simulated town with stores, streets, and even a loading dock.

Technology and Collaboration

Technology allows digital collaboration to occur. **Digital collaboration** is the use of technology to enhance and extend employees' abilities to work together regardless of their geographic proximity.[6] Digital collaboration includes electronic messaging systems, electronic meeting systems, online communities of learning organized by subject where employees can access interactive discussion areas and share training content and Web links, and document-handling systems with collaboration technologies that allow interpersonal interaction. For example, at www.buzzsaw.com, contractors, suppliers, and engineers can buy and sell products and services as well as exchange blueprints, designs, and other data to cut building time. Digital collaboration requires a computer, but collaborative applications for handheld devices and personal digital assistants are becoming available that will allow employees to collaborate anytime or anywhere. Digital collaboration can be synchronous or asynchronous.[7] In **synchronous communication,** trainers, experts, and learners interact with each other live and in real time the same way they would in face-to-face classroom instruction. Technologies such as video teleconferencing and live online courses (virtual classrooms) make synchronous communication possible. **Asynchronous communication** refers to non–real-time interactions. That is, persons are not online and cannot communicate with each other without a time delay, but learners can still access information resources when they desire them. E-mail, self-paced courses on the Web or on CD-ROM, discussion groups, and virtual libraries allow asynchronous communication.

The Shoney's and Captain D's restaurant chains have more than 350 restaurants in more than 20 states.[8] Over 8,000 employees each year must be trained on the basics of the operational parts of the business, including how to make french fries, hush puppies, and coleslaw. Also, each year 600 new managers must be trained in business issues and back-office operations of the restaurants. The biggest challenge that Shoney's faced was how to consistently train geographically dispersed employees. Shoney's solution was to implement OneTouch, a live integrated video and two-way voice and data application that combines synchronous video, voice, and data and live Web pages so that team members can interact with trainers. OneTouch can be delivered to desktop PCs as well as to warehouses and repair bays. Desktop systems can be positioned in any appropriate locations in the restaurant. Individuals or a group of employees can gather around the PC for training. The training modules include topics such as Orientation, Kitchen, and Dining Room. Each module is interactive. Topics are introduced and are followed up by quizzes to ensure that learning occurs. For example, the coleslaw program shows trainees what the coleslaw ingredients are and where they can be found in the restaurant. The coleslaw program includes a video that trainees can watch and refer to as they practice. After they practice, they have to complete a quiz, and their manager has to verify that they completed the topic before they move on to the next program. The training is consistent and easy to update. The program also allows kitchen and counter staff to learn each other's skills, which gives Shoney's flexibility in its staffing (e.g., counter employees who know how to cook).

Technology and Learning Environment

The Internet is primarily responsible for creating our revolution in learning. Internet technology has permitted the development of electronic networks that integrate voice, video, and data connections among learners, instructors, and experts. Figure 8.1 shows three different types of learning environments. Learning used to be a very linear process. That is, instructors presented information to the learners; practice and applications then occurred after instruction was completed (see the classroom learning environment in Figure 8.1). Traditionally, the learning environment included only the instructor or trainer and the learners. The trainer was responsible for delivering content, answering questions, and testing learning. Trainees played a passive role in learning. Communication on course content was one-way: from the instructor to the learner. Experts and resource materials were separate from the learning environment. Contact with resource materials and experts beyond the instructor and course materials assigned for the course required learners to go outside the formal learning environment. Also, learners had to wait to access resource materials and experts until instruction was completed. Interaction among learners occurred primarily outside the training room and tended to be limited to those who worked in the same geographic area.

Technology has allowed learning to become a more dynamic process. As shown on the right side of Figure 8.1, the learning environment can be expanded to include greater interaction between learners and the training content as well as between learners and the instructor. The trainer may help design the instruction, but the instruction is primarily delivered to the learners through technology such as online learning, simulations, or iPods. The instructor becomes more of a coach and resource person to answer students' questions and is less involved in delivery of training content. Learning occurs primarily through communicating with other learners, working on virtual team projects, participating in games, listening, exchanging ideas, interacting with experts (engineers, managers, etc.), and discovering ideas and applications using hyperlinks that take the learner to other Web sites. Experts and resource materials may be part of the learning environment. While learners interact with the training content through exercises, applications, and simulations, they can discuss what they are learning with other learners or access experts or resource materials available on the Internet. Training delivery and administration (e.g., tracking learner progress) is all done by the computer. In the blended learning environment, shown at the bottom of Figure 8.1, trainees have access to a blended training curriculum that consists of both online and classroom instruction. Collaboration can occur between learners, between learners and instructors, and between learners and experts. Although new technologies

FIGURE 8.1 **Types of Learning Environments**

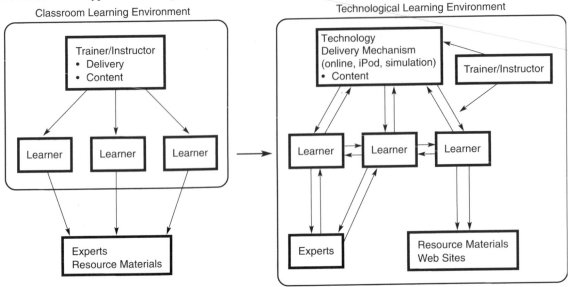

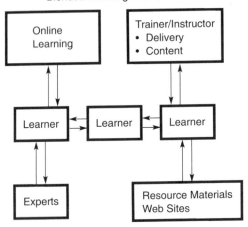

allow for the creation of a dynamic learning environment, it is important to include collaboration, active learner involvement, and access to other resources in the design and development of the training program. Use of new technology requires building these capabilities into the training program. For example, **Web 2.0** refers to user-created social networking features on the Internet, including blogs, wikis, and Twitter.[9] Qualcomm's initiative, Learning 2.0, involves the use of Web 2.0 technologies such as social bookmarking/tagging, blogs, and tools similar to those found on Facebook and YouTube to build relationships between trainees and between trainees and training content.

Technology has enabled training to be delivered to different geographical locations, to accompany trainees whether they are at work or at home (mobile technology), and to be completed online using a personal computer. Many of the training methods discussed in this chapter have these features. For example, online learning, or e-learning, includes instruction and delivery of training using the Internet or Web. Distance learning typically involves videoconferencing and/or computers for delivery of instruction from a trainer to trainees who are not in the same location as the trainer. Mobile technologies allow training to be delivered through iPods, personal data assistants (PDAs), and handheld computers that allow trainees to tune in to training programs at any time or place.

Web-based training and e-learning support virtual reality, animation, interactions, communications among trainees and real-time audio and video. As Figure 8.2 shows, there are six levels of technology-based training. The difference between the highest and lowest levels is that at the higher levels, technology methods allow learning to become more job-related and directly meet a business need. For example, employees can access expert systems while they work. The simplest level facilitates communications among trainers and trainees. More complex uses of technology involve the actual delivery of training, and trainees are very actively involved in learning. Sound, automation, and video are used in Web-based training. In addition, trainees are linked to other resources on the Web. They are also required to share information with other trainees and to deposit knowledge and their insights from the training (such as potential applications of the training content) into a database that is accessible to other company employees. At the highest level—electronic performance support systems—employees receive training on an as-needed basis while they perform their jobs.

TECHNOLOGY AND MULTIMEDIA

Technology developments allow the use of a number of different media for training. **Multimedia training** combines audiovisual training methods with computer-based training.[10] Multimedia training methods include computer-based training, CD-ROM, e-interactive video, the Internet, video, virtual reality, and simulations. Multimedia training integrates text, graphics, animation, video, and audio, and often the trainee can interact with the content. How prevalent is multimedia training? According to a survey by *Training* magazine, 54 percent of companies report they often or always use the Internet or intranet, 37 percent use CD-ROMS, 43 percent use Web-based self study, 10 percent use computer-based games, and 2 percent use virtual reality programs.

FIGURE 8.2 **Levels of Technology-Based Training**

Source: Based on K. Kruse, "Five Levels of Internet-Based Training," *Training and Development* (February 1997): 60–61; R. Clark and C. Lyons, "Using Web-Based Training Wisely," *Training* (July 1999): 51–56; J. Cone and D. Robinson, "The Power of E-Performance," *T&D* (August 2001): 32–41.

Communications	Online referencing	Testing Assessment	Delivery of computer-based training and multimedia (synchronous or asynchronous) Mobile technology	Online learning Blended learning Simulations	Expert systems Electronic performance support systems
1	2	3	4	5	6

Table 8.2 shows the major advantages and disadvantages of multimedia training. Multimedia training motivates trainees to learn, provides immediate feedback and guidance (through online help), tests employees' level of mastery, and allows employees to learn at their own pace.[11] A major disadvantage of multimedia training is the cost. Initial development costs for a computerized version of training can range from $25,000 to $250,000 depending on the complexity of material and media used.[12] These costs can be recovered over time by savings gained from reductions in travel costs and instruction costs if the content does not require frequent updating.[13] Multimedia training may also be difficult to use for training interpersonal skills, especially if the learner needs to recognize and/or practice subtle behavioral cues or cognitive processes.

Medtronic is a 12,000-employee company based in Minneapolis, Minnesota, that specializes in developing and selling medical technology. Multimedia was first used at Medtronic purely for marketing purposes. Salespeople used a laptop personal computer equipped with a CD player to show physicians the benefits and correct usage of heart valves. When the interactive program was introduced at a national sales meeting, demand for the CD exceeded supply.

Medtronic is now using multimedia for training as well as marketing. Medtronic extensively uses classroom-based training for salespeople. Although the product CDs are being used as a learning tool by staff preparing for sales presentations, the CDs are only one step the company is taking toward the goal of enhancing learning. The manager of sales training has expanded use of multimedia training because it cuts salespeople's time in the classroom. The manager believes that multimedia training has increased the consistency and efficiency of training and has provided salespeople with feedback regarding which dimensions of the product they "know." CD-based product programs work best for experienced salespeople who already are familiar with the product. New salespeople need feedback and help screens, available from multimedia applications. New salespeople need to be able to interact with the product at their own pace, so that they are comfortable explaining and demonstrating all aspects of the product to physicians. Salespeople's time is also in great demand. Multimedia provides accessibility to training wherever and whenever salespeople can access their laptop computer. Multimedia also has helped the entire sales force learn about new products as quickly as possible.[14]

TABLE 8.2
Advantages and Disadvantages of Multimedia Training

Source: Based on S.V. Bainbridge, "The Implications of Technology-Assisted Training," *IHRIM-Link* (December 1996/January 1997): 62–68; M. Hequet, "How Does Multimedia Change Training?" *Training* (February 1997): A20–A22.

Advantages	Disadvantages
Is self-paced	Is expensive to develop
Is interactive	Is ineffective for certain training content
Has consistency of content	May lead to trainee anxiety with using technology
Has consistency of delivery	Is difficult to quickly update
Offers unlimited geographic accessibility	Can lead to a lack of agreement on effectiveness
Provides immediate feedback	
Has a built-in guidance system	
Appeals to multiple senses	
Can test and certify mastery	
Provides privacy	

COMPUTER-BASED TRAINING

Computer-based training (CBT) is an interactive training experience in which the computer provides the learning stimulus, the trainee must respond, and the computer analyzes the responses and provides feedback to the trainee.[15] CBT includes interactive video, CD-ROM, and other systems when they are computer-driven. The most common CBT programs consist of software on a floppy disk that runs on a personal computer. CBT, one of the first new technologies to be used in training, has become more sophisticated with the development of laser disks, DVDs, and CD-ROMs and with increasing use of the Internet. These technologies allow greater use of video and audio than do technologies that rely solely on the computer.

For example, to teach managers how to complete performance reviews, Vidicon Enterprises, which operates convenience stores in Washington, purchased software called "Performance Now!"[16] Managers learned how to write better performance reviews and to improve their management skills. The program works by asking managers to identify which of several job dimensions they want to evaluate. For the dimension "job quality," the manager is asked to rate the employee in various categories such as "Strives to Achieve Goals." The program automatically summarizes the ratings into a paragraph that the manager can edit. The program teaches the managers effective language to use in performance evaluations. If the manager writes something inappropriate (e.g., "the employee is too young for the position"), a box appears on the screen with a warning not to equate age with experience. Also, use of the categories underlying each job dimension has broadened managers' views of employee performance.

Computer-based training can also involve simulations. For example, during training needs assessment, Bayer Pharmaceuticals discovered that its technical experts needed new skills to manage large projects.[17] These skills related to keeping project managers focused on the task, managing competing priorities, managing large cross-functional teams, and supervising employees who did not report to them. These skills are important to reduce the time needed to bring research discoveries to the marketplace. To train in these skills, Bayer used a computer-based simulation that requires teams of trainees to manage a large-scale project. The management decisions they make impact their odds of being successful. A computer calculates each team's probability of succeeding. The simulation includes obstacles that can negatively impact a project such as unmotivated employees, absenteeism, and projects being completed late. The simulation also includes online work that trainees complete prior to training. The prework provides trainees with an overview of the steps involved in project management. All trainees complete a self-assessment of their team-related behavior (e.g., conflict resolution). The assessments are used for discussing leader/team-member relationships. After completing the simulation, trainees can access a program Web site that includes a newsletter and tips for project management. Employees who have completed the simulation are demonstrating increased confidence in their ability to manage a project and to handle changing priorities, and they are addressing team issues more quickly.

CD-ROM, DVD, Laser Disk

A personal computer enables animation, video clips, and graphics to be integrated into a training session. Also, the user can interact with the training material through use of a joystick or touch-screen monitor. **CD-ROMs** and **DVDs** utilize a laser to read text, graphics, audio, and video off an aluminum disk. A **laser disk** uses a laser to provide high-quality video and sound. A laser disk can be used alone (as a source of video) or as part of a computer-based instruction delivery system.

For example, at Pilgrim Nuclear Power Plant in Plymouth, Massachusetts, a newly hired security guard learns the layout of the facility by using a computer, television, monitor, joystick, and video disk.[18] The new hire can tour the trash-compactor facility, examine the components on a panel of electrical controls, ride elevators, and listen to colleagues discuss machinery, equipment, and high-radiation areas that the new hire should be aware of. With more than 77,000 photos on the laser disk, the new security guard can travel at normal walking speed, look upward or downward, quickly change location, and store images for future reference.

Chiquita, the fresh fruit company, needed to help employees understand how they could contribute to the company's business goals through a new performance management system, Perform to Grow.[19] Although e-learning modules were developed to help employees learn how to practice the tools and steps within the Perform to Grow system, offices in Central America, Africa, Asia, and Eastern Europe did not have the technology that was available in the North American and European offices. As a result, Chiquita burned the e-learning modules and tool kit onto CD-ROMs for distribution to employees in those locations.

Interactive Video

Interactive video combines the advantages of video and computer-based instruction. Instruction is provided one-on-one to trainees via a monitor connected to a keyboard. Trainees use the keyboard or touch the monitor to interact with the program. Interactive video is used to teach technical procedures and interpersonal skills. The training program may be stored on a videodisk or CD.

Apple Computer's and Federal Express's experiences with CD-ROMs provide good examples of how a CD-ROM can provide greater accessibility to consistent training as well as facilitate learning. Apple Computer's managers wanted access to training, but their busy schedules made it difficult for them to leave their jobs to attend training sessions.[20] As a result of this need for an alternative to classroom instruction, Apple connected CD-ROM drives to all its computers. CD-ROM training programs were created for the managers. One CD-ROM–based program covered basics of employment law, offering both narrated text and video. The CD-ROM also allowed the manager to access reference materials included on the CD, such as a list of legal interview questions and demonstrations of violations of law (e.g., sexual harassment).

Federal Express's 25-disk interactive video curriculum includes courses related to customer etiquette, defensive driving, and delivery procedures.[21] As Federal Express discovered, interactive video has many advantages. First, training is individualized. Employees control what aspects of the training program they view. They can skip ahead when they feel competent, or they can review topics. Second, employees receive immediate feedback concerning their performance. Third, training is accessible on a 24-hour basis regardless of employees' work schedules. From the employer's standpoint, the high cost of developing interactive video programs and purchasing the equipment was offset by the reduction in instructor costs and travel costs related to a central training location. At Federal Express, interactive video has made it possible to train 35,000 customer-contact employees in 650 locations nationwide, saving the company millions of dollars. Without interactive video, Federal Express could not deliver consistent high-quality training.

Online Learning: The Internet, Web-Based Training, E-Learning, and Learning Portals

The **Internet** is a widely used tool for communications, a method for sending and receiving communications quickly and inexpensively, and a way to locate and gather resources such as software and reports.[22] To gain access to the Internet, you need a personal computer with a direct connection via an existing network or a modem to dial into the Internet. Educational institutions, government agencies, and commercial service providers such as Microsoft and America Online provide access to the Internet.

Employees can communicate with managers nearby or across the globe, can leave messages or documents, and can gain access to "rooms" designated for conversation on certain topics (the Americans with Disabilities Act, for example). Various newsgroups, bulletin boards, and discussion groups are dedicated to areas of interest. There you can read, post, and respond to messages and articles. Internet sites can have home pages—mailboxes that identify the person or company and contain text, images, sounds, or even video.

The **World Wide Web (WWW)** is a user-friendly service on the Internet.[23] The Web provides browser software (e.g., Microsoft Internet Explorer, Netscape) that enables you to explore the Web. Besides browser software, you also need a search engine (e.g., Yahoo, Google) to find information on topics of your choice. Every home page on the Web has a uniform resource locator (URL), or Web address.

The Internet is a valuable source of information on a wide range of topics. The inside of the front cover of this book provides Internet and Web site addresses related to training topics. For example, one manager at Hydro Quebec, a large Canadian utility, used the Internet to research topics related to TQM and business process reengineering. When the company wanted information on diversity and women's issues, the manager logged onto a Cornell University Web site and quickly downloaded two dozen reports on the topic. When the company needed to develop a satisfaction survey, the manager used the Internet to identify similar-sized companies that had conducted comprehensive surveys. Within one day, 30 human resource professionals, including managers at Federal Express and United Parcel Service, responded. The Hydro Quebec manager has also networked with human resource managers at Motorola, IBM, and other companies.[24]

Online learning, or **e-learning,** refers to instruction and delivery of training by computer online through the Internet or the Web.[25] Online learning includes Web-based training, distance learning, and virtual classrooms; it may involve a CD-ROM. Online learning can include task-based support, simulation-based training, distance learning, and learning portals. There are three important characteristics of online learning. First, online learning involves electronic networks that enable information and instruction to be delivered, shared, and updated instantly. Second, online learning is delivered to the trainee using computers with Internet technology. Third, it focuses on learning solutions that go beyond traditional training by including the delivery of information and tools that improve performance.

Internet-based, or **Web-based, training** refers to training that is delivered on public or private computer networks and displayed by a Web browser.[26] **Intranet-based training** refers to training that uses the company's own computer network. The training programs are accessible only to the company's employees, not to the general public. Both Internet-based and intranet-based training are stored in a computer and accessed using a computer network. The two types of training use similar technologies. The major difference is that access to the intranet is restricted to a company's employees. For example, Amdahl Corporation (a mainframe computer manufacturer) has set up an intranet.[27] Employees use Netscape to browse the Web along with a company-developed Web browser. Every department at Amdahl has its own Web home page. The home page describes what services the department provides. Many employees also have their own personal home pages. The training department home page includes a list of courses offered by the training department. The manufacturing department gives employees access to technical manuals via the intranet.

Potential Features of Online Learning

In online learning it is possible to enable learners to interact with the training content and other learners and to decide how they want to learn.[28] Figure 8.3 shows the possible features that can be built into online learning. These features include content, collaboration and sharing, links to resources, learner control, delivery, and administration. It is important to note that not all these features are incorporated into online learning methods. One reason is that certain methods make it difficult to incorporate some of these features. For example, as you will see later in the chapter, distance learning that involves teleconferencing may limit the amount of collaboration between trainees and the instructor. Also, in distance learning, trainees do not have control over the content, practice, and speed of learning. Another reason why a feature may not be incorporated is that the designers may have chosen not to include it. Although e-learning *can* include all the features to facilitate learning that are shown in Figure 8.3, it may fall short of its potential because, for example, program developers do not include opportunities for trainees to collaborate. As Figure 8.3 shows, not only can online learning provide the trainee with content, but it also can give learners the ability to control what they learn, the speed at which they progress through the program, how much they practice, and even when they learn. In addition, online learning can allow learners to collaborate or interact with other trainees and experts and can provide links to other learning resources such as reference materials, company Web sites, and other training programs. Text, video, graphics, and sound can be used to present course content. Online learning may also include various aspects of training administration such as course enrollment, testing and evaluating trainees, and monitoring of trainees' learning progress.

Advantages of Online Learning

The possible features that can be built into online learning give it potential advantages over other training methods. The advantages of e-learning are shown in Table 8.3. E-learning initiatives are designed to contribute to a company's strategic business objectives.[29] E-learning supports company initiatives such as expanding the number of customers, initiating new ways to carry out business such as e-business, and speeding the development of new products or services. E-learning may involve a larger audience than traditional training programs that focus on employees. E-learning may involve partners, suppliers, vendors, and potential customers. For example, Lucent Technologies, which designs and delivers communications network technologies, has devoted significant resources to ensure that customers and business partners have access to e-learning.[30] Training affects customer satisfaction with Lucent's products and solutions. It also influences employees' ability to sell to and service customers. Product training courses that deal with installing, repairing, and operating Lucent equipment are available to customers on the company's Web site. Users can take the courses, register and pay for the classes, and track their progress. Lucent also provides training to its business partners, who are required to be certified in Lucent's products before they can receive special discounts. As Lucent increases its electronically

FIGURE 8.3   Potential Features of E-Learning

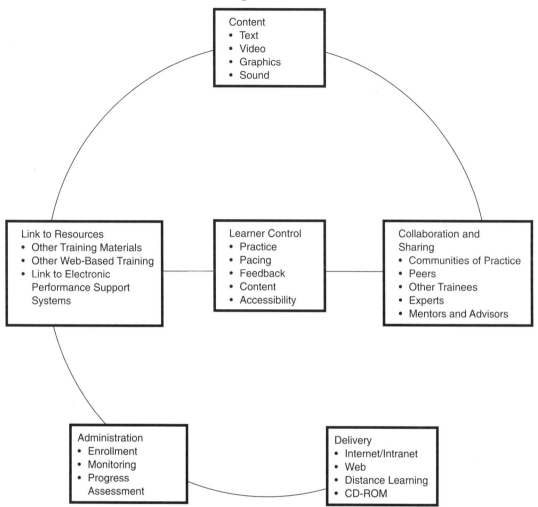

TABLE 8.3
Advantages of E-Learning

Source: Based on D. Hartley, "All Aboard the E-Learning Train," *Training and Development* (July 2000): 37–42; V. Beer, *The Web Learning Field Book: Using the World Wide Web to Build Workplace Learning Environments* (San Francisco: Jossey-Bass, 2000).

It supports the company's business strategy and objectives.
It is accessible at any time and any place.
The audience can include employees and managers as well as vendors, customers, and clients.
Training can be delivered to geographically dispersed employees.
Training can be delivered faster and to more employees in a shorter period of time.
Updating is easy.
Practice, feedback, objectives, assessment, and other positive features of a learning environment can be built into the program. Learning is enhanced through use of multiple media (sound, text, video, graphics) and trainee interaction.
Paperwork related to training management (enrollment, assessment, etc.) can be eliminated.
It can link learners to other content, experts, and peers.

delivered courses, the company is also trying to increase the percentage of learners who take courses online. Today, about half the users attend classroom-based training.

E-learning allows training to be delivered faster and to more employees in a shorter period of time. Ritz Camera Centers uses an e-learning program to help keep its employees up to date on product information and enhance their selling skills.[31] E-learning was selected because the company needed a systematic way to reach all associates quickly with materials that could be easily managed and updated. Ritz Camera employees can access short training courses online on a wide variety of technologies and brands. Each module provides insight into product features, competitive differences, and benefits. Training modules are created monthly and can stay live for up to a year based on product cycles. The modules feature training assessments in the form of a quiz that employees must complete successfully. In addition, Ritz can track employees' participation through a Web portal.

E-learning offers training to geographically dispersed employees at their own locations, reducing travel costs associated with bringing trainees to a central location. This is one reason why online learning is the second most popular approach to training (after print-based materials) for small businesses.[32] For small businesses, online learning helps reduce travel costs related to bringing employees to a central location for training and gives employees flexibility as they try to fit training into their work schedules. Golden Harvest Seeds Inc. found that its sales training program for 250 employees and 2,000 independent crop-seed dealers was not well attended and the training sessions took too much valuable work time. To overcome the attendance problem and increase training effectiveness, Golden Harvest hired a company to produce and post online videos for teaching salespersons how to sell Golden Harvest seeds. Golden Harvest found that employees were watching the videos, sales and the demand for more courses increased, and training costs per person were reduced from over $175 to less than $100.

In another example, Nike was challenged to design a training program for retailers with stores throughout the country and high levels of staff turnover.[33] Nike wanted a program to deliver information in short time periods to make it easier for salespeople to learn but not keep them off the sales floor. Nike developed the Sports Knowledge Underground, which looks like a subway map in which different stations represent different product training. For example, the Apparel Union Station branches off to the apparel technologies line, the running products line, and the Nike Pro products line. Each segment lasts no more than five minutes and gives the salesperson the needed product knowledge. Salespersons are tested at the end of the training and are asked for feedback about the program, which is sent to the e-learning program developers. The program is currently used by more than 20,000 sales associates, and more are expected to complete the training as it becomes available in more stores. The program appears to be having a positive impact on the business—stores that have the program have seen a 4 percent increase in sales.

Some companies have training requirements that all employees have to complete for the company to meet quality or legal requirements. Online learning allows more employees to gain access to these types of programs in a quicker time period than if face-to-face instruction is used. For example, financial services companies are often challenged to keep their global employees up to date on constant changes in products, policies, and government regulations. Face-to-face training is not timely or cost-efficient. As a result, Capital One, Wachovia, and Wells Fargo are using e-learning for training and for tracking and documenting which employees have been trained.[34] E-learning allows retailers, to track every employee's course performance and match it with his or her sales performance.[35] Product lines are tied to specific certificate tracks. To sell those products, employees must first complete the learning for that track and pass the certification exam. The more training employees take, the more products they can sell. At Continental Airlines, e-learning modules have been especially helpful for bringing staff up to speed on new security regulations.[36] "It's hard to have someone away from their job for a whole day," says Jennifer Boubel, senior manager of airport services training for Continental Airlines. "This way, they can spend 30 minutes here and 45 minutes there to complete the modules."

E-learning is also easy to update, thanks to user-friendly authoring languages such as HTML. Changes can be made on the server that stores the e-learning program. Employees worldwide can access the updated program. The administrative features of e-learning make training management a more efficient, paperless process. For example, CCH developed Shared Learning, an online administration module that allows companies to monitor employees' completion of e-learning. It tracks how many times employees complete the same class and how much time employees spend per class, and it bookmarks the point at which trainees leave an online class so they can enter the program at the place they left it when they again begin training.[37]

Effectiveness of Online Learning

Is e-learning effective for all types of learning outcomes and trainees? Both research and company experiences suggest that e-learning is effective for a wide range of outcomes, including knowledge, skills, and behaviors.[38] Table 8.4 shows some of the research results regarding the effectiveness of online learning compared to other training methods. Online learning may be most effective for training that emphasizes cognitive outcomes such as declarative and procedural knowledge (recall the discussion of learning outcomes in Chapters 4 and 6). Online learning may facilitate greater social interaction between trainees than face-to-face learning methods because other trainees are equally accessible or more accessible than the instructor and there are more methods available that allow learners to interact, such as e-mail, group projects, whiteboards, wiki documents, and chat rooms.[39] Also, trainees may be more motivated to participate because they avoid

TABLE 8.4 **Research Results Regarding the Effectiveness of Online Learning**

- Online instruction is more effective than face-to-face classroom instruction for teaching declarative knowledge (cognitive knowledge assessed using written tests designed to measure whether trainees remember concepts presented in training).
- Web-based instruction and classroom instruction are equally effective in teaching procedural knowledge (the ability of learners to perform the skills taught in training).
- Learners are equally satisfied with Web-based and classroom instruction.
- Web-based instruction appears to be more effective than classroom instruction (1) when learners are provided with control over content, sequence, and pace, (2) in long courses, and (3) when learners are able to practice the content and receive feedback.
- Web-based instruction and classroom instruction are equally effective when similar instructional methods are used (for example, both approaches use video, practice assignments, and learning tests).
- The employees who learn most from online learning are those who complete more of the available practice opportunities and take more time to complete the training.
- E-learning is not effective for all learners, especially those with low computer self-efficacy.

Source: Based on K. Kraiger, "Transforming Our Models of Learning and Development: Web-Based Instruction as Enabler of Third-Generation Instruction," *Industrial Organizational Psychology* 1 (2008): 454–467; T. Sitzmann, K. Kraiger, D. Stewart, and R. Wisher, "The Comparative Effectiveness of Web-Based and Classroom Instruction: A Meta-Analysis," *Personnel Psychology* 59 (2006): 623–634; E. Welsh, E. C. Wanberg, K. Brown, and M. Simmering, "E-Learning: Emerging Uses, Empirical Results and Future Directions," *International Journal of Training and Development* 7 (2003): 245–258.

feelings of inadequacy and low self-confidence, which can hinder participation in face-to-face learning. Delaware North Companies (DNC), a hospitality and food services company based in Buffalo, New York, provides hospitality and food services to national parks, stadiums, and airports. DNC delivers self-paced interactive training via the Web, followed by virtual classes.[40] At DNC, soft skills, such as managing a team, effective communication techniques, delegation, empowerment, and conflict resolution, have been identified as best for online training. Functional and technical skills have been found to be best suited for on-the-job training.

Despite the increasing popularity of online learning, many companies such as Home Depot Inc., Recreational Equipment Inc., and Qwest Communications International still prefer face-to-face training methods for teaching skills for complex jobs involving selling and repairing equipment.[41] Online learning is used to train employees when their job requires them to use a standard set of facts or procedures. For example, Recreational Equipment Inc., uses role playing between new employees and trainers who simulate a wide range of customer behaviors, helping them understand the difference between customers who want a specific product and customers who want to discuss different product choices. Qwest Communications estimates that 80 percent of training in its network department is completed face-to-face, compared to 20 percent online. To learn how to fix and install equipment, the company believes employees must have hands-on experience that is similar to what they will encounter working in homes and commercial locations. Online learning may be valuable, but it is insufficient for teaching complex analytical, conceptual, and interpersonal skills.[42] This may be because online learning lacks communication richness, some online learners may be reluctant to interact with other learners, and, although online learning increases accessibility to training, employees with busy work schedules have a greater opportunity to more easily delay, fail to complete, or poorly perform on learning activities. Later in the chapter we discuss how online learning can be combined with face-to-face instruction, known as blended learning, to take advantage of the strengths of both methods. Learning can be enhanced by combining face-to-face instruction and e-learning because learners are more engaged; the use of video, graphics, sound, and text is combined with active learning experiences such as cases, role plays, and simulations. Also, blended learning provides opportunities for learners to practice, ask questions, and interact with other learners and peers both face-to-face and online.

Table 8.5 lists factors that have limited companies' use of e-learning. Approximately one-third of the companies participating in a survey reported that significant factors in not using e-learning were that it cost too much, that employees were not motivated to learn online, and that management had not bought into the idea of e-learning.[43] Twenty-five percent of the companies reported that their use of e-learning was limited because employees lacked intranet access and the company lacked evidence showing e-learning's return on investment. The following sections discuss some ways to overcome these problems.

DEVELOPING EFFECTIVE ONLINE LEARNING

Table 8.6 provides tips for developing effective online learning.[44] Needs assessment, design and method, and evaluation are three central issues that need to be addressed for effective online learning, including Web-based training.

TABLE 8.5 **Factors Limiting the Use of E-Learning**	Cost Lack of motivation among employees to learn online Lack of management buy-in Lack of employee intranet access Lack of proof concerning return on investment Lack of high-quality content
Source: Based on M. Hequet, "The State of the E-Learning Market," *Training* (September 2003): 24–29.	

TABLE 8.6   Tips for Developing Effective Online Learning

Needs assessment	Identify the connection between online learning and the business's needs. Get management to buy in. Make sure employees have access to technology and technology support. Consult with information technology experts about system requirements. Identify specific training needs (knowledge, skills, competencies, behaviors). If needed, train learners on computer and Internet basics.
Design/Method	Incorporate learning principles (practice, feedback, meaningful material, an appeal to active learner involvement, an appeal to multiple senses). Design the course for the available bandwidth or increase the bandwidth. Consider blended instruction. Use games and simulations, which are attractive to learners. Structure materials properly. Allow trainees the opportunity to communicate and collaborate with each other and with the trainer, experts, or facilitators. Make the program user-friendly: Learning modules should be kept short, the content should not overload trainees, and Web pages should not be confusing. Keep each instructional segment self-contained. Create smooth transitions between instructional segments. Provide learners with control, including the opportunity to skip sections or modules and the ability to pause, bookmark, review, and return to where they left off. Learners often need to deal with interruptions and distractions. Any audio, video, or animation should be useful to the learner, otherwise it is a waste of time and bandwidth. Provide the developer/producer with clear specifications regarding required file formats, maximum file sizes, window and image dimensions, navigation, and screen fonts. Provide writers and instructional designers with clear guidelines for the maximum number of words per screen, how many interactive exercises to include, and which exercises are best suited for the content.
Evaluation	Make trainees and managers accountable for course completion and learning. Conduct a formative evaluation (pilot test) before large-scale use of online learning.

Source: Based on K. Dobbs, "What the Online World Needs Now: Quality," *Training* (September 2000): 84–94; P. Galagan, "Getting Started with E-Learning." *Training and Development* (May 2000): 62–64; D. Zielinski, "Can You Keep Learners Online?" *Training* (March 2000): 65–75; V. Beer, *The Web Learning Field Book: Using the World Wide Web to Build Workplace Learning Environments* (San Francisco Jossey-Bass, 2000); E. Zimmerman, "Better Training Is Just a Click Away," *Workforce* (January 2001): 36–42; R. Clark and R. Mayer, *E-Learning and the Science of Instruction* (San Francisco: John Wiley, 2003); E. Salas, R. DeRouin, and L. Littrell, "Research-Based Guidelines for Designing Distance Learning: What We Know So Far," in *The Brave New World of eHR,* ed. H. Gueutal and D. Stone (San Francisco: Jossey-Bass, 2005): 104–37; S. Boehle, "Putting the Learning Back into E-Learning," *Training* (January 2006): 29–35; A Rossett and L. Schafer, "What to Do about E-Dropouts," *T + D* (June 2003): 40–46; M. Morrison, "Leaner E-Learning," *Training* (January 2008): 16–18.

Needs Assessment

The information technology department needs to be involved in the design of any Web-based program to ensure that the technology capabilities of the company network are understood, to guarantee that trainees can get access to the browsers and connections they need to participate in e-learning and utilize all of the tools (e.g., e-mail, chat rooms, hyperlinks) that may accompany it, and to get technical support when needed. Online tutorials may be needed to acquaint trainees with the capabilities of the e-learning system and how to navigate through the Web. Recall from Chapter 3 that a needs assessment determines the company's resources for training and the tasks to be trained for, and it analyzes the employees who may need training. The needs assessment process for Web-based training or any other type of online learning should include a technology assessment (as part of the organizational analysis) and an assessment of the skills that users need for online training (person analysis). Needs assessment also includes getting management to support online learning.

Grant Thornton, a global accounting, tax, and business advisory firm, created Grant Thornton University (GTU), one place for all of its employees' training needs.[45] Through GTU, employees can register for any course, whether it is classroom-based or online, and have access to more than 1,000 hours of self-paced live Webcasts and virtual classroom courses. To ensure that GTU was successful, the company investigated its business learning needs and the best delivery method for each topic (a needs assessment). Learning paths are broken down by competencies and skill requirements and are related to job performance. For example, if employees receive performance feedback suggesting that they need to improve their teamwork skills, managers can identify an appropriate course by position and required competencies. A combination of self-paced lessons and live virtual classroom is the optimal instructional method. The self-paced lessons deliver content, and the live training is used for question-and-answer sessions and case studies. Live training also provides trainees with the opportunity to interact with peers and course experts. To obtain support for GTU, the company's chief learning officer invited managers to participate in a virtual kickoff from their desktop personal computers. The kickoff covered the strategic goals of the initiative, showed managers how the technology worked, and let them sample various content.

Design

Recall the learning process discussed in Chapter 4. E-learning should be designed to minimize content or work that is not related to the learning objectives. Extraneous content or work may take up trainees' limited cognitive processing resources, resulting in less learning. Table 8.7 provides several design principles that should be considered in the design of e-learning. These design principles are based on research regarding multimedia learning—that is, learning that involves words (whether printed or audio text) and pictures (charts, diagrams, photographs, animation, or video). Remember that just putting text online isn't necessarily an effective way to learn. **Repurposing** refers to directly translating an instructor-led face-to-face training program to an online format. Online learning that involves merely repurposing an ineffective training program will still result in ineffective training. Unfortunately, in their haste to develop online learning, many companies are repurposing bad training. The best e-learning uses the advantages of the Internet in combination with the principles of a good learning environment. Effective online learning takes advantage of

TABLE 8.7
Principles for Designing E-Learning

Source: Based on R. Clark and R. Mayer, "Learning by Doing: Evidence-Based Guidelines for Principled Learning Environments," *Performance Improvement* 47 (2008): 5–13; R. Mayer, "Applying the Science of Learning: Evidence-Based Principles for the Design of Multimedia Instruction," *American Psychologist* (November 2008): 760–769; R. Clark and R. Mayer, *E-Learning and the Science of Instruction,* 2nd ed. (San Francisco: Jossey-Bass/Pfeiffer, 2008).

Instruction includes relevant visuals and words.
Text is aligned close to visuals.
Complex visuals are explained by audio or text rather than by both text and audio that narrates the text.
Extraneous visuals, words, and sounds are omitted.
Learners are socially engaged through conversational language agents.
Key concepts are explained prior to the full process or task associated with the concepts.
Content is presented in short sequences over which learners have control.
Activities and exercises that mimic the context of the job are provided.
Explanations are provided for learner responses to quizzes and exercises.
Exercises are distributed within and among the module(s) rather than in a single place.

the Web's dynamic nature and ability to use many positive learning features, including linking to other training sites and content through the use of hyperlinks, providing learner control, and allowing the trainee to collaborate with other learners. Effective online learning uses video, sound, text, and graphics to hold learners' attention. Effective online learning provides trainees with meaningful content related to realistic on-the-job activities, relevant examples, and the ability to apply content to work problems and issues. Also, trainees have opportunities to practice and receive feedback through the use of problems, exercises, assignments, and tests.

To ensure that materials are not confusing or overwhelming to the learner, online learning content needs to be properly arranged.[46] Materials in online learning need to be organized in small, meaningful modules of information. Each module should relate to one idea or concept. The modules should be connected in a way that encourages the learner to be actively involved in learning. Active involvement may include asking trainees to find resources on the Internet, try quizzes or games, make choices between alternative actions, or compare what they know to the knowledge of an expert or model. Objectives, videos, practice exercises, links to material that elaborates on the module content, and tests should be accessible within each module. The modules should be linked in an arrangement that makes sense, such as by importance or by the order in which content has to be learned (prerequisites). Trainees can choose to skip over material that they are familiar with or that they are competent in, based on a test of the content, or they can return to modules they need more practice in.

One of the Web's major potential advantages is that it gives learners control. **Learner control** refers to the ability of trainees to actively learn though self-pacing, exercises, exploring links to other material, and conversations with other trainees and experts. That is, online learning allows activities typically led by the instructor (presentation, visuals, slides) or trainees (discussion, questions) as well as group interaction (discussion of application of training content) to be incorporated into training without trainees or the instructor having to be physically present in a training room. Simply providing learner control does not ensure that trainees will use all the features provided by online learning (e.g., practice exercises).[47] Companies must communicate the importance and meaningfulness of the training content for employees' jobs and must hold employees accountable for completing the training.

Research provides several recommendations for maximizing the benefits of learner control.[48] Training programs should not allow trainees to control the amount of feedback they receive because they may rely too much on the feedback, reducing their long-term retention of the training material. The program should offer practice on each topic repeatedly throughout the program so that trainees will not forget topics they have already completed. The program should provide practice to trainees using different examples to help transfer of training content (skills, knowledge) not only to the full range of situations that trainees may encounter on the job but also to unexpected situations. Trainees should be allowed to control the sequence in which they receive instruction but not be able to skip practice.

Online learning blurs the distinction between training and work. Expectations that trainees will be motivated and able to complete Web-based training during breaks in their normal workday or on their personal time are unrealistic.[49] Companies need to ensure that employees are given time and space for e-learning to occur.[50] That is, employees need dedicated time, protected from work tasks, for learning to occur. As with other training programs, employees need to understand why they should attend e-learning and the benefits they will receive so as to enhance their motivation to learn. Accurate communications about the content and types of learning activities in e-learning courses need to be provided to employees.[51] Managers need to give employees time in their schedules, and employees need to schedule "training time" to complete training and avoid interruptions that can interfere with learning. Some companies are moving away from their initial expectation that online learning can be completed at the employee's desktop without time away from the job; instead they are setting up learning labs for online learning to occur without the distractions of the workplace. "Chunking," or using one- to two-hour training modules, helps trainees learn and retain more than they might in a standard full-day or half-day training class. Training can also be more easily integrated into the typical workday. Trainees can devote one to two hours to a learning session from their office and then return to their work responsibilities. Using formative evaluation of prototypes of Web training can be helpful in identifying the appropriate length and time of modules (formative evaluations were discussed in Chapter 6). End users (managers, potential trainees) should be involved in a formative evaluation to ensure that music, graphics, icons, animation, video, and other features facilitate rather than interfere with learning. Also, end users need to test the content, the navigator, or the site map to guarantee that they can easily move through the learning module and access resources and links to other Web sites as needed.

Technology for Collaboration and Linking

Technology limitations and preferences need to be taken into account. Web-based training must be designed for the bandwidth that is available. **Bandwidth** refers to the number of bytes and bits (information) that can travel between computers per second. Graphics, photos, animation, and video in courses can be slow to download and can "crash" the system. Online learning courses should be designed for the available bandwidth on the company's system. Bandwidth can be increased by upgrading access speed on the users' computers, buying and installing faster servers and switches (computer hardware) on the company's network, or encouraging trainees to access the Web when demand is not high.[52] Soon bandwidth may not be an issue because computer servers will be able to transfer more data faster, personal computers will have greater processing speed, and cables and wireless communications systems that carry data will have greater capacity. Online learning should also try to build in interactivity without requiring the use of plug-ins. **Plug-ins** refer to additional software that needs to be loaded on the computer to listen to sound or watch video. Plug-ins can be expensive because they may require the company to pay licensing fees. Plug-ins also can affect how the computer processes tasks. If trainees experience repeated technology problems (such as slow download times, network downtimes, or plug-in difficulties), they are likely to lose patience and be reluctant to participate in online learning.

Chapter 4 emphasized that learning often occurs as a result of interaction or sharing between employees. Employees learn by informal, unstructured contact with experts and peers. Collaboration can involve an exchange among two or more trainees or among the trainer or other experts. Some of the more common ways that trainees can collaborate in online learning are shown in Table 8.8. Berlitz International's worldwide learning system uses communication technology to enhance and reinforce employee learning.[53] When language instructors take a course, they have to access an electronic bulletin board in order to answer three posted questions and give three new ones. Berlitz uses its communications technology to enhance communications, encourage information sharing, and create a sense of online community. Berlitz employees share ideas in online live chats, threaded discussions, or electronic bulletin boards, giving e-learners the opportunity to meet classmates online to discuss assignments, ask instructors questions, or participate in virtual roundtables. Employees can share ideas and experiences—an important way to learn from others.

Hyperlinks are links that allow a trainee to access other Web sites that include printed materials as well as communications links to experts, trainers, and other learners. Owens Corning's learning resource home page has hyperlinks to all available forms of training

TABLE 8.8
Common Ways of Collaboration in Online Learning

Source: Based on R. Clark and R. Mayer, *E-Learning and the Science of Instruction* (San Francisco: John Wiley, 2003); J. Cone and D. Robinson, "The Power of E-Performance," *T & D* (August 2001): 32–41; "Learning Circuits: Lexicon update," *T + D* (October 2008): 18–20; www.twitter.com.

Chat rooms	Trainees communicate at the same time by text or audio. Chat rooms may be moderated by a facilitator.
Message boards	Trainees communicate at different times by typing comments that remain on the board for others to read and respond to.
Threaded discussion	Trainees communicate via a message board in which related comments appear together. A discussion occurs over time.
Online conferencing	Trainees are online with a moderator. They can hear comments, send messages, display visuals, vote, or work together on a project.
E-mail	Trainees communicate at different times. Communications are received and managed at each trainee's mail site.
List-servs	In these group e-mails, trainees comment on a topic, and comments are sent to everyone on the mailing list.
Blogs (Weblogs)	These journal-like entries are posted on trainees' Web pages for public viewing. Also, blogs typically have links to other Web sites, along with the trainee's personal thoughts and comments.
Wikis	These Web pages are designed to enable trainees who access them to modify their content.
Social networking	Trainees can share information through connections with other trainees, trainers, friends, and family through online communities and message services such as MySpace, Facebook, and Twitter.

information, including CD-ROM, Web-based, and trainer-led programs. The site supports online course registration and allows tests to be sent to trainees, scored, and used to register trainees in appropriate courses.[54]

Research suggests that the reason some employees fail to complete online learning and prefer instructor-led face-to-face instruction over online learning is that they want to be able to learn and network with their peers.[55] Effective online learning connects trainees and facilitates interaction and sharing through the use of chat rooms, e-mail, electronic bulletin boards, and discussion groups. Other methods for learner interaction and sharing include having trainees participate in collaborative online projects and receive tutoring, coaching, and mentoring by experts. Online learning also should provide a link between the trainees and the "instructor," who can answer questions, provide additional learning resources, and stimulate discussion between trainees on topics such as potential applications of the training content and common learning problems.

Given the work demands that employees face, trainees need incentives to complete online learning. Some companies present cash awards and merchandise to employees who pass online competency tests that show they have completed and learned online course content. Other companies use certification programs to ensure that online courses are completed. For example, at Symbol Technologies, a manufacturer of handheld bar-code scanners and computers, sales trainees must complete online courses to be certified as salespersons.[56] If they don't complete the training, they can't continue into other training programs needed to be a successful salesperson. Aventis Pharma AG, a pharmaceutical company, has simply eliminated other training options such as classroom learning. If employees want training, their only option is online learning.

Learning portals are Web sites or online learning centers that provide, via e-commerce transactions, access to training courses, services, and online learning communities from many sources.[57] Learning portals provide not only one-stop shopping for a variety of training programs from different vendors but also access to online classes. Learning portals may also offer services to track employees' enrollment and progress in training programs. They were initially set up with the idea that an individual purchaser (an employee or other "customer") could purchase training using a credit card. The characteristics of learning portals vary.[58] Some allow users to pay, register, and attend courses online; others offer access only to classroom training programs at colleges or universities. In addition to instruction, some sites provide mentors who can tutor students as well as discussion groups where students can communicate with each other. W. R. Grace, a specialty chemicals company, uses its online learning center to support employee development, to link learning to performance and talent management, and to improve communications.[59] The learning center is organized around a set of core competencies that define the knowledge, skills, and abilities all employees are expected to achieve. A search option is provided so that employees can explore and access resources relevant to a specific topic. The learning center includes training sessions, recommended readings, a rental library (providing videotapes and CD-ROMs for self-paced learning), and a strategy guide (providing quick ideas and learning assignments to develop a competency). Every six weeks the learning center sends an electronic newsletter to every employee's personal computer. The newsletter keeps employees up to date on the latest learning center offerings, reports on how employees are effectively using the learning center, and encourages employees to use the center. Ford Motor Company has developed the Ford Learning Network (FLN), which includes 48,000 twenty-minute pieces of information using different media.[60] The FLN has more than 400,000 titles, including 1,500 online courses, 800 classroom courses, 1,900 e-books, and numerous internal resources from Web sites, journals, and industry periodicals. The learning can occur when the employee needs it or as a refresher that can be accessed at the employee's convenience. Ford is adding an automated survey tool that tracks the value of training received to see how training is being used and applied on the job. Ford also hopes that the network can make it possible for novices to gain access to expert employee information. For example, the knowledge and skills of experts in braking systems can be made available throughout the company. Ford's goal is to capture the intellectual property of in-house experts via video and other media and to make that information searchable on the FLN.

BLENDED LEARNING

Because of the limitations of online learning related to technology (e.g., insufficient band-with, lack of high-speed Web connections), trainee preference for face-to-face contact with instructors and other learners, and employees' inability to find unscheduled time during their workday to devote to learning from their desktops, many companies are moving to a hybrid, or blended, learning approach. **Blended learning** combines online learning, face-to-face instruction, and other methods for distributing learning content and instruction. Blended learning courses provide learners with the positive features of both face-to-face instruction and technology-based delivery and instructional methods (such as online learning, distance learning, or mobile technologies like iPods and PDAs) while minimizing the negative features of each.[61] In comparison to classroom delivery, blended learning provides increased learner control, allows for self-directedness, and requires learners to take more responsibility for their learning—all factors consistent with the recommendations of adult learning theory.[62] In comparison to pure online learning, blended learning provides more face-to-face social interaction and ensures that at least some of the instruction is presented in a dedicated learning environment. Blended learning uses the classroom to allow learners to learn together and to discuss and share insights, which helps bring learning to life and make it meaningful. Live feedback from peers is preferable to feedback received online.[63] Blended learning has been found to be more effective than face-to-face instruction for motivating trainees to learn and for teaching declarative knowledge or information about ideas or topics.[64] It appears that blended learning capitalizes on the positive learning features inherent in both face-to-face and Web-based instruction. Interestingly, learners react more favorably toward classroom instruction than blended learning. This may be because blended learning courses are more demanding, requiring a greater time commitment because of the use of two learning approaches. Research suggests that the most significant issues or problems with blended learning are fast-changing technology, insufficient management support and commitment to blended learning, and a lack of understanding of what blended learning really is and how to implement it.[65]

Cisco Systems offers "Management 101," a foundational program for management development.[66] Cisco used to offer seven separate courses to its managers. The current program integrates the management development curriculum. In phase 1, for the first nine weeks, a different topic that managers need to know is covered online each week. The online learning includes testing to ensure that the managers have gained knowledge, multimedia exercises, case studies, and weekly facilitated online discussions. In phase 2, managers attend a four-day program in which they come together in a classroom to discuss and build on what they have learned online. Phase 3 involves each manager learning alongside his or her own manager. At the conclusion of the program, each manager receives a 360-degree feedback evaluation. This evaluation is used to tailor each manager's development plan. Gilbane Building Company offers a change management course that includes an eight-hour face-to-face class combined with a two-hour online prerequisite module presenting change management principles. The face-to-face class allows trainees to apply the change management principles to possible project scenarios. Gilbane also includes a performance support system that trainees can refer to when they return to their jobs.

Express Personnel Services, a staffing company, found that managers can benefit from online material about hiring principles but need classroom instruction to learn how to apply those skills.[67] Also, when they attend courses at one of the company's training centers, managers learn from others doing the same job at a different location. The company tried to use online forums to promote discussions among managers at different locations but found that the managers were too busy to participate. IBM uses a four-tier learning approach that includes e-learning in the first two tiers, blended learning in the third tier, and classroom learning in the fourth tier.[68] In the first tier, knowledge or information is provided to trainees (what IBM calls information transfer). The second tier involves e-based testing of the concepts learned in the first tier. In the third tier, called collaborative learning, both e-learning and the classroom are used to create an environment that facilitates collaboration among colleagues and between learners and experts. The fourth tier includes face-to-face workshops, case studies, and problem discussions in which the skills learned in earlier stages are mastered through application and interaction with other learners.

SIMULATIONS

Simulators were introduced as a traditional training method in Chapter 7. This chapter discusses how development in software and computer technology has improved the learning and transfer that can result from simulators. Table 8.9 shows four different types of simulations. Rogers Wireless Communications, a cell phone company, uses the branching story simulation to teach sales skills and product knowledge.[69] An online role-playing simulator presents a variety of animated customers such as a busy mother and a punk rocker, each

TABLE 8.9
Types of Simulations

Source: Based on C. Cornell, "Better Than the Real Thing?" *Human Resource Executive* (August 2005): 34–37; S. Boehle, "Simulations: The Next Generation of E-Learning," *Training* (January 2005): 22–31.

Type of Simulation	Description
Branching story	Trainees are presented with a situation and asked to make a choice or decision. Trainees progress through the simulation on the basis of their decisions.
Interactive spreadsheet	Trainees are given a set of business rules (usually finance-based) and asked to make decisions that will affect the business. The decisions are entered into a spreadsheet that shows how the decisions affect the business.
Game-based	Trainees play a video game on a computer.
Virtual lab	Trainees interact with a computer representation of the job for which they are being trained.

providing a different customer service challenge. The simulation training has helped improve ratings by mystery shoppers at Rogers retail stores. Pitney Bowes, a mail equipment and service company, uses an interactive spreadsheet program to simulate the company's product lines, key processes, and business culture. Executive teams are given a set of monthly revenue and product goals and are told to make a series of decisions such as how many sales representatives to hire and how much time to invest in finding new clients. The decisions are plugged into the spreadsheet, and both short- and long-term financial results are provided. The simulation has helped executives develop innovative ideas for transforming the sales organization with positive bottom-line dollar results.

At NetApp Inc., 25 managers participated in a game in which they played the role of top executives in an imaginary company modeled after their employer.[70] The managers worked in five-person teams and competed to produce the strongest sales and operating profit. They were faced with challenges such as balancing long-term investments against short-term results. Managers received information including market analyses based on actual NetApp data and a menu of strategic initiatives such as improving college recruiting. The teams had to choose strategies and allocate employees and money. They were given scenarios such as an important customer seeking to add last-minute product features; in responding, they had to decide whether to add the features (which included determining their related costs) or refuse and risk angering an important client. The teams saw the consequences of their decisions. For example, one team declined to add the product features, which resulted in a decline in customer satisfaction and market share. At the end of the simulation, the sales and total profits of each team, as well as the effects of their strategies, were discussed.

Miller Brewing Company is testing a mini-game, "Tips on Tap," to help teach bartenders how to serve the perfect beer, card customers, and provide good service to increase their tips.[71] "Tips on Tap" includes simulations such as Score Your Pour, which teaches how to pour beer using the proper angle and height. Trainees move the glass using a computer mouse and measure the distance and angle of the glass to the beer tap to create the proper "head" (the foam on top of a glass of beer). Points are subtracted if the tap is hit while pouring or if the beer is spilled. Feedback is provided to trainees after each session. Mini-games are becoming increasingly popular for a number of reasons. At Miller, the online game does a better job of replicating how to correctly pour a beer than traditional classroom instruction; it is more convenient and accessible for trainee practice; and the real product is not used, thus eliminating waste and reducing costs. Also, mini-games are easy to access, engage the learner with music and graphics, require less than 20 minutes of student participation, and have low development costs. Mini-games may be most appropriate for learning skills that can be taught and learned through repetition, such as pouring beer or conducting emergency procedures.

Before launching its new product, Rapid Release Gelcaps, Tylenol used a game called, "The Need for Speed Trivia," to help salespersons learn about the product.[72] The game was burned onto a CD-ROM for salespersons to play either by themselves or online against their peers. The game used a timer and scoring system. Salespersons who played against each other raced to see who could answer the most questions in the shortest time. A high-score system was posted so that anyone who played the game could see who had the leading score. Questions about the product were designed to reinforce the information sales reps had received about the new gelcaps at a national sales meeting. The results suggest the game was an effective training tool. Each salesperson played an average of 47 games and interacted with the program for 71 minutes. Feedback from the sales reps indicates that they learned about the product and enjoyed playing the game.

Avatars are computer depictions of humans that are used as imaginary coaches, co-workers, and customers in simulations.[73] Typically, trainees can see the avatar, who appears throughout the training course. For example, a sales training course at CDW Corporation, a technology products and service company, guides trainees through mock interviews with customers. The avatar introduces the customer situation, and trainees hear the customer speaking to them in a simulated phone conversation. Trainees have to "read" the customer's voice, with help from the avatar, to determine what is happening in the sales process. Lowes hotel chain uses Virtual Leader, a program that helps participants learn how to be effective in meetings (e.g., how to build alliances, how to get a meeting agenda approved). As trainees attend the simulated meetings, what they say (or do not say) results in scores that relate to their influence in the meeting.

As you can see from these examples, simulations can be effective for several reasons.[74] First, trainees can use them on their desktop computer, eliminating the need to travel to a central training location. Second, simulations are meaningful, they get trainees involved in learning, and they are emotionally engaging (they can be fun!). This increases employees' willingness to practice, encourages retention, and improves their skills. Third, simulators provide a consistent message of what needs to be learned; trainees can work at their own pace; and, compared to face-to-face instruction, simulators can incorporate more situations or problems that a trainee might encounter. Fourth, simulations can safely put employees in situations that would be dangerous in the real world. Fifth, simulations have been found to result in such positive outcomes as shorter training times and increased return on investment.

Simulations do have some disadvantages. The use of simulations has been limited by their development costs. A customized simulation can cost between $200,000 and $300,000, while a simulation purchased from a supplier without any customization typically costs $100 to $200 per trainee.[75] However, although they continue to be an expensive training method, development costs for simulations continue to decrease, making them a more popular training method. Also, the use of simulations as a training method is likely to increase as technology development allows more realism to be built into simulations. Finally, trainees may not be comfortable in learning situations that lack human contact.

Virtual Reality

Virtual reality is a computer-based technology that provides trainees with a three-dimensional learning experience. Virtual reality allows simulations to become even more realistic. Using specialized equipment or viewing the virtual model on the computer screen, trainees move through the simulated environment and interact with its components.[76] Technology is used to stimulate multiple senses of the trainee.[77] Devices relay information from the environment to the senses. For example, audio interfaces, gloves that provide a sense of touch, treadmills, or motion platforms are used to create a realistic, artificial environment. Devices also communicate information about the trainee's movements to a computer. These devices allow the trainee to experience **presence** (the perception of actually being in a particular environment). Presence is influenced by the amount of sensory information available to the trainee, control over sensors in the environment, and the trainees' ability to modify the environment.

For example, Motorola uses virtual reality in its advanced manufacturing courses for employees learning to run the Pager Robotic Assembly facility. Employees are fitted with a head-mount display that allows them to view the virtual world, which includes the actual lab space, robots, tools, and assembly operation. Trainees hear and see the actual sounds and sights as if they were using the real equipment. Also, the equipment responds to the employees' actions (e.g., turning on a switch or moving a dial).

One advantage of virtual reality is that it allows trainees to practice dangerous tasks without putting themselves or others in danger. Research suggests that virtual reality training is likely to have the greatest impact on complex tasks or tasks that involve extensive use of visual cues.[78] The virtual reality environment can be virtually identical to the actual work environment. Another potential advantage relates to the cognitive processing required by the learner. The use of such a realistic environment in training may make more memory available for learning. Memory that was previously used to convert one- or two-dimensional training scenarios into three-dimensional space can now be used for processing information.

Obstacles to developing effective virtual reality training include poor equipment that results in a reduced sense of presence (e.g., poor tactile feedback and inappropriate time lags between sensing and responding to trainees' actions). Poor presence may result in the trainee experiencing vomiting, dizziness, and headaches (simulator sickness) because senses are distorted.

Virtual Worlds

Second Life is a computer-based, simulated online virtual world that includes a three-dimensional representation of the real world and a place to host learning programs or experiences. In Second Life, trainees use an avatar to interact with each other in classrooms, "webinars" (Web-based seminars), simulations, or role-play exercises. The virtual world of Second Life allows for learning to be real without being dangerous or risky for patients, employees, or customers. Second Life allows employees to learn alone, with their peers, or in teams. Second Life can be used to create virtual classrooms but its strength is its ability to create virtual reality simulations that actively involve the learner, such as putting the trainee's avatar in a realistic role play in which it has to deal with an upset customer. Stapoil, a Norwegian oil company, has an oil platform in Second Life that allows trainees to walk around it. Stapoil uses the oil platform for safety training. It catches fire and employees have to find lifeboats to safely exit the platform.[79]

Employees at Silicon Image learn about making silicon chips in Second Life by exploring a virtual world that represents a corporate campus and interacting with avatars.[80] Employees can visit the company's departments while watching videos and slide shows explaining what type of work is done within each unit. British Petroleum uses Second Life to train new gas station employees in the safety features of gasoline storage tanks and piping systems.[81] BP's virtual world includes three-dimensional replicas of the tank and pipe systems at a gas station. Trainees are able to see the underground storage tanks and piping systems and observe how safety devices control gasoline flow—something they could never do in real life.

Besides Second Life, ProtoSphere, Forterra, and Virtual Heroes are other providers of virtual worlds.[82] Paidera, a technology company that provides English-as-second-language training, uses Forterra to teach English. Trainees create avatars and then enter the virtual world to practice language skills in real situations. Trainees are placed in a virtual environment, such as talking to a cab driver or ordering food at a restaurant, that requires use of their language skills. The cost to rent space from a virtual-world program's campus within a public space is $200–$300 per day; it costs $1,000 to $2,000 for a customized simulation within the space.[83] Leased space in a virtual world can range from $5,000 to $100,000 annually, depending on the size and type of the space leased ($10,000–$20,000 is required for a private space on a public server or a private, customized island).

Advantages of Virtual Worlds

There are several advantages of using a virtual world for training.[84] The virtual environment can imitate an actual workplace such as a lab, processing plant, or hospital emergency room, allowing trainees to both practice their skills without harming products or patients and at the same time see the real-life consequences of their actions and decisions. It also provides a place to meet with trainers, managers, or other employees who can serve as teachers. Virtual worlds also can be useful for teaching interpersonal skills such as time management, communications, leadership, and working under pressure. Teamwork exercises and group problem solving are possible because avatars can be created to simulate other trainees or other trainees can simultaneously be involved in the simulation. Second Life and other virtual worlds motivate learners by making learning fun and interactive. Second Life also can enhance transfer of training because the virtual world used for training can replicate the real-life work environment (identical elements). Second Life can be used for e-learning, collaboration, and meetings. As with other technology-based training methods, it is an especially effective way for employees who are not in the same location or country to have access to training.

Disadvantages of Virtual Worlds

Despite the seemingly unlimited potential for training and development in virtual worlds such as Second Life, this method also has significant disadvantages. Research suggests that disadvantages include lack of ease of use for first-time users; the potential risk of a difficult keyboard and mouse interface, which can demotivate learners; the high investment of time and money required for programming content; and the lack of evidence supporting its effectiveness for learning.[85] The novelty of experiences in a three-dimensional virtual world such as Second Life and the appearance of the avatars may help trainees recall the experience, but they may also interfere with retention and transfer of the training content to the job.

MOBILE TECHNOLOGY AND TRAINING METHODS: IPODS, PDAS

Mobile technology allows learning to occur anywhere at anytime. Mobile technology consists of[86]

- Wireless transmission systems such as Wi-Fi and Bluetooth that allow transmission of data without the need for physical connections between devices or between a device and an Internet connection.
- Mobile devices such as personal digital assistants (PDAs), MP3 players, portable computers, iPods, global positioning system (GPS) devices, and radio frequency identification chips (RFID).
- Software applications related to processing audio files, word processing, spreadsheets, Internet, e-mail, and instant messaging.

GPS and RFID devices are used for tracking customers, employees, and property. For example, many cars and trucks are equipped with GPS devices to allow operators to locate drivers. Trucking companies use GPS devices to track loads and to determine expected arrival times. RFID chips are embedded in products to track their movement and to help in inventory control. Hotels are providing mobile devices such as PDAs to allow customers to access information about guest services, dining, entertainment, and accommodations anywhere on the hotel property.

PDAs, MP3 players, portable computers, and iPods are just starting to be used for training, for needs analysis, or as job aids that employees can access on an as-needed basis. Through mobile technologies, training and learning can occur naturally throughout the work day or at home, employees can be connected to communities of learning, and employees are given the ability to learn at their own pace by reviewing material or skipping over content they know.[87] The typical users for mobile learning include employees who spend most of their time traveling—visiting customers, clients, or various company locations (such as sales people, security officers, executives, or inspectors)—and have limited time available to spend in traditional training activities or e-learning.

Some companies are using PDAs as their primary method for delivering training or as a follow-up to training programs delivered face-to-face or online. At Tyco International Ltd., a safety products producer, service technicians use PDAs to manage service orders, conduct inspections, and generate quotes for customers.[88] Tyco is using the PDAs to deliver a short course that teaches sales technicians how to program and set a burglar alarm. The course includes a simulation of an alarm panel. The ability to use their PDAs for learning is perfect for Tyco's sales technicians; because they are constantly traveling, responding to service requests, they have little time for traditional training or online learning. The PDAs are also used for electronic performance support, providing technicians with access to job aids and procedure guides for tasks such as how to remove and replace a failed alarm or how to troubleshoot a specific piece of equipment. This is important because with the more than 200 categories of equipment serviced by Tyco, it is difficult for the technicians to recall all of the necessary procedures and programming, even when they have been were reviewed in earlier training courses.

Capital One, a financial services company, is one of the first companies to extensively use iPods for training. Capital One provides iPods to employees enrolled in training courses.[89] More than 400 iPods have been distributed as part of the courses offered through Capital One University that have an audio component. The iPods can be used for business or personal reasons, such as listening to music. Capital One decided that it needed a new way to deliver training after employee surveys suggested that employees did not have the time at work to attend classroom training. As a result, Capital One experimented with an audio channel for learning and found that employees liked learning on iPods and were able to gain access to programs that they would have been unable to attend in a classroom. Employees can access digitized audio files, such as MP3 files, that are downloaded to their computers and can be transferred to their iPods. Capital One limits audio learning to 20 courses that fall into the career development category (leadership, management, and competency-based courses), although it is considering expansion to include job-specific courses. Employees can access such programs as leadership development and workshops on conflict management. Textbooks and Harvard Business School cases are provided to employees on the iPod and have been used in executive-level programs to discuss leadership, new-hire issues, and customer service. Some programs use the iPod not only to deliver training content but also to provide employees with books or articles for pre-work before attending a classroom program. Other training programs use the iPod to enhance transfer of training. For example, scenarios and role plays that take place in classroom training are recorded and available for iPod upload. Employees listen to the role plays, which reinforces use of the training content on the job and motivates them to think about using what they have learned. Capital One has determined that, despite the costs related to purchasing and providing each employee with an iPod, if employees are listening to four to six hours of training content outside the classroom, the company is breaking even. Some of the benefits of the iPod programs are increased employee enthusiasm for learning (attending courses that use the iPod), greater ownership of learning among employees, willingness by employees to take on new roles and broader job responsibilities, time savings over traditional learning methods, and greater flexibility for employees to learn at their own pace while they travel.

Some of the challenges of using mobile technology for learning include ensuring that employees know when and how to take advantage of the technology; encouraging communication, collaboration, and interaction with other employees in communities of practice; and ensuring that employees can connect to a variety of networks no matter their location or mobile device.[90] Also, simply repurposing lectures by digitizing them and distributing them to employees will not facilitate learning. For example, Capital One creates simulated radio shows with phone-in questions and answers given by announcers to create an audio learning environment that is enjoyable and interesting. As with e-learning, training that uses mobile technology may be most effective if it is part of a blended learning approach that involves face-to-face interaction among trainees as well as audio learning.

INTELLIGENT TUTORING SYSTEMS

Intelligent tutoring systems (ITS) are instructional systems that use artificial intelligence.[91] There are three types of ITS environments: tutoring, coaching, and empowering. Tutoring is a structured attempt to increase trainee understanding of a content domain. Coaching provides trainees with the flexibility to practice skills in artificial environments. Empowering refers to the student's ability to freely explore the content of the training program. The five components of ITS are shown in Figure 8.4. The ITS has information about the content domain as well as expectations about the trainee's level of knowledge.

ITS can be distinguished from other new training technologies in several ways:[92]

- ITS has the ability to match instruction to individual student needs.
- ITS can communicate and respond to the student.
- ITS can model the trainee's learning process.
- ITS can decide, on the basis of a trainee's previous performance, what information to provide.
- ITS can make decisions about the trainee's level of understanding.
- ITS can complete a self-assessment resulting in a modification of its teaching process.

ITS has been used by NASA in astronaut training.[93] For example, the Remote Maneuvering System ITS was used to teach astronauts how to use the robotic arm on the space shuttle. Astronauts had to learn to complete tasks and procedures related to grappling a payload. The ITS generated processes that were matched to individual astronauts. Feedback

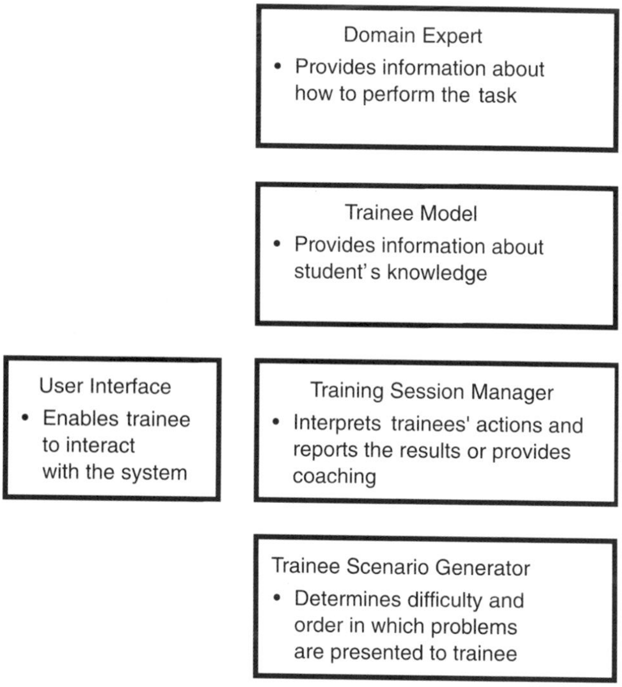

FIGURE 8.4
Components of Intelligent Tutoring Systems

Source: Based on D. Steele-Johnson and B. G. Hyde, "Advanced Technologies in Training: Intelligent Tutoring Systems and Virtual Reality," in *Training for a Rapidly Changing Workplace,* ed. M. A. Quinones and A. Ehrenstein (Washington, DC: American Psychological Association, 1997): 225–48.

Domain Expert
• Provides information about how to perform the task

Trainee Model
• Provides information about student's knowledge

User Interface
• Enables trainee to interact with the system

Training Session Manager
• Interprets trainees' actions and reports the results or provides coaching

Trainee Scenario Generator
• Determines difficulty and order in which problems are presented to trainee

was matched to their pattern of success and failure in learning the tasks. The system recorded performance data for each astronaut, made decisions regarding the student's level of understanding, and used those decisions to provide appropriate feedback.

DISTANCE LEARNING

Distance learning is used by geographically dispersed companies to provide information about new products, policies, or procedures as well as deliver skills training and expert lectures to field locations.[94] Distance learning can include virtual classrooms, which have the following capabilities: projection of still, animated, and video images; instructor-participant audio discussion; sharing of computer software applications; interactions using instant polling technology; and whiteboard marking tools.[95] Distance learning features two-way communications between people, and it currently involves two types of technology.[96] The first technology is teleconferencing. **Teleconferencing** refers to synchronous exchange of audio, video, and/or text between two or more individuals or groups at two or more locations. Trainees attend training programs in training facilities in which they can communicate with trainers (who are at another location) and other trainees using the telephone or personal computer. The second type of distance learning also includes individualized, personal computer–based training.[97] Employees participate in training anywhere they have access to a personal computer. This type of distance learning may involve multimedia training methods such as Web-based training. Course material and assignments can be distributed using the company's intranet, video, or CD-ROM. Trainers and trainees interact using e-mail, bulletin boards, and conferencing systems.

Teleconferencing usually includes a telephone link so that trainees viewing the presentation can call in questions and comments to the trainer. Also, satellite networks allow companies to link up with industry-specific and educational courses for which employees receive college credit and job certification. IBM, Digital Equipment, and Eastman Kodak are among the many firms that subscribe to the National Technological University, which broadcasts courses throughout the United States that technical employees need to obtain advanced degrees in engineering.[98]

Interactive distance learning (IDL) refers to the latest generation of distance learning, which uses satellite technology to broadcast programs to different locations and allows trainees to respond to questions posed during the training program using a keypad.[99] IDL is being used by companies that have employees in many different locations and who lack computers or online access. IDL allows employees in different locations to see behaviors and how to get things done rather than just read or hear about them. For example, JCPenney Company, which produces more than 200 different IDL programs each year, uses distance learning to reach every associate. Each store has a training room where up to 12 employees can sign on to the program and watch on a large television screen. Each employee has his or her own keypad to interact with the program. Employees are able to watch the satellite broadcast live or view a tape of the program later. Regardless of whether watching the program live or via tape, employees can answer questions such as, "How many square feet does your store have for lingerie?" At the end of the program, managers and trainers can access a report on how every store answered. Evaluations of the interactive distance learning program have been positive. IDL has allowed JCPenney to deliver training to every employee in the company. Eight-six percent of its employees report that they have the training needed to effectively perform their jobs.

An advantage of distance learning is that the company can save on travel costs. It also allows employees in geographically dispersed sites to receive training from experts who would not otherwise be available to visit each location. Intuit finds that a traditional classroom environment is good for introducing software and providing trainees with the opportunity to network. Virtual classroom training is used for courses on special software features, for demonstrations, and for troubleshooting using application-sharing features. General Mills uses virtual classrooms at smaller plants where offering a class on-site is not cost effective.[100] Employees have access to courses in product-specific knowledge (e.g., cereal production), general technical skills (e.g., food chemistry), and functional-specific knowledge (e.g., maintenance). FileNeT Corporation was concerned with how its sales force was going to keep up with new software and software updates.[101] FileNeT tried self-paced online learning but discovered that salespeople did not like to read a lot of material about new products on the Web. Enrollment in online courses dwindled, and salespeople flooded the company's training department with requests for one-on-one assistance. To solve the training problem, the company decided to use webcasting. **Webcasting** involves classroom instruction that is provided online through live broadcasts. Webcasting helped spread the sales force training throughout the year rather than cramming it into twice-a-year sales meetings. Webcasting also helped ensure that the salespeople all received the same information. The salespeople liked the webcasts because of the timely information that helped them have conversations with customers. The live sessions were also popular because participants could ask questions. Webcasting has not replaced face-to-face training at FileNeT; classroom training is still about 80 percent of training, but that percentage has decreased by 10 percent. Webcasting has also resulted in savings of $500,000 annually (one of the twice-yearly sales meetings was canceled).

The major disadvantages of distance learning are the lack of interaction between the trainer and the audience, technology failures, and unprepared trainers. A high degree of interaction among trainees or between the trainees and the trainer is a positive learning feature that is missing from distance learning programs that use the technology only to broadcast a lecture to geographically dispersed employees. All this does is repurpose a traditional lecture (with its limitations for learning and transfer of training) for a new training technology. To engage trainees in a distance learning environment, it is useful to limit online sessions to 60 to 90 minutes in length, maintain a good instructional pace, avoid presenting unnecessary text, use relevant and engaging visuals (e.g., graphs, animation), and allow trainees to participate using polling devices and small-group breakout rooms for discussion and projects.[102] A group spokesperson can be assigned to summarize and communicate the group's ideas. Weather conditions and satellite glitches can occur at any time, disconnecting the instructor from the audience or making it difficult to show video or other multimedia presentations. Instructors need backup plans for dealing with technical issues. Because many instructors have difficulty speaking to trainees in another location without a live group of trainees in front of them, it is important to prepare instructors for distance delivery. For example, a producer who is familiar with the technology can work with the instructor and help facilitate the training session.

TECHNOLOGIES FOR TRAINING SUPPORT

Technologies such as expert systems, groupware, and electronic support systems are being used to support training efforts. Training support means that these technologies are helping to capture training content so that it is available to employees who may not have attended training. Training support also means that these technologies provide information and decision rules to employees on an as-needed basis (i.e., they are job aids). Employees can access these technologies in the work environment.

Table 8.10 shows when training support technologies are most needed. Many conditions shown in the table relate to characteristics of the task or the environment that can inhibit transfer of training. For example, employees may work some distance away from their manager, the manager may be difficult to contact, or employees may need special expertise that the manager lacks. These situations make it difficult for employees to find answers to problems that arise on the job. Training support technologies can assist in transfer of training by helping employees generalize training content to the work environment and by providing employees with new information (not covered in training).

TABLE 8.10
Conditions When Training Support Technologies Are Most Needed

Source: Based on A. Rossett, "Job Aids and Electronic Performance Support Systems," in *The ASTD Training and Development Handbook,* 4th ed., ed. R. L. Craig (New York: McGraw-Hill, 1996): 554–77.

- Performance of task is infrequent.
- The task is lengthy, difficult, and information-intensive.
- The consequences of error are damaging.
- Performance relies on knowledge, procedures, or approaches that frequently change.
- There is high employee turnover.
- Little time is available for training, or resources for training are few.
- Employees are expected to take full responsibility for learning and performing tasks.

Expert Systems

Expert systems refer to technology (usually software) that organizes and applies the knowledge of human experts to specific problems.[103] Expert systems have three elements:

1. A knowledge base that contains facts, figures, and rules about a specific subject.
2. A decision-making capability that, imitating an expert's reasoning ability, draws conclusions from those facts and figures to solve problems and answer questions.
3. A user interface that gathers and gives information to the person using the system.

Expert systems are used as a support tool that employees refer to when they have problems or decisions they feel exceed their current knowledge and skills. For example, a large international food processor uses an expert system called Performer, which is designed to provide training and support to its plant operators. One problem the company was facing was determining why potato chips were being scorched in the fryer operation. An operator solved the problem using Performer. He selected the Troubleshooting menu, then Product Texture/Flavor, then Off Oil Flavor. The program listed probable causes, beginning with high oxidation during frying. The operator chose that cause, and the system recommended adjusting the cooking line's oil flush, providing detailed steps for that procedure. Following those steps resolved the problem.[104]

Although expert systems are discussed as a technology that supports training, expert systems can also be used as a delivery mechanism. Expert systems can be used to train employees in the decision rules of the experts. For example, a financial company dramatically increased the portfolio of products that it offered to customers.[105] The sales force needed to be prepared to introduce these products to clients and to make sales. The company developed an expert system to capture the sales processes used by top sales performers. This Web-based expert system allowed salespersons to access information on each financial product, alerted salespersons to information they needed from the customer, and used expert logic to identify opportunities to introduce new products to customers based on data entered by the salesperson (the expert system matches general client characteristics with specific customer characteristics).

Expert systems can deliver both high quality and lower costs. By using the decision processes of experts, the system enables many people to arrive at decisions that reflect experts' knowledge. An expert system helps avoid the errors that can result from fatigue and decision biases. The efficiencies of an expert system can be realized if it can be operated by fewer or less skilled (and likely less costly) employees than the company would otherwise require.

Groupware

Groupware (electronic meeting software) is a special type of software application that enables multiple users to track, share, and organize information and to work on the same document simultaneously.[106] A groupware system combines such elements as e-mail, document management, and an electronic bulletin board. Popular brands of groupware are Lotus Notes and Domino.

Companies have been using groupware to improve business processes such as sales and account management and to improve meeting effectiveness as well as to identify and share knowledge in the organization. (See Chapter 5's discussion of creating a learning organization.) Vernon Carus Limited, based in Preston, England, manufactures infection control and wound health care products.[107] With a subsidiary company in Malta, the organization employs approximately 400 people. Business managers at Vernon Carus were acutely aware of the need to capture more accurate data on customer interactions and to present a stronger brand image. The 40-strong field sales team, the face of the company, had largely stopped using the corporate e-mail system, complaining that it was unreliable. Also, the company had no way to capture or share customer data among teams or with the head office. Vernon Carus installed Lotus software so as to make the same information available to everyone; as a result, the company was better able to react and adapt to customer needs.

As noted earlier in the chapter, many companies are creating their own intranets. Intranets are cheaper and simpler to use than groupware programs but pose potential security problems because of the difficulty of keeping persons out of the network.[108]

Electronic Performance Support Systems

An **electronic performance support system (EPSS)** is an electronic infrastructure that captures, stores, and distributes individual and corporate knowledge assets throughout an organization to enable individuals to achieve required levels of performance in the fastest possible time and with a minimum of support from other people.[109] An EPSS includes all the software needed to support the work of individuals (not just one or two specific software applications). It integrates knowledge assets into the interface of the software tools rather than separating them as add-on components. For example, company policy information may be presented in a dialog box message rather than in a separate online document. The typical EPSS includes:

- An "assistant" to automate tasks and lighten the work load.
- A "librarian" to provide task-specific information.
- A "teacher" to guide the user through the process step by step.
- An "advisor" to provide expert advice.

Chapter 5 discussed EPSS as a means to help training transfer. EPSS can also be used as a substitute for training. Microsoft's Office software has "wizards," a help function that recognizes the task that the user is starting to perform (e.g., writing a letter) and offers information related to that task. At Reuters, the news and financial information company, employees who deal with orders for financial systems information and data needed a way to get their questions answered on an as-needed basis because they did not have time to attend training sessions.[110] Typical questions included how to register financial traders to access Reuters's information and systems and how to coordinate installation of Reuters's technology on the trading floor. Reuters purchased an EPSS that provides employees with help tabs on their computer screens as they perform tasks. The help tabs provide answers to questions about the steps required to complete different processes such as user registration.

To use EPSS as a substitute for training, trainers must determine whether problems and tasks require employees to actually acquire knowledge, skill, or ability (learned capability) and whether periodic assistance through an EPSS is sufficient.

TECHNOLOGIES FOR TRAINING ADMINISTRATION

New technology is making training administration more efficient and effective. Training administration includes record keeping, employee enrollment in courses, and testing and certification. Interactive voice technology, imaging, and software applications have made it easier to track training information. They also provide easy access to training information for trainers to use in decision making.

Interactive Voice Technology

Interactive voice technology uses a conventional personal computer to create an automated phone response system. This technology is especially useful for benefits administration. For example, at Hannaford Brothers—a supermarket chain spread through the northeastern United States—the human resource department installed an interactive voice response system that allows employees to get information on their retirement accounts, stock purchases, and benefit plans by using the push buttons on their phones.[111] Employees can also directly enroll in training programs and speak to a human resource representative if they have questions. As a result of the technology, the company has been able to reduce its human resource staff and more quickly serve employees' benefit needs.

Imaging

Imaging refers to scanning documents, storing them electronically, and retrieving them.[112] Imaging is particularly useful because paper files take a large volume of space and are difficult to access. Training records can be scanned and stored in a database for access at a later date. Some software applications allow the user to scan documents based on key words such as *job history, education,* and *experience.* This is a valuable feature when answering managers' and other customers' questions regarding employees' training and skills. For example, inquiries such as "I need an engineer to take an expatriate assignment in France. Do we have any engineers who speak French?" can be easily and quickly answered by scanning training databases. Imaging can also help a training department better serve its customers by reducing the time needed to locate a file or service a phone inquiry from an employee, providing the ability for employee training records to be shared simultaneously, eliminating the need to refile, and reducing the physical space needed to store training records.

Training Software Applications

Training software applications can be used to track information related to training administration (e.g., course enrollments, tuition reimbursement summaries, and training costs), employee skills, employees' training activities, online learning, and transfer of training. Important database elements for training administration include training courses completed, certified skills, and educational experience. Georgia Power uses a database system that tracks internal training classes, available classroom space, instructor availability, costs, and the salaries of training class members.[113] Table 8.11 shows a screen illustrating an employee's training activity. Some applications provide cost information that can be used by managers to determine which departments are exceeding their training budgets. This information can be used to reallocate training dollars during the next budget period. Other databases give access to summaries of journal articles,

TABLE 8.11
Example of an Employee Training Progress Report

Source:
www.trainersoft.com..
"Trainersoft Manager Demo" (January 29, 2001).

Progress Report for: Joe Trainee					
Course Name	**ID**	**Completed**	**Length**	**Score**	**Manager**
Customer Service Level 1	CUST1	01/12/2000	60:00	98%	dcutter@rd.com
Customer Service Level 2	CUST2	02/03/2000	60:00	No	ldelkin@rd.com
Delivering Value—The RD Way	VALU1	02/08/2000	20:00	No	dcutter@rd.com
Employee Orientation 1	ORIEN1	02/18/2000	30:00	No	ldelkin@rd.com
Employee Orientation—Benefits	ORIEN2	03/07/2000	20:00	No	acarter@rd.com
Managing Conflict	CONF1	03/19/2000	20:00	97%	ldelkin@rd.com

legal cases, and books to help professional employees such as engineers and lawyers keep up to date.[114]

Software applications can be useful for decision making. Companies are showing increased interest in skills databases that can be used to track employee talent and identify skill shortages.[115] These databases keep track of the skills and credentials of each employee, such as prior jobs, training, technical certification, geographical and cultural experiences, spoken languages, and career interests. Managers and trainers can use the database to identify strengths and weaknesses of the company's work force. Using skill inventories, managers can determine which employees need training and can suggest training programs to them that are appropriate for their job and skill levels. Skill inventories are also useful for identifying employees who are qualified for promotions and transfers. Finally, they can also be useful for helping managers quickly build employee teams with the necessary skills to respond to customer needs, product changes, international assignments, or work problems. Dell used its database to locate a sales executive who could work in China. The database helped identify a sales manager who was finishing an assignment in Australia, had experience working in the Asia-Pacific region, and had the skills needed for the job. Geisinger Health Systems has been tracking which training courses employees have completed. Now the company is interested in software that can forecast potential skill gaps due to retirements.

Software known as authoring tools can also be useful for developing online learning programs.[116] **Authoring tools** are used to create presentations, surveys, quizzes, animation, and graphics and to provide sound, video, and text for online learning. One authoring tool is Macromedia Flash MX 2004, which can be used for creating customized e-learning. Software is also available to help trainees transfer training. For example, ActionPlan Mapper helps trainees enter their action plans into an online database that can be accessed by their manager and trainer.[117] Participants receive automatic e-mail reminders asking them to create reports on their use of training content at work.

LEARNING MANAGEMENT SYSTEMS: SYSTEMS FOR TRAINING DELIVERY, SUPPORT, AND ADMINISTRATION

A **learning management system (LMS)** is a technology platform that can be used to automate the administration, development, and delivery of all of a company's training programs. LMSs can provide employees, managers, and trainers with the ability to manage, deliver, and track learning activities. Some of the features of LMSs are shown in Table 8.12. New developments in LMSs include providing the ability for users to simultaneously search the

TABLE 8.12

Features of Learning Management Systems (LMSs)

Source: Based on "Learning Management Systems: An Executive Summary," *Training* (March 2002): 4.

Trainee Management and Reporting	Track and report on trainee progress and activity.
Training Event and Resource Management	Organize courses and learning events in catalogs; manage and track course resources such as classrooms and instructors; support communications among administrators and students.
Online Course Delivery Infrastructure	Deliver online courses; register and track trainees.
Authoring Tools	Create new courses; promote consistency in courses.
Skill Assessment	Create, edit, distribute, and deliver assessment tests; review trainee achievements.
Professional Development Management	Track and compare trainee learning against goals, based on the trainee's job or function.
Knowledge Bases	Integrate links to learning references that supplement online learning.
Personalization	Engage employees in learning through the use of target courses, references, e-mails.

database as well as their company's intranet for information on training courses, contact experts who are identified by the company as topic experts, enroll in all courses related to a certification or particular training topic at one time, and use simulations to determine whether employees are complying with ethical standards and skills they have been trained in using by the LMS.[118]

There are a number of reasons LMSs are becoming more popular. An LMS can help a company reduce travel and other costs related to training, reduce time for program completion, increase employees' accessibility to training across the business, and provide administrative capabilities to track program completion and course enrollments. LMSs allow companies to track all learning activity in the business. For example, FedEx Office (formerly FedEx Kinko's) has document and shipping centers around the world and employs more than 20,000 people. The LMS at FedEx includes a software package that creates individualized training for each employee, schedules classrooms, tracks employee progress, manages all aspects of the training curriculum, and delivers e-learning courses.[119] Employees have access via their personal computer to their personal learning plan, which is based on their job, what their manager requires, and their own personal interests.

Why Develop an LMS?

Tracking the learning activity in a business is important for human capital management. **Human capital management** integrates training with all aspects of the human resource function (e.g., performance evaluation, human resource planning) to determine how training dollars are spent and how training expenses translate into business dollars for the company. The major reasons that companies adopt an LMS are to centralize management of learning activities, track regulatory compliance, measure training usage, and measure employee performance.[120] Thirty-eight percent of companies report integrating an LMS with human resource information systems.[121]

LMSs are also important for companies to be able to track the number of employees who have completed courses that are required to meet state, federal, or professional regulations (compliance training).[122] These courses cover a wide range of topics including financial integrity, health and safety, environmental protection, and employee rights. For example, various regulations mandate that companies be able to prove that employees have completed courses in sexual harassment or defensive driving. Employees from a variety of for-profit businesses, including financial services, oil refining, and pharmaceuticals, as well as employees in nonprofit organizations such as government agencies and hospitals have to complete certain required courses. The Gunderson Lutheran Health System includes hospitals, community clinics, nursing homes, home care, pharmacies, ambulances, mental health services, and vision centers.[123] Employees are required to take courses to comply with national standards on protecting patient privacy as well as courses related to providing a safe and healthy work environment. Gunderson developed an LMS that includes all mandatory compliance courses as well as other courses. Employees can access courses on the LMS through computers located at their desks, in computer labs, or at health sciences libraries. Gunderson has realized many benefits from the LMS. The LMS has been useful in reducing the time employees spend on compliance courses (for example, safety courses now take 20 minutes compared to the two hours required for classroom training). The online courses provide employees with flexibility to fit learning into their schedules. For example, nurses can leave their online course to visit patients and then return to continue learning right where they left off. The online courses offer more interactivity through the use of exercises, assessments, and role plays than did the classroom training, and such interactivity holds employees' interest. Finally, since the LMS was developed, the demand for learning has increased: Departments want more classroom courses to be converted to online courses.

An LMS can help companies understand the strengths and weaknesses of their employees, including where talent gaps exist.[124] Also, an LMS can be linked to other human resource systems, such as performance management or employee development systems, to identify learning opportunities for employees to strengthen their performance weaknesses. Turner Construction has a competency model that divides jobs into nine job families and divides the families into job levels (senior management, administrative/clerical, and management). Employees receive an online performance evaluation of their skills based on their job family and level. The performance management system links to the company's LMS. The LMS analyzes the employees' skill weaknesses and provides recommendations of courses that can improve those skills. The LMS system allows Turner Construction to identify skill gaps for entire levels, job families, or business units. The results can be used to identify where to spend monies allocated for training to develop new courses.

Developing an LMS

How does a company go about developing an LMS? First, senior management needs to be convinced that an LMS will benefit employees, improve business functions, and contribute to overall business strategies and goals. At Glaxo-SmithKline, a research-based pharmaceutical and health care company, most training takes place on the LMS. Training covers important areas such as reporting of adverse medical events with patients, medicine safety, and management certification of business ethics. Providing around-the-clock access to learning and certification along with securing and providing access to training records and certification data is considered critical to the business.[125] The CEO of CitiGroup, a financial services company, plans to use the company's LMS to provide ethics training for all employees, part of the CEO's plan to restore respect in the company. The LMS at United

Airlines has given the company the tools it needs to help boost the company's readiness for change and transformation. The company's training and learning function has obtained more visibility and recognition of its ability to partner with the business units through technology that supports performance improvement.

Second, a company that wants to develop an LMS must have an e-learning culture that supports online learning and encourages employee participation. Third, the online learning environment needs to be under the control of the learner. Learners require not just choices in what and when to learn but also involvement in learning (practice, feedback, appeals to multiple senses).[126]

To maximize its effectiveness, an LMS should be integrated with human resource systems. The interfaces between the systems will provide basic employee information such as business unit, geographic location, and job title. Information about which courses employees have completed should also be stored in the LMS. To develop an LMS for the Internal Revenue Service (IRS), a group known as Strategic Human Resources, which is responsible for establishing human resource policy across the IRS, has developed a partnership with IRS business units and technology staff.[127] In meeting with business units to identify their training needs, the Strategic Human Resources unit determined that the LMS needed to support content from different sources, including e-learning courses purchased from vendors as well as those developed internally, and needed to integrate with the IRS's existing information technology infrastructure. E-learning courses and classroom instruction all have to be managed through a single system. Strategic Human Resources has had to implement specific requirements, standards, and specifications for e-learning administration, scheduling, enrollment, and product development and design. The LMS developed by the Strategic Human Resources unit is being implemented in three phases. Phase 1 involves building the technology infrastructure and establishing product development standards and policies. Phase 2 requires the organization of learning and knowledge content for accessibility by the LMS. In Phase 3 the IRS will integrate learning with actual work performance, enabling employees to access training as they need it.

CHOOSING NEW TECHNOLOGY TRAINING METHODS

Table 8.13 compares technology-based training methods based on the same characteristics used to compare traditional training programs in Chapter 7. Several trends are apparent in this table. First, these methods require considerable investment in development. Development costs are related to purchasing hardware and software as well as developing programs and transferring programs to new media (e.g., CD-ROM). However, although development costs are high, costs for administering the program are low. Advantages of these methods include (1) cost savings due to training being accessible to employees at their home or office, (2) reduced number of trainers needed, and (3) reduced costs associated with employees traveling to a central training location (e.g., airfare, food, lodging). Moreover, with the exception of distance learning, most of the important characteristics needed for learning to occur (practice, feedback, etc.) are built into these methods. Note that limited studies of the effectiveness of several methods (e.g., virtual reality, intelligent tutoring) are available because companies are just starting to use these technologies for training. However, their effectiveness is likely to be high if characteristics of a positive learning environment and learner control, sharing, and linking are built into these methods.

TABLE 8.13   Comparison of Technology-Based Training Methods

	Computer-Based Training	CD-ROM	Internet	Intranet	E-Learning	Distance Learning	Intelligent Tutoring	Simulations and Virtual Reality
Learning Outcome								
Verbal information	Yes	Yes	Yes	Yes	Yes	Yes	Yes	Yes
Intellectual skills	Yes	Yes	Yes	Yes	Yes	Yes	Yes	Yes
Cognitive strategies	Yes	Yes	Yes	Yes	Yes	Yes	Yes	Yes
Attitudes	No	Yes	No	No	Yes	No	No	Yes
Motor skills	No	No	No	No	No	No	Yes	Yes
Learning Environment								
Clear objective	Medium	High	High	High	High	Medium	High	High
Practice	Medium	High	Medium	Medium	High	Low	High	High
Meaningfulness	Medium	High	High	High	High	Medium	High	High
Feedback	Medium	High	Medium	Medium	High	Low	High	High
Observation and interaction with others	Low	High	Medium	Medium	High	Low	Low	Low
Transfer of Training	Medium	High	Medium	Medium	High	Low	High	High
Cost								
Development	High	High	High	High	High	Medium	High	High
Administrative	Low	Low	Low	Low	Low	Low	Low	Low
Effectiveness	Medium	High	?	?	High	Medium	?	High

Recall Chapter 6's discussion of how to determine the costs and benefits of training programs. Caterpillar has found that it spends approximately one-third as much for e-learning as for classroom instruction because of the reduced number of instructors, the lower costs associated with course materials, and the reduced travel expenses.[128] For a one-hour course with a class size of 100 trainees, e-learning is 40 percent less expensive than classroom training ($9,500 versus $17,062, or $76 per trainee). As the number of trainees increases to, for example, 40,000 trainees (Caterpillar has more than 70,000 employees worldwide), the company's cost savings are 78 percent ($1.1 million versus $5 million, or $99 per trainee).[129]

You might assume that Web-based training and e-learning are superior to other methods, but this is not necessarily the case. A comparison between Web-based training and CD-ROM highlights that both methods have distinct advantages (and disadvantages). Two advantages that the CD-ROM has over Web-based training are the CD's greater ability for interaction between the learner and the material in the training program and its greater use of audio and video. Web-based training, in turn, has several advantages over the CD-ROM.

Its major advantage is that Web-based programs offer collaboration and sharing (connecting trainees to other trainees, experts, and chat rooms) and links to resources available on the Web. Web-based training also allows the learner to be given assignments requiring open-ended responses (e.g., write a report on a customer's needs) rather than only yes/no or multiple-choice responses. In Web-based training, the instructor can read the assignment and provide detailed feedback. CD-ROMs can only score close-ended questions with true/false, yes/no, or multiple-choice answers. Finally, Web-based training is easier to update and change than a CD-ROM. If a company's e-learning program has complex simulations requiring a high degree of interaction with the trainee, the company will likely provide the trainee with a CD-ROM for the simulation and will rely on the Web for linking to resources, collaboration and sharing, and testing trainees.

How do new technology training methods relate to traditional training methods discussed in Chapter 7? Virtual reality and intelligent tutoring systems are best suited for teaching complex processes related to operating machinery, tools, and equipment. These methods are an extension of simulations. CD-ROMs, the Internet, the intranet, and e-learning are best suited for teaching facts, figures, cognitive strategies (e.g., how to hold an effective meeting), and interpersonal skills (e.g., closing a sale). These methods are technological extensions of traditional training methods such as behavior modeling, on-the-job training, and apprenticeship. Although traditional training methods can be effective, managers and trainers should consider using new technology training methods under certain conditions:[130]

1. Sufficient budget and resources will be provided to develop and support the use of new technology.
2. Trainees are geographically dispersed and travel costs related to training are high.
3. Trainees are comfortable using technology, including the Web, personal computers, and CD-ROMs.
4. The increased use of new technology is part of the company's business strategy. New technology is being used or implemented in manufacturing of products or service processes.
5. Employees have a difficult time attending scheduled training programs.
6. Current training methods allow limited time for practice, feedback, and assessment.
7. Use of new technology fits into the organizational culture or business strategy.

The best uses for classroom instruction may be when trainees need interaction, instructor support, or visual cues. It is important to note that many companies recognize the strengths and weaknesses of both face-to-face instruction and technology-based training methods and are using both in a blended learning approach. Technology-based training can be used to provide consistent delivery of training content involving transfer of information (knowledge and skills) to geographically dispersed employees who work at their own pace, practice, and collaborate with the trainer and other trainees online. Then trainees can be brought to a central location for face-to-face training (classroom, action learning, games, and role plays) that emphasizes through the use of cases and problems the application of the recently acquired knowledge and skills. Face-to-face instruction is also more useful for facilitating interaction among trainees as well as collaboration, networking, and discussion. For example, at Pitney Bowes, a mailing equipment provider, e-learning is used for content that many geographically dispersed employees must know, such as legal compliance requirements or new product training.[131] Learning that requires interaction with others—such as leadership management training, problem solving, or decision making—requires face-to-face classroom instruction or a blended learning approach.

Summary

This chapter provided an overview of the use of new technologies in training delivery, support, and administration. Many new technologies have features that help to ensure learning and transfer of training (e.g., multimedia training methods such as CD-ROM and e-learning). These technologies appeal to multiple senses and allow employees to pace themselves, receive feedback and reinforcement, and find information from experts on an as-needed basis. New mobile training methods (such as iPods) allow employees to participate in training from home or work on a 24-hour basis. Employees control not only the presentation of training content but also when and where they participate in training. Simulations and virtual reality also can create a more realistic training environment, which can make the material more meaningful and increase the probability that training will transfer to the job. Expert systems and electronic support systems are tools that employees can access on an as-needed basis to obtain knowledge and information. Groupware and intranets help to capture the knowledge that employees gain from training and facilitate their sharing of information. Interactive voice technologies, imaging, and software applications especially designed for training make it easier to store and record training information such as course enrollments and employee training records. This technology also makes it easier to retrieve training-related information for managerial decision making. More companies are investing in learning management systems, which provide training administration, delivery, and support.

Most new technology training methods are superior to traditional methods because a positive learning environment can be built into the method. But development costs of new technology training methods are high. Considerations include monies for development, geographic dispersion of employees, employees' difficulty in attending training, and whether new technologies are part of the company's business strategy. Rather than choosing between face-to-face and technology-based training methods, companies are often choosing to use both.

Key Terms

digital collaboration, *298*
synchronous communication, *298*
asynchronous communication, *298*
web 2.0, *300*
multimedia training, *301*
computer-based training (CBT), *303*
CD-ROM, *303*
DVD (digital video disk), *303*

laser disk, *303*
interactive video, *304*
Internet, *305*
World Wide Web (WWW), *305*
online learning, *305*
e-learning, *305*
Internet-based training, *305*
Web-based training, *305*
intranet-based training, *305*
repurposing, *312*

learner control, *313*
bandwidth, *314*
plug-in, *314*
hyperlink, *315*
learning portal, *316*
blended learning, *317*
avatar, *320*
virtual reality, *320*
presence, *320*
Second Life, *321*
intelligent tutoring systems (ITS), *324*

distance learning, *325*
teleconferencing, *325*
interactive distance
learning (IDL), *326*
webcasting, *326*
expert systems, *328*
groupware (electronic
meeting software), *328*

electronic performance
support system
(EPSS), *329*
interactive voice
technology, *330*
imaging, *330*
authoring tools, *331*

learning management
system (LMS), *331*
human capital
management, *332*

Discussion Questions

1. Explain how technology has changed the learning environment.
2. What are some advantages and disadvantages of multimedia training?
3. What are the differences between expert systems and electronic performance tools?
4. Are training support technologies always needed? Justify your answer.
5. Discuss how new technologies make it easier to learn. How do they facilitate transfer of training?
6. Is all Internet training the same? Explain.
7. What are some potential problems with using virtual reality technology for training?
8. How can interactive voice technology and imaging help with training administration?
9. Explain learner control, sharing, and linking. How do they contribute to the effectiveness of e-learning?
10. What is repurposing? How does it affect the use of new technologies in training?
11. Distance learning can be used to deliver a lecture to geographically dispersed trainees. How might distance learning be designed and used to avoid some of the learning and transfer of training problems of the traditional lecture method?
12. Why would a company use a combination of face-to-face instruction and Web-based training?

Application Assignments

1. Using only the Web, further investigate any new technology discussed in this chapter. Utilizing any search engine on the Web (e.g., Google, Yahoo), conduct a search for information about the technology you have chosen. Find information describing the technology, hints for developing or purchasing the technology, and examples of companies marketing and/or using the technology. Include Web addresses in your summary.
2. The Interactive Patient is a realistic interactive computer simulation of a patient's visit to a physician's office. The Interactive Patient is a Web-based training program used to train medical students at Marshall University and to provide continuous education credits to practicing physicians. Visit and review the Interactive Patient at <u>medicus.marshall.edu/</u>.
   a. What are the program's strengths and weaknesses?
   b. How would you improve the program?

3. Go to www.skillsoft.com, the Web site for Skillsoft, a company that specializes in providing e-learning solutions. Move the cursor over Info Center, then over Demos. Click on Business Skills Demos. View one of the e-learning courses. Does the program create a positive learning environment? How? What suggestions do you have for improving the program?

4. Go to www.mzinga.com. Mzinga provides software solutions for learning. Click on Technology. Then click on Mzinga Social Learning Suite. What learning solutions are provided by the Social Learning Suite? Do you believe that these solutions are effective? Why?

5. Go to www.isense.com, the Web site for InterSense, a company that develops and markets motion tracking projects used for commercial applications. Click on either Military or Industrial markets. Click on Learn More and then review the simulation. What are the advantages of the simulation you reviewed? What are the potential weaknesses?

6. Go to www.capellauniversity.edu, the Web site for Capella University—a university that offers online courses. Click on Online Learning on the left side of the page. View the short course demo and watch the video "Night in the Life of a Capella Learner." Based on the video and course demo, what are the strengths and weaknesses of online courses? What will be most effective for helping students learn?

7. 8. Go to www.youtube.com. Search for "Training in Second Life" or "Training Simulation sin Second Life." Choose and review a video of one of the many different types of training offered in Second Life (e.g., medicine, nursing, management). Provide a brief description of the training and the URL for the video. Discuss the strengths and weaknesses of the training. Based on the video you reviewed, do you think that companies, interest in Second Life for training will increase or decrease in the future? Why?

Case: *Cisco Systems Account Managers Are Too Busy for Training*

Cisco Systems of San Jose, California, helps people make connections in business, education, philanthropy, or creativity. Cisco hardware, software, and service offerings are used to create the Internet solutions that make networks possible—providing easy access to information anywhere, at any time. Cisco's account managers are the company's frontline sales force. A needs assessment found that account managers were concerned because learning content was not being delivered to them in a way that fit their work patterns or learning styles. Because account managers spend a lot of time traveling, they wanted to get on the Internet, find what they needed, and get out again. They preferred not to sit in front of a personal computer for a long e-learning course.

As a result, Cisco is creating the Account Manager Learning Environment (AMLE). The AMLE is intended to be a development tool and performance support system based on four business objectives: increase sales, increase revenue, increase speed at which account managers become competent in a topic, and reduce travel and costs. Cisco's goal in developing the AMLE is to create a learning environment that will motivate account managers to use it.

What new technology training methods would you recommend including in Cisco's AMLE? Why? Discuss the knowledge, skills, behavior, or competencies that your training method(s) would focus on.

Source: Based on M. Delahoussaye and R. Zemke, "Ten Things We Know for Sure About Learning On-line," Training (September 2001): 48–59; P. Galayan, "Delta force," T + D (July 2002): 21–28.

Endnotes

1. L. Hurtubise, "iPod Adds a Touch of Education Innovation," *Insight* (December 2008): 1.

2. J. McCallister, "The Popular Online World Inspires New Ways to Teach and Learn," *onCampus* (January 24, 2008): 1–14; D. Naraghi, "Brave New (Virtual) World," *Ohio State University Alumni Magazine* (May/June 2008): 24–29.

3. M. Van Buren and W. Woodwell Jr., *The 2000 ASTD Trends Report: Staying Ahead of the Winds of Change* (Alexandria VA: American Society for Training and Development, 2000).

4. P. Shank; "When to Use Instructional Technology," *T + D* (September 2004): 30–37; S. E. O'Connell, "New Technologies Bring New Tools, New Rules," *HR Magazine* (December 1995): 43–48; S. E. O'Connell, "The Virtual Workplace Moves at Warp Speed," *HR Magazine* (March 1996): 51–57.

5. M. Weinstein, "Virtually Integrated," *Training* (April 2007): 10; A. Hira, "The Making of a UPS Driver," *Fortune* (November 12, 2007): 118–129; P. Ketter, "What Can Training Do for Brown?" *T + D* (May 2008): 30–36.

6. J. Salopek, "Digital Collaboration," *Training and Development* (June 2000): 39–43.

7. V. Beer, *The Web Learning Fieldbook* (New York: John Wiley, 2000); A. Chute, P. Sayers, and R. Gardner, "Network Learning Environments," *New Directions for Teaching and Learning* 71 (1997): 75–83.

8. E. Hollis, "Shoney's: Workforce Development on the Side," *Chief Learning Officer* (March 2003): 32–34.

9. "Qualcomm, Inc: Learning 2.0," *Training* (February 2009): 100.

10. J. J. Howell and L. O. Silvey, "Interactive Multimedia Systems," in *The ASTD Training and Development Handbook,* 4th ed., ed. R. L. Craig (New York: McGraw-Hill, 1996): 534–53.

11. R. Zemke and J. Armstrong, "Evaluating Multimedia," *Training* (August 1996): 48–52.

12. K. Murphy, "Pitfalls vs. Promise in Multimedia Training," May 6, 1996 (from *The New York Times* Web site, www.nytimes.com).

13. Howell and Silvey, "Interactive Multimedia Systems."

14. W. Webb, "High-Tech in the Heartland," *Training* (May 1997): 51–56.

15. W. Hannum, *The Application of Emerging Training Technologies* (Alexandria, VA: American Society for Training and Development, 1990).

16. A. Field, "Class Act," *Inc.* (January 1997): 55–57.

17. "Project Leadership," *Human Resource Executive* (2000): A16.

18. S. Greengard, "How Technology Is Advancing HR," *Personnel Journal* (September 1993): 80–90.

19. M. Weinstein, "Satellite Success," *Training* (January 2007): 36–38.

20. L. Keegan and S. Rose, "The Good News about Desktop Learning," *Training and Development* (June 1997): 24–27.

21. F. Filipowski, "How Federal Express Makes Your Package Its Most Important," *Personnel Journal* (February 1992): 40–46.

22. S. Greengard, "Catch the Wave as HR Goes Online," *Personnel Journal* (July 1995): 54–68; M. I. Finney, "It's All in the Knowing How," *HR Magazine* (July 1995): 36–43; "A Survey of the Internet" (special section), *The Economist* (July 1, 1995): 3–18; A. Doran, "The Internet: The New Tool for the HR Professional," *The Review* (August/September 1995): 32–35.

23. S. Greengard, "Leverage the Power of the Internet," *Workforce* (March 1997): 76–85.

24. Greengard, "Catch the Wave as HR Goes Online."

25. M. Rosenberg, *E-Learning: Strategies for Delivering Knowledge in the Digital Age* (New York: McGraw-Hill, 2001).

26. "What Is Web-Based Training?" (from www.clark.net/pub/nractive/fl.html).

27. B. Filipczak, "An Internet of Your Very Own," in *Using Technology-Delivered Training,* ed. D. Zielinski (Minneapolis, MN: Lakewood, 1997): 127–28.

28. M. Moore, "Three Types of Interaction," *American Journal of Distance Education* 3, no.2 (1989): 1–6.

29. P. Galagan, "The E-Learning Revolution," *Training and Development* (December 2000): 24–30; D. Khirallah, "A New Way to Learn," *Information Week Online,* May 22, 2000; G. Wang, R. Von Der Linn,

D. Facar-szocki, O. Griffin, and E. Sceiford, "Measuring the Business Impact of E-Learning—An Empirical Study," *Performance Improvement Quarterly* 16 (2003): 17–30.

30. M. Gold, "E-Learning, the Lucent Way," *T&D* (July 2003): 46–50.

31. S. Murphy, "Ritz Camera Focuses on Web-Based Teaching Tools," *Chain Store Age* (December 23, 2008).

32. R. Flandez, "Firms Go Online to Train Employees," *The Wall Street Journal* (August 14, 2007): B4.

33. J. Marquez, "Faced with High Turnover, Retailers Boot Up E-Learning Programs for Quick Training," *Workforce Management* (August 2005): 74–75.

34. D. Sussman, "Dividends Paid," *T + D* (January 2006): 26–29.

35. S. Gale, "Making E-Learning More Than 'Pixie Dust,' " *Workforce* (March 2003): 58–62.

36. H. Baldwin, *Q Magazine* (May/June 2003) at *cisco.com/en/us/strategy/index.html* ("The Travel Industry's Journey Forward").

37. Shared learning demo, January 24, 2001 (from CCH Web site, *hr.cch.com*).

38. K. Brown, "Using Computers to Deliver Training: Which Employees Learn and Why?" *Personnel Psychology* 54 (2001): 271–96; E.T. Welsh, C.R. Wanberg, K.G. Brown, and M.J. Simmering, "E-Learning: Emerging Uses, Empirical Results, and Future Directions," *International Journal of Training and Development* 7, no. 4 (2003): 245–58; T. Sitzmann, K. Kraiger, D. Stewart, and R. Wisher, "The Comparative Effectiveness of Web-Based and Classroom Instruction: A Meta-analysis," *Personnel Psychology* 59(2006): 623–624.

39. K. Kraiger, "Transforming Our Models of Learning and Development: Web-Based Instruction as Enabler of Third-Generation Instruction," *Industrial Organizational Psychology* 1, no.4 (December 2008): 454–67.

40. B. Roberts, "Hard Facts about Soft-Skills E-Learning," *HR Magazine* (January 2008): 76–78.

41. G. Anders, "Companies Find On-Line Training Has Its Limits," *The Wall Street Journal* (March 26, 2007): B3.

42. Welsh, Wanberg, Brown, and Simmering, "E-Learning: Emerging Uses, Empirical Results, and Future Directions."

43. M. Hequet, "The State of the E-Learning Market," *Training* (September 2003): 24–29.

44. K. Kiser, "10 Things We Know So Far about Online Training," *Training* (November 1999): 66–70; R. Wells, "Back to the (Internet) Classroom," *Training* (March 1999): 50–54; L. Martins and F. Kellermans, "A Model of Business School Students' Acceptance of a Web-Based Course Management System," *Academy of Management Learning and Education* 3 (2004): 7–26; H. Klein, R. Noe, and C. Wang, "Motivation to Learn and Course Outcomes: The Impact of Delivery Mode, Learning Goal Orientation, and Perceived Barriers and Enablers," *Personnel Psychology* 59 (2006): 665–702.

45. S. Gale, "Making E-Learning More Than 'Pixie Dust.' "

46. K. Brown and J. Ford, "Using Computer Technology in Training: Building an Infrastructure for Active Learning," in *Creating, Implementing, and Managing Effective Training and Development,* ed. K. Kraiger (San Francisco: Jossey-Bass, 2002): 192–233.

47. S. Boehle, "Putting the Learning Back in E-Learning," *Training* (January 2006): 29–35; Brown, "Using Computers to Deliver Training: Which Employees Learn and Why?"

48. R. DeRouin, B. Fritzsche, and E. Salas, "Learner Control and Workplace Learning: Design, Person, and Organizational Issues," *Research in Personnel and Human Resource Management,* vol. 24, ed. J. Martocchio (New York: Elsevier, 2005): 181–214.

49. D. Zielinski, "The Lie of Online Learning," *Training* (February 2000): 38–40; D. Zielinski, "Can You Keep Learners On-Line?" *Training* (March 2000): 65–75.

50. K. Brown, "A Field Study of Employee E-Learning Activity and Outcomes," *Human Resource Development Quarterly* (Winter 2005): 465–80.

51. S. Chyung and M. Vachon, "An Investigation of the Profiles of Satisfying and Dissatisfying Factors in E-Learning," *Performance Improvement Quarterly* 18 (2005): 97–113.

52. D. Schaaf, "Bandwidth Basics," *Training* (September 1999): OL23–OL37; J. Adams, "Rapid Talent Development," *T + D* (March 2008): 68–73.

53. C. Osberg, "How to Keep E-Learners Online," *T&D* (October 2002): 45–46.

54. C. Pollack and R. Masters, "Using Internet Technologies to Enhance Training," *Performance Improvement* (February 1997): 28–31.

55. Zielinski, "Can You Keep Learners On-Line?"; Brown and Ford, "Using Computer Technology in Training."

56. Zielinski, "Can You Keep Learners On-Line?"

57. J. Armstrong, "The Biggest, Baddest Learning Portals," *Training* (June 2000): 61–63.

58. Ibid.; B. Hall, "One-Stop Shopping: Learning Portals Proliferate," 1999–2000 (from Web site www .internetconnect.net/bhall/portals/portals.html).

59. K. Boxer and B. Johnson, "How to Build an Online Learning Center," *T&D* (August 2002): 36–42.

60. T. Sosbe, "Ed Sketch: Ford's Drive toward Quality Education," *Chief Learning Officer* (May 2003): 36–39.

61. S. J. Hysong and L. M. Mannix, "Learning Outcomes in Distance Education versus Traditional and Mixed Environments" (paper presented at the annual conference of the Society for Industrial and Organizational Psychology, Orlando, FL, 2003).

62. M. Knowles, *The Adult Learner,* 4th ed. (Houston, TX: Gulf Publishing, 1990).

63. M. Weinstein, "Got Class," *Training* (December 2005): 29–32.

64. Sitzmann, Kraiger, Stewart, and Wisher, "The Comparative Effectiveness of Web-Based and Classroom Instruction: A Meta-analysis"; Klein, Noe, and Wang, "Motivation to Learn and Course Outcomes."

65. K. Kim, C. Bonk, and E. Oh, "The Present and Future of Blended Learning in Workplace Settings in the United States," *Performance Improvement* (September 2008): 5–14.

66. M. Weinstein, "A Better Blend," *Training* (September 2008): 30–39.

67. J. Mullich, "A Second Act for E-Learning," *Workforce Management* (February 2004): 51–55.

68. Ibid.; Weinstein, "Got Class."

69. C. Cornell, "Better Than the Real Thing?" *Human Resource Executive* (August 2005): 34–37.

70. P. Dvorak, "Theory & Practice: Simulation Shows What It Is Like to Be the Boss; Middle Managers at NetApp Receive Useful Taste of Reality," *The Wall Street Journal* (March 31, 2008): B7.

71. C. Aldrich, "Engaging Minigames Find Niche in Training," *T + D* (July 2007): 22–24.

72. M. Weinstein, "Winning games," *Training* (April 2007): 16–18.

73. J. Borzo, "Almost Human," *The Wall Street Journal,* May 24, 2004: R1, R10; J. Hoff, "My Virtual Life," *BusinessWeek,* May 1, 2006: 72–78.

74. Cornell, "Better Than the Real Thing?"; E. Frauenheim, "Can Video Games Win Points as Teaching Tools?" *Workforce Management* (April 10, 2006): 12–14; Boehle, "Simulations: The Next Generation of E-Learning"; Borzo, "Almost Human."

75. L. Freifeld, "Solid Sims," *Training* (October 2007): 48.

76. N. Adams, "Lessons from the Virtual World," *Training* (June 1995): 45–48.

77. D. Steele-Johnson and B. G. Hyde, "Advanced Technologies in Training: Intelligence Tutoring Systems and Virtual Reality," in *Training for a Rapidly Changing Workplace,* ed. M. A. Quinones and A. Ehrenstein (Washington, DC: American Psychological Association, 1997): 225–48.

78. Ibid.

79. H. Dolezalek, "Virtual Vision," *Training* (October 2007): 40–46.

80. R. Flandez, "Small Business Link: Chip Maker Trains in the Virtual World," *The Wall Street Journal* (April 3, 2008): B6.

81. P. Galagan, "Second That," *T + D* (February 2008): 34–37.

82. H. Dolezalek, "Virtual Vision."

83. What things cost: "What Does It Cost to Use a Virtual World Learning Environment?" *T + D* (November 2008): 88.

84. A. Nancheria, "Robots in the Room," *T + D* (November 2008): 18.

85. K. Taylor and S. Chyung, "Would You Adopt Second Life as a Training and Development Tool?" *Performance Improvement* (September 2008): 17–25.

86. D. Gayeski, "Goin' Mobile," *T + D* (November 2004): 46–51; D. Gayeski and M. Petrillose, "No Strings Attached," *Performance Improvement* (February 2005): 25–31; D. Hartley, "Pick Up Your PDA," *T + D* (February 2004): 22–24.

87. E. Wagner and P. Wilson, "Disconnected," *T + D* (December 2005): 40–43; J. Bronstein and A. Newman, "IM Learning," *T + D* (February 2006): 47–50.

88. M. Weinstein, "Mobility Movement," *Training* (September 6, 2007): 15–16

89. M. Weinstein, "Ready or Not, Here Comes Podcasting," *Training* (January 2006): 22–23; D. Sussman, "Now Here This," *T + D* (September 2005): 53–54; J. Pont, "Employee Training on iPod Playlist," *Workforce Management* (August 2005): 18; S. Boehle, "iPod Corporation," *Training* (September 6, 2007): 17–19

90. Wagner and Wilson, "Disconnected."

91. Steele-Johnson and Hyde, "Advanced Technologies in Training: Intelligent Tutoring Systems and Virtual Reality."

92. R. J. Seidel, O. C. Park, and R. S. Perez, "Expertise of ICAI: Developmental Requirements," *Computers in Human Behavior* 4 (1988): 235–56.

93. Steele-Johnson and Hyde, "Advanced Technologies in Training: Intelligent Tutoring Systems and Virtual Reality."

94. "Putting the Distance into Distance Learning," *Training* (October 1995): 111–18.

95. R. Clark, "Harnessing the Virtual Classroom," *T + D* (November 2005): 40–45.

96. D. Picard, "The Future Is Distance Training," *Training* (November 1996): s3–s10.

97. A. F. Maydas, "On-Line Networks Build the Savings into Employee Education," *HR Magazine* (October 1997): 31–35.

98. J. M. Rosow and R. Zager, *Training: The Competitive Edge* (San Francisco: Jossey-Bass, 1988).

99. M. Weinstein, "Satellite Success."

100. "Training Top 100 Best Practices 2006: General Mills," *Training* (March 2006): 61.

101. S. Alexander, "Reducing the Learning Burden," *Training* (September 2002): 32–34.

102. Clark, "Harnessing the Virtual Classroom"; R. Clark and R. Mayer, *E-Learning and the Science of Instruction* (San Francisco: John Wiley, 2003).

103. Hannum, *The Application of Emerging Training Technologies.*

104. P. A. Galagan, "Think Performance: A Conversation with Gloria Gery," *Training and Development* (March 1994): 47–51.

105. "Module Example: Financial Products Sales Applications," from PortBlue Web site, www.portblue.com/pub/solutions-sales-marketing (April 24, 2006).

106. J. Clark and R. Koonce, "Meetings Go High-Tech," *Training and Development* (November 1995): 32–38; A. M. Townsend, M. E. Whitman, and A. R. Hendrickson, "Computer Support Adds Power to Group Processes," *HR Magazine* (September 1995): 87–91.

107. "Vernon Carus Transforms Its Branding with IBM Lotus Notes and Domino," from www-306.ibm.com/software/success/ (January 11, 2006).

108. B. Ziegler, "Internet Software Poses Big Threat to Notes, IBM's Stake in Lotus," *The Wall Street Journal* (November 7, 1995): A1, A8.

109. S. Caudron, "Your Learning Technology Primer," *Personnel Journal* (June 1996): 120–36; A. Marquardt and G. Kearsley, *Technology-Based Learning* (Boca Raton, FL: St. Lucie Press, 1999).

110. M. Weinstein, "Wake-Up Call," *Training* (June 2007): 48–50.

111. Greengard, "How Technology Is Advancing HR."

112. A. L. Lederer, "Emerging Technology and the Buy-Wait Dilemma: Sorting Fact from Fantasy," *The Review* (June/July 1993): 16–19.

113. S. E. Forrer and Z. B. Leibowitz, *Using Computers in Human Resources* (San Francisco: Jossey-Bass, 1991); V. R. Ceriello and C. Freeman, *Human Resource Management Systems* (Lexington, MA: Lexington Books, 1991).

114. L. Granick, A. Y. Dessaint, and G. R. VandenBos, "How Information Systems Can Help Build Professional Competence," in *Maintaining Professional Competence,* ed. S. L. Willis and S. S. Dubin (San Francisco: Jossey-Bass, 1990): 278–305.

115. E. White, "Skills Tracking Lets Firms Measure Bench Strength," *The Wall Street Journal* (February 13, 2006): B3; J. Meade, *The Human Resources Software Handbook* (San Francisco: Jossey-Bass, 2003).

116. B. Hall, "How to Select the Right Authoring Tool," *Training* (May 2005): 46–61; H. Singh, "On-Line Training with a Distributed Learning Framework," in *The ASTD Handbook of Training Design and Delivery*, ed. G. Piskurich, P. Beckschi, and B. Hall (New York: McGraw-Hill, 2000): 356–67.

117. "The Wired Taskmaster: Making Learning Stick," *Training* (June 2005): 10.

118. S. Boehle, "LMS Leaders," *Training* (October 2008): 30–34.

119. D. Sussman, "The LMS Value," *T + D* (July 2005): 43–45.

120. "LMS Survey Results," from www.learningcircuits.org/2005/jun2005/LMS_survey.htm (July 7, 2006).

121. E. Cohen, "At the Ready," *Human Resource Executive* (August 2003): 40–42.

122. K. Oakes, "Mission Critical," *T + D* (September 2005): 25–28; Sussman, "The LMS Value"; H. Johnson, "Prescription for Success," *Training* (October 2003): 52.

123. Johnson, "Prescription for Success."

124. J. Barbian, "Great Expectations," *Training* (September 2002): 10–12; Sussman, "The LMS Value."

125. Oakes, "Mission Critical."

126. K. Dobbs, "Take the Gamble out of an LMS," *Workforce* (November 2002): 52–58.

127. M. Gold, "IRS Goes E," *T + D* (May 2003): 76–82.

128. I. Speizer, "Value-Minded," *Workforce Management* (July 2005): 55–58.

129. Weinstein, "Got Class."

130. Shank, "When to Use Instructional Technology"; H. Dolezalek, "Dose of Reality," *Training* (April 2004): 28–34; E. Salas, R. DeRouin, and L. Littrell, "Research-Based Guidelines for Designing Distance Learning," in *The Brave New World of eHR*, ed. H. Gueutal and D. Stone (San Francisco: Jossey-Bass, 2005): 104–37; G. Piskurich, "E-Learning: Fast, Cheap, Good," *Performance Improvement* (January 2006): 18–24.

131. Weinstein, "Got Class."

Employee Development

Objectives

After reading this chapter, you should be able to

1. Discuss current trends in using formal education for development.
2. Relate how assessment of personality type, work behaviors, and job performance can be used for employee development.
3. Describe the benefits that protégés and mentors receive from a mentoring relationship.
4. Explain the characteristics of successful mentoring programs.
5. Tell how job experiences can be used for skill development.
6. Explain how to train managers to coach employees.
7. Explain the key features of an effective development strategy and how e-learning incorporates them.
8. Describe the steps in the development planning process.
9. Discuss the employee's and company's responsibilities in the development planning process.

Randstad's Partnering Program Develops Employees

Randstad USA is one of the largest recruiting agencies in the United States, with over 600 branch offices. Randstad USA encourages its younger employees to pair with older, more experienced employees. New sales agents are assigned a partner to work with until their business has grown to a specific size, and then they serve as a partner for someone who has just joined the company. Randstad uses this approach to help 20-something employees identify with their jobs and reduce new employee turnover. Randstad managers believe that when Generation Y employees share a job with someone whose own success depends upon their success they get the support they need. So far, the partnering program has been successful. It has improved employee retention rates 10 percent above the industry standard.

Randstad has been pairing people since the company was started nearly 40 years ago. Based on the company founder's motto that, "Nobody should be left alone," the original goal was to increase productivity by having sales agents share one job and trade off responsibilities. Currently, the way the pairing works is that each week one person goes out making sales calls and the other stays in the office handling paperwork and interviewing potential workers. Then the partners switch responsibilities. One of the most important aspects of the partnering program is that neither person is the boss and both are expected to teach each other. For example, one 60-year-old senior agent is paired with a 28-year-old partner who is working in her first office job. The senior partner is helping the new agent understand how to ask clients the right questions and not be timid when giving job applicants advice (such as appropriate apparel for a job interview). The senior employee has gained a new perspective from the younger employee about how to relax at work. Working with his younger partner encouraged another senior partner to overcome his hesitation in using the electronic payroll system that Randstad offers to save time and reduce paperwork. Randstad also encourages the partners to solve their own problems and dissolves partnerships only when major problems are occurring, such as when one person is sabotaging the other or productivity is suffering. In these cases—which occur infrequently—the uncooperative partner usually leaves the company.

Randstad doesn't just pair employees together and expect that the partnering relationship will be successful. The company selects employees based on extensive interviews and requires job candidates to shadow a sales agent for half a day. Interview questions focus on the ability of the job candidate to work in teams and groups as opposed to wanting to be the star employee and relishing personal achievement.

Source: Based on S. Berfield, "Bridging the Generation Gap," *BusinessWeek* (September 17, 2007): 60–61; www.randstadusa.com, Web site for Randstad USA.

INTRODUCTION

As the Ranstad USA vignette illustrates, employee development involves more than a training program. Employee development often has its roots in the company's mission, goals, and values and is related to important business outcomes such as employee retention and the creation of an agile and talented management team and work force. Traditionally, development has focused on management-level employees, while line employees received training designed to improve a specific set of skills needed for their current job. However, with the increased need to engage employees and the focus on talent management, development is becoming more important for all employees. **Development** refers to formal education, job experiences, relationships, and assessments of personality and abilities that help employees perform effectively in their current or future job and company.[1] Many companies use a combination of development activities. For example, the Washington Division of URS provides engineering, construction, and technical services for environmental management, industrial/process, infrastructure, mining, and power projects. The Washington Division deals with difficult projects such as nuclear waste disposal and the upgrading of coal-fired power plants.

The Division's Washington Group's development efforts include formal courses, job experiences, and mentoring.[2] An important focus in the company's employee development program is training in management skills such as controlling costs and time management. Also, technical training is combined with job experiences to help employees better understand construction projects. One project manager worked on the construction of six auto plants, which helps him better understand each stage of the project. Several times each year managers are invited to the company's Leaders Forum. At the Leaders Forum, executives present current business challenges that the company is facing and ask participants to work in teams to generate solutions. For example, participants were presented with a business acquisition proposal. The experience gave managers the opportunity to understand how things work at the top of the company and to visualize all the issues involved in decision making, such as considering labor unions and local government. The company's Leadership Excellence Program involves pairing managers with executive mentors for one year. For example, one manager who wants to develop his financial knowledge and presentation skills is working with his mentor to create a financial plan for another business unit and present it to financial executives.

Steve Hanks, former CEO of the Washington Division, believed in being involved in every aspect of employee development, from reviewing courses to monitoring employee attendance and reviewing employee course feedback. Hanks believed that the Washington Division should be a constant learning organization, which was sufficient justification for the company's financial commitment to employee development. He was not concerned that competitors would lure his employees; instead he worried that if the Washington Division didn't train its employees it would be stuck with unskilled and poorly performing employees.

Because development is future oriented, it involves learning that is not necessarily related to the employee's current job. Table 9.1 shows the differences between training and development. It is important to note that although training and development are similar, there are important differences between them. Traditionally, training is focused on helping improve employees' performance in their current jobs. Development helps prepare them for other positions in the company and increases their ability to move into jobs that may not yet exist.[3] Development also helps employees prepare for changes in their current job that may result from new technology, work designs, customers, or product markets. Because training often focuses on improving employees' performance in their current jobs, attendance at training programs is required. Development may be mandatory for employees who have been identified to have managerial potential. However, most employees must take the initiative to become involved in development. Chapter 2 emphasized the strategic role of training. Note that as training continues to become more strategic (more related to business goals), the distinction between training and development will blur. Both training and development will be required and will focus on current and future personal and company needs.

Why is employee development important? Employee development is a necessary component of a company's efforts to improve quality, meet the challenges of global competition and social change, and incorporate technological advances and changes in work design. Development is also important for talent management, particularly for senior managers and employees with leadership potential (recall the discussion of attracting and retaining talent in Chapter 1). Companies report that the most important talent management challenges they face are developing existing talent and attracting and retaining

TABLE 9.1 Comparison between Training and Development		Training	Development
	Focus	Current	Future
	Use of Work Experiences	Low	High
	Goal	Preparation for current job	Preparation for changes
	Participation	Required	Voluntary

leadership talent.[4] Increased globalization of product markets compels companies to help their employees understand cultures and customs that affect business practices. For high-involvement companies and work teams to be successful, their employees need strong interpersonal skills. Employees must also be able to perform roles traditionally reserved for managers. Legislation (such as the Civil Rights Act of 1991), labor market forces, and a company's social responsibility dictate that employers provide women and minorities with access to development activities that will prepare them for managerial positions. Companies must help employees overcome stereotypes and attitudes that inhibit the innovative contributions that can come from a work force made up of employees with diverse ethnic, racial, and cultural backgrounds.

As noted in Chapter 1, employees' commitment and retention are directly related to how they are treated by their managers. Managers need to be able to identify high-potential employees, make sure that their talents are used, and reassure them of their value before they become dissatisfied and leave the company. Managers also must be able to listen. While new employees need strong direction and a boss who can make quick decisions, they expect to be able to challenge a manager's thinking and be treated with respect and dignity. Because of their skills, many employees are in high demand and can easily leave for a competitor. Development activities can help companies reduce turnover in two ways: (1) by showing employees that the company is investing in the employees' skill development, and (2) by developing managers who can create a positive work environment that makes employees want to come to work and contribute to the company goals. One of the major reasons that good employees leave companies is poor relationships with their managers. Companies need to retain their talented employees or risk losing their competitive advantage. Development activities can help companies with employee retention by developing managers' skills. Sprint PCS used 360-degree feedback as a way to help develop people skills in the managers of its customer contact centers.[5] That is, the company wanted its managers to develop skills in communication, creating trust, coaching, and other interpersonal actions that would help the company retain good employees. Managers who scored high on the 360-degree assessment were also ranked by their employees as high in providing career development help and support (key reasons employees stayed with Sprint). The 360-degree assessment was linked to a development plan, and each interpersonal skill could be developed through online training. Sprint set a goal to reduce turnover to 48 percent. Every Sprint location that completed the 360-degree assessment met the goal!

This chapter discusses approaches that companies use to develop employees as well as the development process itself. The chapter begins by exploring development approaches including formal education, assessment, job experiences, and interpersonal relationships. The chapter emphasizes the types of skills, knowledge, and behaviors that are strengthened by each development method. Developmental approaches are one part of the development planning process. Before one or multiple developmental approaches are used, the employee and the company must have an idea of the employee's development needs and the purpose of development. Identifying needs and the purpose of development is part of the development planning process. The chapter provides an overview of the development planning process, including a discussion of the roles of the employee and the company. The chapter concludes with a discussion of employee development strategies, including the use of e-learning.

APPROACHES TO EMPLOYEE DEVELOPMENT

Four approaches are used to develop employees: formal education, assessment, job experiences, and interpersonal relationships.[6] Many companies use a combination of these approaches. A recent survey of use of company employee development practices found that 84 percent use training other than leadership training, 70 percent use development planning, 55 percent use formal coaching, 47 percent use job assignments, 30 percent use job rotation, and 25 percent use formal internal mentoring programs.[7] Larger companies are more likely to use leadership training and development planning more frequently than smaller companies.

Hindustan Unilever is India's largest consumer products company.[8] The company has 15,000 employees, including 10,000 production employees. Each of the company's 45 plants has three human resource leaders who spend half their time on leadership development. These leaders are directly accountable for "hot jobs, hot people." The hot jobs are the 50 most strategic positions in the company and the hot people are the 50 people with the most potential. The objective is that hot people must be in 90 percent of the hot jobs. The goal is to maximize the movement of the hot people into the hot jobs. Hindustan Unilever uses job rotation and mentoring as development activities. Every year the management committee meets to discuss the top 200 people in the company. The management committee discusses each employee and his or her development plans.

Regardless of the approach used to ensure that development programs are effective, the programs should be developed through the same process used for training design: assessing needs, creating a positive development environment, ensuring employees' readiness for development, identifying the objectives for development, choosing a combination of development activities that will help achieve the objectives, ensuring that the work environment supports development activities and the use of skills and experiences acquired, and evaluating the program. To determine the development needs of an individual, department, or company, an analysis of strengths and weaknesses needs to be completed so that appropriate development activities can be chosen. Many companies have identified key competencies for successful managers. Recall from the discussion in Chapter 3 that competencies are areas of personal capability that enable employees to successfully perform their jobs. Competencies can include knowledge, skills, abilities, or personal characteristics.

Two companies that first determined the need for development and then used assessment to determine appropriate development activities are Schwan and General Physics. Schwan, a Minnesota-based frozen food delivery service, created its own corporate university.[9] As part of the process, the company had to determine what kind of managers it wanted and how they were supposed to perform. Schwan identified 15 important competencies, including "managing vision and purpose," and "developing direct reports." After the competencies were identified, the company used 360-degree feedback to measure managers' competency strengths and weaknesses and created development activities related to strengthening the competencies (e.g., coaches, training programs, job experiences).

General Physics (GP), a training and work force development company, believed that the company's managers needed development.[10] GP assessed its current leaders before determining what type of development activity was appropriate and what skills needed to be developed. GP used 360-degree feedback to evaluate managers' competencies in managing change, leadership, motivation, managing conflict, performance, and empowerment.

GP also developed an organizational climate survey that was completed by other employees in the company. The climate survey measured the same competencies that the 360-degree assessment did. Based on the results of the 360-degree assessment and the climate survey, GP determined that all of the competencies needed development. GP management also decided that a nontraditional approach was needed to get managers to change, so it adopted a "boot camp" philosophy. The official announcement of the new program was made at a business meeting attended by GP directors and other top-level managers. One of the members of the management team in charge of development initiatives described the program while dressed in battle fatigues. Many in the audience applauded the program, signifying important support from top management. The two-day intensive leadership development program included physically challenging teamwork exercises, motivational speakers, classroom training, and action learning in which teams of program participants worked on issues affecting corporate human performance and briefed senior management on how to deal with them. To reinforce the importance of the program, participants remained at the camp away from business activities and ate all meals together. All participants were issued uniforms. Did the program result in improved leadership competencies? In a follow-up climate survey that was completed six months after the program, employees indicated an improvement in the managers: there was a 17 percent to 25 percent improvement in all of the competencies.

Keep in mind that although the large majority of development activity is targeted at managers, all levels of employees may be involved in one or more development activities. Specific issues related to developing managers (succession planning, dealing with dysfunctional managers, creating more opportunities for women and minorities to become managers) are discussed in Chapter 10.

Formal Education

Formal education programs include off-site and on-site programs designed specifically for the company's employees, short courses offered by consultants or universities, executive MBA programs, and university programs in which participants actually live at the university while taking classes. These programs may involve lectures by business experts or professors, business games and simulations, adventure learning, and meetings with customers. For example, Harvard University offers several different programs for executives, high-potential upper-level managers, and general managers (e.g., an advanced management program). Harvard also offers programs on managerial issues such as negotiations and programs for specific audiences (e.g., Senior Executive Program for South Africa).

Many companies primarily rely on in-house development programs offered by training and development centers or corporate universities rather than sending employees to programs offered by universities.[11] Companies rely on in-house programs because these programs can be tied directly to business needs, can be easily evaluated using company metrics, and can involve senior-level management.

At Paducah Bank & Trust Company, a community bank with 140 employees, most of the management jobs are filled by current employees.[12] Employees wanting a management job can apply for a leadership development program. Six to eight employees are selected for the program, which teaches the fundamentals of banking (such as liability management), sends employees to conferences and schools to learn more about leadership skills and banking, and requires them to complete a project. One class developed a plan to better market the bank to women. These development opportunities are intended to help the employees feel valuable to the company and feel and think like owners on the job. Verizon Wireless has started on-site college degree programs at 14 of its corporate offices. Each program offers classes for associate, bachelor's and MBA degree programs.[13] Verizon's program has an 18 percent participation rate. MBAs are not necessary for every position, but the degree provides employees with a broader understanding of business and business results and helps to prepare potential future leaders of the business. Compared to the overall work force, employees who earn their degrees are almost one and one-half times more likely to receive a promotion or lateral move within the company.

General Electric (GE) has one of the oldest and most widely known management development centers in the world. GE develops managers at the John F. Welch Leadership Center at Crotonville, New York.[14] GE invests approximately $1 billion each year in training and education programs for its employees.[15] Over the last 15 years, the 189 most senior executives in the company have spent at least 12 months in training and professional development. In addition to classrooms, GE's leadership facility has residence buildings in which participants stay while attending programs. Every year GE employees, chosen by their managers based on their performance and potential, attend management development programs. The programs include professional skills development and specialized courses in areas such as risk analysis and loan structuring. All the programs emphasize theory and practical application. Course time is spent discussing business issues facing GE. The programs are taught by in-house instructors, university faculty members, and even CEO Jeff Immelt. Examples of management development programs available at GE are shown in Table 9.2. As you can see, GE uses a combination of coursework and job experiences to

TABLE 9.2   **Examples of Leadership Development Programs at General Electric**

Program	Summary	Qualifications to Attend
Commercial Leadership Program: Sales and Marketing	Formal courses, including Selling@GE, Marketing@GE, and negotiation skills. Challenging assignments in key sales and marketing roles within a business.	Bachelor's degree in engineering or industrial distribution, minimum 3.0 GPA; willingness to relocate; interest in sales; career- and results-oriented.
Experienced Commercial Leadership Program (ECLP): Sales and Marketing	Four 6-month business rotations within the sales and marketing functions of a GE business. Every three months, complete self-assessment and receive manager evaluation. Develop key marketing, sales, and leadership skills in 6 weeks of intensive training.	MBA candidate with 4–6 years marketing or sales experience; demonstrated leadership and achievement in sales and marketing, communications, and analytical skills; willingness to relocate.

Source: Based on "Leadership Programs," www.gecareers.com (February 25, 2009).

develop entry-level and top-level management. Other programs, such as the Business Manager Course and the Executive Development Course, utilize action learning (discussed in Chapter 7). Program participants are assigned a real problem that GE is facing and must present their recommendations to Jeff Immelt. Besides programs and courses for management development, GE also holds seminars to help employees better understand customer expectations and holds leadership conferences designed specifically for African American, female, and Hispanic managers.

Most formal education programs actively involve the employees in learning. Separate programs are usually offered for supervisors, middle managers, and executives. Special programs for particular jobs (such as engineer) are also available. At Whirlpool, the largest manufacturer of large home appliances in the world, the company's leadership development program focuses on 12 critical attributes: (1) character and enduring values, (2) communications, (3) customer champion, (4) confidence, (5) developing talent, (6) diversity with inclusion, (7) driver of change/transformation, (8) extraordinary results, (9) management skills, (10) strategy, (11) thought leadership, and (12) vision.[16] The leadership development program is organized into three tiers. The first tier (Leadership Development Programs) includes programs to train new graduates for higher-level positions in the functional areas such as marketing, engineering, finance, or human resources. Each program runs three to four years and includes formal training, mentoring, and rotations through job assignments. One hundred new employees attend the program each year with over 300 involved in the rotations at any one time. The second tier of programs (Leading the Whirlpool Enterprise), required for the top 700 company leaders, involves two one-week classes. One class includes a 360-degree assessment evaluating each executive's attributes and providing feedback. The second week focuses on asking the executives to consider the company's strategic objectives, identify the most important business issue, and develop a plan to solve the issue. The third tier (Leaders Developing Leaders) includes the 20 top company executives from around the world. These executives are given an intensive assessment of their skills and personality and they are matched with a coach who works with them to help improve their weaknesses and capitalize on their strengths. To ensure that the company's investment in the leadership development program is well-spent, managers and company leaders are held accountable for developing future leaders by serving as teachers in the courses. Also, managers' and company leaders' performance evaluations include objectives related to leadership development as well as financial results.

Leadership, entrepreneurship, and e-business are the most important topics in executive education programs. Programs directed at developing executives' understanding of global business issues and management of change are other important parts of executive development.[17] Also, there is a movement toward custom courses designed to meet business needs as well as gain an understanding of global business and culture.

Xerox Corporation's Emerging Leaders Program (ELP) is a five-month program that includes a two-hour program kickoff using Web-based conferencing, e-modules that employees complete at their own pace, face-to-face meetings, online assessment, coaching, and mentoring.[18] Employees from North America and Europe have participated in ELP. Each session in the European ELP includes high-potential managers from 14 countries who work in different functions and speak different languages. The most challenging part of ELP involves working as a cross-functional, cross-cultural, geographically dispersed team to identify, plan, and begin a business project based on the strategic initiatives. Each team presents its results to vice presidents and executives at the conclusion of the program.

Table 9.3 shows examples of institutions that provide executive education. There are several important trends in executive education. Increasingly, many companies and universities are using distance learning (which was discussed in Chapter 8) to reach executive audiences.[19] Many business schools have begun offering companies in-house custom programs to help managers gain real-world skills and study problems in real-world environments without having to disrupt their work with travel to a campus. For example, Duke Corporate Education conducts custom programs for ArcelorMittal, which was formed by the merger of two steel companies.[20] One of the challenges the company faces is how to get its managers to understand the global challenges facing the steel industry. As a result, the program involves middle managers visiting steel plants in both mature and emerging markets to gain an understanding of the technology and management processes of a more established steel plant compared to a growing steel plant. The managers are asked to develop proposals for improving the growing plant, such as how to identify environmental problems and expand health and safety features. The Haas School of Business at the University of California, Berkeley, has worked with StatoilHydro, the Norwegian oil and gas company, to develop a program that focuses on preparing employees to work in different cultures. The program includes challenges, such as working with contractors who may not have the necessary employees or equipment to complete a project on time or learning to deal with local government officials.

Another trend in executive education is to supplement formal courses from consultants or university faculty with other types of training and development activities. Avon Products has used action learning for management development. Its Passport Program is targeted at employees the company thinks can become general managers.[21] The program brings a team of employees together for six-week periods spread over 18 months. To learn Avon's global strategy, these employees meet for each session in a different country. Participants are provided with a general background of a functional area by university faculty and consultants. Then teams work with senior executives on a country project such as how to penetrate a new market. The team projects are presented to Avon's top managers.

Managers who attend the Center for Creative Leadership development program in Greensboro, North Carolina, take psychological tests; receive feedback from managers, peers, and direct reports; participate in group building activities (like adventure learning, discussed in Chapter 7) or simulations; receive counseling; set improvement goals; and write development plans.[22]

TABLE 9.3
Examples of Institutions That Provide Executive Education

Source: Based on "2008 Business School Rankings and Profiles," www.BusinessWeek.com, February 28, 2009.

Provider (Location)	2006–07 Revenue (millions)	Open Programs Offered	Clients Served for Customized Courses
Harvard (Boston)	90.8	113	39
INSEAD (France; Singapore)	73.6	341	112
IMD (Lausanne, Switzerland)	73.2	132	100
Stanford (Stanford, California)	22.8	42	11
Columbia (New York)	13.1	73	22

Many companies and their employees are looking to reduce the time it takes to complete an advanced business degree. As a result, universities are offering miniature MBA programs that allow employees to earn the MBA in less than two years, the time needed to earn an MBA in a full-time program.[23] For example, Drexel University and Ohio University offer intensive, accelerated MBA programs that can be completed in just over a year's time.

Given the costs of executive education programs, companies are asking for evaluation data that show the value of the program. As a result, many universities that offer executive education programs are beginning to measure their programs' return on investment. For example, Columbia Business School uses performance measures to track the success of program participants.[24] Leadership skills, team building, and strategic thinking are measured via self-assessments, manager evaluations, and peer reviews collected before the participant attends the program as well as up to a year following program completion. To judge its programs' practical value, the Darden Graduate School of Business Administration at the University of Virginia asks participants in executive education programs to complete surveys three months after attending programs. Some of the Darden School's programs use action learning in which employees make presentations to top-level managers, thereby showing how their participation in the program has helped them successfully deal with work problems. This demonstrates how learning has benefited the company.

Enrollment in executive education programs or MBA programs may be limited only to managers or employees identified to have management potential. As a result, many companies also provide tuition reimbursement as a benefit for all employees to encourage them to develop. **Tuition reimbursement** refers to the practice of reimbursing employees' costs for college and university courses and degree programs. Companies spend about $10 billion on tuition reimbursement for courses offered by nonprofit colleges and universities as well as for-profit universities like Capella University.[25] These courses include face-to-face classroom instruction, online learning, and blended learning. For example, United Technology's Employee Scholar Program allows employees to receive 100 percent tuition reimbursement of all educational costs including tuition, registration fees, and books. Courses do not have to be related to the employee's job. Employees are allowed three hours each week to study or attend class. Employees who earn a degree receive $10,000 in company stock. The company has paid out over $60 million for the program. About 15 percent of employees use the program.

Despite the large investment in tuition reimbursement, many companies have not attempted to identify the value of such programs. Companies that have evaluated tuition reimbursement programs have found that the programs increase employee retention rates, increase employees' readiness for promotion, and improve job performance.[26] United Technology sees no need for a cost-benefit analysis because it believes that a better educated work force is likely to be more productive. However, some companies at least require employees to achieve a minimum course grade or maintain a minimum grade point average to receive reimbursement. Other companies require employees to remain with them for a certain period of time after receiving a degree through a tuition reimbursement program. Employees who leave early are responsible for reimbursing tuition costs to the company. Kum and Go, a large convenience store chain, has a tuition reimbursement program that allows employees to obtain their college degrees while working full-time. The program reimburses students 100 percent of their tuition if they receive either an A or B and 50 percent if they receive a C.[27]

Assessment

Assessment involves collecting information and providing feedback to employees about their behavior, communication style, values, or skills.[28] The employees, as well as their peers, managers, and customers, may be asked to provide information. Assessment is most frequently used to identify employees with managerial potential and to measure current managers' strengths and weaknesses. Assessment is also used to identify managers with the potential to move into higher-level executive positions, and it can be used with work teams to identify individual team members' strengths and weaknesses as well as the decision processes or communication styles that inhibit the team's productivity.

Companies vary in the methods and sources of information they use in developmental assessment. Many companies provide employees with performance appraisal information. Companies with sophisticated development systems use psychological tests to measure employees' skills, personality types, and communication styles. These types of assessments can help employees understand their tendencies, needs, the type of work environment they prefer, and the type of work for which they are best suited.[29] This type of information, along with information they receive from the company about their performance (from performance appraisals) and their potential, can help employees decide what type of development goals might be most appropriate for them (e.g., a leadership position or an increase in the scope of their current position). Examples of personality assessment tools include the NEO Personality Inventory (or NEO PI-R), DiSC, and Myers-Briggs. The NEO PI-R measures five factors of personality (also known as the Big Five): conscientiousness, extroversion, adjustment, agreeableness, and openness to experience. DiSC provides classifications of four aspects of behavior (dominance, influence, steadiness, and conscientiousness).

For example, Carmeuse North American uses personality assessments in its leadership development program. The personality assessments for employees who have been identified as having high potential for top management positions are used to guide employees into development activities such as coaching and formal courses.[30] Edward Jones, the brokerage and investment advisory firm, uses personality assessment to assess the leadership potential of financial advisors working outside its St. Louis, Missouri, headquarters.[31] The personality assessment is combined with 360-degree feedback from peers to provide the company with an idea of employees' leadership skills. Employees and their managers receive the results, which are used to determine if employees possess the personality needed to take a leadership role at headquarters. In addition to peers, companies may also collect self and manager's ratings of employees' interpersonal styles and behaviors. The following sections look at several popular assessment tools.

Myers-Briggs Type Indicator

The **Myers-Briggs Type Indicator (MBTI)** is the most popular psychological test for employee development. As many as 2 million people take the MBTI in the United States each year. The test consists of more than 100 questions about how the person feels or prefers to behave in different situations (e.g., "Are you usually a good 'mixer' or rather quiet and reserved?"). The MBTI is based on the work of psychologist Carl Jung, who believed that differences in individuals' behavior resulted from people's preferences in decision making, interpersonal communication, and information gathering.

The MBTI identifies individuals' preferences for energy (introversion versus extroversion), information gathering (sensing versus intuition), decision making (thinking versus feeling), and lifestyle (judging versus perceiving).[32] The energy dichotomy determines where individuals gain interpersonal strength and vitality. Extroverts (E) gain energy through interpersonal relationships. Introverts (I) gain energy by focusing on personal thoughts and feelings. The information-gathering dichotomy relates to the actions individuals take when making decisions. Individuals with a Sensing (S) preference tend to gather facts and details. Intuitives (I) tend to focus less on facts and more on possibilities and relationships between ideas. Differences in decision-making styles are based on the amount of consideration the person gives to others' feelings in making a decision. Individuals with a Thinking (T) preference tend to be very objective in making decisions. Individuals with a Feeling (F) preference tend to evaluate the impact of potential decisions on others and be more subjective in making a decision. The lifestyle dichotomy reflects an individual's tendency to be flexible and adaptable. Individuals with a Judging (J) preference focus on goals, establish deadlines, and prefer to be conclusive. Individuals with a Perceiving (P) preference tend to enjoy surprises, like to change decisions, and dislike deadlines.

Sixteen unique personality types result from the combination of the four MBTI preferences (see Table 9.4). Each of us has developed strengths and weaknesses as a result of our

TABLE 9.4   Personality Types Used in the Myers-Briggs Type Indicator Assessment

	Sensing Types (S)		Intuitive Types (N)	
	Thinking (T)	Feeling (F)	Feeling (F)	Thinking (T)
Introverts (I) Judging (J)	**ISTJ** Quiet, serious, earn success by thoroughness and dependability. Practical, matter-of-fact, realistic, and responsible. Decide logically what should be done and work toward it steadily, regardless of distractions. Take pleasure in making everything orderly and organized—their work, their home, their life. Value traditions and loyalty.	**ISFJ** Quiet, friendly, responsible, and conscientious. Committed and steady in meeting their obligations. Thorough, painstaking, and accurate. Loyal, considerate, notice and remember specifics about people who are important to them, concerned with how others feel. Strive to create an orderly and harmonious environment at work and at home.	**INFJ** Seek meaning and connection in ideas, relationships, and material possessions. Want to understand what motivates people and are insightful about others. Conscientious and committed to their firm values. Develop a clear vision about how best to serve the common good. Organized and decisive in implementing their vision.	**INTJ** Have original minds and great drive for implementing their ideas and achieving their goals. Quickly see patterns in external events and develop long-range explanatory perspectives. When committed, organize a job and carry it through. Skeptical and independent, have high standards of competence and performance—for themselves and others.
Perceiving (P)	**ISTP** Tolerant and flexible, quiet observers until a problem appears, then act quickly to find workable solutions. Analyze what makes things work and readily get through large amounts of data to isolate the core of practical problems, interested in cause and effect, organize facts using logical principles, value efficiency.	**ISFP** Quiet, friendly, sensitive, and kind. Enjoy the present moment, what's going on around them. Like to have their own space and to work within their own time frame. Loyal and committed to their values and to people who are important to them. Dislike disagreements and conflicts, do not force their opinions or values on others.	**INFP** Idealistic, loyal to their values and to people who are important to them. Want an external life that is congruent with their values. Curious, quick to see possibilities, can be catalysts for implementing ideas. Seek to understand people and to help them fulfill their potential. Adaptable, flexible, and accepting unless a value is threatened.	**INTP** Seek to develop logical explanations for everything that interests them. Theoretical and abstract, interested more in ideas than in social interaction. Quiet, contained, flexible and adaptable. Have unusual ability to focus in depth to solve problems in their area of interest. Skeptical, sometimes critical, always analytical.

TABLE 9.4   *(concluded)*

	Sensing Types (S)		Intuitive Types (N)	
	Thinking (T)	**Feeling (F)**	**Feeling (F)**	**Thinking (T)**
Extroverts (E) **Perceiving (P)**	**ESTP** Flexible and tolerant, they take a pragmatic approach focused on immediate results. Theories and conceptual explanations bore them—they want to act energetically to solve the problem. Focus on the here-and-now, spontaneous, enjoy each moment that they can be active with others. Enjoy material comforts and style. Learn best through doing.	**ESFP** Outgoing, friendly, and accepting. Exuberant lovers of life, people, and material comforts. Enjoy working with others to make things happen. Bring common sense and a realistic approach to their work, and make work fun. Flexible and spontaneous, adapt readily to new people and environments. Learn best by trying a new skill with other people.	**ENFP** Warmly enthusiastic and imaginative. See life as full of possibilities. Make connections between events and information very quickly, and confidently proceed based on the patterns they see. Want a lot of affirmation from others, and readily give appreciation and support. Spontaneous and flexible, often rely on their ability to improvise and their verbal fluency.	**ENTP** Quick, ingenious, stimulating, alert, and outspoken. Resourceful in solving new and challenging problems. Adept at generating conceptual possibilities and then analyzing them strategically. Good at reading other people. Bored by routine, will seldom do the same thing the same way, apt to turn to one new interest after another.
Judging (J)	**ESTJ** Practical, realistic, matter-of-fact. Decisive, quickly move to implement decisions. Organize projects and people to get things done, focus on getting results in the most efficient way possible. Take care of routine details. Have a clear set of logical standards, systematically follow them and want others to also. Forceful in implementing their plans.	**ESFJ** Warmhearted, conscientious, and cooperative. Want harmony in their environment, work with determination to establish it. Like to work with others to complete tasks accurately and on time. Loyal, follow through even in small matters. Notice what others need in their day-by-day lives and try to provide it. Want to be appreciated for who they are and for what they contribute.	**ENFJ** Warm, empathetic, responsive, and responsible. Highly attuned to the emotions, needs, and motivations of others. Find potential in everyone, want to help others fulfill their potential. May act as catalysts for individual and group growth. Loyal, responsive to praise and criticism. Sociable, facilitate others in a group, and provide inspiring leadership.	**ENTJ** Frank, decisive, assume leadership readily. Quickly see illogical and inefficient procedures and policies, develop and implement comprehensive systems to solve organizational problems. Enjoy long-term planning and goal setting. Usually well informed, well read, enjoy expanding their knowledge and passing it on to others. Forceful in presenting their ideas.

preferences. For example, individuals who are Introverted, Sensing, Thinking, and Judging (known as ISTJs) tend to be serious, quiet, practical, orderly, and logical. They can organize tasks, be decisive, and follow through on plans and goals. ISTJs have several weaknesses because they have not used the opposite preferences of Extroversion, Intuition, Feeling, and Perceiving. Potential weaknesses for ISTJs include problems dealing with unexpected opportunities, appearing too task-oriented or impersonal to colleagues, and being overly quick to make decisions. Visit the Web site www.keirsey.com for more information on the personality types.

The MBTI is used for understanding such things as communication, motivation, teamwork, work styles, and leadership. For example, it can be used by salespeople or executives who want to become more effective at interpersonal communication by learning about their own personality styles and the way they are perceived by others. The MBTI can help a company develop teams by matching team members with assignments that allow them to capitalize on their preferences and by helping employees understand how the different preferences of team members can lead to useful problem solving.[33] For example, employees with an Intuitive preference can be assigned brainstorming tasks. Employees with a Sensing preference can be given the responsibility of evaluating ideas.

People who take the MBTI find it a positive experience and say it helps them change their behavior. MBTI scores appear to be related to one's occupation. Analysis of managers' MBTI scores in the United States, England, Latin America, and Japan suggests that a large majority of all managers have certain personality types (ISTJ, INTJ, ESTJ, or ENTJ). However, MBTI scores are not necessarily stable or reliable over time. Studies administering the MBTI at two different times found that as few as 24 percent of those who took the test were classified as the same type the second time.[34]

The MBTI is a valuable tool for understanding communication styles and the ways people prefer to interact with others. Because it does not measure how well employees perform their preferred functions, it should not be used as the only means to appraise performance or evaluate employees' promotion potential. Furthermore, MBTI types should not be viewed as unchangeable personality patterns.

Assessment Center

The **assessment center** is a process in which multiple raters or evaluators (also known as assessors) evaluate employees' performance on a number of exercises.[35] An assessment center is usually held at an off-site location such as a conference center. From 6 to 12 employees usually participate at one time. Assessment centers are primarily used to identify if employees have the personality characteristics, administrative skills, and interpersonal skills needed for managerial jobs. They are also increasingly being used to identify if employees have the necessary skills to work in teams.

The types of exercises used in assessment centers include leaderless group discussions, interviews, in-baskets, and role plays.[36] In a **leaderless group discussion,** a team of five to seven employees must work together to solve an assigned problem within a certain time period. The problem may involve buying and selling supplies, nominating a subordinate for an award, or assembling a product. An **in-basket** is a simulation of the administrative tasks of the manager's job. The exercise includes a variety of documents that may appear in the in-basket on a manager's desk. The participant is asked to read the materials and decide how to respond to them. Responses might include delegating tasks, scheduling meetings, writing replies, or completely ignoring the memo!

In **role plays,** participants take the part or role of a manager or other employee. For example, an assessment center participant may be asked to take the role of a manager who has to give a negative performance review to a subordinate. The participant is provided with information regarding the subordinate's performance. The participant is asked to prepare for and actually hold a 45-minute meeting with the subordinate to discuss the performance problems. The role of the subordinate is played by a manager or other member of the assessment center design team or the company. The assessment center might also include testing. Interest and aptitude tests may be used to evaluate employees' vocabulary, general mental ability, and reasoning skills. Personality tests may be used to determine if employees can get along with others, their tolerance for ambiguity, and other traits related to success as a manager.

The exercises in the assessment center are designed to measure employees' administrative and interpersonal skills. Skills that are typically measured include leadership, oral communication, written communication, judgment, organizational ability, and stress tolerance. Table 9.5 shows an example of the skills measured by the assessment center. Each exercise allows participating employees to demonstrate several skills. For example, the exercise requiring scheduling to meet production demands evaluates employees' administrative and problem-solving abilities. The leaderless group discussion measures interpersonal skills such as sensitivity toward others, stress tolerance, and oral communications skills.

Managers are usually used as assessors. The managers are trained to look for behaviors related to the skills that will be assessed. Typically, each assessor is assigned to observe and record one or two employees' behaviors in each exercise. The assessors review their notes and rate the employee's level of skills. (For example, a rating of 5 equals a high level of leadership skills, 1 equals a low level of leadership skills.) After all employees have completed the exercises, the assessors meet to discuss their observations of each employee. They compare their ratings and try to agree on each employee's rating for each skill.

Research suggests that assessment center ratings are related to performance, salary level, and career advancement.[37] Assessment centers may also be useful for development purposes because employees who participate in the process receive feedback regarding their attitudes, skill strengths, and weaknesses.[38] For example, Steelcase, the office furniture manufacturer based in Grand Rapids, Michigan, uses assessment centers for first-level managers.[39] The assessment center exercises include in-basket, interview simulation, and a timed scheduling exercise requiring participants to fill positions created by absences. Managers are also required to confront an employee on a performance issue, getting the employee to commit to improve. Because the exercises relate closely to what managers are required to do at work, feedback given to managers based on their performance in the assessment center can target specific skills or competencies that they need to be successful managers.

TABLE 9.5 **Examples of Skills Measured by Assessment Center Exercises**

	Exercises				
Skills	**In-Basket**	**Scheduling Exercise**	**Leaderless Group Discussion**	**Personality Test**	**Role Play**
Leadership (Dominance, coaching, influence, resourcefulness)	X		X	X	X
Problem solving (Judgment)	X	X	X		X
Interpersonal (Sensitivity, conflict resolution, cooperation, oral communication)			X	X	X
Administrative (Organizing, planning, written communications)	X	X	X		
Personal (Stress tolerance, confidence)			X	X	X

Note: An "X" indicates that the skill is measured by the exercise.

Benchmarks

Benchmarks is an instrument designed to measure important factors in being a successful manager. Items measured by Benchmarks are based on research that examines the lessons executives learn at critical events in their careers.[40] Items that are measured include dealing with subordinates, acquiring resources, and creating a productive work climate. Table 9.6 shows the 16 skills and perspectives believed to be important in becoming a successful manager. These skills and perspectives have been shown to relate to performance evaluations, bosses' ratings of promotability, and actual promotions received.[41] To get a complete picture of managers' skills, the managers' supervisors, their peers, and the managers themselves all complete the instrument. A summary report presenting the self-ratings and ratings by others is provided to the manager along with information about how the ratings compare with those of other managers. Also available is a development guide with examples of experiences that enhance each of the skills and how successful managers use the skills.

Performance Appraisals and 360-Degree Feedback Systems

Performance appraisal is the process of measuring employees' performance. There are several different approaches for measuring performance, including ranking employees, rating their work behaviors, rating the extent to which employees have desirable traits believed to be necessary for job success (e.g., leadership), and directly measuring the results of work performance (e.g., productivity).

TABLE 9.6   **Skills Related to Managerial Success**

Resourcefulness	Can think strategically, engage in flexible problem-solving behavior, and work effectively with higher management.
Doing Whatever It Takes	Has perseverance and focus in the face of obstacles.
Being a Quick Study	Quickly masters new technical and business knowledge.
Building and Mending Relationships	Knows how to build and maintain working relationships with co-workers and external parties.
Leading Subordinates	Delegates to subordinates effectively, broadens their opportunities, and acts with fairness toward them.
Compassion and Sensitivity	Shows genuine interest in others and sensitivity to subordinates' needs.
Straightforwardness and Composure	Is honorable and steadfast.
Setting a Developmental Climate	Provides a challenging climate to encourage subordinates' development.
Confronting Problem Subordinates	Acts decisively and fairly when dealing with problem subordinates.
Team Orientation	Accomplishes tasks through managing others.
Balance between Personal Life and Work	Balances work priorities with personal life so that neither is neglected.
Decisiveness	Prefers quick and approximate actions to slow and precise ones in many management situations.
Self-Awareness	Has an accurate picture of strengths and weaknesses and is willing to improve.
Hiring Talented Staff	Hires talented people for his or her team.
Putting People at Ease	Displays warmth and a good sense of humor.
Acting with Flexibility	Can behave in ways that are often seen as opposites.

Source: Adapted from C. D. McCauley, M. M. Lombardo, and C. J. Usher, "Diagnosing Management Development Needs: An Instrument Based on How Managers Develop," *Journal of Management* 15 (1989): 389–403.

These approaches can be useful for employee development under certain conditions.[42] The appraisal system must give employees specific information about their performance problems and ways they can improve their performance. Appraisals should provide a clear understanding of the differences between current performance and expected performance, identify the causes of the performance discrepancy, and develop action plans to improve performance. Managers must be trained in providing performance feedback and must frequently give employees performance feedback. Managers also need to monitor employees' progress in carrying out the action plan.

Consider how Just Born, the company that makes Mike and Ike, Hot Tamales, and Marshmallow Peeps, uses performance appraisals for evaluation and development.[43] The appraisal starts with a planning meeting between employee and manager. The strategic initiatives of the department are discussed along with the employee's role. The employee and manager agree on four personal objectives that will help the department reach its goals, and they choose key performance outcomes related to the employee's job description. The two identify competencies that the employee needs in order to reach the personal objectives. The manager and employee jointly develop a plan for learning or improving the competencies. During the year, the manager and employee monitor the progress toward reaching the performance and personal objectives and achievement of the learning plan. Pay decisions made at the end of each year are based on the achievement of both performance and learning objectives. General Electric reviews its top managers in a unique process known as Session C.[44] Session C includes full-day reviews at all major business locations and follow-up sessions. The sessions focus on evaluating a manager's strengths and weaknesses. They also include presentations of business results and reviews of accomplishments.

A trend in the use of performance appraisals for management development is the upward feedback and 360-degree feedback process. Dow Chemical, Hallmark, The Limited stores, Raychem, and AT&T, for example, use this type of appraisal process. In **upward feedback,** the appraisal process involves collecting subordinates' evaluations of managers' behaviors or skills. The **360-degree feedback** process (see Figure 9.1) is a special version of the upward feedback process. In 360-degree feedback systems, employees' behaviors or skills are evaluated not only by subordinates but also by peers, customers, their boss, and themselves. The raters complete a questionnaire that rates the person on a number of different dimensions. Table 9.7 provides an example of the types of competencies that are rated in a 360-degree feedback questionnaire. This example evaluates the management competency of decision making. Each of the five items relates to a specific aspect of decision making (e.g., takes accountability for results of individual and team decisions). Typically, raters are asked to assess the manager's strength in a particular item or whether development is needed. Raters may also be asked to identify how frequently they observe a competency or skill (e.g., always, sometimes, seldom, never).

The results of a 360-degree feedback system show managers how they are seen on each item. The results reveal how self-evaluations differ from evaluations from the other raters. Typically, managers are asked to review their results, seek clarification from the raters, and participate in development planning designed to set specific development goals based on the strengths and weaknesses identified.[45] Roadway Express, the motor carrier, has developed a new leadership model that includes a program called Leaders Developing Leaders.[46] One of the first steps in the program was to use a 360-degree feedback tool that provides data on skills, behavior, and development needs. The 360-degree evaluation was administered to 200 division managers as well as to supervisors with the goal of helping to

FIGURE 9.1
360-Degree
Feedback
System

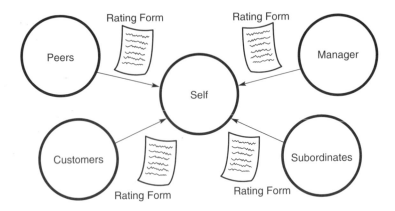

develop leaders at both levels. The 360-degree evaluation helped identify the management skills that would be the focus of training and development activities. The evaluation helped identify the need to develop managers' information-sharing, communications, delegation, and conflict-management skills.

Table 9.8 shows the types of activities involved in development planning using the 360-degree feedback process.[47] The first step for the manager being rated is to gain an understanding of skill strengths and weaknesses. This includes comparing self-ratings to other ratings (i.e., manager, peers, customers, subordinates) to identify areas of agreement and disagreement. A manager may overrate herself (rate herself too high) in comparison to the other raters. This means that the manager believes she has greater skill than the other raters believe. The manager may also underrate herself (rate herself too low) in comparison to the other raters. This suggests that the manager may lack confidence in her skills. The second step is for the manager to identify a skill or behavior to develop. Third, the manager needs to identify how she will determine her progress toward meeting her development goal. The final step in the process is to provide the manager with strategies for reaching her goal. This includes three components. First, the manager needs to identify specific actions she can take to reach her goal (e.g., job experiences, courses). Next, the manager needs to identify whom she will ask to provide feedback about her progress. Third, the manager needs to consider how she will find reinforcement for her progress. Recall from Chapter 5's discussion of transfer of training that it is often difficult to receive reinforcement for using trained skills in the workplace. Similarly, the manager needs to consider self-reinforcement for development progress. This reinforcement could involve buying herself a gift or rewarding herself with a night out on the town.

TABLE 9.7
Sample
Competency
and Items
from a 360-
Degree
Feedback
Instrument

Decision Making

Identifies the key decisions that have the greatest impact on business goals.
Understands and integrates conflicting or contradictory information.
Balances business sense with data and logic to make effective decisions.
Takes accountability for results of individual and team decisions.
Makes appropriate trade-offs between complete analysis and speed when making decisions.

TABLE 9.8
Development-Planning Activities from 360-Degree Feedback

1. **Understand strengths and weaknesses.**
   Review ratings for strengths and weaknesses.
   Identify skills or behaviors where self and others' (managers', peers', customers') ratings agree and disagree.

2. **Identify a development goal.**
   Choose a skill or behavior to develop.
   Set a clear, specific goal with a specified outcome.

3. **Identify a process for recognizing goal accomplishment.**

4. **Identify strategies for reaching the development goal.**
   Establish strategies such as reading, job experiences, courses, and relationships.
   Establish strategies for receiving feedback on progress.
   Establish strategies for receiving reinforcement for the new skill or behavior.

Benefits of 360-degree feedback include collecting multiple perspectives of managers' performance, allowing employees to compare their own personal evaluation with the views of others, and formalizing communications between employees and their internal and external customers. For example, a high-level executive now more freely airs his opinions in executive committee meetings based on the feedback he received from his subordinates as part of a 360-degree feedback system. Several studies have shown that performance improvement and behavior change occur as a result of participation in upward feedback and 360-degree feedback systems.[48] The most change occurs in individuals who receive lower ratings from others than they gave themselves (overraters).

Potential limitations of 360-degree feedback systems include the time demands placed on the raters to complete the evaluation, managers seeking to identify and punish raters who provided negative information, the need to have a facilitator to help interpret results, and companies' failure to provide ways that managers can act on the feedback they receive (e.g., development planning, meeting with raters, taking courses).

In developing (or hiring a consultant to develop) a 360-degree feedback system, several factors are necessary for the system to be effective. The system must provide reliable or consistent ratings; feedback must be job-related (valid); the system must be easy to use, understandable, and relevant; and the system must lead to managerial development. Important issues to consider include[49]

- Who will the raters be?
- How will you maintain confidentiality of the raters?
- What behaviors and skills are job-related?
- How will you ensure full participation and complete responses from every employee who is asked to be a rater?
- What will the feedback report include?
- How will you ensure that managers receive and act on the feedback?

Both Capital One and World Bank have developed effective 360-degree feedback systems.[50] Capital One, a consumer credit company, has included a number of features in its 360-degree feedback system to minimize the chance that the ratings will be used as a way to get back at an employee or be turned into a popularity contest. The 360-degree assessments are based on the company's competency model, so raters are asked for specific feedback on a competency area. Rather than a lengthy form that places a large burden on raters to assess many different competencies, Capital One's assessment asks the raters to concentrate on three or four strengths or development opportunities. It also seeks comments rather than limiting raters to merely circling numbers corresponding to how much of each competency the employee has demonstrated. These comments often provide specific information about what aspect of a competency needs to be developed or identifies work situations in which a competency needs to be improved. This comment system helps tailor development activities to fit competency development. To increase the chances that the assessment will result in change, the feedback from the 360-degree assessment is linked to development plans, and the company offers coaching and training to help employees strengthen their competencies. Employees are encouraged to share feedback with their co-workers. This creates a work environment based on honest and open feedback that helps employees personally grow. The World Bank's 360-degree feedback system offers anonymity to raters, but employees who are being assessed are responsible for nominating those who provide feedback. Similar to Capital One's approach, the World Bank system encourages written commentary along with ratings. Although the bank leaves it up to each employee to make use of the 360-degree feedback, it does link development opportunities directly to the items included in the assessment. The bank also helps facilitate the feedback of the assessment information, either in person or through video conferencing.

New technology has allowed 360-degree questionnaires to be delivered electronically to the raters via their personal computers or to be completed on a Web site. This increases the number of completed questionnaires, makes it easier to process the information, and speeds delivery of feedback reports to managers.

Regardless of the assessment method used, the information must be shared with the employee for development to occur. Along with the assessment information, the employee needs suggestions for correcting skill weaknesses and using skills already learned.[51] These suggestions might be to participate in training courses or develop skills through new job experiences. Based on the assessment information and available development opportunities, employees should develop an action plan to guide their self-improvement efforts.

Job Experiences

Most employee development occurs through job experiences.[52] **Job experiences** refer to relationships, problems, demands, tasks, or other features that employees face in their jobs. A major assumption of using job experiences for employee development is that development is most likely to occur when there is a mismatch between the employee's skills and past experiences and the skills required for the job. To be successful in their jobs, employees must stretch their skills—that is, they must be forced to learn new skills, apply their skills and knowledge in a new way, and master new experiences.[53] At Dave and Busters, which runs several large-volume restaurant-entertainment complexes across the United States, the company uses job experiences to strengthen employees' management competencies.[54] Employees are placed in departments in which they have to cope with real-life issues such as working with the kitchen staff or dealing with difficult customers.

Most of what is known about development through job experiences comes from a series of studies conducted by the Center for Creative Leadership in Greensboro, North Carolina.[55] Executives were asked to identify key events in their careers that made a difference in their managerial styles and the lessons they learned from these experiences. The key events included those involving the job assignment (e.g., fixing a failing operation), interpersonal relationships (e.g., getting along with supervisors), and making transitions (e.g., handling situations in which the executive did not have the necessary education or work background). Job demands and what employees can learn from them are shown in Table 9.9. One concern regarding the use of demanding job experiences for employee development is whether they are viewed as positive or negative stressors. Job experiences that are seen as positive stressors challenge employees to stimulate learning. Job challenges viewed as negative stressors create high levels of harmful stress for employees who are exposed to them. Research suggests

TABLE 9.9   **Job Demands and the Lessons Employees Learn from Them**

Making Transitions	*Unfamiliar responsibilities:* The manager must handle responsibilities that are new, very different, or much broader than previous ones. *Proving yourself:* The manager has added pressure to show others she can handle the job.
Creating Change	*Developing new directions:* The manager is responsible for starting something new in the organization, making strategic changes in the business, carrying out a reorganization, or responding to rapid changes in the business environment. *Inherited problems:* The manager has to fix problems created by his predecessor or take over problem employees. *Reduction decisions:* Decisions about shutting down operations or staff reductions have to be made. *Problems with employees:* Employees lack adequate experience, are incompetent, or are resistant.
Having High Level of Responsibility	*High stakes:* Clear deadlines, pressure from senior managers, high visibility, and responsibility for key decisions make success or failure in this job clearly evident. *Managing business diversity:* The scope of the job is large with responsibilities for multiple functions, groups, products, customers, or markets. *Job overload:* The sheer size of the job requires a large investment of time and energy. *Handling external pressure:* External factors that affect the business (e.g., negotiating with unions or government agencies; working in a foreign culture; coping with serious community problems) must be dealt with.
Being Involved in Nonauthority Relationships	*Influencing without authority:* Getting the job done requires influencing peers, higher management, external parties, or other key people over whom the manager has no direct authority.
Facing Obstacles	*Adverse business conditions:* The business unit or product line faces financial problems or difficult economic conditions. *Lack of top management support:* Senior management is reluctant to provide direction, support, or resources for current work or new projects. *Lack of personal support:* The manager is excluded from key networks and gets little support and encouragement from others. *Difficult boss:* The manager's opinion or management style differs from that of the boss, or the boss has major shortcomings.

Source: C. D. McCauley, L. J. Eastman, and J. Ohlott, "Linking Management Selection and Development through Stretch Assignments," *Human Resource Management* 84 (1995): 93–115. Copyright © 1995 John Wiley and Sons, Inc. Reprinted by permission of John Wiley and Sons, Inc.

that all job demands, with the exception of obstacles, are related to learning.[56] Managers reported that obstacles and job demands related to creating change were more likely to lead to negative stress than were other job demands. This suggests that companies should carefully weigh the potential negative consequences before placing employees in development assignments involving obstacles or creation of change.

Although research on development through job experiences has focused on executives and managers, line employees can also learn from job experiences. As was noted earlier, for a work team to be successful, its members now need the kinds of skills that only managers were once thought to need (e.g., dealing directly with customers, analyzing data to determine product quality, resolving conflict among team members). Besides the development that occurs when a team is formed, employees can further develop their skills by switching work roles within the team.

Figure 9.2 shows the various ways that job experiences can be used for employee development. These include enlarging the current job, job rotation, transfers, promotions, downward moves, and temporary assignments, projects, and volunteer work.

Enlarging the Current Job

Job enlargement refers to adding challenges or new responsibilities to an employee's current job. This could include special project assignments, switching roles within a work team, or researching new ways to serve clients and customers. For example, an engineering employee may be asked to join a task force charged with developing new career paths for technical employees. Through this project work, the engineer may be asked to take leadership for certain aspects of career path development (such as reviewing the company's career development process). As a result, the engineer has the opportunity not only to learn about the company's career development system but also to use leadership and organizational skills to help the task force reach its goals.

FIGURE 9.2

How Job Experiences Are Used for Employee Development

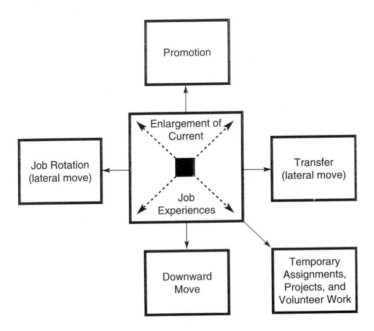

Some companies are allowing their employees to redesign their jobs. Rainforest Alliance is an international nonprofit organization with 265 employees that helps product makers employ sustainable land practices. Challenged by quick growth (it has doubled in size since 2003), Rainforest needed to identify and develop managerial staff.[57] The organization gives many junior employees the chance to lead research and other initiatives and, if they are successful, promotes them to manage the initiatives. For example, one employee, who is now the coordinator of a new climate initiative, started with the company as an administrative assistant but was asked to take on more responsibilities, including researching climate change. Junior employees also can take part in internship programs in foreign offices to learn more about the organization and work on the "front lines" implementing sustainable land practices.

A new practice is to give two managers the same responsibilities and job title and allow them to divide the work (two-in-a-box).[58] This helps managers learn from a more experienced employee, helps companies fill jobs that require multiple skills, and, for positions requiring extensive travel, ensures that one employee is always on-site to deal with work-related issues. For example, at Cisco Systems, the head of Cisco's routing group, who was trained as an engineer but now works in business development, shares a job with an engineer. Both employees are exposed to each other's skills, which has helped them both perform their jobs better.

Job Rotation

Job rotation involves providing employees with a series of job assignments in various functional areas of the company or movement among jobs in a single functional area or department. Regions Financial has job rotation programs in information technology and regional banking.[59] The two full-time positions in the information technology program involve a 12- to 18-month job rotation within the six information technology departments to work on special projects. Employees participating in the company's Retail Leadership Development Program work as tellers, financial service representatives, and branch sales managers to complement instructor-led and computer-based training that focuses on developing service, sales, branch operations, and leadership skills. India-based Tata Consultancy Services's job rotation program sends native employees to operations in China, Hungary, and South America.[60] The program helps the company develop skilled employees who are prepared to work in any of the company's offices in 42 countries, while employees gain an understanding of the culture of the country in which they work. The program also helps improve customer service because the company can draw on the strength of its entire work force, rather than just relying on employees who are located close to the customer. The assignments typically last 18 to 24 months and involve learning from both the customers and the local employees based at the location. After their assignment is complete, employees usually work on the same kinds of projects they worked on in their overseas assignment, which helps to transfer the knowledge gained to the employees' home operations.

Job rotation helps employees gain an overall appreciation of the company's goals, increases their understanding of different company functions, develops a network of contacts, and improves their problem-solving and decision-making skills.[61] Job rotation has also been shown to be related to skill acquisition, salary growth, and promotion rates. However, there are several potential problems with job rotation from both the employee's and the work unit's point of view. The rotation may create a short-term perspective of problems and solutions in the employees being rotated and their peers. Employees' satisfaction and motivation may be adversely affected because they may find it difficult to develop functional specialties and because they may not spend enough time in one position to receive a challenging assignment. Productivity losses and work load increases may be experienced by both the department gaining a rotating employee and the department losing the employee due to training demands and the loss of a resource.

Top-level managers may rotate jobs to acquire the experiences they need to prepare for the top management job in the company—chief executive officer. For example, two top Citigroup managers—the chief financial officer and head of strategy, and the chairman and chief executive of SmithBarney, Citigroup's stock research and brokerage group—swapped jobs so that both could get the experiences they needed to become top leaders in the company.[62] One manager needed financial experience and the other needed operations experience. Promotion of a chief financial officer to the company's top job requires experience in running a business unit.

Table 9.10 shows characteristics of effective job rotation systems. Effective job rotation systems are linked to the company's training, development, and career management systems. Also, job rotation is used for all types of employees, not just those with managerial potential.

Transfers, Promotions, and Downward Moves

Upward, lateral, and downward mobility is available for development purposes in most companies.[63] In a **transfer,** an employee is given a different job assignment in a different area of the company. Transfers do not necessarily involve increased job responsibilities or compensation. They are likely lateral moves (a move to a job with similar responsibilities). **Promotions** are advancements into positions with greater challenges, more responsibility, and more authority than in the previous job. Promotions usually include pay increases.

Transfers may involve relocation within the United States or to another country, which can be stressful for a number of reasons. The employee's work role changes. If the employee has a family, they have to join a new community. Employed spouses may have to find new employment. Transfers disrupt employees' daily lives, interpersonal relationships, and work habits.[64] Employees have to find new housing as well as new shopping, health care, and leisure facilities, and they may be many miles from the emotional support

**TABLE 9.10
Characteristics of Effective Job Rotation Systems**

Source: Based on L. Cheraskin and M. Campion, "Study Clarifies Job Rotation Benefits," *Personnel Journal* (November 1996): 31–38; M. Fiester, A. Collis, and N. Cossack, "Job Rotation, Total Rewards, Measuring Value," *HR Magazine* (August 2008): 33–34.

1. Job rotation is used to develop skills as well as give employees experience needed for managerial positions.
2. Employees understand specific skills that will be developed by rotation.
3. Job rotation is used for all levels and types of employees.
4. Job rotation is linked with the career management process so employees know the development needs addressed by each job assignment.
5. Benefits of rotation are maximized and costs are minimized through timing the rotations to reduce work load costs and help employees understand the job rotation's role in their development plans.
6. All employees have equal opportunities for job rotation assignments, regardless of their demographic group.

of friends and family. They have to learn a new set of work norms and procedures as well as develop interpersonal relationships with their new managers and peers, and they are expected to be as productive in their new jobs as they were in their old jobs even though they may know very little about the products, services, processes, or employees for whom they are responsible.

Because transfers can be anxiety provoking, many companies have difficulty getting employees to accept them. Research has identified the employee characteristics associated with a willingness to accept transfers:[65] high career ambitions, a belief that one's future with the company is promising, and a belief that accepting a transfer is necessary for success in the company. Employees who are not married and not active in the community are most willing to accept transfers. Among married employees, the spouse's willingness to move is the most important influence on whether an employee will accept a transfer.

A **downward move** occurs when an employee is given a reduced level of responsibility and authority.[66] This may involve a move to another position at the same level but with less authority and responsibility (lateral demotion), a temporary cross-functional move, or a demotion because of poor performance. Temporary cross-functional moves to lower-level positions, which give employees experience working in different functional areas, are most frequently used for employee development. For example, engineers who want to move into management often take lower-level positions (e.g., shift supervisor) to develop their management skills.

Because of the psychological and tangible rewards of promotions (e.g., an increased feeling of self-worth, high salary, and higher status in the company), employees are more willing to accept promotions than they are to accept lateral or downward moves. Promotions are most readily available when a company is profitable and growing. When a company is restructuring and/or experiencing stable or declining profits, promotion opportunities may be limited, especially if a large number of employees are interested in promotions and if the company tends to rely on the external labor market to staff higher-level positions.[67]

Unfortunately, many employees have difficulty associating transfers and downward moves with development. They see them as punishments rather than as opportunities to develop skills that will help them achieve long-term success with the company. Many employees decide to leave a company rather than accept a transfer. Companies need to successfully manage transfers not only because of the costs of replacing employees but because of the costs directly associated with managing them. For example, GTE spends approximately $60 million a year on home purchases and other relocation costs such as temporary housing and relocation allowances.[68] One challenge companies face is learning how to use transfers and downward moves as development opportunities—convincing employees that accepting these opportunities will result in long-term benefits for them.

To ensure that employees accept transfers, promotions, and downward moves as development opportunities, companies can provide[69]

- Information about the content, challenges, and potential benefits of the new job and location.

- Involvement in the transfer decision by sending the employees to preview the new locations and giving them information about the community and other employment opportunities.

- Clear performance objectives and early feedback about their job performance.

- A host at the new location who will help them adjust to the new community and workplace.
- Information about how the job opportunity will affect their income, taxes, mortgage payments, and other expenses.
- Reimbursement and assistance in selling, purchasing, and/or renting a place to live.
- An orientation program for the new location and job.
- A guarantee that the new job experiences will support employees' career plans.
- Assistance for dependent family members, including helping to identify schools as well as child and elder care options.
- Help for spouses in identifying and marketing their skills and finding employment.

Externships allow employees to take full-time, temporary operational roles at another company. Mercer Management, a consulting firm, uses its externship program to develop employees who have an interest in gaining experience in a specific industry.[70] Mercer Management promises to re-employ the externs after their assignments end. For example, one employee who has been a consultant for Mercer for five years is now vice president of Internet services for Binney and Smith, the maker of Crayola crayons. A year ago he was working on an Internet consulting project for Binney and Smith, but he wanted to actually implement his recommendations rather than just provide them to the client and move on to another project. As a result he started working at Binney and Smith. He remains on Mercer Management's payroll, though his salary comes from Binney and Smith. Mercer believes that employees who participate in the externship program will remain committed to the company because they have had the opportunity to learn and grow professionally and have not had to disrupt their personal and professional lives with a job search. Although externships provide employees with new employment options and although some employees leave, Mercer believes that the program is not only a good development strategy but also helps in recruitment. The externship program signals to potential employees that Mercer is creative and flexible with its employees.

Temporary Assignments, Projects, and Volunteer Work

Employee exchange is one example of temporary assignments in which two companies agree to exchange employees. Procter & Gamble (P&G) and Google have began to swap employees.[71] Employees from the two companies participate in each other's training programs and attend meetings in which business plans are discussed. Both companies hope to benefit from the employee swap. Procter & Gamble is trying to increase its understanding of how to market laundry detergent, toilet paper, and skin cream products to a new generation of consumers who spend more time online than watching television. Google wants to gain more ad revenue by persuading companies to shift from showcasing their brands on television to using video-sharing sites such as YouTube. The idea of the employee swap occurred when Procter & Gamble recognized that a switch to a smaller Tide laundry soap bottle with a more concentrated formula didn't include an online campaign where buyers could find answers as to why the bottle decreased in size. Employees of both companies have benefited from the swap. Google employees have learned that Tide's bright orange packaging is a critical part of the brand and have adopted P&G's marketing language. P&G employees have recognized that online ad campaigns can increase brand awareness even for products such as diapers that are not purchased online. P&G has invited mommy-bloggers to visit its baby division to better understand how its diapers can meet their needs.

Volunteer assignments can also be used for development. As part of its leadership development, PNC Financial Services Group has a volunteerism program that includes partnerships with over 200 nonprofit organizations.[72] Employees can choose assignments to improve their skills or projects unrelated to their jobs. An associate marketing analyst at Target led a volunteer effort assembling safety kits for the American Red Cross and the Salvation Army involving 350 PNC employees at the company's headquarters in Minneapolis. As a result, she got to work with the company's vice presidents and several other managers she would not have otherwise had the chance to meet.

At General Mills, volunteer assignments and involvement with community projects is one of the ways the company lives up to its corporate values.[73] Employees work in a wide variety of charities, with duties ranging from serving meals to the homeless, to painting child-care center rooms, to serving as corporate board members. Besides providing valuable services to community organizations, General Mills believes volunteer assignments help employees improve team relationships and develop leadership and strategic thinking skills. Volunteer assignments may offer employees opportunities to manage change, to teach, to take on a higher level of responsibility, or to be exposed to other job demands, such as those shown in Table 9.9.

Interpersonal Relationships

Employees can also develop skills and increase their knowledge about the company and its customers by interacting with a more experienced organizational member. Mentoring and coaching are two types of interpersonal relationships used to develop employees.

Mentoring

A **mentor** is an experienced, productive senior employee who helps develop a less experienced employee (the protégé). Most mentoring relationships develop informally as a result of interests or values shared by mentor and protégé. Research suggests that employees with certain personality characteristics (e.g., high needs for power and achievement, emotional stability, ability to adapt their behavior based on the situation) are more likely to seek a mentor and be an attractive protégé for a mentor.[74]

Mentoring relationships can also develop as part of a planned company effort to bring together successful senior employees with less experienced employees (a formal mentoring program).

KLA-Tencor, a supplier of process control solutions for the semiconductor industry, uses mentoring to improve senior managers' skills.[75] The senior managers receive mentoring from company board members as well as retired company executives. The senior managers are expected to increase their functional expertise, identify specific performance goals and developmental activities to address job-related weaknesses, and increase their understanding of the company's culture, vision, and political structure. KLA-Tencor also has an online mentoring program for managers identified as having high potential for upper-level positions. The program includes an automated relationship pairing function and a 360-degree assessment that is used in the mentoring relationship to improve skill weaknesses.

Developing Successful Mentoring Programs   Although many mentoring relationships develop informally, one major advantage of formalized mentoring programs is that they ensure access to mentors for all employees, regardless of gender or race. An additional advantage is that participants in the mentoring relationship tend to know what is expected of them.[76] One limitation of formal mentoring programs is that mentors may not be able to provide counseling and coaching in a relationship that has been artificially created.[77] To overcome this limitation, it is important that mentors and protégés spend time discussing their work styles, personalities, and backgrounds, which helps to build the trust that is needed for both parties to be comfortable with their relationship.[78]

Table 9.11 presents characteristics of a successful formal mentoring program. A key to successful mentoring programs is that the mentor and protégé actually interact with each other face to face or virtually. Companies are using Web-conferencing and video teleconferencing solutions to bring together mentors who are geographically separate, as well as collaboration software so mentors and protégés can meet and review assignments.[79] Software is also available to track mentors and protégés' work, help build development plans, and schedule mentor and protégé meetings. For example, at SAIC, a company specializing in technology solutions, a Web-based tool is used to provide online forms, make calendar appointments, set goals for mentoring relationships, and outline an action plan to ensure that protégé needs are discussed.

Web-based matching systems also are available to help match mentors and protégés. For example, both Dow Chemical and Intel have a Web system that allows protégés to input the

TABLE 9.11 **Characteristics of Successful Formal Mentoring Programs**	1. Mentor and protégé participation is voluntary. Relationship can be ended at any time without fear of punishment. 2. Mentor-protégé matching process does not limit the ability of informal relationships to develop. For example, a mentor pool can be established to allow protégés to choose from a variety of qualified mentors. 3. Mentors are chosen on the basis of their past record in developing employees, their willingness to serve as a mentor, and evidence of positive coaching, communication, and listening skills. 4. Mentor-protégé matching is based on how the mentor's skills can help meet the protégé's needs. 5. The purpose of the program is clearly understood. Projects and activities that the mentor and protégé are expected to complete are specified. 6. The length of the program is specified. Mentor and protégé are encouraged to pursue the relationship beyond the formal time period. 7. A minimum level of contact between the mentor and protégé is specified. Mentors and protégés need to determine the mechanics of the relationship: when they will meet, how often, and how they will communicate outside of the meetings. 8. Protégés are encouraged to contact one another to discuss problems and share successes. 9. The mentor program is evaluated. Interviews with mentors and protégés are used to obtain immediate feedback regarding specific areas of dissatisfaction. Surveys are used to gather more detailed information regarding benefits received from participating in the program. 10. Employee development is rewarded, which signals managers that mentoring and other development activities are worth their time and effort.

qualities they want in a mentor. Similar to the results of a Google search, the list of names they are given presents the closest match to their qualities at the top.[80] Wyndham's hotel chain has found that a Web-based matching system tripled the number of employees participating in mentoring. After Wyndham generates a list of mentor names, protégés have seven days to select the mentor who they believe is the best fit and to contact the mentor to arrange a meeting to decide if it is a good match. The mentor and protégé then sign a contract committing to meeting a certain amount of time each month. The system sends reminders of planned meetings to both the mentor and the protégé.

Professional services firm Ernst & Young has mentoring programs that pair high-potential employees with executive mentors (Executive Mentoring Program) and minority employees with senior leaders (Learning Partnerships). Mentors are not forced to serve; they volunteer their time. The programs require mentors and protégés to meet in person four times a year, once to set goals, once for a six-month review, once at a year-end evaluation session, and one other time.[81] Any topics can be discussed in these confidential conversations, including career goals, work-life balance, performance issues, and problems with managers. The mentors also introduce their protégés to senior managers whom they otherwise would not meet. Protégés grade their mentors using the company's performance appraisal system. The company has adjusted salaries and denied promotions to managers who were poor mentors.

Mentors should be chosen based on interpersonal and technical skills, and they need to be trained.[82] For example, New York Hospital–Cornell Medical Center developed a mentoring program for housekeeping employees. Each mentor has 5 to 10 protégés who meet on a quarterly basis. To qualify as mentors, employees must receive outstanding performance evaluations, demonstrate strong interpersonal skills, and be able to perform basic cleaning tasks and essential duties of all housekeeping positions including safety procedures (such as handling infectious waste). Mentors undergo a two-day training program that emphasizes communication skills. They are taught how to convey information about the job and give directions effectively without criticizing employees.[83]

Fannie Mae provides financial products and services that make it possible for families to purchase homes. At Fannie Mae, the company's mentoring program is designed to encourage the advancement of high-potential employees, especially women and minorities.[84] To ensure that the mentor and protégé are compatible, a pairing committee conducts detailed screening and matching based on the mentor's and protégé's interests and expectations (e.g., What skills, experiences, and knowledge would you like your mentor to possess?). Fannie Mae provides guidelines to both mentors and protégés that identify what is expected of the relationship. Orientation sessions help the mentor and protégé become acquainted with each other. Both mentor and protégé sign a confidentiality agreement to build trust between the parties. To help ensure the success of the mentoring program, Fannie Mae uses surveys to conduct formal and informal evaluations that help the company understand the strengths and weaknesses of the program.

Benefits of Mentoring Relationships Both mentors and protégés can benefit from a mentoring relationship. Research suggests that mentors provide career and psychosocial support to their protégés. **Career support** includes coaching, protection, sponsorship, and providing challenging assignments, exposure, and visibility. **Psychosocial support** includes serving as a friend and a role model, providing positive regard and acceptance, and providing an outlet for the protégé to talk about anxieties and fears. Additional benefits for protégés include skill development, higher rates of promotion, larger salaries, and greater organizational influence.[85]

Mentoring relationships provide opportunities for mentors to develop their interpersonal skills and increase their feelings of self-esteem and worth to the organization. Adobe Systems, located in San Jose, California, provides digital imaging, design, and document technology for consumers and businesses (you may have read a document using Adobe's PDF file format). For example, Melissa Dyrdahl, a manager at Adobe Systems, and Bruce Chizen, a senior vice president at Adobe, have multiple mentors that they benefit from.[86] Chizen considers the founders of Adobe as mentors. The founders have taught him how to preserve the company's culture by hiring people smarter than he is. The founders' technical creativity has inspired him to offer new ideas to engineers at the company. He knows that the founders care about him personally but are honest in their opinions. Dyrdahl considers one of the Abode board members a mentor. She asked the mentor for career advice and exposure to new ideas without changing jobs. Her mentor encouraged her to pursue a seat on a public company board of directors, especially a company needing her marketing skills. Another of Dyrdahl's mentors, who works for a marketing agency, has encouraged her to advance her career by highlighting her accomplishments to others.

For mentors in management positions as well as technical fields such as engineering and health services, the protégé may help them gain knowledge about important new scientific developments in their field and therefore prevent them from becoming technically obsolete. For example, General Electric launched an initiative in e-business. However, many veteran managers faced the challenge of trying to understand how to effectively use the Internet. John Welch, then CEO of General Electric, created a mentoring program for his top 600 managers in which younger employees who were experienced with the Internet served as mentors for the top managers.[87] Welch generated interest in the program by getting his own mentor, who was approximately half his age and had much less business experience than he does. However, she was a Web expert who ran the company's Web site! The purpose of the program was to help managers become familiar with competitors' Web sites, to experience the difficulty of ordering products online, and to understand what the best Web sites were doing well. Welch started the program believing that e-business knowledge is generally inversely related to age and position in the company hierarchy—younger employees at the lower levels of the organization are more Web-savvy. GE managers meet with their younger mentors for Web lessons, where they critique Web sites, discuss assigned articles and books about e-commerce, and ask questions. The sessions benefit both the mentors and the protégés. The protégés learn about the Web, and the mentoring sessions make the younger employees feel more comfortable talking to their bosses while learning about the skills that a manager needs to run a large business operation (e.g., ability to communicate with different people).

Purposes of Mentoring Programs One estimate is that about 20 percent of companies have a formal mentoring program.[88] The purpose of these programs varies. Mentoring programs are used to socialize new employees and to increase the likelihood of skill transfer from training to the work setting. Mentoring programs may also be developed specifically for women and minorities to enable them to gain the experience and skills needed for managerial positions. Mentoring is part of Deloitte and Touche's Women's Initiative Program, designed to help women successfully deal with the barriers they may face in advancing to senior level management positions.[89] Research also shows that the promotion rate of women who have had a mentor is greater than for women who have not had a mentor.[90] Mentoring programs can be used to develop managers for top-level management positions or to help them acquire specific skills. Consider the New York Hospital–Cornell Medical Center mentoring program just discussed. The program is designed to help new employees more quickly learn housekeeping duties and understand the culture of the hospital. One benefit of the program is that new employees' performance deficiencies are more quickly corrected. Although formal mentoring of new employees lasts only two weeks, mentors are available to provide support many months later.

Mentoring can also occur between mentors and protégés from different organizations and allow small business owners access to experienced mentors they might not otherwise meet.[91] Web sites such as MicroMentor are available to help small business owners find online mentors. For example, Sturdy McKee wanted to expand his physical therapy practice but needed help understanding financial statements in order to plan the growth of his business and seek outside funding. Using MicroMentor, he completed a personal profile, listed his goals, and searched potential mentor profiles. Sturdy and his mentor had weekly phone conversations discussing the basics of balance sheets and financial vocabulary. As a result of his positive experience, Sturdy has mentored other entrepreneurs seeking help on how to start their own physical therapy practices.

Group mentoring programs have been initiated by some companies that lack potential mentors or a formal reward system supporting mentoring or that believe that the quality of mentorships developed in a formal program is poorer than informal mentoring relationships. Group mentoring acknowledges the reality that it is difficult for one mentor to provide an employee with all the guidance and support he needs. Group mentoring provides a development network for employees: a small group that an employee can use for mentoring support that also has an interest in the employee's learning and development. In **group mentoring programs,** a successful senior employee is paired with four to six less experienced protégés. One potential advantage of the mentoring group is that protégés can learn from each other as well as from a more experienced senior employee. The leader helps protégés understand the organization, guides them in analyzing their experiences, and helps them clarify career directions. Each member of the group may have specific assignments to complete, or the group may work together on an issue.[92]

Coaching Relationships

A **coach** is a peer or manager who works with employees to motivate them, help them develop skills, and provide reinforcement and feedback. There are three roles that a coach can play.[93] Part of coaching may be one-on-one with an employee, providing feedback based on psychological tests, 360-degree assessment, or interviews with bosses, peers, and subordinates. A second role is to help employees learn for themselves by putting them in touch with experts who can help them with their concerns and by teaching them how to obtain feedback from others. Third, the coach may provide the employee with resources such as mentors, courses, or job experiences that the employee may not otherwise have access to. For example, at National Semiconductor, managers participate in a 360-degree feedback program. Each manager selects another manager as a coach. They both attend a coaching workshop that focuses on skills such as active listening. The workshop presents a coaching process that includes creating a contract outlining members' roles and expectations, discussing 360-degree feedback, and identifying specific improvement goals and a plan for achieving them. After each pair works alone for six to eight months, they evaluate their progress.

Becton Dickinson, the medical technology company, uses peer coaching as part of its leadership development programs.[94] The topics discussed include job challenges as a development method, ambiguity as a change agent, and how to influence others. Evaluation of the peer coaching has found that the coaches gain confidence in their abilities and the participants learn about the topics discussed.

Research has provided some insight into coaching relationships.[95] Coaching typically occurs during a 7- to 12-month period. The main reasons why coaches are used include: to develop high-potential managers, to act as a sounding board for managers, or to specifically try to change behaviors that are making managers ineffective. The most important factors in a successful coaching relationship include a good manager-coach, relationship, a high motivation (on the manager's part) to change, and the existence of a strong commitment by top company management to develop the manager. The most important qualifications to look for when hiring a coach are experience, the use of a clearly defined coaching method (such in-depth psychological interviews or use of 360-degree feedback), and the quality of the coach's client list.

The best coaches are empathetic, supportive, practical, and self-confident but do not appear to know all the answers or want to tell others what to do.[96] Employees who are going to be coached need to be open-minded and interested, not defensive, close-minded, or concerned with their reputation. Both coaches and employees to be coached take risks in the relationship. Coaches are offering their expertise and experience to help an employee. Employees are vulnerable because they must speak honestly about their weaknesses. Coaches need to be able to suggest effective improvement actions and must respect employee confidentiality. If assessment instruments are part of the coaching process, the coach must be familiar with them.

Some companies are using coaching specifically to help groom current and future executives.[97] Wachovia Corporation, a financial services company, has an executive coaching program that uses both internal and external coaches.[98] Participants in the executive leadership development program receive 360-degree assessments that they take to their internal coaches, who are from a different division in the company. Together the manager and coach review the assessment results and agree on an action plan. The coaches are trained in how to coach and in understanding the positive and negative aspects of 360-degree feedback. Wachovia hires external coaches for top executives who have been identified as high-potential leaders who are facing a specific job challenge or problem, such as moving into a new position after a merger. The coaching lasts nine months to a year and includes 360-degree assessments, interviews, and psychological tests. Research suggests that coaching improves managers' use of 360-degree feedback by helping them set specific improvement goals and solicit ideas for improvement, which results in improved performance.[99]

Training programs that develop coaching skills need to focus on four issues related to managers' reluctance to provide coaching.[100] First, managers may be reluctant to discuss performance issues even with a competent employee because they want to avoid confrontation—especially if the manager is less of an expert than the employee. Second, managers may be better able to identify performance problems than to help employees solve them. Third, managers may feel that the employee might interpret coaching as criticism. Fourth, as companies downsize and operate with fewer employees, managers may feel that there is not enough time for coaching. For example, a middle manager at PG&E, an energy company, was hurting her relationships with her associates, and her career, due to her brash personality.[101] PG&E hired a coach to work with her. The coach videotaped her as she role-played an actual clash that she had had with another manager over a new information system. During the confrontation (and the role play), she was aloof, abrasive, cold, and condescending. The coach helped her see the limitations of her approach. She apologized to the colleague and listened to the colleague's ideas. Coaching helped this manager learn how to maintain her composure and focus on what is being said rather than on the person.

THE DEVELOPMENT PLANNING PROCESS

The **development planning process** involves identifying development needs, choosing a development goal, identifying the actions that need to be taken by the employee and the company to achieve the goal, determining how progress toward goal attainment will be measured, investing time and energy to achieve the goal, and establishing a timetable for development.[102] Table 9.12 shows the development planning process, identifying responsibilities of the employee and the company. An emerging trend in development is that the employee must initiate the development planning process.[103] Note that the development approach is dependent on the needs and developmental goal. To identify development needs, employees must consider what they want to do, what they are interested in doing, what they can do, and what others expect of them. A development need can result from gaps between current capabilities and/or interests and the type of work or position that the employee wants in the future. Some ways that employees can identify opportunities for development include looking at the strengths and weaknesses listed on their most recent performance appraisal and looking at their progress on skills needed to achieve personal goals or their mastery of competencies that the company may have identified.[104] Also, asking peers and friends and using 360-degree feedback data can be useful for identifying development opportunities.

TABLE 9.12   **Responsibilities in the Development Planning Process**

Development Planning Process	Employee Responsibility	Company Responsibility
Opportunity	How do I need to improve?	Company provides assessment information to identify employee's strengths, weaknesses, interests, and values.
Motivation	Am I willing to invest the time and energy to develop?	Company assists employee in identifying personal and company reasons for change. Manager discusses steps for dealing with barriers and challenges to development.
Goal Identification	What do I want to develop?	Company provides development planning guide. Manager has developmental discussion with employee.
Criteria	How will I know I am making progress?	Manager provides feedback on criteria.
Actions	What will I do to reach my development goal?	Company provides assessment, courses, job experiences, and relationships.
Accountability	What is my timetable? How can I ask others for feedback on progress toward my goal?	Manager follows up on progress toward development goal and helps employee set a realistic timetable for goal achievement.

The company responsibility is primarily taken by the employee's manager. The role of the manager in development planning is to provide coaching, communicate information about development opportunities (e.g., job experiences, courses), help eliminate barriers to development, and refer the employee to other people (human resources) and resources (assessment tools). Managers must also help employees set realistic development goals, establish checkpoints for evaluating progress toward meeting those goals, and ensure that the time requirements for completing the plan are realistic given the employee's job demands.

How might the development planning process work? Take the example of Robert Brown, a program manager in an information systems department. He needs to increase his knowledge of available project management software. His performance appraisal indicates that only 60 percent of the projects he is working on are being approved due to incomplete information. (Assessment has identified his development need.) As a result, Robert and his manager agree that his development goal is to increase his knowledge of available project management software. This software can increase his effectiveness in project management. To boost his knowledge of such software, Robert will read articles (formal education), meet with software vendors, and contact vendors' customers for their evaluations of the project management software they have used (job experiences). His manager will provide the names of customers to contact. Robert and his manager set six months as the target date for completing these activities.

COMPANY STRATEGIES FOR PROVIDING DEVELOPMENT

There are several company strategies for providing development. One strategy is to provide development only for top-level executives, senior managers, and employees identified as having high potential. Lower-level managers who play a critical role in motivating and retaining employees are neglected. Another strategy is to require all employees to devote a specific number of hours or spend a certain amount of money on development. While this approach guarantees that employees will partake in development, it tends to emphasize formal courses as the only viable development method. This is counter to adult learning theory (see Chapter 4), which emphasizes that adults want to interact in the learning process and are more motivated to learn when they get to choose the learning topics and the delivery method (e.g., classroom, mentoring, job experiences).

The most effective development strategies involve individualization, learner control, and ongoing support.[105] Individualization makes sure that development efforts are directed at capitalizing on the employee's strengths and improving weaknesses. Personality and interest inventories as well as 360-degree feedback provide information about an employee's interests, values, strengths, and weaknesses. Instead of requiring employees to attend courses or workshops, companies should offer a menu of development options. These might include courses offered in the classroom or on the Web, mentoring, discussion groups, support networks, and job experiences.

Sprint's individual development plans are based on five core competencies: act with integrity, focus on the customer, deliver results, build relationships, and develop leadership.[106] These competencies are used by each business unit to establish its strategy as well as by each manager and employee in creating development plans. The competencies are the foundation for development conversations between managers and employees. Resources are available to support the development plan, including a development activities guide that includes audiotapes, books, and specific courses designed to improve each of the competencies and a Web site at which employees can learn about the process. General Mills's development plan follows the development planning process shown in Table 9.12. Each employee completes a development plan that asks employees to consider four areas:

1. *Professional goals and motivation:* What professional goals do I have? What excites me to grow professionally?
2. *Talents and strengths:* What are my talents and strengths?
3. *Development opportunities:* What development needs are important for me to improve?
4. *Development objectives and action steps:* What will be my objective for this plan? What steps can I take to meet the objective?

Managers and employees are encouraged to discuss the development plan at least once a year. Speakers, online tools, and workshops—which serve to help employees complete the development plan and prepare for development discussions with their managers—increase the visibility of and emphasize the importance of the development planning process.

Booz Allen Hamilton, a strategy and technology consulting company headquartered in McLean, Virginia, uses a program it calls the Development Framework to help managers and employees choose the right combination of development activities to strengthen competencies.[107] The Development Framework consists of four sections:

1. *Development roles:* Managers, mentors, development staff, and other roles in the development process.
2. *Performance expectations:* A description of competencies, performance results, and major job experiences required to succeed at each level of the company.
3. *Development needs:* Needs that frequently occur at each career level, those that vary by individual, and the derailers that can stall career progress and negatively affect performance. Ways to prevent or deal with derailers are provided.
4. *Development road map:* Descriptions of development activities that should occur at each career level and that support development needs and prevent derailers. These activities include job experiences, training and education, coaching and mentoring, and self-directed experiences.

Employees can access the Development Framework online via the company's virtual campus and Web site. Managers can use the tool to discuss development needs in their departments. The framework includes the competencies for each staff level and for each employee, which allows employees to view their personal development needs online. By identifying the competencies that employees want to strengthen, the framework provides a list of activities employees can use to develop those competencies. Employees can use the Development Framework to take charge of their own careers. The framework helps employees answer questions such as, "I'm at this level and this person is above me; how can I get there?"

The framework was provided by Booz Allen Hamilton to help employees better understand how to develop themselves. Booz Allen views development as a shared responsibility between employees and the company. The framework helps employees realize that development can occur through activities other than training classes. The framework makes a strong business case for employee development by aligning development to the business strategy and to different levels of the company; as such, the program provides a process for simultaneously building the company's intellectual capital and helping employees build successful careers. The framework also provides a map for preparing potential leaders, which is important because the company is growing 20 percent per year. The framework also provides a map for preparing new leaders. Leadership development takes a blended approach that includes formal courses and small-group activities such as leadership and mentoring. Leaders can also develop their skills through community activities, such as board memberships, that are tied to the company's leadership competencies.

E-Learning and Employee Development

With the development of e-learning, many companies are moving development activities online. Consider IBM's programs for new and experienced managers.[108] IBM's Basic Blue for Managers program replaces a widely successful New Manager School. The yearlong program includes a combination of online self-study, simulations, competency assessment, coaching, and classroom experience. The program helps managers understand their responsibilities in managing performance, employee relations, diversity, and multicultural issues. It moves the learning of all basic management skills to the Web, using classroom experiences for more complex management issues. It also gives managers and their bosses greater responsibility for development, while the company provides support in the form of unlimited access to development activities and support networks. The learning model includes four levels:

1. *Management Quick Views:* Management Quick Views provide practical information on more than 40 common management topics related to business, leadership/management competencies, productivity, and HR issues.
2. *Interactive Learning Modules and Simulations:* These interactive simulations emphasize people and task management. Employees learn by viewing videos; interacting with models and problem employees; making decisions on how to deal with the problem, issue, or request; and getting feedback on their decision. Case studies are also available for review.
3. *Collaborative Learning:* The learner can connect via the company intranet with tutors, team members, customers, or other learners to discuss problems, issues, and approaches and to share what has been learned.
4. *Learning Labs:* These five-day in-class workshops build on the learning acquired during the previous phases of e-learning. The workshops emphasize peer learning and the development of a learning community. Through challenging activities and assignments, managers gain increased self-awareness of themselves, their work teams, and IBM.

Management Quick Views, Interactive Learning Modules and Simulations, and Collaborative Learning are delivered by technology. Learning Labs is a face-to-face classroom experience. The Basic Blue for Managers program recognizes the role of the boss as coach, supporter, and role model. The boss is involved in the program through coaching and feedback, on-the-job learning experiences, assessment of the manager's development needs and progress, and assistance in completing individual development plans.

The Role of the Manager@IBM is a program that targets all managers at IBM using face-to-face instruction and technology. The program is an expert system that provides a customized learning portfolio for each manager based on his or her background, training, and management style. The expert system also helps guide managers through pre-work that has to be completed prior to attending Learning Labs. Learning is reinforced through use of a knowledge management system. The system allows managers to share ideas and post suggestions to senior management.

IBM believes that utilization of e-learning and the classroom environment enables managers to participate in self-directed learning, try out skills in a "safe" environment, gain access to communities of learning, and use just-in-time learning. The advantages of e-learning are complemented by the strengths of an interactive classroom experience and support from the manager's boss to create the best development program possible.

Evaluations of both programs have been positive. Participants in the Basic Blue for Managers program report satisfaction with program content and delivery. Nearly all the participants have achieved mastery in the 15 subject areas included in the program. Program alumni report that business value related to leadership skill improvement averages $450,000 per employee. Managers who have been through the Role of the Manager@IBM program have been ranked as better leaders than managers yet to complete the program. Action plans developed by program participants have generated revenues of $184 million.

Summary

This chapter emphasized that there are several development methods: formal education, assessment, job experiences, and interpersonal relationships. Most companies use one or more of these approaches to develop employees. Formal education involves enrolling employees in courses or seminars offered by the company or educational institutions. Assessment involves measuring the employees' performance, behavior, skills, and/or personality characteristics. Job experiences include job enlargement, rotating to a new job, promotions, downward moves, temporary assignments, and transfers. A more experienced senior employee (a mentor) can help employees understand the company and gain exposure and visibility to key persons in the organization. Part of a manager's job responsibility may be to coach employees. Regardless of the development approach used, employees need a development plan to identify the type of development needed, development goals, the best approach for development, and a means to determine whether development goals have been reached. For development plans to be effective, the employee, the company, and the manager all have responsibilities that need to be completed. An effective development strategy involves individualization, learner control, and support. Development programs based on e-learning can provide these features.

Key Terms

Discussion Questions

1. What role does assessment have in employee development? Can assessment alone be effective for development? Why or why not?

2. How can competencies be used in employee development?

3. List and explain the characteristics of effective 360-degree feedback systems.

4. Why do companies develop formal mentoring programs? What are the potential benefits for the mentor and for the protégé? What is the best way to match mentors and protégés?

5. Your boss is interested in hiring a consultant to help identify potential managers from current employees of a fast-food restaurant. The manager's job is to help wait on customers and prepare food during busy times, oversee all aspects of restaurant operations (including scheduling, maintenance, on-the-job training, and food purchase), and motivate employees to provide high-quality service. The manager is also responsible for resolving disputes between employees. The position involves working under stress and coordinating several activities at one time. Your boss asks you to outline the type of assessment program you believe would best identify employees who could be successful managers. What will you tell your boss?

6. Many employees are unwilling to relocate geographically because they like their current community and because spouses and children prefer not to move. As a result, it is difficult to develop employees through job experiences that require relocation (e.g., transfer to a new location). How could an employee's current job be changed to develop that employee's leadership skills?

7. What is coaching? Is there only one type of coaching? Explain.

8. Discuss reasons why many managers are reluctant to coach their employees.

9. Discuss the characteristics of the most effective company development strategies. Which characteristic do you believe is most important? Why?

10. How do volunteer assignments and job experiences contribute to employee development?

11. What can companies do to ensure that tuition reimbursement programs are worth the investment?

Application Assignments

1. Your manager wants you to create a one-page form for development planning. Create the form, and provide a rationale for each category you include on it.

2. Read the article, "Baby Boomers Seek New Ways to Escape Career Claustrophobia," in *The Wall Street Journal,* June 24, 2003: B1. It describes the challenges of motivating managers who have limited opportunities for advancement. Write a two-page memo outlining your recommendations for developing managers who are stuck in their jobs or feel underutilized.

3. Go to General Electric's Web site at www.gecareers.com. Review the entry-level leadership and experienced leadership programs. Overall, what type of development activities are included in these programs? Choose one program and describe it (development activities, length, participants). Compare the development activities used in the entry-level

and experienced leadership programs. How are they similar? How are they different? Why might they differ?

4. Go to www.keirsey.com. Complete the Keirsey Temperament Sorter or the Keirsey Character Sorter. (You will have to register first.) These are examples of assessment instruments that can be used for development. What did you learn about yourself? How could the instrument you completed be useful for management development? What might be some disadvantages of using this instrument?

5. Go to www.dukece.com, a provider of custom corporate education programs. Click on Client stories and read one of the client success stories. Prepare a brief summary of the business issue, approach, learning experience, execution, and outcome. Why do you think the program was successful?

Case: *Mentoring Is Not Always a Positive Experience*

On the second day of his job, Bob was introduced to his mentor and shown his office. His mentor was an electrical engineer who had been on the job before Bob was born. Bob's first interaction with his mentor involved the mentor showing him where the pens and paper were stored in the supply cabinet. Over the next year, Bob did not have a chance to speak to his mentor. The only time he heard from him was when his manager told the mentor that he had chosen the wrong size parts for a circuit he was working on.

Is this a successful mentoring relationship? What steps should the company take in the future to ensure that its formal mentoring relationships are more successful? How would you determine if a formal mentoring program was successful? What would you measure? Who would be involved?

Source: Based on E. Holmes, "Career Mentors Today Seem Short on Advice but Give a Mean Tour," *The Wall Street Journal* (August 28, 2007): B1.

Endnotes

1. M. London, *Managing the Training Enterprise* (San Francisco: Jossey-Bass, 1989); C. McCauley and S. Heslett, "Individual Development in the Workplace," in *Handbook of Industrial, Work, and Organizational Psychology*, vol. 1, ed. N. Anderson, D. Ones, H. Sinangil, and C. Viswesvaran (London: Sage Publications, 2001): 313–35; D. Day, *Developing Leadership Talent* (Alexandria, VA: SHRM Foundation, 2007).

2. J. Marquez, "Building Knowledge," *Workforce Management* (February 2006): 24–30; www.urscorp.com, Web site for URS Corporation.

3. R. W. Pace, P. C. Smith, and G. E. Mills, *Human Resource Development* (Englewood Cliffs, NJ: Prentice-Hall, 1991); W. Fitzgerald, "Training versus Development," *Training and Development Journal* (May 1992): 81–84; R. A. Noe, S. L. Wilk, E. J. Mullen, and J. E. Wanek, "Employee Development: Issues in Construct Definition and Investigation of Antecedents," in *Improving Training Effectiveness in Work Organizations*, ed. J. K. Ford (Mahwah, NJ: Lawrence Erlbaum, 1997): 153–89.

4. Towers-Perrin, *Talent Management: The State of the Art* (Towers-Perrin, 2005).

5. C. Taylor, "Focus on Talent," *T&D* (December 2002): 26–31.

6. R. J. Campbell, "HR Development Strategies," in *Developing Human Resources*, ed. K. N. Wexley (Washington, DC: BNA Books. 1991): 5–1 to 5–34; M. A. Sheppeck and C. A. Rhodes, "Management Development: Revised Thinking in Light of New Events of Strategic Importance," *Human Resource Planning* 11 (1988): 159–72; B. Keys and J. Wolf, "Management Education: Current Issues and Emerging Trends," *Journal of Management* 14 (1988): 205–29; L. M. Saari, T. R. Johnson, S. D. McLaughlin, and D. Zimmerle, "A Survey of Management Training and Education Practices in U.S. Companies," *Personnel Psychology* 41 (1988): 731–44.

7. E. Esen and J. Collison, *Employee Development* (Alexandria, VA: SHRM Research, 2005).

8. F. Hansen, "Building Better Leaders . . . Faster," *Workforce Management* (June 9, 2008): 25–28.

9. C. Cornell, "Fail Safe," *Human Resource Executive* (June 2, 2003): 33–36.

10. J. Ronan, "A Boot to the System," *T&D* (March 2003): 38–45.

11. C. Waxer, "Course Review," *Human Resource Executive* (December 2005): 46–48.

12. *The Wall Street Journal* (October 13, 2008): R8. K. Spors "Top Small Workplaces 2008: Paducah Bank & Trust Co".

13. B. Yovovich, "Golden Opportunities," *Human Resource Executive* (August 2008): 30–34.

14. R. Knight, "GE's Corporate Boot Camp Cum Talent Spotting Venue," *Financial Times Business Education* (March 20, 2006): 2; J. Durett, "GE Hones Its Leaders at Crotonville," *Training* (May 2006): 25–27.

15. www.ge.com/company/culture/leaderhip_learning.html, retrieved January 15, 2009.

16. F. Hansen, "Building Better Leaders . . . Faster."

17. J. Bolt, *Executive Development* (New York: Harper Business, 1989); H. S. Jonas, R. E. Fry, and S. Srivasta, "The Office of the CEO: Understanding the Executive Experience," *Academy of Management Executive* 4 (1990): 36–48; J. Noel and R. Charam, "GE Brings Global Thinking to Light," *Training and Development Journal* (July 1992): 29–33; B. O'Reilly, "How Execs Learn Now," *Fortune* (April 5, 1993); M. A. Hitt, B. B. Tyler, C. Hardee, and D. Park, "Understanding Strategic Intent in the Global Marketplace," *Academy of Management Executive* 9 (1995): 12–19.

18. Center for Creative Leadership, "Xerox Corporation" (2007), from Web site, www.ccl.org.

19. J. A. Byrne, "Virtual Business Schools," *BusinessWeek* (October 23, 1995): 64–68.

20. "Client Stories," www.dukece.com, Web site of Duke Corporate Education.

21. J. Reingold, "Corporate America Goes to School," *BusinessWeek* (October 20, 1997): 66–72.

22. L. Bongiorno, "How'm I Doing," *BusinessWeek* (October 23, 1995): 72, 74; Leadership Development Programs Overview, Center for Creative Leadership Web site at www.ccl.org, retrieved January 17, 2009.

23. L. Gerdes, "Programs: Picking Up the Pace," *BusinessWeek Online,* October 24, 2005, special report on executive education, www.businessweek.com.

24. C. Waxer, "Course Review."

25. A. Meisler, "A Matter of Degree," *Workforce Management* (May 2004): 32–38; K. Merriman, "Employers Warm Up to Online Education," *HR Magazine* (January 2006): 79–82.

26. R. Johnson, "The Learning Curve: The Value of Tuition Reimbursement," *Training* (November 2005): 30–33; G. Benson, D. Finegold, and S. Mohrman, "You Paid for the Skills, Now Keep Them: Tuition Reimbursement and Voluntary Turnover," *Academy of Management Journal* 47 (2004): 315–31.

27. "Flexibility Fuels Employee Development," *T + D* (April 2006): 96–97.

28. A. Howard and D. W. Bray, *Managerial Lives in Transition: Advancing Age and Changing Times* (New York: Guilford, 1988); Bolt, *Executive Development;* J. R. Hinrichs and G. P. Hollenbeck, "Leadership Development," in K. N. Wexley (ed), *Developing Human Resources,* 5-221 to 5-237.

29. M. Weinstein, "Personalities & Performance," *Training* (July/August 2008): 36–40.

30. E. Krell, "Personality Counts," *HR Magazine* (November 2005): 47–52.

31. Weinstein, "Personalities & Performance."

32. S. K. Hirsch, *MBTI Team Member's Guide* (Palo Alto, CA: Consulting Psychologists Press, 1992); A. L. Hammer, *Introduction to Type and Careers* (Palo Alto, CA: Consulting Psychologists Press, 1993).

33. A. Thorne and H. Gough, *Portraits of Type* (Palo Alto, CA: Consulting Psychologists Press, 1991).

34. D. Druckman and R. A. Bjork, *In the Mind's Eye: Enhancing Human Performance* (Washington, DC: National Academy Press, 1991); M. H. McCaulley, "The Myers-Briggs Type Indicator and Leadership," in *Measures of Leadership,* eds. K. E. Clark and M. B. Clark (West Orange, NJ: Leadership Library of America, 1990): 381–418.

35. G. C. Thornton III and W. C. Byham, *Assessment Centers and Managerial Performance* (New York: Academic Press, 1982); L. F. Schoenfeldt and J. A. Steger, "Identification and Development of Management Talent," in *Research in Personnel and Human Resource Management,* vol. 7, eds. K. N. Rowland and G. Ferris (Greenwich, CT: JAI Press, 1989): 151–81.

36. Thornton and Byham, *Assessment Centers and Managerial Performance.*

37. B. B. Gaugler, D. B. Rosenthal, G. C. Thornton III, and C. Bentson, "Meta-analysis of Assessment Center Validity," *Journal of Applied Psychology* 72 (1987): 493–511; D. W. Bray, R. J. Campbell, and D. L. Grant, *Formative Years in Business: A Long-Term AT&T Study of Managerial Lives* (New York: Wiley, 1974).

38. R. G. Jones and M. D. Whitmore, "Evaluating Developmental Assessment Centers as Interventions," *Personnel Psychology* 48 (1995): 377–88.

39. J. Schettler, "Building Bench Strength," *Training* (June 2002): 55–58.

40. C. D. McCauley and M. M. Lombardo, "Benchmarks: An Instrument for Diagnosing Managerial Strengths and Weaknesses," in Clark and Clark, *Measures of Leadership,* 535–45.

41. C. D. McCauley, M. M. Lombardo, and C. J. Usher, "Diagnosing Management Development Needs: An Instrument Based on How Managers Develop," *Journal of Management* 15 (1989): 389–403.

42. S. B. Silverman, "Individual Development through Performance Appraisal," in K. N. Wexley (ed), *Developing Human Resources,* 5-120 to 5-151.

43. M. Sallie-Dosunmu, "Born to Grow," *T + D* (May 2006): 34–37.

44. "Master of HR at GE," *Human Resource Executive* (October 2004): 16–24.

45. J. S. Lublin, "Turning the Tables: Underlings Evaluate Bosses," *The Wall Street Journal* (October 4, 1994): B1, B14; B. O'Reilly, "360 Feedback Can Change Your Life," *Fortune* (October 17, 1994): 93–100; J. F. Milliman, R. A. Zawacki, C. Norman, L. Powell, and J. Kirksey, "Companies Evaluate Employees from All Perspectives," *Personnel Journal* (November 1994): 99–103.

46. Center for Creative Leadership, "Roadway Express" (2007), from Web site, www.ccl.org.

47. Center for Creative Leadership, *Skillscope for Managers: Development Planning Guide* (Greensboro, NC: Center for Creative Leadership, 1992); G. Yukl and R. Lepsinger, "360 Feedback," *Training* (December 1995): 45–50.

48. L. Atwater, P. Roush, and A. Fischthal, "The Influence of Upward Feedback on Self- and Follower Ratings of Leadership," *Personnel Psychology* 48 (1995): 35–59; J. F. Hazucha, S. A. Hezlett, and R. J. Schneider, "The Impact of 360-Degree Feedback on Management Skill Development," *Human Resource Management* 32 (1993): 325–51; J. W. Smither, M. London, N. Vasilopoulos, R. R. Reilly, R. E. Millsap, and N. Salvemini, "An Examination of the Effects of an Upward Feedback Program Over Time," *Personnel Psychology* 48 (1995): 1–34; J. Johnson and K. Ferstl, "The Effects of Interrater and Self-Other Agreement on Performance Improvement Following Feedback," *Personnel Psychology* 2 (1999): 271–303; J. Smither and A. Walker, "Are the Characteristics of Narrative Comments Related to Improvements in Multirater Feedback Ratings over Time?" *Journal of Applied Psychology* 89 (2004): 575–81; J. Smither, M. London, and R. Reilly, "Does Performance Improve Following Multisource Feedback? A Theoretical Model, Meta-analysis, and Review of Empirical Findings," *Personnel Psychology* 58 (2005): 33–66.

49. D. Bracken, "Straight Talk about Multirater Feedback," *Training and Development* (September 1994): 44–51; K. Nowack, J. Hartley, and W. Bradley, "How to Evaluate Your 360 Feedback Efforts," *Training and Development* (April 1999): 48–52.

50. A. Freedman, "The Evolution of 360s," *Human Resource Executive* (December 2002): 47–51.

51. C. Seifert, G. Yukl, and R. McDonald, "Effects of Multisource Feedback and a Feedback Facilitator on the Influence Behavior of Managers toward Subordinates," *Journal of Applied Psychology* 88 (2003): 561–69.

52. M. W. McCall Jr., M. M. Lombardo, and A. M. Morrison, *Lessons of Experience* (Lexington, MA: Lexington Books, 1988).

53. R. S. Snell, "Congenial Ways of Learning: So Near Yet So Far," *Journal of Management Development* 9 (1990): 17–23.

54. C. Cornell, "Fail Safe."

55. McCall, Lombardo, and Morrison, *Lessons of Experience;* M. W. McCall, "Developing Executives through Work Experiences," *Human Resource Planning* 11 (1988): 1–11; M. N. Ruderman, P. J. Ohlott, and C. D. McCauley, "Assessing Opportunities for Leadership Development," in Clark and Clark, *Measures of Leadership,* 547–62; C. D. McCauley, L. J. Estman, and P. J. Ohlott, "Linking Management Selection and Development through Stretch Assignments," *Human Resource Management* 34 (1995): 93–115.

56. C. D. McCauley, M. N. Ruderman, P. J. Ohlott, and J. E. Morrow, "Assessing the Developmental Components of Managerial Jobs," *Journal of Applied Psychology* 79 (1994): 544–60.

57. *The Wall Street Journal* (October 13, 2008): R9. K. Spors "Top Small Workplaces 2008: Rainforest Alliance."

58. S. Thurm, "Power-Sharing Prepares Managers," *The Wall Street Journal* (December 5, 2005): B4.

59. "Training Top 100 Best Practices: Regions Financial," *Training* (March 2006): 61.

60. M. Weinstein, "Foreign but Familiar," *Training* (January 2009): 20–23.

61. M. London, *Developing Managers* (San Francisco: Jossey-Bass, 1985); M. A. Campion, L. Cheraskin, and M. J. Stevens, "Career-Related Antecedents and Outcomes of Job Rotation," *Academy of Management Journal* 37 (1994): 1518–42; M. London, *Managing the Training Enterprise* (San Francisco: Jossey-Bass, 1989); M. Fiester, A. Collis, and N. Cossack, "Job Rotation, Total Rewards, Measuring Value," *HR Magazine* (August 2008): 33–34.

62. M. Pacelle, "Job Swap Is Meant to Groom 'Next Generation,'" *The Wall Street Journal* (September 28, 2004): C1, C4.

63. D. C. Feldman, *Managing Careers in Organizations* (Glenview, IL: Scott-Foresman, 1988).

64. J. M. Brett, L. K. Stroh, and A. H. Reilly, "Job Transfer," in *International Review of Industrial and Organizational Psychology: 1992,* eds. C. L. Cooper and I. T. Robinson (Chichester, England: John Wiley and Sons, 1992); D. C. Feldman and J. M. Brett, "Coping with New Jobs: A Comparative Study of New Hires and Job Changers," *Academy of Management Journal* 26 (1983): 258–72.

65. R. A. Noe, B. D. Steffy, and A. E. Barber, "An Investigation of the Factors Influencing Employees' Willingness to Accept Mobility Opportunities," *Personnel Psychology* 41 (1988): 559–80; S. Gould and L. E. Penley, "A Study of the Correlates of Willingness to Relocate," *Academy of Management Journal* 28 (1984): 472–78; J. Landau and T. H. Hammer, "Clerical Employees' Perceptions of Intraorganizational Career Opportunities," *Academy of Management Journal* 29 (1986): 385–405; R. P. Duncan and C. C. Perruci, "Dual Occupation Families and Migration," *American Sociological Review* 41 (1976): 252–61; J. M. Brett and A. H. Reilly, "On the Road Again: Predicting the Job Transfer Decision," *Journal of Applied Psychology* 73 (1988): 614–20.

66. D. T. Hall and L. A. Isabella, "Downward Moves and Career Development," *Organizational Dynamics* 14 (1985): 5–23.

67. H. D. Dewirst, "Career Patterns: Mobility, Specialization, and Related Career Issues," in *Contemporary Career Development Issues,* ed. R. F. Morrison and J. Adams (Hillsdale, NJ: Lawrence Erlbaum, 1991): 73–108.

68. N. C. Tompkins, "GTE Managers on the Move," *Personnel Journal* (August 1992): 86–91.

69. J. M. Brett, "Job Transfer and Well-Being," *Journal of Applied Psychology* 67 (1992): 450–63; F. J. Minor, L. A. Slade, and R. A. Myers, "Career Transitions in Changing Times," in Morrison and Adams, *Contemporary Career Development Issues,* 109–20; C. C. Pinder and K. G. Schroeder, "Time to Proficiency Following Job Transfers," *Academy of Management Journal* 30 (1987): 336–53; G. Flynn, "Heck No—We Won't Go!" *Personnel Journal* (March 1996): 37–43.

70. R. E. Silverman, "Mercer Tries to Keep Employees through Its 'Externship' Program," *The Wall Street Journal,* November 7, 2000: B18.

71. E. Byron, "A New Odd Couple: Google, P&G Swap Workers to Spur Innovation," *The Wall Street Journal* (November 19, 2008): A1, A18.

72. S. Needleman, "The Latest Office Perk: Getting Paid to Volunteer," *The Wall Street Journal* (April 29, 2008): D1, D5.

73. M. Weinstein, "Charity Begins @ Work," *Training* (May 2008): 56–58; K. Ellis, "Pass It On," *Training* (June 2005): 14–19.

74. D. B. Turban and T. W. Dougherty, "Role of Protégé Personality in Receipt of Mentoring and Career Success," *Academy of Management Journal* 37 (1994): 688–702; E. A. Fagenson, "Mentoring: Who Needs It? A Comparison of Protégés' and Nonprotégés' Needs for Power, Achievement, Affiliation, and Autonomy," *Journal of Vocational Behavior* 41 (1992): 48–60.

75. T. Galvin, "Best Practices: Mentoring, KLA-Tencor Corp," *Training* (March 2003): 58.

76. A. H. Geiger, "Measures for Mentors," *Training and Development Journal* (February 1992): 65–67; K. Dunham, "Mentors May Not Help," *The Wall Street Journal* (September 23, 2003): B8.

77. K. E. Kram, *Mentoring at Work: Developmental Relationships in Organizational Life* (Glenview, IL: Scott-Foresman, 1985); L. L. Phillips-Jones, "Establishing a Formalized Mentoring Program," *Training and*

Development Journal 2 (1983): 38–42; K. Kram, "Phases of the Mentoring Relationship," *Academy of Management Journal* 26 (1983): 608–25; G. T. Chao, P. M. Walz, and P. D. Gardner, "Formal and Informal Mentorships: A Comparison of Mentoring Functions and Contrasts with Nonmentored Counterparts," *Personnel Psychology* 45 (1992): 619–36; B. Ragins, J. Cotton, and J. Miller, "Marginal Mentoring: The Effects of Type of Mentor, Quality of Relationship, and the Program Design on Work and Career Attitudes," *Academy of Management Journal* 43 (2000): 1177–94.

78. E. White, "Making Mentorships Work," *The Wall Street Journal* (October 23, 2007): B11; E. Holmes, "Career Mentors Today Seem Short on Advice but Give a Mean Tour"; J. Sandberg, " With Bad Mentors It's Better to Break Up than to Make Up," *The Wall Street Journal* (March 18, 2008): B1; T. Allen, L. Finkelstein, & M. Poteet, *"Designing Workplace Mentoring Programs* (Chichester, westsussex, United Kingdom: Wiley—Blackwell, 2009).

79. M. Weinstein, "Tech connects," *Training* (September 2008): 58–59.

80. E. Tahmincioglu, "Looking for a Mentor? Technology Can Help Make the Right Match," *Workforce Management* (December 2004): 63–65; D. Owens, "Virtual Mentoring," *HR Magazine* (March 2006): 105–7.

81. M. Boyle, "Most Mentoring Programs Stink—But Yours Doesn't Have To," *Training* (August 2005): 12–15.

82. L. Eby, M. Butts, A. Lockwood, and A. Simon, "Protégés Negative Mentoring Experiences: Construct Development and Nomological Validation," *Personnel Psychology* 57 (2004): 411–47; T. DeLong, J. Gabarro, and R. Lees, "Why Mentoring Matters in a Hypercompetitive World," *Harvard Business Review* (January 2008): 115–121.

83. C. M. Solomon, "Hotel Breathes Life into Hospital's Customer Service," *Personnel Journal* (October 1995): 120.

84. A. Poe, "Establishing Positive Mentoring Relationships," *HR Magazine* (February 2002): 62–69.

85. T. Allen, L. Eby, M. Poteet, E. Lenz, and L. Lima, "Benefits Associated with Mentoring for Protégés: A Meta-analysis," *Journal of Applied Psychology* 89 (2004): 127–36; G. F. Dreher and R. A. Ash, "A Comparative Study of Mentoring among Men and Women in Managerial, Professional, and Technical Positions," *Journal of Applied Psychology* 75 (1990): 539–46; J. L. Wilbur, "Does Mentoring Breed Success?" *Training and Development Journal* 41 (1987): 38–41; R. A. Noe, "Mentoring Relationships for Employee Development," in *Applying Psychology in Business: The Handbook for Managers and Human Resource Professionals,* ed. J. W. Jones, B. D. Steffy, and D. W. Bray (Lexington, MA: Lexington Books, 1991): 475–82; M. M. Fagh and K. Ayers Jr., "Police Mentors," *FBI Law Enforcement Bulletin* (January 1985): 8–13; Kram, "Phases of the Mentoring Relationship"; R. A. Noe, "An Investigation of the Determinants of Successful Assigned Mentoring Relationships," *Personnel Psychology* 41 (1988): 457–79; B. J. Tepper, "Upward Maintenance Tactics in Supervisory Mentoring and Nonmentoring Relationships," *Academy of Management Journal* 38 (1995): 1191–205; B. R. Ragins and T. A. Scandura, "Gender Differences in Expected Outcomes of Mentoring Relationships," *Academy of Management Journal* 37 (1994): 957–71; M. Lankau and T. Scandura, "An Investigation of Personal Learning in Mentoring Relationships: Content, Antecedents, and Consequences," *Academy of Management Journal* 45 (2002): 779–90.

86. J. Lublin, "Even Top Executives Could Use Mentors to Benefit Careers," *The Wall Street Journal* (July 1, 2003): B1.

87. M. Murray, "GE Mentoring Program Turns Underlings into Teachers of the Web," *The Wall Street Journal* (February 15, 2000): B1, B16.

88. C. Douglas and C. McCauley, "Formal Development Relationships: A Survey of Organizational Practices," *Human Resource Development Quarterly* 10 (1999): 203–21.

89. J. Barbian, *Training* (May 2002): 39–42.

90. *Women of Color in Corporate Management: Three Years Later* (New York: Catalyst, 2002).

91. K. Spors, "Websites Offer Access to Mentors," *The Wall Street Journal* (June 3, 2008): B7.

92. B. Kaye and B. Jackson, "Mentoring: A Group Guide," *Training and Development* (April 1995): 23–27; K. Kram and M. Higgins, "A New Approach to Mentoring," *The Wall Street Journal* (September 22, 2008): R10.

93. D. B. Peterson and M. D. Hicks, *Leader as Coach* (Minneapolis, MN: Personnel Decisions, 1996); L. Thach and T. Heinselman, "Executive Coaching Defined," *Training and Development* (March 1999): 200–4; D. Cole, "Even Executives Can Use Help from the Sidelines," *The New York Times,* November 5, 2002, www.nytimes.com/2002/10/29/business/businessspecial/29COLE.html.

94. J. Toto, "Untapped World of Peer Coaching," *T + D* (April 2006): 69–71.

95. D. Coutu and C. Kauffman, "What Can Coaches Do for You?" *Harvard Business Review* (January 2009): 91–97; J. Bono, R. Purvanova, A. Towter, & D. Peterson, "A Survey of Executive Coaching Practices," *Personnel Psychology* 62 (2009): 361–397.

96. Toto, "Untapped World of Peer Coaching."

97. J. S. Lublin, "Building a Better CEO," *The Wall Street Journal* (April 14, 2000): B1, B4; J. W. Smither and S. Reilly, "Coaching in Organizations: A Social Psychological Perspective," in *How People Evaluate Others in Organizations,* ed. M. London (Mahwah, NJ: Erlbaum, 2001).

98. H. Johnson, "The Ins and Outs of Executive Coaching," *Training* (May 2004): 36–41.

99. J. Smither, M. London, R. Flautt, Y. Vargas, and L. Kucine, "Can Working with an Executive Coach Improve Multisource Ratings Over Time? A Quasi-experimental Field Study," *Personnel Psychology* 56 (2003): 23–44.

100. R. Zemke, "The Corporate Coach," *Training* (December 1996): 24–28.

101. J. Lublin, "Did I Just Say That?! How You Can Recover from Foot-in-Mouth," *The Wall Street Journal* (June 18, 2002): B1.

102. L. Summers, "A Logical Approach to Development Planning," *Training and Development* 48 (1994): 22–31; D. B. Peterson and M. D. Hicks, *Development First* (Minneapolis, MN: Personnel Decisions, 1995); D. Peterson, "Management Development," in *Creating, Implementing, and Managing Effective Training and Development,* ed. K. Kraiger (San Francisco: Jossey-Bass, 2002): 160–91.

103. D. T. Jaffe and C. D. Scott, "Career Development for Empowerment in a Changing Work World," in *New Directions in Career Planning and the Workplace,* ed. J. M. Kummerow (Palo Alto, CA: Consulting Psychologists Press, 1991): 33–60.

104. D. Grote, "Driving True Development," *Training* (July 2005): 24–29.

105. S. Caudron, "Building Better Bosses," *Workforce* (May 2000): 33–39.

106. K. Ellis, "Individual Development Plans: The Building Blocks of Development," *Training* (December 2004): 20–25.

107. G. Johnson, "The Development Framework," *Training* (February 2003): 32–36; J. Kornik, "Booz Allen Hamilton Puts People First," *Training* (March 2006): 11–12, 14.

108. N. Lewis and P. Orton, "The Five Attributes of Innovative E-Learning," *Training and Development* (June 2000): 47–51; K. Mantyla, *Blending E-Learning* (Alexandria, VA: ASTD, 2001); T. Barron, "IBM's New-Fangled, Old-Fashioned Pep," *T + D* (April 2004): 64–65.

Special Issues in Training and Employee Development

Objectives

After reading this chapter, you should be able to

1. Discuss the potential legal issues that relate to training.
2. Develop a program for effectively managing diversity.
3. Design a program for preparing for cross-cultural assignments.
4. Make recommendations on steps to take to "melt the glass ceiling."
5. Discuss what a trainer needs to do to ensure that school-to-work and hard-core–unemployed training programs are effective.
6. Describe the necessary steps in a program for helping dysfunctional managers.
7. Discuss the implications of a skill-based pay plan for training.

Successful Management Requires International Experience

As companies become increasingly global, economic patterns and business practices in one area of the world can determine the success of a company on the other side of the world. At Procter & Gamble (P&G), being a successful global leader requires an international background. A majority of P&G's 140,000 employees work outside the United States. P&G uses international assignments to teach employees how business is conducted in another country. Lessons learned are then applied at home or in another region. Only a quarter of relocations originate in the United States; the majority are from place to place across the world. An important goal for employees who receive international assignments is to develop local talent to replace themselves.

For example, a manager who is being prepared to take over a top finance position in Russia might go to Britain to gain experience working in a more structured and complex market. P&G managers in Europe must learn to keep the company's products on the shelves of big-box stores such as Carrefour, the European supermarket

389

and discount chain and one of the largest retailers in the world. P&G might send junior U.S. managers to work with European managers who are responsible for products at Carrefour, expecting them to transfer the skills they learn back in the U.S. when dealing with product placement in big-box retail stores such as Wal-Mart and Costco. As Poland, Hungary, and the Czech Republic integrate into the European Union, their economies may become similar to those of England and Germany. Managers who have gained experience in Western Europe can transfer that knowledge to jobs in Eastern Europe.

As a result of its emphasis on international experience, 39 of P&G's top 44 global officers have had an international assignment, and 22 of the 44 have been born outside the United States. This has produced a deep pool of internationally saavy managers who have produced results such as increasing P&G business in China from less than $90 million to nearly $1 billion dollars!

Source: Based on M. Schoeff, "P&G Places a Premium on International Experience," *Workforce Management* (April 10, 2006): 28.

INTRODUCTION

The opening vignette illustrates that for companies to become successful globally they must develop managers who have a global perspective. Procter & Gamble uses international assignments to help managers gain a broad perspective on effective business practices. Such development programs are one example of how understanding the larger environment (e.g., global markets and cultures) relates to successful training initiatives.

Other environmental pressures that influence companies include legal issues, partnering with the community to train a qualified, commited work force and provide local jobs, and an increasingly diverse work force. Both trainers and managers who purchase training services must be aware of how legal issues relate to training practices, cross-cultural preparation, diversity training, and school-to-work and hard-core–unemployed training programs. These issues are covered in the first part of this chapter.

The second part of the chapter covers issues that result from pressures from the company's internal environment. These pressures include the need to train managerial talent, provide training and development opportunities for all employees (regardless of their personal characteristics), and motivate employees to learn through the company's compensation system. Specifically, the second half of the chapter covers basic skills training, life-long learning, melting the glass ceiling, joint union–management training programs, succession planning programs, training dysfunctional managers, and skill-based pay systems.

TRAINING ISSUES RESULTING FROM THE EXTERNAL ENVIRONMENT

Legal Issues

Table 10.1 shows potential training activities and situations that can make an employer vulnerable to legal actions and harm the company's reputation. The following sections describe each situation and potential implications for training.[1]

TABLE 10.1

Situations That May Result in Legal Action

- Failing to provide required training or providing inadequate training
- Incurring employee injury during a training activity
- Incurring injuries to employees or others outside the training session
- Incurring breach of confidentiality or defamation
- Reproducing and using copyrighted material in training classes without permission
- Excluding women, minorities, and older Americans from training programs
- Not ensuring equal treatment while in training
- Requiring employees to attend training programs they may find offensive
- Revealing discriminatory information during a training session
- Not accommodating trainees with disabilities
- Incorrectly reporting training as an expense or failing to report training reimbursement as income

Failing to Provide Training or Providing Inadequate Training

To comply with a wide range of laws and regulations, companies are required to show that employees not only have completed training programs but also are applying their new knowledge on the job. Most companies provide training to reduce the potential for a hostile work environment for employees protected by Title VII of the Civil Rights Act (race, color, gender, religion, nationality, national origin), the Age Discrimination in Employment Act (age), or the Americans with Disabilities Act (disability).[2] For example, the U.S. Supreme Court considers sexual harassment training to be an important factor for companies that wish to avoid punitive damages in sexual harassment cases. Employers must also train employees to comply with practices designed to prevent harassment of any class protected by Title VII.

Federal laws may require a certain number of training hours and types of training for employees in certain industries. For example, initial training for flight attendants must include how to handle passengers, use galley equipment, evacuate the airplane, and use the public address system. The safe landing of US Airways Flight 1549 on the Hudson River was one of the rare moments when a U.S. passenger plane completed a forced landing without loss of life of passengers or crew. As a result, the Federal Aviation Administration is proposing new training regulations and rules for airlines, calling for hands-on drills on the use of emergency equipment and procedures for all flight attendants.[3]

In congressional hearings, the Federal Aviation Administration (FAA) has been accused of providing inadequate training for air traffic controllers, resulting in near collisions between aircraft.[4] As a result, the FAA has upgraded training by purchasing simulators that use voice-recognition technology and allow trainees to instruct simulated aircraft on takeoff and landing procedures in all types of weather conditions. This allows better training of air traffic controllers who otherwise would have to wait for inclement weather to conduct on-the-job training.

Companies in health care are required to comply with the Health Insurance Portability and Accountability Act (HIPPA); companies in finance are required to comply with the Bank Secrecy Act; and companies in the gaming industry (such as casinos) are required to train employees on how to handle money and how to report suspicious activity.[5] In several states, candidates interested in being hired as full-time police officers must complete approved police training. Legislation can also require training that is related to providing a drug-free workplace (e.g., training about drug abuse and making counseling available) and a safe workplace (e.g., training about the handling of hazardous materials and the use of safety equipment as dictated by the Occupational Safety and Health Act).

Due to recent corporate scandals, compliance examiners are now more rigorously reviewing the quality of training by evaluating whether employees understand how regulations apply to their jobs.[6] This has resulted in a change in the methods used for compliance training. Traditionally, compliance training used passive learning methods such as lectures, handouts, or e-mail attachments with PowerPoint slides. Now, companies are using training methods that enhance both learning and transfer of training—such as e-learning, business games, and role playing—to ensure that employees not only understand regulations but can also apply them. For example, Tufts Health Plan uses a game-show format for awareness training, and Ho-Chunk Casino uses scenarios to teach casino employees specific behaviors to watch for.

Incurring Employee Injury during a Training Activity

On-the-job training and simulations often involve the use of work tools and equipment (e.g., welding machinery, printing press) that could cause injury if incorrectly used. Workers' compensation laws in many states make employers responsible for paying employees their salary and/or providing them with a financial settlement for injuries received during any employment-related activity such as training. Managers should ensure that (1) employees are warned of potential dangers from incorrectly using equipment and (2) safety equipment is used.

Incurring Injuries to Employees or Others Outside a Training Session

Managers should ensure that trainees have the necessary level of competence in knowledge, skills, and behaviors before they are allowed to operate equipment or interact with customers. Even if a company pays for training to be conducted by a vendor, it is still liable for injuries or damages resulting from the actions of poorly, incorrectly, or incompletely trained employees. A company that contracts out training to a vendor or consultant should ensure that it has liability insurance, be sure that the trainers are competent, and determine if there has been previous litigation against the trainer or the vendor providing the training. Also, trainers should be sure to keep copies of notes, activities, and training manuals that show that training procedures were correct and followed the steps provided by licensing or certification agencies (if appropriate).

Incurring Breach of Confidentiality or Defamation

Managers should ensure that information placed in employees' files regarding performance in training activities is accurate. Also, before discussing an employee's performance in training with other employees or using training performance information for promotion or salary decisions, managers should tell employees that training performance will be used in that manner.

Reproducing and Using Copyrighted Material in Training Classes without Permission

Copyrights protect the expression of an idea (e.g., a training manual for a software program) but not the ideas that the material contains (e.g., the use of help windows in the software program).[7] Copyrights also prohibit others from creating a product based on the original work and from copying, broadcasting, or publishing the product without permission.

The use of videotapes, learning aids, manuals, and other copyrighted materials in training classes without obtaining permission from the owner of the material is illegal. Managers should ensure that all training materials are purchased from the vendor or consultant who developed them or that permission to reproduce materials has been obtained. Material on Internet sites is not necessarily free from copyright law.[8] Many Web sites are governed by the fair use doctrine, which means that you can use small amounts of copyrighted material without asking permission or paying a fee as long as the use meets four standards. The standards relate to (1) the purpose for which the copyrighted materials are being used, (2) what the copyrighted work is, (3) the proportion of the copyrighted material you are using, and (4) how much money the copyright owner can lose as a result of the use. Republishing or repackaging under your own name material that you took from the Internet can be a violation of copyright law. For example, the CEO of Crisp Learning frequently finds his small company in court defending copyright issues. Crisp Learning develops and sells video and training courses that deal with skills such as business report writing and time management. The series of courses, known as the Fifty-Minute series, is popular because it is easily applied and can be completed in a short period of time. Crisp Learning has found that copyright violators have actually retyped its books and sold them as their own work. Violating copyright can be expensive. Copyright violators can end up paying expensive legal fees and paying damages that are more expensive than what it would have cost to legally purchase the training materials. To obtain copyright permission, you need to directly contact the owners of the material and explain how the material will be used and how ownership will be cited. Another way to get copyright permission is to seek permission from organizations such as the Copyright Clearance Center (www.copyright.com) or iCopyright.com.

Excluding Women, Minorities, and Older Employees from Training Programs

Two pieces of legislation make it illegal for employers to exclude women, minorities, or older persons from training programs. Title VII of the Civil Rights Act of 1964 (amended in 1991) makes it illegal to deny access to employment or deprive a person employment because of the person's race, color, religion, gender, or national origin. The Age Discrimination in Employment Act (ADEA) prohibits discrimination against persons who are age 40 or older. The Equal Employment Opportunity Commission (EEOC) is responsible for enforcing both the Civil Rights Act and the ADEA.

Although these two pieces of legislation have existed for several years, a study by the U.S. Department of Labor found that training experiences necessary for promotion are not as available or accessible to women and minorities as they are to white males.[9] Women, minorities, and older employees can be illegally excluded from training programs either by not being made aware of opportunities for training or by purposeful exclusion from enrollment in training programs. Denial of training opportunities and better treatment of younger employees can be used to support claims of age discrimination.[10] Older employees may bring lawsuits against companies based on a denied promotion or discharge. As evidence for age discrimination, the courts will investigate whether older workers were denied training opportunities that were provided to younger workers. To avoid age discrimination in training, managers and trainers need to ensure that the organization's culture and policies are age-neutral. Decisions about training and development opportunities should not be made on the basis of stereotypes about older workers and should take into account job-relevant factors such as performance. Managers should be held accountable for fair training and development practices and for ensuring that all employees have development plans. Finally, all employees should receive training on the ADEA and on how age stereotypes can affect treatment of older employees. Stereotypes such as "older workers are resistant to change" may result in exclusion of older workers from training and development programs.

The University of Phoenix had to pay over $1 million for demonstrating a religious bias against non-Mormon employees who worked as enrollment counselors in the university's Online Division.[11] The bias included denying tuition waivers to non-Mormon employees for failing to meet student registration goals while granting similar waivers to Mormon employees. In another example, Coca-Cola settled out of court a discrimination suit in which African American employees were excluded from programs needed to receive promotions in the company. Four current and former Coke employees filed a lawsuit alleging race discrimination in pay, promotions, and performance evaluations within the Coca-Cola company.[12] Rather than face continued legal and public scrutiny and to move forward on initiatives to correct the perceived racial discrimination, Coca-Cola agreed to pay $113 million in cash to the plaintiffs, $3.5 million to adjust salaries of African American employees during the next 10 years, and $36 million to implement various diversity initiatives. The goal of the settlement is to change the company culture. Coke's employment practices have been reviewed by a task force consisting of experts in civil rights, diversity, labor, employment, and business. The task force also reviews Coke's human resource practices. The settlement required more oversight of managers' decisions on promotions, more mentoring programs, and regular diversity training for all employees. Coke has made progress in complying with the requirements of the settlement agreement.[13] Coke's external recruiting of minorities has increased, and the company has sent all its managers and half its employees to two-day diversity awareness training. However, according to employee surveys, Coke's African American employees are, on average, less positive about fairness within the company than are white employees, particularly about fairness related to advancement and career opportunities.

Not Ensuring Equal Treatment of All Employees While in Training

Equal treatment of all trainees means that conditions of the learning environment, such as opportunities for practice, feedback, and role playing, are available for all trainees regardless of their background. Also, trainers should avoid jokes, stories, and props that might create a hostile learning environment. For example, because of claims that female employees were being harassed at air traffic control centers, the Federal Aviation Administration (FAA) required employees to attend diversity training. The diversity training required male employees to experience what it felt like to be taunted and jeered at as you walked down the aisle in an air traffic control facility (known as "walking the gauntlet"). One of the male employees found the experience to be distasteful and psychologically stressful, sued the FAA, and won.

Requiring Employees to Attend Programs That Might Be Offensive

Allstate Insurance has been the focus of several religious discrimination lawsuits brought by insurance agents who have found the Scientology principles emphasized in agent training programs offensive and counter to their religious beliefs. For example, the program taught concepts such as the "tone scale" which catalogs emotions and scientologists believe can influence behavior.[14]

Revealing Discriminatory Information during a Training Session

At Lucky Store Foods, a California supermarket chain, notes taken during a diversity training program were used as evidence of discrimination.[15] In the training session, supervisors were asked to verbalize their stereotypes. Some comments ("women cry more," "black women are aggressive") were derogatory toward women and minorities. The plaintiff in the case used the notes as evidence that the company conducted the training session to avoid an investigation by the Equal Employment Opportunity Commission. The case was settled out of court.

Not Accommodating Trainees with Disabilities

The **Americans with Disabilities Act (ADA)** of 1990 prohibits individuals with disabilities from being discriminated against in the workplace. The ADA prohibits discrimination based on disability in employment practices including hiring, firing, compensation, and training. The ADA defines a disability as a physical or mental impairment that substantially limits one or more major life activities, a record of having an impairment, or being regarded as having such an impairment. This includes serious disabilities such as epilepsy, blindness, or paralysis as well as persons who have a history of heart disease, mental illness, or cancer that is currently in remission.

The ADA requires companies to make "reasonable accommodation" to the physical or mental condition of a person with a disability who is otherwise qualified unless it would impose an "undue hardship" on the organization's operations. Determination of undue hardship is made by analyzing the type and cost of the accommodation in relation to the company's financial resources. Even if the undue hardship can be justified, the ADA requires that the person with the disability be provided the option of paying that part of the cost that causes the undue hardship.

In the context of training, **reasonable accommodation** refers to making training facilities readily accessible to and usable by individuals with disabilities. Reasonable accommodation may also include modifying instructional media, adjusting training policies, and providing trainees with readers or interpreters. Employers are not required to make reasonable accommodation if the person does not request them. Employers are also not required to make reasonable accommodation if persons are not qualified to participate in training programs (e.g., they lack the prerequisite certification or educational requirements).

One example of how the ADA might influence training activities involves adventure learning. Some adventure learning experiences demand a high level of physical fitness. Employees who have a disability cannot be required to attend adventure learning training programs.[16] If it does not cause an undue hardship, employees should be offered an alternative program for developing the learned capabilities emphasized in the adventure learning program.

It is impossible to give specific guidelines regarding the type of accommodations that trainers and managers should make to avoid violating the ADA. It is important to identify if the training is related to "essential" job functions. That is, are the tasks or knowledge, skills, and abilities that are the focus of training fundamental to the position? Task analysis information (discussed in Chapter 3) can be used to identify essential job functions. For example, tasks that are frequently performed and critical for successful job performance would be considered essential job functions. If training relates to a function that may be performed in the job but does not have to be performed by all persons (a marginal job function), then a disability in relation to that function cannot be used to exclude that person from training. To the extent that the disability makes it difficult for the person to receive the training necessary to complete essential job functions, the trainer must explore whether it is possible to make reasonable accommodations.

Incorrectly Reporting Training as an Expense or Failing to Report Training Reimbursement as Income

The cost of training is covered by Internal Revenue code. Companies can often deduct the cost of training provided to employees as a business expense. The Employer Assistance Program allows an employer to pay an employee up to $5,250 per year for certain educational expenses. This amount can be deducted by the employer as a business expense without adding the payment to the employee's yearly gross income. In other programs (e.g., the Educational Reimbursement Program), the employer can decide which training is paid for and how it is funded. Reimbursement for training expenses that an employee incurs may be considered part of the employee's taxable income. Employees may be able to deduct work-related educational expenses as itemized deductions on their income taxes. To be deductible, the expenses must be for training that maintains or improves skills required in the job or that serves a business purpose of the company and is required by the company, or by law or regulations, in order for employees to keep their present salary, status, or job. See www.irs.org for more information about business and individual reporting of educational expenses.

Cross-Cultural Preparation

As mentioned in Chapter 1, companies today are challenged to expand globally. Because of the increase in global operations, employees often work outside their country of origin or work with employees from other countries. Top managers who obtain experience through international assignments contribute to their global company's successful performance. Table 10.2 shows the different types of employees in global companies. **Expatriates** work in a country other than their country of origin. The most frequently selected locations for expatriate assignments include the United States, China, the United Kingdom, Singapore, Germany, and Japan.[17] Many U.S. companies are using international rotational assignments as a training tool. For example, at Microsoft, 14 divisions use international rotational programs. Companies are also increasing the movement of employees from one global location to another. These relocations involve the movement of management or technical positions from one country to another, such as from India to China or Vietnam. This type of relocation is less expensive than moving a U.S.-based manager (who would have to be paid wages comparable to what he or she would earn in the U.S.) to China. Unfortunately, only about 25 percent of companies make cultural training mandatory for international assignments.[18] This

TABLE 10.2 **Types of Employees in Global Companies**	*Parent-country national:* Employee whose country of origin is where the company has its headquarters *Host-country national:* Employee from the host country *Third-country national:* Employee who has a country of origin different from both the parent country and host country where he or she works

may be because of the mistaken belief that employees who have already been on international assignments or who have traveled internationally will be able to adapt to a new culture.

Because of a growing pool of talented labor around the world, greater use of host-country nationals is occurring.[19] (**Host-country nationals** are employees with citizenship in the country where the company is located.) A key reason is that a host-country national can more easily understand the values and customs of the work force than an expatriate can. Also, training and transporting U.S. employees and their families to a foreign assignment and housing them there tends to be more expensive than hiring a host-country national.

Cross-cultural preparation involves educating employees (expatriates) and their families who are to be sent to a foreign country. To successfully conduct business in the global marketplace, employees must understand the business practices and the cultural norms of different countries. Table 10.3's "impression shock" column shows the typical impressions that a Japanese manager may have of the U.S. culture. The "integration shock" column describes the typical American interpretation of Japanese managers' style. Clearly, for American and Japanese managers to have successful business discussions, they need to be prepared to deal with cultural differences!

Cross-cultural preparation is important for the success of the assignment, which can be very expensive. The annual cost of sending an employee overseas has been estimated to be three to seven times the employee's salary. Besides salary, expenses include taxation,

TABLE 10.3   **Negative Surprises Facing the Newly Arrived Japanese Manager**

	Impression Shock— Japanese Perceptions of American Ways	Integration Shock— American Responses to Japanese Ways
Community Life	Social diversity	Aloof/clannish community
	Violence and crime	Misunderstood customs
	Poverty and homelessness	Economic takeover
	Education problems	Lingering resentment
	Ignorance of foreign ways	Self-serving conduct
Business Practice	Different operations	Vagueness and delay
	Shortsightedness	Overworked employees
	Lackluster service	Unfair industrial groups
	Hasty dealmaking	Ethical violations
	Legal minefields	Influence peddling
Organizational Dynamics	No spiritual quality	Management inexperience
	Individual careerism	Avoided accountability
	Narrow job focus	Closed inner circle
	Political confrontation	Stifled employees
	Employee disloyalty	Discriminatory practices
Interpersonal Dealings	Assertiveness	Distrust/secrecy
	Frankness	Arrogance/hubris
	Egoism	Withheld sentiments
	Glibness	Cautious intimacy
	Impulsiveness	Excessive sensitivity

Note: The individual entries in the two columns are not aligned to correspond to one another. They merely list the major surprises experienced by visitors.
Source: Richard G. Linowes, "The Japanese Manager's Traumatic Entry into the United States: Understanding the American-Japanese Cultural Divide," *Academy of Management Executive* 7, no. 4 (1993): 26.

housing, and education.[20] Most companies offer tax equalization to expatriates. That is, the company will either pay taxes, offer additional salary, or provide other goods and services, depending on tax laws, so that the employee does not incur additional tax expenses by living abroad. For example, expatriates in Germany may have twice the income tax they would have in the United States, and they are taxed on their housing and cost-of-living allowances. Most employees expect to duplicate their U.S. housing arrangements, and expatriates with families may expect that they will be able to send their children to English-speaking schools, which adds considerable expense. Unfortunately, 10 to 50 percent of expatriates return early from their assignments, costing companies between $250,000 and $1 million![21] Even if they do not return early, expatriates who are not adequately prepared for the assignments can still hurt the company through damaged relations, poor productivity, or lost business opportunities.

Dimensions of Cultural Differences

Many cultural characteristics influence employee behavior. Keep in mind that there are national cultures as well as company cultures. A **culture** refers to the set of assumptions that group members share about the world and how it works and the ideals worth striving for.[22] Culture is important because it influences the effectiveness of different behaviors and management styles. A management style that seems friendly to some employees might offend others who would rather maintain distance and respect toward their bosses.

In Germany, managers achieve their status by demonstrating technical skills, and employees look to managers to assign tasks and resolve technical problems. In the Netherlands, managers focus on seeking agreement, exchanging views, and balancing the interests of people affected by a decision.[23] Indians may shake hands rather limply and avoid eye contact. This is not a sign of dislike or disrespect. In Indian culture, a soft handshake conveys respect, and lack of eye contact is a sign of deference.[24] Consider how cultural differences affect European managers' perceptions of American managers.[25] European managers admire the financial results of many American companies. But they also believe that American managers do not know how to eat and drink properly and do not understand European history. One German manager was embarrassed when managers from an Indiana company to whom he was recently introduced called him by his first name. In Germany, such informality occurs only after long-term relationships have been established. Other work style differences include the American emphasis on monthly and quarterly business results versus the European focus on yearly and longer-term profits.

Research conducted by G. Hofstede identified five dimensions of national culture: individualism-collectivism, uncertainty avoidance, masculinity-femininity, power distance, and time orientation.[26] Figure 10.1 shows the locations of selected countries on these dimensions. Awareness of these dimensions can help trainers develop cross-cultural preparation programs that include meaningful information regarding the culture the expatriates will find themselves working in. Awareness of these dimensions can also help trainers adapt their training styles to employees in non-U.S. locations. But note that individuals differ within any culture, so these generalizations describe some members of a culture better than others.

The degree to which people act as individuals rather than as members of a group is the cultural dimension known as **individualism-collectivism**. In an individualistic culture like the United States, employees expect to be hired, evaluated, and rewarded based on their

FIGURE 10.1   **Cultural Dimensions with Relative Standing of Selected Countries**

Source: From P. M. Wright and R. A. Noe, *Management of Organizations* (Burr Ridge, IL: Irwin/McGraw-Hill, 1996).

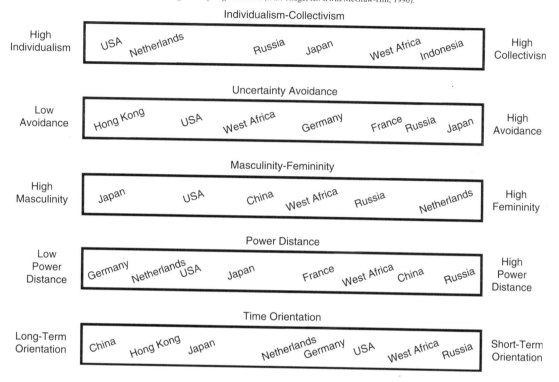

personal skills and accomplishments. In a collectivist culture, employees are more likely to have a voice in decisions. As you saw in Table 10.3, Japanese managers, who tend to have a collectivist orientation, can be shocked by the apparent self-interest of their American colleagues!

Uncertainty avoidance refers to the degree to which people prefer structured rather than unstructured situations. Cultures with a strong uncertainty avoidance orientation (e.g., Japan, Russia) favor structured situations. Religion, law, or technology in these countries socialize people to seek security through clear rules on how to act. In a culture with weak uncertainty avoidance (e.g., Jamaica, Hong Kong), employees cope by not worrying too much about the future.

Masculinity-femininity refers to the extent to which the culture values behavior considered traditionally masculine (competitiveness) or feminine (helpfulness). Examples of "masculine" cultures include Japan, Germany, and the United States. Here assertiveness and competitiveness are valued. In contrast, in a culture such as the Netherlands, a higher value is likely placed on quality of life, helping others, and preserving the environment.

Power distance refers to expectations for the unequal distribution of power in a hierarchy. India, Mexico, and Russia, for example, have great power distance. This means that people attempt to maintain differences between various levels of the hierarchy. One illustration of differences in power distance is how people talk to one another. In high power distance countries such as Mexico and Japan, people address each other with titles (Señor Smith, Smith-san). At the other extreme, in most situations in the United States people use first names—behavior that would be disrespectful in other countries.

Time orientation refers to the degree to which a culture focuses on the future rather than the past and present. In cultures with a short-term orientation, such as the United States, Russia, and West Africa, the orientation is toward the past and present. These cultures tend to emphasize respect for tradition and social obligations. A culture with a long-term orientation, such as Japan and China, values such traits as thrift and persistence, which pay off in the future rather than the present.

In a Mexican slipper-manufacturing plant (a culture with high power distance), an effort to expand the decision-making authority of production workers was derailed when the workers rebelled at doing what they saw as the manager's work.[27] Realizing they had moved too quickly, the managers narrowed the scope of the workers' decision-making authority. On the other hand, Mexico's high collectivism culture supported worker empowerment. The employees liked discussing team-related information and using the information to benefit the entire team.

Implications for Expatriates and Their Families: Cross-Cultural Training

To prepare employees for cross-cultural assignments, companies need to provide cross-cultural training. To be successful in overseas assignments, expatriates (employees on foreign assignments) need to be

1. Competent in their area of expertise.
2. Able to communicate verbally and nonverbally in the host country.
3. Flexible, tolerant of ambiguity, emotionally stable, outgoing and agreeable, and sensitive to cultural differences.
4. Motivated to succeed, able to enjoy the challenge of working in other countries, and willing to learn about the host country's culture, language, and customs.
5. Supported by their families.[28]

Studies have found that personality characteristics were related to expatriates' desire to terminate the assignment as well as to their performance in the assignment.[29] Expatriates who were extroverted (outgoing), agreeable (cooperative, tolerant), and conscientious (dependable, achievement-oriented) were more likely to want to stay on the assignment and perform well. This suggests that cross-cultural training may be effective only when an expatriate's personality predisposes him or her to be successful in assignments in other cultures.

One reason for U.S. expatriates' high failure rate is that companies place more emphasis on developing employees' technical skills than on preparing them to work in other cultures. Research suggests that the comfort of an expatriate's spouse and family is the most important determinant of whether the employee will complete the assignment.[30]

One key to successful foreign assignment appears to be a combination of training and career management for employees and their families. Foreign assignments involve three phases: predeparture, on-site, and repatriation (preparing to return home). Training is necessary in all three phases.

Predeparture Phase In the predeparture phase, employees need to receive language training and an orientation in the new country's culture and customs. It is critical that the family be included in the orientation programs.[31] Expatriates and their families need information about housing, schools, recreation, shopping, and health care facilities in the area where they will live. Expatriates also must discuss with their managers how the foreign assignment fits into employees' career plans and what type of position expatriates can expect upon return. Although English is the common business language in many countries, failing to speak the native language may keep the expatriate from informal conversations and increase the risk of being misinterpreted.[32] For example, a manager at ABB Ltd. oversees 7,000 employees in China and speaks only basic Mandarin. He is having difficulty conducting business with his Chinese employees because they are reluctant to say no to managers. Because he isn't fluent in Chinese languages, he tries to read employees' body language but often reaches the wrong conclusions.

Cross-cultural training methods range from presentational techniques, such as lectures that expatriates and their families attend on the customs and culture of the host country, to actual experiences in the home country in culturally diverse communities.[33] Experiential exercises, such as miniculture experiences, allow expatriates to spend time with a family in the United States that is from the ethnic group of the host country.

Research suggests that the degree of difference between the United States and the host country (cultural novelty), the amount of interaction with host country citizens and host nationals (interaction), and the familiarity with new job tasks and work environment (job novelty) all influence the "rigor" of the cross-cultural training method.

Rigor here refers to the degree to which the training program emphasizes knowledge about the culture as well as behavior and skills needed to effectively live in the culture. Less rigorous training methods such as lectures and briefings focus on communicating factual material about the country and culture to trainees. More rigorous methods not only offer factual material but also help expatriates and their families develop communication skills and behavior needed to interact in another country. Figure 10.2 shows the relationship between training rigor and training focus (characteristics that a training program needs to be effective).[34] Experiential training methods are most effective (and most needed) in assignments with a high level of cultural and job novelty that require a good deal of interpersonal interaction with host nationals. A trainer from India took 20 managers from Advanced Micro Devices on a two-week immersion trip during which the group traveled to New Delhi, Bangalore, and Mumbai, meeting with businesspersons and government officials.[35] The program, which required six months of planning, provided the executives with information on foods to eat, potential security issues, and how to interact in business meetings. For example, Indians prefer to indirectly enter into business discussions, so the managers were advised to first discuss current events and other subjects before talking business.

On-Site Phase On-site training involves continued orientation to the host country and its customs and cultures through formal programs or through a mentoring relationship. Expatriates and their families may be paired with a mentor from the host country who helps them understand the new, unfamiliar work environment and community.[36] Companies are also using the Web to answer questions from employees on expatriate assignments.[37] Expatriates can access a Web site for answers to questions such as, "How do I conduct a meeting here?" or "What religious philosophy might have influenced today's negotiation behavior?" Knowledge management software allows employees to contribute, organize, and access knowledge specific to their expatriate assignment.

A major reason that employees refuse expatriate assignments is that they can't afford to lose their spouse's income or are concerned that their spouse's career could be derailed by

FIGURE 10.2

Relationship between Training Methods and Training Rigor

Source: Based on L. Littrell and E. Salas, "A Review of Cross-Cultural Training: Best Practices, Guidelines, and Research Needs," *Human Resource Development Review* 4 (2005): 305–34; M. Mendenhall, E. Dunbar, and G. Oddou, "Expatriate Selection, Training, and Career-Pathing: A Review and Critique," *Human Resource Management* 26 (1987): 331–45.

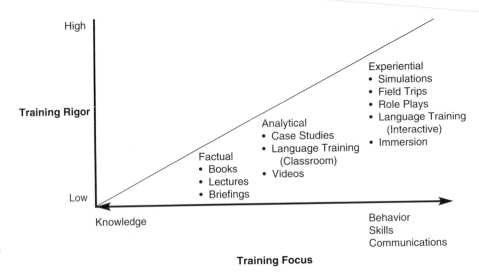

being out of the work force for a few years.[38] Spouses may be unable to work in the host country because of difficulties in obtaining a work permit. Some "trailing" spouses decide to use the time to pursue educational activities that could contribute to their long-term career goals. But it is difficult to find these opportunities in an unfamilar place. Pfizer, the pharmaceutical firm, is taking action to help trailing spouses. It provides a $10,000 allowance that the spouse can use in many different ways. A person at the expatriate location is assigned to help the spouse with professional development and locating educational or other resources. In countries where spouses are allowed to work, Pfizer tries to find them jobs within the company. Pfizer also provides cross-cultural counseling and language assistance. The company tries to connect the family with the expatriate community. Several multinational companies, including Hewlett-Packard, Axalto, and Group Danon, have worked together to develop partnerjob.com, an online employment resource that helps trailing spouses find work by posting job openings at other member companies.[39] However, a major restriction to spouse employment is work permit rules requiring potential employers to demonstrate that the spouse possesses skills that are not locally available.

Research suggests that companies should offer support for expatriates.[40] Services such as career counseling for expatriates are important for reducing stress and anxiety. Support from the foreign facility (either one person or a department) is also important for work and interaction adjustment. Expatriates who have high-quality relationships with their supervisors are more effective in completing job responsibilities.

Repatriation Phase **Repatriation** prepares expatriates for return to the parent company and country from the foreign assignment. Expatriates and their families are likely to experience high levels of stress and anxiety when they return because of the changes that have occurred since their departure. This shock can be reduced by providing expatriates with company newsletters and community newspapers and by ensuring that they receive personal and work-related mail from the United States while they are on foreign assignment. It is also not uncommon for employees and their families to have to readjust to a lower standard of living in the United States than they enjoyed in the foreign country, where they may have had maid service, a limousine, private schools, and clubs. Salary and other compensation arrangements should be worked out well before employees return from overseas assignments.

Aside from reentry shock, many expatriates decide to leave the company because the assignment they are given upon returning to the United States has less responsibility, challenge, and status than the foreign assignment.[41] Experts suggest that companies can minimize turnover by offering the expatriates recognition, career support, a choice in the assignment they are given upon return, and opportunities to use their international experience.[42] As noted earlier, career planning discussions need to be held before the employees leave the United States to ensure that they understand the positions they will be eligible for upon repatriation.

Employees should be encouraged to self-manage the repatriation process.[43] Before they go on the assignment, they need to consider what skills they want to develop and the types of jobs that might be available in the company for an employee with those skills. Because the company may undergo changes and because colleagues, peers, and managers may leave while the expatriate is on assignment, he or she needs to maintain contact with key company and industry people. Otherwise, the employee's reentry shock will be heightened from having to deal with new colleagues, a somewhat changed job, and a company culture that may have shifted.

Royal Dutch Shell, a joint Dutch and United Kingdom oil and gas company, has one of the world's largest expatriate work forces.[44] To avoid expatriates who feel undervalued and leave the company, Royal Dutch gets involved with expatriates and their careers. Resource planners track workers abroad, helping to identify their next assignment. Most expatriates know their next assignment three to six months before the move, and all begin the next assignment with a clear job description. Expatriates who have the potential to reach top-level management positions are placed in the home office every third assignment to increase their visibility to company executives. Expatriates are also assigned technical mentors who evaluate their skills and help them improve their skills through training at Royal Dutch's training center.

Because of the difficulty in getting employees to accept foreign assignments and the low success rate of expatriate assignments, companies are creating "virtual" expatriate positions and using short-time assignments.[45] **Virtual expatriates** are assigned an operation abroad to manage without being located permanently in that country. The employees periodically travel to the overseas location, return, and later use videoconferencing and communications technology to manage the operation. Virtual expatriates eliminate exposing the family to the culture shock of an overseas move. This setup also allows the employee to manage globally while keeping in close touch with the home office. Virtual expatriates are less expensive than traditional expatriates, who can cost companies over three times as much as a host-country national employee. One major disadvantage of virtual expatriates is that visiting a foreign operation on a sporadic basis may lengthen the time needed to build a local management team, so it will take longer to solve problems because of the lack of a strong personal relationship with local employees.

Because of family issues, poor economic times, and security issues, many companies are reducing the number of expatriates and relying more on short-time assignments, frequent business travel, and international commutes in which an employee lives in one country and works in another.[46] Companies such as Wal-Mart Stores and NCR have reduced the number of expatriate assignments, but they still believe that long-term expatriate assignments are necessary in order to develop key talent possessing global responsibilities and experience. One of the potential difficulties of short-term international assignments is that employees may be perceived as foreigners rather than colleagues because they haven't had the time to build relationships and develop trust among co-workers in their short-term location. Another is that traveling can take a physical and emotional toll on employees as they try to juggle business responsibilities with maintaining contact with family and friends. Procter & Gamble helps employees on short-term assignments by providing a trip fund that is based on the length of time an employee is on an extended business trip. For example, a U.S.-based employee working in western Europe for six months would get a fund containing the cost of five business-class round-trips. The employee can use money from the fund to take trips home or to cover family visits to the employee's location.

Implications of Cultural Differences for Training

Table 10.4 presents the implications of each of the cultural dimensions for training. In the United States, interaction between the trainer and the trainees is viewed as a positive characteristic of the learning environment. However, in other cultures, this type of learning environment may not be familiar to the trainee or may violate expected norms of good instruction. For example, consider the cultural differences that exist when conducting training programs in China compared to Brazil.[47] In China, trainers are highly respected. Because education is valued, trainees are most likely motivated to learn. Because China is a culture high on power distance, trainees expect the trainer to lead the class as an expert, lecture is the preferred delivery method, and it is difficult for trainees to question the trainer. Harmony is valued in China because the culture is low on individualism. Therefore, trainers should focus on group performance and not highlight the performance of individual trainees. In Brazil, on the other hand, trainers need to build a personal relationship with trainees, so trainers should share their experiences and background. Power distance in Brazil is accepted and respected. Popular training methods in Brazil include lecture and small group work. Group discussion of issues may be uncomfortable for trainers because the trainees may seem like they are arguing and angry with each other; however, they are engaging in acceptable communication behavior in Brazil.

TABLE 10.4
Implications of Cultural Dimensions for Training Design

Source: Based on B. Filipczak, "Think Locally, Train Globally," *Training* (January 1997): 41–48.

Cultural Dimension	Implications
Individualism	Culture high in individualism expects participation in exercises and questioning to be determined by status in the company or culture.
Uncertainty Avoidance	Culture high in uncertainty avoidance expects formal instructional environments; less tolerance for impromptu style.
Masculinity	Culture low in masculinity values relationships with fellow trainees; female trainers less likely to be resisted in low-masculinity cultures.
Power Distance	Culture high in power distance expects trainer to be expert; trainers expected to be authoritarian and controlling of session.
Time Orientation	Culture with a long-term orientation will have trainees who are likely to accept development plans and assignments.

Expectations regarding the environment in which training is to occur may also differ from U.S. culture. On-the-job training may be viewed skeptically by Russian employees because historically most workers are expected to have been formally trained by attending lectures at an institute or university.[48] Because Russian culture values family relationships (Russian culture is more "feminine" than American culture), the meaningfulness of training materials is likely to be enhanced by using examples from employees' work and life situations.

Besides cultural dimensions, trainers must consider language differences in preparing training materials. If an interpreter is used, it is important to conduct a practice session with the interpreter to evaluate pacing of the session and whether the amount of topics and material is appropriate. Training materials, including videos and exercises, need to be translated well in advance of the training session.

Consider the Deloitte Touche Tohmatsu (DTT) ethics training.[49] DTT must establish, sustain, and communicate high ethical standards to clients worldwide. Nine ethical principles are required by all the member firms: honesty and integrity, professional behavior, competence, objectivity, confidentiality, fair business practices, responsibility to society, respect and fair treatment of colleagues, and leading by example. DTT provides Web-based training through a program it calls the Integrity Compass. The company has a chief ethics partner for at least one member firm in each country it operates in. A toll-free telephone hotline is available for employees to report evidence of unethical conduct. The hotline presents a cultural challenge. In some countries, history and values make the hotline unacceptable. For example, in France and Italy, anonymous tips are associated with memories of people collaborating with the enemy during World War II. In parts of the Middle East, employees might accept the idea of making reports to a local office but not to an international headquarters. In addition to addressing the value differences, DTT faces the challenge of providing understandable and accurate ethics materials in several languages. Examples used in training materials also need to be realistic for the different cultures. As a result, although the nine ethical principles are shared globally, DTT has customized various elements of the ethics program to match the culture of each country.

The key to success in a foreign training session is preparation! The needs assessment must include an evaluation of cultural dimensions and the characteristics of the audience (such as language ability, trainees' company, and cultural status).

Managing Work Force Diversity

Despite the efforts of many companies to embrace diversity, women and minorities continue to report many barriers to feeling valued and advancing in their careers.[50] A survey by the Society for Human Resource Management revealed barriers including stereotyping and preconceptions, corporate culture, exclusion from informal networks, and lack of mentors and role models. That is, anyone who is perceived as "different" is likely to have a difficult time contributing to company goals and experiencing personal growth.

What Is Diversity? Why Is It Important?

Diversity can be considered any dimension that differentiates one person from another.[51] For example, at Verizon, diversity means embracing differences and variety, including age, ethnicity, education, sexual orientation, work style, race, gender, and more. The goals of diversity training are (1) to eliminate values, stereotypes, and managerial practices that inhibit employees' personal development and therefore (2) to allow employees to contribute to organizational goals regardless of their race, age, physical condition, sexual orientation, gender, family status, religious orientation, or cultural background.[52] Because of equal opportunity employment laws, companies have been forced to ensure that women and minorities are adequately represented in their labor force. That is, companies are focused on ensuring equal access to jobs. Also, as was discussed in Chapter 1, the impact of culture on the workplace, and specifically on training and development, has received heightened attention. Cultural factors that companies need to consider include the terrorist attacks of 9/11; employees' fear of discussing cultural differences; more work being conducted in teams whose members have many different characteristics; the realization that people from diverse cultures represent an important customer market; and, especially for professional and technical jobs, the availability of highly trained employees that has many companies seeking workers from overseas. These new immigrants need diversity training to help them understand such facets of American culture as obsession with time, individualistic attitudes, and capitalistic ideas.[53]

Managing diversity involves creating an environment that allows all employees to contribute to organizational goals and experience personal growth. This environment includes access to jobs as well as fair and positive treatment of all employees. The company must develop employees who are comfortable working with people from a wide variety of ethnic, racial, and religious backgrounds. Managing diversity may require changing the company culture. It includes the company's standards and norms about how employees are treated, competitiveness, results orientation, innovation, and risk taking. The value placed on diversity is grounded in the company culture.

Table 10.5 shows how managing diversity can help companies gain a competitive advantage. Various customer groups appreciate doing business with employees like themselves.

TABLE 10.5   **How Managing Diversity Can Provide a Competitive Advantage**

Argument	Rationale
Cost	As organizations become more diverse, the cost of a poor job in integrating workers will increase. Organizations that handle integration well will thus create cost advantages over those that don't.
Employee Attraction and Retention	Companies develop reputations as favorable prospective employers for women and ethnic minorities. Those with the best reputations for managing diversity will win the competition for the best personnel. As the labor pool shrinks and changes composition, this edge will become increasingly important.
Market Share	For multinational organizations, the insight and cultural sensitivity that members with roots in other countries bring to the marketing effort should improve these efforts in important ways. The same rationale applies to marketing to subpopulations within domestic operations.
Creativity	Diversity of perspectives and less emphasis on conformity to norms of the past (which characterize the modern approach to management of diversity) should improve the level of creativity.
Problem Solving	Heterogeneity in decisions and problem-solving groups potentially produces better decisions through a wider range of perspectives and more thorough critical analysis of issues.
Flexibility	Organizations that become more diverse will experience greater adaptability in a rapidly changing market.

Source: Based on N. Lockwood, *Workplace Diversity: Leveraging the Power of Difference for Competitive Advantage* (Alexandria, VA: Society for Human Resource Management, 2005); T. H. Cox and S. Blake, "Managing Cultural Diversity: Implications for Organizational Competitiveness," *Academy of Management Executive* 5 (1991): 47.

Also, diverse employees can contribute insights into customers and product markets. For example, Hispanic, African American, and other employee groups at Bausch & Lomb have helped the company better understand employees as well as customers.[54] Bausch & Lomb is now doing more consumer marketing and targeting more advertising at specific groups, such as gays, who are more likely to use new procedures like Lasik eye surgery. Also, the company is looking at the rates of eye diseases in Hispanics and African Americans to see if customer needs match current product offerings. Companies also need creativity and innovation to cope with the rapid pace of change. Research supports the view that these traits are more likely to exist in a company whose employees come from a variety of backgrounds.[55]

Capitalizing on diversity also plays a major role in the success of work teams.[56] Diversity goes beyond differences in race, physical appearance, ethnicity, and sexual orientation to include differences in communication and problem-solving style and professional and functional expertise (e.g., marketing versus engineering). When teams don't capitalize on differences but instead get caught up in identifying differences, distrust and unproductive teams usually result. Many companies (e.g., IBM, Colgate-Palmolive) have used a strategy that focuses on awareness of differences and on providing the skills that successful team members need. Team mission statements should reflect not only what the team is supposed to accomplish but also how interpersonal conflict should be handled. Some companies even require rotation of responsibilities so each person has a chance to demonstrate his or her abilities (and show that stereotypes based on race or function are not valid).

Diversity can enhance company performance when organizations have an environment that promotes learning from diversity. The link between diversity and company performance is both direct and indirect. The diversity–financial success relationship is not always directly observable.[57] For example, a Hispanic manager at DuPont Merck recommended labeling a drug in Spanish. This significantly improved sales.[58] Harley-Davidson has added more female and minority managers and has created a work environment to retain them.[59] The company believes that more visible female and minority employees will attract more female and minority customers. Currently, women make up 10 percent of Harley-Davidson customers, and people of color account for 7 percent. IBM, by adding more female and minority managers, has increased its amount of business with small and mid-size minority-owned companies from $10 million in 1998 to $300 million. For a company to see the success of its diversity efforts, it must make a long-term commitment to managing diversity. Successful diversity requires that it be viewed as an opportunity for employees to (1) learn from each other how to better accomplish their work, (2) be provided with a supportive and cooperative organizational culture, and (3) be taught leadership and process skills that can facilitate effective team functioning. Diversity is a reality in labor and customer markets and is a social expectation and value. Managers should focus on building an organizational environment, human resource practices, and managerial and team skills that all capitalize on diversity. As you will see in the discussion that follows, managing diversity requires difficult cultural change, not just slogans on the wall!

Managing Diversity through Adherence to Legislation

One approach to managing diversity is through affirmative action policies and human resource practices that meet standards of equal employment opportunity laws.[60] This approach rarely results in changes in employees' values, stereotypes, and behaviors, which can inhibit productivity and personal development. Figure 10.3 shows the cycle of disillusionment that

FIGURE 10.3
Cycle of
Disillusionment
That Results
from Managing
Diversity
through
Adherence to
Legislation

Source: C. Torres and
M. Bruxelles,
"Capitalizing on
Global Diversity"
HR Magazine
(December 1992):
30–33. Reprinted with
the permission of
HR Magazine.
Published by the
Society for Human
Resource
Management,
Alexandria, VA.

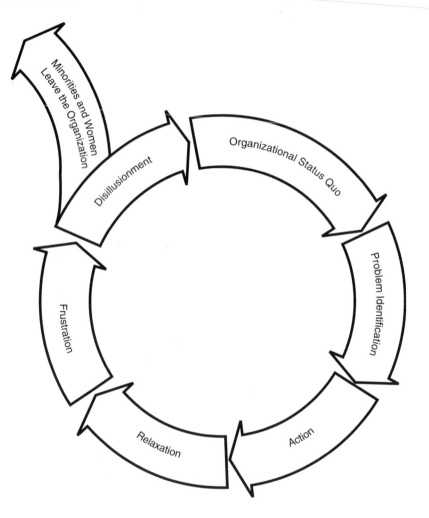

results from managing diversity by relying solely on adherence to employment laws. The cycle
begins when the company realizes that it must change policies regarding women and minorities because of legal pressure or a discrepancy between the number or percentage of women
and minorities in the company's work force and the number available in the broader labor
market. To address these concerns, a greater number of women and minorities are hired by the
company. Managers see little need for additional action because women and minority employment rates reflect their availability in the labor market. However, as women and minorities
gain experience in the company, they likely become frustrated. Managers and co-workers may
avoid providing coaching or performance feedback to women and minorities because they are
uncomfortable interacting with individuals from different gender, ethnic, or racial backgrounds. Co-workers may express the belief that women and minorities are employed only
because they have received special treatment (e.g., hiring standards were lowered).[61] As a
result of their frustration, women and minorities may form support groups to voice their concerns to management. Because of the work atmosphere, women and minorities may fail to
fully utilize their skills and may leave the company.

Managing Diversity through Diversity Training Programs

The preceding discussion is not to suggest that companies should be reluctant to engage in affirmative action or pursue equal opportunity employment practices. However, affirmative action without additional supporting strategies does not deal with issues of assimilating women and minorities into the work force. To successfully manage a diverse work force, companies need to ensure that

- Employees understand how their values and stereotypes influence their behavior toward people of a different gender, ethnicity, race, or religion.
- Employees gain an appreciation of cultural differences among themselves.
- Behaviors that isolate or intimidate minority group members improve.

These goals can be accomplished through diversity training programs. **Diversity training** refers to training designed to change employee attitudes about diversity and/or to help employees develop the skills needed to work with a diverse work force. Diversity training programs differ according to whether attitude or behavior change is emphasized.[62] Some research suggests that composition of the training group and prior experience with diversity training may affect attitudinal and behavior change.[63] Diversity training programs purchased off the shelf or developed without taking into account the company's needs, history, and culture will likely be unsuccessful.[64]

Attitude Awareness and Change Programs   **Attitude awareness and change programs** focus on increasing employees' awareness of differences in cultural and ethnic backgrounds, physical characteristics (e.g., disabilities), and personal characteristics that influence behavior toward others. Awareness training covers questions such as, What is diversity? Who am I? and stereotypes, assumptions and biases regarding different ethnic groups. The assumption underlying these programs is that by increasing their awareness of stereotypes and beliefs, employees will be able to avoid negative stereotypes when interacting with employees of different backgrounds. The programs help employees consider the similarities and differences between cultural groups, examine their attitudes toward affirmative action, or analyze their beliefs about why minority employees are successful or unsuccessful in their jobs. Many of these programs use videotapes and experiential exercises to increase employees' awareness of the negative emotional and performance effects of stereotypes, values, and behaviors on minority group members. Sodexo serves millions of customers each day in the cafeterias it operates in companies and universities.[65] As a result, Sodexo believes that it is important for its managers to understand the needs of a diverse customer base. The company has mandatory classes that provide managers with an overview of equal opportunity and affirmative action laws. As you will see later in the chapter, these classes are part of the company's larger effort to manage diversity. The classes relate to other initiatives, which include courses on generational differences and body language that can be offensive. The courses use group dialogues and scenarios. One game requires participants to wear labels such as "hearing impaired" and interact with others based on that description.

The attitude awareness and change approach has been criticized for several reasons.[66] First, by focusing on group differences, the program may communicate that certain stereotypes and attitudes are valid. For example, in diversity training a male manager may learn that female employees prefer to work by building consensus rather than by arguing until others agree with their point. He might conclude that the training has validated his stereotype. As a result, he will continue to fail to give women important job responsibilities that involve "heated" negotiations with customers or clients. Second, encouraging employees to share their attitudes, feelings, and stereotypes toward certain groups may cause employees to feel discriminated against, guilty, angry, and less likely to see the similarities among racial, ethnic, or gender groups and the advantages of working together. (Consider the discussion of Lucky Store Foods earlier in the chapter.) Third, if diversity training only covers issues such as race, gender, ethnicity, or sexual orientation, some employees may feel that their interests are not represented in the program.[67]

Behavior-Based Programs **Behavior-based programs** focus on changing the organizational policies and individual behaviors that inhibit employees' personal growth and productivity.

One approach of these programs is to identify incidents that discourage employees from working up to their potential. Groups of employees are asked to identify specific promotion opportunities, sponsorships, training opportunities, or performance management practices that they believe were handled unfairly. The program may collect employees' views regarding how well the work environment and management practices value employee differences and provide equal opportunity. Specific training programs may be developed to address the issues presented in the focus groups.

Another approach is to teach managers and employees basic rules of behavior in the workplace.[68] These lessons include behavior toward peers and managers as well as customers. For example, managers and employees should learn that it is inappropriate to use statements and engage in behaviors that have negative racial, sexual, or cultural content. Companies that have focused on teaching rules and behavior have found that employees react less negatively to this type of training than to other diversity training approaches. All 11,000 employees at Saks Fifth Avenue, the New York–based retailer, have received diversity training that focuses on providing customer service to a diverse customer base. The training is video-based and shows actual employees interacting with customers in various situations. Saks Fifth Avenue estimates that every customer interaction is worth about $250, so treating customers inappropriately can cost the company a lot of money.[69]

A third approach is cultural immersion. **Cultural immersion** refers to the process of sending employees directly into communities where they have to interact with persons from different cultures, races, and/or nationalities. The degree of interaction varies, but it may involve talking with community members, working in community organizations, or learning about religious, cultural, or historically significant events. For example, the United Parcel Service (UPS) Community Internship Program is a management development program designed to help UPS senior managers understand the needs of diverse customers and a diverse work force through exposure to poverty and inequality.[70] UPS is the world's largest package delivery company and a leading global provider of transportation and logistic services. Since 1968, over 1,200 senior managers have completed the program, an internship that typically lasts four weeks. The internships take the managers to cities throughout the United States, where they work on the problems facing local populations. UPS managers may find themselves serving meals to the homeless, working in AIDS centers, helping migrant farm workers, building temporary housing and schools, and managing children in a Head Start program. These experiences take the managers outside their comfort zones, and the problems that they encounter—from transportation to housing to education to health care—help them better understand the issues that many UPS employees face daily. This enlightenment is a business necessity for UPS because three out of four managers are white, whereas 35 percent of the employees are minorities. UPS has not formally evaluated the program, but the company continues to invest $10,000 per intern. The company has invested more than $13.5 billion in the program since its start in 1968. Despite the lack of hard evaluation data, UPS managers report that the program helps them look for unconventional solutions to problems. One manager who spent a month working at a halfway house in New York was impressed by the creative ideas of uneducated addicts for keeping teens away from drugs. The manager realized that she had failed to capitalize on the creativity of the employees she supervised. As a result, when she returned to her job and faced problems, she started brainstorming with her entire staff, not just senior managers. Other managers report that the experience helped them empathize with employees facing crises at home.

Characteristics of Successful Diversity Efforts

Which is most effective, a behavior-based program or an attitude awareness and change program? Increasing evidence shows that attitude awareness programs are ineffective and that one-time diversity training programs are unlikely to succeed. Effective diversity training programs are part of a broader company strategy to manage diversity and make capitalizing on diversity a business goal.

For example, R. R. Donnelley & Sons suspended its diversity awareness training program even though the company spent more than $3 million on it as a result of a racial discrimination lawsuit.[71] At various R. R. Donnelley training sessions, participants were encouraged to voice their concerns. Many said that they were experiencing difficulty in working effectively because of abuse and harassment. The managers who were attending the training disputed those concerns. Also, after training, an employee who applied for an open position was rejected because, she was told, she was too honest in expressing her concerns during the diversity training session. Although R. R. Donnelley held many diversity training sessions, little progress was made in increasing the employment and promotion rates of women and minorities. Because of the low ratio of black employees to white employees, many black employees were asked to attend multiple training sessions to ensure diverse groups, which they resented. The company declined to release to shareholders data that it provided to the Equal Employment Opportunity Commission regarding female and minority representation in jobs throughout the company. The firm also failed to act on recommendations made by company-approved employee "diversity councils."

More generally, surveys of diversity training efforts have found that

- The most common area addressed through diversity is the pervasiveness of stereotypes, assumptions, and biases.
- Fewer than one-third of the companies do any kind of long-term evaluation or follow-up. The most common indicators of success are reduced number of grievances and lawsuits, increased diversity in promotions and hiring, increased self-awareness of biases, and increased consultation of human resource specialists on diversity-related issues.
- Most programs last only one day or less.
- Three-fourths of the survey respondents indicate that they believe the typical employee leaves diversity training with positive attitudes toward diversity. However, over 50 percent report that the programs have no effect over the long term.[72]

• Twenty-nine percent of survey respondents report that no tools are provided to reinforce diversity training and 22 percent report that no development or advancement issues are addressed.

Table 10.6 shows the characteristics associated with the long-term success of diversity programs. It is critical that the diversity program be tied to business objectives. For example, cultural differences affect the type of skin cream consumers believe they need or the fragrance they may be attracted to. Understanding cultural differences is part of understanding the consumer (which is critical to the success of companies such as Avon). Top management support can be demonstrated by creating a structure to support the initiative. For example, Pepsi's president believes that the full potential of diversity cannot be realized unless employees are "comfortable being uncomfortable" so that they are willing to share difficult issues in the workplace.[73] As a result, members of the senior management team have been named as sponsors for specific employee groups, including African Americans, Latinos, Asians, women, women of color, white males, people with disabilities, and people who are gay, lesbian, and transgendered. The managers are expected to understand their group members' needs, identify talent, and mentor at least three employees in their group. Also, they are expected to provide updates to the president on their progress.

Another important characteristic of diversity programs is that managers are rewarded for progress toward meeting diversity goals.[74] Allstate Insurance Company surveys all 50,000 of its employees four times a year. The survey asks employees to evaluate how well the company is satisfying customers and employees. Several questions are used as a "diversity index." Employees are asked questions about the extent to which managers' racial or gender biases affect development opportunities, promotions, and service to customers. Twenty-five percent of a manager's yearly bonus is determined by how employees evaluate him or her on the diversity index.

TABLE 10.6   **Characteristics Associated with Diversity Programs' Long-Term Success**

- Top management provides resources, personally intervenes, and publicly advocates diversity.
- The program is structured.
- Capitalizing on a diverse work force is defined as a business objective.
- Capitalizing on a diverse work force is seen as necessary to generate revenue and profits.
- The program is evaluated using metrics such as sales, retention, and promotion rates.
- Manager involvement is mandatory.
- The program is seen as a culture change, not a one-shot program.
- Managers and demographic groups are not blamed for problems.
- Behaviors and skills needed to successfully interact with others are taught.
- Managers are rewarded on progress toward meeting diversity goals.
- Management collects employee feedback and responds to it.
- The company fosters a safe and open culture to which all employees want to belong and in which all employees can discover and appreciate the differences and benefits of diversity.

Source: R. Anand and M. Winters, "A Retrospective View of Corporate Diversity Training from 1964 to the Present," *Academy of Management Learning & Education* 7: 356–372; C. Chavez and J. Weisinger, "Beyond Diversity Training: A Social Infusion for Cultural Inclusion," *Human Resource Management* 47 (2008): 331–350; M. Jayne and R. Dipboye, "Leveraging Diversity to Improve Business Performance: Research Findings and Recommendations for Organizations," *Human Resource Management* 43 (2004): 409–24; S. Rynes and B. Rosen, "What Makes Diversity Programs Work?" *HR Magazine* (October 1994): 67–73; S. Rynes and B. Rosen, "A Field Survey of Factors Affecting the Adoption and Perceived Success of Diversity Training," *Personnel Psychology* 48 (1995): 247–70; Corporate Leadership Council, *The Evolution of Corporate Diversity* (Washington, DC: Corporate Executive Board, 2002).

Consider Sodexo's diversity effort.[75] Sodexo is the leading food and facilities management company in the U.S. Canada, and Mexico, serving 10 million customers daily. Diversity is seen as being important for the company to meet its business growth targets. As a result, diversity and inclusion are core elements of Sodexo's business strategy. The objectives of the company's efforts to manage diversity are related to the business, its employees, its shareholders, and the community. For example, some of the company's objectives include understanding and living the business case for diversity and inclusion; increasing awareness of how diversity relates to business challenges; creating and fostering a diverse work environment by developing management practices that drive hiring, promotion, and retention of talent; engaging in relationship management and customer service to attract and retain diverse clients and customers; and partnering with women and minority businesses to deliver food and facility management services.

Sodexo separates equal employment opportunity (EEO) and legal compliance training from diversity education. Every three years, employees are required to take EEO and affirmative action refresher courses. Top management is also involved in and committed to managing diversity. The senior executives' program includes ongoing classroom training that is reinforced with community involvement, sponsorship of employee groups, and the mentoring of diverse employees. Executives are engaged in learning the business case for diversity and are accountable for the company's diversity agenda. Every manager takes an eight-hour introductory class (Spirit of Diversity). Other learning opportunities are also available, including three-to four-hour learning labs that include topics such as cross-cultural communications, sexual orientation in the workplace, generations in the workplace, and gender in the workplace. The company's learning and development team develops customized learning solutions for different functions and work teams. For example, a course related to selling to a diverse client base was developed and offered to the sales force and a cross-cultural communications program was provided for recruiters.

In addition to diversity training activities, Sodexo has six employee network groups, such as the African American Leadership Forum and People Respecting Individuality, Diversity and Equality, that provide a forum for employees' professional development and the sharing of ideas to support the company's diversity efforts. Sodexo's "Champions of Diversity" program rewards and recognizes employees who advance diversity and inclusion.

To emphasize the importance of diversity for the company, at Sodexo each manager has a diversity scorecard which evaluates their success in the recruitment, retention, promotion, and development of all employees. The scorecard includes both quantitative goals as well as an evaluation of specific behaviors such as participating in training, mentoring, and community outreach. A portion of managers' pay bonuses is determined by success in these areas.

Sodexo has found that its diversity training and efforts to manage diversity are having a positive impact on business results. Its mentoring program has led to the increased productivity, engagement, and retention of women and people of color. There has been an estimated return on investment of $19 for every $1 spent on the program. Sodexo also has been awarded several new business contracts and has retained clients because of its involvement in managing diversity.

Most effective programs to manage diversity, such as Sodexo's diversity program, include the key components shown in Table 10.7. Other companies, such as Denny's (in response to a lawsuit) and Weyerhaeuser (in response to a retiring work force and survey

TABLE 10.7 Key Components of Effective Managing Diversity Programs

Top Management Support
- Make the business case for diversity.
- Include diversity as part of the business strategy and corporate goals.
- Participate in diversity programs and encourage all managers to attend.
- Form an executive management team that mirrors the diversity of the work force.

Recruitment and Hiring
- Ask search firms to identify a wider array of candidates.
- Enhance the interviewing, selection, and hiring skills of managers.
- Expand college recruitment at historically minority colleges.

Identifying and Developing Talent
- Form a partnership with INROADS, a nationwide internship program that targets minority students for management careers.
- Establish a mentoring process.
- Refine the company's global succession planning system to improve identification of talent.
- Improve the selection and development of managers and leaders to help ensure that they are capable of maximizing team performance.
- Ensure that all employees, especially women and minorities, have access to management development and leadership programs.

Employee Support
- Form resource groups or employee network groups that include employees with common interests (e.g., Asian Pacific employees, women, gays, Native American employees, veterans, Hispanic employees) and use them to help the company develop business goals and understand the issues with which they are concerned.
- Celebrate cultural traditions, festivities, and holidays.
- Make work/life balance initiatives, such as flextime, telecommuting, and eldercare, available to all employees.

Ensuring Fair Treatment
- Conduct extensive diversity training.
- Implement an alternative dispute resolution process.
- Include women and minorities on all human resource committees throughout the company.

Holding Managers Accountable
- Link managers' compensation to their success in meeting diversity goals and creating openness and inclusion in the workplace.
- Use employee attitude or engagement surveys to track employees' attitudes regarding inclusion, fairness, opportunities for development, work/life balance, and perceptions of the company's culture.

Improving Relationships with External Stakeholders
- Increase marketing to diverse communities.
- Provide customer service in different languages.
- Broaden the company's base of suppliers and vendors to include businesses owned by minorities and women.
- Provide scholarships and educational and neighborhood grants to diverse communities and their members.

Source: Based on R. Anand and M. Winters, "A Retrospective View of Corporate Diversity Training from 1964 to the Present," *Academy of Management Learning & Education* 7: 356–72; C. Chavez and J. Weisinger, "Beyond Diversity Training: A Social Infusion for Cultural Inclusion," *Human Resource Management* 47 (2008): 331–50; V. Smith, "Texaco Outlines Comprehensive Initiatives," *Human Resource Executive* (February 1997): 13, Also see Verizon's diversity program available at the company's Web site, www.verizon.com.

results that suggested the need for a more accepting workplace), have established diversity programs that include some of the same features as Sodexo's program.[76] As should be apparent from this discussion, successful diversity programs involve more than just an effective training program. They require an ongoing process of culture change that includes top management support as well as diversity policies and practices in the areas of recruitment and hiring; training and development; administrative structures, such as conducting diversity surveys and evaluating managers' progress on diversity goals; and improved relationships with minority customers, vendors, and suppliers.[77]

School-to-Work Transition

Industry and education experts agree that a system is needed for training students who do not attend college directly after high school. **School-to-work transition programs** combine classroom experiences with work experiences to prepare high school graduates for employment. Many school districts have changed their curriculum to include more work experience as part of the traditional classroom-based educational experience. The federal government, recognizing a need for this type of program, has helped fund local government efforts. The **School-to-Work Opportunities Act** is designed to assist the states in building school-to-work systems that prepare students for high-skill, high-wage jobs or future education. The act encourages partnerships between educational institutions, employers, and labor unions. The act requires that every school-to-work system include work-based learning, school-based learning, and connecting activities that match students with employers and bring classrooms and workplaces together. For example, a high school in Wisconsin has a program that combines engineering classes at school with paid, on-the-job engineering experience.[78] Wisconsin has one of the most fully developed school-to-work programs. Apprenticeships are offered in 13 fields ranging from tourism to engineering. Committees of employers and educators developed the skill sets to be covered and identified appropriate classroom and work experiences.

Federal Tool & Engineering, a customized metal stamping company based in Wisconsin, received a $1.5 million order because the company had taken the time and invested the money to get several employees certified in advanced manufacturing skills.[79] Because of grants made by the state of Wisconsin to technical college and work-force development boards, four employees were able to obtain certification by attending a standardized training program that focuses on quality practices and measurement, safety, process and production, and maintenance awareness. The program also helps employees develop math, science, communications, computing, problem-solving, and teamwork skills. Wisconsin's governor has made a commitment to have 40 percent of the state's manufacturing work force complete at least one part of the certification by 2016.

Universities and colleges have begun developing or have restarted nuclear-education programs, often working with energy companies concerned about a potential shortage of engineers in anticipation of new plants going online to meet increasing electricity demand.[80] The median age of an employee in the nuclear-energy field is 48, and up to 35 percent of the industry's workers may be eligible to retire within five years. The energy provider Dominion recently approached Virginia Commonwealth University (VCU) with concerns about its aging work force. In response, the university has added a nuclear track to its master's of engineering program. The bulk of the program's 20 students are Dominion employees who are taking courses taught by mechanical- and electrical-engineering professors and Dominion engineers and scientists.

Company-sponsored mentoring programs are also used to link companies to students.[81] Leadership Connections matches mentors with female high school students who are recruited through churches, schools, and juvenile courts. The students come from poor, rural North Carolina. The volunteer mentors are women from more than 40 companies, including Sara Lee and Carolina Power and Light. The only requirement is that the women be willing to commit to improving the mentee's well-being. The mentoring program gives students an awareness of the expectations of the working world. The mentors help at-risk students develop self-esteem and confidence and stay out of trouble. Most of the students have improved their school grades since joining the program, and many go on to college.

Training's Role in Welfare-to-Work and Other Public-Private Sector Programs

Companies are seeking to hire people from nontraditional sources such as welfare roles and prisons to meet labor needs and give hard-to-employ persons a second chance. Also, the welfare reform act passed by Congress in 1996 (the Personal Responsibility and Work Opportunity Act) increased the pressure on welfare recipients to find jobs, through either public employment agencies or other ways. Under the law, most people have a five-year limit on benefits and must find jobs within two years. The law also gives employers incentives (tax credits) for each welfare recipient they hire. Training plays an important part in helping these employees succeed on the job.

Mark Goldsmith, a former Revlon executive, started his own nonprofit organization called Getting Out and Staying Out (GOSO).[82] GOSO is currently working with over 200 inmates serving prison sentences in New York. GOSO works with young prisoners who are attending school and have been in prison for only a short time. It provides individual job and education counseling and interview preparation, maintains a job bank of openings from employers willing to hire former inmates, provides educational scholarships, and holds seminars. One seminar taught by a retired construction company executive focused on the skills required to become a successful tradesperson. GOSO has been successful. Fewer than 10 percent of the 400 released inmates GOSO has worked with have been arrested again, compared with two-thirds of prisoners nationwide who have been rearrested following their release. Seventy-five percent of the former prisoners in GOSO are employed or attending school. Former inmates stop by to share good news about a job, discuss problems they are having at home or at work, or return for counseling if they lose or don't get a job, want to change jobs, or decide to go back to school.

At the Greater Chicago Food Depository, a nonprofit food bank, the primary mission has been to feed the hungry.[83] The Chicago food bank—and others around the country affiliated with America's Second Harvest—has been offering 30 chef training classes to about 1,000 students. These programs teach low-income students the basics of cooking, such as slicing, dicing, sizing, and fricasseeing, as well as advanced skills—with the goal of getting each student a job. Also, the program teaches the students life skills, such as punctuality, responsibility, teamwork, and commitment. As one of the executive chef instructors told her 17 students on the first day of class, "When you're out there working and you're 15 minutes late, I'm already calling someone to do your job." Seventy percent of program graduates find jobs within one month and more than 65 percent retain their first job for at least six months. For students who succeed, the program helps them escape the cycle of poverty.

There are two methods for training welfare recipients.[84] In the first method, government agencies refer welfare recipients to a company-sponsored training program subsidized with money and tax credits from the government.

The second method is for state and local governments to provide life and skills training directly to welfare recipients. The skills developed are often based on the needs of local employers. For example, in Oregon, the Department of Human Resources' JOBS training program has helped 19,000 people find work. Participants attend training sessions on basic work habits and learn to interview, write résumés, and manage their personal lives. The welfare-to-work transition is facilitated by a state law that requires welfare recipients to find work or risk losing their benefits. Another program requires the state to reimburse companies for the wages of welfare recipients for six months, while the employers provide meaningful work experiences and training. In one program for clerical workers, 85 percent of those who stayed in the program for four months were hired by the employers and still had jobs even after the state subsidy ended.

One problem facing welfare-to-work programs is that as unemployment rises, welfare recipients face competition against an increased number of job seekers who have greater experience, fewer problems finding child care, and better access to transportation.[85] For example, Cleveland Track Material, which makes railroad track equipment, has 14 Center for Employment Training alumni in its work force of 220 employees. Cleveland Track Material would like to hire more workers from the employment center, but when business dropped, the company reduced all hiring.

The **Workforce Investment Act of 1998** created a comprehensive work force investment system. The reformed system is intended to be customer focused, help Americans manage their careers through information and high-quality services, and help U.S. companies find skilled workers. The cornerstone of the new system is One-Stop service delivery, which unifies numerous training, education, and employment programs into a single, customer-friendly system in each community. The underlying notion of One-Stop is the coordination of programs, services, and governance structures so that the customer has access to a seamless system of work force investment services. It is envisioned that a variety of programs could utilize One-Stop's common intake, case management, and job development services in order to take full advantage of One-Stop's potential for efficiency and effectiveness. A wide range of services, including training and employment programs, will be available to meet the needs of employers and job seekers. The challenge in helping One-Stop live up to its potential is to make sure that the state and local boards can effectively coordinate and collaborate with the network of other service agencies, including Temporary Assistance for Needy Families agencies, transportation agencies and providers, metropolitan planning organizations, child care agencies, nonprofit and community partners, and the broad range of partners who work with youth.

O*NET, the Occupational Information Network, is a unique, comprehensive database and directory of occupational titles, worker competencies, and job requirements and resources.[86] O*NET, which supports One-Stop service delivery, is the primary source of occupational information in the United States. The O*NET database includes information on skills, abilities, knowledge, work activities, and interests associated with occupations. O*NET information can be used to facilitate career exploration, vocational counseling, and a variety of human resource functions, such as developing job orders, creating position descriptions, and aligning training with current workplace needs. Job seekers can use

O*NET to find out which jobs fit with their interests, skills, and experience and to identify the skills, knowledge, and abilities needed for their dream job.

TRAINING ISSUES RELATED TO INTERNAL NEEDS OF THE COMPANY

Basic Skills Training

Chapter 1 highlighted employers' difficulty in finding competent entry-level job candidates—persons with appropriate reading, writing, and arithmetic skills. Chapter 3 emphasized the relationship between cognitive ability, reading skills, and training success. Also, Chapter 3 discussed how basic skills can be identified during needs assessment. Because employers have not been successful at finding job candidates with appropriate levels of basic skills (a recruiting and selection issue), employers have been forced to develop basic skills training programs. Also, as companies move toward high-performance workplace systems, they may find that current employees lack the skills needed to realize these systems' benefits. Basic skills include the ability to read instructions, write reports, and do math at a level needed to perform job duties.

As explained in Chapter 3, basic skills programs involve several steps. First, the necessary skill level needs to be identified. That is, what level of basic skills do employees need to be successful in their jobs? Second, employees' current skill levels must be assessed. The training programs that are developed will be based on the gap between current skill level and desired skill level. Training programs need to include an emphasis on basic skills in the context of work problems to increase their meaningfulness to trainees. In 24-hour operations (such as manufacturing plants) that use several shifts of employees, basic skills training needs to be available to employees during their off-shift times. Finally, many employees who lack basic skills do not want their peers to be aware of these deficiencies. Participation in basic skills training needs to be as private as possible. If privacy cannot be guaranteed, those employees who most need basic skills training may not participate.

Consider how Smith & Wesson dealt with its need for qualified workers.[87] Smith & Wesson, the firearms manufacturer, reorganized its production department. The reorganization made jobs more interesting and challenging by requiring employees to interpret process control statistics and operate in work teams. The reorganization revealed that some employees' basic skills deficiencies kept them from being successful in the new production environment. Smith & Wesson conducted an assessment of the skills that employees needed in the new production environment. This assessment identified three skills: higher math skills for understanding numerical control equipment, better reading and writing skills, and better oral communication skills for working in teams and interacting with other employees. A literacy audit showed that employees needed to have at least an eighth-grade reading level. To determine which employees needed training, Smith & Wesson used tests. To ensure employee confidentiality, the test results were sent to employees' home addresses. Thirty percent of employees scored below the eighth-grade level in either reading or math. These employees were told that they would not lose their jobs, but they were expected to take basic skills classes on company time, paid for by the company. Management presentations on the business benefits of the classes helped encourage employees who were reluctant to participate.

Evaluations of the first classes were very positive. Seventy percent of employees who attended the classes improved their reading skills to the eighth-grade level or higher. A company survey found that the program helped employees improve their writing and ability to read charts, graphs, and bulletin boards; increased their ability to use fractions and decimals; and improved their self-confidence.

Public Service Enterprise Group (PSEG) was trying to recruit new technicians and linemen to replace retiring employees.[88] However, PSEG found that many new recruits could not pass the math section on pre-employment tests. As a result, PSEG joined six New Jersey community colleges and technical high schools to create a new degree program in energy technology. Since starting the new degree program, PSEG has hired almost all of the 85 program graduates. The company has saved money hiring low-level employees since it no longer needs to advertise or spend money and time training new hires in basic skills. Likewise, Bristol-Myers Squibb has started a relationship with a technical school and community college located near its new manufacturing plant. Bristol-Myers is working with the educational institutions to train students in the maintenance and mechanical skills, technical writing, and Food and Drug Administration–approved manufacturing practices they need to work in the new plant.

Life Long Learning

A **Lifelong Learning Account** (LiLA) refers to an account for adult education into which both the employee and the company contribute and the employee keeps—even if he or she leaves the company. The money in the LiLA can be used to pay for a range of educational expenses, including tuition, books, fees, supplies, and non-job-specific certification courses. The money in the account can be rolled over from year to year. Maine and Washington were the first states to create LiLAs. The federal Lifelong Learning Accounts Act of 2008 (proposed but not yet voted on) would allow individuals to contribute up to $5,250 to LiLA accounts each year and the contributions would be excluded from their gross incomes for federal tax purposes. Employers could match the contributions and receive tax credits for each dollar matched, up to $500 per year for each employee.[89]

Some companies have taken the initiative to introduce their own type of LiLA to make continuing education a priority.[90] IBM's Matching Accounts for Learning Initiative program allows employees to contribute up to $1,000 per year into a portable, interest-bearing account with a 50 percent company match. Employees can use the money to gain skills not directly related to their current jobs, such as learning a new language. University of California at San Francisco (UCSF) Medical Center set up a small pilot LiFA program that was so successful it is being expanded. During the pilot phase of the program, employees took training in health care–related skills as well as real estate, finance, and word processing. Managers at UCSF Medical Center believe that, although employees are using the LiLA accounts to learn skills unrelated to their jobs, they are unlikely to leave for other job opportunities because of the investment that UCSF has made in their careers.

Melting the Glass Ceiling

A major training and development issue facing companies today is how to move women and minorities into upper-level management positions—how to break the glass ceiling. Although women represent half of all managers and professionals, they hold only approximately 10–15 percent of corporate officer positions.[91] Seventy-four of the top 500 companies have no female corporate officers. The **glass ceiling** is a barrier to advancement to the higher levels of the organization. This barrier may be due to stereotypes or company systems that adversely affect the development of women or minorities.[92] The glass ceiling is likely caused by lack of access to training programs, by lack of access to appropriate developmental job experiences, by lack of access to developmental relationships such as mentoring and informal social networks, and by an organizational culture that may work against women.[93] Male managers' development experiences tend to be given to them; female managers have to be more proactive about getting development assignments. Research has found no gender differences in access to job experiences involving transitions such as handling new job responsibilities or creating change such as fixing business problems or making strategic changes in the business.[94] However, male managers received significantly more assignments involving high levels of responsibility (high stakes, international assignments managing business diversity, handling external pressure) than did female managers of similar ability and managerial level. Also, female managers reported experiencing more challenge because of lack of personal support (a type of job demand considered to be an obstacle that has been found to relate to harmful stress). Career encouragement from peers and senior managers does help women advance to the highest management levels.[95] Managers making developmental assignments must carefully consider whether gender biases or stereotypes are influencing the types of assignments given to women versus men.

Consider Safeway's efforts to melt the glass ceiling.[96] Safeway has 1,775 grocery stores in the U.S. and Canada. To meet the challenges of specialty grocers and big-box, low-price competitors such as Wal-Mart and Target, and recognizing that 70 percent of its customers are women, Safeway has taken steps to help develop women for advancement into management. Safeway's women's initiative, "Championing Change for Women: An Integrated Strategy," includes programs that focus on leadership development, mentoring, and work-life balance. One example is the Retail Leadership Development (RLD) program. Safeway typically promotes from within and has focused on the retail level as a source for potential managers through the RLD program. Ninety percent of Safeway's 1,800 store managers have moved up through the company's management ranks through the RLD program and all but one of the company's 10 division presidents began their career working in one of the stores.

The RLD program is helping women and minorities achieve top level management positions. Those who complete the program are assigned to a store or an assistant manager position that can lead to corporate-level leadership positions. To help support women's efforts to gain leadership positions, Safeway ensures that women who work part-time and use flexible schedules have similar opportunities for coaching, advancement, and development as those employees who are on traditional work schedules. The company also has realized that frequent relocations don't work for some employees, especially women. As a result, rejecting a relocation assignment is no longer considered a career-busting decision.

Safeway also provides a women's leadership network for women interested in advancing into management. The network sponsors events such as presentations at different company locations that highlight the success of Safeway women and provide learning opportunities. Executives who attend these presentations meet with women who have been identified as candidates for management positions and are targeted for development opportunities in stores. These discussions focus on the women's career interests and the executives suggest job opportunities and encourage them to apply for positions that can help them advance to the next management level. Safeway's mentoring program emphasizes that a manager's first protégé should be a woman because of the lack of female mentors. Safeway's work-life balance program includes flextime and encourages all women, regardless of their family status, to have a healthy balance between work and life. Safeway realizes that its managers are responsible for helping women reach management positions. As a result, all managers attend a Managing Diversity Workshop. Managers are evaluated on their success in meeting diversity goals. Managers who reach their targets can increase their bonus pay by 10 percent.

Safeway's women's initiative has been successful. Since 2000 the number of female store managers has increased by 42 percent. The number of women who have qualified for and completed the RLD program has increased 31 percent during the past five years. A research report prepared by Lehman Brothers shows that the program has increased the company's sales and earnings. By enhancing its reputation as an employer of choice for women and minorities, Safeway has received the Catalyst Award, which is presented annually to outstanding companies that promote the career advancement of women and minorities. Table 10.8 provides recommendations for melting the glass ceiling and retaining talented women.

Like Safeway, other companies are also working to melt the glass ceiling. Although most of LeasePlan USA's 450 employees were women, the majority of the company's top managers were men.[97] To help promote more women to management positions, LeasePlan USA hired a consultant to develop a program that focused on skill assessment, career guidance, and communication. The program also featured networking events and a panel discussion with female executives from other companies. For every five women participating in the program, one has been promoted. In addition, 6 of the company's top 14 managers are now women, an increase of our women from two years ago. The program is also improving job satisfaction and engagement among women employees. Survey results show that one year after the program's implementation, the number of women who feel that management supports their efforts to manage their careers and who think that positions at LeasePlan are fairly awarded has increased by 12 percent.

Women and minorities often have trouble finding mentors because of their lack of access to the "old boy network," managers' preference to interact with other managers of similar status rather than with line employees, and intentional exclusion by managers who have negative stereotypes about women's and minorities' abilities, motivation, and job preferences.[98] Potential mentors may view minorities and women as a threat to their job security because they believe affirmative action plans give those groups preferential treatment. Wal-Mart's strong corporate culture—emphasizing leadership, trust, willingness to

TABLE 10.8
Recommendations for Melting the Glass Ceiling

Source: Based on D. McCracken, "Winning the Talent War for Women," *Harvard Business Review* (November–December 2000): 159–67.

Make sure that senior management supports and is involved in the program.
Make a business case for change.
Make the change public.
Using task forces, focus groups, and questionnaires, gather data on problems causing the glass ceiling.
Create awareness of how gender attitudes affect the work environment.
Create accountability through reviews of promotion rates and assignment decisions.
Promote development for all employees.

relocate on short notice, and promotion from within—may have unintentionally created a glass ceiling.[99] Eighty-six percent of store manager positions were held by men. More than two-thirds of Wal-Mart managers start as hourly employees. Hourly job openings are posted at each store, but Wal-Mart never posted openings for management training positions that allowed hourly employees to move up into salaried, management positions. Part of the reason for this practice was that Wal-Mart values efficiency and never saw the need for job postings to fill open management positions. The other reason is that Wal-Mart trusts its managers to promote individuals who deserve promotion. However, women who work at Wal-Mart claimed that it was difficult to find out about manager jobs. Male employees had more access to information about management job openings because they spent more time socializing and talking with management employees (who were primarily male). Wal-Mart's corporate attitude that managers had to be willing to relocate on short notice resulted in management opportunities that accommodated men more than women. Wal-Mart has taken many steps to ensure that the company remains a good place to work. For example, to give women more opportunities for management positions, Wal-Mart developed a posting system for all management jobs. Through Women in Leadership seminars, Wal-Mart has been able to help its female employees improve those skills required for management positions. The company also provides employees with a database that notifies them of job openings at stores across the country. As a result of its efforts, Wal-Mart's board of directors now includes three women and more than 40 percent of the company's officials and managers are women. The company has received a number of arrivals for its development of women (e.g., *Working Mother* magazine's 2007 Best Company for Multicultural Women).

Many companies, as part of their approach to managing a diverse work force, are using mentoring programs to ensure that women and minorities gain the skills and visibility needed to move into managerial positions. Procter & Gamble (P&G) has a unique program called Mentoring Up, which asks mid- and junior-level female managers to mentor senior-level male managers to raise their awareness of work-related issues affecting women.[100] The goals of the program are to reduce turnover of promising female managers, to give female managers greater exposure to P&G's top decision makers, and to improve cross-gender communications. Mentoring Up was developed because of the turnover of high-potential female employees who in exit interviews cited not feeling valued (rather than money, promotions, or better assignments) as the reason they were leaving the company. Although the program was designed to help upper-level male managers better understand how to work with women, the program also includes five upper-level female managers who participate as protégés.

The Mentoring Up program incorporates many characteristics of effective mentoring programs. All eligible junior-level female managers and senior-level male managers are expected to participate. The female managers must have at least one year of tenure and be good performers. Junior mentors are matched with senior mentors based on their responses to a questionnaire. Both mentors and protégés attend an orientation session that includes a panel discussion by past participants in the program and a series of exercises probing women's workplace issues and reasons for success at P&G. The mentor-protégé pairs are required to meet at least once every two months. Mentors and protégés receive discussion guides designed to facilitate dialogue. For example, one guide asked the mentor-protégé pairs to explore the keys to success and failure for women and men in company leadership positions. The discussion guides also include questions designed to elicit attitudes about when women feel valued. The mentor and protégé explore differences and similarities in responses to these questions to identify how people like to be recognized. Two issues have frequently been raised in the mentor-protégé relationships: the barriers that women face in achieving a balance between work and life, and differences in managerial and decision-making styles between men and women.

One of the biggest benefits of the program has been that mentors and protégés have shared advice and perspectives and feel comfortable using each other to test out new ideas. Junior female managers also get exposure to the top executives who make promotion and succession-planning decisions. The program has reduced the turnover rate of female managers. Turnover of female managers whom the company wanted to retain is down 25 percent and is now at the same rate as male manager turnover.

Joint Union-Management Programs

To be more competitive, U.S. industries that have lost considerable market share to foreign competition (e.g., the auto industry) have developed joint union-management training. Both labor and management have been forced to accept new roles. Employees need to become involved in business planning and strategic decision making, and management needs to learn how to share power and allow worker participation in decision making.

The initial goal of these programs was to help displaced employees find new jobs by providing skill training and outplacement assistance. Currently, **joint union-management training programs** provide a wide range of services designed to help employees learn skills that are directly related to their job and also develop skills that are "portable"—that is, valuable to employers in other companies or industries.[101] Both employers and unions contribute money to run the programs, and both oversee their operation. Major joint efforts include the United Auto Workers (UAW) with Ford, General Motors, and DaimlerChrysler; and the Communications Workers of America (CWA) with Qwest Communications and Verizon Communications.

The National Coalition for Telecommunications Education and Learning (NACTEL) is a partnership between telecommunications companies, including AT&T, Qwest Communications, and Verizon Communications, and labor unions (CWA and International Brotherhood of Electrical workers) that has developed online education programs.[102] NACTEL includes courses that allow employees to work toward associate degrees (e.g., Telecommunications) and certificate programs (e.g., Introduction to Telecommunications). The NACTEL programs are offered by Pace University's School of Computer Science and Information Systems. The curriculum is based on training programs offered by Qwest and Verizon.

The UAW-Ford joint effort offers a number of programs, including a technical skills program that helps employees gain skills needed to function in the high-performance workplace and including UAW-Ford University, which offers online courses from accredited universities that can be taken by employees for credit toward certificate programs and toward associate, bachelor's, master's, and even doctoral degrees.[103] A negotiated central fund and local training funds support the joint training efforts. Program administration is provided by the first national training center ever negotiated in a labor contract in the United States and by a network of local committees at each UAW-Ford location in the United States. At both the national and local levels, the programs address issues in product quality, education and development, team structures, health and safety, and employee assistance (e.g., counseling, help with care of elders). For example, the UAW-Ford "Best in Class" Quality Program established a new certification training for quality representatives, established a review process for quality concerns, and helped employees work together to improve quality.

Union-management partnerships are also providing education and training programs that help less skilled workers advance and increase productivity. The Farmworker Institute for Education and Leadership Development (FIELD) was founded by the United Farm Workers union to help low-income and low-skilled Latino and other workers.[104] One of FIELD's employer partners is Monterey Mushrooms, a California-based distributor of mushroom products. FIELD designed a training program for Monterey Mushrooms that encouraged collaboration, conflict resolution, and safety. These partnerships help the United States stay competitive in the worldwide agriculture market. Traditionally, U.S. farm workers have relied on a technological advantage to sell and distribute their products. In the current market, productivity and quality can make the difference against foreign competition.

Yes, these programs are costly (General Motors has spent over $1.6 billion jointly with the UAW), and employees may get trained in skills that are not directly related to their current jobs. But both labor and management believe that these programs improve the literacy levels of the work force and contribute to productivity. Both parties want to encourage life-long learning as a key aspect of a work force that can adapt to new technologies and global competition.

Succession Planning

Many companies are losing a sizable number of upper-level managers because of retirement and company restructurings that reduce the number of potential upper-level managers. Companies are finding that their middle managers are not ready to move into upper management positions because of skill weaknesses or lack of experience. One estimate is that less than half of today's companies have succession plans in place.[105] Succession plans are needed long before there is a need to fill an open position. Otherwise, when managers and executives leave, the company must hire outsiders who likely need time to understand markets and customers, the business strategy, key employees, and the company culture. Also, if companies have to resort to hiring chief executives from the outside, they pay a premium. One study found that CEOs hired from outside the company receive 65 percent more compensation in their first year than internally promoted CEOs.[106] These issues create the need for succession planning.

Succession planning refers to the process of identifying and developing the future leadership of the company. Succession planning is especially important given that the baby boomers are preparing to retire or reduce their participation in organizations, creating vacancies at all management levels. Succession planning helps organizations in several different ways.[107] It requires senior management to systematically conduct a review of leadership talent in the company. It ensures that top-level managerial talent is available. It provides a set of development experiences that managers must complete to be considered for top management positions, which avoids the premature promotion of managers who are not ready for upper-management ranks. Succession planning systems also help attract and retain managerial employees by providing them with development opportunities that they can complete if upper-level management is a career goal for them. For example, at Xerox, Chairman and CEO Anne Mulcahy named Ursula Burns as her successor.[108] Ms. Burns was an engineer who had managed Xerox's operations and research. To prepare Ms. Burns for the CEO position, Ms. Mulcahy gave her responsibilities for marketing and human resources and invited her to collaborate on solutions to problems facing Xerox as they occurred.

High-potential employees are employees that the company believes are capable of being successful in higher-level managerial positions such as general manager of a strategic business unit, functional director (e.g., director of marketing), or chief executive officer (CEO).[109] Replacements for top-level managers are usually made from the pool of high-potential employees. The activities discussed in Chapter 9 are used to develop high-potential employees. High-potential employees typically complete an individualized development program that involves education, executive mentoring and coaching, and rotation through job assignments.[110] Job assignments are based on the successful career paths of the managers that the high-potential employees are being prepared to replace. High-potential employees may also receive special assignments, such as making presentations and serving on committees and task forces.

Research suggests that the development of high-potential employees involves three stages.[111] A large pool of employees may initially be identified as high-potential employees, but the numbers are reduced over time because of turnover, poor performance, or a personal choice not to strive for a higher-level position. In Stage 1, high-potential employees are selected. Those who have completed elite academic programs (e.g., an MBA at Stanford) or who have been outstanding performers are identified. Psychological tests—such as those done at assessment centers—may also be used.

In Stage 2, high-potential employees receive development experiences. Those who succeed are the ones who continue to demonstrate good performance. A willingness to make sacrifices for the company is also necessary (e.g., accepting new assignments or relocating to a new location). Good oral and written communication skills, ease in interpersonal relationships, and talent for leadership are a must. In what is known as a tournament model of job transitions, high-potential employees who meet the expectations of their senior managers in this stage are given the opportunity to advance into the next stage of the process.[112] Employees who do not meet the expectations are ineligible for higher-level managerial positions in the company.

To reach Stage 3, high-potential employees usually have to be viewed by top management as fitting into the company's culture and having the personality characteristics needed to successfully represent the company. These employees have the potential to occupy the company's top positions. In Stage 3, the CEO becomes actively involved in developing the employees, who are exposed to the company's key personnel and given a greater understanding of the company's culture. Note that the development of high-potential employees is a slow process. Reaching Stage 3 may take 15 to 20 years.

Table 10.9 shows the steps that a company takes to develop a succession planning system. The first step is to identify what positions are included in the succession plan, such as all management positions or only certain levels of management. The second step is to identify which employees are part of the succession planning system. For example, in some companies only high-potential employees are included in the succession plan. Third, the company needs to identify how positions will be evaluated. For example, will the emphasis

TABLE 10.9

The Succession Planning Process

Source: Based on R. Barnett and S. Davis, "Creating Greater Success in Succession Planning," *Advances in Developing Human Resources* 10 (2008): 721–739; B. Dowell, "Succession Planning," in *Implementing Organizational Interventions,* ed. J. Hedge and E. Pulaskos (San Francisco: Jossey-Bass, 2002): 78–109.

1. Identify what positions are included in the plan.
2. Identify the employees who are included in the plan.
3. Develop standards to evaluate positions (e.g., competencies, desired experiences, desired knowledge, developmental value).
4. Determine how employee potential will be measured (e.g., current performance and potential performance).
5. Develop the succession planning review.
6. Link the succession planning system with other human resource data and systems, including training and development, compensation, and staffing systems.
7. Determine what feedback is provided to employees.
8. Measure the effectiveness of the succession planning process.

be on competencies needed for each position or on the experiences an individual needs to have before moving into the position? Fourth, the company should identify how employee potential will be measured. That is, will employees' performance in their current jobs as well as ratings of potential be used? Will employees' position interests and career goals be considered? Fifth, the succession planning review process needs to be developed. Typically, succession planning reviews first involve employees' managers and human resources. A talent review could also include an overall assessment of leadership talent in the company, an identification of high-potential employees, and a discussion of plans to keep key managers from leaving the company. Sixth, succession planning is dependent on other human resource systems, including compensation, training and development, and staffing. Incentives and bonuses may be linked to completion of development opportunities. Activities such as training courses, job experiences, mentors, and 360-degree feedback can be used to meet development needs. Companies need to make such decisions as whether to fill an open management position internally with a less-experienced employee who will improve in the role over time or to hire a manager from outside the company who can immediately deliver results. Seventh, employees need to be provided with feedback on future moves, expected career paths, and development goals and experiences. Finally, the succession planning process needs to be evaluated. This includes identifying and measuring appropriate results outcomes (such as reduced time to fill manager positions, increased use of internal promotions) as well as collecting measures of satisfaction with the process (reaction outcomes) from employees and managers. Also, modifications that will be made to the succession planning process need to be identified, discussed, and implemented.

Software or Web-based solutions that allow companies to manage large amounts of data regarding the requirements of various positions and the strengths and weaknesses of employees are critical for the success of succession planning systems.[113] The software also gets employees involved in succession planning by giving them responsibility for updating information about their education, experience, and interests. With succession planning software, companies can quickly view information on the strengths, weaknesses, and development plans for individual employees and can obtain analyses of succession gaps and strengths in departments, work groups, or level hierarchies. For example, Pep Boys, an auto parts and service company, needed a system that could track all 20,000 of its employees.[114] The system chosen by Pep Boys eliminated the previous multiple databases for performance information and succession plans that had made it difficult to analyze data for different parts of the company. The new system automatically provides performance and potential evaluations for every employee, and it can create an organizational chart that shows each employee's performance level, his or her risk of turnover, the impact of turnover, whether that person has a successor, and the time frame for when that successor can take over the position. Pep Boys's new system has allowed for better managerial talent discussions and individual career discussions with employees.

Another example of an effective succession planning system is the system at Well-Point, a health care company headquartered in Thousand Oaks, California.[115] WellPoint has a Web-based corporate database that identifies employees for management jobs throughout the company and tracks the development of employee talent. WellPoint has operations across the United States, including locations in California and Georgia. The succession planning system includes 600 managers and executives across five levels of the company. The Human Resource Planning System (HRPS) has detailed information on possible candidates, including performance evaluations, summaries of the candidates' accomplishments at the company, self-evaluations, information about career goals, and personal data such as the candidates' willingness to relocate to another part of the company. Part of the development of HRPS involved identifying the company's strengths and weaknesses at each position. Senior management team members developed standards, or benchmarks, to use to identify the best candidates for promotion. The HRPS system allows managers and the human resource team to identify and evaluate candidates for every management position in the company. It helps identify and track the development of promising internal candidates and also identifies areas where internal candidates are weak, so that (1) external candidates can be recruited, (2) a special development program can be initiated to develop employee talent, and (3) the company can place more emphasis on developing the missing skills and competencies in internal candidates. For example, because WellPoint lacked candidates for two levels of management, the company created a special training program that used business case simulations for 24 managers and executives who had been identified as high-potential candidates for upper-level management positions.

WellPoint's process of succession planning includes several steps. Each employee who is eligible for succession planning is asked to enter into the HRPS such information as educational background and preferences in types of jobs and company locations. That employee's manager adds a performance appraisal, a rating on the employee's core competencies, and a promotion assessment, that is, an assessment of the employee's potential for promotion. The promotion assessment includes the manager's opinion regarding what positions the employee might be ready for and when the employee should be moved. It also includes the manager's view on who might fill the open position if the employee is promoted. The information from the employee and the manager is used to create an online résumé for each eligible employee. The company holds "talent calibration" meetings that provide preparation for departures as well as development of leaders. The system has benefited the company's bottom line. WellPoint has realized an 86 percent internal promotion rate, which exceeds its goal of filling 75 percent of management positions from within. By improving employees' opportunities for promotion, WellPoint has reduced its turnover rate by 6 percent since 1997 and has saved $21 million on recruitment and training expenses. The time to fill open management positions has been reduced from 60 days to 35 days.

Developing Managers with Dysfunctional Behaviors

A number of studies have identified managerial behaviors that can cause an otherwise competent manager to be a "toxic" or ineffective manager. These behaviors include insensitivity to others, inability to be a team player, arrogance, poor conflict-management skills, inability to meet business objectives, and inability to change or adapt during a transition.[116] For example, a skilled manager who is interpersonally abrasive, aggressive, and autocratic may find it difficult to motivate subordinates, may alienate internal and external customers, and may have trouble getting ideas accepted by superiors. These managers are in jeopardy of losing their jobs and have little chance of future advancement because of their dysfunctional behaviors. Typically, a combination of assessment, training, and counseling is used to help managers change dysfunctional behavior. For example, a chief technical officer at TaylorMade-addidas Golf (TMaG), a golf equipment company and U.S.-based subsidiary of adidas Group, had decades of experience, and his education and technical abilities were sufficient to effectively manage the more than 100 engineers and other staff who reported to him.[117] However, his people-skills needed improvement. In meetings he made cynical comments and quickly reviewed technical information with his staff, not taking time to answer their questions. His lack of people-skills caused a high turnover rate in his department. To improve his people-skills, the manager began working with a coach to help him identify his strengths and weaknesses. Now he meets his coach twice a month to develop his people-skills based on a set of clearly defined improvement objectives which they developed together. As a result of the coaching, employees now come to him first with their issues and problems because he is a good listener.

One example of a program designed specifically to help managers with dysfunctional behavior is the Individual Coaching for Effectiveness (ICE) program.[118] Although the effectiveness of these types of programs needs to be further investigated, initial research suggests that managers' participation in these programs results in skill improvement and reduced likelihood of termination.[119] The ICE program includes diagnosis, coaching, and support activities. The program is tailored to the manager's needs. Clinical, counseling, or industrial/organizational psychologists are involved in all phases of the ICE program. They conduct the diagnosis, coach and counsel the manager, and develop action plans for implementing new skills on the job.

The first step in the ICE program, diagnosis, involves collecting information about the manager's personality, skills, and interests. Interviews with the manager and the manager's supervisor and colleagues plus psychological tests are used to determine whether the manager can actually change the dysfunctional behavior. For example, personality traits such as extreme defensiveness may make it difficult for the manager to change the problem behavior. If it is determined that the manager can benefit from the program, then typically the manager and the manager's supervisor set specific developmental objectives tailored to the manager's needs.

In the coaching phase of the program, the manager is first presented with information about the targeted skills or behavior. This information may be about principles of effective communication or teamwork, tolerance of individual differences in the workplace, or methods for conducting effective meetings. The second step is for the manager to participate in behavior-modeling training, which was discussed in Chapter 7. The manager also receives psychological counseling to overcome beliefs that may inhibit learning the desired behavior.

The support phase of the program involves creating conditions to ensure that on the job the manager is able to use the new behaviors and skills acquired in the ICE program. The supervisor provides feedback to the manager and the psychologist about progress the manager has made in using the new skills and behavior. The psychologist and manager identify situations in which the manager may tend to rely on dysfunctional behavior. The coach and manager also develop action plans that outline how the manager should try to use new behavior in daily work activities.

Training and Pay Systems

Compensation refers to pay and benefits that companies give to employees in exchange for performing their jobs. Companies use compensation systems to achieve many objectives, including attracting talented employees to join the company, motivating employees, and retaining employees by paying wages and benefits that meet or exceed those the employee might receive from other companies in the labor market (local as well as national or even international companies). As was discussed in Chapter 1, to remain competitive, companies need employees who possess a wide range of skills and are willing and able to learn new skills to meet changing customer service and product requirements.

Training is increasingly linked to employees' compensation through the use of skill-based pay systems. In **skill-based** or **knowledge-based pay systems,** employees' pay is based primarily on the knowledge and skills they possess rather than the knowledge or skills necessary to successfully perform their current job.[120] The basic idea is that to motivate employees to learn, pay is based on the skills that employees possess. Why would a company do this? The rationale is that this type of system ensures that employees are learning and gives the company additional flexibility in using employees to provide products and services. Skill-based pay has been found to be related to an increase in employees' skills and their maintenance of skill proficiency over time.[121] Skill-based pay systems are often used to facilitate cross-training. Cross-training involves training employees to learn the skills of one or several jobs. This system is especially critical for work teams in which employees need to be able to rotate between jobs or substitute for employees who are absent.

The skill-based pay approach contributes to better use of employees' skills and ideas. It also provides the opportunity for leaner staffing levels because employee turnover or absenteeism can be covered by employees who are multiskilled. Multiskilled employees are important where different products require different manufacturing processes or where supply shortages call for adaptive or flexible responses. These are characteristics typical of many so-called advanced manufacturing environments (e.g., flexible manufacturing or just-in-time systems).[122]

Table 10.10 shows a skill-based pay system. In this example, skills are grouped into skill blocks. Employees' compensation increases as they master each skill block. Entry-level employees begin at $15 per hour and can progress to $25 per hour by mastering other skill blocks.

Skill-based pay systems have implications for needs assessment, delivery method, and evaluation of training.[123] Since pay is directly tied to the amount of knowledge or skill employees have obtained, employees will be motivated to attend training programs. This means that the volume of training conducted as well as training costs will increase. Although employee motivation to attend training may be high, it is important to conduct a thorough needs assessment (e.g., using testing) to ensure that employees have the prerequisite knowledge needed to master the new skills.

TABLE 10.10   **Example of a Skill-Based Pay System**

Skill Block	Description	Pay Rate
A	*Molding:* Operates molding machines and performs machine setup	$15 per hour
B	*Finishing:* Operates finishing machine and performs finishing machine setup function	$20 per hour
	Inspection: Operates both inspection machines and makes scrap/rework decisions	
	Packaging: Operates packaging equipment and performs inventory and shipping functions	
C	*Quality control:* Performs quality control functions	$25 per hour

Source: Based on R. L. Bunning, "Models for Skill-Based Pay Plans," *HR Magazine* (February 1992): 62–64.

Training must also be accessible to all employees. For example, if the company manufactures products and provides services on a 24-hour basis, training must be available for employees working all shifts. Computer-assisted instruction or intranet-based training are ideal for skill-based pay systems. Training can be easily offered at all hours on an as-needed basis—employees only need access to a computer! Also, computer-based instruction can automatically track an employee's progress in training.

In skill-based pay systems, managers and/or peers usually serve as trainers. Training involves a combination of on-the-job training and use of presentation techniques such as lectures or videos. As a result, employees need to be trained in how to be trainers.

Finally, a key issue in skill-based pay systems is skill perishability—ensuring that employees have not forgotten the skills when it comes time to use them. Skill-based pay systems require periodic evaluation of employees' skills and knowledge using behavior and learning outcomes. Although employees may be certified that they have mastered skills, many skill-based pay programs require them to attend refresher sessions on a periodic basis to remain certified (and receive the higher wage).

Summary

This chapter explored special training and development issues relating to pressures that companies face from the external and internal company environments. External environmental pressures include legal compliance, globalization, an increasingly diverse work force, and lack of skills in the labor market. The chapter addressed these environmental pressures by presenting information on legal issues in training, cross-cultural preparation, diversity training, school-to-work transition, and hard-core–unemployed training programs.

Internal issues that companies face relate to preparing the company's current work force for the future, helping dysfunctional managers, and motivating employees to learn. The chapter discussed succession planning systems, basic skills training, life-long learning, joint union-management training programs, and methods to ensure that women and minorities receive equal opportunities for training and development (melting the glass ceiling). The chapter also covered skill-based pay systems that directly link training to employees' wage rates to encourage employees to learn.

Note that for many issues discussed in this chapter, training is only one part of the solution. For example, trainers and managers can take steps to ensure that women and minorities are not excluded from training programs, but this action alone will not solve the broader issue of discrimination in our society. Similarly, companies are using training to provide welfare recipients with employment. However, training cannot overcome broader societal ills that have resulted in persons being overly dependent on the welfare system. Only through partnerships among education, private sector training practices, and government legislation can societal problems of discrimination and hard-core unemployment be resolved.

Key Terms

copyrights, *392*

Americans with Disabilities Act (ADA), *395*

reasonable accommodation, *395*

expatriates, *396*

host-country nationals, *397*

cross-cultural preparation, *397*

culture, *398*

individualism-collectivism, *398*

uncertainty avoidance, *399*

masculinity-femininity, *399*

power distance, *399*

time orientation, *400*

rigor, *401*

repatriation, *402*

virtual expatriate, *403*

diversity, *405*

managing diversity, *406*

diversity training, *409*

attitude awareness and change programs, *409*

behavior-based programs, *410*

cultural immersion, *410*

school-to-work transition programs, *415*

School-to-Work Opportunities Act, *415*

Workforce Investment Act of 1998, *417*

Lifelong Learning Account (LiLA), *419*

glass ceiling, *419*

joint union-management training programs, *423*

succession planning, *424*

high-potential employee, *425*

skill-based pay systems, *429*

knowledge-based pay systems, *429*

Discussion Questions

1. What are some potential legal issues that a trainer should consider before deciding to run an adventure learning program?

2. Discuss the steps in preparing a manager to go overseas.

3. List the five dimensions of culture. How does each of the dimensions affect employee behavior?

4. What does the "rigor" of a cross-cultural training program refer to? What factors influence the level of training rigor needed?

5. What are virtual expatriates? What are their advantages and disadvantages for the company and the manager?

6. The director of sales and marketing for a Warner Brothers theme park has been working in Madrid. She is getting ready to return to the United States. What should Warner Brothers do to ensure her successful repatriation?

7. What does "managing diversity" mean to you? Assume you are in charge of developing a diversity training program. Who would be involved? What would you include as the content of the program?

8. What are school-to-work transition programs? Why are they needed? How do they benefit companies?

9. What are some potential advantages and disadvantages of attitude-awareness-based diversity training programs?

10. Discuss the implications of a skill-based pay system for training practices.

11. List and discuss the steps involved in developing a succession planning system. How might a succession planning system differ between high-potential employees and employees with midlevel managerial talent?

12. How can companies ensure that talented women have access to development programs?

13. What are Lifelong Learning Accounts? Do you think they help retain employees or encourage them to train and then leave the company? Explain your rationale.

Application Assignments

1. Go to the Web site for Hewlett-Packard (HP) at www.hp.com. Click on About US, and then, click on Diversity Inclusion. Hewlett-Packard is known for its commitment to diversity. How does HP demonstrate this commitment? What is the diversity value chain? What are the implications of the value chain for managing diversity?

2. The Big Brothers/Big Sisters of America is the oldest teen mentor organization in the country. Go to its Web site at www.bbbsa.org. Read about the corporate partners; read the newsletters and press releases on the news stories in the News Room. Identify the benefits that a company receives by working with this organization.

3. You are in charge of preparing a team of three managers from the United States to go to Ciudad Juarez, Mexico, where you have recently acquired an auto assembly plant. The managers will be in charge of reviewing current plant operations and managing the plant for the next three years. You have one month to prepare them to leave on assignment. What will you do? Use the following resources to help develop your plan: M. Gowan, S. Ibarreche, and C. Lackey, "Doing the Right Things in Mexico," *Academy of Management Executive* 10, no. 1 (1996): 74–81; and M. de Forest, "Thinking of a Plant in Mexico?" *Academy of Management Executive* 8, no. 1 (1994): 33–40.

4. Go to fairuse.stanford.edu, a Web site called Copyright and Fair Use created by Stanford University Libraries. How does work fall into the public domain? That is, how can you use someone else's work for free without having to obtain permission to use it?

5. Go to www.walmartstores.com, the Web site for Wal-Mart. Click on Careers and then click on Diversity. Review Wal-Mart's diversity efforts. What has Wal-Mart done to strengthen its diversity? Rate the company's diversity efforts in the following categories: Top Management Support, Employee Support, Recruitment and Hiring, Identifying and Developing Talent, Ensuring Fair Treatment, Holding Managers Accountable, and Improving Relationships with External Shareholders. What other recommendations would you make to Wal-Mart for improving its diversity efforts? Be as specific as possible.

6. Go to www.uawford.com, the Web site for the UAW-Ford National Programs Center. Choose one of the joint programs to investigate. Search the Web site to find information about the program. What is the purpose of the program? What activities does the program include? Who participates in the program?

7. The Department of Labor's Occupational Information Network (O*NET) is designed to meet the goal of promoting the education, training, counseling, and employment needs of the American work force. Go to online.onetcenter.org/. Choose a job family and then select a job within the family. What types of information are provided? Discuss the different ways that this information could be useful for training and development.

Case: *Melting the Glass Ceiling for Accountants*

In the accounting profession, both men and women have excellent career opportunities with major firms. However, in a classic case of the glass ceiling, women make up half of the entry-level jobs but just one-fifth of most firms' partners. Firms are concerned because they want to find and keep the best people, regardless of their gender. Also, experienced accountants are retiring while the demand for accounting services is rising. Firms need to find and keep the best employees.

Ernst & Young has found that attractive career paths can help retain female accountants. Many female accountants are juggling work with the need to care for elderly parents or children, putting them at a potential disadvantage compared to their male counterparts who may be on the management fast track. Traditionally firms have avoided assigning top clients to accountants who want to limit their hours. Ernst & Young has been defining career opportunities more flexibly, offering reduced schedules, flexible hours, and telecommuting. To help ensure that these career opportunities are as interesting as those offered to employees on traditional schedules and to ensure that assignments given to high-potential women and minorities include top clients, Ernst & Young has established leadership teams.

The firm makes a special effort to develop female and minority employees identified as having high-potential. Members of the executive board are assigned to serve as mentors to high-potential employees. The mentors offer the wisdom of their experience but also help make the women and minority candidates more visible when the firm is looking for candidates to take on important assignments. Ernst & Young has taken steps to ensure that the firm's partners, usually males, are comfortable mentoring female accountants. The senior partner in charge of the firm's gender-equity strategy helps the partners develop in the mentoring role. For example, she advises partners to invite women along to meetings, rather than expecting them to speak up and ask to attend. She encourages the partners to be direct if they have to provide negative feedback to their female protégés. She also helps uncover the unspoken expectations of the mentors. In one situation, a manager had more talented women available than openings for partner. He didn't offer transfers to some of the women because he admitted that he assumed the women's husbands would object to moving. She suggested he let the candidates address those concerns themselves. The manager tried and reported that he had a win–win situation: a new senior manager who was delighted to relocate and pursue a career that offered a future as a partner.

Why is breaking the glass ceiling an important business issue for Ernst & Young? Which approach to development does Ernst & Young use to address the challenge of the glass ceiling? What recommendations would you give Ernst & Young to help it ensure that its mentoring program for high-potential employees is successful?

Sources: Based on C. Hymowitz, "Coaching Men on Mentoring Women Is Ernst & Young Partner's Mission," *The Wall Street Journal* (June 14, 2007), http://online.wsj.com; "Leadership Drivers," *Training* (June 1, 2007); J. Cavaluzzi, "Women Are Not on Par(tner) with Male Colleagues," *Crain's New York Business* (September 14, 2007); "Accounting for Good People: Talent Management," *Economist* (July 21, 2007).

Endnotes

1. J. Sample, *Avoiding Legal Liability for Adult Educators, Human Resource Developers, and Instructional Designers* (Malabar, FL: Krieger Publishing, 2007); A. Cardy, "The Legal Framework of Human Resource Development: Overview, Mandates, Strictures, and Financial Implications," *Human Resource Development Review* 2 (2003): 26–53; A. Cardy, "The Legal Framework of Human Resource Development, Part II: Fair Employment, Negligence, and Implications for Scholars and Practitioners," *Human Resource Development Review* 2 (2003): 130–54; A. Cardy, "Reputation, Goodwill, and Loss: Entering the Employee Training Audit Question," *Human Resource Development Review* (September 2005): 279–304.

2. W. Turner and C. Thrutchley, "Employment Law and Practices Training: No Longer the Exception—It's the Rule," in *Legal Report* (Alexandria, VA: Society for Human Resources Management, July–August 2003): 1–4.

3. A. Pasztor and S. Carey, "Rescue Renews Focus on Training," *The Wall Street Journal* (January 17–18, 2009): A3.

4. B. Shutan, "Unfriendly Skies," *Human Resource Executive* (September 2008): 64–67.

5. D. Zielinski, "A Closer Look," *Training* (November 2005): 16–22.

6. Ibid.

7. G. Kimmerling, "A Licensing Primer for Trainers," *Training and Development* (January 1997): 30–35; M. Partridge, "Copyrights and Wrongs," *HR Magazine* (November 2008): 101–104.

8. R. Ganzel, "Copyright or Copywrong?" *Training* (2002): 36–44.

9. U.S. Department of Labor, *A Report on the Glass Ceiling Initiative* (Washington, DC: U.S. Government Printing Office, 1991); C. Petrini, "Raising the Ceiling for Women," *Training and Development* (November 1995): 12.

10. T. Maurer and N. Rafuse, "Learning, Not Litigating: Managing Employee Development and Avoiding Claims of Age Discrimination," *Academy of Management Executive* 15 (2001): 110–21.

11. "University of Phoenix to Pay $1,875,000 for Religious Bias against Non-Mormons," November 10, 2008, press release from www.eeoc.gov, the Web site for the Equal Employment Opportunity Commission.

12. B. McKay, "Coke Settles Bias Suit for $192.5 Million," *The Wall Street Journal* (November 17, 2000): A3, A8.

13. D. Morse, "Coke Rated 'Acceptable' on Diversity," *The Wall Street Journal* (September 26, 2002): A6.

14. R. Sharpe, "In Whose Hands? Allstate and Scientology," *The Wall Street Journal* (March 22, 1995): A1, A4.

15. Bureau of National Affairs, "Female Grocery Store Employees Prevail in Sex-Bias Suit against Lucky Stores," *BNAs Employee Relations Weekly* 10 (1992): 927–38; *Stender* v. *Lucky Store Inc.,* DCN California, No. C-88-1467, 8/18/92.

16. J. Sample and R. Hylton, "Falling Off a Log—and Landing in Court," *Training* (May 1996): 67–69.

17. I. Speizer, "Rolling through the Downturn," *Workforce Management* (August 11, 2008): 31–37.

18. Speizer, "Rolling through the Downturn."

19. B. Ettorre, "Let's Hear It for Local Talent," *Management Review* (October 1994): 9; S. Franklin, "A New World Order for Business Strategy," *Chicago Tribune,* May 15, 1994: 19–7 to 19–8.

20. S. Gale, "Taxing Situations for Expatriates," *Workforce* (June 2003): 100–04.

21. D. Eschbach, M. Parker, and P. Stoeberl, "American Repatriate Employees' Retrospective Assessments of the Effects of Cross-Cultural Training on Their Adaptation to International Assignments," *International Journal of Human Resource Management* 12 (2001): 270–87.

22. V. Sathe, *Culture and Related Corporate Realities* (Homewood, IL: Richard D. Irwin, 1985); M. Rokeach, *Beliefs, Attitudes, and Values* (San Francisco: Jossey-Bass, 1968).

23. G. Hofstede, "Cultural Constraints in Management Theories," *Academy of Management Executive* 7 (1993): 81–90.

24. P. Tam, "Culture Course," *The Wall Street Journal* (May 25, 2004): B1, B12.

25. C. Hymowitz, "Companies Go Global, but Many Managers Just Don't Travel Well," *The Wall Street Journal* (August 15, 2000): B1.

26. G. Hofstede, "Dimensions of National Cultures in Fifty Countries and Three Regions," in *Expectations in Cross-Cultural Psychology*, ed. J. Deregowski, S. Dziurawiec, and R. C. Annis (Lisse, Netherlands: Swet and Zeitlinger, 1983); G. Hofstede, "Cultural Constraints in Management Theories."

27. W. Randolph and M. Sashkin, "Can Organizational Empowerment Work in Multinational Settings?" *Academy of Management Executive* 16 (2002): 102–15.

28. W. A. Arthur Jr. and W. Bennett Jr., "The International Assignee: The Relative Importance of Factors Perceived to Contribute to Success," *Personnel Psychology* 48 (1995): 99–114; G. M. Spreitzer, M. W. McCall Jr., and Joan D. Mahoney, "Early Identification of International Executive Potential," *Journal of Applied Psychology* 82 (1997): 6–29; R. Garonzik, J. Brockner, and P. Siegel, "Identifying International Assignees at Risk for Premature Departure: The Interactive Effect of Outcome Favorability and Procedural Fairness," *Journal of Applied Psychology* 85 (2000): 13–20; P. Caligiuri, I. Tarique, & R. Jacobs, "Selection for International Assignments", Human Resource Management Review, 19 (2009): 251–262.

29. P. Caligiuri, "The Big Five Personality Characteristics as Predictors of Expatriates' Desire to Terminate the Assignment and Supervisor-Rated Performance," *Personnel Psychology* 53 (2000): 67–88; M. Shaffer, D. Harrison, H. Gregersen, J. Black, and L. Ferzandi, "You Can Take It with You: Individual Differences and Expatriate Effectiveness," *Journal of Applied Psychology* 91 (2006): 109–25.

30. J. S. Black and J. K. Stephens, "The Influence of the Spouse on American Expatriate Adjustment and Intent to Stay in Pacific Rim Overseas Assignments," *Journal of Management* 15 (1989): 529–44.

31. E. Dunbar and A. Katcher, "Preparing Managers for Foreign Assignments," *Training and Development Journal* (September 1990): 45–47.

32. K. Kranhold, D. Bilefsky, M. Karnitschnig, and G. Parker, "Lost in Translation," *The Wall Street Journal* (May 18, 2004): B1, B6.

33. J. S. Black and M. Mendenhall, "A Practical But Theory-Based Framework for Selecting Cross-Cultural Training Methods," in *Readings and Cases in International Human Resource Management*, ed. M. Mendenhall and G. Oddou (Boston: PWS-Kent, 1991): 177–204.

34. S. Ronen, "Training the International Assignee," in *Training and Development in Organizations*, ed. I. L. Goldstein (San Francisco: Jossey-Bass, 1989): 417–53.

35. Tam, "Culture Course."

36. P. R. Harris and R. T. Moran, *Managing Cultural Differences* (Houston: Gulf Publishing, 1991).

37. J. Carter, "Globe Trotters," *Training* (August 2005): 22–28.

38. C. Solomon, "Unhappy Trails," *Workforce* (August 2000): 36–41.

39. J. Ramirez, "Lost in the Shuffle," *Human Resource Executive* (January 2006): 54–57.

40. M. Kraimer, S. Wayne, and R. Jaworski, "Sources of Support and Expatriate Performance: The Mediating Role of Expatriate Adjustment," *Personnel Psychology* 54 (2001): 71–99; D. Jack and V. Stage, "Success Strategies for Expatriates," *T+D* (September 2005): 48–51.

41. Solomon, "Unhappy Trails."

42. GMAC Global Relocation Services, "2003–2004 Global Relocation Trends Survey," www.gmacglobalrelocation.com.

43. H. Lancaster, "Before Going Overseas, Smart Managers Plan Their Homecoming," *The Wall Street Journal* (September 28, 1999): B1; A. Halcrow, "Expats: The Squandered Resource," *Workforce* (April 1999): 42–48.

44. J. Barbian, "Return to Sender," *Training* (January 2002): 40–43.

45. J. Flynn, "E-Mail, Cellphones, and Frequent-Flier Miles Let 'Virtual' Expats Work Abroad but Live at Home," *The Wall Street Journal* (October 25, 1999): A26; J. Flynn, "Multinationals Help Career Couples Deal with Strains Affecting Expatriates," *The Wall Street Journal*, (August 8, 2000:) A19; C. Solomon, "The World Stops Shrinking," *Workforce* (January 2000): 48–51.

46. J. Cook, "Rethinking Relocation," *Human Resources Executive* (June 2, 2003): 23–26.

47. N. Orkin, "Focus on Brazil," *Training* (May 2008): 20; N. Orkin, "World View: Focus on China," *Training* (August 2008): 13; B. Filipczak, "Think Locally, Train Globally," *Training* (January 2007): 41–48.

48. L. Thach, "Training in Russia," *Training and Development* (July 1996): 34–37.

49. K. Maher, "Global Companies Face Reality of Instituting Ethics Program," *The Wall Street Journal* (November 9, 2004): B8; Deloitte Touche Tohmatsu, "About Us," www.deloitte.com.

50. P. Sappal, "Women and Minorities Continue to Take a Backseat in Business," *The Wall Street Journal* (October 17, 2000): B22.

51. H. Dolezalek, "The Path to Inclusion," *Training* (May 2008): 52–54.

52. S. E. Jackson and Associates, *Diversity in the Workplace: Human Resource Initiatives* (New York: Guilford Press, 1992); A. Wellner, "How Do You Spell Diversity?" *Training* (April 2000): 34–38.

53. M. Lee, "Post-9/11 Training," *T&D* (September 2002): 33–35.

54. J. Gordon, "Diversity as a Business Driver," *Training* (May 2005): 24–29.

55. R. M. Kanter, "When a Thousand Flowers Bloom: Structural, Collective, and Social Conditions for Innovations in Organizations," in *Research in Organizational Behavior,* vol. 10, ed. L. L. Cummings and B. M. Staw (Greenwich, CT: JAI Press, 1988): 169–211; W. Watson, Kamalesh Kumar, and L. K. Michaelsen, "Cultural Diversity's Impact on Interaction Process and Performance: Comparing Homogeneous and Diverse Task Groups," *Academy of Management Journal* 36 (1993): 590–602.

56. S. Caudron, "Diversity Ignites Effective Work Teams," *Personnel Journal* (September 1994): 54–63.

57. T. Kochan, K. Bezrukova, R. Ely, S. Jackson, A. Joshi, K. Jehn, J. Leonard, D. Levine, and D. Thomas, "The Effects of Diversity on Business Performance: Report of the Diversity Research Network," *Human Resource Management* 42 (2003): 3–21; F. Hansen, "Diversity's Business Case Just Doesn't Add Up," *Workforce* (June 2003): 29–32.

58. N. Lockwood, *Workplace Diversity: Leveraging the Power of Difference for Competitive Advantage* (Alexandria, VA: Society for Human Resource Management, 2005).

59. C. Hymowitz, "The New Diversity," *The Wall Street Journal* (November 14, 2005): R1, R3; D. Thomas, "Diversity as Strategy," *Harvard Business Review* (September 2004): 98–108.

60. R. R. Thomas, "Managing Diversity: A Conceptual Framework," in *Diversity in the Workplace,* ed. S. Jackson and Associates (New York: Guilford Press, 1992): 306–18.

61. M. E. Heilman, C. J. Block, and J. A. Lucas, "Presumed Incompetent? Stigmatization and Affirmative Action Efforts," *Journal of Applied Psychology* 77 (1992): 536–44.

62. B. Gerber, "Managing Diversity," *Training* (July 1990): 23–30; T. Diamante, C. L. Reid, and L. Ciylo, "Making the Right Training Moves," *HR Magazine* (March 1995): 60–65.

63. L. Roberson, C. Kulik, and M. Pepper, "Designing Effective Diversity Training: Influence of Group Composition and Trainee Experience," *Journal of Organizational Behavior* 22 (2001): 871–85.

64. A. Aparna, "Why Diversity Training Doesn't Work . . . Right Now," *T+D* (November 2008): 52–57.

65. L. Egodigwe, "Back to Class," *The Wall Street Journal* (November 14, 2005): R4.

66. S. M. Paskoff, "Ending the Workplace Diversity Wars," *Training* (August 1996): 43–47; H. B. Karp and N. Sutton, "Where Diversity Training Goes Wrong," *Training* (July 1993): 30–34.

67. Aparna, "Why Diversity Training Doesn't Work . . . Right Now."

68. Paskoff, "Ending the Workplace Diversity Wars."

69. J. Barbian, "Moving toward Diversity," *Training* (February 2003): 44–48.

70. L. Lavelle, "For UPS Managers, a School of Hard Knocks," *BusinessWeek* (July 22, 2002): 58–59; M. Berkley, "UPS Community Internship Program (CIP) Fact Sheet" (Atlanta, GA: United Parcel Service, 2003).

71. A. Markels, "Diversity Program Can Prove Divisive," *The Wall Street Journal* (January 30, 1997): B1–B2; "R. R. Donnelley Curtails Diversity Training Moves," *The Wall Street Journal* (February 13, 1997): B3.

72. S. Rynes and B. Rosen, "What Makes Diversity Programs Work?" *HR Magazine* (October 1994): 67–73; S. Rynes and B. Rosen, "A Field Survey of Factors Affecting the Adoption and Perceived Success of Diversity Training," *Personnel Psychology* 48 (1995): 247–70; A. Nancheria, "Nobody's Perfect: Diversity Training Study Finds Common Flaws," *T+D* (May 2008): 20.

73. C. Terhune, "Pepsi, Vowing Diversity Isn't Just Image Polish, Seeks Inclusive Culture," *The Wall Street Journal* (April 19, 2005): B1.

74. L. E. Wynter, "Allstate Rates Managers on Handling Diversity," *The Wall Street Journal* (November 1, 1997): B1.

75. R. Anand and M. Winters, "A Retrospective View of Corporate Diversity Training from 1964 to the Present," *Academy of Management Learning & Education* 7: 356–372; Dolezalek, "The Path to Inclusion." Also, see www.sodexousa.com.

76. I. Speizer, "Diversity on the Menu," *Workforce Management* (November 2004): 41–45; F. Jossi, "Cultivating Diversity," *Human Resource Executive* (December 2004): 37–40.

77. C. T. Schreiber, K. F. Price, and A. Morrison, "Workforce Diversity and the Glass Ceiling: Practices, Barriers, Possibilities," *Human Resource Planning* 16 (1994): 51–69; Lockwood, *Workplace Diversity;* M. Jayne and R. Dipboye, "Leveraging Diversity to Improve Business Performance: Research Findings and Recommendations for Organizations," *Human Resource Management* 43 (2004): 409–24.

78. D. Stamps, "Will School-to-Work Transition Work?" *Training* (June 1996): 72–81.

79. J. Dresang, "Factory Workers' New Skills Help Lure Business," *Columbus Dispatch* (August 24, 2008): D3.

80. "Nuclear-Education Programs Mushroom in U.S. Classrooms," *Virginian-Pilot* (December 27, 2008): D3.

81. R. Ganzel, "Reaching Out to Tomorrow's Workers," *Training* (June 2000): 71–75.

82. C. Hymowitz, "Executives Teach Inmates How to Be Employees," *The Wall Street Journal* (March 17, 2008): B1, B3.

83. R. Thurow, "To Tackle Hunger, a Food Bank Tries Training Chefs," *The Wall Street Journal* (November 28, 2006): A1, A13.

84. F. Jossi, "From Welfare to Work," *Training* (April 1997): 45–50; A. Pomeroy, "Welfare-to-Work: A Work in Progress," *HR Magazine* (February 2008): 34–39.

85. C. Tejada, "Lack of Jobs Is Complicating Welfare Rules," *The Wall Street Journal* (March 11, 2003): B1, B10.

86. See http//online.onetcenter.org/.

87. D. Baynton, "America's 60 Billion Dollar Problem," *Training* (May 2001): 50–52, 54, 56; Johnson, "Grab Your Partner."

88. M. Korn, "Firm's New Training Methods," *The Wall Street Journal* (November 7, 2007): B5A.

89. "Lifelong Learning Accounts, Summary of the Lifelong Learning Accounts Act of 2007" (2007 The Council for Adult and Experiential Learning) at www.cael.org. Also see www.thomas.gov and search 110th Congress, Bill Number s.26.

90. S. Ladika, "When Learning Lasts a Lifetime," *HR Magazine* (May 2008): 56–60.

91. *Women in U.S. Corporate Leadership: 2003* (New York: Catalyst, 2003); C. Hymowitz, "On Diversity, America Isn't Putting Its Money Where Its Mouth Is," *The Wall Street Journal* (February 25, 2008): B1.

92. N. Lockwood, *The Glass Ceiling* (Alexandria, VA: Society For Human Resource Management, 2004); J. Lubin, "Women Aspire to Be Chief as Much as Men Do," *The Wall Street Journal* (June 23, 2004): D2; U.S. Department of Labor, *A Report on the Glass Ceiling Initiative.*

93. P. J. Ohlott, M. N. Ruderman, and C. D. McCauley, "Gender Differences in Managers' Developmental Job Experiences," *Academy of Management Journal* 37 (1994): 46–67; K. Lyness and D. Thompson, "Climbing the Corporate Ladder: Do Female and Male Executives Follow the Same Route?" *Journal of Applied Psychology* 85 (2000): 86–101.

94. L. A. Mainiero, "Getting Anointed for Advancement: The Case of Executive Women," *Academy of Management Executive* 8 (1994): 53–67; J. S. Lublin, "Women at Top Still Are Distant from CEO Jobs," *The Wall Street Journal* (February 28, 1995): B1, B5; P. Tharenou, S. Latimer, and D. Conroy, "How Do You Make It to the Top? An Examination of Influences on Women's and Men's Managerial Advancement," *Academy of Management Journal* 37 (1994): 899–931.

95. P. Tharenou, "Going Up? Do Traits and Informal Social Processes Predict Advancing in Management?" *Academy of Management Journal* 44 (2001): 1005–17.

96. A. Pomeroy, "Cultivating Female Leaders," *HR Magazine* (February 2007): 44–50.

97. C. Tuna, "Initiative Moves Women Up Corporate Ladder," *The Wall Street Journal* (October 20, 2008): B4.

98. U.S. Department of Labor, *A Report on the Glass Ceiling Initiative;* R. A. Noe, "Women and Mentoring: A Review and Research Agenda," *Academy of Management Review* 13 (1988): 65–78; B. R. Ragins and J. L. Cotton, "Easier Said Than Done: Gender Differences in Perceived Barriers to Gaining a Mentor," *Academy of Management Journal* 34 (1991): 939–51.

99. C. Daniels, "Women vs. Wal-Mart," *Fortune* (July 21, 2003): 78–82; Advancement of Women Fact Sheet, "Wal-Mart's Diversity Commitment Translates into Support for Women at All Levels," and "*Working Mother* Magazine Names Wal-Mart a 2007 Best Company for Multicultural Women," from www.walmartstores.com, accessed March 25, 2009.

100. D. Zielinski, "Mentoring Up," *Training* (October 2000): 136–40.

101. M. Hequet, "The Union Push for Lifelong Learning," *Training* (March 1994): 26–31; S. J. Schurman, M. K. Hugentoble, and H. Stack, "Lessons from the UAW-GM Paid Education Leave Program," in *Joint Training Programs*, ed. L. A. Ferman, M. Hoyman, J. Cutcher-Gershenfeld, and E. J. Savoie (Ithaca, NY: ILR Press, 1991): 71–94. Also see www.cwa-union.org, the Web site for Communications Workers of America (accessed March 25, 2009).

102. See www.nactel.org, the Web site for the National Coalition for Telecommunications Education and Learning (accessed March 25, 2009).

103. See www.uawford.com, the Web site for UAW-Ford National Programs Center (accessed March 25, 2009).

104. Johnson, "Grab Your Partner."

105. C. Hymowitz, "Too Many Companies Lack Succession Plans, Wasting Time, Talent," *The Wall Street Journal* (November 26, 2007): B1.

106. C. Tuna, "Hiring a CEO from the Outside Is More Expensive," *The Wall Street Journal* (July 28, 2008): B5.

107. W. J. Rothwell, *Effective Success in Planning*, 3d ed. (New York: Amacom, 2005).

108. Hymowitz, "Too Many Companies Lack Succession Plans."

109. C. B. Derr, C. Jones, and E. L. Toomey, "Managing High-Potential Employees: Current Practices in Thirty-Three U.S. Corporations," *Human Resource Management* 27 (1988): 273–90.

110. H. S. Feild and S. G. Harris, "Entry-Level, Fast-Track Management Development Programs: Developmental Tactics and Perceived Program Effectiveness," *Human Resource Planning* 14 (1991): 261–73.

111. Derr, Jones, and Toomey, "Managing High-Potential Employees"; K. M. Nowack, "The Secrets of Succession," *Training and Development* 48 (1994): 49–54; J. S. Lublin, "An Overseas Stint Can Be a Ticket to the Top," *The Wall Street Journal* (January 29, 1996): B1–B2.

112. Ibid.

113. J. Lorenzetti, "Gap Management," *Human Resource Executive* (October 2005): 36–39.

114. D. Robb, "Succeeding with Succession," *HR Magazine* (January 2006): 89–92.

115. P. Kiger, "Succession Planning Keeps WellPoint Competitive," *Workforce* (April 2002): 50–54; E. Fravenheim, "Succession Progression," *Workforce Management* (January 2006): 31–34.

116. M. W. McCall, Jr., and M. M. Lombardo, *Off the Track: Why and How Successful Executives Get Derailed*, Technical Report no. 21 (Greensboro, NC: Center for Creative Leadership, 1983); E. V. Veslor and J. B. Leslie, "Why Executives Derail: Perspectives across Time and Cultures," *Academy of Management Executive* 9 (1995): 62–72.

117. S. Boehle, "Crafting a Coaching Culture," *Training* (May 18, 2007): 22–24.

118. L. W. Hellervik, J. F. Hazucha, and R. J. Schneider, "Behavior Change: Models, Methods, and a Review of Evidence," in *Handbook of Industrial and Organizational Psychology*, 2d ed., ed. M. D. Dunnette and L. M. Hough (Palo Alto, CA: Consulting Psychologists Press, 1992), 3: 823–99.

119. D. B. Peterson, "Measuring and Evaluating Change in Executive and Managerial Development." Paper presented at the annual conference of the Society for Industrial and Organizational Psychology, (Miami, FL, 1990).

120. G. E. Ledford, "Paying for the Skills, Knowledge, Competencies of Knowledge Workers," *Compensation and Benefits Review* (July–August 1995): 55.

121. E. Dierdorff and E. Surface, "If You Pay for Skills, Will They Learn? Skill Change and Maintenance under a Skill-Based Pay System," *Journal of Management* 34 (2008): 721–743.

122. E. E. Lawler III, *Strategic Pay* (San Francisco: Jossey-Bass, 1990).

123. D. Feuer, "Paying for Knowledge," *Training* (May 1987): 57–66.

Secrets of an HR Superstar

General Electric Co.'s (*GE*) legendary reputation in talent management owes much to one man: William J. Conaty. In his 40 years at GE, including 13 as head of human resources, he helped to shape the modern face of HR. "The guy is spectacular," says former Chief Executive and *BusinessWeek* columnist Jack Welch. "He has enormous trust at every level. The union guys respect him as much as the senior managers."

Conaty took a department that's often treated as a support function and turned it into a high-level business partner, fostering a deep bench of talent and focusing attention on the need for continuous leadership development. Among other things, he helped manage the seamless transition from Welch to Jeffrey R. Immelt in 2001 and was critical in shaping a new vision of global leadership that emphasizes such traits as imagination and inclusiveness. At 61, Conaty is now easing into retirement, having passed the top job over to long-time HR colleague John Lynch earlier this year while agreeing to stay on to handle GE's labor union negotiations this summer. As he winds up affairs at GE, Conaty shared his advice for nurturing leaders.

DARE TO DIFFERENTIATE

Relentlessly assessing and grading employees build organizational vitality and foster a true meritocracy, in Conaty's view. Employees must be constantly judged, ranked, and rewarded or punished for their performance. Welch famously talked about cutting the bottom 10 percent of employees. Immelt doesn't like to fixate on hard targets. But Conaty insists that differentiation "is what still drives this company." There's nothing like a bit of anxiety and the knowledge that you're being measured against peers to boost performance. "We want to create angst in the system," he says. "We have evolved from being anal about what percent have to fall into each category.

But you have to know who are the least effective people on your team—and then you have to do something about them."

CONSTANTLY RAISE THE BAR

Leaders continually seek to improve performance, both their own and their team members'. "The one reason executives fail at GE is they stop learning," says Conaty. "The job grows, the accountability grows, and the people don't grow with it." Continuous learning is so valued that GE training courses are considered high-profile rewards. Getting tapped to go to Crotonville, the 53-acre executive training center in New York's Hudson River Valley, is a signal that someone is poised to go to the next level. "Crotonville is one of the best tools we have in our arsenal," says Conaty. The company's extensive training programs are a powerful recruitment tool and help to stimulate midcareer employees. Moreover, GE uses Crotonville and other training centers worldwide as a way to recognize valued customers and business partners.

DON'T BE FRIENDS
WITH THE BOSS

Too often, says Conaty, HR executives make the mistake of focusing on the priorities and needs of the CEO. That diminishes the powerful role of being an employee advocate. "If you just get closer to the CEO, you're dead," says Conaty. "The HR leader locks in with the CEO, and the rest of the organization thinks the HR leader isn't trustworthy and can't be a confidant."

Conaty tries to counteract that risk by distancing himself from Immelt in public settings. While few people spend more time with Immelt than Conaty, he deliberately socializes with other colleagues at functions. Moreover, Conaty says he is the one to "purposely throw the daggers at Jeff that the other guys don't dare do. He knows what I'm doing. I need to be independent. I need to be credible." He also makes a point of being candid with leaders in private. As Immelt recently remarked: "I call Bill the 'first friend'. . . the guy that could walk in my office and kick my butt when it needed to be."

BECOME EASY TO REPLACE

Great leaders develop great succession plans. Insecure leaders are intimidated by them. "I can go business by business and tell you where we're strongest and weakest on succession. It all comes down to having an executive who doesn't want to admit someone else could do their job," says Conaty. "If they kill two or three viable successors along the way, you have to start looking at the person who's doing the killing." At GE, leaders are judged on the strength of their team and are rewarded for mentoring people throughout the organization. Conaty, for one, takes pride in the fact that his own successor is someone that he helped develop within the HR function at GE.

BE INCLUSIVE

Within every organization, there's a tendency to favor people you know. That can undermine success. Conaty winces at the memory of GE's acquisition of Borg-Warner's chemical business in 1988. "We figured that their sales force didn't look quite as spiffy and energized as our GE team," he says. The top management jobs went to GE folks, marginalizing the existing team. "We ended up losing most of their sales force, and lost the business with it."

Now, GE rigorously assesses the talent within companies before they're even acquired. It's a critical form of due diligence. "We find there are generally half a dozen people that we've got to have on the team of that company, and we need them there for a few years," he says. "Now we make special provisions to make them feel financially welcome—as well as emotionally welcome. Our GE people can't be the victors in these deals."

FREE UP OTHERS TO DO THEIR JOBS

When it comes to the CEO, says Conaty, "one of my jobs is to take things off his desk, not put things on his desk." Ram Charan, a management consultant who has worked with GE executives, says Conaty "has the intensity to look at the nuances of issues and take these things off the CEO plate. He solves things and goes forward."

That attitude extends to giving people the tools and permission to work on their own terms, and even GE has become much better about letting people step off the track for a while. "That used to be the kiss of death," says Conaty. He points to someone like Sharon R. Daley, a senior HR executive who turned down a promotion to spend more time with her kids. GE kept her in a part-time job until she was ready to take on new challenges. Today she's a company officer and the top HR person in the energy business. Conaty does draw limits. "I'm still cynical about seeing 'WFH' [working from home] on a calendar, especially on a Friday," he notes. "But we're much more open and flexible because you see the payoff."

KEEP IT SIMPLE

Most organizations require simple, focused, and disciplined communications. "You can't move 325,000 people with mixed messaging and thousands of initiatives," notes Conaty. Leaders succeed by being consistent and straightforward about a handful of core messages. And the best don't get derailed when times turn tough. "I'd say 70 percent of our leaders handle adversity well, and 30 percent let it overwhelm them," says Conaty. "If you can't take a punch and you don't have a sense of humor, you don't belong in this company. Everyone experiences failure now and then. It's how you handle it that matters."

Questions

1. One of Bill Conaty's tips for developing leadership is "Be Inclusive." Based on what was discussed in Chapters 7, 8, 9, and 10, what does "Be Inclusive" mean to you?

2. How does "Dare to Differentiate" relate to succession planning? What role does assessment play in differentiate between employees?

3. How can employees and their managers determine whether they are interested and qualified for leadership positions?

Source: D. Brady, "Secrets of an HR Superstar," *Business Week* (April 9, 2007). Copyright 2000–2009, by the McGraw-Hill Companies Inc.

Careers and Career Management

All of us will likely experience at least one, if not several, careers in our working lives. Chapter 11, Careers and Career Management, discusses the most current perspective on careers, why companies should be interested in helping employees manage their careers, the career management process, and the employee's, the manager's, and the company's responsibility for effective career management. Chapter 12, Special Challenges in Career Management, discusses important issues that employees may face throughout the span of a career as they join companies, change jobs, employers, or careers, or stop working. Special challenges discussed include socializing and orienting employees, career paths and job sharing, avoiding technical obsolescence, career plateauing, dealing with work-life conflicts, outplacement, and retirement.

Part Four concludes with a case that chronicles the experiences of two women who decide to job share.

Careers and Career Management

Objectives

After reading this chapter, you should be able to

1. Identify the reasons why companies should help employees manage their careers.
2. Discuss the protean career and how it differs from the traditional career.
3. Explain the development tasks and activities in the career development process.
4. Design a career management system.
5. Discuss the role of the Web in career management.
6. Effectively perform the manager's role in career management.

Managing Careers Helps Accenture Reach Out to Its Virtual Work Force

Accenture, a global management consulting firm, has offices in 150 cities across the globe, including Argentina, Botswana, South Korea, Poland, and the U.S., but it encourages employees to spend time with clients while *not* in their offices. If employees want to spend time in one of the consulting firm's offices, they have to make a reservation for a desk! Accenture has a virtual management work force of 178,000 employees who at any one time are working at different times and places around the world. Accenture's consultants analyze clients' business needs and design and implement solutions. The consultants work in teams depending on the size of the client and the project. While the work and travel can be exciting, they also can take a heavy toll on the consultants, many of whom at some point in their careers choose to take a more stable job, often with one of the clients with whom they have worked. A consultant who decides to work for a client cannot be considered completely disloyal; in fact, it can help Accenture keep and maybe even add new business. However, a serious downside is that Accenture loses money when talented employees leave.

Accenture has taken several steps to reduce turnover by helping consultants recognize and take advantage of opportunities within the company. For example, after orientation, every new hire is assigned a career counselor, a more senior Accenture employee in the same line of business who is available to meet face-to-face or electronically to discuss the new employee's current work as well as potential career opportunities. Accenture's performance and compensation system encourages senior employees to make time in their schedules for career counseling. Every employee at Accenture is evaluated on people development skills as part of their annual performance review; this evaluation is tied to a percentage of their pay increase. To encourage career development, Accenture's human resource department is focusing on how to communicate more effectively the different career paths available to employees. Also, the company's career counselors attend mandatory one-day training on the different career paths at Accenture. Accenture has replaced the old "get promoted or leave" philosophy with one that emphasizes how its multiple work forces each contribute to the business in a different but complementary way. Accenture's business strategy depends on these different work forces blending together as an integrated whole, to help the company and its clients achieve higher levels of performance. As a result, Accenture now has many different opportunities that vary in both the type of work (consulting, technology, and outsourcing) and the type of client being served (for-profit and not-for-profit businesses).

A Web site known as Careers Marketplace was developed by Accenture to provide employees with information about changing careers within the company. It also provides links to unfilled positions. For example, one of the videos on the Web site explains how one employee has moved within the company from consulting to business operations work to human resources. The employee discusses how each move has helped her develop her skills and experience. Accenture also recognizes the important role of nonwork life in a successful career. For example, Accenture has a leave program (Future Leave) through which employees can arrange for part of their paychecks to be set aside for up to three months of time off in the future. The company also asks employees to evaluate how well the company is doing in providing them with a high quality life as well as to rank issues such as diversity, reputation, work, rewards, and career development in order of personal importance. This helps Accenture determine the work-life balance of employees. The surveys are also used by career counselors in their discussions with employees.

Source: Based on J. Marquez, "Accentuating the Positive," *Workforce Management* (September 22, 2008): 18–25. Also, see Accenture's Web site at www.accenture.com; S. Needleman, "New Career, Same Employer," *The Wall Street Journal* (April 21, 2008): B9.

INTRODUCTION

Career development is important for companies to create and sustain a continuous learning environment. A study conducted by PricewaterhouseCoopers of companies in finance, online services, hospitality, real estate, and high-tech industries suggests that companies that are successful at managing the employee growth that accompanies business expansion and increased demand for their products and services focus on recruitment, career development, culture orientation, and communications.[1] These companies emphasize that employees are responsible for career management. But they also provide company resources that support careers, such as career counselors, development opportunities, mentoring, and managerial training in how to coach employees. The opening vignette about

Accenture shows the value of career management for both employees and their employer. The biggest challenge companies face is how to find a balance between advancing current employees' careers while simultaneously attracting and acquiring employees with new skills. For example, T. Rowe Price created task forces and councils across the company that were charged with looking at the role of career management in employee attraction and retention. One program focused on a career path for new phone representatives. The program helped identify and quickly bring development opportunities to promising new employees by offering them financial incentives and advancement opportunities directly related to training and job experiences.[2]

Another factor influencing the concept of careers is the growing use of teams to produce products and provide services. Teams give companies the flexibility to bring talented persons both inside the company (full-time employees) and outside the company (temporary and contract employees) to work on services and products on an as-needed basis. In some cases, careers are viewed as project careers. **Project careers** are a series of projects that may not be in the same company. These changes are altering the career concept and increasing the importance of career management from both the employee's and the company's perspective.

Because many persons spend a large amount of their lives working, work provides a place where employees look to satisfy a number of needs, such as affiliation, achievement, power, and growth. Career management can help employees satisfy these needs. Career management is becoming important also because the workplace is an area in which social equality, workplace diversity, and personal liberation can be achieved.[3] To melt the glass ceiling and to manage diversity, companies have to pay more attention to the career experiences provided to all employees. With the increased use of contingent employees such as independent contractors and temporary employees (recall the discussions in Chapter 1), career management has become more of a challenge. A related issue is that some employees (especially independent contractors and temporary employees) choose to frequently change jobs and careers for personal interests or to avoid becoming obsolete or expendable by specializing in one job as technology, the economy, or business changes. For example, a senior consultant at New York's Health and Human Services Department has worked on many different jobs, some of which she designed.[4] She also networks with professionals outside the agency. She says the contacts and exposure keep her "thinking about new ideas and different approaches." Many employees do not want to sacrifice personal lives and their family lives for their careers. For example, some employees are seeking jobs that provide shorter and more flexible work hours, attractive work environments, relaxed dress codes, and benefits such as child care, elder care, and concierge services, which help employees better balance their work and nonwork lives.

You may wonder why a training book covers career and career management. It is important to recognize that employees' motivation to attend training programs, the outcomes they expect to gain from attendance, their choice of programs, and how and what they need to know have been affected by changes in the concept of a "career." For example, an employee's career may not entirely be with one company. Career management is not something that companies do for employees. Rather, employees have to take the initiative to manage their career by identifying the type of work they want, their long-term work interests, and the skills they would like to develop. As you will learn in this chapter, because of the changing expectations that employers and employees have for one another (referred to as the psychological contract), more emphasis is being placed on using job experiences and relationships for learning rather than formal training courses and seminars. Also, trainers may be responsible for designing programs to help managers play an effective role in career management systems.

This chapter begins with a discussion of why career management is important. The second part of the chapter introduces changes in the concept of a career. The implications of these changes for career management are emphasized. The chapter presents a model of career development that is based on the new career concept and that highlights the developmental challenges employees face and how companies can help employees meet these challenges. The chapter concludes by examining the specific components of career management systems and by discussing the roles played by employees, managers, and companies in successful career management systems.

WHY IS CAREER MANAGEMENT IMPORTANT?

Career management is the process through which employees

- Become aware of their own interests, values, strengths, and weaknesses.
- Obtain information about job opportunities within the company.
- Identify career goals.
- Establish action plans to achieve career goals.[5]

Career management is important from both the employees' perspective and the company's perspective.[6] From the company's perspective, the failure to motivate employees to plan their careers can result in a shortage of employees to fill open positions, lower employee commitment, and the inappropriate use of monies allocated for training and development programs. From the employees' perspective, lack of career management can result in frustration due to lack of personal growth and challenge at work, feelings of not being valued in the company, and an inability to find suitable employment should a job change (internal or with another company) be necessary due to mergers, acquisitions, restructuring, or downsizing. For example, consider American Infrastructure, a civil construction, mining, and materials company with more than 1,700 employees. American Infrastructure developed a Career Development Roadmap as part of its efforts to increase employee satisfaction and reduce turnover.[7] The Career Development Roadmap includes a menu of development activities such as assessments, coaching, programs, skills training, and job shadowing. Manager and employee mentors are trained to help them work with employees to create a three- to five-year career roadmap. As a result, retention among high-potential employees has increased 92 percent.

Career Management's Influence on Career Motivation

Companies need to help employees manage their careers to maximize their career motivation. **Career motivation** refers to employees' energy to invest in their careers, their awareness of the direction they want their careers to take, and their ability to maintain energy and direction despite barriers they may encounter. Career motivation has three aspects: career resilience, career insight, and career identity.[8] **Career resilience** is the extent to which employees are able to cope with problems that affect their work. **Career insight** involves (1) how much employees know about their interests and their skill strengths and weaknesses and (2) their awareness of how these perceptions relate to their career goals. **Career identity** is the degree to which employees define their personal values according to their work.

Figure 11.1 shows how career motivation can create value for both the company and employees. Career motivation likely has a significant relationship to the extent to which a company is innovative and adaptable to change. Employees who have high career resilience are able to respond to obstacles in the work environment and adapt to unexpected events (such as changes in work processes or customer demands). They are dedicated to continuous learning, they are willing to develop new ways to use their skills, they take responsibility for career management, and they are committed to the company's success.[9] Research suggests that low career motivation may be especially detrimental for older, more experienced employees.[10]

Employees with high career insight set career goals and participate in development activities that help them reach those goals. They tend to take actions that keep their skills from becoming obsolete. Employees with high career identity are committed to the company; they are willing to do whatever it takes (e.g., work long hours) to complete projects and meet customer demands. They also take pride in working for the company and are active in professional and trade organizations. Research suggests that both career identity and career insight are related to career success.[11]

Career motivation is positively influenced by the extent to which companies provide opportunities for achievement, encouragement for development, and information about career opportunities. Career management systems help identify these opportunities and provide career information. Career management systems that give employees flexibility to make career choices based on both their work and life interests and demands may be especially useful for employee motivation and retention. For example, Deloitte LLP has designed a framework, known as Mass Career Customization (MCC), that aligns current and future career development options for employees with current and future business requirements so that both parties can benefit.[12] The MCC framework includes a set of options along four career dimensions or "dials": pace (rate of career progression), workload (quantity of work output), location/schedule (when and where work is performed), and choice (choice of positions or responsibility). Tradeoffs for each choice are specified

FIGURE 11.1
The Value of Career Motivation

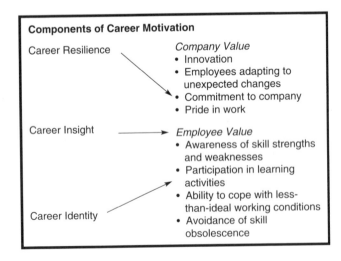

and choices are allowed to be changed over time to match employees' career needs. Employees and their managers discuss how to customize their career by selecting the option from each of the dimensions that matches their career objective, taking into account their individual circumstances and the needs of the business. For example, an employee who is hired into a fast-track program out of business school might be on an accelerated pace toward promotion, full workload, and unrestricted travel and schedule activity. The birth of a child may make it necessary to make changes to pace, workload, and location (perhaps less travel, taking on important work but not geared toward promotion). Use of MCC gives employees the ability to adjust the "dials" to achieve the best career-life fit while still contributing to the business. Using the MCC has allowed Deloitte to design a career development system that makes a long-term deal with the employee and therefore helps with retention; Deloitte realizes that some years an employee may work harder than others, but the employee will be working in ways that benefit both the company and themselves. Deloitte has found positive results from using MCC. Ninety percent of its employees believe it has positively influenced their decision to stay with the company, satisfaction with life and career fit has improved, client service standards have been maintained, and employees have not immediately asked to cut back on their workloads.

WHAT IS A CAREER?

Four different meanings can be applied to the concept of careers.[13] First, careers have been described as advancement. That is, careers are described as a sequence of promotions or upward moves in a company during the person's work life. Second, careers have been described as a profession. This definition suggests that careers occur only in certain occupations in which there is a clear pattern of advancement. For example, doctors, professors, businesspersons, lawyers, and other professionals have a path of career movement. University faculty members can hold positions as assistant, associate, and full professor. Managers can start in management trainee jobs, become supervisors, and then move to positions as managers and executives. Employees in jobs that do not lead to a series of related positions, such as waiters and maintenance employees, are not considered to have careers. Third, careers can be considered a lifelong sequence of jobs. A person's career is the series of jobs held during the course of that person's life, regardless of occupation or job level. According to this description, all persons have careers. Fourth, careers can be described as a lifelong sequence of role-related experiences. Careers represent how persons experience the sequence of jobs and assignments in their work history. This definition includes positions held and job moves as well as a person's feelings and attitudes about their jobs and their life.

This book uses Hall's definition of careers.[14] A **career** refers to the individual sequence of attitudes and behavior associated with work-related experiences and activities over the span of the person's life. This definition does not imply career success or failure based on promotion or advancement, and it recognizes that a career is a process, that is, a series of work-related experiences that all persons have, not just employees in professional careers. Work experiences, which include the employee's position, job experiences, and tasks, are influenced by the employee's values, needs, and feelings. Employees' values, needs, and feelings vary, depending on their stage of career development and biological age. As a result, managers and human resource development professionals must understand the career development process and the differences in employee needs and interests at each stage of development.

The Protean Career

Today's careers are known as protean careers.[15] A **protean career** is based on self-direction with the goal of psychological success in one's work. Protean employees take major responsibility for managing their careers. For example, an engineering employee may take a sabbatical from her engineering position to work at the United Way Agency for a year in a management position. The purpose of this assignment is to develop her managerial skills as well as to enable her to personally evaluate whether she likes managerial work more than engineering.

Traditional Career versus Protean Career

Table 11.1 compares the traditional organizational career to the protean career on several dimensions. Changes in the psychological contract between employees and companies have influenced the career concept.[16] A **psychological contract** refers to the expectations that employers and employees have about each other. Traditionally, the psychological contract emphasized that the company would provide continued employment and advancement opportunities if the employee remained with the company and maintained a high level of job performance. Pay increases and status were linked directly to vertical movement in the company (promotions).

However, the psychological contract between employees and employers has changed. Why? One reason is the change in companies' organizational structures. Because companies' structures tend to be "flat" (meaning the structure has fewer layers of management), authority is decentralized, and more of employees' responsibilities are organized on a project or customer basis rather than a functional basis. Flat structures are found especially in small and midsize organizations such as e-businesses. As a result, employees are expected to develop a wide variety of skills (recall the forces that affect work and learning discussed in Chapter 1). Another reason the psychological contract has changed is that, due to increased domestic and global competition as well as mergers and acquisitions, companies cannot offer job security and may have to downsize. Instead of offering job security, companies can offer employees opportunities to attend training programs and participate in work experiences that can increase their employability with their current and future employers.

TABLE 11.1 **Comparison of Traditional Career and Protean Career**

Dimension	Traditional Career	Protean Career
Goal	Promotions Salary increase	Psychological success
Psychological Contract	Security for commitment	Employability for flexibility
Mobility	Vertical	Lateral
Responsibility for Management	Company	Employee
Pattern	Linear and expert	Spiral and transitory
Expertise	Know how	Learn how
Development	Heavy reliance on formal training	Greater reliance on relationships and job experiences

Source: Based on D. T. Hall, "Protean Careers of the 21st Century," *Academy of Management Executive* 10 (1996): 8–16; N. Nicholson, "Career Systems in Crisis: Change and Opportunity in the Information Age," *Academy of Management Executive* 10 (1996): 40–51; K. Brousseau, M. J. Driver, K. Eneroth, and R. Larsson, "Career Pandemonium: Realigning Organizations and Individuals," *Academy of Management Executive* 10 (1996): 52–66; D. Hall, *Careers In and Out of Organizations* (Thousand Oaks, CA: Sage, 2002).

For example, the term *blue-collar work* has always meant manufacturing work, but technology has transformed the meaning dramatically.[17] Traditional assembly-line jobs that required little skill and less education have been sent overseas. Today's blue-collar workers are more involved in customized manufacturing. At U.S. Steel, employees make more than 700 different kinds of steel, requiring greater familiarity with additives and more understanding of customers and markets. Jobs once considered as lifetime employment are now more temporary, forcing employees to adapt by moving from one factory to another or by changing work shifts. Employees are taking classes to keep up with the latest developments in steelmaking, such as lathes and resins. Despite the lack of guaranteed lifetime employment, many blue-collar jobs are safer and better paying than they were 10 years ago.

The goal of the protean career is psychological success. **Psychological success** is the feeling of pride and accomplishment that comes from achieving life goals that are not limited to achievements at work (e.g., raising a family, good physical health). Psychological success is more under the control of the employee than were traditional career goals, which were not only influenced by employee effort but also controlled by the availability of positions in the company. Psychological success is self-determined rather than determined solely through signals the employee receives from the company (e.g., salary increase, promotion). Psychological success appears to be especially prevalent among the new generation of persons entering the work force. For example, consider Jacqueline Strayer. After graduating from college in 1976, she has held a series of positions with different companies including General Electric, GTE, United Technologies, and William Mercer.[18] While she worked, she earned a master's degree in professional studies in film and television, and she is currently working on a doctorate in management. Her motivation has come from finding interesting, challenging positions rather than trying to be promoted to a top management position. She is also passionate about running, so she wants to work with an employer that has a fitness center. Research suggests that individuals who embrace the protean career appear to engage in more activities that provide career insight, which in turn is related to career success.[19]

An important difference between the traditional career and the protean career is the need for employees to be motivated and able to learn rather than to rely on a static knowledge base. This difference has resulted from companies' need to be more responsive to customers' service and product demands. The types of knowledge that an employee must possess to be successful have changed.[20] In the traditional career, "knowing how"—having the appropriate skills and knowledge to provide a service or produce a product—was critical. Although knowing how remains important, employees need to "know why" and "know who." *Knowing why* refers to understanding the company's business and culture so that the employee can develop and apply knowledge and skills that can contribute to the business. *Knowing who* refers to relationships that the employee may develop to contribute to company success. Employees may network with vendors, suppliers, community members, customers, or industry experts. Learning who and why requires more than formal courses and training programs.

Consider the growing use of consultants in the information services area.[21] Internal information processing staffs have been downsized as companies have decided that they do not need internal staffs and can find talented employees on an as-needed basis. Many companies have an overabundance of experienced information systems staff who are solid performers but who do not bring to the job the ambition, experience, and ideas that consultants have developed by working with different clients.

Learning and development in the protean career are increasingly likely to involve relationships and job experiences rather than formal courses. For example, as was mentioned in Chapter 9, through mentoring relationships employees can gain exposure and visibility to a wide range of persons inside and outside the company. Job experiences involving project assignments and job rotation can improve employees' understanding of the business strategy, functions, and divisions of the company as well as help them develop valuable contacts.

The emphasis on continuous learning and learning beyond knowing how as well as changes in the psychological contract are resulting in changes in direction and frequency of movement within careers (career pattern).[22] Traditional career patterns consisted of a series of steps arranged in a linear hierarchy, with higher steps in the hierarchy related to increased authority, responsibility, and compensation. Expert career patterns involve a lifelong commitment to a field or specialization (e.g., law, medicine, management). These types of career patterns will not disappear. Rather, career patterns involving movement across specializations or disciplines (spiral career patterns) will become more prevalent. Also, careers in which the person moves from job to job every three to five years (transitory career patterns) are likely to become more common. For many employees, changing jobs can be satisfying because it offers them an opportunity for new challenges and skill development.

The most appropriate view of today's careers is that they are "boundaryless" and often change.[23] Boundaryless means that careers may involve identifying more with a job or profession than with the present employer. A career can also be considered boundaryless in the sense that career plans or goals are influenced by personal or family demands and values. One way that employees cope with changes in their personal lives and their employment relationships is by rearranging and shifting their roles and responsibilities. Employees can change their careers throughout their lives based on an awareness of their strengths and weaknesses, the perceived need to balance work and life, and the need to find stimulating and exciting work.[24] Career success may be tied to achieving goals that are personally meaningful to the employee rather than promotions or goals set by parents, peers, or the company. As we will discuss later in the chapter, careers are best managed through employee–company partnerships in which employees are committed to the organization but take personal control for managing their own careers to benefit themselves and company.

Career Needs and Interests of Different Generations

Different generations of employees (or employee cohorts) likely have different career needs and interests. Understanding generational differences is important if a company wants to provide the work conditions that will contribute to employee satisfaction and retention of good employees. Gen Xers, more so than previous generations, appear to place higher importance on work-life balance, opportunities for growth, and good work relationships.[25] Baby boomers appear to want meaningful work rather than flexibility in work scheduling. The baby boom generation has supplied companies with a well-educated, knowledgeable, hardworking, and career-oriented work force. As the baby boomers age and eventually retire, there are concerns that they will be discriminated against based on inappropriate stereotypes that they are unable or unwilling to learn, less productive, and would prefer to stop working.[26] As mentioned in Chapter 1, older workers do have valuable explicit and tacit knowledge that companies would be wise to "capture" and share with less experienced employees. Table 11.2 shows some of the personal characteristics of so-called

TABLE 11.2 **Suggested Characteristics of Different Generations of Employees**

Generation	Age	Traits
Millennium	9 to late 20s (Born 1982–2000)	Are independent spenders Are globally concerned Are health conscious Accept nontraditional families Accept constant change Understand need for training to remain employable Are cyber-savvy Have high expectations Want challenging work Need help managing constructive criticism and managing conflict Good at multitasking but unaware that it could be perceived as offensive by others Interested in frequent coaching and support
Generation X	Mid 20s to early 40s (Born 1965–1981)	Are experienced and confident using new technologies Are diverse Are independent Are entrepreneurial Are flexible Are team players Expect more feedback than older workers do Have a hard time accepting authority Don't want to have to hold people accountable Consider work-life balance to be critical Want status, prestige, authority, and rewards in jobs that make them more marketable and employable Willing to change jobs to acquire new skills and experience (free agents)
Baby Boomers	Mid 40s to mid 50s (Born 1946–1964)	Are idealistic Are competitive Question authority Are members of the "me" generation Want flexible retirement Want meaningful work
Traditionalists	Late 50s to early 80s (Born in 1945 or before)	Are patriotic Are loyal Are fiscally conservative Have faith in institutions Want their experience to be valued Respect previous generations, business leaders

Source: Based on J. Salopek, "The Young and the Rest of Us," *Training and Development* (February 2000): 26–29; M. Alch, "Get Ready for the Net Generation," *Training and Development* (February 2000): 32–34; N. Woodward, "The Coming of the Managers," *HR Magazine* (March 1999): 75–80; C. Solomon, "Ready or Not, Here Come the Net Kids," *Workforce* (February 2000): 62–68; P. Harris, "Boomer vs. Echo Boomer: The Work War," *T + D* (May 2005): 44–48; H. Dolezalek, "X-Y Vision," *Training* (June 2007): 22–27; K. Tyler, "Generation Gaps," *HR Magazine* (January 2008): 69–72.

millenniums (also known as Generation Y or Nexten), Gen Xers, baby boomers, and traditionalists. Some traits, such as health consciousness, may be present in all cohorts but are more important to some cohorts than others. Millenniums and Gen Xers are more used to change and job insecurity than are baby boomers and traditionalists. According to a recent study, 60 percent of employees of all ages rated time and flexibility as very important reasons for staying with a company.[27] But Gen Xers were more likely to leave a job than were baby boomers. Fifty-one percent of employees under age 40 reported that they were going to look for a new job within the next year, but only 25 percent of employees 40 or older said the same thing. Gen Xers are loyal to their own skills, and they change jobs to develop them.[28] They seek achievement of their own goals and value personal relationships. Gen Xers tend to perform several tasks quickly and often have to balance competing work demands. They respond best to short-deadline, multifaceted projects. Gen Xers are looking for meaning in their work. They want to see the company commit resources for career management. They do not believe the company is responsible for their careers. The millennium generation may be the first to embrace diversity and demand social responsibility in the workplace.[29] Because millenniums have been exposed to sophisticated technologies most of their lives, they are not afraid to use, learn about, and develop innovative ideas for new technology. Millenniums are able to shift attention from one task to another compared to other generations. They welcome feedback as a way to help them improve. Many millenniums may not understand the importance that their managers place on the unwritten rules of the workplace, such as spending time in the office. However, they want to perform well and understand why their work is important and how it relates to the company's goals. A recent survey of recruiters found that millenniums are seen as the weakest performers among the four generations that make up the U.S. work force. Although they are the most technology-proficient generation, they are often seen as being unmotivated and entitled to high salaries and great work environments.

An important difference between Gen Xers and baby boomers is that many baby boomers worked during a time when companies tended to reward years of service with promotions, job security, and benefits. Gen Xers work in a still-turbulent business environment characterized by swings between business growth and downsizing. Baby boomers may be more willing to relocate for a promotion or new assignment than younger employees. Gen Xers are more likely to stay in an area where they have formed social and work relationships. Many boomers view the younger generations as being lazy or unmotivated and fail to consider that Gen Xers and millenniums grew up during a time when layoffs were common.[30] Witnessing the layoffs of parents and friends may have caused these generations to place less importance on company commitment. Baby boomers also often criticize the younger generations for inappropriate dress, for spending too much time on cell phones, and for a lack of manners. Wendel Woodford is a Gen Xer who works as a copywriter at an ad agency.[31] This is the fourth company that he has worked for, and he realizes that he will make future job changes. He has never believed that he would stay at one ad agency and receive the job security that previous generations of workers enjoyed. Woodford considers himself a free agent, working hard for his current employer but recognizing that he will be moving on in the future. In contrast, despite the turbulent nature of business today, many baby boomers and traditionalists still expect companies to provide clearly defined career paths and reward good performance with promotions. Charles Coffey, a traditionalist, has worked for the Royal Bank of Canada (RBC) for 42 years.[32] In 1962, Coffey hoped that in return for his commitment and good performance, RBC would provide promotions and an exciting career. The company has required a strong commitment from Coffey. He and his family had to relocate across Canada several times, and he even had to ask for company permission to marry. As a result of his commitment and performance, Coffey has become executive vice president at RBC. Given the changes in the business environment and psychological contract, today's companies need to communicate to all employees, especially baby boomers and traditionalists, about the need to self-manage their careers and to reconsider linking their personal career success to promotions and salary increases.

It is important to realize that although differences in population size, diversity, education rates, and economic conditions likely affect generations in different ways, research suggests that younger and older generations share many similar values related to family, respect, and trust.[33] Differences in values and attitudes across generations may be the result of different work and life-stage contexts (such as position in the organization) rather than age. Most employees, regardless of age, want security and the ability to balance their work and personal lives through job flexibility or paid time off. However, for older employees, feeling secure about the future many mean working for a company that provides retirement benefits while for younger workers who have college debt and high living costs it may mean earning a good wage.

Companies today are reviewing their career management systems to ensure that they meet the needs of all generations of employees. For example, United Stationers Supply Company, a wholesale distributor of office products in Deerfield, Illinois, has reconsidered its career development opportunities based on generational differences.[34] The company's career bands are structured so that employees can move laterally to new jobs more easily and obtain new skills, knowledge, and experience without having to wait for a promotion or leave the company. The company is also trying to offer more flexible work schedule options, knowing that Gen Xers are interested in work-life balance.

A MODEL OF CAREER DEVELOPMENT

Career development is the process by which employees progress through a series of stages, each characterized by a different set of developmental tasks, activities, and relationships.[35] There are several career development models. Although it is widely accepted that the concept of a career has changed, the research literature does not agree on which career development model is best.[36]

The **life-cycle models** suggest that employees face certain developmental tasks over the course of their careers and that they move through distinct life or career stages. The **organization-based models** also suggest that careers proceed through a series of stages, but these models propose that career development involves employees' learning to perform certain activities. Each stage involves changes in activities and relationships with peers and managers. The **directional pattern model** describes the form or shape of careers.[37] Table 11.3 presents a model that incorporates the important contributions that the life-cycle, organization-based, and directional pattern models make to understanding career development. As noted in the discussion of the changing career concept, these models suggest that employees make decisions about how quickly they want to progress through the career stages and at what point they want to return to an earlier career stage. For example,

TABLE 11.3 **A Model of Career Development**

	Career Stage			
	Exploration ↓	**Establishment** ↓	**Maintenance** ↓	**Disengagement** ↓
Developmental Tasks	Identify interests, skills, fit between self and work	Advancement, growth, security, develop lifestyle	Hold on to accomplishments, update skills	Retirement planning, change balance between work and nonwork
Activities	Helping Learning Following directions	Making independent contributions	Training Sponsoring Policy making	Phasing out of work
Relationships to Other Employees	Apprentice	Colleague	Mentor	Sponsor
Typical Age	Less than 30	30–45	45–60	61+
Years on Job	Less than 2 years	2–10 years	More than 10 years	More than 10 years

some employees plan on staying in a job or occupation their entire lives and have well-thought-out plans for moving within the occupation (this career has a linear shape). Other employees view their careers as having a spiral shape. The spiral career form is increasing as many employees work on projects or in jobs for a specific period of time and then take a different job or project within or outside their current employer. As discussed in Chapter 9, employees may actually accept a job in another functional area that is lower in status than their current job (known as a downward move) in order to learn the basic skills and obtain the experiences needed to be successful in this new function.

Career Stages

Table 11.3 shows the four career stages: exploration, establishment, maintenance, and disengagement. Each career stage is characterized by developmental tasks, activities, and relationships. Employee retention, motivation, and performance are affected by how well the company addresses the development tasks at each career stage.

Research suggests that employees' current career stage influences their needs, attitudes, and job behaviors. For example, one study found that salespersons in the exploration career stage tended to change jobs and accept promotions more frequently than did salespersons in other career stages.[38] Another study found that the degree to which employees identify with their job is affected more by the job's characteristics (e.g., variety of tasks, responsibility for task completion) in early career stages than in later career stages.[39]

Exploration Stage

In the **exploration stage,** individuals attempt to identify the type of work that interests them. They consider their interests, values, and work preferences, and they seek information about jobs, careers, and occupations from co-workers, friends, and family members. Once they identify the type of work or occupation that interests them, individuals can begin pursuing the needed education or training. Typically, exploration occurs in the mid-teens to early-to-late 20s (while the individual is still a student in high school, college, or technical school). Exploration continues when the individual starts a new job. In most cases, employees who are new to a job are not prepared to take on work tasks and roles without help and direction from others. In many jobs, the new employee is considered an apprentice. An **apprentice** is an employee who works under the supervision and direction of a more experienced colleague or manager. From the company's perspective, orientation and socialization activities are necessary to help new employees get as comfortable as possible with their new jobs and co-workers so they can begin to contribute to the company's goals.

Establishment Stage

In the **establishment stage,** individuals find their place in the company, make an independent contribution, achieve more responsibility and financial success, and establish a desirable lifestyle. Employees at this stage are interested in being viewed as contributors to the company's success. Employees who have reached the establishment stage are considered to be colleagues. **Colleagues** are employees who can work independently and produce results. They are less dependent on more experienced employees than those in the exploration stage. They learn how the company views their contributions from informal interactions with peers and managers and from formal feedback received through the performance appraisal system. For employees in this stage, the company needs to develop policies that help balance work and nonwork roles. Also, employees in this stage need to become more actively involved in career-planning activities.

Maintenance Stage

In the **maintenance stage,** the individual is concerned with keeping skills up to date and being perceived by others as someone who is still contributing to the company. Individuals in the maintenance stage have many years of job experience, much job knowledge, and an in-depth understanding of how the company expects business to be conducted. Employees in the maintenance stage can be valuable trainers or mentors for new employees. A **mentor** is an experienced employee who teaches or helps less experienced employees.

Maintenance-stage employees may be asked to review or develop company policies or goals. Their opinions about work processes, problems, and important issues that the work unit is facing may be solicited. From the company's perspective, a major issue is how to keep employees in the maintenance stage from plateauing. Also, the company needs to ensure that employees' skills do not become obsolete.

To keep its employees from plateauing, General Electric emphasizes career development during its annual performance reviews.[40] During the reviews, employees discuss their goals with their managers. Those discussions are reviewed by operations and human resources personnel, who try to match employees' career goals (e.g., seeking job changes) with job openings. For example, older and more experienced managers who have knowledge about General Electric and about the people in the business may change jobs to help integrate newly acquired businesses into General Electric. Other managers who have new mobility when their children leave home may be encouraged to take advantage of overseas assignments.

Disengagement Stage

In the **disengagement stage,** individuals prepare for a change in the balance between work and nonwork activities. They may take on the role of sponsor. A **sponsor** provides direction to other employees, represents the company to customers, initiates actions, and makes decisions.

Disengagement typically refers to older employees electing to retire and concentrate entirely on nonwork activities such as sports, hobbies, traveling, or volunteer work. However, a survey conducted by Watson Wyatt, an international human resources consulting company, found that three out of four older employees preferred to reduce their work hours gradually rather than face the traditional all-work or no-work type of retirement.[41] For many employees, the disengagement phase means a gradual reduction in work hours. Phased retirement programs help both the employee and the company. The company gets to take advantage of the experienced employees' knowledge and specialized skills, which might be difficult to replace, while reducing the costs related to hiring and training a new employee.[42] For employees, phased retirement means that they have the opportunity to choose retirement in a way that meets their financial and emotional needs. To capitalize on older employees' talents, companies need to be flexible—for example, they might offer part-time and consulting work.

Also, keep in mind that regardless of age, employees may elect to leave a company to change occupations or jobs. Some may be forced to leave the company because of downsizing or mergers. Others may leave because of their interests, values, or abilities.

Employees who leave the company often recycle back to the exploration stage. They need information about potential new career areas, and they have to reconsider their career interests and skill strengths. From the company's perspective, the major career management activities in the disengagement stage are retirement planning and outplacement. Downsizing, outplacement, and retirement are discussed more in Chapter 12.

As Table 11.3 shows, an employee's age and length of time on the job are believed to be good signals of his or her career stage. However, relying strictly on these two characteristics could lead to erroneous conclusions about the employee's career needs. For example, many changes that older employees make in their careers involve recycling back to an earlier career stage.[43] **Recycling** involves changing one's major work activity after having been established in a specific field. Recycling is accompanied by a reexploration of values, skills, interests, and potential employment opportunities. For example, the global entertainment company Cirque du Soleil has a career transition program that helps artistic staff plan for their post-performing years.[44] The program relies on Cirque's expertise of what skills are needed to work backstage in the entertainment business. Cirque can help artists obtain the training they need for careers as fitness coaches, naturopaths, or makeup artists. A mid-50s corporate manager at General Electric started a new career and a lifelong dream of becoming a fashion designer as a result of taking early retirement.[45] One woman gave up her five-year career teaching fifth graders to work with the importer of Zyr Vodka.[46] While on vacation, this woman agreed to help a friend market a new Russian vodka during a business trip to Las Vegas. The work was very different from what she had been doing, but she found the work interesting and exciting. After the trip, her friend asked her to join the company as vice president. The job did not offer the woman the same security as the teaching job, and she would be taking a pay cut. Despite those negative aspects of the job, she accepted the position and has been working hard to build the brand by meeting with restaurant owners, liquor distributors, and club owners. She finds that working for a small distributor gives her a sense of ownership in the success (or failure) of the business. Also, she enjoys being accountable for all her decisions.

Recycling is not just limited to older employees who are nearing retirement. Many companies that face a serious shortage of qualified employees are developing retraining programs in hopes of filling labor shortages with employees from other fields.[47] Companies are using these training programs to help recycle employees into new jobs and careers. For example, in the computer-help-desk field, companies face a shortage of qualified staff for internal help desks and customer service. Also, many persons with computer skills who seek these positions lack the interpersonal skills needed to give counsel and advice to users of software, databases, and company intranets. The computer consulting industry is training former stockbrokers, flight attendants, and bank tellers to work at help desks. These training programs are referred to as "boot camps" because the training emphasizes total immersion in the job, one-on-one supervision, and cramming into a short training program what knowledge and skills the employee needs to have.

It is also not uncommon for employees who are considering recycling to conduct informational interviews with managers and other employees who hold jobs in functional areas they believe may be congruent with their interests and abilities. Employees conduct **informational interviews** with managers or other employees to gather information about the skills, job demands, and benefits of their jobs. A 30-year-old manager at Intel Corporation was unhappy with her job as a consumer marketing manager.[48] To find new job opportunities, she conducted informational interviews with managers and had discussions with colleagues at work. She also researched different departments, such as corporate communications, and searched Intel's intranet for job information. Because she was interested in education, she also looked outside Intel for opportunities at universities, educational software firms, and toy companies. She found a job as a program marketing manager with Intel's worldwide education group.

Stan Alger provides a good example of the concept of recycling in the career stage model. For 30 years, Alger worked as a factory sales representative for a bicycle company in the San Francisco area.[49] However, Alger often thought about working for Home Depot, the home improvement retailer. Alger enjoyed looking at the gadgets in the Home Depot store in his area and finding materials for his home projects. After his employer changed ownership, Alger quit his job. At age 59, he now works part-time at Home Depot. He enjoys helping people learn to use tools. "When you tell them how, and you see that light click on in their eyes, it's kind of fun," he says.

Employees bring a range of career development issues to the workplace. Specific career development issues (e.g., orientation, outplacement, work, and family) are discussed in Chapter 12. Besides developing policies and programs that will help employees deal with their specific career development issues (in order to maximize their level of career motivation), companies need to provide a career management system to identify employees' career development needs. A **career management system** helps employees, managers, and the company identify career development needs. Research shows that career management systems that provide employees with career advice and help them meet important people in the company can lead to employees who are more committed to the company and can have a positive influence on employees' job performance.[50]

CAREER MANAGEMENT SYSTEMS

Companies' career management systems vary in the level of sophistication and the emphasis they place on the different components of the process. However, all career management systems include the components shown in Figure 11.2: self-assessment, reality check, goal setting, and action planning.

The four steps in the career management process use the development activities (assessment, job experiences, formal courses, relationships) that were discussed in Chapter 9. The career management process is similar to the development planning process. Assessment information from psychological tests, performance evaluations, assessment centers, or 360-degree feedback can be used as part of the self-assessment or reality check steps. Employees engaged in action planning may use job experiences, relationships (mentoring or coaching), or formal courses to reach their short- and long-term career goals.

Self-Assessment

Self-assessment refers to the use of information by employees to determine their career interests, values, aptitudes, and behavioral tendencies. It often involves psychological tests such as the Strong-Campbell Interest Inventory and the Self-Directed Search. The former helps employees identify their occupational and job interests; the latter identifies employees' preferences for working in different types of environments (e.g., sales, counseling, landscaping). Tests may also help employees identify the relative value they place on work and leisure activities. Self-assessment can also involve exercises such as the one in Table 11.4. This type of exercise helps employees consider where they are now in their careers, identify future plans, and assess how their career fits with their current situation and available resources. Career counselors are often used to assist employees in the self-assessment process and interpret the results of psychological tests.

Verizon Wireless provides employees an online tool that allows them to assess their current skills and abilities in order to benchmark themselves against job openings throughout the company. This self-assessment tool allows employees to identify capabilities they are lacking and provides them with specific information about what they can do to develop skills through training, job experiences, or enrolling in an academic program.[51] As part of Caterpillar's performance management process, employees and their managers discuss career development. To facilitate this discussion, employees complete a data sheet that serves as an internal résumé. The data sheet includes information about the employee's skills, education, academic degrees, languages spoken, and previous positions. Managers are expected to indicate the employee's readiness for a new job, whether the job will be a promotion or lateral move, and what education or training will be needed for the employee to be ready for the move. Managers discuss with employees where they might go next and what they should do to prepare themselves for the next position. Managers also identify where they think the employee has the best opportunities in different functional areas and provide an overall rating of potential and promotability. At IBM, employees are offered a skills evaluation tool that recommends jobs and career areas where they best fit.[52]

FIGURE 11.2
The Career Management Process

Self-Assessment ⟶ Reality Check ⟶ Goal Setting ⟶ Action Planning

TABLE 11.4 **Example of a Self-Assessment Exercise**

Activity (Purpose)

Step 1: *Where am I? (Examine current position of life and career.)*
Think about your life from past and present to the future. Draw a time line to represent important events.

Step 2: *Who am I? (Examine different roles.)*
Using 3 × 5 cards, write down one answer per card to the question "Who am I?"

Step 3: *Where would I like to be and what would I like to happen?*
 (This helps in future goal setting.)
Consider your life from present to future. Write an autobiography answering three questions: What do you want to have accomplished? What milestones do you want to achieve? What do you want to be remembered for?

Step 4: *An ideal year in the future* (Identify resources needed.)
Consider a one-year period in the future. If you had unlimited resources, what would you do? What would the ideal environment look like? Does the ideal environment match step 3?

Step 5: *An ideal job* (Create current goal.)
In the present, think about an ideal job for you with your available resources. Consider your role, resources, and type of training or education needed.

Step 6: *Career by objective inventory* (Summarize current situation.)
• What gets you excited each day?
• What do you do well? What are you known for?
• What do you need to achieve your goals?
• What could interfere with reaching your goals?
• What should you do now to move toward reaching your goals?
• What is your long-term career objective?

Source: Based on J. E. McMahon and S. K. Merman, "Career Development," in *The ASTD Training and Development Handbook,* 4th ed., ed. R. L. Craig (New York: McGraw-Hill, 1996): 679–97.

Psychological tests can be helpful in choosing between equally appealing career options. For example, a man who had served as a branch manager at Wells Fargo Bank for 14 years enjoyed both working with computers and researching program development issues.[53] He was experiencing difficulty in choosing whether to pursue further work experiences with computers or enter a new career in developing software applications. Psychological tests that he completed as part of the company's career assessment program confirmed that he had strong interests in research and development. As a result, he began his own software design company.

Reality Check

Reality check refers to the information employees receive about how the company evaluates their skills and knowledge and where they fit into the company's plans (e.g., potential promotion opportunities, lateral moves). Usually, this information is provided by the employee's manager as part of the performance appraisal process. It is not uncommon in well-developed career planning systems for the manager to hold separate performance appraisals and career development discussions. For example, in Coca-Cola USA's career planning system, employees and managers have a separate meeting after the annual performance review to discuss the employee's career interests, strengths, and possible development activities.[54]

Goal Setting

In **goal setting,** employees develop short- and long-term career objectives. These goals usually relate to desired positions (e.g., to become sales manager within three years), level of skill application (e.g., to use one's budgeting skills to improve the unit's cash flow problems), work setting (e.g., to move to corporate marketing within two years), or skill acquisition (e.g., to learn how to use the company's human resource information system). These goals are usually discussed with the manager and written into a development plan. Figure 11.3 shows a development plan for a project manager. Development plans usually

FIGURE 11.3   Career Development Plan

Name: **Title:** Project Manager   **Immediate Manager:**

Competencies
Please identify your three greatest strengths and areas for improvement.
Strengths:
Strategic thinking and execution (confidence, command skills, action orientation)
Results orientation (competence, motivating others, perseverance)
Spirit for winning (building team spirit, customer focus, respect for colleagues)

Areas for Improvement
Patience (tolerance of people or processes and sensitivity to pacing)
Written communications (ability to write clearly and succinctly)
Overly ambitious (too much focus on successful completion of projects rather than developing relationships
   with individuals involved in the projects)

Career Goals
Please describe your overall career goals.
Long-term: Accept positions of increased responsibility to a level of general manager (or beyond). The areas of specific interest include but are not limited to product and brand management, technology and development, strategic planning, and marketing.
Short-term: Continue to improve my skills in marketing and brand management while utilizing my skills in product management, strategic planning, and global relations.

Next Assignments
Identify potential next assignments (including timing) that would help you develop toward your career goals.
Manager or director level in planning, development, product, or brand management. Timing estimated to be spring 2008.

Training and Development Needs
List both training and development activities that will either help you to develop in your current assignment or provide overall career development.
Master's degree classes will allow me to practice and improve my written communications skills. The dynamics of my current position, teamwork, and reliance on other individuals allow me to practice patience and to focus on individual team members' needs along with the success of the projects.

Employee _____   **Date** _____
Immediate Manager _____   **Date** _____
Mentor _____   **Date** _____

include descriptions of strengths and weaknesses, career goals, and development activities (assignments, training) for reaching the career goals.

Just Born, the candy company that makes Mike and Ike, Hot Tamales, and Peeps, offers a program called the Career Development Process (CDP) that is used by high-performing employees to decide on their career path with the company and to ready themselves for their next position.[55] The CDP helps employees identify both short- and long-term career goals, and employees commit to two goals to help them progress in their career. Just Born provides a competency dictionary on the company's intranet that can be used for identifying development needs. The CDP gives both employees and their managers the opportunity to discuss future career plans, and the exercise becomes a reality check for employees by raising company expectations and increasing performance standards. Employees initiate the CDP program by defining future job interests, indicating a long-term career goal, and identifying work experiences that would serve as preparation for the future job. Employees then discuss the CDP with their manager. The manager can support the CDP or can suggest changes. If employees' future job interests are outside their current department, those interests are communicated to the manager of the desired department.

Action Planning

In **action planning,** employees determine how they will achieve their short- and long-term career goals. Action plans may involve enrolling in training courses and seminars, conducting informational interviews, or applying for job openings within the company. Fresh assignments allow employees to take advantage of their existing skills, experiences, and contacts while helping them develop new ones.[56] At Wachovia, employees in the information technology department occasionally find themselves between projects. Wachovia's hGrid program allows IT employees the opportunity to work on new tasks and projects that interest them but that lie outside their current position.[57] Employees log into the hGrid Web site and create a profile where they can post the types of projects or experiences they are interested in. After they create their profile, they can explore projects that are posted online and use an online discussion area to exchange ideas in order to form bids to work on the project. Before employees can bid on a project, they must have their manager's approval. Wachovia benefits from the program by having new IT projects completed. Employees benefit by having the opportunity to try other types of projects to see if they want to pursue other types of jobs and skills, without risking their current position.

Some companies are lending out employees to nonprofits and small businesses to provide accounting, marketing, and other professional services.[58] In these assignments, often called *employee volunteerism programs,* employees have the opportunity to use and expand their skills and at the same time reach career goals and address a social problem. These programs may be especially important for millenniums (workers born after 1980) who want to work for companies that are socially responsible. For example, an employee at Ernst & Young left her Washington, D.C., office to spend 12 weeks in Buenos Aires providing free accounting services to a small publishing company. Her travel and housing expenses were covered during the assignment and she was on the company payroll for the entire time she was away from her job. In her volunteer assignment, she gained the satisfaction of helping others while at the same time facing the challenge of having more autonomy in her work than she had experienced in her company assignments. As a result, when she returned to her Washington office, the partners began letting her work more independently because they knew that she now had experience in taking a project from start to finish.

The career development system established by United Parcel Service (UPS) illustrates the career planning process and the strategic role it can play in ensuring that staffing needs are met.[59] UPS has 285,000 employees in 185 nations and territories who are responsible for making sure that packages are picked up and delivered in a timely fashion. UPS wanted to put together a management development system that would ensure that managers' skills were up-to-date and that would link the system to selection and training activities. As a result, UPS designed a career management process. The manager starts the process by identifying the skills, knowledge, and experience required by the work team to meet current and anticipated business needs. Gaps between needs and relevant qualifications of the team are pinpointed. The manager then identifies the development needs of each team member. Next, the team members complete a series of exercises that help them with self-assessment, goal setting, and development planning (self-assessment). The manager and each employee work together to create an individual development plan. In the discussion, the manager shares performance appraisal information and analysis of team needs with the employee (reality check). The plan includes the employee's career goals and development actions during the next year (goal setting and action planning). To ensure that the career management process helps with future staffing decisions, divisionwide career development meetings are held. At these meetings managers report on the development needs and plans as well as capabilities of their work teams. Training and development managers attend to ensure that a realistic training plan is created. The process is repeated at higher levels of management. The ultimate result is a master plan with training activities and development plans that are coordinated among the functional areas.

The UPS system includes all the steps in the career planning process. The most important feature of the system is the sharing of information about individual employees, districts, and functional development and training needs and capabilities. This use of information at all three levels allows UPS to be better prepared to meet changing staffing needs and customer demands.

Table 11.5 shows several important design factors that should be considered in developing a career management system. Tying development of the system to business needs

TABLE 11.5
Design Factors of Effective Career Management Systems

Source: Based on B. Baumann, J. Duncan, S. E. Former, and Z. Leibowitz, "Amoco Primes the Talent Pump," *Personnel Journal* (February 1996): 79–84; D. Hall, *Careers In and Out of Organizations* (Thousand Oaks, CA: Sage, 2002).

1. System is positioned as a response to a business need or supports a business strategy.
2. Employees and managers participate in development of the system.
3. Employees are encouraged to take active roles in career management.
4. Evaluation is ongoing and used to improve the system.
5. Business units can customize the system for their own purposes (with some constraints).
6. Employees need access to career information sources (including advisors and positions available).
7. Senior management supports the career system.
8. Career management is linked to other human resource practices such as performance management, training, and recruiting systems.
9. System creates a large, diverse talent pool.
10. Information about career plans and talent evaluation is accessible to all managers.

and strategy, obtaining the support of top management, and having managers and employees participate in building the system are especially important factors in overcoming resistance to the system.

Career Management Systems on the Web

Many companies are developing career management Web sites that provide employees with self-assessment tools, salary information for jobs within the company, career management advice, and training resources. Similarly, many companies in the employee recruitment business (such as monster.com) provide similar resources for job seekers and employers. Table 11.6 presents the elements of career management Web sites. As the left side of Table 11.6 shows, users or employees need access to self-assessment tools, training resources, job data, salary information, and career management advice. The right side of Table 11.6 shows the features the company needs to include in the Web site design (e.g., jobs database, tools, and services). Users may include employees, managers, recruiters, or human resource managers. Both the users and the company gain valuable information from these systems—information that is useful for ensuring that employees' abilities, skills, and interests match their jobs. If there is a mismatch, these sites provide links to assessment tools so employees can determine what type of work best suits them as well as training and development resources for them to develop their skills. The company benefits from such systems in several ways. First, it can quickly post job openings and reach a large number of potential job seekers. Second, such Web sites provide detailed accessible information about jobs and careers within the company, which facilitates employee development. Employees are aware of what knowledge and skills are needed for jobs and careers in the company. Third, online systems encourage employees to be responsible for and take an active role in career management. This benefit is congruent with the new psychological contract and protean career discussed earlier in this chapter.

John Deere, the consumer and residential equipment provider, has an online career development program that encourages employees to manage their careers.[60] The online system includes a job-fit analysis that allows employees to compare their current competencies with the job competencies of positions they would like to have in the future. This program gives employees control and responsibility for identifying skill deficiencies and encourages them to discuss with their managers a development plan that helps them reach their career goals. Employees can also prepare an online internal résumé for the company's job posting system. With these résumés, managers throughout the company have access to employees' credentials. In the first three months that the online system was available, employees made more than 10,000 hits on the job catalog. More than 6,000 internal résumés are posted in the system.

TABLE 11.6
Elements of Career Management Web Sites

User Access	Web Site Features
Self-assessment tools	Jobs database
Training resources	Employee profile database
Job data	Matching engine
Salary information	Tools and services such as assessment, online
Career management advice	training programs, development resources

Dow Chemical has created an online tool, called My Profile, that allows all employees to share their job interests and goals and other career-related perspectives, such as willingness to relocate.[61] This profile information can be viewed by employees' managers and used to develop job opportunities for employees. It also helps facilitate career development dialogue between employees and their managers. The profiles give both current and future managers a living, up-to-date narrative of their employees' goals and aspirations.

ROLES OF EMPLOYEES, MANAGERS, HUMAN RESOURCE MANAGERS, AND THE COMPANY IN CAREER MANAGEMENT

Employees, their managers, human resource managers, and the company share the responsibility for career management.[62] Figure 11.4 shows the roles of employees, managers, human resource managers, and the company in career management.

Employee's Role

The new psychological contract and the protean career mentioned earlier in the chapter suggest that employees can increase their value to their current employer (increase their employment opportunities and take change of their careers) by taking responsibility for career planning. Companies with effective career management systems expect employees to take responsibility for their own career management. At IBM, Blue Opportunities reinforces to employees that growing their careers is an important step in obtaining challenging and interesting work. Employees are encouraged to take responsibility, working with their manager, for identifying training and development activities that interest them.[63] Blue Opportunities highlights the company's training and development opportunities—such as short- and long-term job rotation, on-site job shadowing, and cross-functional projects—on an employee-only Internet site that is accessible by IBM employees in the U.S. and other global locations. The goals of Blue Opportunities are to develop employees' skills and knowledge and offer them potential job or career changes. Blue Opportunities provides a way for employees to develop skills across business units and explore career options that they may not have previously considered. For example, a Brazilian employee worked on a project with a manager in Ireland. As a result, he learned more about the opportunities available in another business unit. An employee in India completed a short-term assignment with customers in Italy and used the new skills acquired to train less experienced engineers. Managers also benefit from

FIGURE 11.4
Shared
Responsibility:
Roles in
Career
Management

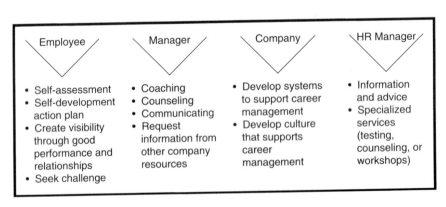

Employee	Manager	Company	HR Manager
• Self-assessment • Self-development action plan • Create visibility through good performance and relationships • Seek challenge	• Coaching • Counseling • Communicating • Request information from other company resources	• Develop systems to support career management • Develop culture that supports career management	• Information and advice • Specialized services (testing, counseling, or workshops)

Blue Opportunities. The program helps managers assist their employees in developing competencies and careers and provides a way to share expertise across departments and multiple lines of business.

Regardless of how sophisticated the company's career planning system is, employees should engage in several career management actions:[64]

- Take the initiative to ask for feedback from managers and peers regarding skill strengths and weaknesses.
- Identify stage of career development and development needs.
- Seek challenges by gaining exposure to a range of learning opportunities (e.g., sales assignments, product design assignments, administrative assignments).
- Interact with employees from different work groups inside and outside the company (e.g., professional associations, task forces).
- Create visibility through good performance.

Manager's Role

Regardless of the type of formal career management system in place at the company, managers play a key role in the process. In most cases, employees look to their managers for career advice. Why? Because managers typically evaluate employees' readiness for job mobility (e.g., promotions). Also, managers are often the primary source of information about position openings, training courses, and other developmental opportunities. Unfortunately, many managers avoid becoming involved in career planning activities with employees because they do not feel qualified to answer employees' career-related questions, they have limited time for helping employees deal with career issues, and they lack the interpersonal skills needed to fully understand career issues.[65]

To help employees deal with career issues, managers need to be effective in four roles: coach, appraiser, advisor, and referral agent.[66] The responsibilities of each of these roles is shown in Table 11.7. Managers are responsible for helping employees manage their career through meeting personal needs as well as company needs. Coaching,

TABLE 11.7
Managers' Roles in Career Management

Source: Based on Z. B. Leibowitz, C. Farren, and B. L. Kaye, *Designing Career Development Systems* (San Francisco: Jossey-Bass, 1986).

Role	Responsibilities
Coach	Probe problems, interests, values, needs
	Listen
	Clarify concerns
	Define concerns
Appraiser	Give feedback
	Clarify company standards
	Clarify job responsibilities
	Clarify company needs
Advisor	Generate options, experiences, and relationships
	Assist in goal setting
	Provide recommendations
Referral Agent	Link to career management resources
	Follow up on career management plan

appraising, advising, and serving as a referral agent are important roles for managers to play for employees in all stages of their careers. Employees early in their career may need information related to how well their performance is meeting customer expectations. Employees in both establishment and maintenance stages may use the manager as a sounding board for ideas and perspectives on job changes and career paths. Managers need to understand employees' interests by discussing with employees their job likes and dislikes.[67] One way to initiate this discussion is to ask employees to write up the characteristics of a satisfying career. This exercise helps employees better understand what they want from work in both the short term and long term. Only after understanding employees' interests can managers match employees to job experiences related to their interests.

To understand the manager's role in career management, consider the case of José, who works in the oil and chemical industry. José is an industrial hygienist at a chemical plant, where safety is critical. He is unhappy about what he thinks is a lack of career development at the company. As a result, he is considering leaving the company. José has been at a refinery in Texas the past year, but he wants to move back to Utah for family reasons. He was denied a lateral move to a plant in Utah. He made the request at a time when the company was downsizing and seeking voluntary retirements. The company understands that José wants to return to Utah, but it does not feel he is ready for another move. José considers his career stunted, and he thinks that the company does not care about him. Although he is unhappy, his performance is acceptable.

How can José's manager help him deal with this career issue to avoid losing a solid performer? José and his manager need to sit down and discuss his career. Table 11.8 presents the results that a manager should try to achieve in a career discussion. José's manager needs to clarify José's career concerns (coaching role). The manager also needs to make sure that José understands that although his job performance is acceptable, the company believes he needs to gain more experience at the Texas facility (appraiser role). Third, José's manager needs to discuss with José what can be done now to help him feel better about his job and the company and also help him understand how the company's need for a hygienist with his qualifications at the Texas refinery fits into the larger picture of his career development (advisor role). José and his manager should discuss and agree on a timetable for his next possible move (which could be to a position in Utah). The manager may give José advice concerning the correct timing for requesting a transfer, given the company's financial situation. Finally, José's manager should let him know about career counseling or other career management resources available within the company (role of referral agent).

TABLE 11.8
Characteristics of Successful Career Discussions

Source: Adapted from F. L. Otte and P. G. Hutcheson, *Helping Employees Manage Careers* (Englewood Cliffs, NJ: Prentice-Hall, 1992): 57–58.

Manager gains an awareness of employee's work-related goals and interests.
Manager and employee agree on the next developmental steps.
Employee understands how the manager views his or her performance, developmental needs, and options.
Manager and employee agree on how the employee's needs can be met on the current job.
Manager identifies resources to help the employee accomplish the goals agreed on in the career discussion.

Human Resource Manager's Role

Human resource managers should provide information or advice about potential career paths and training and development opportunities. Also, human resource managers may provide specialized services such as testing to determine employees' values, interests, and skills; preparing employees for job searches; and offering counseling on career-related problems. Hewlett-Packard's "People Promise" program was begun to show employees that they can build a career at the company.[68] The HR department now categorizes jobs into 400 job families, which makes it easier for employees to research online how to plan career moves within the company. Job openings are first posted internally, and the internal database is used to match employees with job openings before looking outside the company. The program also allows employees to complete their own career development plans so they can grow within their current job or prepare for other jobs in the company.

Company's Role

Companies are responsible for providing employees with the resources needed to be successful in managing their careers. These resources include specific programs as well as processes for career management:

- Career workshops (seminars on topics such as how the career management system works, self-assessment, goal setting, and helping managers understand and perform their roles in career management).
- Information on career and job opportunities (places such as a career center or newsletters, electronic databases, or Web sites where employees can find information about job openings and training programs).
- Career planning workbooks (printed guides that direct employees through a series of exercises, discussions, and guidelines related to career planning).
- Career counseling (advice from a professionally trained counselor who specializes in working with employees seeking assistance with career issues).
- Career paths (planning job sequences and identifying skills needed for advancement within and across job families, such as moving from technical jobs to management jobs).

The company also needs to monitor the career management system to (1) ensure that managers and employees are using the system as intended and (2) evaluate whether the system is helping the company meet its objectives (e.g., shortening the time it takes to fill positions).

For example, American Express conducted a survey of its 8,000 customer service representatives to better understand their career issues. The survey results showed that they wanted more training, the ability to develop their careers, pay based on performance, and flexible work schedules.[69] In responding to those needs, American Express developed a new career development effort involving a four-tier career path. An Internet site provides a way for call center representatives to review job opportunities and learn about promotional opportunities. Inexperienced new employees work at level one and deal with generic customer calls. Experienced employees working at level four interact with the most important clients and handle complex calls. As a result of American Express's efforts to meet employees' needs, the company estimates it has saved approximately $9 million in turnover costs. Employee engagement survey results have also improved.

Ohio Savings Bank developed a formal career counseling program to identify and develop employee talent and to give employees the tools and training they need to direct their own careers. Career development counselors play an important role in the program. Employees can meet with a career development counselor to discuss career paths and training requirements for positions within Ohio Savings Bank. Information sessions are available for employees who are thinking about changing divisions within the company. During these sessions, managers from different divisions provide information about current or future job openings. The career development counselor also meets with managers to discuss employees' career plans. Managers and counselors might discuss high-potential employees or action plans for employees to reach their career goals. Ohio Savings Bank also has a Career Development Services Web page that employees can access. This Web page has more hits than any other internal Web page![70] At Ernst & Young, each employee is assigned a career counselor who conducts the employee's annual performance evaluation, helps set improvement goals, and provides career counseling. Each employee-counselor pair develops a learning plan that identifies the employee's strengths and development needs. The counselor also provides feedback throughout the year.[71]

EVALUATING CAREER MANAGEMENT SYSTEMS

Career management systems need to be evaluated to ensure that they are meeting the needs of employees and the business. The outcomes, methods, and evaluation study designs that were discussed in Chapter 6 relating to training evaluation are relevant for career management system evaluation.

Several types of outcomes can be used to evaluate career management systems. First, the reactions of the customers (employees and managers) who use the career management system can be determined through surveys. For example, employees who use the services (planning, counseling, etc.) can be asked to evaluate the information's timeliness, helpfulness, and quality. Managers can provide information regarding how the system affected the time needed to fill open positions in their department as well as the quality of the job candidates and the employees selected for the positions. Second, more objective information related to the retention rates of key employees or managers of the career management system can be tracked, such as actual time to fill open positions, employee use of the system (including contact with career counselors, use of career libraries, or inquiries on job postings), or number of employees identified as ready for management positions. If the goals of the system relate to diversity, the number of women and minorities promoted into management positions may be an appropriate measure.

Evaluation of a career management system should be based on its objectives. If improving employee morale is the system's goal, then attitudes should be measured. If the system objectives are more concrete and measurable (as with a system designed to retain employees with high potential for management), then appropriate data (turnover rates) should be collected.

Summary   This chapter explained the concept of a career and career management. It began by discussing career management's importance for the company and employees. The chapter described the changing nature of the career concept. Today, careers are more flexible and more likely to be evaluated on psychological success than on salary increases or promotions. The chapter introduced a career development model based on the new career concept and on life-cycle, organizational, and directional pattern perspectives of careers. It suggested that employees face different developmental tasks depending on their career stage (exploration, establishment, maintenance, disengagement). The actions that companies can take to help employees deal with these developmental tasks were highlighted. The career management process consists of self-assessment, reality check, goal setting, and action planning. For career management to be successful, employees, managers, and the company must all be actively involved.

Key Terms

project career, *446*
career management, *447*
career motivation, *447*
career resilience, *447*
career insight, *447*
career identity, *448*
career, *449*
protean career, *450*
psychological contract, *450*
psychological success, *451*
career development, *455*

life-cycle models, *455*
organization-based
model, *455*
directional pattern model,
455
exploration stage, *456*
apprentice, *457*
establishment stage, *457*
colleague, *457*
maintenance stage, *457*
mentor, *457*

disengagement stage, *457*
sponsor, *457*
recycling, *458*
informational
interview, *459*
career management
system, *459*
self-assessment, *460*
reality check, *461*
goal setting, *462*
action planning, *463*

Discussion Questions

1. What stage of career development are you in? What career concerns are most important to you? Are these concerns consistent with any one of the development models presented in the chapter?

2. Discuss the implications that the career development model presented in this chapter may have for training and development activities.

3. Why should companies be interested in helping employees plan their careers? What benefits can companies gain? What are the risks?

4. What are the three components of career motivation? Which is most important? Which is least important? Why?

5. How does the protean career concept differ from the traditional career concept on the following dimensions: pattern, development sources, goal, and responsibility for management?

6. What is a psychological contract? How does the psychological contract influence career management?

7. What are the manager's roles in a career management system? Which role do you think is most difficult for the typical manager? Which is easiest? List the reasons why managers might resist involvement in career management.

8. How has the Web influenced career management for employees? For companies?

9. If you were asked to develop a career management system, what would it look like? How might you evaluate whether it was effective? What information would you use to develop the system?

Application Assignments

1. Go to www.thomsonreuters.com, the part of the Web site for the Thomson Corporation that provides career assistance for current Thomson employees and job seekers. Click on Career. What does Thomson Reuters provide on the site that helps prospective and current employees? Be specific and explain how each part of the site helps in career management.

2. Go to www.monster.com. Roll over to Career Tools. Review Career Snapshot, Career Benchmark, and Career Mapping. How are each of these tools helpful for career management?

3. Go to www.ncsu.edu/careerkey, the Web site for Career Key, an assessment tool that can be used for self-assessment and career management. Roll the cursor over Your Personality, and click on Holland's Theory of Career Choice and You. According to Holland's theory, when will people be most successful and satisfied? Read the description of each of the six personality types. Which one best fits you? What jobs or careers best match your personality type? Explain.

4. The World Wide Web is increasingly being used by companies to list job openings and by individuals to find jobs. Using the Web sites listed here (or sites you find yourself by surfing the Web), find two job openings that you may be qualified for. The Web sites include

   www.collegerecruiter.com

   www.careerbuilder.com

   www.monster.com

   www.vetjobs.com

   www.dice.com

   Choose one of these Web sites and describe the career resources it provides. From the company's perspective, what are the advantages of using the Web to recruit new employees? What are the advantages from the job searcher's perspective?

5. Go to online.onetcenter.org. Click on Skills Search. Complete the skills search, and click Go. What occupations match your skills? How might Skills Search be useful for career management?

6. Complete the self-assessment exercise in Table 11.4. What changes would you make in the exercise to improve it?

Case: *Generation X Values Have Implications for Career Management*

Some experts argue that the same career management approaches that work with baby boomers don't work with Generation Xers. Gen Xers don't have the same values as baby boomers. Teen experiences as latch-key kids and watching their parents get laid off from corporations helped to shape Gen Xers' belief that one of their most important priorities is to take care of themselves under any circumstances. Many Gen Xers feel that the traditional corporate career path is too narrow, emphasizing an "up or out" mentality. Gen Xers view the availability of multiple career paths as creating options and providing them with an opportunity to gain a broad set of business skills. Companies that are known as good places to make personal contacts are valued by Gen Xers. Gen Xers also value their children and their family relationships. This means that they have strict standards about how many hours they will work or the amount of business travel they will accept. As a result of the incompatibility between their values and those of large companies, many Gen Xers have left "Corporate America" for smaller companies or to start their own businesses.

Consider the question: "A career is . . .?" How would Gen Xers define a career? How would Baby Boomers define a career? What are the similarities and differences? Do you think that differences in how a career is defined between generations (e.g., Baby Boomers vs. Gen Xers) are greater than differences that might exist within any one generation? That is, are there really generational differences in how a career is defined?

How can companies use their career management systems to attract, retain, and motivate talented Gen X employees? Consider each step in the career management process and provide recommendations for what managers and the company should do to appeal to Gen Xers' values.

Source: Based on T. Erickson, "Don't Treat Them Like Baby Boomers," *BusinessWeek* (September 1, 2008): 64; K. Auby, "A Boomer's Guide to Communication with Gen X and Gen Y," *BusinessWeek* (September 1, 2008): 63; P. O'Connell, "What's Eating Gen X," *BusinessWeek* (September 1, 2008): 61.

Endnotes

1. P. Weber, "Getting a Grip on Employee Growth," *Training and Development* (May 1999): 87–94.

2. Ibid.

3. D. Hall, *Careers In and Out of Organizations* (Thousand Oaks, CA: Sage, 2002).

4. C. Hymowitz, "Baby Boomers Seek New Ways to Escape Career Claustrophobia," *The Wall Street Journal,* (June 24, 2003): B1.

5. D. C. Feldman, *Managing Careers in Organizations* (Glenview, IL: Scott-Foresman, 1988).

6. J. E. Russell, "Career Development Interventions in Organizations," *Journal of Vocational Behavior* 38 (1991): 237–87; T. C. Gutteridge, "Organizational Career Development Systems: The State of the Practice," in *Career Development in Organizations,* ed. D. T. Hall and Associates (San Francisco: Jossey-Bass, 1986): 50–94.

7. "American Infrastructure: A Cornerstone for Learning," *T + D* (October 2008): 66–68.

8. V. Sessa and M. London, *Continuous Learning in Organizations* (Mahwah, NJ: Lawrence Erlbaum, 2006); M. London and E. M. Mane, *Career Management and Survival in the Workplace* (San Francisco: Jossey-Bass, 1987); M. London, "Toward a Theory of Career Motivation," *Academy of Management Review* 8 (1983): 620–30.

9. R. H. Waterman Jr., J. A. Waterman, and B. A. Collard, "Toward a Career-Resilient Workforce," *Harvard Business Review* (July–August 1994): 87–95.

10. G. Wolf, M. London, J. Casey, and J. Pufahl, "Career Experience and Motivation as Predictors of Training Behaviors and Outcomes for Displaced Engineers," *Journal of Vocational Behavior* 47 (1995): 316–31.

11. L. Eby, M. Butts, and A. Lockwood, "Predictors of Success in the Era of the Boundaryless Career," *Journal of Organizational Behavior* 24 (2003): 689–708.

12. "Relatively Few Dial-Down Their Careers," *HR Magazine* (March 2008): 10; C. Benko and A. Weisberg, "Implementing a Corporate Career Lattice: The Mass Career Customization Model," *Strategy & Leadership* 35 (2007): 29–36.

13. Hall, *Careers In and Out of Organizations.*

14. Ibid.

15. D. T. Hall, "Protean Careers of the 21st Century," *Academy of Management Executive* 10 (1996): 8–16; Hall, *Careers In and Out of Organizations.*

16. D. M. Rousseau, "Changing the Deal While Keeping the People," *Academy of Management Executive* 10 (1996): 50–61; D. M. Rousseau and J. M. Parks, "The Contracts of Individuals and Organizations," in *Research in Organizational Behavior* 15, ed. L. L. Cummings and B. M. Staw (Greenwich, CT: JAI Press, 1992): 1–47.

17. C. Ansberry, "A New Blue-Collar World," *The Wall Street Journal,* (June 30, 2003): B1.

18. K. Kathryn, "Three Generations, Three Perspectives," *The Wall Street Journal,* (March 29, 2004): R8.

19. A. DeVos and N. Soens, "Protean Attitude and Career Success: The Mediating Role of Self-Management," *Journal of Vocational Behavior* (December 2008): 449–56.

20. M. B. Arthur, P. H. Claman, and R. J. DeFillippi, "Intelligent Enterprise, Intelligent Careers," *Academy of Management Executive* 9 (1995): 7–20.

21. B. Wysocki Jr., "High Tech Nomads Write New Program for Future Work," *The Wall Street Journal,* (August 19, 1996): A1, A6.

22. K. R. Brousseau, M. J. Driver, K. Eneroth, and R. Larsson, "Career Pandemonium: Realigning Organizations and Individuals," *Academy of Management Executive* 10 (1996): 52–66.

23. M. B. Arthur, "The Boundaryless Career: A New Perspective of Organizational Inquiry," *Journal of Organization Behavior* 15 (1994): 295–309; P. H. Mirvis and D. T. Hall, "Psychological Success and the Boundaryless Career," *Journal of Organization Behavior* 15 (1994): 365–80; M. Lazarova and S. Taylor, "Boundaryless Careers, Social Capital, and Knowledge Management: Implications for Organizational Performance," *Journal of Organizational Behavior* 30 (2009): 119–39; D. Feldman and T. Ng, "Careers: Mobility, Embeddedness, and Success," *Journal of Management* 33 (2007): 350–77.

24. L. Mainiero and S. Sullivan, "Kaleidoscope Careers: An Alternative Explanation for the "Opt-Out" Revolution," *Academy of Management Executive* 19 (2005): 106–123; S. Sullivan and L. Mainiero, "Benchmarking Ideas for Fostering Family-Friendly Workplaces," *Organizational Dynamics* 36 (2007): 45–62.

25. L. Chao, "What Gen Xers Need to Be Happy at Work," *The Wall Street Journal,* (November 29, 2005): B6; E. Kaplan-Leiserson, "The Changing Workforce," *T + D* (February 2005): 10–11.

26. G. Callahan and J. Greenhaus, "The Babyboomer Generation and Career Management: A Call to Action," *Advances in Developing Human Resources* 10 (2008): 70–85.

27. "2005 Emerging Workforce Study," Spherion, www.spherion.com.

28. P. Sellers, "Don't Call Me a Slacker," *Fortune* (December 12, 1994): 181–96.

29. M. Laff, "The New Face of Data Collection," *T + D* (October 2008): 13; M. O'Brien, "Generation Y Not," *Human Resource Executive* (January 2009): 29.

30. H. Dolezalek, "Boomer Reality," *Training* (May 10, 2007); 16–21 R. Grossman, "Mature Workers: Myths and Realities," *HR Magazine* (May 2008): 40–41.

31. Kathryn, "Three Generations, Three Perspectives."

32. Ibid.

33. *"Generational Differences: Myths and Realities,"* 4 (Alexandria, VA: Society for Human Resource Management, 2007).

34. H. Dolezalek, "X-Y Vision," *Training* (June 2007): 22–27.

35. J. H. Greenhaus and G. A. Callanan, *Career Management,* 2d ed. (Fort Worth, TX: Dryden Press, 1994).

36. D. Brown, L. Brooks, and Associates, *Career Choice and Development,* 3d ed. (San Francisco: Jossey-Bass, 1996).

37. D. E. Super, *The Psychology of Careers* (New York: Harper and Row, 1957); G. Dalton, P. Thompson, and R. Price, "The Four Stages of Professional Careers," *Organizational Dynamics* (Summer 1972): 19–42; M. J. Driver, "Career Concepts—A New Approach to Career Research," in *Career Issues in Human Resource Management,* ed. R. Katz (Englewood Cliffs, NJ: Prentice-Hall, 1982): 23–34; D. T. Hall, *Careers in Organizations* (Pacific Palisades, CA: Goodyear, 1976); M. B. Arthur, D. T. Hall, and B. S. Lawrence, *Handbook of Career Theory* (New York: Cambridge University Press, 1989).

38. J. W. Slocum and W. L. Cron, "Job Attitudes and Performance during Three Career Stages," *Journal of Vocational Behavior* 26 (1985): 126–45.

39. S. Rabinowitz and D. T. Hall, "Changing Correlates of Job Involvement," *Journal of Vocational Behavior* 18 (1981): 138–44.

40. Hymowitz, "Baby Boomers Seek New Ways."

41. D. Fandray, "Gray Matters," *Workforce* (July 2000): 26–32.

42. P. Dvorak, "Set to Be Put Out to Pasture? Think Again," *The Wall Street Journal,* (February 21, 2006): B8.

43. F. L. Otte and P. G. Hutcheson, *Helping Employees Manage Careers* (Englewood Cliffs, NJ: Prentice-Hall, 1992).

44. C. Waxer, "Life's a Balancing Act for Cirque du Soleil's Human Resource Troupe," *Workforce Management* (January 2005): 52–53.

45. D. Carpenter, "Baby Boomers 'Retire' to New Careers," *Columbus Dispatch* (October 16, 2005): F2.

46. C. Berk, "Now for Something Completely Different . . . ," *The Wall Street Journal,* (March 19, 2004): R5.

47. A. Karr, "Boot Camp for Job Hoppers," *The Wall Street Journal,* (July 11, 2000): B1, B14.

48. C. Hymowitz and K. Dunham, "How to Get Unstuck," *The Wall Street Journal,* (March 29, 2004): R1, R4.

49. S. Shellenbarger, "Seeking Part-Time Work: 60-Something Former Exec Will File, Answer Phones," *The Wall Street Journal,* (August 14, 2003): D1.

50. J. Sturges, N. Conway, D. Guest, and A. Liefooghe, "Managing the Career Deal: The Psychological Contract as a Framework for Understanding Career Management, Organizational Commitment, and Work Behavior," *Journal of Organizational Behavior* 26 (2005): 821–38.

51. B. Yovovich, "Golden Opportunities," *Human Resource Executive* (August 2008): 30–34.

52. S. Needleman, "New Career, Same Employer," *The Wall Street Journal* (April 21, 2008): B9.

53. Consulting Psychologists Press, "Wells Fargo Helps Employees Change Careers," *Strong Forum* 8, no. 1 (1991): 1.

54. L. Slavenski, "Career Development: A Systems Approach," *Training and Development Journal* (February 1987): 56–60.

55. M. Sallie-Dosunmu, "Born to Grow," *T + D* (May 2006): 34–37.

56. R. Morrison, T. Erickson, and K. Dychtwald, "Managing Middlescence," *Harvard Business Review* (March 2006): 78–86.

57. M. O'Brien, "Flight of the High Performers," *Human Resource Executive* (July 2008): 42–49.

58. S. Needleman, "The Latest Office Perk: Getting Paid to Volunteer," *The Wall Street Journal* (April 29, 2008): D1, D5.

59. Z. Leibowitz, C. Schultz, H. D. Lea, and S. E. Forrer, "Shape Up and Ship Out," *Training and Development* (August 1995): 39–42.

60. R. Davenport, "John Deere Champions Workforce Development," *T + D* (April 2006): 40–43.

61. O'Brien, "Flight of the High Performers."

62. D. T. Jaffe and C. D. Scott, "Career Development for Empowerment in a Changing Work World," in *New Directions in Career Planning and the Workplace,* ed. J. M. Kumerow (Palo Alto, CA: Consulting Psychologists Press, 1991): 33–59; F. J. Minor, "Computer Applications in Career Development Planning," in Hall, *Career Development in Organizations:* 202–35.

63. N. Davis, "One-on-One Training Crosses Continents," *HR Magazine* (November 2007): 54–56.

64. S. Sherman, "A Brave New Darwinian Workplace," *Fortune* (January 25, 1993): 50–56.

65. B. M. Moses and B. J. Chakins, "The Manager as Career Counselor," *Training and Development Journal* (July 1989): 60–65.

66. Z. B. Leibowitz, C. Farren, and B. L. Kaye, *Designing Career Development Systems* (San Francisco: Jossey-Bass, 1986).

67. T. Butler and J. Waldrop, "Job Sculpting: The Art of Retaining Your Best People," *Harvard Business Review* (September–October 1999): 144–52.

68. O'Brien, "Flight of the High Performers."

69. J. Marquez, "American Express," *Workforce Management* (October 20, 2008): 18.

70. T. Galvin, "Ohio Savings Bank," *Training* (March 2003): 60–61; Ohio Savings Bank Web site, www.ohiosavings.com.

71. "Top 100 Best Practices: Career Counseling," *Training* (March 2005): 68.

Special Challenges in Career Management

Objectives

After reading this chapter, you should be able to

1. Design an effective socialization program for employees.
2. Discuss why a career path is necessary for all employees and why dual-career paths are important for professional and managerial employees.
3. Provide advice on how to help a plateaued employee.
4. Develop policies to help employees and the company avoid technical obsolescence.
5. Develop policies to help employees deal with work-life conflicts.
6. Select and design outplacement strategies that minimize the negative effects on displaced employees and "survivors."
7. Explain why retirees may be valuable as part-time employees.

Nonwork Lives Are Important Food for Thought

General Mills markets consumer brands across a wide range of food categories, including cereals, meals, baking products, snacks, and yogurt. The General Mills work environment is dynamic and high-energy. Expectations for employees' performance are high. But General Mills does not ignore employees' lives outside work. The company wants employees to be challenged and to succeed, but it also wants them to have time for family and hobbies. General Mills's CEO believes that flexible work arrangements and family leaves contribute positively to the company's bottom line by reducing expensive turnover. In poor economic times, it might seem surprising to see a company dedicate time and money to helping employees balance their work and nonwork lives. But General Mills believes that these programs will benefit the company in the future. Its philosophy is that it is better to allow someone to take a leave of absence and keep that person with the company. That way, the employee will still be making contributions 15 or 20 years from now for General Mills and not a competitor. As part of this philosophy, employees are eligible for a 4- to 12-week sabbatical after every seven years of service with General Mills.

Employees at the General Mills locations in Minneapolis and Saint Paul have access to valuable lifestyle benefits. The company's family-friendly workplace initiatives include flexible work arrangements, an on-site infant care center, and health care, backup child care, sick child care, and two weeks of paid leave for new fathers and employees who are adopting children. In addition, the company reimburses adoption expenses up to $5,000. General Mills also provides many services that make it easier to balance work and nonwork life, such as dry cleaning and laundry services, photo developing, hair salon services, and an automotive service center. Many employees consider the best benefit of all to be a 12:30 P.M. quitting time on Fridays between Memorial Day and Labor Day.

For example, the company's marketing director took an 18-month leave of absence for travel and volunteer work. She started a book club for African American professional women and middle-school girls. When she was ready to return to the company, she learned she was pregnant. The company brought her back into a newly created position exploring cereal growth opportunities and held the job open while she took a three-month maternity leave. Two years later, she took an eight-month leave with her second child. In the meantime, she was promoted to vice president of marketing for Cheerios and Wheaties. She believes the company understands that having to devote time to nonwork issues does not mean employees are not committed. She says, "No one ever asked, Are you committed? After ten years with the company this was a given." A senior vice president of external relations says, "It [General Mills] understands that it's not just your work half that shows up at the office." General Mills has been recognized as one of the 100 best companies to work for by both *Fortune* magazine and *Working Mother* magazine. The lifestyle benefits at General Mills not only keep its current employees happy but also make the company an attractive employer for job seekers.

Source: Based on "2008 100 Best Companies" and B. Rubin, "Think Outside the (Cereal) Box," both from the Web site for *Working Mother* magazine, www.workingmother.com; and the Lifestyle and Benefits section on the General Mills Web site, www.generalmills.com.

INTRODUCTION

As the chapter opening vignette highlights, many companies believe that helping employees balance work and life benefits both the business and employees' personal lives. Work-life balance from the employee's perspective means trying to manage work obligations as well as family and life responsibilities. From the company's perspective, work-life balance is the challenge of creating a supportive company culture where employees can focus on their jobs while at work. A **supportive work-life culture** is a company culture that acknowledges and respects family and life responsibilities and obligations and encourages managers and employees to work together to meet personal and work needs.[1] Work-life initiatives such as those at General Mills have been shown to have a positive relationship to shareholder returns, low absenteeism, motivation, decreased health care costs and stress-related illnesses, and retention.[2]

This chapter discusses a wide range of companies' special challenges in career management, including emphasizing work-life balance, socializing and orienting new employees, developing career paths, avoiding skill obsolescence, helping employees cope with job loss, and preparing employees for retirement. These issues are considered career challenges because they tend to be challenges that employees and companies face at one point in employees' careers (e.g., retirement), throughout their careers (e.g., work-life balance), or at different points in their careers (e.g., socialization and orientation to new jobs). These challenges also affect a company's ability to attract, retain, and motivate talented employees. As this chapter explains, training programs and development activities are usually part of a company's solution to the career challenges of socialization, orientation, and skill obsolescence. It is important to emphasize that solving all the challenges discussed in this chapter requires a collaborative effort among trainers, line managers, human resource managers, and counselors as well as support from the company's top level.

SOCIALIZATION AND ORIENTATION

Organizational socialization is the process by which new employees are transformed into effective members of the company. As Table 12.1 shows, the purpose of orientation is to prepare employees to perform their jobs effectively, learn about the organization, and establish work relationships. The three phases of the socialization process are anticipatory socialization, encounter, and settling in.[3]

Anticipatory Socialization

Anticipatory socialization occurs before the individual joins the company. Through **anticipatory socialization,** employees develop expectations about the company, job, working conditions, and interpersonal relationships. These expectations are developed through interactions with representatives of the company (e.g., recruiters, prospective peers, and managers) during the recruitment and selection process. The expectations are also based on prior work experiences in similar jobs.

Potential employees need to be provided with realistic job information. A **realistic job preview** provides accurate information about the attractive and unattractive aspects of the job, working conditions, company, and location to ensure that employees develop appropriate expectations. This information needs to be provided early in the recruiting and selection process. It is usually given in brochures, in videos, or by the company recruiter during an

TABLE 12.1 **What Employees Should Learn and Develop through Socialization**

History	The company's goals, values, traditions, customs, and myths; background of members
Company Goals	Rules or principles directing the company
Language	Slang and jargon unique to the company; professional technical language
Politics	How to gain information regarding the formal and informal work relationships and power structures in the company
People	Successful and satisfying work relationships with other employees
Performance Proficiency	What needs to be learned; effectiveness in using and acquiring the knowledge, skills, and abilities needed for the job

Source: Based on G. T. Chao, A. M. O'Leary-Kelly, S. Wolf, H. Klein, and P. D. Gardner, "Organizational Socialization: Its Content and Consequences," *Journal of Applied Psychology* 79 (1994): 730–43.

interview. Although research specifically investigating the influence of realistic job previews on employee turnover is weak and inconsistent, we do know that unmet expectations resulting from the recruitment and selection process have been shown to relate to dissatisfaction and turnover.[4] Employees' expectations about a job and a company may be formed by interactions with managers, peers, and recruiters rather than from specific messages about the job.

Encounter

The **encounter phase** occurs when the employee begins a new job. No matter how realistic the information was that they were provided during interviews and site visits, individuals beginning new jobs will experience shock and surprise.[5] Employees need to become familiar with job tasks, receive appropriate training, and understand company practices and procedures.

Challenging work plus cooperative and helpful managers and peers have been shown to enhance employees' learning a new job.[6] New employees view managers as an important source of information about their job and the company. Research evidence suggests that the nature and quality of a new employee's relationship with the manager has a significant impact on socialization.[7] In fact, the negative effects of unmet expectations can be reduced if new employees have a high-quality relationship with the manager! Managers can help create a high-quality work relationship by helping new employees understand their role, by providing information about the company, and by being understanding regarding the stresses and issues that new employees are experiencing.

Settling In

In the **settling-in phase,** employees begin to feel comfortable with their job demands and social relationships. They start resolving work conflicts (e.g., too much work to do, conflicting demands of the job) and conflicts between work and nonwork activities. Employees become interested in the company's evaluation of their performance and in learning about potential career opportunities within the company.

Employees need to complete all three phases of the socialization process to fully contribute to the company. For example, employees who do not feel that they have established good working relationships with co-workers will likely spend time and energy worrying about relationships with other employees rather than worrying about product development or customer service. Employees who experience successful socialization are more motivated, more committed to the company, and more satisfied with their jobs.[8]

Socialization and Orientation Programs

Socialization and orientation programs play an important role in socializing employees. As shown in Table 12.1, effective socialization and orientation programs focus on providing the employee with a broad understanding of the history of the company, the company goals, and day-to-day interpersonal relationships as well as performance requirements. Effective socialization programs result in employees who have strong commitment and loyalty to the company, which reduces turnover.[9] Orientation involves familiarizing new employees with company rules, policies, and procedures. Table 12.2 shows the content of orientation programs. Typically, a program includes information about the company, the department in which the employee will be working, and the community.

TABLE 12.2
Content of Orientation Programs

Source: J. L. Schwarz and M. A. Weslowski, "Employee Orientation: What Employers Should Know," *The Journal of Contemporary Business Issues* (Fall 1995): 48.

I. Company-Level Information
Company overview (e.g., values, history, mission)
Key policies and procedures
Compensation
Employee benefits and services
Safety and accident prevention
Employee and union relations
Physical facilities
Economic factors
Customer relations

II. Department-Level Information
Department functions and philosophy
Job duties and responsibilities
Policies, procedures, rules, and regulations
Performance expectations
Tour of department
Introduction to department employees

III. Miscellaneous
Community
Housing
Family adjustment

While the content of orientation programs is important, the process of orientation cannot be ignored. Too often, orientation programs consist of completing payroll forms and reviewing personnel policies with managers or human resource representatives. The new employee is a passive recipient of information and has little opportunity to ask questions or interact with peers and managers. Software and online tools are now available to make it easier for companies and their new employees to complete the ordinary tasks related to a new job: setting up e-mail accounts, distributing online employee handbooks, completing important documents such as tax and benefit forms, and scheduling orientation meetings. This allows the new employee more time for interacting with new peers and managers and learning about the company culture and products and services. For example, Pinnacle Entertainment used a Web-based system to create online files for newly hired casino employees.[10] The system allows employees to go online to complete forms and to schedule two days of orientation. The new employees like the system because it eliminates the need for them to rewrite their personal information on multiple forms. The company has found that the system reduces the time, paperwork, and hassles related to hiring new employees.

Effective orientation programs include active involvement of the new employee. To learn the orientation content shown in Table 12.2, new employees need social networks that provide both information and the feeling that the new employee is an important part of the company.[11] Social networks can be established through company orientation programs that provide new employees with opportunities to meet other new employees as well as employees in different parts of the company; social events that allow new employees to meet other people and develop networks; and mentors who can help new employees develop relationships with managers and other higher-level employees. Table 12.3 shows the characteristics of effective orientation programs.

TABLE 12.3
**Characteristics
of Effective
Orientation
Programs**

Employees are encouraged to ask questions.
Program includes information on both technical and social aspects of the job.
Orientation is the responsibility of the new employee's manager.
New employees are not debased or embarrassed.
Formal and informal interactions with managers and peers occur.
Programs involve relocation assistance (e.g., house hunting, information session on the community for employees and their spouses).
Employees are provided with information about the company's products, services, and customers.

Robert W. Baird, a financial services company, combines learning requirements with activities designed to help new employees feel at home in the company culture.[12] For example, new financial advisors participate in a six-month program involving both in-class and field assignments. Advisors also attend the Professional Business Forum at the company's Milwaukee headquarters. In addition, new hires attend panel discussions with Baird's senior management from all business units, sessions devoted to topics such as communications and project management, and a question-and-answer session with Baird's chairman, president, and chief executive officer.

Monster, the leader in online recruitment, uses a day-long orientation session in which education is mixed with fun, games, and prizes.[13] During the first part of the orientation session, new employees meet each other and discuss how they chose a job at Monster. Monster's founder and the North American president as well as other executives personally welcome the new hires either in person or via videotape. New employees receive information about Monster's business philosophy, its customers, and its products and services. New employees receive specialized badges and fun Monster prizes. The meeting room is decorated in Monster colors and includes a list of the company values. The second part of the orientation program helps employees get off to a good start in their new job. Each new employee's manager receives a list of things that need to be done before the new employee arrives (such as setting up the work area) and during the employee's first four weeks at Monster (such as training, completing paperwork, identifying peers). All new employees are also assigned departmental mentors. Mentors greet the new hires at the end of the orientation, introduce them to their managers, and serve as their key contact person until the new employee is comfortable. New hires' reactions to the program have been positive.

Several companies are using technology to make orientation more interactive and reduce travel costs. For example, consider Arrow Electronics, an electronics component and computer products company with 11,000 employees in over 200 locations in 53 countries. Arrow used to have a five-day orientation that introduced the industry and Arrow's culture, values, and history to new employees.[14] However, the program was not cost effective because it was limited to the company's North American employees and meant all new employees had to travel to one location to attend the program. Arrow now delivers the same content through an interactive computer game. New employees can view modules on industry basics, corporate history, and corporate culture. Each module is followed by a quiz show-based game that assesses what employees have learned and provides immediate feedback. The program is self-paced, can be accessed around the world, and can be completed in several different languages. The program has saved Arrow money. Total costs for game development were approximately 10 percent of what was traditionally spent on classroom orientation. As discussed in Chapter 8, IBM uses Second Life to teach its new hires about corporate culture and business processes. Employees' avatars attend meetings, watch presentations, and interact with other avatars in a virtual IBM community.

An example of how orientation and socialization can reduce turnover and contribute to business, consider Clarkston Consulting's program. Clarkston Consulting, a management and technology consulting company with approximately 300 employees, has an orientation program that includes learning about the company after accepting a job offer as well as during the first days on the job.[15] An onboarding team (discussed below) consisting of trainers, recruiters, human resource representatives, and current employees maintains contact with each new employee using a wiki. The wiki provides information about the company culture and a discussion blog is also accessible. Once they join the company, employees have eight weeks of instructor-led and e-learning training, a book assignment with a discussion, and individual and team assignments simulating actual projects with clients. Biweekly conference calls are arranged for new employees so they can share their knowledge and experiences. Farmers Insurance involves its 2,000 new field employees in an immersion program that provides industry and job knowledge, group discussion and peer interaction, job shadowing, and peer mentoring, along with live, supervised interactions with customers. As a result of the program, new-hire turnover has decreased 4 percent in one year, saving the company $1.96 million. Also, employees' quality scores in the areas of accuracy, efficiency, and service have improved from 87 to 92 percent on their 90-day evaluations.

Onboarding refers to the orientation process for newly hired managers. Onboarding gives new managers an introduction to the work they will be supervising and an understanding of the culture and operations of the entire company. For example, at Pella Corporation, an Iowa-based manufacturer of windows and doors, new managers are sent on a tour of production plants, meeting and observing employees and department heads. These tours ensure that the managers will get a better sense of the market and how the company's products are designed, built, and distributed.[16] At The Limited, the Columbus, Ohio, retail clothing company, new vice presidents and regional directors spend their days talking to customers, reading company history, working the floor of retail stores, investigating the competition, and studying the company's current and past operations. They spend a month with no responsibilities for the tasks related to their new positions. Limited's philosophy is that managers are better able to perform their job by first taking time to understand the people, customers, company, and operations they will be working with.

CAREER PATHS, DEVELOPING DUAL-CAREER PATHS, AND CAREER PORTFOLIOS

A **career path** is a sequence of job positions involving similar types of work and skills that employees move through in the company.[17] Career paths are important for attracting, retaining, and developing employees. They help companies offer career options to their employees that help them make job choices that best fit their life situation. Also, career paths help companies build employees' skills through a series of jobs or roles. This maximizes their value to the company Figure 12.1 shows the career paths in Whole Foods Market stores and communicates the company's perspective of career management.

FIGURE 12.1

Career Paths in Whole Foods Market Stores

Source: From http://www.wholefood smarket.com/career/ paths.html (June 11, 2009).

Career Paths

Whole Foods Market seeks individuals who believe in our mission of Whole Foods, Whole People, Whole Planet — people who are enthusiastic about food and our products, and who want to join a culture of shared fate.

We mentor our team members through education and on-the-job experience. We encourage participation and involvement at all levels of our business. Team expertise is developed by fostering creativity, self-responsibility and self-directed teamwork, and by rewarding productivity and performance.

Opportunities That Grow With You

We encourage all qualified team members to apply for any available opportunity in their store or facility, their region or the company as they expand their product knowledge, develop their skills and enhance their value to their teams. To support advancement from within, all openings for positions at team leader level and higher are listed on our internal job site. Many other openings are posted as well, from all around the company.

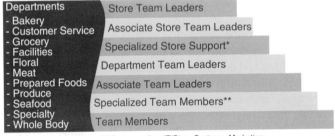

Developing career paths involves analyzing work and information flows, important development experiences, qualifications and the types of tasks performed across jobs, similarities and differences in working environments, and the historical movement patterns of employees into and out of jobs (i.e., where in the company employees come from and what positions they take after leaving the job).[18]

Dual-Career Path

For companies with professional employees such as engineers and scientists, an important issue is how to ensure that they feel valued. Many companies' career paths are structured so that the only way engineers and scientists (individual contributors) can advance and receive certain financial rewards (such as stock options) is by moving into managerial positions. Figure 12.2 shows examples of traditional career paths for scientists and managers. Advancement opportunities within a technical career path are limited. Individual contributors who move directly into management may lack the experience and/or competencies needed to be successful. Managerial career paths may be more highly compensated

FIGURE 12.2
Traditional
Career Paths
for Scientists
and Managers

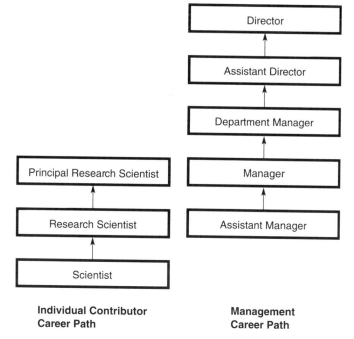

than technical career paths. A career path system such as the one in Figure 12.2 can have negative consequences for the company. Scientists may elect to leave the company because of lower status, less salary, and fewer advancement opportunities than managers enjoy. Also, if scientists want to gain status and additional salary, they must choose to become managers. Scientists who cannot meet the challenges of a managerial position may leave the company.

Many companies are using multiple- or dual-career-path systems to give scientists and other individual contributors additional career opportunities. A **dual-career-path system** enables employees to remain in a technical career path or move into a management career path.[19] Figure 12.3 shows a dual-career-path system. Research scientists have the opportunity to move into three different career paths: a scientific path and two management paths. It is assumed that because employees can earn comparable salaries and have similar advancement opportunities in all three paths, they will choose the path that best matches their interests and skills.

Effective dual-career paths have several characteristics:[20]

- Salary, status, and incentives for technical employees compare favorably with those of managers.
- Individual contributors' base salary may be lower than that of managers, but they are given opportunities to increase their total compensation through bonuses (e.g., for patents and developing new products).
- The individual contributor career path is not used to satisfy poor performers who have no managerial potential. The career path is for employees with outstanding technical skills.

FIGURE 12.3

Example of Dual-Career-Path System

Source:
Z. B. Leibowitz,
B. L. Kaye, and
C. Farren, "Multiple
Career Paths,"
*Training and
Development Journal*
(October 1992):
31–35.

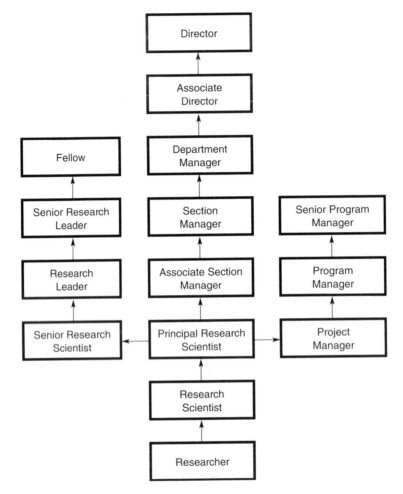

- Individual contributors are given the opportunity to choose their career path. The company provides assessment resources (such as psychological tests and developmental feedback, as discussed in Chapters 9 and 11). Assessment information enables employees to see how similar their interests, work values, and skill strengths are to those of employees in technical and managerial positions.

A good example of the process used to develop an effective dual-career-path system is found at British Petroleum Exploration (BPX).[21] BPX's individual contributors could not move to higher positions in the company without assuming managerial responsibility. After individual contributors reached the top job in the career path, their choices were to stop progressing upward or leave the company. BPX decided to develop a dual-career-path system similar to that in Figure 12.3. One path was for managers, the other for individual contributors. The paths were comparable in terms of responsibility, rewards, and influence.

Managers, individual contributors, and human resource staff all contributed to the development of the dual-career-path system. The first step in the process was to create descriptions of skills and performance levels that applied to managerial and individual contributor positions. Skill matrices were constructed for the two career paths. Each skill matrix described the skills needed for each position within each career path. The skill matrices were distributed to all employees so that they were aware of the skills they needed in their current job and the skills they needed to develop to change jobs. The skill matrices were integrated with other human resource systems including performance management, reward, and training. For example, the skill matrices served as a source of information for BPX's development program. The matrices were used to determine what performance improvement, training, or experience employees needed to meet current job responsibilities and to prepare for their next job experience. Employees could move from the individual contributor to the management career path based on their performance, their qualifications, and business need (e.g., turnover).

BPX believes that innovation is enhanced by providing employees with career paths that reward individual contributors as well as management contributors. Also, BPX believes that it will be easier to recruit and keep talented scientists and engineers because the dual-career-path system demonstrates the company's interest in satisfying employees' career interests.

Career Portfolio

A **career portfolio** consists of multiple part-time jobs that together make up a full-time position. This creates a distinct career path that allows individuals to combine their interests. Companies' interest in and acceptance of multiple job career paths is increasing; in many cases, there is a demand for specialists who can do project or consulting work on an as-needed basis without being hired as full-time employees. For example, Dr. Gold is the medical director and head of medical affairs at the Rebekah Rehabilitation and Extended Care Center in the Bronx, New York, and a senior vice president and medical director for Grey Healthcare Group in Manhattan.[22] These two half-time positions satisfy his desire to work with patients and be part of a marketing team that creates advertisements for pharmaceutical products. He is one of a number of professionals who have decided to opt out of the traditional career path and instead craft a career portfolio. As another example, Karl Hampe spent nine years working at BDO Seidman, an accounting and consulting firm. He decided he wanted to pursue one of his other interests, cartooning, as a second career. BDO accepted his request to cut back to a three-day work schedule, taking a 25 percent pay cut. On the other two days of the week and weekends he works on his comic strip, The Regulars, which appears on the Web. Although pursuing a career portfolio can help increase job satisfaction and provide companies with flexibility, it also can have disadvantages, such as stalled earnings and trouble maintaining company-sponsored health care. Also, there is a readjustment each time the employee moves from one job to the other.

Skill-based pay systems (discussed in Chapter 10) are also used by companies to reward employees who are unlikely to move into managerial positions. In these systems, part of employees' pay is based on their level of knowledge or skills rather than the requirements of their current job. These systems (1) motivate employees to broaden their skill base and (2) reduce the differential in pay rates between managerial and nonmanagerial positions.

PLATEAUING

Plateauing means that the likelihood of the employee receiving future job assignments with increased responsibility is low. Compared to employees in other career stages, mid-career employees are most likely to plateau. Consider, for example, a 54-year-old manager who once specialized in marketing production. He has since had to learn finance, marketing, and purchasing. He works 12 hours a day doing the same job he did 10 years ago. The salary and status of his job have not changed much, but the knowledge and skills needed and the time demands have increased dramatically. He used to manage people, but now he spends most of his time managing information. He is given fewer resources to accomplish more work. He once had his own secretary to manage his schedule and handle phone calls, but not any more. His phone is constantly ringing, and his e-mail box is filled with messages.

Plateauing is not necessarily bad for the employee or the company. A plateaued employee may not desire increased job responsibilities. A plateaued employee's job performance may meet the minimum acceptable standards. Plateauing becomes dysfunctional when the employee feels stuck in a job that offers no potential for personal growth. Such frustration results in poor job attitude, increased absenteeism, and poor job performance.[23]

Employees can plateau for several reasons:[24]

- Discrimination based on, for example, age, gender, or race.
- Lack of ability.
- Lack of training.
- Low need for achievement.
- Unfair pay decisions or dissatisfaction with pay raises.
- Confusion about job responsibilities.
- Slow company growth resulting in reduced development opportunities.

Table 12.4 provides several means to help plateaued employees. Employees need to understand why they are plateaued. Being stuck in a position is not necessarily the employee's fault. Plateauing may be due to restructuring of the company that has eliminated many potential positions. (This situation is known as structural plateauing.) If plateauing is due to a performance problem, employees need to be aware of this so they can correct the problem.

Plateaued employees should be encouraged to become involved in developmental opportunities, including training courses, job exchanges, and short-term assignments in which they can use their expertise outside their departments. Participating in developmental opportunities may prepare employees for more challenging assignments in their current job or may qualify them for new positions within the company. Plateaued employees may need career counseling to help them understand why they are plateaued

TABLE 12.4
Possible Remedies for Plateaued Employees

Employee understands the reasons for plateauing.
Employee is encouraged to participate in development activities.
Employee is encouraged to seek career counseling.
Employee does a reality check on his or her solutions.

and their options for dealing with the problem. For example, to cope with stress the 54-year-old manager mentioned earlier meets with a group of middle-aged men twice a month. Discussions often revolve around the difficulty of keeping up with new products and the relentless pressure to produce. Many discussions focus on retirement or finding new careers such as consulting or working with the needy. The group's underlying feelings are clear. They feel they have peaked in their careers but not in life. They have been caught unexpectedly by the erosion of the relationship between natural talent, hard work, good morals, job security, and stability.[25] Employees should be encouraged to do a reality check on their plateauing solutions through discussions with their manager, co-workers, and human resource manager. A reality check is necessary to ensure that their solutions are realistic given the resources available in the company. At times it may be in the best interest of the employee and the company if the employee is encouraged to leave the company.

SKILLS OBSOLESCENCE

Obsolescence is a reduction in an employee's competence resulting from a lack of knowledge of new work processes, techniques, and technologies that have developed since the employee completed his or her education.[26] Avoiding skills obsolescence has traditionally been a concern of employees in technical and professional occupations such as engineering and medicine. However, rapid technological change affects all aspects of business from manufacturing to administration, so all employees are at risk of becoming obsolete. Also, obsolescence needs to be avoided if companies are trying to become learning organizations. If employees' skills become obsolete, both the employee and the company suffer. The company will be unable to provide new products and services to customers, losing its competitive advantage. As was mentioned in the discussion on plateauing, lack of up-to-date skills is one reason why employees become plateaued. For example, a secretary who fails to keep up with developments in word processing software (e.g., merging text with figures, tables, charts, and pictures) will soon be unable to produce state-of-the-art documents for the secretary's internal customer, the advertising manager. The advertising manager's clients may view the company's material as outdated and therefore give their advertising business to a competitor. The secretary will be given more mundane and uninteresting work and will likely become an outplacement candidate.

What can be done to avoid skills obsolescence? Examine Figure 12.4. As was mentioned in Chapter 5, the company culture plays an important role in encouraging employees to develop their skills. Through implementing a climate for continuous learning, many companies combat skills obsolescence by encouraging employees to attend courses, seminars, and programs and to consider how to do their jobs better on a daily basis. Obsolescence can also be avoided by:[27]

- Providing employees with the opportunity to exchange information and ideas.
- Giving employees challenging job assignments early in their careers.
- Providing job assignments that challenge employees and require them to "stretch" their skills.
- Providing rewards for updating behaviors (such as taking courses), suggestions, and customer service and product innovations.

FIGURE 12.4
Factors
Related to
Updating
Skills

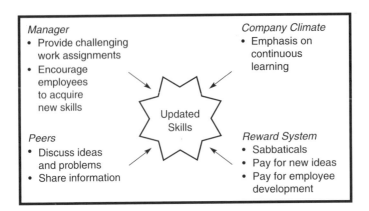

- Allowing employees to attend professional conferences, subscribe to professional journals and magazines, or enroll in university, technical school, or community center courses at low or no cost.
- Encouraging employees to interact in person or electronically to discuss problems and new ideas.

Sabbaticals are one method to help employees avoid obsolescence. A **sabbatical** refers to a leave of absence from the company to renew or develop skills. Employees on sabbatical often receive full pay and benefits. Sabbaticals allow employees to get away from their day-to-day job stresses and acquire new skills and perspectives. Sabbaticals also allow employees more time for personal pursuits such as writing a book or raising young children. Sabbaticals are common in a variety of industries ranging from consulting firms to the fast-food industry. Fallon Worldwide, an advertising agency, offers a program called Dreamcatchers to staff members who want to work on a project or travel.[28] Dreamcatchers was developed by the agency to avoid having employees burn out and lose their creative edge. Fallon employees have taken time off to write novels, kayak, and motorcycle through the Alps. Fallon matches employee contributions of up to $1,000 annually for two years and offers up to two extra weeks of paid vacation. The agency partners believe that the program has helped in the retention of key employees and the recruiting of new ones. The partners also believe that the program helps recharge employees' creativity, an important factor in the field of advertising.

Sabbaticals are available to all Intel employees after seven years with the company.[29] Employees may take up to eight weeks off, and some employees have added sabbaticals and vacation time together for a three-month break. Employees like Clifton Corpus find that the time off improves their perspective: "Before my sabbatical, I wasn't proactive. I just wanted to do a good job. Now I want to take more responsibility in order to advance." Intel's program also benefits the employees who handle the absent person's work, because they receive valuable cross-training and new job experiences. The sabbatical program at Xerox encourages community service. Employees must apply to be selected for the program, in which they can serve up to one year. One Xerox sales manager chosen for the program worked with a residential program for troubled children; projects included rebuilding a worn-out tractor. Xerox's sabbatical program benefits the community organization, the company, and the employee. Employees who participate gain a sense of satisfaction and purpose and also develop leadership skills. Because employees join the nonprofit organizations as volunteers, not managers, they have to accomplish goals through interpersonal skills rather than position power, which makes them more effective managers.

Key issues that need to be addressed for a sabbatical program to work include employees' worries about their financial security; concerns that clients, contacts, and subordinates will be well taken care of; helping employees adjust to a slower lifestyle while still staying stimulated; and ensuring that employees' job responsibilities are covered. For example, in 2004, more than 4,000 Intel workers were on sabbatical at some point. Managers and employees must work together closely to schedule these extended absences and to plan how the work flow will be maintained.

COPING WITH CAREER BREAKS

Both men and women face major problems in trying to return to work after taking several months or years off for family or other reasons.[30] Since 2001, approximately 1.4 million U.S. forces have been deployed in Iraq and Afghanistan.[31] The **Uniformed Services Employment and Reemployment Rights Act** covers deployed employees' rights, such as guaranteeing jobs when they return, except under special circumstance. Reservists are often not given much advance warning of their mobilizations, which can last for a few weeks or several years. Peers are often asked to take over the work load of the reservists, which can mean longer work hours, a larger work load, and more time at work on weekends and evenings. These disruptions are worse for small companies than for large companies because the loss of a few employees can have a greater impact on the other employees. Although federal law requires employers to hold reservists' jobs, the job they return to might be different from the one they left and could even be in a different location. Even reservists who return to the same job will likely experience some career disruption because they may not be running the same projects or have the same leadership roles. Reservists who return to work after active duty have to prove themselves all over again. Companies must ensure that returning reservists are provided with career counseling and information on jobs and career opportunities in order to minimize the negative career influence of having to leave their job. For example, for one member of the Army National Guard, the transition of returning to his job as a manager overseeing an 80-person call center for Allianz Life Insurance Company after spending 22 months in Iraq was made easier because the company spent time preparing him to leave and reorienting him to new products and new peers who had joined his team when he returned from deployment.[32] He gave all of his responsibilities to another manager within a week of receiving his orders so he could spend as much time as possible with his wife and three young daughters. When he returned, he went through a manager training program to familiarize himself with new procedures and systems. The company also used e-mail to keep in touch with him while he was in Iraq.

Women are more likely than men to leave jobs for family reasons. Women trying to return to work often find that their skills and knowledge are out-of-date and that they have lost their professional network. Because of the need to retain skilled employees in the areas of accounting, finance, and consulting, many companies are helping women cope during their family leave by offering special work arrangements, such as small project work, training, and mentoring.[33] Booz Allen Hamilton provides small work contracts that can be done at home. The contracts include proposal writing, idea development, and client contact.

Deloitte & Touche's Personal Pursuits Program provides leave for up to 10 years, with mentoring, training, and the opportunity to accept paying projects. Women who have participated in such programs believe that the programs have helped them keep their skills up-to-date and have increased the likelihood that they will return to their employer. Other types of alternative work arrangements and programs that help employees balance work and nonwork are discussed later in the chapter.

BALANCING WORK AND LIFE

Families with a working husband, homemaker wife, and two or more children account for only 7 percent of American families. Typically, work and family research and practice has focused on men and women who are married or living with a partner and who have children.[34] But work-life balance is also a concern of single-earner mothers and fathers, single and childless employees, blended families with children from both marriages, families with shared custody of children, grandparents raising their grandchildren, and employees with responsibility for elder care. Research suggests that employees need to have support networks at home, at work, and in the community.[35] The influence of partner support is greater when employees feel that their employers are unsupportive of their nonwork lives. For employees with unsupportive partners, company nonwork policies reduce conflict. One way that companies can help employees balance work and life is to provide support for employees who are concerned with simultaneously meeting the needs of work and family. Work and family needs are likely to conflict because employees are forced to take on several different roles (e.g., parent, spouse, employee) in a number of different environments (e.g., workplace, home, community). Many working mothers feel that they are failures both at home and at work. To fit into the "ideal worker" mold (an employee who works at least eight hours a day, 40 hours a week and longer), women often feel that they have to sacrifice being good mothers. One study even suggested that to reach high-level managerial jobs, women must sacrifice having children![36] Research suggests that dual-career families, single-parent families, and families with children under age five are likely to experience the most work and family conflict.[37]

Social legislation has been approved to help employees balance work and family. The **Family and Medical Leave Act (FMLA)** is a federal law that provides for up to 12 weeks of unpaid leave for parents with new infants or newly adopted children. The FMLA also covers employees who must take a leave of absence from work to care for a family member who is ill or to deal with a personal illness. Companies are required to provide the employee with health care benefits during their leave of absence.

Maintaining a healthy work-life balance is a concern for all employees, even those without families or dependents. Flexibility in when and where work is performed and support services are valuable for helping all employees deal with the stresses and strains related to work and nonwork conflicts. Employees with dependents struggle with child care and elder care. All employees struggle with finding time to participate in nonwork activities when they have increasing work demands.

Training can play two roles in balancing work and nonwork. First, trainers and managers may be responsible for developing policies and procedures. Second, trainers may be responsible for developing training programs to teach managers their role in administering and overseeing the use of work-life policies.

Types of Work-Life Conflict

Employees often feel that their work and life are out of balance because of conflicts between the two. Feelings of frustration are only one outcome of work and nonwork conflict. Work-life conflict has also been found to be related to increased health risks, decreased productivity, tardiness, turnover, and poor mental health.[38] All employees have nonwork roles and activities that may conflict with work. Three types of work-family conflict have been identified: time-based conflict, strain-based conflict, and behavior-based conflict.[39]

Time-based conflict occurs when the demands of work and nonwork interfere with each other. For example, jobs that demand late evenings at the office, overtime work, or out-of-town travel conflict with family activities and team-sport schedules. **Strain-based conflict** results from the stress of work and nonwork roles. For example, a newborn child deprives parents of sleep; as a result, it is difficult for them to concentrate at work. **Behavior-based conflict** occurs when employees' behavior in work roles is not appropriate for their behavior in nonwork roles. For example, managers' work demands that they be logical, impartial, and authoritarian. At the same time, these same managers are expected to be warm, emotional, and friendly in their relationships with their family members or friends.

Employees who work on nonstandard shifts are especially vulnerable to these types of conflict.[40] One estimate is that 20 percent of the U.S. work force does not have the traditional day-shift (9 to 5) work schedule. These employees may suffer from lack of sleep (making them irritable). Nonstandard shifts also cause them to miss special events and meals. Family life can be disrupted as the shiftworker, spouse, and children all lead separate lives. For example, a data processing supervisor for an insurance company spent 10 years rotating every 12 to 18 months among day, evening, and overnight shifts. Communication with her husband, who worked a day shift, was difficult, and she missed her children's after-school events. The stress affected her ability to sleep. She would wake up and not know what time of day it was. Working nonstandard shifts, however, sometimes enables parents to be part of their children's lives in ways that they could not be with a 9-to-5 work schedule.

COMPANY POLICIES TO ACCOMMODATE WORK AND NONWORK

Besides following the FMLA, many companies are responding to work and nonwork issues by developing policies designed to reduce the potential for work-life conflict. These policies emphasize the communication of realistic information about the demands of jobs and careers, flexibility in where and when work is performed, job redesign, and support services such as child care and elder care programs. The top five nonwork-friendly benefits offered by companies are dependent care flexible spending accounts, flextime, family leave above FMLA requirements, telecommuting, and compressed workweeks.[41] Research suggests that company policies that help employees manage work and nonwork conflicts enhance employees' job performance, lower costs associated with disability leave, and reduce turnover and absenteeism.[42] For example, Lost Arrow Corporation, the manufacturer of Patagonia clothing, spends about $530,000 a year on family-friendly benefits, including an on-site child care facility.[43] The company receives more than $190,000 in federal and state tax breaks and estimates that it saves $350,000 in recruiting, training, and productivity costs because the programs help reduce turnover. Table 12.5 provides examples of some companies' work-life programs. Note that the programs shown in Table 12.5 are relevant and accessible for all employees, not just those with children.

Consider the actions taken by the National Association of Insurance Commissioners—a Kansas City–based nonprofit group that supports the 50 state insurance commissioners—to help employees balance work and life. The company was losing employees to competitors who were offering 50 percent salary increases.[44] Turnover had reached 30 percent. Unable to offer higher salaries, the company began to offer benefits that would give employees more flexibility and a higher quality of life. The benefits included an infants-in-the-workplace program that allowed employees to bring babies up to the age of six months to their offices. Parents had to sign a liability release and designate a co-worker to serve as a care provider when the employee was in meetings. Changing tables were installed in all restrooms, and a quiet room with soft lights, crib, and rocking chair were available for parents. The company established a grievance procedure for other employees to complain about distractions as a result of infants in the workplace (no one has ever used the process). Other benefits included a four-day compressed workweek, flextime, telecommuting, a sick-leave pool that enables employees to donate unused sick days to a peer with a serious illness, a zero-interest computer purchase program for employees to buy a personal computer for their home, and one day off each year to participate in Habitat for Humanity. The program has been successful—turnover has been reduced to 7 percent.

Identifying Work and Life Needs and Communicating Information about Work and Nonwork Policies and Job Demands

Companies have to understand employees' needs, solicit their input, and make work-life benefits accessible to everyone. To do so, companies need to comprehend the diversity, complexity, and reality of employees' lives. Programs should be designed to provide as

TABLE 12.5
Example Work-Life Programs

Source: "2008 100 Best Companies," *Working Mother* magazine Web site, www.workingmother.com.

Company	Program
Mariott International	To encourage employees to take summer vacation, management discourages meetings and conference calls on Fridays between May 21 and September 1.
American Electric Power	Parents can use back-up child care that offers subsidized babysitting at home or in a local child-care center.
Genentech	Busy employees can order healthy dinners online and pick them up at work.
Patagonia	Pays for children (and their caregivers) to accompany parents on business trips. Parents can take up to seven paid days to care for an ill child. Hires a surfing instructor for employees at headquarters.
Bank of America	Created the "My Work" program, which allows associates to work at home. Company will outfit a home office or associates can work from a fully equipped satellite office.
Moffitt Cancer Center	Leave policy gives all new moms 16 job-guaranteed weeks off, including four paid; Fathers, domestic partners, and secondary adoptive caregivers receive one paid week. Moms-to-be receive two weeks of prematernity leave at full pay.

many benefits as possible to meet the needs of as many people as possible. For example, at Hartford Insurance, employees could take time off for vacation, personal time, or sick days. But these options did not relate to employees' lives. Through surveys and focus groups, the company learned that employees with families, especially single parents, wanted a more liberal unscheduled-absence policy. As a result, the company designed a paid-time-off program that provides a specific number of days for employees to use as they wish.

Work-life program benefits need to be communicated and available to all employees whether they are married or single, parents or childless.[45] At Deloitte Touche, benefits are not dependent on parental status. Employees who request a flexible work arrangement are not asked for their marital or family status or to explain why they are making the request. The employees only need to prove they can meet the job requirements. Intel makes sure that benefits are publicized in as many ways as possible, including the intranet and in-house newsletters, and the company shares stories of how various benefits are being used. For example, an employee who loves to paint as a hobby does his best work in the early morning, and he was able to rearrange his schedule to arrive at work a few hours late. Kodak has a program known as Unique Personal Opportunity Leave, which allows employees to take up to 52 weeks for personal, humanitarian, or educational needs. This program helps parents, but it also allows nonparents opportunities to travel, go on a mission, sail, or do whatever they feel would benefit them. For both parents and nonparents, the manager has to approve the leave request.[46]

Employees need to be made aware of the time demands and the stress related to jobs within the company. This information should be part of a realistic job preview that employees receive during the recruitment process (both when they first join the company and for jobs within the company). This information helps employees choose career opportunities that match the importance they place on work.

Flexibility in Work Arrangements and Work Schedules

There are two ways to deal with work-life conflicts. The first way is to provide employees with more flexibility about when work is performed (work schedules) and where it is performed (work arrangements). To help employees with their work schedules, companies should educate them about the positives and negatives of various schedules, allow them to participate in choosing their schedules, and train them in handling the physical, family, and social effects of their work schedule. For example, when Sawtek, a producer of microelectronic filters, expanded operations from five days a week to 24 hours a day, seven days a week, focus groups of employees met to design different scheduling choices (e.g., 8- and 12-hour shifts).[47] Some employees chose the 12-hour shift, which caused severe changes to their life schedules, but they accepted those changes because they had an active role in choosing their own schedule. The company also hired consultants to train employees (and their spouses) in how to deal with sleep problems. Other companies (such as Cinergy, an energy company) allow employees to swap shifts, with the manager's approval, to accommodate personal needs.

The second method for dealing with work-life conflicts is to reduce the pressure on employees to work long hours. Work-family conflict can be reduced by increasing employees' control over work and family demands.[48] One way many companies have provided employees with additional control is through alternative work schedules involving flextime or part-time work. In Utah, the state is experimenting with a mandatory four-day work week involving 17,000 employees who work from 7 A.M. to 6 P.M. Monday through Thursday.[49] Utah implemented the change to become more energy-efficient but it has found unexpected benefits, such as longer hours to serve the public and higher employee satisfaction. Table 12.6 presents examples of alternative work arrangements and work schedules. These work arrangements provide employees with some control over their work schedule by giving them time to deal with family demands (e.g., paying bills, caring for infants and small children). Some of these arrangements also help employees avoid the difficulties of commuting (e.g., traffic, high fuel costs). For example, a nurse and clinical care manager for United Health travels and visits patients in their homes several days a week and finishes paperwork and makes phone calls from her home.[50] This gives her the flexibility to see her two children off to school every day. At Abbott Laboratories's nutrition unit in Columbus, Ohio, 75 percent of its employees are on flexible work schedules and the rest have day-to-day flexibility. Wednesday is the only day everyone has to be in the office. Alternative work arrangements reduce stress and absenteeism.[51] Home-based work is dominated by individuals in educational, professional, business, repair, and social service occupations.

Organizations are responding to employees' need for more flexible working hours to help cope with work-life conflicts. A survey by the Families and Work Institute found that 68 percent of all organizations polled offer flextime, but 79 percent of employees say they need more flexibility.[52] Another study by the National Study of the Changing Workforce revealed the same results, with 67 percent of the 2,810 employees polled complaining they do not spend enough time with their children, and 63 percent saying they do not spend enough time with their spouse. Of the employees that were offered extended flextime, 68 percent of men and 79 percent of women avail themselves of it. The study found that organizations with flexible work schedules tend to operate more efficiently and have a

TABLE 12.6   Alternative Work Schedules and Work Arrangements

	Where	When
Traditional	Place of employment	5 days, 40 hours per week
Flextime	Place of employment	40 hours per week but allows choice of when to start and end work; may require work during certain core hours
Compressed Workweek	Place of employment	4 days, 10-hour workdays
Temporary Work	Place of employment	On as-needed basis
Job Sharing	Place of employment	Split 5-day, 40-hour workweek with another employee
Part-Time Work	Place of employment	Less than 8 hours a day or 5 days a week
Shift Work	Place of employment	Morning, afternoon, or overnight shifts sometimes on a rotating basis
Telecommuting	Varies; typically home	Varies; could be one or more days during normal business hours
Reduced Work Hours	Place of employment; home	Varies; could include reduced number of meetings, no weekend work, work maximum of 8 hours per day
Hoteling	Shared office space in a company location designed for use on a drop-in basis	Varies

higher rate of retention than companies with rigid business hours. At companies that are the most flexible, 66 percent of employees report high rates of job engagement and commitment, and 72 percent plan to stay with their employer. In addition to retaining top talent, the Families and Work Institute's survey found that flexible business practices attract new talent, improve productivity, raise morale and job satisfaction, and reduce stress or burnout.

Role of Technology

Technology can both help and interfere with the work-life balance. The explosion of data capabilities related to the availability of high-speed Internet connections and the increased use of e-mail, beepers, and cell phones has bombarded employees with demands and information in both their work and nonwork lives. In the car, at home, on vacation, and even in the bathroom, employees can be reached and asked to respond to work demands. However, technology can also provide employees with flexibility to balance work and life. It can remove the need for face-time with peers or customers. Being in the office as a demonstration that an employee is working hard was once the accepted norm—it is now outdated. Employees do not have to be in the office to be responsive to peers, managers, and customers. Office computers can be operated by remote connection and e-mail timers let employees send e-mails at any time of the day. For example, the manager of a trucking company took a cruise to Acapulco, but his clients never knew he left the office.[53] He used software to manipulate his computer by remote connection. He could even check on the position of each of his trucks by using global positioning systems. If an employee was not on the correct route, he could send a text message to the truck. The flexibility that technology provides can also be misused by workers who are shirking their duties. Technology allows employees to make it look like they are working when they are not. One technology worker was fired because he manipulated his computer from a diner so he could take three-hour lunches.

Telecommuting

Technology has made telecommuting a more realistic work arrangement for employees in many different jobs. **Telecommuting,** or **telework,** refers to a work arrangement that gives employees flexibility in both location and hours. Approximately 40 percent of U.S. companies offer some type of telecommuting option.[54] As the need for customer service call centers has increased, so has the technology that allows agents to work at home. Telecommuting benefits both companies and employees. At Hartford Customer Services Group, the turnover rate for home-based agents is four times lower than for agents who work in the office.[55] In addition, less office space is required. An employee who works part-time as a member of JetBlue Airway's reservation staff lists several advantages to telecommuting: "I like the flexibility. You can trade shifts. And when the weather is bad, you don't have to go out in the snow. You save on gas, wardrobe, wear and tear on your car. It makes you feel more free, more on your own." In a survey of 10,000 U.S. employees, 73 percent who worked from home said they are satisfied with their company as a place to work; in contrast, only 64 percent of employees who work in the office reported being satisfied with their company.[56] Also, compared to office workers, more of the employees who worked at home said they were not considering leaving the company.

About 80 percent of the employees at Sun Microsystems, which manufactures computer workstations and software, are connected to the company remotely.[57] The iWork program is based on the idea that flexibility in where and when people work can contribute to success and productivity. Sun has created flexible work spaces and drop-in centers to help employees connect from home and on the road. Employees can access Sun's network via a personal computer using a smart card to view files and applications from anywhere in the world. Sun also provides collaboration tools and video conferencing. Assessment tools are available to help employees determine if working from home is appropriate for them. Managers receive training in how to get the most out of the iWork program. Program results have been positive. The company has saved money by eliminating the need for 7,700 cubicles and workstations. It has also saved $24 million annually in power and information technology costs. About 43 percent of Sun's 35,000 employees are able to use iWork up to two days per week. Employees who use the drop-in centers report drive-time savings of 90 minutes.

In some cases, employees use shared office space, particularly in urban areas where employees live in apartments that are too small for home offices.[58] For example, Chris Jurney, a senior videogame programmer with Relic Entertainment, tried to telecommute from his home office in Philadelphia after relocating there for his wife's work, but he missed the personal contact with other employees. He found a place 30 minutes from his home where he could share office space and also have his own desk, free Internet access, and a conference room. Relic is paying the costs for his new office space. His co-working arrangement allows him to interact with other programmers located in the same office, which he could not have done from home. He is connected to his peers at Relic through a video camera that sits on his old desk in Vancouver, British Columbia.

Many companies are trying new work schedules and paid-time-off policies that give employees more control over their jobs. Companies such as Earthlink and Nationwide Mutual Insurance are combining vacation and sick days into a single bank of paid time off and giving employees the freedom to decide when to use it.[59] The paid-time-off system allows companies to more accurately track employees' use of time off. From the employees' perspective, the system removes feelings of guilt (or lying) to get a day off. At Earthlink, managers receive an accounting of employees' use of time off. They encourage employees to take some days off if they have worked a large number of days or hours without taking a break. At SC Johnson, the company in Racine, Wisconsin, that makes floor waxes, window cleaner, and storage bags, meetings by its 3,500 U.S. employees are banned twice a month. Meeting-Free Fridays help employees avoid taking work home on weekends.[60] Prior to the new policy, employees often were in meetings the entire workday, forcing them to work on a weekend that they needed for rest. Intel encourages employees to tell managers to stop calling them at home or at night. Both Radio Shack and iVillage have policies stating that employees should not call the office while on vacation. Consulting firm Deloitte & Touche eliminated Sunday business trips for its consultants. Consultants leave Monday to spend three nights and four days at clients' offices and return the fifth day to work at their office at Deloitte & Touche. The company estimates that the flexible work arrangements— compressed workweeks, reduced hours, and telecommuting—made available to its 30,000 employees have saved the company $41 million in turnover costs![61]

Some of the difficulties posed by alternative work schedules and work arrangements include communication problems (employees may be at different locations and on different work schedules), a lack of necessary supplies and equipment, and family interruptions.[62] For example, a senior mutual fund analyst at Morningstar in Chicago has telecommuted from his home in Rochester, Michigan, for the past six years, going to the office only two to three days each month.[63] The perks of the job include time saved not commuting, meals with his family, and working without interruptions. The downsides include not getting to know his colleagues well and family distractions. He feels positively about Morningstar because it is willing to trust its employees to get their jobs done without direct supervision and accommodate family needs. To avoid potential difficulties, some companies are allowing flexible schedules only if certain conditions are met. At Chubb Corporation, for example, employees were offered control over their hours if they took responsibility for helping complete their team's work. With this incentive, employees improved the work flow and speeded claims processing. As a result, employees were able to work compressed workweeks or have flexible lunch hours or starting and quitting times.[64] PrinterForLess.com, a commercial printer, requires client service employees to cross-train other employees at multiple jobs. The cross-training allows three-person teams with trained backup employees to schedule their own work weeks. At Kodak, flexible work arrangements can involve working at any location, at any hour, or on any schedule as long as two conditions are met.[65] First, the flexible arrangement cannot have a negative impact on business operations. Second, the manager must approve the plan. Managers are trained in how to work with flexible work arrangements without having them adversely affect business operations. It is the employee's responsibility to make the business case for the flexible arrangement and convince the manager that it can work. Employees use a booklet provided by Kodak to create their proposals for flexible arrangements. The manager and employee discuss the proposal and identify advantages and disadvantages of different work arrangements.

Employees who choose to work evenings, weekends, overnights, or rotating work schedules may be susceptible to health problems, including chronic fatigue and depression.[66] For example, an oncology nurse who works 12 overnight shifts at the Weill Cornell Medical Center in Manhattan likes working only three nights a week and being able to run errands during the day. However, she hates working weekends because she can't go out with her friends.

Job Sharing

Job sharing might be the most challenging work option because it requires more attention, flexibility, and communication than do other alternative work options. Job sharing is offered by only 19 percent of companies, less than other options such as flextime, telecommuting, and compressed workweeks.[67] Job sharing is attractive to parents of small children and to employees nearing retirement who want to balance their careers with nonwork interests. **Job sharing** refers to having two employees divide the hours, the responsibilities, and the benefits of a full-time job. Companies may also use two job-sharing part-time employees to fill a full-time position. The company gains the expertise of two employees (rather than one) and can save substantial costs because part-time employees may not be eligible for health care and retirement benefits.

Charlotte Schutzman and Sun Manix share the job of vice president of public affairs and communications at Verizon Communications.[68] Their work schedule allows each of them to work two days a week and on alternate Wednesdays. They talk by phone on Wednesdays and Sundays to discuss their lists of issues to be aware of and work that needs to be done. Job sharing has allowed these two workers to raise their children, and Verizon has retained two highly motivated and experienced employees who might otherwise have left the company.

For job sharing to be effective,

- The impact of job sharing on clients and customers must be determined. If satisfying client and customer needs is compromised (if customers want one consistent contact person, for example), job sharing is likely to be an unattractive option.
- The employee interested in job sharing must find another employee performing the same job who wants reduced work hours.
- The job sharers need to have similar work values and motivations. Otherwise, interpersonal conflicts will interfere with the completion of assignments.
- The job sharers must be good employees who have excellent communications skills and are cooperative and flexible.
- The manager must actively communicate with the job sharers and accept the fact that they might not be immediately available for consultation.
- Meeting schedules, work assignments, and vacation schedules need to be carefully coordinated. Job sharers should plan overlap times during which to meet and communicate.
- Performance evaluations of job sharers need to include both an individual and a team appraisal.
- A job-sharing agreement should be written that clearly spells out performance expectations, work schedules for each employee, and any other management concerns.

Redesigning Jobs

As companies move away from traditional job descriptions and toward cross-functional teams and more contingent employees (e.g., consultants, temporary employees), it becomes less clear who is responsible for work. As a result, work assignments can be given to anyone, including those people who are already overworked. Companies need to review employees' work loads and identify what work is necessary and what work is not.[69] For example, at Merck, a pharmaceutical company, employees were complaining about work schedules and overwork. Merck assigned groups of employees to teams who analyzed and reorganized work so that employees had more control over their work loads and schedules. In one area, employees were not happy with the large number of overtime hours they had to work. The employee teams realized that much of their work was most critical early in the week. Solutions included reducing employees' commute time by allowing them to work at home more often, and providing compressed workweeks. Some of the work load was adjusted by outsourcing (giving the work to other companies). Another approach to redesigning work is to focus on identifying core competencies. (Recall the discussion of competencies in Chapter 3.) For example, the Massachusetts Housing Finance Agency identified eight core competencies that relate to what employees in each of five roles (e.g., business leader, individual contributor) are expected to accomplish at work. By focusing on competencies, the company is eliminating extraneous work.

Managerial Support for Work-Life Policies

Many employees are concerned about using flexible work arrangements and schedules because they fear that managers will view them as uninterested in their careers and accuse them of shirking their job responsibilities. They fear that managers may not provide them with development opportunities and will evaluate their performance less favorably. Companies need to train managers to understand that employees' use of work-family policies should not be punished. The more supportive the manager is (e.g., willing to listen to employees' family-related work problems and offer solutions based on the company's program), the less work-family conflict employees will experience.[70]

By supporting work-life policies, top-level managers can reduce employees' anxiety. For example, General Mills's CEO, as the chapter opening vignette showed, is an avid supporter of work-life policies. Kenneth Lewis, CEO of Bank of America, believes that the company's work-life policies help make the company the best place to work, which means that customers have the best place to do business.

Dependent Care Support: Child and Elder Care and Adoption Support

Companies can help employees deal with child care demands in a number of ways. The child care services that companies most frequently provide include help in identifying child care resources and flexible benefit plans that allow employees to pay for child care with pretax dollars. In addition, because restrictions on overseas adoptions have made the process more difficult, causing stress and work disruptions for parents, companies are increasingly offering adoption benefits including paid leave and reimbursement for adoption costs.[71] For example, Eli Lilly provides employees with a $10,000 adoption reimbursement to help them realize their dream of adopting an infant. Companies such as Deutsche Bank, Pfizer, and Texas Instruments offer paid leave for adoptive parents.

Child care services need to be flexible to meet the needs of a diverse work force. A single parent may need more assistance than does an employee with a spouse who works part-time. Employees with infants may want to take parental leave or work part-time or at home. Although more than half of companies offer flextime, less than one-third offer child care referral services or parental leave beyond that allowed by the FMLA.[72] The lack of child care likely has the greatest impact on low-income parents, who cannot afford to pay for child care services. These parents face the difficult decision of working (and leaving children unattended) or not working and staying home with their children.

A growing concern for many employees is elder care—how to care for aging parents. At least 20 percent of all employees currently care for a parent. The care of elderly persons will only increase in importance in the United States because 13 percent of Americans are age 65 or older, and by 2030, 20 percent of Americans will be more than 65 years old. The population age 85 and older is the fastest-growing segment of the older population, growing by 274 percent over the past 25 years.[73] The stresses of elder care result in problems similar to working parents' difficulties: absenteeism, work interruptions, negative attitudes toward work, and lack of energy.[74] Elder care may be even more demanding than child care if the elder person has a debilitating disease such as Alzheimer's.

Plante and Moran, an accounting and management consulting firm, provides every expectant mother with an experienced parent to ease her transition into leave and then back to work. The parenting "buddy" helps the new mother step out of the job and ensures that the company's clients are serviced.[75] Lancaster Laboratories, a provider of chemical and biological laboratory services, has approximately 700 employees.[76] The company has an on-site child care program for 161 children, from infant to school age, along with a full-time kindergarten program and summer day care. Lancaster created the physical space and partnered with an external provider that runs other child care centers. Employees receive discounts on these services that average 25 percent. Lancaster also has an adult day care center for elder care. The child care and adult care centers were developed based on surveys and awareness that the company's work force was more than half female and that many employees were planning to start families. Lancaster wanted to ensure the retention of employees that it had relocated, employed, and trained. Besides keeping turnover rates low (8 percent) and reducing the time it takes new mothers to return to work (96 percent return in three months), Lancaster believes that the child care and adult care centers send a message to potential employees about the company's character, giving Lancaster a recruiting edge. Small companies also offer flexible work arrangements and dependent care programs. For example, Fulcrum Analytics, with 48 employees, develops marketing solutions through analytics and database management. Many of its employees work full time out of home offices equipped by Fulcrum; other employees have flexible schedules or telecommute one or two days each week. Birth and adoptive parents receive two weeks of their leave at full pay.[77]

The Bon Secours Richmond Health System found that the costs for helping employees with elder care so employees could remain on the job were less than what the company would pay for temporary workers to fill in while the caregivers were absent.[78] Bon Secours Richmond provides half the cost of in-home care, up to 10 days per year, for employees' elderly relatives. If the employee's obligations take him or her away from the elderly relative, the company places the elder in one of the company's assisted-living facilities. Fannie Mae, a mortgage financing company, offers elder care benefits that include flexible work options, employee assistance program consultations, and reimbursement for a portion of backup dependent care costs (e.g., when a scheduled caregiver is not available). A counselor is available at the company's Washington, D.C., headquarters to help employees find resources, arrange consultations, and help with other caregiving needs. Fannie Mae also offers employees a discount on long-term care insurance.

Table 12.7 provides recommendations for companies that want to develop dependent care (elder or child care) assistance programs. The first step is to determine if employees perceive a need for assistance and in what form they need assistance (e.g., on-site child care, referrals for elder care, flexible schedules). Communication of dependent care benefits is critical to ensure that employees are aware of the types of assistance available. As mentioned earlier, managers need to be trained as to the purpose and use of the program. Finally, ongoing evaluation is needed to ensure that the program is satisfying both the employees' and the company's needs.

Dependent programs will fail if the needs assessment is not accurate. Consider what happened to Marriott International.[79] Five hotels in the Atlanta area worked together to build a child care facility that would be available to employees at all work hours. The center is open 24 hours a day, seven days a week. Tuition is tied to the family's income. The center is within walking distance of several downtown hotels. Although the center is a valuable asset to the community, it doesn't meet hotel employees' needs. Only about one-third of the center's enrollees are children of hotel employees. Many hotel employees are uncomfortable about

TABLE 12.7
Recommendations for the Development of Dependent Care Assistance Programs

Source: Based on E. E. Kossek, B. J. DeMarr, K. Backman, and M. Kollar, "Assessing Employees' Emerging Eldercare Needs and Reactions to Dependent Care Benefits," *Public Personnel Management* (Winter 1993): 617–38.

Use surveys and focus groups to determine need.
Develop a philosophy or rationale related to business objectives.
Solicit employees' participation in designing and implementing the program.
Allocate resources for communicating the program to employees and managers.
Request feedback from users to make adjustments to the program.

going outside their families and neighborhoods to find child care. Although the cost of care is tied to income, the tuition is still too high for many hotel employees.

COPING WITH JOB LOSS

Coping with job loss is an important career development issue because of the increased use of downsizing to deal with excess staff resulting from corporate restructurings, mergers, acquisitions, and takeovers. Research suggests that layoffs do not result in improved profits, they have mixed effects on productivity, and they have adverse effects on the morale, work load, and commitment of employees who remain with the company.[80] Job loss also causes stress and disrupts the personal lives of laid-off employees.[81] Because of the potential damaging effects of downsizing, companies should first seek alternative ways to reduce head count (the number of employees) and lower labor costs. These alternatives may include asking employees to work fewer hours, offering early retirement plans, delaying wage increases, and deciding not to fill position openings created by turnover and retirements. However, job loss may be inevitable in the case of mergers or acquisitions (which may create redundant positions and an excess of employees with similar skills) or downturns in business that force the company to reduce labor costs by eliminating employees in order to survive.

Job loss is especially traumatic for older workers. They may find it difficult to find a job because of their age. For example, a middle manager who had been making $65,000 a year was laid off from his job at Boston Mutual Life Insurance Company.[82] He and his wife are down to their last $2,500 after using up all his unemployment benefits. He now finds himself standing on a street corner with a sign that says "I need a job . . . 36 yrs exper; Insur/mngmnt" and includes his phone number. He has no pension, and he cannot live on the $1,200 per month that Social Security would pay. Pillowtex Corporation, a North Carolina–based textile company, recently laid off 5,500 employees.[83] Ruth Jones, an 83-year-old employee with over 50 years of service at Pillowtex, doesn't know how she will meet her expenses. She gets unemployment benefits and Social Security benefits, but she is unlikely to get severance pay from Pillowtex. She does get two small pensions from two companies that preceded Pillowtex (Cannon Mills and Fieldcrest Cannon), and her home is paid off. She plans to seek other jobs at the local grocery store or the gas station.

From a career management standpoint, companies and managers have two major responsibilities. First, they are responsible for helping employees who will lose their jobs. Second, steps must be taken to ensure that the "survivors" of the layoff (the remaining employees) remain productive and committed to the organization.

To prepare employees for layoffs and reduce their potential negative effects, companies need to provide outplacement services. Outplacement services should include[84]

- Advance warning and an explanation for the layoff.
- Psychological, financial, and career counseling.
- Assessment of skills and interests.
- Job campaign services such as résumé-writing assistance and interview training.
- Job banks where job leads are posted and where out-of-town newspapers, phones, and books regarding different occupations and geographic areas are available.
- Electronic delivery of job openings, self-directed career management guides, and values and interest inventories.

Some companies are providing training and education to assist outplaced employees. Ford Motor Company closed several of its North American factories and cut more than 34,000 jobs.[85] Ford has offered its Educational Opportunity Program to laid-off workers at these factories. Under the program, Ford will pay as much as $15,000 per year in tuition for United Auto Workers (UAW) members who go to school full time to earn a degree, certificate, or license. Employees receive half their usual hourly salary plus medical benefits. Workers also can decide instead to stay in the JOBS Bank program, a program negotiated with the UAW in which employees receive full pay and benefits if their jobs are eliminated. Each UAW employee in the JOBS Bank costs Ford approximately $130,000. Employees in the JOBS Bank must report to the plant for 40 hours per week, where they may or may not be given work. Boeing Company, the aircraft manufacturer in Washington, worked with the state of Washington and local business and government officials to offer a small business training program to outplaced employees.[86] Selection for the program—which involved classes, reviews of business plans, and consultation—was rigorous. Applicants had to have a viable business idea, identify competitors and customers, and indicate how they would support themselves until the business made a profit. Laid-off workers started such businesses as restaurants, bookstores, and accounting offices. Besides helping former employees, the program allowed Boeing to hold down its unemployment insurance contributions and improve its image in the community. Many laid-off workers, frustrated by long job searches and craving independence, have started their own businesses despite high odds against success.[87] For example, when Michele Free, a technical writer, was laid off and unable to find a job, she started an online literary agency. Her agency helps writers find publishers. She has nine clients on contract and has sold a fantasy trilogy and a Civil War history book. Free is much happier, although to make ends meet she has had to sell food grown on her property and to cash in stock that she received from her last job.

Employees in upper-level managerial and professional positions typically receive more personalized outplacement services (e.g., office space, private secretary) than do lower-level employees.[88] Outplacement also involves training managers in how to conduct termination meetings with employees. Table 12.8 presents guidelines for such meetings. Providing counseling for laid-off employees is critical because employees first have to deal with the shock of the layoff and their feelings of anger, guilt, disbelief, and blame. Many outplaced employees also experience mood swings, question their self-worth, experience mild depression, and may be indecisive and pessimistic about the future.[89] Trained counselors can help employees work through these concerns so that they can focus full attention on conducting a campaign to find a new job.

Typically, companies devote more resources to outplacing employees who have lost their jobs than to employees who remain. Although losing a job causes grief and denial in employees, once employees have worked through their emotions, they are capable of carrying on a campaign to find a new job. Laid-off employees are certain of their future in that they know that they need to seek alternative employment. However, for the **survivors** (employees who remain with the company following a downsizing), uncertainty about their future remains. Survivors feel some sense of gratification because they have kept their jobs. However, they do not know how safe their current job is nor do they know in what direction the company is heading. Also, in many cases, survivors are expected to perform the work of

TABLE 12.8   **Guidelines for Termination Meetings with Employees**

1. Planning
- Alert outplacement firm that termination will occur (if appropriate).
- Prepare severance and benefit packages.
- Prepare public statement regarding terminations.
- Prepare statement for employees affected by terminations.
- Have telephone numbers available for medical or security emergencies.
- Consider security issues (software, documents, facility access, badges).

2. Timing
- Terminations should not occur on Friday afternoon, very late on any day, or before a holiday.
- Terminate employees early in the week so employees can receive counseling and outplacement assistance.

3. Place
- The termination meeting usually occurs in the employee's office.
- A human resource representative may need to be present to explain the severance and outplacement package.
- In sensitive cases in which severe emotional reaction is expected, a third party is needed.

4. Length
- The meeting should be short and to the point. The termination should occur within the first two minutes. The remainder of the time should be spent explaining separation benefits and allowing the employee to express feelings.

5. Approach
- Provide a straightforward explanation, stating the reasons for termination.
- A statement should be made that the decision to terminate was made by management and is irreversible.
- Do not discuss your feelings, needs, or problems.

6. Benefits
- A written statement of salary continuation, benefits continuation, outplacement support (e.g., office arrangements, counseling), and other terms and conditions should be provided and discussed with the employee.

Source: Adapted from R. D. Sommer, "How to Implement Organizational Resizing," in *Resizing the Organization*, ed. K. De Meuse and M. Marks (San Francisco: Jossey-Bass, 2003): 246–74; R. J. Lee, "Outplacement Counseling for the Terminated Manager," in *Applying Psychology in Business*, ed. J. W. Jones, B. D. Steffy, and D. W. Bray (Lexington, MA: Lexington Books, 1991): 489–508.

the laid-off employees as well as their own. As a result, survivors experience considerable anxiety, anger toward top-level managers, cynicism toward reorganization and new business plans, resentment, and resignation.[90]

Research suggests that survivors' attitudes and productivity are influenced by their beliefs regarding the fairness of the layoffs and the changes in working conditions.[91] Survivors are more likely to view layoffs as fair if employees are asked to cut costs to avoid layoffs, if the factors used to decide whom to lay off (e.g., performance, seniority) are applied equally to line and staff employees, if advance notice is provided, and if clear and adequate explanations are given for the layoffs. Survivors need to be trained to deal with increased work loads and job responsibilities due to the consolidation and loss of jobs. The company also needs to provide survivors with realistic information about their future with the company.

DEALING WITH OLDER WORKERS

A survey of 150 Fortune 500 companies found that one-third expect some of their executives to leave within the next five years, and the companies lack confidence that they will be able to find talented people to replace them.[92] As was discussed in Chapter 1, this shortage of talented employees goes beyond the managerial ranks. Because of the shortage of skilled and experienced employees in many industries, companies are likely to try to keep talented older employees working. Also, many potential retirees plan to cut back on work but not completely quit working. The AARP/Roper Report has found that 80 percent of baby boomers plan to work at least part time during their retirement.[93] This is due to both personal preferences and economic reasons. Because of the stock market plunge and the decrease in home values, many recent retirees are finding themselves low on money and looking to reenter the work force. For example, a 71-year-old retiree who gave up a long career in the defense industry and retired in the mild weather of Tucson, Arizona, is looking for work at local hardware stores and considering filing for bankruptcy.[94] To meet the needs of older workers and to avoid skill shortages, companies are offering alternative work schedules and arrangements including part-time work, rehiring of retirees, and phased retirement programs in which employees gradually reduce their work hours.

When are employees considered "older" employees? Mandatory retirement varies according to occupation; for air traffic controllers it is age 56, for pilots it is age 65, and for federal law enforcement officers it is age 57. Professional football players are considered "old" at age 30. As mentioned in Chapter 10, the federal **Age Discrimination in Employment Act** begins protecting workers at age 40. This includes denying access to training programs and forcing the retirement of employees (without a legitimate reason) who are covered by the act. Older employees do not have higher absenteeism rates and are not more likely to put less effort into work as they approach retirement. However, they do require more help in learning new technology and prefer hands-on practice during training.[95] Older employees are as productive and customer-saavy as younger employees and they have valuable experience. Border's has found that its stores with older workers have much lower turnover and better financial returns.[96] Its employees age 50 or older are more satisfied, have higher retention rates, and provide better customer service compared to employees under 30. As a result, Border's has tripled the number of older employees working at its stores. Two-thirds of its employees are between 50 and 60.

Consider what the Tennessee Valley Authority (TVA) is doing to reduce the impact of retirements. TVA, located in Knoxville, Tennessee, has a highly skilled and experienced work force, but the average age of the work force is nearly 47, and almost one-third of the employees plan to retire in the next five years.[97] TVA is concerned that these workers will take with them knowledge that is critical to the future of the company. TVA is developing a process to identify this critical knowledge and retain it. TVA's problem is a special situation of knowledge management that was discussed in Chapters 2 and 5. To identify the potential for lost knowledge through retirements, TVA interviews line managers each year to identify what knowledge will be lost, what the consequences are of losing knowledge, and the line managers' suggestions of how to retain the knowledge. Employees who are planning to retire and who have important knowledge are asked to take on roles as consultants, instructors, and mentors as ways to pass on their knowledge to other employees. In other cases, the employee knowledge is based on a process and a procedure that is written down. TVA also looks at whether a retired employee's knowledge is based on technology or equipment that needs to be updated. If so, the retirement is regarded by TVA as an opportunity to update systems or reengineer processes. IBM is encouraging employees to post descriptions of their job experiences in an online directory so that other employees can find knowledge before these experienced workers retire.[98]

Meeting the Needs of Older Workers

Companies can take several actions to meet the needs of older employees. First, flexibility in scheduling allows older employees to take care of sick spouses, go back to school, travel, or work fewer hours. For example, Home Depot allows older employees to work in stores based in Florida during the winter and then relocate to stores in the northeastern United States during the warmer summer months.[99] Southern Company, an electric utility, found that many of its employees were planning to retire in the next 5 to 10 years but were also interested in coming back to work on a part-time basis. The company created a "retired reservists pool" consisting of retired employees who can be called back during hurricanes and other emergencies to train new employees and to staff short-term projects.[100] Second, research suggests that the probability of receiving company-sponsored training peaks at age 40 and declines as an employee's age increases.[101] Companies need to ensure that older employees receive the training they need to avoid obsolescence and to be prepared to use new technology. Third, older employees need resources and referral help that addresses long-term health care and elder care. Fourth, assessment and counseling are necessary to help older employees recycle to new jobs or careers, or transition to less secure positions whose responsibilities are not as clearly defined. Fifth, it is important to recognize that as older employees' physical and mental abilities decline they can rely on experience and motivation to avoid poor performance. Companies should consider moving valuable older employees who are suffering skill deterioration to other jobs. Bon Secours Richmond Health System in Richmond, Virginia, credits the company's success to its older employees. Because 30 percent of Bon Secours's employees are over 50, the company tries to accommodate them. For example, a licensed practical nurse at Bon Secours found the physical aspects of her job (walking, lifting, and helping patients to stand up) too demanding. In response, the company moved her to the employee wellness program, where she gives innoculations and performs less strenuous duties.[102] Finally, companies need to ensure that employees do not hold inappropriate stereotypes about older employees (e.g., that they fear new technology or cannot learn new skills).

Preretirement Socialization

Preretirement socialization is the process of helping employees prepare to exit from work. It encourages employees to learn about retirement life; plan for adequate financial, housing, and health care resources; and form accurate expectations about retirement. Employees' satisfaction with life after retirement is influenced by their health, their feelings about their jobs, and their level of optimism. Employees who attend preretirement socialization programs have fewer financial and psychological problems and experience greater satisfaction with retirement compared to employees who do not attend these programs. These programs typically address the following topics:[103]

- Psychological aspects of retirement, such as developing personal interests and activities.
- Housing, including a consideration of transportation, living costs, and proximity to medical care.

- Health during retirement, including nutrition and exercise.
- Financial planning, insurance, and investments.
- Health care plans.
- Estate planning.
- The collection of benefits from company pension plans and Social Security.

Preretirement socialization or retirement planning can help employees avoid being forced to return to work because of poor financial planning. For example, a 58-year-old retiree took an early retirement package from GTE, the telecommunications company.[104] He accepted a buyout from GTE after its merger talks with Bell Atlantic. Stock market losses and his decision to withdraw $2,000 from his retirement account each month have made it necessary for him to seek employment again. He now works for $10.50 per hour at a car dealership chain, loading and delivering car parts. After paying his bills, he is able to save $100 per week in a savings account. He is considering retirement again at age 60 when he will begin collecting his military pension. But the turbulence in the stock market and rising health insurance expenses (which have increased between $150 and $450 per quarter) may make it difficult for him to retire until he reaches age 62, when he can collect Social Security benefits.

Many companies are also using phased retirement and alternative work arrangements such as rehiring retired employees to help employees make the transition into retirement while at the same time continuing to utilize their talents. In a **phased retirement,** older employees gradually reduce their work hours, which helps them transition into retirement.[105] Monsanto Corporation has a program called the Resource Re-Entry Center (RRC) that is open to all employees who leave the company.[106] Through RRC, retired employees who want to work part time may do so on a temporary basis. As many as 200 retired secretaries, accountants, and engineers are now working at Monsanto. Managers turn to retirees for job sharing, to meet cyclical increases in work, and for temporary positions when unplanned leaves occur. Monsanto's retirees return to work for a number of reasons, but most retirees focus on quality of life. The retirees want time for bridge, golf, and grandchildren but also want to enjoy work. Managers submit specific requests to the business leader of RRC, who recruits the best person for the job. Managers tend to be flexible about dealing with a retiree's work schedule preferences because they would rather work with a retired Monsanto worker (who knows the company and its systems) than with someone from an outside employment agency.

Monsanto's program is successful because (1) senior management encourages the full use of older workers; (2) more than 2,500 retirees live within commuting distance of company headquarters, so there is a large labor pool; (3) detailed information about the program is made available as part of the career management process for employees nearing retirement; and (4) feedback is provided on a retiree's performance on the temporary job. Monsanto has gained a number of benefits from rehiring its retirees: These employees are dependable and mature, able to handle responsibilities, and familiar with how the company operates. Returning retirees can get to work on the task faster than would inexperienced new employees who are unfamiliar with the company culture and policies.

Formal preretirement socialization programs are primarily for employees who are considering retirement, but financial planning, estate planning, and purchasing insurance need to be done much earlier in their career to ensure that employees will have the financial resources necessary to live comfortably during retirement.

Retirement

Retirement involves leaving a job and a work role and making a transition into life without work. For some employees, retirement involves making a transition out of their current job and company and seeking full- or part-time employment elsewhere. This concept of recycling was discussed in Chapter 11.

By 2014, one out of five employees of the U.S. labor force will be over 55 years of age. Recent changes in the Social Security system have led to no mandatory retirement age for most jobs, and financial needs suggest that employees may elect to work longer.[107] The oldest members of the baby boom generation should be retiring soon because they are reaching age 62, the earliest age for collecting Social Security benefits.[108] However, many employees are postponing retirement because of economic reasons, including the shrinking value of investment portfolios, falling housing prices, and the reduction or loss of health care benefits upon retirement. For example, a 63-year-old project manager was laid off last year from a company that makes medical devices and has been looking for part-time work as a grant writer in a nonprofit organization. He recently shifted his job search to full-time employment after realizing that his 401(k) retirement account had lost 16 percent of its value, translating into a loss of four years of retirement income.[109] A couple who recently retired from SAP AG, the German software company, thought they had done a good job of planning for their financial needs during retirement. However, the husband of the couple is now interviewing for a new full-time job, because declines in the stock market have resulted in substantial declines in the available assets they have to live on during retirement. Although delayed retirement is disappointing for employees, it is potentially good news for many companies, particularly those in knowledge-based industries, which are predicted to suffer from retirements due to the loss of experienced, expert employees.

Despite the need for employees to work longer because of economic reasons, historically over half of all employees retire before age 63, and 80 percent leave by the time they are 70. This may be because employees accept companies' offers of early retirement packages, which usually include generous financial benefits. Also, employees may find work less satisfying and be interested in pursuing primarily nonwork activities as a source of satisfaction.

The aging work force and the use of early retirement programs to shrink companies' work forces have three implications. First, companies must meet the needs of older employees. Second, companies must take steps to prepare employees for retirement. Third, companies must be careful that early retirement programs do not unfairly discriminate against older employees.

Early Retirement Programs

Early retirement programs offer employees financial benefits to leave the company. These programs are usually part of the company's strategy to reduce labor costs without having to lay off employees. Financial benefits usually include a lump sum of money and a percentage of salary based on years of service. These benefits can be quite attractive to employees, particularly those with long tenure with the company. Eligibility for early retirement is usually based on age and years of service. Ford is offering its workers several different early retirement programs, including a special retirement incentive in which employees with 30 years of service or more receive $35,000 to retire with full retiree benefits. Workers 55 years or older with at least 10 years on the job can leave and receive lifetime retiree benefits, and in another plan, workers with 28 years of service but not yet 30 years can leave and receive 85 percent of their pay until they reach 30 years.[110]

Early retirement programs have two major problems. First, employees who may be difficult to replace may elect to leave the company. Second, older employees may believe that early retirement programs are discriminatory because they feel they are being forced to retire. To avoid costly litigation, companies need to make sure that their early retirement programs contain the following features:[111]

- The program is part of the employee benefit plan.
- The company can justify age-related distinctions for eligibility for early retirement.
- Employees are allowed to voluntarily choose early retirement.

Eligibility requirements should not be based on stereotypes about ability and skill decrements that occur with age. Research suggests that age-related declines in specific abilities and skills have little effect on job performance.[112] Employees' decisions are considered voluntary if they can refuse to participate, if they are given complete information about the plan, and if they receive a reasonable amount of time to make their decisions.

Training plays an important role in early retirement programs. Companies teach employees to understand the financial implications of early retirement. Training programs are also used to help employees understand when and in what forms health benefits and retirement savings can be received. For example, retirement savings can often be distributed to retirees either as a one-time lump sum of money or as a payout of a specific amount of money each month, quarter, or year.

Summary

This chapter presented several career management challenges that trainers and managers need to be prepared to deal with. The challenges include new employee orientation and socialization, career paths, dual-career paths, and career portfolios, plateauing, obsolescence, career breaks, balance of work and nonwork, job loss, and retirement. The chapter includes specific practices of companies that have successfully dealt with these issues.

Key Terms

supportive work-life culture, 478
organizational socialization, 479
anticipatory socialization, 479
realistic job preview, 479
encounter phase, 480
settling-in phase, 480
onboarding, 483
career path, 483
dual-career-path system, 485
career portfolio, 487

plateauing, 488
obsolescence, 489
sabbatical, 490
Uniformed Services Employment and Reemployment Rights Act, 491
Family and Medical Leave Act (FMLA), 492
time-based conflict, 493
strain-based conflict, 493
behavior-based conflict, 493

telecommuting (telework), 497
job sharing, 499
survivors, 504
Age Discrimination in Employment Act, 506
preretirement socialization, 507
phased retirement, 508
retirement, 509
early retirement programs, 509

Discussion Questions

1. Describe the stages of organizational socialization. What are the employees' needs at each stage?

2. Why are content and process important in the design of employee orientation programs? What content should an effective orientation program include? What process should be used?

3. How are career paths useful for employees? How can they contribute to company effectiveness?

4. What is a dual-career path? What are the characteristics of an effective dual-career path?

5. Why do employees plateau? How could you help a plateaued employee? Discuss the characteristics of a plateaued employee who might resist your help.

6. Why should managers be trained as part of establishing supportive work-life policies?

7. How could you help downsized survivors remain motivated and productive? Rank your recommendations in order of importance. Provide a rationale for your ranking.

8. What advantages and disadvantages might a company gain by rehiring retired employees?

9. Are work-family programs the same as work-life programs? Explain.

10. What are the advantages and potential disadvantages of telecommuting for employees? For companies?

Application Assignments

1. Interview a relative or friend who is currently employed. The interview should
   a. Identify her current career development stage.
   b. Identify a special career management challenge she faces.
   c. Find out how her current employer is helping her deal with the career management challenge.
   d. Evaluate her employer's response to the career management issue.
   e. Suggest how the company might better help her deal with the issue.
   Write a paper summarizing your interview.

2. Go to www.workingmother.com, the Web site for *Working Mother* magazine. Review any five of the "2008 100 Best Companies" for work-life policies. What common practices do they use to help employees balance work-life conflicts? What important practices are missing from the five companies you chose? Why do you feel the missing practices are important?

3. Visit the Web site www.careerjournal.com. This *Wall Street Journal* Web site has articles related to career issues.
   a. Click on the tab titled Career Strategies. Choose an article to read.
   b. Write a one-page paper or send an e-mail to your professor (per your professor's preference) summarizing the article and your evaluation of its implications for companies or its impact on how employees manage their careers.

4. Several Web sites provide guidance to working and nonworking parents: www .en-parent.com (for the entrepreneurial parent), www.wahm.com (for work-at-home moms), and www.AtHomeDad.com for stay-at-home dads. Visit one of these sites. Summarize the resources available at the site. Evaluate the recommendations provided. Are they realistic? Explain.

5. Go to www.aoa.gov, the Web site for the Administration on Aging (AoA). Review the Web site. Is this site useful for employees seeking information about elder care? Explain the type of information available and how it is useful.

6. Go to www.eldercare.gov, the Eldercare Locator, a public service of the U.S. Administration on Aging. What resources are available on this Web site? What topics do these resources cover?

Case: *Do We Have to Cut Jobs to Reduce Costs?*

Some companies are trying unusual tactics to downsize their workforce without the drastic job cuts that result in "survivor" syndrome for the remaining employees. Vermont's Rhino Foods, maker of the cookie dough for Ben and Jerry's ice cream, sent 15 factory workers to a nearby lip balm factory to help with the holiday rush. The employees were paid by Rhino, which then billed the factory for the hours worked. Nucor Steel has cut time in the factory for its hourly employees. On the days they are not in the factory, employees are paid their base salary to perform maintenance work or to take classes. Luxury Retreats, a villa rental agency, decided to help train existing staff to learn more skills by moving employees from product development to sales areas rather than hiring new employees. Ernst & Young gave 9,000 of its mainland China and Hong Kong employees the opportunity to take one month of unpaid leave during the first half of 2009. Almost 90 percent of the firm's auditors agreed to take the unpaid leave.

Why would companies put in the time and effort to develop alternative strategies in order to avoid cutting jobs and laying off employees? Consider economic reasons as well as social responsibility. Do you think that companies should avoid layoffs at all costs? Can job losses and layoffs ever be beneficial for companies? For employees? Can training and development help reduce or eliminate the need for layoffs? Explain the rationale for your answers.

Source: Based on M. Boyle, "Cutting Costs without Cutting Jobs," *BusinessWeek* (March 9, 2009): 55.

Endnotes

1. N. Lockwood, *Work/Life Balance: Challenges and Solutions* (Alexandria, VA: SHRM Research Quarterly, 2003).

2. J. Landauer, "Bottom Line Benefits of Work/Life Programs," *HR Focus* 74 (1997): 3–4.; M. Arthur, "Share Price Reactions to Work Family Initiatives: An Institutional Perspective," *Academy of Management Journal* 46 (2003): 497–505.

3. D. C. Feldman, "A Contingency Theory of Socialization," *Administrative Science Quarterly* 21 (1976): 433–52; D. C. Feldman, "A Socialization Process That Helps New Recruits Succeed," *Personnel* 57 (1980): 11–23; J. P. Wanous, A. E. Reichers, and S. D. Malik, "Organizational Socialization and Group Development: Toward an Integrative Perspective," *Academy of Management Review* 9 (1984): 670–83; C. L. Adkins, "Previous Work Experience and Organizational Socialization: A Longitudinal Examination," *Academy of Management Journal* 38 (1995): 839–62; E. W. Morrison, "Longitudinal Study of the Effects of Information Seeking on Newcomer Socialization," *Journal of Applied Psychology* 78 (1993): 173–83.

4. G. M. McEnvoy and W. F. Cascio, "Strategies for Reducing Employee Turnover: A Meta-Analysis," *Journal of Applied Psychology* 70 (1985): 342–53.

5. M. R. Louis, "Surprise and Sense Making: What Newcomers Experience in Entering Unfamiliar Organizational Settings," *Administrative Science Quarterly* 25 (1980): 226–51.

6. R. F. Morrison and T. M. Brantner, "What Enhances or Inhibits Learning a New Job? A Basic Career Issue," *Journal of Applied Psychology* 77 (1992): 926–40.

7. D. A. Major, S. W. J. Kozlowski, G. T. Chao, and P. D. Gardner, "A Longitudinal Investigation of Newcomer Expectations, Early Socialization Outcomes, and the Moderating Effect of Role Development Factors," *Journal of Applied Psychology* 80 (1995): 418–31.

8. D. C. Feldman, *Managing Careers in Organizations* (Glenview, IL: Scott-Foresman, 1988).

9. H. Klein and N. Weaver, "The Effectiveness of an Organizational-Level Orientation Program in the Socialization of New Hires," *Personnel Psychology* 53 (2000): 47–66.

10. M. Kirk, "E-Orientation," *Human Resource Executive* (October 2005): 40–43.

11. Feldman, *Managing Careers in Organizations;* D. Reed-Mendenhall and C. W. Millard, "Orientation: A Training and Development Tool," *Personnel Administrator* 25, no. 8 (1980): 42–44; M. R. Louis, B. Z. Posner, and G. H. Powell, "The Availability and Helpfulness of Socialization Practices," *Personnel Psychology* 36 (1983): 857–66; C. Ostroff and S. W. J. Kozlowski Jr., "Organizational Socialization as a Learning Process: The Role of Information Acquisition," *Personnel Psychology* 45 (1992): 849–74; D. R. France and R. L. Jarvis, "Quick Starts for New Employees," *Training and Development* (October 1996): 47–50; E. Morrison, "Newcomers' Relationships: The Role of Social Network Ties During Socialization," *Academy of Management Journal* 45 (2002): 1149–60.

12. Robert W. Baird & Company, *T + D* (October 2008): 88.

13. D. Sussman, "A Monstrous Welcome," *T + D* (April 2005): 40–41.

14. J. Arnold, "Gaming Technology Used to Orient New Hires," *SHRM 2009 HR Trendbook* (Alexandria, VA: Society for Human Resource Management): 36–38.

15. Clarkston Consulting, *T + D* (October 2008): 73.

16. K. Rhodes, "Breaking In the Top Dogs," *Training* (February 2000): 67–71.

17. G. Carten, K. Cook, and D. Dorsey, *Career Paths* (Chichester, West Sussex: United Kingdom, 2009). J. Greenhaus and G. Callanan, *Career Management,* 2d ed. (Fort Worth, TX: Dryden Press, 1994).

18. R. H. Vaughn and M. C. Wilson, "Career Management Using Job Trees: Charting a Path through the Changing Organization," *Human Resource Planning* 17 (1995): 43–55.

19. H. D. Dewirst, "Career Patterns: Mobility, Specialization, and Related Career Issues," in *Contemporary Career Development Issues,* ed. R. F. Morrison and J. Adams (Hillsdale, NJ: Lawrence Erlbaum, 1991): 73–107.

20. Z. B. Leibowitz, B. L. Kaye, and C. Farren, "Multiple Career Paths," *Training and Development Journal* (October 1992): 31–35.

21. M. Moravec and R. Tucker, "Transforming Organizations for Good," *HR Magazine* (October 1991): 74–76; R. Tucker, M. Moravec, and K. Ideus, "Designing a Dual Career Track System," *Training and Development Journal* (June 1991): 55–58.

22. T. Gutner, "Doubling Up on Careers Suits More Workers," *The Wall Street Journal* (February 5, 2008): B4.

23. D. C. Feldman and B. A. Weitz, "Career Plateaus Reconsidered," *Journal of Management* 14 (1988): 69–80; Feldman, *Managing Careers in Organizations;* J. P. Near, "A Discriminant Analysis of Plateaued versus Nonplateaued Employees," *Journal of Vocational Behavior* 26 (1985): 177–88; S. K. Stout, J. Slocum Jr., and W. L. Cron, "Dynamics of the Career Plateauing Process," *Journal of Vocational Behavior* 22 (1988): 74–91.

24. Feldman and Weitz, "Career Plateaus Reconsidered"; B. Rosen and T. H. Jerdee, "Managing Older Working Careers," in *Research in Personnel and Human Resource Management,* vol. 6, ed. F. R. Ferris and F. M. Rowland (Greenwich, CT: JAI Press, 1988): 37–74.

25. J. Kaufman, "A Middle Manager, 54 and Insecure, Struggles to Adapt to the Times," *The Wall Street Journal* (May 5, 1997): A1, A6.

26. S. S. Dubin, "Maintaining Competence through Updating," in *Maintaining Professional Competence,* ed. S. L. Willis and S. S. Dubin (San Francisco: Jossey-Bass, 1990): 9–43.

27. J. A. Fossum, R. D. Arvey, C. A. Paradise, and N. E. Robbins, "Modeling the Skills Obsolescence Process: A Psychological/Economic Integration," *Academy of Management Review* 11 (1986): 362–74; S. W. J. Kozlowski and B. M. Hults, "An Exploration of Climates for Technical Updating and Performance," *Personnel Psychology* 40 (1988): 539–64.

28. F. Jossi, "Taking Time Off from Advertising," *Workforce* (April 2002): 15.

29. C. Larson, "Time Out," *U.S. News and World Report* (February 28, 2005): EE2–EE8.

30. A. Chaker and H. Stout, "After Years Off, Women Struggle to Renew Their Careers," *The Wall Street Journal* (May 4, 2004): A1, A8; S. Shellenbarger, "Rewriting the Rulebook on When Mothers Work," *The Wall Street Journal;* E. Simon, "Smoothing War-to-Work Shift Takes Care," *Columbus Dispatch* (October 21, 2007): D3.

31. K. Stringer, A. Carrns, and C. Binkley, "Reporting for Duty," *The Wall Street Journal* (February 18, 2003): B1, B6.

32. E. Simon, "Smoothing War-to-Work Shift Takes Care."

33. S. Shellenbarger, "Employers Step Up Efforts to Lure Stay-at-Home Mothers Back to Work," *The Wall Street Journal* (February 9, 2006): D1; Chaker and Stout, "After Years Off, Women Struggle."

34. S. Parasuraman and J. Greenhaus, "Toward Reducing Some Critical Gaps in Work-Family Research," *Human Resource Management Review* 12 (2002): 299–312.

35. S. Friedman and J. Greenhaus, *Work and Family—Allies or Enemies? What Happens When Business Professionals Confront Life Choices* (New York: Oxford University Press, 2000).

36. S. Garland, "The New Debate over Working Moms," *BusinessWeek* (September 18, 2000): 102–16.

37. C. Lee, "Balancing Work and Family," *Training* (September 1991): 23–28; D. E. Super, "Life Career Roles: Self-Realization in Work and Leisure," in *Career Development in Organizations,* ed. D. T. Hall (San Francisco: Jossey-Bass, 1986): 95–119; P. Voydanoff, "Work Role Characteristics, Family Structure Demands, and Work/Family Conflict," *Journal of Marriage and the Family* 50 (1988): 749–62; R. F. Kelly and P. Voydanoff, "Work/Family Role Strain among Employed Parents," *Family Relations* 34 (1985): 367–74.

38. J. H. Greenhaus and N. Beutell, "Sources of Conflict between Work and Family Roles," *Academy of Management Review* 10 (1985): 76–88; J. H. Pleck, *Working Wives/Working Husbands* (Newbury Park, CA: Sage, 1985); Kelly and Voydanoff, "Work/Family Role Strain"; J. Quick, A. Henley, and J. Quick, "At Work and at Home," *Organizational Dynamics* 33 (2004): 426–38.

39. Greenhaus and Beutell, "Sources of Conflict between Work and Family Roles"; R. G. Netemeyer, J. S. Boles, and R. McMurrian, "Development and Validation of Work-Family Conflict and Family-Work Conflict Scales," *Journal of Applied Psychology* 81 (1996): 401–10.

40. S. Shellenbarger, "Some Employees Begin to Find What Helps Shiftworker Families," *The Wall Street Journal* (September 20, 2000): B1.

41. Society for Human Resource Management, *SHRM 2003 Benefits Survey* (Alexandria, VA: Society for Human Resource Management, 2003).

42. J. H. Greenhaus, "The Intersection of Work and Family Roles: Individual, Interpersonal, and Organizational Issues," in *Work and Family,* ed. E. B. Godsmith (Newbury Park, CA: Sage, 1987): 23–44; Bureau of National Affairs, "Measuring Results: Cost-Benefit Analyses of Work and Family Programs," *Employee Relations Weekly* (Washington, DC: Bureau of National Affairs, 1993); L. T. Thomas and D. C. Ganster, "Impact of Family-Supportive Work Variables on Work-Family Conflict and Strain: A Control Perspective," *Journal of Applied Psychology* 80 (1995): 6–15; New York Times News Service, "Many Americans Shelve Job Success to Be with Family, Study Says," *Chicago Tribune* (Sunday, October 29, 1995): section 1, 17; S. Hand and R. A. Zawacki, "Family Friendly Benefits: More Than a Frill," *HR Magazine* (October 1994): 79–84.

43. E. Demby, "Do Your Family-Friendly Programs Make Cents?" *HR Magazine* (January 2004): 74–78.

44. M. Hammers, "Babies Deliver a Loyal Workforce," *Workforce* (April 2003): 52.

45. M. Hammers, "A 'Family Friendly' Backlash," *Workforce Management* (August 2003): 77–79.

46. J. Spencer, "Shirk Ethic: How to Fake a Hard Day at the Office," *The Wall Street Journal* (May 15, 2003): D1, D3.

47. Shellenbarger, "Some Employees Begin to Find What Helps Shiftworker Families."

48. L. E. Duxbury and C. A. Higgins, "Gender Differences in Work-Family Conflict," *Journal of Applied Psychology* 76 (1991): 60–74.

49. T. Grant, "Four-Day Workweek Catching on Slowly," *Columbus Dispatch* (August 24, 2008): D3.

50. S. Shellenbarger, "Good News for Professionals Who Want to Work at Home," *The Wall Street Journal* (November 15, 2007): D1.

51. B. Baltes, T. Briggs, J. Huff, J. Wright, and G. Neuman, "Flexible and Compressed Workweek Schedules: A Meta-analysis of Their Effects on Work-Related Criteria," *Journal of Applied Psychology* 84 (2000): 496–513; J. Schramm, "Fuel Economy," *HR Magazine* (December 2005): 120.

52. "Work-Life Balance: Making Flextime Work for Your Firm," *Managing Benefits Plans* (December 12, 2008).

53. Spencer, "Shirk Ethic."

54. B. Foss, "Millions Agree: Telecommuting's the Way to Go," *Columbus Dispatch* (March 19, 2006): G2; S. Wells, "Making Telecommuting Work," *HR Magazine* (October 2001): 34–46.

55. C. Patton, "Home Work," *Human Resource Executive* (May 16, 2006): 34–36.

56. A. Coombes, "Seeking Loyal, Devoted Workers? Let Them Stay Home," *The Wall Street Journal* (September 11, 2007): B4.

57. S. Greengard, "Sun's Shining Example," *Workforce Management* (March 2005): 48–49.

58. J. Marquez, "Corporations Picking Up Bill for Co-Working," *Workforce Management* (August 11, 2008): 10.

59. S. Shellenbarger, "Companies Retool Time-Off Policies to Prevent Burnout, Reward Performance," *The Wall Street Journal* (January 5, 2006): D1.

60. J. S. Lublin, "Memo to Staff: Stop Working," *The Wall Street Journal* (July 6, 2000): B1, B4.

61. E. Demby, "Do Your Family Friendly Programs Make Cents?"

62. J. L. Pierce, J. W. Newstrom, R. B. Dunham, and P. E. Barber, *Alternative Work Schedules* (Boston: Allyn and Bacon, 1989); F. W. Horvath, "Work at Home: New Findings from the Current Population Survey," *Monthly Labor Review* 109, no. 11 (1986): 31–35; J. R. King, "Working at Home Has Yet to Work Out," *The Wall Street Journal* (December 22, 1989): B1–B2.

63. A. Coombes, "Seeking Loyal, Devoted Workers? Let Them Stay Home."

64. S. Shellenbarger, "Fairer Flextime: Employers Try New Policies for Alternative Schedules," *The Wall Street Journal* (November 17, 2005): D1.

65. C. Solomon, "Workers Want a Life! Do Managers Care?" *Workforce* (August 1999): 58–67; J. Cook, "No Kidding," *Human Resource Executive* (May 6, 2002): 32–36; F. Hansen, "Truth and Myths about Work/Life Balance," *Workforce* (December 2002): 34–39; C. Hirschman, "Share and Share Alike," *HR Magazine* (September 2005): 53–57; C. Larson, "Family Balance," *U.S. News and World Report* (March 21, 2005): 44–45.

66. T. Rivas, "Atypical Workdays Becoming Routine," *The Wall Street Journal* (April 4, 2006).

67. C. M. Solomon, "Job Sharing: One Job, Double Headache?" *Personnel Journal* (September 1994): 88–96; Society for Human Resource Management, *SHRM 2005 Benefits Survey* (Alexandria, VA: Society for Human Resource Management, 2005).

68. Hirschman, "Share and Share Alike."

69. J. Laabs, "Overload," *Workforce* (January 1999): 30–37.

70. F. S. Rodgers and C. Rodgers, "Business and the Facts of Family Life," *Harvard Business Review* (November–December 1989): 121–29; S. J. Goff, M. K. Mount, and R. L. Jamison, "Employer Support Child Care, Work/Family Conflict, and Absenteeism: A Field Study," *Personnel Psychology* 43 (1990): 793–809; A. Ryan and E. Kossek, "Work-Life Policy Implementation: Breaking Down or Creating Barriers to Inclusiveness?" *Human Resource Management* 47 (2008): 295–310.

71. S. Shellenbarger, "For Some, Job Benefits Ease Growing Hassles of Adoption," *The Wall Street Journal* (August 30, 2007): D1.

72. M. Burke, E. Esen, and J. Collison, *SHRM Foundation 2003 Benefits Survey* (Alexandria, VA: Society for Human Resource Management, 2003).

73. Society for Human Resource Management, "Work-Life Balance," *Workplace Visions* 4 (2002): 1–8.

74. E. E. Kossek, B. J. DeMarr, K. Backman, and M. Kollar, "Assessing Employees' Emerging Elder Care Needs and Reactions to Dependent Care Benefits," *Public Personnel Management* 22 (1993): 617–37.

75. J. McGregor, "Balance and Balance Sheets," *Fast Company* (May 2004): 96–97.

76. V. Powers, "Keeping Work and Life in Balance," *T + D* (July 2004): 32–35.

77. "2006 Best Small Companies," *Working Mother* magazine, www.workingmother.com.

78. T. Shea, "Help with Elder Care," *HR Magazine* (September 2003): 113–18.

79. E. Graham, "Marriott's Bid to Patch the Child Care Gap Gets a Reality Check," *The Wall Street Journal* (February 2, 2000): B1.

80. W. Cascio, *Responsible Restructuring: Creative and Profitable Alternatives to Layoffs* (San Francisco: Berrett-Koehler, 2002).

81. J. Brockner, "The Effects of Work Layoffs on Survivors: Research, Theory, and Practice," in *Research in Organizational Behavior,* vol. 10, ed. B. M. Staw and L. L. Cummings (Hillsdale, NJ: Lawrence Erlbaum, 1988): 45–95; L. Greenhalgh, A. T. Lawrence, and R. I. Sutton, "Determinants of Workforce Reduction Strategies in Declining Organizations," *Academy of Management Review* 13 (1988): 241–54; J. Nocera, "Living with Layoffs," *Fortune* (April 1, 1996): 69–71; J. Martin, "Where Are They Now?" *Fortune* (April 1, 1996): 100–8.

82. J. Pereira, "A Worker's Quest for a Job Lands on a Street Corner," *The Wall Street Journal* (March 5, 2003): A1, A7.

83. D. Morse, "Older Workers in the Lurch," *The Wall Street Journal* (August 20, 2003): B1, B10.

84. J. C. Latack and J. B. Dozier, "After the Ax Falls: Job Loss as Career Transition," *Academy of Management Review* 11 (1986): 375–92; J. Brockner, "Managing the Effects of Layoffs on Survivors," *California Management Review* (Winter 1992): 9–28; S. L. Guinn, "Outplacement Programs: Separating Myth from Reality," *Training and Development Journal* 42 (1988): 48–49; D. R. Simon, "Outplacement: Matching Needs, Matching Services," *Training and Development Journal* 42 (1988): 52–57; S. Rosen and C. Paul, "Learn the Inner Workings of Outplacement," *The Wall Street Journal* (July 31, 1995): editorial page; S. Spera, E. D. Buhrfeind, and J. P. Pennebaker, "Expressive Writing and Coping with Job Loss," *Academy of Management Journal* 37 (1994): 722–33.

85. J. McCracken and J. White, "Ford Will Shed 28% of Workers in North America," *The Wall Street Journal* (January 24, 2006): A1, A16; J. McCracken, "To Shed Idled Workers, Ford Offers to Foot the Bill for College," *The Wall Street Journal* (January 18, 2006): B1, B3.

86. J. Cole, "Boeing Teaches Employees How to Run Small Business," *The Wall Street Journal* (November 7, 1995): B1–B2.

87. K. Dunham, "Frustrated Laid-Off Workers Take Risk of Entrepreneurship," *The Wall Street Journal* (July 8, 2003): B10.

88. E. B. Picolino, "Outplacement: The View from HR," *Personnel* (March 1988): 24–27.

89. B. Z. Locker, "Job Loss and Organization Change: Psychological Perspectives," in *Special Challenges in Career Management,* ed. A. J. Pickman (Mahwah, NJ: Lawrence Erlbaum, 1997): 13–24.

90. H. M. O'Neill and D. J. Lenn, "Voices of Survivors: Words That Downsizing CEOs Should Hear," *Academy of Management Executive* 9 (1995): 23–34.

91. Brockner, "Managing the Effects of Layoffs on Survivors"; J. Brockner, M. Konovsky, R. Cooper-Schneider, R. Folger, C. Martin, and R. J. Bies, "Interactive Effects of Procedural Justice and Outcome Negativity on Victims and Survivors of Job Loss," *Academy of Management Journal* 37 (1994): 397–409.

92. W. Byham, "Grooming Next-Millennium Leaders," *HR Magazine* (February 1999): 46–53.

93. S. Brown, "Staying Ahead of the Curve 2003: The AARP Working in Retirement Study," American Association for Retired Persons (September 2003). Available in the Policy and Research Section of the AARP Web site at www.aarp.org.; H. Dolezalek, "Boomer Reality," *Training* (May 10, 2007): 16–21.

94. H. Green, "The Unretired," *BusinessWeek* (December 15, 2008): 46–49.

95. R. Grossman, "Mature Workers: Myths and Realities," *HR Magazine* (May 2008): 40–41; G. Callahan and J. Greenhaus, "The Babyboomer Generation and Career Management: A Call to Action," *Advances in Developing Human Resources* 10 (2008): 70–85.

96. R. Grossman, "Keep Pace with Older Workers," *HR Magazine* (May 2008): 38–46.

97. B. Leonard, "Taking HR to the Next Level," *HR Magazine* (July 2003): 57–63.

98. K. Greene, "Bye-Bye Boomers," *The Wall Street Journal* (September 20, 2005): B1, B6.

99. M. Freudenheim, "More Help Wanted: Older Workers Please Apply," *The New York Times* (March 23, 2005): A1.

100. Greene, "Bye-Bye Boomers."

101. C. A. Olson, "Who Receives Formal Firm-Sponsored Training in the U.S.?" October 15, 1996, National Center for the Workplace, Institute of Industrial Relations, University of California (Berkeley). Document at http://violet.lib.berkeley.edu/~ iir/.

102. R. Grossman, "Keep Pace with Older Workers."

103. A. L. Kamouri and J. C. Cavanaugh, "The Impact of Preretirement Education Programs on Workers' Preretirement Socialization," *Journal of Occupational Behavior* 7 (1986): 245–56; N. Schmitt and J. T. McCune, "The Relationship between Job Attitudes and the Decision to Retire," *Academy of Management Review* 24 (1981): 795–802; N. Schmitt, B. W. Coyle, J. Rauschenberger, and J. K. White, "Comparison of Early Retirees and Non-retirees," *Personnel Psychology* 32 (1981): 327–40; T. A. Beehr, "The Process of Retirement," *Personnel Psychology* 39 (1986): 31–55; S. M. Comrie, "Teach Employees to Approach Retirement as a New Career," *Personnel Journal* 64, no. 8 (1985): 106–8; L. Grensing-Pophal, "Departure Plans," *HR Magazine* (July 2003): 83–86.

104. K. Greene, "Back on an Early Shift, But at Half the Pay," *The Wall Street Journal* (March 5, 2003): B1, B2.

105. R. Hutchens, "Phased Retirement," in J. Greenhaus and G. Callahan (eds.), *Encyclopedia of Career Development* 2 (Thousand Oaks, CA: Sage, 2006).

106. K. Dychtwald, T. Erickson, and B. Morison, "It's Time to Retire Retirement," *Harvard Business Review* (March 2004): 48–57; L. Phillon and J. Brugger, "Encore! Retirees Give Top Performance as Temporaries," *HR Magazine* (October 1994): 74–77; B. Gerber, "Who Will Replace Those Vanishing Execs," *Training* (July 2000): 49–53; G. Callahan and J. Greenhaus, "The Babyboomer Generation and Career Management: A Call to Action."

107. K. Greene, "Many Older Workers to Delay Retirement Until After Age 70," *The Wall Street Journal* (September 23, 2003): D2.

108. J. Levitz, "Americans Delay Retirement as Housing, Stocks, Swoon," *The Wall Street Journal* (April 1, 2008): A1, A13.

109. K. Greene, "Baby Boomers Delay Retirement," *The Wall Street Journal* (September 22, 2008): A4.

110. McCracken, "To Shed Idled Workers, Ford Offers."

111. M. L. Colusi, P. B. Rosen, and S. J. Herrin, "Is Your Early Retirement Package Courting Disaster?" *Personnel Journal* (August 1988): 60–67.

112. B. Rosen and T. Jerdee, "Managing Older Workers' Careers," in *Research in Personnel and Human Resources Management,* vol. 6, ed. G. Ferris and K. Rowland (Greenwich, CT: JAI Press, 1998): 37–74.

Two for the Cubicle

They share a title and a salary, a desk, a phone, and an e-mail account. Their résumés are nearly identical: For the past 15 years, Sharon Cercone, 48, and Linda Gladziszewski, 45, have been partners in seven human resources jobs at three different companies. They are now compensation consultants at PNC Financial Services Group Inc. (**PNC**) in Pittsburgh, where one executive describes them in a way that might unnerve even the most collaborative among us: "I think of them as a single individual," says Valentine Przezdecki.

Successfully sharing a job is more demanding than pretty much any other flexible work arrangement. Partners have to trust each other with their careers. They receive the same recognition, and if one falters, both take the blame. They have to communicate the details of their days precisely and without fail. Theirs is an intricate pas de deux, requiring a certain familiarity and ease, and like most things in life, it can't be forced. "All of the stars have to be aligned. You have to be able to complete each other's sentences and have a manager who doesn't mind adding another level of complexity," says Kathleen C. D'Appolonia, a senior vice-president at PNC. "When it doesn't work, it is very disruptive, and it can not work for all kinds of reasons. It's sort of like marriage." She says that nearly half of PNC's 25,000 employees have some kind of flexible arrangement; a total of 12 share jobs.

The decision to share a job is usually the result of a cool appraisal of the workplace: that the arrangement confers more status than a part-time job does. "If the position is full-time, it's less likely that the contribution will be marginalized," says Pat Katepoo, the founder of WorkOptions.com.

No one has an estimate of how many workers share jobs nowadays. But as companies try to retain talented women (and men) with young families as well as those baby boomers who want more time to themselves, the number that offer job shares is rising.

The 2005 National Study of Employers by the Families and Work Institute found that 44 percent of businesses allow some employees to share jobs; in 1998, 38 percent did.

CEMENTING THE BOND

Sharon and Linda happened upon the idea at a time of transition in their home and work lives. In the late 1980s, Mellon Financial Corp., where they were full-time compensation consultants, was in turmoil. The bank had cut 20 percent of its work force and was looking for ways to encourage its most talented employees to stay. After the birth of her first child, Sharon proposed sharing her job and was matched with another woman. When her partner left Mellon to teach, Sharon asked Linda, who had just returned from maternity leave and wanted more time with her son, to apply for the job. In October 1991, they began to work together.

The practice of constant communication and intense organization that they developed then remains intact today, though made vastly easier by mobile phones and e-mail. Sharon works Mondays and Tuesdays, Linda Thursdays and Fridays; they alternate Wednesdays. They talk or exchange text messages several times a day, and more often on Wednesdays. They check in at night. They keep project notes and a phone log, and even describe the body language of those with whom they meet. "We overcompensate so people understand that we don't let anything fall through the cracks," says Sharon. "We make references to our notes when talking to others." The back-and-forth can add up to three hours to their workweeks, but, says Linda, "We know the arrangement could end at any time, so whatever we can do, we do." They even schedule face time; colleagues tease them about planning lunches weeks ahead.

In the early days of their job share, co-workers weren't always supportive. "People would try to drive a wedge between us," says Sharon. They'd say, 'Yesterday, Linda told me this.' And I would know she hadn't. Or people would say, 'Wow, you're so lucky.' And I would say, 'You do realize we only get half pay.'"

JOINED AT THE HIP

The pair moved from compensation to recruiting at Mellon in 1995, a job that proved far more demanding on their time than they'd expected, with a boss who was less comfortable with the arrangement than they'd hoped. "We were told that if we wanted to be on the A-team, we needed to work full-time," says Sharon. "So we decided to look elsewhere."

It didn't take them long to find another compensation consultant job to share. The financial-services industry in Pittsburgh is relatively small: Sandy Short, a colleague at Mellon who'd helped set up Sharon and Linda's job share, had moved to PNC and was hiring. But even Short needed some convincing. PNC was in the midst of a reorganization, and she wondered about having to manage two people instead of one. Sharon and Linda assured her that they would manage each other. In 2002, after five years on the job, they moved to another that was created for them but soon eliminated in a restructuring.

Following a two-year turn at Crown Castle International Corp., which leases cell tower space, they were rehired at PNC by Renee Rossi, a senior human resources manager who initially was unsure that two people could share the position. Sharon and Linda's work as compensation consultants didn't require daily interaction with colleagues outside their department. The role of a human resources generalist would be different, and the finance managers who Sharon and Linda would be advising worried that the job share would complicate their lives. As Rossi says: "They had to be reassured that if they had a conversation about an employee issue with Sharon on Tuesday that they wouldn't have to start over with Linda on Wednesday." After extensive interviews and reference checks, Rossi could tell the managers they wouldn't.

By then, Sharon and Linda were expert at one of the most important things anyone can do for their career: managing a boss's expectations. As Rossi recalls: "Sharon warned me, 'Remember that you didn't hire two people who are on call all the time.' And I did find myself excited that I had two people. I had to remind myself that they were really one person." Rossi also had to resist the tendency to divide assignments based on each one's strengths. Sharon is very organized, Linda less so. Sharon is a confident public speaker who likes leading group training sessions; Linda prefers one-on-one interactions.

A year and a half ago, Linda and Sharon's position was eliminated. They returned to dealing with compensation at PNC, their seventh job together. As is often the case with them, the move was lateral. As Linda says: "Would we be in the same place if we both worked full-time? No." But over the years they have rejected offers of full-time jobs. "There may be certain situations we don't like, but we're willing to do pretty much anything because we treasure working with each other," says Sharon.

This spring, Sharon began working at home on her days off on an independent project for PNC. Her department is short-staffed, and she is ready to work more now that her kids are older. But she's uneasy about the new situation. "I'm not used to it, and I don't really like it," she says. "Linda and I are not as connected."

Questions

1. From a careers perspective, why would two employees decide to job share?
2. What are the advantages and disadvantages of job sharing from the company's perspective?
3. Are certain kinds or types of jobs better for job sharing? Do the characteristics of the job, the manager, or the employees sharing the job have the most important influence on the effectiveness of job sharing? Explain.

Source: S. Berfield, "Two for the Cubicle," *BusinessWeek* (July 24, 2006). Copyright 2000–2009 by the McGraw-Hill Companies Inc.

The Future

Chapter 13 discusses the future of training and development. Many factors will influence the future of training and development, including the development of new technology, which can affect how training is delivered and the quality and realism of instruction; the increased emphasis on just-in-time learning; and the increased value placed on intellectual capital, which can be developed through social relationships and networks.

Part Five concludes with a case that explores how one company is using technology to facilitate mentoring on the Web.

The Future of Training and Development

Objectives

After reading this chapter, you should be able to

1. Identify the future trends that are likely to influence training departments and trainers.

2. Discuss how these future trends may impact training delivery and administration as well as the strategic role of the training department.

3. Discuss how rapid instructional design differs from traditional training design.

4. Describe the components of the change model and how they can be used to introduce a new training method.

5. Benchmark current training practices.

6. Discuss how process reengineering can be used to review and redesign training administration practices (e.g., enrollment in training).

7. Discuss the advantages of embedded learning.

Training for Sustainability

Sustainability refers to a company's ability to make a profit without sacrificing the resources of its employees, the community, or the environment. A growing number of companies have made sustainability an important part of their business strategy. Training and development is helping them reach their sustainability goals.

For example, the pharmaceutical company Novartis supports the Regional Psychosocial Support Initiative (REPSSI), an African-based philanthropic organization that provides emotional and psychological support to children affected by the HIV/AIDS epidemic. The company's trainers provide REPSSI's employees with leadership development training. The charity wants to grow from servicing 500,000 children to helping 5 million children by 2011. However, to meet this service goal, REPSSI managers need training in communication skills, providing feedback, intercultural skills, and project management. Novartis has transformed its corporate training programs into a form useful for REPSSI. The training content is delivered through instructor-led courses and e-learning. Novartis and training vendor partners, including business schools, send speakers at their own expense to Africa. Instructors are also available for follow-up after each course is completed.

DHL Express Europe has launched GoGreen, a carbon-neutral product line. After GoGreen shipments are delivered, their environmental impact—including truck transport, sorting, long-distance flights, and distribution—is calculated using software that accounts for all of the carbon emissions released during the shipments. Customers are charged a fee to offset the emissions. The fee is then used to fund carbon reduction projects such as the development of alternative fuel vehicles and solar cells and the planting of trees. DHL Express Europe uses e-learning to help its salesforce understand the facts about global warming, why it is a concern for the company, and the company programs in place to reduce its impact on global warming. The company also has an environmental training program for all employees, including the GoGreen Academy, which includes numerous assignments on global business practices.

Gilbane Building Company is a family-owned construction business headquartered in Rhode Island. Concerns about building in a environmentally friendly way have been an important part of the company culture for many years, and recently customers have been showing more interest in "green buildings." Green buildings are buildings that have been designed so that construction wastes fewer materials and uses less electricity. Customers enjoy the energy cost savings and the available tax breaks for green buildings. As a result of adopting environmentally friendly building practices, Gilbane can be both socially responsible and profitable.

Training plays an important role in helping Gilbane exceed customer expectations and provide the greener buildings that customers desire. Gilbane University includes instructor-led and online courses as well as distance learning and a virtual classroom. Gilbane offers certification and training for employees in the LEED (Leadership in Energy and Environmental Design) rating system. LEED is a set of standards for constructing buildings in an environmentally responsible way with minimal waste. The standards were developed by the U.S. Building Green Council, which consists of building product managers, owners, utilities, and government agencies in the construction trade. Buildings that are built according to the LEED standards become LEED-certified. One course at Gilbane University helps employees prepare for the LEED exam. The course covers the LEED scorecard, reviews design decisions, and explains the documentation that a builder must keep for the building to be LEED-certified. Course participants can also use Gilbane's green portal, a page on the company's intranet that includes course resources such as study guides and practice exams. Another course offered by Gilbane University, New Construction Success, teaches construction managers how to work with all departments (such as purchasing) to produce a LEED-certified building. For example, if a builder wants to use a high level of recycled material in a building, steel may be the choice. However, it is important to know that steel takes longer to deliver. The manager needs to be sure that the building schedule takes into account the longer lead time. Besides offering training, Gilbane also positions green teams in each of the company's nine operating regions to help the region develop and use sustainable business practices and to keep the region up-to-date on the latest green construction methods and materials.

Source: Based on M. Weinstein, "Charity Begins @ Work," *Training* (May 2008): 56–58; A. Fox, "Get in the Business of Being Green," *HR Magazine* (June 2008): 45; J. Jarventaus, "Training a Green Workforce," *T + D* (September 2007): 28–34; H. Dolezalek, "Good News: Training Can Save the World," *Training* (May 2006): 28–33; Gilbane Building Company Web site, www.gilbanebuilding.com.

INTRODUCTION

Many companies are beginning to use training to help meet sustainability goals. This relates to an increased emphasis on performance analysis and learning for business enhancement, one of the future's training trends. The previous 12 chapters discussed training design and delivery as well as employee development and career management. This chapter looks toward the future by discussing trends that are likely to influence the future of training and development and your future as a trainer. Table 13.1 presents the future trends that will affect training.

INCREASED USE OF NEW TECHNOLOGIES FOR TRAINING DELIVERY

The use of online learning, mobile learning (iPods), and other new technologies will likely increase in the future for several reasons. First, the cost of these technologies will decrease. Second, companies can use technology to better prepare employees to serve customers and generate new business. Third, use of these new technologies can substantially reduce training costs related to bringing geographically dispersed employees to one central training location (e.g., travel, food, housing). Fourth, these technologies allow trainers to build into training many of the desirable features of a learning environment (e.g., practice, feedback, reinforcement). Fifth, as companies employ more contingent employees (e.g., part-timers, consultants) and offer more alternative work arrangements (e.g., flexible work schedules), technology will allow training to be delivered to any place and at any time.

New technology also makes it possible to create "smart" products.[1] For example, packages sent by UPS leave an electronic trail that can be used to improve shipping and delivery processes. In the future, training products may also leave an electronic trail that will enable trainers and managers to better understand how these products are being used. New technologies that combine computer science, instructional design, and graphic interfaces have the potential to increase our ability to learn.[2] Employees may soon learn in their sleep. One device detects when a person is dreaming, which is a good time to acquire new skills. Teleimmersion—which is a technology that provides realistic, life-sized holographic projections in which employees can hear and see collaborators as if they were physically present in the office—can be used to create a holographic training room in the office with virtual trainees beamed in from other locations. Virtual retinal display is a technology that projects images directly on the retina of the eye. Virtual retinal display allows real-time, on-site

TABLE 13.1 **Future Trends** **That Will** **Affect Training**	• Increased use of new technologies for training delivery. • Increased demand for training for virtual work arrangements. • Increased emphasis on speed in design, focus in content, and use of multiple delivery methods. • Increased emphasis on capturing and sharing intellectual capital. • Increased use of true performance support. • Increased emphasis on performance analysis and learning for business enhancement. • Increased use of training partnerships and outsourcing training. • A change model perspective to training and development.

performance support. The technology takes what is shown on a computer monitor and reduces it through special glasses directly onto the retina in full color. The image looks like it is floating in air about two feet away. Digital Avatar is an animated virtual teacher. With this technology, corporate trainers can create animated versions of themselves for online instruction. Training in the future will also include greater use of two- and three-dimensional simulations and virtual worlds such as Second Life that feature interactions between employees and between employees and customers (such as pharmaceutical salespersons interacting with physicians, pharmacists, and other health care professionals).[3] The content of the simulations can be changed quickly to make it appropriate for global audiences. Instant messaging, PDAs, networking Web sites, blogs, and social software such as Meetup and MySpace are making collaboration very easy.[4] The knowledge exchanged through these types of collaboration may be tacit knowledge that is difficult to communicate through other methods.

INCREASED DEMAND FOR TRAINING FOR VIRTUAL WORK ARRANGEMENTS

Virtual work arrangements include virtual teams as well as **telecommuting,** work that is conducted in a remote location (distant from central offices) where the employee has limited contact with peers but is able to communicate electronically. The critical feature of virtual work arrangements is that location, organization structure, and employment relationships are not limiting factors.[5] For example, employees from two or three organizations may work together on projects designed to meet the strategic and operational needs of their organizations. Similarly, employees within a single organization may work with peers from different units or functions on a project team. Virtual knowledge teams have members that are distributed across multiple time zones, countries, and/or companies. They are more diverse than other knowledge teams, with team members representing different specialties and perhaps different cultures, languages, and organizational allegiances. These teams do not have constant membership. Team members may move onto and off the team at different points in a project. Some members may participate in all team tasks, whereas others may work only on some. Successful virtual knowledge teams need structure (e.g., reporting relationships, membership), leadership (empowered, shared leadership, integration with other teams), shared values (what do we value as a team, how will we run meetings, make decisions, and solve problems?), and rewarded goals (what are our key goals, what do customers need from us, and how will we reward goal accomplishment?). If team members are from different cultures, working from a distance can make language and cultural differences even more difficult to deal with. For example, teams responsible for evaluating business opportunities for Shell Technology Ventures, a subsidiary of Royal Dutch/Shell found that it was challenging to create a team process structured so that team members who prefer structure can move forward without creating so much bureaucracy that it inhibits team members who do best in an unstructured environment. Dutch team members prefer more details about how a process works, who will make a decision, and what the next steps are than do their colleagues from the United States.

There are two training challenges for virtual work arrangements. First, companies have to invest in training delivery methods that facilitate digital collaboration.[6] **Digital collaboration** refers to an interaction between two or more people mediated by a computer. The Web, intranet, and learning portals enable employees to access training from their desktops and to collaborate with others on an as-needed basis. Virtual work arrangements rely on digital collaboration. Virtual team members need training in team work skills and understanding cultural differences as well as in technical skills and competencies needed to perform their jobs. Second, for companies with virtual work arrangements, having knowledge, knowing which employees possess it, and sharing knowledge within and across functions, teams, and individuals are critical for effectiveness. Teams and employees must be provided with the tools that they need for finding knowledge—knowledge that can be used to provide a service, develop or manufacture a product, or refine a process.

INCREASED EMPHASIS ON SPEED IN DESIGN, FOCUS IN CONTENT, AND USE OF MULTIPLE DELIVERY METHODS

Because of new technology, trainers are being challenged to find new ways to use instructional design.[7] Shifts are taking place in who is leading the learning (from instructor to the employee) as well as where learning is taking place (from workplace to mobile learning). Trainers need to determine, for example, the best way to design an effective training course using podcasting. Despite the use of new technology for learning, the fundamental questions remain: Why is training occurring? Who is the audience? What resources are necessary so that employees can learn what they need to know?

As discussed in Chapter 1, the traditional training design model has been criticized for several reasons. First, it is a linear approach driven by subject-matter experts. Second, the Instructional System Design model uses a rational, step-by-step approach that assumes that the training content is stable. Third, given the accelerated demand for training to be delivered just in time, traditional training takes too long. **Rapid instructional design (RID)** is a group of techniques that allows training to be built more quickly. RID modifies the training design model that consists of needs analysis, design, development, implementation, and evaluation (recall the discussion of training design in Chapter 1). There are two important principles in RID.[8] One is that instructional content and process can be developed independently of each other. The second is that resources that are devoted to design and delivery of instruction can be reallocated as appropriate. *Design* includes everything that happens before the training experience; *delivery* is what happens during the training experience. For example, if a company has limited resources for training delivery, such as large groups of trainees and a tight schedule, extra time should be allocated to the design process. Table 13.2 lists RID strategies. For example, learning style differences make it difficult to develop a training program that maximizes learning for all employees. As a result, if possible, training content can be offered through books, manuals, audiotapes, videotapes, and online learning. It may also be possible to combine steps of the design process, such as analyses and evaluation. For example, knowledge tests and other evaluation outcomes may be based on task analysis and other needs analysis results. There is no need to conduct separate analyses of training needs and learning outcomes. If the client is convinced that there is a training need and if the trainer can quickly confirm the need, then there is no reason to conduct a full needs analysis (e.g., new regulations that affect business transactions in financial services, or product changes). Job aids such as checklists, worksheets, and performance support tools can be provided to employees based on the results of a task analysis to identify activities and decisions needed to complete a procedure. Job aids can be chosen to help employees complete the procedure, and training can

TABLE 13.2

Examples of RID Strategies

Source: Based on S. Thiagarajan, "Rapid Instructional Development," in *The ASTD Handbook of Training Design and Delivery,* ed. G. Piskurich, P. Beckschi, and B. Hall (New York: McGraw-Hill, 2000): 54–75.

Focus on accomplishment and performance.
Develop a learning system instead of an instructional system.
Use shortcuts (e.g., use existing records for needs assessment; conduct focus groups).
Combine different steps of the instructional design process.
Implement training and continuously improve it.
Skip steps in the instructional design process.
Use existing course materials that can be customized with examples, exercises, and assignments.
Develop instruction around job aids.
Use recording equipment, Internet, and e-mail to collect data and exchange information with subject matter experts.

be provided to teach employees how to use the job aid. The point to keep in mind is that use of a training design process (or instructional design process), as discussed in Chapter 1, should not be abandoned! Rather, now and in the future trainers will further develop RID techniques to reduce the time and cost and to increase the efficiency of training design in order to better meet business needs.

Managers are demanding training courses that are shorter and that focus on the necessary content.[9] Training departments will be expected to reduce the number of courses and programs that are offered without directly addressing a business issue or performance problem. Subject matter experts used as trainers will be expected to focus their presentations on information that is directly relevant to trainees. Seminars and classes that take place over several days or half-days will have to be retooled to be more accessible and individualized. At Hartford Life Company, training managers are receiving more requests for shorter training sessions.[10] To ensure that learning and transfer of training occur in the shorter courses, trainers have asked managers to act as coaches to supplement the training and have created more on-the-job learning opportunities. Other companies are asking trainees to complete more pre-class assignments and are using more post-course job aids. The development of focused content will become easier because of blogs and podcasts that allow training content to be developed without programming languages such as HTML. Content-developed authoring tools will likely continue to become more user-friendly.

In the future, companies will need to recognize that different employees prefer different types of delivery methods.[11] MP3 players and iPods can be used to deliver audio and video content. Training departments can use learning management systems to develop different versions of the same training content to address differences in trainees' learning styles. There will also be a greater emphasis on informal learning. Tools are being developed to measure and quantify informal learning so its effectiveness can be determined and it can be categorized in an online library and made accessible to all employees.

Also in the future, employees will become more involved in managing their own personal learning and building their own learning environments using Web tools.[12] As employees and teams address their own needs, there may be a decline in companywide learning systems that monitor, test, and track usage of more formal learning content and an increase in the development and use of systems that provide customizable Web tools for learning design and delivery.

INCREASED EMPHASIS ON CAPTURING AND SHARING INTELLECTUAL CAPITAL

Companies that recognize the strategic value of becoming a learning organization and are concerned about the loss of valuable knowledge because their baby boomer employees are retiring (see the discussions in Chapters 1 and 5) will continue to seek ways to turn employees' knowledge (human capital) into a shared company asset. As emphasized in Chapter 2, training functions will focus on learning, with an emphasis on employee training and development and the management and coordination of organizational learning. Sharing knowledge and contributing to the company's intellectual capital is going to become more common as collaborative social networking technology and Web 2.0 tools make this simpler to implement. The rise of intelligent tutors and on-demand learning technologies will make connections to information faster, more current and accurate, and more easily customizable to employees' needs and work. More teams and groups of employees will make use of social media and Web 2.0 tools to share links and content with each other, participate in discussions, collaborate, and create learning content.

For example, to improve productivity at MWH, an engineering firm specializing in water projects, employees are asked to indicate which employees they talk to and ask for help.[13] This information is used to create a "map" of connections. The map shows communications gaps, places where information gets stuck, and employees who are not connected to their colleagues. MWH's purpose in developing the map of informal connections between employees, known as **social network analysis,** was to reduce costs and improve communications between its seven technology centers. MWH found that information flowed well within each center but not between centers. For example, employees in Denver had little contact with employees in California and the least amount of contact with employees in New Zealand. To remove communication barriers, U.S. employees were sent to fill vacation openings in the United Kingdom. Top managers were trained to become less authoritarian and more collaborative, therefore helping to facilitate information flow. After five years, the employees within MWH are now more closely connected with each other. It takes employees 2.4 steps on average to get the information they need, down from 3.2 in 2004.

The increasing use of new technologies to deliver training and to store and communicate knowledge means that trainers must be technologically literate. That is, they must understand the strengths and weaknesses of new technologies and implementation issues such as overcoming users' resistance to change (which is discussed later in this chapter). Also, many companies have created positions such as knowledge manager or chief information officer whose job is to identify reliable knowledge and make sure it is accessible to employees.

INCREASED USE OF TRUE PERFORMANCE SUPPORT

Companies are moving away from courseware and classes as a performance improvement method and are instead adopting true performance support that is available during the work process.[14] **Embedded learning** refers to learning that occurs on the job as needed;

it involves collaboration and nonlearning technologies such as instant messaging, and it is integrated with knowledge management.[15] Embedded learning may become increasingly prevalent in the future because companies can no longer have employees attend classroom instruction or spend hours on online learning that is not directly relevant to their current job demands. Formal training programs and courses will not disappear but will focus more on development of competencies that can benefit the employee and the company over the long term, whereas embedded learning will focus on providing the learning that the employee needs to complete key job tasks. Embedded-learning products include task-specific, real-time content and simulation that are accessible during work as well as real-time collaboration in virtual workspaces. Recent and rapid adoption of wireless technology is connecting employees directly to business processes. For example, radio frequency identification chips are implanted in products such as clothing, tires, and mechanical parts. These chips contain information that is beamed via radio waves to employees processing handheld wireless devices. The device, the task context, and the performance environment are not compatible with classroom or courseware-based learning but with performance support. Learning is a business process that is integrated with several other business processes. Learning is expected as a result of collaboration with employees and machines in the work process. Employees can be provided with real-time performance support through communications with experts and through automated coaching.

One vision of the future is that employees will be presented with short learning episodes embedded in their work, will be alerted when the learning episodes are needed, will have direct connections to experts, will be continuously connected online wirelessly, and will have simulations for guidance.[16] Every employee will have a dynamic display (a personalized "dashboard") that provides a unique view into the company. The display will be customized to each employee's role and background and will give the employee a current picture of specific job responsibilities within the scope of the entire work flow. The dashboard will allow the employee to collaborate with others, request information, or participate in a simulation to deal with a problem. Another vision is that the personal computer will be the hub that allows employees not only to share data but also to access training content and subject matter experts automatically, on an as-needed basis. This will occur through the interface of e-mail, instant messaging, virtual offices supplied through 3D environments, video conferencing, wikis, and shared meetings applications.[17]

Figure 13.1 shows the four functional areas and applications of real-time extended business, in which employees and systems work together in a process to produce products and services. The four areas are resource management, collaboration management, product management, and process management. Resource management includes applications designed to create inventories and map resources. Resources include people, property, machines, systems, and learning content. Collaboration management includes events, processes, and experiences that characterize work. Collaboration involves the exchange of information and knowledge. Process management includes analysis of the work flow and of people and systems in the work flow. Product management includes the links among employees, products, partners, and customers. E-learning can be used to integrate the four quadrants.

FIGURE 13.1
Functional Areas and Applications of Real-Time Extended Business

Source: Based on S. Adkins, "The Brave New World of Learning," *T&D* (June 2003): 28–37.

Resource Management	Collaboration Management
• Human capital development • Enterprise resource management • Employee resource management • Learning management systems	• Structured knowledge management • Instant messaging • Collaborative Web-conferencing
Product Management	Process Management
• Product life-cycle management • Supply chain management • Work force management • Customer relations management	• Work flow management • Customer analytics • Work force analytics • Business process management

Technology available for collaboration includes (1) virtual classroom software that facilitates distance learning by allowing trainees to meet together and hold conversations and (2) asynchronous tools such as discussion boards. Through collaboration, software can be used to build knowledge bases or expert systems that are available to all employees.[18] Dell, the computer maker, uses collaborative software along with its learning management system (LMS). The LMS is used to automate the administration of training (recall the discussion of LMSs in Chapter 8). Employees can look for, register for, pay for, and take classes all through the same Web site. The collaborative software allows Dell employees to experience a virtual classroom setting in which they can hear and talk to the trainer. After the course, employees can use learning labs to practice what they have learned.

INCREASED EMPHASIS ON PERFORMANCE ANALYSIS AND LEARNING FOR BUSINESS ENHANCEMENT

Because of an increasing focus on contributing to the company's competitive advantage, training departments will have to ensure that they are seen as helping the business functions (e.g., marketing, finance, production) meet their needs. Also, the work force will continue to be more global and diverse, making diversity training and the management of diversity important learning initiatives, along with understanding how to teach managers how to lead a global work force.[19] Trainers will have to become more aware of cultural norms in other countries. Consider how companies in three different industries expect training to influence their bottom line.[20] The training offered at TRX, a company that provides transaction processing and data integration services, is expected to have a direct influence on boosting customer satisfaction scores and agents' productivity. Metrics such as hours of training delivered are not as important as showing how training is contributing to customer service, productivity, and profitability. Supply-chain training for Coca-Cola must be tied in some way to the company's three-year business plan or it will not be supported. At Ho-Chunk Casino in Wisconsin, the director of training spends time educating managers on how the training unit adds value to the business. One of the director's biggest challenges is convincing first-line supervisors to support transfer of training. The training director has found that explaining Kirkpatrick's evaluation model (discussed in Chapter 6: reaction, learning, behavior, results) to the supervisors helps them understand that training is a process and not a one-time event and that they play an important role in determining the success or failure of training. Training departments must shift the focus from training as *the* solution to business problems to a performance analysis approach. A **performance analysis approach** involves identifying performance gaps or deficiencies and examining training as one possible solution for the business units (the customers). Training departments will need to continue instructing managers to consider all potential causes of poor performance before deciding that training is the solution. Poor employee performance may be due to poor management, inefficient technologies, or outdated technology rather than deficiencies in skill or knowledge (recall the discussion of person analysis in Chapter 3). Three ways that training departments will need to be involved are (1) focusing on interventions related to performance improvement, (2) providing support for high-performance work systems, and (3) developing systems for training administration, development, and delivery that reduce costs and increase employees' access to learning.

Training departments' responsibilities will likely include a greater focus on systems that employees can use for information (such as expert systems or electronic performance support systems) on an as-needed basis. This need is driven by the use of contingent employees and the increased flexibility necessary to adapt products and services to meet customers' needs. For example, companies do not want to spend money to train employees who may be with the company only a few weeks. Instead, through temporary employment agencies, companies can select employees with the exact skill set needed. Training departments need to provide mechanisms to support the temporary employees once they are on the job and encounter situations, problems, rules, and policies they are unfamiliar with because they are not yet knowledgeable about the company.

As was discussed in Chapter 1, more companies are striving to create high-performance workplaces because of the productivity gains that can be realized through this type of design. High-performance work requires that employees have the interpersonal skills necessary to work in teams. High-performance work systems also require employees to have high levels of technical skills. Employees need to understand statistical process control and the Total Quality Management philosophy. Employees also must understand the entire production and service system so they can better serve both internal and external customers. As more companies move to high-performance work systems, training departments will need to be prepared to provide effective training in interpersonal, quality, and technical skills as well as to help employees understand all aspects of the customer-service or production system.

Business competitiveness can be realized by quick change, speed in delivery, and reductions in costs and time constraints. Cypress Semiconductors, a supplier of integrated circuits for network equipment that is based in San Jose, California, utilizes competency models that are linked to success profiles that detail employees' roles, activities, responsibilities, career development initiatives, and training options.[21] The profiles are used for employee performance evaluations, and they are also used in the hiring process. For example, a training plan can be developed for new hires as soon as they are on the job so that they can be successful as quickly as possible.

Just-in-time learning is many companies' answer to quick learning and the quick application of learning to the business.[22] Memorial Sloan Kettering Cancer Center developed a set of simulation tools that are integrated with the implementation of several clinical support systems (order management, electronic medical records, picture archival and communications, and disease management) available to the entire medical center. IBM Global Services has moved its training from three days in the classroom to just-in-time on the Web. E-business consultants can now access a Web site that provides them with the training they need or with information or case studies from which the training was built. They can also collaborate with other consultants to share knowledge.

Because the direction in training is away from learning as the primary outcome and more toward learning as a way to enhance business performance, companies have started to purchase learning management systems (LMSs) that provide training administration, development tools, and online training. (LMSs are discussed in Chapter 8.) LMS software contains learning analytics, or analysis tools, that can track learning activity and costs and can relate learning results to product revenues or sales goals.[23]

INCREASED USE OF TRAINING PARTNERSHIPS AND OUTSOURCING TRAINING

Chapter 2 discussed several reasons for companies to outsource their training. Two main reasons were that employees need to learn specialized new knowledge and that companies want to gain access to best practices and cost savings. External suppliers may be consultants, academics, graduate students, or companies in the entertainment and mass communications industries. External suppliers can be partners or be sole providers of training services. The key decision for companies will not be whether to outsource but rather how much training to outsource.

BellSouth developed a new training program on the basics of wireless communications for its own employees. Members of the training team believed that if employees within BellSouth could benefit from knowing more about how wireless communications work, then key suppliers, end-user customers, and companies that sell the wireless products would also benefit. This type of training might give BellSouth an advantage over its competitors. As a result, BellSouth's Intro to Wireless Communications training is being offered both within the company and to companies that sell BellSouth's products, such as Best Buy. Best Buy is making the training available to their customers. BellSouth is also providing training that can help make its networks of suppliers and customers more knowledgeable in other areas, such as basic personal computer skills for managing computer networks. BellSouth offers courses from training suppliers on its company Web site. The company charges a fee for the training.

Why train suppliers, customers, and vendors? The intent is to build a broad understanding of what wireless technology does, how it works, where it works, why it works, its strengths and weaknesses, and its potential applications. Providing training also enhances the value of BellSouth's services. That customers, vendors, and suppliers are learning more about BellSouth's products and services translates into higher sales. For example, the more that salespeople understand the products and the technology they are selling, the better they can match customer needs and product capabilities. This knowledge increases customer satisfaction and word-of-mouth advertising, and it lowers the number of returns and complaints—thus cutting the costs of doing business.[24]

Training departments will be increasing their partnerships with academic institutions (e.g., community colleges, universities) to provide basic skills training and to develop customized programs. In addition, there will be an increased emphasis on retraining employees from labor-intensive industries that are experiencing layoffs, such as textiles and automobile manufacturing, and moving them into industries that have labor shortages. This will involve cooperation between companies, state governments, and educational institutions, including universities, community colleges, and technical schools. For example, in school-to-work transition programs (which were discussed in Chapter 10), companies are actively involved in designing curricula and providing experiences for students to help ensure that they are competent to enter the work force. Another use of academic partners is as subject-matter experts. The academics evaluate current training practices and modify training programs to increase their effectiveness. Academic partners may also work with training departments to develop specialized programs for employees at all levels in the company. For example, Westcott Communication is working with eight business schools to provide executive education for several companies, including Kodak, Disney, and Texas Instruments.[25] Sematech, the semiconductor industry association, is working with community colleges in the Phoenix, Arizona, area to develop a curriculum for training entry-level manufacturing technicians.[26] Displaced auto workers in Michigan have been recruited to fill nursing positions.[27] Oakland University recruits auto workers into a one-year nursing program. After completing the program, participants can gain employment with St. John Health, the largest health network in Detroit. In San Francisco, material handlers who have lost jobs in the aviation industry have been retrained to work for Genentech, a biotechnology company. The Integrated Basic Education and Skills Training (IBEST) offered by the state of Washington allows participants to receive training for jobs in nursing, hospitality, corrections, and welding. The program is targeted to the underemployed and the unemployed. Completion of the one-year program prepares participants with sufficient skills to obtain an entry-level job in their chosen field with the opportunity to return for additional training.

As the role of external suppliers of training increases, trainers will need to become more savvy in contract negotiations and make-versus-buy analysis.[28] Trainers will need to know how to identify and select training vendors. Trainers may be called on to support managers and employees who will actually conduct the training. Rather than developing training programs, trainers increasingly are likely to need competency in designing train-the-trainer programs.

For example, Motorola outsourced its training to ACS to create ACS Global HR Solutions, which manages all human resource and training activities worldwide for the company.[29] Motorola transferred 650 key human resource and learning employees to ACS. Motorola decided it wanted world-class management of administrative and transactional human resource functions, including training and development. Outsourcing also allowed Motorola to reduce costs during a downsizing. ACS gained Motorola's service center, employee portal, and employees. Motorola will retain control over strategic areas, assessment, and customer interface. It will also have the final decision on whether to design training or buy it from an outside supplier. Motorola believes that the careers of its former employees will be enhanced, because training is a primary business of ACS whereas it was only a support function at Motorola.

One type of training outsourcing involves the use of an application service provider. An **application service provider (ASP)** is a company that rents out access to software for a specific application.[30] Some ASPs have relationships with courseware developers that provide online learning. These relationships allow the ASP to offer structured courses as well as custom options. The major benefit is that company resources are not used to purchase or maintain an internal network or intranet. Also, companies save the costs associated with building, renting, or maintaining a training facility. Typically, the company pays for a license along with a maintenance contract. Training delivery and administration programs are run on the ASP's computers. The ASP can track how many employees use the software contracted for, which areas are accessed the most, and how employees perform on post-training tests. The ASP also provides technical support, including software upgrades. The company pays the ASP a fee. For example, KPMG Consulting challenged its e-learning department to develop a program that would train 8,500 employees worldwide in e-business.[31] The national director of e-learning recognized that he had to ensure that the program didn't overload KPMG's computer system. The solution was to use an ASP to host the company's computer-based training program, providing access to employees worldwide while using none of KPMG's computer resources. The use of an ASP allowed KPMG to quickly develop and make the training available to its work force.

Implications of Future Trends for Trainers' Skills and Competencies

A recent study found that the competencies and expertise included in the ASTD competency model (see Figure 1.4) are likely to be needed in the future. However, increased emphasis will also be placed on the ability of trainers to more effectively use technology. Also, as companies become more global, they will need to adapt training methods and content to local cultures.[32] Table 13.3 shows the skills that trainers will need to develop in the future.

TRAINING AND DEVELOPMENT FROM A CHANGE MODEL PERSPECTIVE

Although the concept of change is usually addressed in an organizational behavior course, the reality is that for new training or development practices to be successfully implemented, they must be accepted by the customer (manager, upper management, employees).

The specific process that should be used to determine and implement change varies by company and by types of problems and opportunities. Four conditions are necessary for

TABLE 13.3
Skills for Future Trainers

Source: Based on M. Laff, "Trainers Skills 2020," *T + D* (December 2008): 42.

- Matching training content and methods to the local culture of the work force.
- Designing learning space as well as content in technology-driven learning environments.
- Use of multimedia tools, including audio, video, Webcasts, and live action.
- Delivering and packaging training in different formats for beginners and experts.
- Use of assessments to determine trainees' learning styles.
- Developing search-and-identify techniques so employees can find information and training when they need it.
- Facilitating learning and staying in touch with employees, managers, and business units to identify what they need and making suggestions regarding tools, processes, or procedures that could help them work more effectively.
- Developing and delivering learning that is integrated with the job.

change to occur: (1) Employees must understand the reasons for change and agree with those reasons, (2) employees must have the skills needed to implement the change, (3) employees must see that managers and other employees in power positions support the change, and (4) organizational structures such as compensation and performance management systems must support the change.[33] For managers and employees, change is not easy. Even when employees know that a practice or program could be better, they have learned to adapt to its inadequacies. Therefore, resistance to new training and development practices is likely. Prior to implementing a new training or development practice, trainers should consider how they can increase the likelihood of its acceptance.

Figure 13.2 provides a model of change. The process of change is based on the interaction among four components of the organization: task, employees, formal organizational arrangements (structures, processes, systems), and informal organization (communication patterns, values, norms).[34] As shown in the figure, different types of change-related problems occur depending on the organizational component that is influenced by the change. For example, introducing new technology for training into a company (such as multimedia training using the Internet) might cause changes in the organization's power structure. With the new technology, managers may have less control over access to training programs than they had with traditional methods of training. The result is tension related to the power imbalance created by the new system. If these issues are not dealt with, the managers will not accept the new technology or provide support for transfer of training.

The four change-related problems that need to be addressed before implementation of any new training practice are resistance to change, loss of control, power imbalance, and task redefinition. **Resistance to change** refers to managers' and employees' unwillingness

FIGURE 13.2
A Change Model

Source: David A. Nadler and Michael L. Tushman, "A Congruence Model for Diagnosing Organizational Behavior," in *Organizational Psychology: A Book of Readings,* ed. D. Rabin and J. McIntyre (Englewood Cliffs, NJ: Prentice Hall, 1979), as reprinted in David A. Nadler, "Concepts for the Management of Organizational Change," in *Readings in the Management of Innovation,* 2d ed., ed. M. L. Tushman and N. Moore (Cambridge, MA: Ballinger Publishing Co., 1988): 722.

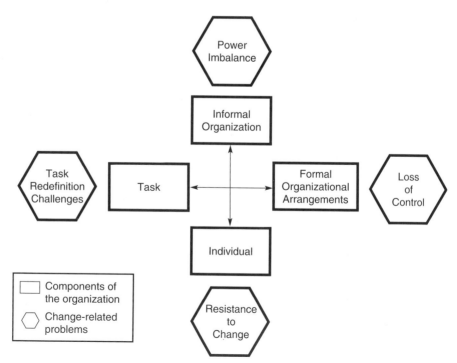

to change. Managers and employees may be anxious about change, feel they will be unable to cope, value the current training practice, or not understand the value of the new practice. **Control** relates change to managers' and employees' ability to obtain and distribute valuable resources such as data, information, or money. Changes can cause managers and employees to have less control over resources. Change can also give managers and employees control over processes that they have not previously been involved in (e.g., choosing which training programs to attend). **Power** refers to the ability to influence others. Managers may lose the ability to influence employees as employees gain access to databases and other information, thus getting more autonomy to deliver products and services. Employees may be held accountable for learning in self-directed training. Web-based training methods such as **task redefinition** create changes in managers' and employees' roles and job responsibilities. Employees may be asked not only to participate in training but also to consider how to improve its quality. Managers may be asked to become facilitators and coaches.

Table 13.4 provides recommendations for a successful change process that will help ensure the presence of the conditions necessary for change to occur. Consider what the United States Postal Service (USPS) has done to successfully manage change at the postal service.[35] The postmaster general introduced the USPS transformation plan that set new expectations about customer focus, the quality of the work environment, market competitiveness, and budget and service goals. The plan has resulted in the elimination of debt, in record service levels, and in the introduction of new products and services (such as Click 'n Ship). Implementation of the plan has led to changes in the postal service. To help top managers lead the people side of change, the USPS (along with the Center for Creative

TABLE 13.4

Steps in a Change Process

Source: Based on C. McAllaster, "Leading Change by Effectively Utilizing Leverage Points within an Organization," *Organizational Dynamics* 33 (2004): 318; L. Freifeld, "Changes with Penguins," *Training* (June 2008): 24–28.

1. **Identify the problem or opportunity and create a sense of urgency.** Is the stated problem actually the real problem facing the company? How does the opportunity fit into the company's business strategy?
2. **Identify possible solutions.** Ask managers and employees to suggest courses of action to deal with the problem or capitalize on an opportunity. Do not ask for ideas or suggestions if they are not going to be seriously considered. Resistance to change can be reduced if employees feel they have genuine input into the solution.
3. **Communicate for buy-in.** Employees need to know what is occurring. Use briefings, newsletters, Web pages, informational meetings.
4. **Choose and announce the action as soon as possible.** Employees affected by the change must hear about it as soon as possible. Employees need to know why and how the final action was selected, how the process has progressed, and what is going to happen in the next days and months. Communicating logic and reasoning can help overcome resistance to change.
5. **Execute and create short-term wins.** Success requires management attention and the desire to do it right. Managers and change leaders must model new behavior and become enthusiastic supporters for the process. Leaders should involve employees and provide them with the necessary training and resources. If a pilot test or beta program is used, employees should be kept informed on its progress and asked for their opinions. Learning should occur from any mistakes.
6. **Follow up, reevaluate, and modify.** Be flexible and make changes if they are needed. Share information about mistakes or issues, and work with the employees affected to fix them.

Leadership) developed the Leading People Through Transformation program. This program provides managers with an experience that helps them rethink their approach to change leadership. Over three years, more than 650 top managers have attended 34 five-day sessions. The postmaster general begins each session with the managers by sharing his vision of transformation, offering encouragement, and answering questions. At the end of the week, five executive officers join the participants. The involvement of the postmaster general and the executives sends a message to the managers that top executives are committed to change and demonstrates an open and honest leadership style that is important for leading change.

The program allows the emotional component of change to be personally experienced by the managers. During the debriefing of the experience, managers realize that their emotional reactions during the program are similar to how their employees will respond in the face of the USPS transformation. With this revelation, managers can openly discuss how to lead change. They see in a new light the operational changes, job relocations, and facilities closings that can result from the transformation. They become interested in how to handle the people side of change, and they consider ways to lead employees through the transition so they can adapt and make long-term contributions to the postal service. The USPS has seen a change in decision making by top managers. Rather than relying on an "I'm paid to make the decisions" leadership style, top managers are now more likely to involve employees in the decision-making process by listening to their concerns and asking questions.

METHODS TO DETERMINE WHETHER CHANGE IS NECESSARY

Viewing training from a systems perspective means that companies and trainers need to understand both internal and external environments.[36] Specifically, they need to understand the effectiveness and efficiency of current training practices. They also need to be aware of other companies' practices to ensure that their training practices are the best possible. Benchmarking provides information about other companies' practices. Process reengineering provides information about the effectiveness and efficiency of training systems within the company.

Benchmarking

As was mentioned in Chapter 3, benchmarking is the practice of finding examples of excellent products, services, or systems (i.e., best practices). Benchmarking is an important component of a company's quality strategy. Benchmarking training practices are useful for several reasons.[37] By looking at how excellent companies conduct training, a company can identify how its training practices compare to the best practices. Benchmarking also helps a company learn from others. A company can see what types of training practices work and how they were successfully implemented. Use of this information can increase the chances that new training practices will be accepted and effective. Learning what other successful companies are doing can help managers create a case for changing current training and development practices in the company (i.e., overcoming resistance to change). Benchmarking can also be used to help establish a training strategy and set priorities for training practices.

Benchmarking was developed by Xerox Corporation in order to compete with the low prices of plain paper copiers made in Japan. Xerox's benchmarking process features the 10 steps shown in Table 13.5. Besides collecting its own benchmarking information, a company

TABLE 13.5

Xerox's Benchmarking Practices

Source: Based on S. Greengard, "Discover Best Pictures through Benchmarking," *Personnel Journal* (November 1995): 62–73.

1. Identify what is to be benchmarked.
2. Identify comparable companies.
3. Determine data collection methods and collect data.
4. Determine current performance levels.
5. Project future performance levels.
6. Communicate benchmark results and gain acceptance.
7. Establish functional goals.
8. Develop action plans.
9. Implement action plans and monitor progress.
10. Recalibrate benchmarks.

may want to subscribe to a service that collects data regarding human resource practices from several companies. For example, the American Society for Training and Development sponsors a benchmarking forum. The 40 companies that belong to the forum are generally large companies such as Xerox. They report information regarding training expenditures, structure of training programs, training design, and delivery practices. This information is shared among forum members; a report summarizing the results is sold to other interested parties. Some estimate that as many as 70 percent of Fortune 500 companies use benchmarking on a regular basis.[38]

Trainers need to take several factors into account when benchmarking.[39] Trainers must gather information about internal processes to serve as a comparison for best practices. It is important to clearly identify the purpose of benchmarking and the practice to be benchmarked.

Upper-level management needs to be committed to the project. Both quantitative (numbers) and qualitative data should be collected. Descriptions of programs and how they operate are as valuable as knowing how best practices contributed to the bottom line. Trainers must be careful to gather data from companies both within and outside their industry. Benchmarking may actually limit a company's performance if the goal is only to learn and copy what other companies have done and not consider how to improve on the process. Trainers should be careful not to view human resource practices in isolation from each other. For example, examining training practices also requires consideration of the company's staffing strategy (use of internal labor market versus the external labor market to fill positions). Benchmarking will not provide a "right" answer. The information collected needs to be considered in terms of the context of the companies. Finally, benchmarking is one part of an improvement process. As a result, use of the information gathered from benchmarking needs to be considered in the broader framework of organization change, which was discussed in the previous section.

Process Reengineering

Trainers need to understand their current training practices and processes and evaluate them to determine what should be changed. **Reengineering** is a complete review of critical processes and the redesign of those processes to make them more efficient and able to deliver higher quality. Reengineering is critical to ensuring that the benefits of new training and development programs will be realized. Reengineering is especially important when trainers attempt to deliver training using new technology. Reengineering is also important when training departments try to streamline administrative processes and improve the services they offer to their "customers." This streamlining can apply to course enrollment processes, processes related to issuing tuition reimbursement, and processes related to employees reviewing their training records. Applying new technology (e.g., interactive voice technology) to a course enrollment process burdened with too many steps will not result in improvements in efficiency or effectiveness. What it will result in is increased product or service costs related to the introduction of the new technology.

Reengineering can be used to review the training department functions and processes or it can be used to review a specific training program or development program practice such as a career management system. The reengineering process involves the four steps shown in Figure 13.3: Identify the process to be reengineered, understand the process, redesign the process, and implement the new process.[40]

Identify the Process

Managers and trainers who control the process or are responsible for functions within the process ("process owners") should be identified and asked to participate on the reengineering team. Team members should include employees involved in the process (to provide expertise) and outside the process, as well as internal or external customers who see the outcome of the process.

Understand the Process

Several factors need to be considered when evaluating a process:

- Can tasks (e.g., course enrollment and pretraining assessment) be combined?
- Can employees be given more autonomy? Can the process be streamlined by building control and decision making into it?
- Are all the steps in the process necessary?
- Are data redundancy or unnecessary checks and controls built into the process?
- How many special cases and exceptions have to be dealt with?
- Are the steps in the process arranged in their natural order?
- What is the desired outcome? Are all the tasks necessary? What is the value of the process?

A number of techniques are used to understand processes. **Data-flow diagrams** show the flow of data between departments. For example, to investigate why tuition reimbursement checks take too long to reach employees, trainers may want to investigate the relationship between the training department (where tuition reimbursement is approved) and accounting (where checks are issued). **Data-entity relationship diagrams** show the types of data used within a business function and the relationship among the different types of data. These diagrams would be especially useful for investigating, for example, the time

FIGURE 13.3
The Reengineering Process

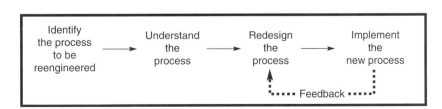

and people within the training department involved in filling employees' requests for their training records. In **scenario analysis,** simulations of real-world issues are presented to data end users. The end users are asked to indicate how a new technology could help address their particular situations and what data should be maintained to deal with those situations. Surveys and focus groups collect information about the data collected, used, and stored in a functional area as well as information about time and data processing requirements. Users may be asked to evaluate the importance, frequency, and criticality of automating specific tasks within a functional area. (For example, how critical is it to have an employee tracking system that maintains data on employees' fluency in foreign languages?) Cost-benefit analyses compare the costs of completing tasks with and without an automated system or software application. For example, the analysis should include (1) the costs in terms of people, time, materials, and dollars, (2) the anticipated costs of software and hardware, and (3) labor, time, and material expenses.[41]

Redesign the Process

The team develops models, tests them, chooses a prototype, and determines how to integrate the prototype into the organization.

Implement the Process

The company tries out the process by testing it in a limited, controlled setting before expanding it companywide.

KEY ISSUES IN IMPLEMENTING CHANGE

As noted in Chapter 1, companies face many forces—including new technologies, globalization, and a diverse work force—that mean they have to change to be successful. **Organization development** is a planned, systematic change process that uses behavioral science knowledge and techniques to improve companies' effectiveness by improving relationships and increasing learning and problem-solving capabilities.[42] Organization development helps create a learning environment through increased trust, confrontation of problems, employee empowerment and participation, knowledge sharing, work design, and cooperation between groups, and by allowing employees to maximize their skills and grow.

Change Management

Change management is the process of ensuring that new interventions such as training practices are accepted and used by employees and managers. Four issues need to be addressed to facilitate the change management process shown in Table 13.4. These issues include overcoming resistance to change, managing the transition to the new practice, shaping political dynamics, and using training to make change stick.

Overcoming Resistance to Change

Resistance to change can be overcome by involving the affected people in planning the change and rewarding them for desired behavior. It is also critical for managers to divide the implementation of the new practice into steps that are understandable and that employees believe they can accomplish. Employees need to understand how new training practices help them meet their needs.[43] These needs may include better-quality training, faster access to descriptions of training programs, a link between training and compensation, and more meaningful training or access to training programs from their personal computers.

For example, 20 different departments within the Pepsi Bottling Group's shared services division had been accustomed to operating independently.[44] They performed the same functions at different Pepsi Groups, but they each had their own practices and procedures for getting work done. A small team of employees tried to create one set of shared practices and procedures, but the departments did not accept them. The next step to persuade the departments to accept the change was to involve as many employees as possible. This larger group of employees came up with a common set of procedures and documented them online. Similarly, Detroit Edison used involvement of as many employees as possible to help determine ways to cut costs. One-third of the entire organization participated in the process. The changes were accepted by employees, and Detroit Edison saved millions of dollars.

Managing the Transition

Tactics for managing the transition include communicating a clear picture of the future and creating organizational arrangements for the transition (e.g., contact person, help line). It might be good to allow an old practice and a new practice to exist simultaneously (run parallel) so that employees can see the benefits and advantages of the new practice. Then, any problems that are identified can be worked out. This parallel process is commonly done when new technology is introduced in companies.

Shaping Political Dynamics

Managers need to seek the support of key power groups including formal and informal leaders. For example, as was mentioned in Chapter 10, successful diversity efforts are characterized by active involvement and endorsement by top managers. Not only do top managers talk about the need to manage diversity, but they also get actively involved through mentoring programs, setting up formal committees and positions to promote diversity, and rewarding managers for their diversity efforts.

Managers of support functions such as human resources that are not directly involved in the design, manufacturing, or delivery of a product or service to the marketplace can shape political dynamics by becoming business partners. The steps to becoming a business partner relate to the discussion of strategic training in Chapter 2. First, the trainer identifies and understands the business problems that the manager is facing. Second, the trainer explains to the manager how training can help solve the problem. Third, the trainer works with the manager to develop the best training solution that meets the manager's needs. The manager should be treated as a customer. Finally, the trainer measures how training has helped overcome or solve the business problem.

Table 13.6 shows several misconceptions that some managers hold about training. These misconceptions are likely due to a lack of understanding of the function and value of the training department. To counter these misconceptions and gain political alliances with managers in the business functions, trainers need to take several actions. As mentioned in Chapters 1 and 2, trainers need to ensure that the training department adds value to the business, builds relationships with functional business managers, and establishes credibility in the company.[45] This reassurance is accomplished through helping functional managers deal with training-related problems, evaluating the effectiveness of training practices, and providing excellent service to the functional managers (e.g., providing

TABLE 13.6
Managers'
Misconceptions
about Training

Source: Based on
R. F. Mager, "Morph-
ing into a . . . 21st
Century Trainer,"
Training (June 1996):
47–54.

- Training is not valuable.
- Training is an expense, not an investment.
- Anybody can be a trainer.
- The training department is a good place to put poor performers.
- Training is the responsibility of trainers.

information and finishing projects in a timely manner, committing only to projects that can be realistically delivered).

Using Training to Make Change Stick

Because many practices involve changes not only in the way the service or process is going to be provided, but also in employees' and managers' roles, training is critical. Managers and employees need to be trained to deal with new systems whether they involve job redesign (e.g., teams), performance management (e.g., use of 360-degree feedback systems), selection systems (e.g., a structured interview), or new technology (e.g., a new computer-based manufacturing system).

For example, these principles helped with the introduction of a computerized flexible manufacturing system at a manufacturer of diesel engines.[46] The computers were to be used to provide instructions for customized orders and to give the order center updates on production status. The production workers were reluctant to use the computers. Their objections included that they did not know how to type and that their jobs made their hands too greasy. To ensure that the production workers would use the new system, the company took several steps. First, an electronic performance support system was placed in the cafeteria to answer employees' questions about the system. Second, the company asked workers for suggestions as they tested prototypes of the system. Third, the touch screen system was modified so that employees could use foot controls, thus alleviating concerns about greasy hands when typing. Twenty months after the process for introducing the new manufacturing system began, the system was in place.

Training plays an important role in ensuring that changes that result from a merger or acquisition are successful. Consider the role of training at PNC Financial Services Group and Wachovia Bank, two companies that have needed to successfully manage change in order to grow through mergers and acquisitions.[47] In 2007, PNC Financial announced its acquisition of Sterling Financial Corporation. Just over one year later, Sterling's offices reopened as PNC retail locations. To facilitate the successful acquisition and integration, current PNC employees were sent to Sterling's work locations to serve as mentors for new employees and to help them learn PNC's systems, policies, and procedures. Each of Sterling's more than 1,000 employees received training from PNC. The training included a mix of classroom, online, and on-the-job experiences. At Wachovia Bank, which has completed more than 100 mergers in less than 20 years, an enterprise merger training team is formed soon after a merger is announced. The team uses the ADDIE model (analysis, design, development, implementation, and evaluation) to analyze the other bank and determine what training is needed. Much of the training focuses on the acquired company's culture. Wachovia designs training to embrace the company's culture and help employees understand and accept the new Wachovia culture. Typically, on the first day of training, the first several hours focus on culture and change and the values of Wachovia. Each newly merged employee is given a booklet that includes an overview of Wachovia's products, how its organizational structure works, its diversity mission, its focus on volunteerism, and its core values. Trainers are prepared to answer questions on a wide range of human resource issues, from number of vacation days to type of health benefits. At Wachovia, training doesn't necessarily lead change management but it supports it. At the end of every merger, a "training cookbook" is created which documents all of the processes, roles, and responsibilities needed to help make the merger successful from a training perspective.

Change Interventions

Besides training, there are several interventions that companies have used successfully to bring about change. These include survey feedback, process consultation, and group interventions.

Survey Feedback

Survey feedback refers to the process of collecting information about employees' attitudes and perceptions using a survey, summarizing the results, and providing employees with feedback to stimulate discussion, identify problems, and plan actions to solve problems. Surveys can be administered via the Web. The goal of survey feedback is to identify issues, solve problems, and improve relationships among work group members through discussion of shared problems.

Process Consultation

In **process consultation,** a consultant works with managers or other employees to help them understand and take action to improve specific events that occur at work. Process consultation may involve analysis of relationships between employees, the work flow, how decisions are made, communication patterns, or other behaviors. The consultant helps employees diagnose what processes need to be improved.

Group Interventions

Large group interventions involve employees from different parts of the organization. They may also involve customers and other important stakeholders from outside the company. The interventions bring together the participants in an off-site setting to discuss problems and opportunities or to plan change. For example, the Work Out program within General Electric (GE) includes six steps:[48]

1. A process or problem for discussion is chosen.
2. A cross-functional team, including customers and others outside GE (e.g., suppliers), is selected.
3. A "champion" is assigned to follow through on recommendations made by the team.
4. Team meetings generate recommendations to improve processes or solve problems.
5. Top managers meet with the teams to review recommendations and evaluate them.
6. Additional meetings are held to pursue the recommendations.

The program grew out of former CEO Jack Welch's desire to motivate the more than 300,000 employees at GE. Welch believed that employees have to be involved in creating change for it to occur.

Large group interventions seek to bring about radical change in the entire company by involving the entire company system (managers, employees, customers) in the change effort. Intergroup activities occur on a much smaller scale. **Intergroup activities** attempt to improve relationships among different teams, departments, or groups. These interventions have been used for labor-management conflicts, to smooth mergers and acquisitions, and to alleviate differences between staff and line functions. One intergroup activity has the involved groups meet separately and list the beliefs they have about themselves and the other group.[49] The groups discuss their similarities and differences and how misperceptions have developed. The groups then discuss possible solutions to their conflict and misperceptions.

Seagate, one of the world's largest manufacturers of computer hard drives, flew 200 employees to New Zealand for its sixth annual Eco Seagate, a week of team building that concludes with an all-day race in which employees have to hike, bike, swim, and rappel down a cliff.[50] The event is designed to break down barriers, increase confidence, and make employees better team members. Seagate wants a culture that is open and honest and that encourages employees to work together. Each morning, one of Seagate's top executives gives a presentation on the characteristics of a strong team. In the afternoon, employees divide into "tribes" and go out for physical training in one of the race events. The week concludes with the teams competing in such events as kayaking, mountain biking, swimming, and hiking.

Summary	This chapter discussed future trends that are likely to influence training and development. These trends relate to training delivery and structure of the training function. Trainers will be asked to design focused content more quickly and to deliver training using multiple methods. New technology will have a growing impact on training delivery in the future. Also, new technology will allow training departments to store and share human capital throughout the company. There will be an increased emphasis on integrating training with other human resource functions and showing how training helps the business. Training departments are more likely to develop partnerships with vendors and other companies in the future. The chapter discussed the importance of viewing training from a change perspective. Benchmarking training practices and reengineering training processes are important prerequisites for creating a need for change. For new training practices to be accepted by employees and managers, trainers need to overcome resistance to change, manage the transition, shape the political dynamics, and use training to redefine the task. Organization development interventions involving consultants, groups, and survey feedback can be used to create change.

Key Terms

virtual work
arrangement, *525*

telecommuting, *525*

digital collaboration, *525*

rapid instructional design
(RID), *526*

social network
analysis, *528*

embedded learning, *528*

performance analysis
approach, *531*

application service provider
(ASP), *533*

resistance to change, *535*

control, *536*

power, *536*

task redefinition, *536*

reengineering, *538*

data-flow diagrams, *539*

data-entity relationship
diagrams, *539*

scenario analysis, *540*

organization
development, *540*

change management, *540*

survey feedback, *543*

process consultation, *543*

large group
intervention, *543*

intergroup activity, *543*

Discussion Questions

1. Discuss how new technologies are likely to impact training in the future.

2. What new skills will trainers need to be successful in the future?

3. What is rapid instructional design? How does it differ from the traditional training design process discussed in Chapter 1? (See Figure 1.1.)

4. How does the use of a learning management system better link training to business strategy and goals?

5. What is benchmarking? Explain the process you would use to benchmark a company's safety training programs.

6. What is process reengineering? Why is it relevant to training?

7. Discuss the steps necessary to introduce a new training practice from a change model perspective.

8. What misconceptions do managers have about training? How could you change those misconceptions?

9. Explain what you believe are the advantages and disadvantages of creating a training consortium or partnership with other companies.

10. What is organization development? Describe the interventions used to create change.

11. What are the implications of virtual work arrangements for training?

Application Assignments

1. Interview a manager. Ask him to evaluate his company's training department in terms of training delivery, service, expertise, and contribution to the business. Ask him to explain the rationale for his evaluation. Summarize this information. Based on the information you gathered, make recommendations regarding how the training department can be improved.

2. This chapter discussed several trends that will influence the future of training. Based on future social, economic, political, or technological factors, identify one or two additional trends that you think will influence training. Write a two- to three-page paper summarizing your ideas. Make sure you provide a rationale for your trends. Many organizations are moving from a training perspective to a performance perspective. That is, they are interested in performance improvement, not training just for the sake of training.

3. GeoLearning is an application service provider (ASP). Visit www.geolearning.com. What services and products does this ASP provide?

4. Go to en.wikipedia.org/wiki/Blog to learn about blogs. What is a blog? How might a blog be useful for training or development?

Case: *Going Paperless Requires a Change Management Process*

Ecology-minded consumers are putting pressure on companies to prove they're doing their best to minimize their environmental impact. "Going green" requires training employees in new business operations and practices as well as overcoming their resistance to change. Cortel, a communications company, decided to go paperless as part of a green initiative. The company hired an outside vendor to automate all human resource functions such as payroll and benefits, but most employees still want to print copies of their pay stubs and performance reviews. Cortel wants employees to retrain from printing out these records as part of the overall transformation of the company into a paperless organization. Going paperless also helps reduce costs. One estimate is that the typical employee prints six wasted pages per day. This and the average cost of a wasted page is $0.06 and adds up to 1,410 wasted pages per year, at a cost of $84 per employee!

What recommendations would you give Cortel for successfully changing into a paperless organization and overcoming employees' resistance?

Source: Based on M. Weinstein, "It's Not Easy Being Green," *Training* (March/April 2008): 20–25.

Endnotes

1. C. E. Plott and J. Humphrey, "Preparing for 2020," *Training and Development* (November 1996): 46–49.
2. J. Barbian, "The Future Training Room," *Training* (September 2001): 40–45.
3. P. Harris, "Immersive Learning Seeks a Foothold," *T + D* (January 2009): 40–45.
4. H. Dolezalek and T. Galvin, "Future Scan," *Training* (September 2004): 30–38; A. Kamenetz, "The Network Unbound," *Fast Company* (June 2006): 68–73.
5. N. Crandall and M. Wallace Jr., *Work and Rewards in the Virtual Workplace* (New York: AMACOM, 1998).
6. J. Salopek, "Digital Collaboration," *Training and Development* (June 2000): 38–43.
7. H. Dolezalek, "Who Has the Time to Design?" *Training* (January 2006): 24–28.
8. S. Thiagarajan, "Rapid Instructional Development," in *The ASTD Handbook of Training Design and Delivery,* ed. G. Piskurich, P. Beckschi, and B. Hall (New York: McGraw-Hill, 2000): 54–75.
9. M. Weinstein, "Six for '06," *Training* (January 2006): 18–22.
10. D. Zielinski, "Wanted: Training Manager," *Training* (January 2006): 36–39.
11. Weinstein, "Six for '06."
12. A. Nancherta, "Tools 2020," *T + D* (December 2008): 34–35; J. Llorens, "Technology 2020," *T + D* (December 2008): 36–37.
13. P. Dvorak, "Engineering Firm Charts Ties," *The Wall Street Journal* (January 26, 2009): B7.
14. S. Adkins, "The Brave New World of Learning," *T&D* (June 2003): 28–37.
15. M. Littlejohn, "Embedded Learning," *T + D* (February 2006): 36–39.
16. J. Cross and T. O'Driscoll, "Workflow Learning gets REAL," *Training* (February 2005): 30–35.
17. A. Nancherta, "Tools 2020," J. Llorens, "Technology 2020."
18. M. Weinstein, "So Happy Together," *Training* (May 2006): 34–39.
19. P. Ketter, "Workforce 2020," *T + D* (December 2008): 40–41.
20. Zielinski, "Wanted: Training Manager."
21. H. Dolezalek, "Mining for Gold," *Training* (September 2003): 36–42.
22. R. Weintraub and J. Martineau, "The Just-in-Time Imperative," *T&D* (June 2002): 50–58.
23. M. Hequet, "The State of the E-Learning Market," *Training* (September 2003): 24–29.
24. D. Garrett, "Crossing the Channel," *Training* (September 1999): OL14–OL20.
25. L. J. Bassi, G. Benson, and S. Cheney, "The Top Ten Trends," *Training and Development* (November 1996): 28–42.
26. S. Jackson, "Your Local Campus: Training Ground Zero," *BusinessWeek* (September 30, 1996): 68.
27. M. Laff, "Switching Gears Leads to New Careers," *T + D* (September 2007): 39–43.
28. C. J. Bachler, "Trainers," *Workforce* (June 1997): 93–105; Bassi, Benson, and Cheney, "The Top Ten Trends."
29. P. Harris, "A New Market Emerges," *T&D* (September 2003): 30–38.
30. D. Schaaf, "ERP or Oops?" *Training* (May 2000): S4–S12; J. Ryder, "Future of HR Technology," *HR Magazine* 50th Anniversary Issue (2005): 67–68.

31. M. Kaeter, "Training for Rent," *Training* (May 2000): S14–S22.

32. J. Salopek, "Keeping It Real," *T + D* (August 2008): 42–45.

33. E. Lawson and C. Price, "The Psychology of Change Management," *The McKinsey Quarterly* 2 (2003).

34. D. A. Nadler, "Concepts for the Management of Organizational Change," in *Readings in the Management of Innovation,* 2d ed., ed. M. L. Tushman and N. L. Moore (Cambridge, MA: Ballinger, 1988): 722.

35. K. Bunker, M. Wakefield, O. Jaehnigen, and B. Stefl, "Transformation Delivered," *T + D* (March 2006): 26–30.

36. A. P. Brache and G. A. Rummler, "Managing an Organization as a System," *Training* (February 1997): 68–74.

37. E. F. Glanz and L. K. Dailey, "Benchmarking," *Human Resource Management* 31 (1992): 9–20; C. E. Schneier and C. Johnson, "Benchmarking: A Tool for Improving Performance Management and Reward Systems," *American Compensation Association Journal* (Spring/Summer 1993): 14–31.

38. S. Greengard, "Discover Best Practices through Benchmarking," *Personnel Journal* (November 1995): 62–73; J. D. Weatherly, "Dare to Compare for Better Productivity," *HR Magazine* (September 1992): 42–46.

39. C. E. Bogan and M. J. English, "Benchmarking for Best Practices," in *The ASTD Handbook for Training and Development,* 4th ed., ed. R. L. Craig (New York: McGraw-Hill, 1996): 394–412.

40. T. B. Kinni, "A Reengineering Primer," *Quality Digest* (January 1994): 26–30; "Reengineering Is Helping Health of Hospitals and Its Patients," *Total Quality Newsletter* (February 1994): 5; R. Recardo, "Process Reengineering in a Finance Division," *Journal for Quality and Participation* (June 1994): 70–73.

41. S. E. O'Connell, "New Technologies Bring New Tools, New Rules," *HR Magazine* (December 1995): 43–48; S. F. O'Connell, "The Virtual Workplace Works at Warp Speed," *HR Magazine* (March 1996): 51–57.

42. "What Is Organization Development?" in *Organizational Development and Transformation: Managing Effective Change,* ed. W. French, C. Bell Jr., and R. Zawacki (Burr Ridge, IL: Irwin/McGraw-Hill, 2000): 16–19.

43. E. Kossek, "The Acceptance of Human Resource Innovation by Multiple Constituencies," *Personnel Psychology* 42 (1989): 263–81.

44. W. Webb, "Winds of Change," *Training* (July 2002): 40–43.

45. J. J. Laabs, "Put Your Job on the Line," *Personnel Journal* (June 1995): 74–88.

46. M. Samuel, "Managing Change: Safety, Accountability, and Some Discomfort Needed," *Total Quality Newsletter* (September 1994).

47. L. Wheeler, "Change Every Day," *Training* (October 2008): 51–53.

48. J. Quinn, "What a Work Out!" *Performance* (November 1994): 58–63; R. Ashkenas and T. Jick, "From Dialogue to Action in GE Work-Out: Developmental Learning in a Change Process," in *Research in Organizational Change and Development,* ed. R. Woodman and W. Pasmore (Greenwich, CT: JAI Press, 1992): 267–87.

49. D. Daft and R. Noe, *Organizational Behavior* (Fort Worth, TX: Harcourt College Publishers, 2001).

50. S. Max, "Seagate's Morale-athon," *BusinessWeek* (April 3, 2006): 110–12.

IBM Reinvents Mentoring, Via the Web

It may be time-tested, but there's something uninspiring about the corporate mentoring protocol, wherein a seasoned veteran gets assigned to impart wisdom to an ambitious young talent. IBM is putting a fresh spin on the practice by democratizing its mentoring program. As of January, the company began empowering employees to reach across its global empire with the click of a button for advice on everything from preparing for a promotion to learning how to innovate.

The changes reflect the company's effort to become a truly global enterprise that relies on cross-border information-sharing and collaboration. "It became obvious that we had to make mentoring a tool for transferring knowledge globally," says Sheila Forte-Trammell, an IBM human resources consultant who helped launch the initiative.

Any IBM employee can now sign up to give or receive advice by filling out a profile in a Web-based employee directory called BluePages. Think of it as Match.com for mentoring. In less than two months, 3,000 people have joined.

Jocelyn Koh McDowell, a 22-year IBM veteran who lives in Houston, sought a mentor who could give her detailed advice on how to qualify for a promotion. Using a Web search tool, she found the right person in minutes: Lisa Squires, a 13-year veteran in Sacramento who oversees a technology certification program McDowell needs to complete. "She had even more experience than I was looking for," says McDowell.

IBM's program earns praise from experts. Belle Rose Ragins, a human resource management professor at the University of Wisconsin at Milwaukee, says IBM has "broken new ground in using the Internet to develop global relationships."

Questions

1. Do you think the advice you can get electronically is just as good as the advice you might get from a mentor in a face-to-face relationship? Explain.

2. What advantages and disadvantages does IBM's program have for mentors? For protégés? For mentees?

3. Is IBM's program really a mentoring program? Why or why not?

4. How would you evaluate the effectiveness of IBM's web-based mentoring program?

Source: S. Hamm, "IBM Reinvents Mentoring Via the Web," *BusinessWeek* (March 12, 2009). Copyright 2000–2009 by the McGraw-Hill Companies Inc.

Glossary

360-degree feedback A special case of the upward feedback system. Here employees' behaviors or skills are evaluated not only by subordinates but also by peers, customers, bosses, and employees themselves via a questionnaire rating them on a number of dimensions.

ability The physical and mental capacity to perform a task.

action learning Training method that involves giving teams or work groups a problem, having them work on solving it and committing to an action plan, and then holding them accountable for carrying out the plan.

action plan A written document detailing steps that a trainee and the manager will take to ensure that training transfers to the job.

action planning An employee's process of determining how the employee will achieve short- and long-term career goals.

advance organizers Outlines, texts, diagrams, and graphs that help trainees organize information that will be presented and practiced.

adventure learning Training method focusing on developing teamwork and leadership skills using structured outdoor activities.

affective outcomes Outcomes including attitudes and motivation.

Age Discrimination in Employment Act A federal law that prohibits discrimination against individuals 40 years of age or older.

alternative work arrangements Independent contributors, on-call workers, temporary workers, and contract company workers.

Americans with Disabilities Act (ADA) A 1990 act prohibiting workplace discrimination against people with disabilities.

andragogy The theory of adult learning.

anticipatory socialization Initial phase in organizational socialization involving the development of an employee's expectations about the company, job, working conditions, and interpersonal relationships.

application assignments Work problems or situations that trainees are asked to apply training content to solve.

application planning The preparing of trainees to use key behaviors on the job.

application service provider (ASP) A company that rents out access to software for specific applications.

apprentice An employee in the exploration stage of his or her career who works under the supervision and direction of a more experienced colleague or manager.

apprenticeship A work-study training method with both on-the-job and classroom training.

assessment The collecting of information and providing of feedback to employees about their behavior, communication style, or skills.

assessment center A process in which multiple raters or evaluators (also known as assessors) evaluate employees' performances on a number of exercises.

asynchronous communication Non–real-time interactions in which people cannot communicate with each other without a time delay.

attitude Combination of beliefs and feelings that predispose a person to behave in a certain way.

attitude awareness and change program Program focusing on increasing employees' awareness of their attitudes toward differences in cultural and ethnic backgrounds, physical characteristics (e.g., disabilities), and personal characteristics that influence behavior toward others.

audiovisual instruction Media-based training that is both watched and heard.

auditing In training, the providing of information related to the frequency of training within a company.

authoring tools Software used to develop online learning programs.

automatization Making performance of a task, recall of knowledge, or demonstration of a skill so automatic that it requires little thought or attention.

avatars Computer depictions of humans that are used as imaginary coaches, co-workers, and customers in simulations.

baby boomers People born between 1945 and 1960.

balanced scorecard A means of performance measurement that allows managers to view the overall company performance or the performance of departments or functions (such as training) from the perspective of internal and external customers, employees, and shareholders.

bandwidth The number of bytes and bits (information) that can travel between computers per second.

basic skills Skills necessary for employees to perform their jobs and learn the content of training programs.

behavior-based conflict   Conflict occurring when an employee's behavior in work roles is not appropriate in nonwork roles.

behavior-based program   Program focusing on changing the organizational policies and individual behaviors that inhibit employees' personal growth and productivity.

behavior modeling   A training method in which trainees are presented with a model who demonstrates key behaviors to replicate and provides them with the opportunity to practice those key behaviors.

benchmarking   The use of information about other companies' training practices to help determine the appropriate type, level, and frequency of training.

Benchmarks   A research instrument designed to measure important factors in being a successful manager.

benefits   The value company gains from a training program.

blended learning   Learning involving a combination of online learning, face-to-face instruction, and other methods.

business-embedded (BE) model   A training function model that aligns closely with the company's business strategy and that is characterized by five competencies: strategic direction, product design, structural versatility, product delivery, and accountability for results.

business game   A training method in which trainees gather information, analyze it, and make decisions.

business process outsourcing   The outsourcing of any business process, such as human resource management, production, or training.

business strategy   A plan that integrates a company's goals, policies, and actions.

career   The pattern of work-related experiences that span the course of a person's life.

career development   The process by which employees progress through a series of stages, each characterized by a different set of developmental tasks, activities, and relationships.

career identity   The degree to which employees define their personal value according to their work.

career insight   The degree to which employees know about their interests as well as their skill strengths and weaknesses; the awareness of how these perceptions relate to their career goals.

career management   The process through which employees (1) become aware of their own interests, values, strengths, and weaknesses, (2) get information about job opportunities within a company, (3) identify career goals, and (4) establish action plans to achieve career goals.

career management system   System that helps employees, managers, and the company identify career development needs; includes self-assessment, reality check, goal setting, and action planning.

career motivation   Employees' energy to invest in their careers, their awareness of the direction they want their careers to take, and their ability to maintain energy and direction despite any barriers that they may encounter.

career path   A sequence of job positions involving similar types of work and skills that employees move through in a company.

career portfolio   Multiple part-time jobs that together make up a full-time position.

career resilience   Employees' ability to cope with problems that affect their work.

career support   Coaching, protection, sponsorship, and provision of challenging assignments, exposure, and visibility to an employee.

case study   A description of how employees or an organization dealt with a situation.

CD-ROM   An aluminum disk from which a laser reads text, graphics, audio, and video.

centralized training   Organizing the training department so that training and development programs, resources, and professionals are primarily housed in one location and decisions about training investment, programs, and delivery are made from that department.

change   The adoption of a new idea or behavior by a company.

change management   The process of ensuring that new interventions such as training practices are accepted and used by employees and managers.

chief learning officer (CLO)   A leader of a company's knowledge management efforts (also called knowledge officer).

climate for transfer   Trainees' perceptions about a wide variety of characteristics of the work environment; these perceptions facilitate or inhibit use of trained skills or behavior.

coach   A peer or manager who works with employees to motivate them, help them develop skills, and provide reinforcement and feedback.

cognitive ability   Verbal comprehension, quantitative ability, and reasoning ability.

cognitive outcomes   Outcomes used to measure what knowledge trainees learned in a training program.

cognitive strategies   Strategies that regulate the learning processes; they relate to the learner's decision regarding what information to attend to, how to remember, and how to solve problems.

cognitive theory of transfer   Theory asserting that the likelihood of transfer depends on the trainee's ability to retrieve learned capabilities.

colleague Employees, generally in the establishment stage of their career, who can work independently and produce results.

combination Systematizing explicit concepts into a knowledge system by analyzing, categorizing, and repurposing information.

community of practice A group of employees who work together, learn from each other, and develop a common understanding of how to get work accomplished.

comparison group A group of employees who participate in an evaluation study but do not attend a training program.

competency An area of personal capability that enables employees to perform their job.

competency model A model identifying the competencies necessary for each job as well as the knowledge, skills, behavior, and personal characteristics underlying each competency.

competitive advantage An upper hand over other firms in an industry.

competitiveness A company's ability to maintain and gain market share in an industry.

computer-based training (CBT) An interactive training experience in which the computer provides the learning stimulus, the trainee must respond, and the computer analyzes responses and provides feedback to the trainee.

concentration strategy Business strategy focusing on increasing market share, reducing costs, or creating a market niche for products and services.

consequences Incentives employees receive for performing well.

continuous learning A learning system in which employees are required to understand the entire work system including the relationships among their jobs, their work units, and the company. Also, employees are expected to acquire new skills and knowledge, apply them on the job, and share this information with fellow workers.

control A manager's or employee's ability to obtain and distribute valuable resources.

coordination training Training a team in how to share information and decision-making responsibilities to maximize team performance.

copyright Legal protection for the expression of an idea.

corporate university model A training model in which the client group includes not only company employees and managers but also stakeholders outside the company.

cost-benefit analysis The process of determining the economic benefits of a training program using accounting methods.

course objectives (lesson objectives) The goals of the training course or the lesson. In terms of the expected behaviors, content, conditions, and standards, these objectives are more specific than program objectives.

criteria relevance The extent to which training outcomes relate to the learned capabilities emphasized in training.

criterion contamination When a training program's outcomes measure inappropriate capabilities or are affected by extraneous conditions.

criterion deficiency The failure to measure training outcomes that were emphasized in training objectives.

cross-cultural preparation The education of employees (expatriates) and their families who are to be sent to a foreign country.

cross training Training method in which team members understand and practice each other's skills so that members are prepared to step in and take another member's place should someone temporarily or permanently leave the team; also, more simply, training employees to learn the skills of one or several additional jobs.

cultural immersion Used to prepare employees for overseas assignments; involves sending employees directly into a community where they have to interact with persons from different cultures, races, and/or nationalities.

culture A set of assumptions group members share about the world and how it works as well as ideals worth striving for.

customer capital The value of relationships with persons or other organizations outside a company for accomplishing the goals of the company (e.g., relationships with suppliers, customers, vendors, government agencies).

customer model A training model in which a training department is responsible for the training needs of one division or function of the company.

data-entity relationship diagram An illustration of the types of data used within a business function and the relationships among the different types of data.

data-flow diagram An illustration of the flow of data between departments.

detailed lesson plan The translation of the content and sequence of training activities into a guide used by the trainer to help deliver training.

development Formal education, job experiences, relationships, and assessments of personality and abilities that help employees prepare for the future.

development planning process Process of identifying development needs, choosing a development goal, identifying actions the employee and company need to take to achieve the goal, determining how progress toward goal attainment will be measured, and establishing a timetable for development.

digital collaboration   An interaction between two or more people mediated by a computer; the use of technology to enhance and extend employees' ability to work together regardless of their geographic proximity.

direct costs   Training costs including salaries and benefits of all employees involved, program supplies, equipment and classroom rental or purchase, and travel costs.

directional pattern model   A model describing the form or shape of careers.

discrimination   The degree to which trainees' performances on an outcome actually reflect true differences in performance.

disengagement stage   Career stage in which an individual prepares for a change in the balance between work and nonwork activities.

disinvestment strategy   Business strategy emphasizing liquidation and divestiture of businesses.

distance learning   Training method in which geographically dispersed companies provide information about new products, policies, or procedures as well as skills training and expert lectures to field locations.

diversity   Any dimension that differentiates one person from another (e.g., age, ethnicity, education, sexual orientation, race, gender, and so on).

diversity training   Training programs designed to change employees' attitudes about diversity and/or to develop skills needed to work with a diverse work force.

downward move   Reduction of an employee's responsibility and authority.

dual-career-path system   A career path system that enables technical employees to either remain in a technical career path or move into a management career path.

DVD (digital video disk)   A technology in which a laser reads text, graphics, audio, and video off an aluminum disk.

early retirement program   A system of offering employees financial benefits to leave the company.

e-commerce   A technology enabling business transactions and relationships to be handled electronically.

elaboration   A learning strategy requiring the trainee to relate the training material to other more familiar knowledge, skills, or behavior.

e-learning   Instruction and delivery of training by computer online through the Internet or Web.

electronic performance support system (EPSS)   Computer application that can provide, as requested, skills training, information access, and expert advice.

embedded learning   Learning that occurs on the job as needed.

employee engagement   The extent to which employees are fully involved in their work and the strength of their commitment to their job and the company.

encounter phase   Middle phase in organizational socialization in which an employee begins a new job.

error management training   Training in which trainees are given opportunities to make errors, which can aid in learning and improve trainees' performance on the job.

establishment stage   Career stage in which an individual finds his or her place in a company, makes an independent contribution, achieves more responsibility and financial success, and establishes a desirable life style.

evaluation design   Designation of what information is to be collected, from whom, when, and how to determine training's effectiveness.

expatriate   A person working in a country other than his or her nation of origin.

expectancy   Belief about the link between trying to perform a behavior (or effort) and actually performing well; the mental state that the learner brings to the instructional process.

experiential learning   A training method in which participants (1) are presented with conceptual knowledge and theory, (2) take part in a behavioral simulation, (3) analyze the activity, and (4) connect the theory and activity with on-the-job or real-life situations.

expert systems   Technology (usually software) that organizes and applies human experts' knowledge to specific problems.

explicit knowledge   Knowledge that can be formalized, codified, and communicated.

exploration stage   Career stage in which individuals attempt to identify the type of work that interests them.

external conditions   Processes in the learning environment that facilitate learning.

external growth strategy   Business strategy emphasizing acquiring vendors and suppliers or buying businesses that allow the company to expand into new markets.

external validity   The generalizability of study results to other groups and situations.

externalization   Translating tacit knowledge into explicit knowledge.

externship   Situation in which a company allows an employee to take a full-time, temporary operational role at another company.

faculty model   A training model that resembles the structure of a college. The training department is headed by director with a staff of experts having specialized knowledge of a particular topic or skill area.

Family and Medical Leave Act (FMLA)   A federal law that provides for up to 12 weeks of unpaid leave for parents with new infants or newly adopted children; also covers employees who must take a leave of absence from work to care for a family member who is ill or to deal with a personal illness.

far transfer Trainees' ability to apply learned capabilities to the work environment even though it is not identical to the training session environment.

feedback Information employees receive while they are performing about how well they are meeting objectives.

fidelity The extent to which a training environment is similar to a work environment.

focus group A face-to-face meeting with subject-matter experts in which specific training needs are addressed.

formal education program Off-site or on-site program designed for a company's employees, short course offered by a consultant or school, an executive MBA program, or university program in which students live at the university while taking classes.

formative evaluation Evaluation conducted to improve the training process; usually conducted during program design and development.

Gen Xers People born between 1961 and 1980.

generalization A trainee's ability to apply learned capabilities to on-the-job work problems and situations that are similar but not identical to problems and situations encountered in the learning environment.

generalizing Adapting learning for use in similar but not identical situations.

glass ceiling A barrier to advancement to an organization's higher levels.

goal What a company hopes to achieve in the medium- to long-term future.

goal orientation A trainee's goals in a learning situation.

goal setting An employee's process of developing short- and long-term career objectives.

goal setting theory A theory assuming that behavior results from a person's conscious goals and intentions.

gratifying The feedback that a learner receives from using learning content.

group building methods Training methods designed to improve team or group effectiveness.

group mentoring program Program in which a successful senior employee is paired with a group of four to six less experienced protégés to help them understand the organization, guide them in analyzing their experiences, and help them clarify career directions.

groupware (electronic meeting software) A special type of software application that enables multiple users to track, share, and organize information and to work on the same document simultaneously.

hands-on method Training method in which the trainee is actively involved in learning.

Hawthorne effect A situation in which employees in an evaluation study perform at a high level simply because of the attention they are receiving.

high-leverage training Training that uses an instructional design process to ensure that it is effective and that compares or benchmarks the company's training programs against those of other companies.

high-potential employee An employee who the company believes is capable of succeeding in a higher-level managerial position.

host-country national An employee with citizenship in the country where the company is located.

human capital The sum of the attributes, life experiences, knowledge, inventiveness, energy, and enthusiasm that a company's employees invest in their work.

human capital management The integration of training with other human resource functions so as to track how training benefits the company.

human resource development The integrated use of training and development, organizational development, and career development to improve individual, group, and organizational effectiveness.

human resource management The policies, practices, and systems that influence employees' behavior, attitudes, and performance.

human resource management (HRM) practices Management activities relating to investments in staffing, performance management, training, and compensation and benefits.

human resource planning The identification, analysis, forecasting, and planning of changes needed in a company's human resources area.

hyperlinks Links that allow a user to easily move from one Web page to another.

imaging Scanning documents, storing them electronically, and retrieving them.

in-basket A training exercise involving simulation of the administrative tasks of the manager's job.

indirect costs Costs not related directly to a training program's design, development, or delivery.

individualism-collectivism The cultural dimension reflecting the degree to which people act as individuals rather than members of a group.

informational interview An interview an employee conducts with a manager or other employee to gather information about the skills, job demands, and benefits of that person's job.

input Instructions that tell employees what, how, and when to perform; also, the resources employees are given to help them perform their jobs.

instruction The characteristics of the environment in which learning is to occur.

Instructional System Design (ISD)   A process for designing and developing training programs.

instructor evaluation   A measurement of a trainer's or instructor's success.

instrumentality   In expectancy theory, a belief that performing a given behavior is associated with a particular outcome.

intellectual capital   The codified knowledge that exists in a company.

intellectual skills   Mastery of concepts and rules.

intelligent tutoring system (ITS)   An instructional system using artificial intelligence.

interactive distance learning (IDL)   The use of satellite technology to broadcast programs to different locations, allowing trainees to respond to questions posed during the training program using a keypad.

interactive video   Training medium, combining video and computer-based instruction, in which the trainee interacts with the program.

interactive voice technology   Technology using a conventional PC to create a phone-response system.

intergroup activity   A change intervention that attempts to improve relationships among different teams, departments, or groups.

internal conditions   Processes within the learner that must be present for learning to occur.

internal growth strategy   Business strategy focusing on new market and product development, innovation, and joint ventures.

internal validity   Establishing that the treatment (training) made a difference.

internalization   Converting explicit knowledge to tacit knowledge.

Internet   A global collection of computer networks that allows users to exchange data and information; a communications tool for sending and receiving messages quickly and inexpensively; a means of locating and gathering resources.

Internet-based training   Training delivered on public or private computer networks and displayed by a Web browser (also called Web-based training).

intranet-based training   Training delivered using a company's own computer network or server.

ISO 10015   A quality management tool designed to ensure that training is linked to a company's needs and performance.

ISO 9000:2000   A family of standards developed by the International Organization for Standardization that includes 20 requirements for dealing with such issues as how to establish quality standards and document work processes.

job   A specific position requiring completion of certain tasks.

job analysis   The process of developing a description of the job (duties, tasks, and responsibilities) and the specifications (knowledge, skills, and abilities) that an employee must have to perform it.

job enlargement   The adding of challenges or new responsibilities to an employee's current job.

job experience   The relationships, problems, demands, tasks, and other features that an employee faces on the job.

job incumbent   An employee currently holding the job.

job rotation   Assigning employees a series of jobs in various functional areas of a company or movement among jobs in a single functional area or department.

job sharing   Work situation in which two employees divide the hours, responsibilities, and benefits of a full-time job.

joint union-management training program   Program created, funded, and supported by both union and management to provide a range of services to help employees learn skills that are directly related to their jobs and that are "portable" (valuable to employers in other companies or industries).

key behaviors   A set of behaviors that is necessary to complete a task. Important part of behavior modeling training.

knowledge   Facts or procedures that individuals or teams of employees know or know how to do (human and social knowledge); also a company's rules, processes, tools, and routines (structured knowledge).

knowledge-based pay system   Pay system based primarily on an employee's knowledge rather than on the job he or she is performing (also called skill-based pay system).

knowledge management   The process of enhancing company performance by designing and implementing tools, processes, systems, structures, and cultures to improve the creating, sharing, and use of knowledge.

knowledge officer   A leader of a company's knowledge management efforts (also called chief learning officer).

knowledge workers   Employees who own the means of producing a product or service. These employees have a specialized body of knowledge or expertise that they use to perform their jobs and contribute to company effectiveness.

lapse   Situation in which a trainee uses previously learned, less effective capabilities instead of trying to apply capabilities emphasized in a training program.

large group intervention   A change intervention that brings together employees from different parts of an organization (and perhaps customers and other stakeholders) in an off-site setting to discuss problems and opportunities or to plan change.

laser disk   A disk that uses a laser to provide video and sound.

leaderless group discussion   A training exercise in which a team of five to seven employees must work together to solve an assigned problem within a certain time period.

lean thinking   Doing more with less effort, equipment, space, and time, but providing customers with what they need and want. Part of lean thinking includes training workers in new skills or how to apply old skills in new ways so they can quickly take over new responsibilities or use new skills to help fill customer orders.

learner control   A trainee's ability to actively learn through self-pacing, exercises, exploring links to other material, and conversations with other trainees and experts.

learning   The acquisition of knowledge by individual employees or groups of employees who are willing to apply that knowledge in their jobs in making decisions and accomplishing tasks for the company; a relatively permanent change in human capabilities that does not result from growth processes.

learning management systems (LMS)   A system for automating the administration of online training programs.

learning organization   A company that has an enhanced capacity to learn, adapt, and change; an organization whose employees continuously attempt to learn new things and then apply what they have learned to improve product or service quality.

learning portal   Web site that provides, via e-commerce transactions, access to training courses, services, and online learning communities from many sources.

lecture   Training method in which the trainer communicates through spoken words what trainees are supposed to learn.

lesson plan overview   A plan matching a training program's major activities to specific times or time intervals.

life-cycle model   A model suggesting that employees face certain developmental tasks over the course of their careers and that they move through distinct life or career stages.

Lifelong Learning Account (LiLA)   An account for adult education to which both the employee and the company contribute and the employee keeps—even if he or she leaves the company.

logical verification   Perceiving a relationship between a new task and a task already mastered.

maintenance   The process of continuing to use newly acquired capabilities over time.

maintenance stage   Career stage in which an individual is concerned about keeping skills up to date and being perceived by others as someone who is still contributing to the company.

Malcolm Baldrige National Quality Award   National award created in 1987 to recognize U.S. companies' quality achievements and to publicize quality strategies.

manager support   Trainees' managers (1) emphasizing the importance of attending training programs and (2) stressing the application of training content on the job.

managing diversity   The creation of an environment that allows all employees (regardless of their demographic group) to contribute to organizational goals and experience personal growth.

masculinity-femininity   The cultural dimension reflecting the degree to which a culture values behavior that is considered traditionally masculine (competitiveness) or feminine (helpfulness).

massed practice   Training approach in which trainees practice a task continuously without rest.

mastery orientation   An effort to increase ability or competence in a task.

matrix model   A training model in which trainers report to both a manager in the training department and a manager in a particular function.

mental requirements   The degree to which a person must use or demonstrate mental skills or cognitive skills or abilities to perform a task.

mentor   An experienced, productive senior employee who helps develop a less experienced employee (a protégé).

metacognition   A learning strategy whereby trainees direct their attention to their own learning process.

millenniums   People born after 1980 (also called nexters).

mission   A company's long-term reason for existing.

modeling   Having employees who have mastered the desired learning outcomes demonstrate them for trainees.

modeling display   Often done via videotape or computer, a training method in which trainees are shown key behaviors, which they then practice.

motivation to learn   A trainee's desire to learn the content of a training program.

motor skills   Coordination of physical movements.

multimedia training   Training that combines audio-visual training methods with computer-based training.

Myers-Briggs Type Indicator (MBTI)   A psychological test for employee development consisting of over 100 questions about how the person feels or prefers to behave in different situations.

near transfer   A trainee's ability to apply learned capabilities exactly to the work situation.

need   A deficiency that a person is experiencing at any point in time.

needs assessment   The process used to determine if training is necessary; the first step in the Instructional System Design model.

nexters People born after 1980 (also called millenniums).

norms Accepted standards of behavior for work-group members.

objective The purpose and expected outcome of training activities.

obsolescence A reduction in an employee's competence resulting from a lack of knowledge of new work processes, techniques, and technologies that have developed since the employee completed his or her education.

offshoring The process of moving jobs from the United States to other locations in the world.

onboarding The orientation process for newly hired managers.

online learning Instruction and delivery of training by computer online through the Internet or Web.

on-the-job training (OJT) Training in which new or inexperienced employees learn through first observing peers or managers performing the job and then trying to imitate their behavior.

opportunity to perform The chance to use learned capabilities.

organizational analysis Training analysis that determines the appropriateness of training, considering the context in which training will occur.

organizational socialization The process of transforming new employees into effective company members. Its phases are anticipatory socialization, encounter, and settling in.

organization-based model A model suggesting that careers proceed through a series of stages with each stage involving changes in activities and relationships with peers and managers.

organization development A planned, systematic change process that uses behavioral science knowledge and techniques to improve a company's effectiveness by improving relationships and increasing learning and problem-solving capabilities.

organizing A learning strategy that requires the learner to find similarities and themes in the training materials.

other In task analysis, a term referring to the conditions under which tasks are performed, for example, physical condition of the work environment or psychological conditions, such as pressure or stress.

output A job's performance standards.

outsourcing The acquisition of training and development activities from outside the company.

overall task complexity The degree to which a task requires a number of distinct behaviors, the number of choices involved in performing the task, and the degree of uncertainty in performing the task.

overlearning Employees' continuing to practice even if they have been able to perform the objective several times.

part practice Training approach in which each objective or task is practiced individually as soon as it is introduced in a training program.

past accomplishments System of allowing employees to build a history of successful accomplishments.

perception The ability to organize a message from the environment so that it can be processed and acted upon.

performance analysis approach An approach to solving business problems that identifies performance gaps or deficiencies and examines training as a possible solution.

performance appraisal The process of measuring an employee's performance.

performance orientation A learner's focus on task performance and how the learner compares to others.

person analysis Training analysis involving (1) determining whether performance deficiencies result from lack of knowledge, skill, or ability or else from a motivational or work-design problem, (2) identifying who needs training, and (3) determining employees' readiness for training.

person characteristics An employee's knowledge, skill, ability, behavior, or attitudes.

phased retirement Phase during which older employees gradually reduce their hours, which helps them transition into retirement.

physical requirements The degree to which a person must use or demonstrate physical skills and abilities to perform and complete a task.

pilot testing The process of previewing a training program with potential trainees and managers or other customers.

plateauing A workplace situation with little likelihood of the employee receiving future job assignments with increased responsibility.

plug-in Extra software that needs to be loaded on a computer, for example, to listen to sound or watch video.

posttest only An evaluation design in which only posttraining outcomes are collected.

posttraining measure A measure of outcomes taken after training.

power The ability to influence others.

power distance Expectations for the unequal distribution of power in a hierarchy.

practicality The ease with which outcome measures can be collected.

practice An employee's demonstration of a learned capability; the physical or mental rehearsal of a task, knowledge, or skill to achieve proficiency in performing the task or skill or demonstrating the knowledge.

preretirement socialization   The process of helping employees prepare for exit from work.

presence   In training, the perception of actually being in a particular environment.

presentation methods   Training methods in which trainees are passive recipients of information.

pretest/posttest   An evaluation design in which both pretraining and posttraining outcome measures are collected.

pretest/posttest with comparison group   An evaluation design that includes trainees and a comparison group. Both pretraining and posttraining outcome measures are collected.

pretraining measure   A baseline measure of outcomes.

process consultation   The use of a consultant to work with managers or other employees to help them understand and take action to improve specific events that take place at work.

program design   The organization and coordination of the training program.

program objectives   Broad summary statements of a training program's purpose. They are usually included on the design template.

project career   A career based on a series of projects that may or may not be in the same company.

promotion   An advancement into a position with greater challenges, more responsibility, and more authority than the previous job provided; usually includes a pay increase.

protean career   A career that is frequently changing based on changes in the person's interests, abilities, and values as well as changes in the work environment.

psychological contract   The expectations that employers and employees have about each other and about the employment relationship.

psychological success   A feeling of pride and accomplishment that comes from achieving life goals.

psychosocial support   Serving as a friend and role model to an employee; also includes providing positive regard, acceptance, and an outlet for the protégé to talk about anxieties and fears.

random assignment   The assignment of employees to training or a comparison group on the basis of chance.

rapid instructional design (RID)   A group of techniques that allows training to be built more quickly; the two principles of RID are that instructional content and process can be developed independently of each other and that resources devoted to design and delivery of instruction can be reallocated as appropriate.

rapid needs assessment   A needs assessment that is done quickly and accurately but without sacrificing the quality of the process or the outcomes.

reaction outcomes   A trainee's perceptions of a training program, including perceptions of the facilities, trainers, and content.

readability   Written materials' level of difficulty.

readiness for training   The condition of (1) employees having the personal characteristics necessary to learn program content and apply it on the job and (2) the work environment facilitating learning and not interfering with performance.

realistic job preview   Stage in which a prospective employee is provided accurate information about attractive and unattractive aspects of a job, working conditions, company, and location to be sure that the employee develops appropriate expectations.

reality check   Information an employee receives about how the company values that employee's skills and knowledge as well as where that employee fits into the company's plans.

reasonable accommodation   In terms of the Americans with Disabilities Act and training, making training facilities readily accessible to and usable by individuals with disabilities; may also include modifying instructional media, adjusting training policies, and providing trainees with readers or interpreters.

recycling   Changing one's major work activity after having been established in a particular field.

reengineering   A complete review and redesign of critical processes to make them more efficient and able to deliver higher quality.

rehearsal   A learning strategy focusing on learning through repetition (memorization).

reinforcement theory   Theory emphasizing that people are motivated to perform or avoid certain behaviors because of past outcomes that have resulted from those behaviors.

reliability   The degree to which outcomes can be measured consistently over time.

repatriation   Preparing expatriates for return to the parent company and country from a foreign assignment.

repurposing   Directly translating a training program that uses a traditional training method onto the Web.

request for proposal (RFP)   A document that outlines for potential vendors and consultants the requirements for winning and fulfilling a contract with a company.

resistance to change   Managers' and/or employees' unwillingness to change.

results   Outcomes used to determine a training program's payoff.

retirement The leaving of a job and work role to make the transition into life without work.

retrieval The identification of learned material in long-term memory and use of it to influence performance.

return on investment (ROI) A comparison of a training program's monetary benefits and costs.

reversal A time period in which training participants no longer receive training intervention.

rigor The degree to which a training program emphasizes behavior and skills needed to effectively accomplish the training's goals.

role play A training exercise in which the participant takes the part or role of a manager or some other employee; training method in which trainees are given information about a situation and act out characters assigned to them.

sabbatical A leave of absence from the company to renew or develop skills.

scenario analysis Simulation of real-world issues presented to data end users.

School-to-Work Opportunities Act (1994) Federal act designed to assist the states in building school-to-work systems that prepare students for high-skill, high-wage jobs or future education.

school-to-work transition program Program combining classroom experience with work experience to prepare high school students for employment after graduation.

Second Life A computer-based, simulated online virtual world that includes a three-dimensional representation of the real world and a place to host learning programs or experiences. In Second Life, trainees use an avatar to interact with each other in classrooms, webinars, simulations, or role-play exercises.

self-assessment An employee's use of information to determine career interests, values, aptitudes, and behavioral tendencies.

self-directed learning Training in which employees take responsibility for all aspects of their learning (e.g., when it occurs, who is involved).

self-efficacy Employees' belief that they can successfully perform their job or learn the content of a training program.

self-management Person's attempt to control certain aspects of his or her decision making and behavior.

semantic encoding The actual coding process of incoming memory.

settling-in phase A phase in the job socialization process in which employees begin to feel comfortable with their job demands and social relationships.

simulation A training method that represents a real-life situation, with trainees' decisions resulting in

outcomes that mirror what would happen if they were on the job.

situational constraints Work environment characteristics including lack of proper equipment, materials, supplies, budgetary support, and time.

Six Sigma process A process of measuring, analyzing, improving, and then controlling processes once they have been brought within the Six Sigma quality tolerances or standards.

skill Competency in performing a task.

skill-based outcomes Outcomes used to assess the level of technical or motor skills or behavior; include skill acquisition or learning and on-the-job use of skills.

skill-based pay system Pay system based primarily on an employee's skills rather than on the job the employee is performing (also called knowledge-based pay system).

social capital The value of relationships among employees within a company.

socialization Sharing tacit knowledge by sharing experiences.

social learning theory Theory emphasizing that people learn by observing other persons (models) who they believe are credible and knowledgeable.

social network analysis A map of employee relationships that can be used to help identify informal employee communications and information- and knowledge-sharing patterns.

social support Feedback and reinforcement from managers and peers.

Solomon four-group An evaluation design combining the pretest/posttest comparison group and the posttest-only control group designs.

spaced practice Training approach in which trainees are given rest intervals within the practice session.

sponsor A staff member who provides direction to other employees, represents the company to customers, initiates actions, and makes decisions.

staffing strategy A company's decisions regarding where to find employees, how to select them, and the mix of employee skills and statuses.

stakeholders The parties with an interest in a company's success (include shareholders, employees, customers, and the community).

stimulus generalization approach The construction of training to emphasize the most important features or general principles.

strain-based conflict Conflict resulting from the stress of work and nonwork roles.

strategic training and development initiatives Learning-related actions that a company takes to achieve its business strategy.

subject-matter expert (SME) Person who is knowledgeable of (1) training issues, (2) knowledge, skills, and abilities required for task performance, (3) necessary equipment, and (4) conditions under which tasks have to be performed.

success cases Concrete examples of the impact of training that show how learning leads to results that the company finds worthwhile and the managers find credible.

succession planning The process of identifying and tracking high-potential employees for advancement in a company.

summative evaluation Evaluation of the extent that trainees have changed as a result of participating in a training program.

supportive work-life culture A company culture that acknowledges and respects family and life responsibilities and obligations and encourages managers and employees to work together to meet personal and work needs.

support network A group of two or more trainees who agree to meet and discuss their progress in using learned capabilities on the job.

survey feedback The process of collecting information about employees' attitudes and perceptions using a survey, summarizing the results, and providing employees with feedback to stimulate discussion, identify problems, and plan actions to solve problems.

survivor An employee remaining with a company after downsizing.

SWOT analysis An identification of a company's operating environment as well as an internal analysis of its strengths and weaknesses. SWOT is an acronym for strengths, weaknesses, opportunities, and threats.

synchronous communication Communication in which trainers, experts, and learners interact with each other live and in real time in the same way that they would in face-to-face classroom instruction.

tacit knowledge Personal knowledge that is based on individual experience and that is difficult to explain to others.

talent management Process of attracting, retaining, developing, and motivating highly skilled employees and managers.

task A statement of an employee's work activity in a specific job.

task analysis Training analysis that involves identifying the tasks and knowledge, skills, and behaviors that need to be emphasized in training for employees to complete their tasks.

task redefinition Changes in managers' and/or employees' roles and methods.

team leader training Training that a team manager or facilitator receives.

team training Training method that involves coordinating the performances of individuals who work together to achieve a common goal.

telecommuting Working in a remote location (distant from a central office), where the employee has limited contact with peers but can communicate electronically (also called teleworking).

teleconferencing Synchronous exchange of audio, video, and/or text between two or more individuals or groups at two or more locations.

teleworking Working in a remote location (distant from a central office), where the employee has limited contact with peers but can communicate electronically (also called telecommuting).

theory of identical elements A theory that transfer of learning occurs when what is learned in training is identical to what the trainee has to perform on the job.

threats to validity Factors that lead one to question either (1) the believability of a study's results or (2) the extent to which evaluation results are generalizable to other groups of trainees and situations.

time-based conflict Situation in which the demands of work and nonwork interfere with each other.

time orientation The degree to which a culture focuses on the future rather than the past and present.

time series An evaluation design in which training outcomes are collected at periodic intervals pre- and posttraining.

Total Quality Management (TQM) A style of doing business that relies on the talents and capabilities of both labor and management to build and provide high-quality products and services and continuously improve them.

traditionalists People born between 1920 and 1944.

trainee characteristics The abilities and motivation that affect learning.

training A company's planned effort to facilitate employees' learning of job-related competencies.

training administration Coordination of activities before, during, and after a training program.

training context The physical, intellectual, and emotional environment in which training occurs.

training design Characteristics of the learning environment.

training design process A systematic approach to developing training programs. Its six steps include conducting needs assessment, ensuring employees' readiness for training, creating a learning environment, ensuring transfer of training, selecting training methods, and evaluating training programs.

training effectiveness Benefits that a company and its trainees receive from training.

training evaluation The process of collecting the outcomes needed to determine whether training has been effective.

training outcomes (criteria) Measures that a company and its trainer use to evaluate training programs.

training site The place where training is conducted.

transfer Giving an employee a different job assignment in a different area of the company.

transfer of training Trainees' applying to their jobs the learned capabilities gained in training.

tuition reimbursement The practice of reimbursing employees the costs for college and university courses and degree programs.

uncertainty avoidance A preference for structured rather than unstructured situations.

Uniformed Services Employment and Reemployment Rights Act An act that covers deployed employees' rights, such as guaranteeing jobs when they return, except under special circumstances.

upward feedback An appraisal process involving the collection of subordinates' evaluations of managers' behaviors or skills.

utility analysis A cost-benefit analysis method that involves assessing the dollar value of training based on estimates of the difference in job performance between trained and untrained employees, the number of individuals trained, the length of time a training program is expected to influence performance, and the variability in job performance in the untrained group of employees.

valence The value that a person places on an outcome.

values Principles and virtues that symbolize the company's beliefs.

verbal information Names or labels, facts, and bodies of knowledge.

verbal persuasion Offering words of encouragement to convince others that they can learn.

vicarious reinforcement Situation in which a trainee sees a model being reinforced for using certain behaviors.

virtual expatriate An employee assigned to work on an operation in another country without being located permanently in it.

virtual reality A computer-based technology that provides trainees with a three-dimensional learning experience.

virtual team A team that is separated by time, geographic distance, culture, and/or organizational boundaries and that relies almost exclusively on technology to interact and complete projects.

virtual work arrangement Work arrangement (including virtual teams as well as teleworking) in which location, organization structure, and employment relationship are not limiting factors.

vision The picture of the future that the company wants to achieve.

Web 2.0 User-created social networking features on the Internet, including blogs, wikis, and Twitter.

Web-based training Training delivered on public or private computer networks and displayed by a Web browser (also called Internet-based training).

webcasting Classroom instructions that are provided online through live broadcasts.

whole practice Training approach in which all tasks or objectives are practiced at the same time.

work environment On-the-job factors that influence transfer of training.

Workforce Investment Act A 1998 federal act that created a new, comprehensive work force investment system that is customer focused, that provides Americans with career management information and high-quality services, and that helps U.S. companies find skilled workers.

working storage The rehearsal and repetition of information, allowing it to be coded for memory.

work team A group of employees with various skills who interact to assemble a product or produce a service.

World Wide Web (WWW) A user-friendly service on the Internet; provides browser software enabling users to explore the Web.

Name Index

Company/Organization Index

Subject Index